C++ Plus Data Structures

FIFTH EDITION

Nell Dale
University of Texas, Austin

JONES & BARTLETT
LEARNING

World Headquarters
Jones & Bartlett Learning
5 Wall Street
Burlington, MA 01803
978-443-5000
info@jblearning.com
www.jblearning.com

Jones & Bartlett Learning books and products are available through most bookstores and online booksellers. To contact Jones & Bartlett Learning directly, call 800-832-0034, fax 978-443-8000, or visit our website, www.jblearning.com.

Substantial discounts on bulk quantities of Jones & Bartlett Learning publications are available to corporations, professional associations, and other qualified organizations. For details and specific discount information, contact the special sales department at Jones & Bartlett Learning via the above contact information or send an email to specialsales@jblearning.com.

Production Credits
Chief Executive Officer: Ty Field
President: James Homer
SVP, Editor-in-Chief: Michael Johnson
SVP, Chief Technology Officer: Dean Fossella
SVP, Chief Marketing Officer: Alison M. Pendergast
Publisher: Cathleen Sether
Senior Acquisitions Editor: Timothy Anderson
Managing Editor: Amy Bloom
Director of Production: Amy Rose
Associate Marketing Manager: Lindsay White
V.P., Manufacturing and Inventory Control: Therese Connell
Composition: Northeast Compositors, Inc.
Cover and Title Page Design: Kristin E. Parker
Cover and Title Page Image: © iStockphoto/Thinkstock
Printing and Binding: Malloy, Inc.
Cover Printing: Malloy, Inc.

Library of Congress Cataloging-in-Publication Data
Dale, Nell B.
C++ plus data structures / Nell Dale. – 5th ed.
p. cm.
Includes bibliographical references and index.
ISBN-13: 978-1-4496-4675-2 (casebound)
ISBN-10: 1-4496-4675-1 (casebound)
1. C++ (Computer program language) 2. Data structures (Computer science) I. Title.
QA76.73.C153D334 2011
005.7'3–dc23

2011028812

6048

Printed in the United States of America
15 14 13 12 11 10 9 8 7 6 5 4 3 2 1

To Alfred George Dale

N. D.

contents

preface

Historically, a course on data structures has been a mainstay of most computer science departments. However, the focus of this course has broadened considerably. The topic of data structures now has been subsumed under the broader topic of *abstract data types* (*ADTs*)—the study of classes of objects whose logical behavior is defined by a set of values and a set of operations.

The term *abstract data type* describes a comprehensive collection of data values and operations. The term *data structures* refers to the study of data and how to represent data objects within a program; that is, the implementation of structured relationships. The shift in emphasis is representative of the move towards more abstraction in computer science education. We now are interested in the study of the abstract properties of classes of data objects in addition to how the objects might be represented in a program. Johannes J. Martin puts it very succinctly: ". . . depending on the point of view, a data object is characterized by its type (for the user) or by its structure (for the implementor)."[1]

Three Levels of Abstraction

The focus of *C++ Plus Data Structures* is on abstract data types as viewed from three different perspectives: their specification, their application, and their implementation. The specification describes the logical or abstract level. This level is concerned with *what* the operations do. The application level, sometimes called the user level, is concerned with how the data type might be used to solve a problem. This level is concerned with *why* the operations do what they do. The implementation level is where the operations are actually coded. This level is concerned with the *how* questions.

Within this focus, we stress computer science theory and software engineering principles, including modularization, data encapsulation, information hiding, data abstraction, object-oriented decomposition, functional decomposition, the analysis of

[1]Johannes J. Martin, *Data Types and Data Structures,* Prentice-Hall International Series in Computer Science, C. A. R. Hoare, Series Editor, Prentice-Hall International, (UK), LTD, 1986, p. 1.

algorithms, and life-cycle software verification methods. We feel strongly that these principles should be introduced to computer science students early in their education so that they learn to practice good software techniques from the beginning.

An understanding of theoretical concepts helps students put the new ideas they encounter into place, and practical advice allows them to apply what they have learned. To teach these concepts to students who may not have completed many college-level mathematics courses, we consistently use intuitive explanations, even for topics that have a basis in mathematics, like the analysis of algorithms. In all cases, our highest goal has been to make our explanations as readable and as easily understandable as possible.

Prerequisite Assumptions

In this book, we assume that the students are familiar with the following C++ constructs.

- Built-in simple data types
- Stream I/O as provided in `<iostream>`
- Stream I/O as provided in `<fstream>`
- Control structures while, do...while, for, if, and switch
- User-defined functions with value and reference parameters
- Built-in array types
- Class construct

We have included sidebars within the text to refresh the student's memory concerning some of the details of these topics.

Updates to the Fifth Edition

Terminology Object-oriented terminology now dominates computing vocabulary. For example, *Put* and *Get* are used to insert and retrieve items in/from a structure. The ADT operation names have been updated to reflect this terminology.

The use of an output parameter to define the meaning of a function return value is common in most language libraries, such as the Standard Template Library and the Java Collections Framework. Although this technique flies in the face of the principle that a function has only one return value, the students need to know this technique in order to read library code. Thus, the list operation *Get* returns the complete list item found or the same item for which it searched, depending on the value of *found*, a Boolean parameter.

The *GetNextItem* operation is now a function rather than a procedure with a return parameter. This structure is more convenient, because the function can appear within a statement that processes the item.

Case Studies A Case Study has been added to Chapter 3 and the Case Studies in Chapters 4 and 5 have been replaced. These three case studies are related in that they refer to a deck of playing cards. The ADTs Card and Deck are introduced in Chapter 3. Chapter 4 uses these ADTs to construct and evaluate Poker hands. Chapter 5 uses these ADTs to simulate a Solitaire game.

Exercises Additional exercises have been added to most chapters.

Content and Organization

Chapter 1 outlines the basic goals of high-quality software and the basic principles of software engineering for designing and implementing programs to meet these goals. Abstraction, functional decomposition, and object-oriented design are discussed. This chapter also addresses what we see as a critical need in software education: the ability to design and implement correct programs and to verify that they are actually correct. Topics covered include the concept of "life-cycle" verification; designing for correctness using preconditions and postconditions; the use of deskchecking and design/code walk-throughs and inspections to identify errors before testing; debugging techniques, data coverage (black box), and code coverage (clear or white box) approaches; test plans, unit testing, and structured integration testing using stubs and drivers. The concept of a generalized test driver is presented and executed in a Case Study that develops the ADT Fraction.

Chapter 2 presents data abstraction and encapsulation, the software engineering concepts that relate to the design of the data structures used in programs. Three perspectives of data are discussed: abstraction, implementation, and application. These perspectives are illustrated using a real-world example (a library), and then are applied to built-in data structures that C++ supports: structs and arrays. The C++ class type is presented as the way to represent the abstract data types we examine in subsequent chapters. The principles of object-oriented programming—encapsulation, inheritance, and polymorphism—are introduced here along with the accompanying C++ implementation constructs. The Case Study at the end of this chapter reinforces the ideas of data abstraction and encapsulation in designing and implementing a user-defined data type representing a date. This class is tested using a version of the generalized test driver.

Chapter 2 includes a discussion of two C++ constructs that help users write better software: namespace and exception handling using the *try/catch* statement. Various approaches to error handling are demonstrated in subsequent chapters.

Because there is more than one way to solve a problem, we discuss how competing solutions can be compared through the analysis of algorithms, using Big-O notation. Throughout the rest of the book, the ADT implementations are compared using Big-O notation.

The Case Study defines the ADT Date, implements the class, defines a test plan, and implements the test plan.

We would like to think that the material in Chapters 1 and 2 is a review for most students. However, the concepts in these two chapters are so crucial to the future of any and all students that we feel that we cannot rely on their having seen the material before.

Chapter 3 introduces the most fundamental abstract data type of them all: the unsorted list. The chapter begins with a general discussion of operations on abstract data types and then presents the framework with which all of the other data types are examined: a presentation and discussion of the specification, a brief application using the operations, and the design and coding of the operations. The specification is of the ADT Unsorted List. An array-based implementation of the specification is developed.

The concept of dynamic allocation is introduced, along with the syntax for using C++ pointer variables. The concept of linking nodes together to form lists is presented in clear detail with many diagrams. This technique is then used to re-implement the unsorted list. The array-based and linked implementations are compared using Big-O notation.

The Case Study designs the ADTs Card and Deck to represent a deck of playing cards. These are implemented as classes and tested.

Chapter 4 introduces the ADT Sorted List and develops the array-based implementation. The binary search is introduced as a way to improve the performance of the search operation in the sorted list. The ADT is then implemented using a linked implementation. These implementations are compared using Big-O notation.

Both the logical and physical distinctions between bound and unbound structures are discussed. The four-phase object-oriented methodology is presented and demonstrated in the Case Study that evaluates hands according to the rules of Texas Hold 'em Poker.

Chapter 5 introduces the ADTs Stack and Queue. Each ADT is first considered from its abstract perspective, and the idea of recording the logical abstraction in an ADT specification is stressed. The operations are used in an application program; then the set of operations is implemented in C++ using an array-based implementation, followed by a linked implementation. The Case Study simulates a Solitaire game, using the classes created in the chapter.

Chapter 6 is a collection of advanced concepts and techniques. Templates are introduced as a way of implementing generic classes. Circular linked lists and doubly linked lists are discussed. The insertion, deletion, and list traversal algorithms are developed and implemented for each variation. An alternative representation of a linked structure, using static allocation (an array of structs), is designed. Class copy constructors, operator overloading, and dynamic binding are covered in detail. The Case Study uses doubly linked lists to implement large integers.

Chapter 7 presents recursion, giving the student an intuitive understanding of the concept, and then shows how recursion can be used to solve programming problems. Guidelines for writing recursive functions are illustrated with many examples. After demonstrating that a by-hand simulation of a recursive routine can be very tedious, a simple three-question technique is introduced for verifying the correctness of recursive functions. Because many students are wary of recursion, the introduction to this material is deliberately intuitive and nonmathematical. A more detailed discussion of how recursion works leads to an understanding of how recursion can be replaced with iteration and stacks. The Case Study develops and implements the process of escaping form a maze.

Chapter 8 introduces binary search trees as a way to arrange data, giving the flexibility of a linked structure with $O(\log_2 N)$ insertion and deletion time. In order to build on the previous chapter and exploit the inherent recursive nature of binary trees, the algorithms first are presented recursively. After all the operations have been implemented recursively, we code the insertion and deletion operations iteratively to show the flexibility of binary search trees. A nonlinked array-based binary tree implementation is described. The Case Study discusses the process of building an index for a manuscript and implements the first phase.

Chapter 9 presents a collection of other branching structures: priority queues (implemented with both lists and heaps), graphs, and sets. The graph algorithms make use of stacks, queues, and priority queues, thus both reinforcing earlier material and demonstrating how general these structures are. Two set implementations are discussed: the bit-vector representation in which each item in the base set is assigned a present/absent flag and the operations are the built-in logic operations, and a list-based representation in which each item in a set is represented in a list of set items. If the item is not in the list, it is not in the set.

Chapter 10 presents a number of sorting and searching algorithms and asks the question: Which are better? The sorting algorithms that are illustrated, implemented, and compared include straight selection sort, two versions of bubble sort, quick sort, heap sort, and merge sort. The sorting algorithms are compared using Big-O notation. The discussion of algorithm analysis continues in the context of searching. Previously presented searching algorithms are reviewed and new ones are described. Hashing techniques are discussed in some detail. Finally, radix sort is presented and analyzed.

Additional Features

Chapter Goals A set of goals presented at the beginning of each chapter helps the students assess what they have learned. These goals are tested in the exercises at the end of each chapter.

Chapter Exercises Most chapters have more than 40 exercises. They vary in levels of difficulty, including short programming problems, the analysis of algorithms, and problems to test the student's understanding of concepts. The answer key for the exercises can be found in the *Instructor's Manual.*

Case Studies There are eight case studies. Each includes a problem description, an analysis of the problem input and required output, and a discussion of the appropriate data types to use. Most of the case studies are completely coded and tested. Two are left partially complete, requiring the student to complete and test the final versions.

Student and Instructor Resources Source code for all programs, partial programs, and case studies within the text are available for student and instructor download at go.jblearning.com/ndale. In addition, instructors may access the following resources:

- Instructor's Manual with goals, teaching notes, workouts (suggestions for in-class activities), programming assignments for each chapter, and answers to the end-of-chapter exercises.
- PowerPoint Presentations
- Test Bank

Acknowledgments

First we would like to thank the twenty-four people who replied to our Web survey concerning this new edition. Respondents included both users and non-users of one of the previous editions. Your comments were invaluable: Thank you.

Thanks to my friends and family, who have been such a support over the last year. Thanks to my tennis friends, who kept me fit, and my bridge friends, who challenged my mind.

A virtual bouquet of roses to the people who have worked on this book: Mike and Sigrid Wile along with our Jones & Bartlett Learning family: Tim Anderson, our editor, and Amy Rose, our production goddess.

N. D.

chapter 1

Software Engineering Principles

Goals

After studying this chapter, you should be able to

- Describe the general activities in the software life cycle
- Describe the goals for "quality" software
- Explain the following terms: software requirements, software specifications, algorithm, information hiding, abstraction, stepwise refinement
- Explain and apply the fundamental ideas of top-down design
- Explain and apply the fundamental ideas of object-oriented design
- Explain how CRC cards and UML diagrams can be used in software design
- Identify several sources of program errors
- Describe strategies to avoid software errors
- Specify the preconditions and postconditions of a program segment or function
- Show how deskchecking, code walk-throughs, and design and code inspections can improve software quality and reduce the software development effort
- Explain the following terms: acceptance tests, regression testing, verification, validation, functional domain, black-box testing, white-box testing
- State several testing goals and indicate when each would be appropriate
- Describe several integration-testing strategies and indicate when each would be appropriate
- Explain how program verification techniques can be applied throughout the software development process
- Create a C++ test driver program to test a simple class

At this point in your computing career, you have completed at least one semester of computer science course work. You can take a problem of medium complexity, write an algorithm to solve the problem, code the algorithm in C++, and demonstrate the correctness of your solution. At least, that's what the syllabus for your introductory class said you should be able to do when you complete the course. Now that you are starting your second (or third?) semester, it is time to stop and review those principles that, if adhered to, guarantee that you can indeed do what your previous syllabus claimed.

In this chapter, we review the software design process and the verification of software correctness. In Chapter 2, we review data design and implementation.

1.1 The Software Process

When we consider computer programming, we immediately think of writing a program for a computer to execute—the generation of code in some computer language. As a beginning student of computer science, you wrote programs that solved relatively simple problems. Much of your initial effort went into learning the syntax of a programming language such as C++: the language's reserved words, its data types, its constructs for selection (`if-else` and `switch`) and looping (`while`, `do while`, and `for`), and its input/output mechanisms (`cin` and `cout`).

You may have learned a programming methodology that took you from the problem description that your instructor handed out all the way through the delivery of a good software solution. Programmers have created many design techniques, coding standards, and testing methods to help develop high-quality software. But why bother with all that methodology? Why not just sit down at a computer and write programs? Aren't we wasting a lot of time and effort, when we could just get started on the "real" job?

If the degree of our programming sophistication never had to rise above the level of trivial programs (like summing a list of prices or averaging grades), we might get away with such a code-first technique (or, rather, *lack* of technique). Some new programmers work this way, hacking away at the code until the program works more or less correctly—usually less.

As your programs grow larger and more complex, you must pay attention to other software issues in addition to coding. If you become a software professional, you may work as part of a team that develops a system containing tens of thousands, or even millions, of lines of code. The successful creation of complex programs requires an organized approach. We use the term software engineering to refer to the discipline concerned with all aspects of the development of high-quality software systems. It encompasses *all* variations of techniques used during the software life cycle plus supporting activities such as documentation and teamwork. A software process is a specific set of inter-related software engineering techniques, used by a person or organization to create a system.

Software engineering The discipline devoted to the design, production, and maintenance of computer programs that are developed on time and within cost estimates, using tools that help to manage the size and complexity of the resulting software products

Software process A standard, integrated set of software engineering tools and techniques used on a project or by an organization

Software engineering is a broad field. Most computing education programs devote one or more advanced courses to the topic. In fact, there are several schools that offer degrees in the discipline. This section provides a brief introduction to this important field.

Software Life Cycles

The term "software engineering" was coined in the 1960s, to emphasize that engineering-like discipline is required when creating software. At that time software development was characterized by haphazard approaches with little organization. The primary early contribution of the disciplined approach was the identification and study of the various activities involved in developing successful systems. These activities make up the "life cycle" of a software project and include

- *Problem analysis* Understanding the nature of the problem to be solved
- *Requirements elicitation* Determining exactly what the program must do
- *Requirements specification* Specifying what the program must do (the functional requirements) and the constraints on the solution approach (non-functional requirements, such as what language to use)
- *High- and low-level design* Recording how the program meets the requirements, from the "big picture" overview to the detailed design
- *Implementation of the design* Coding a program in a computer language
- *Testing and verification* Detecting and fixing errors and demonstrating the correctness of the program
- *Delivery* Turning over the tested program to the customer or user (or instructor!)
- *Operation* Actually using the program
- *Maintenance* Making changes to fix operational errors and to add or modify the function of the program

Classically, these activities were performed in the sequence shown above. Each stage would culminate in the creation of structured documentation, which would provide the foundation upon which to build the following stage. This became known as the "waterfall" life cycle, because its graphical depiction resembled a cascading waterfall, as shown in Figure 1.1a. Each stage's documented output would be fed into the following stage, like water flowing down a river.

The waterfall approach was widely used for a number of years, and was instrumental in organizing software development. However, software projects differ from one another in many important ways, for example size, duration, scope, required reliability, and application area. It is not reasonable to expect that one life cycle approach is best for all projects. The waterfall approach's inflexible partitioning of projects into separate stages and its heavy emphasis on documentation caused it to lose popularity. It is still useful when requirements are well understood and unlikely to change, but that is often not the case for modern software development.

Alternate life cycle approaches evolved for projects that did not conform well to the waterfall cycle. For example, the Spiral Model depicted in Figure 1.1b directly addresses major risks inherent in software development, for example the risk of creating an

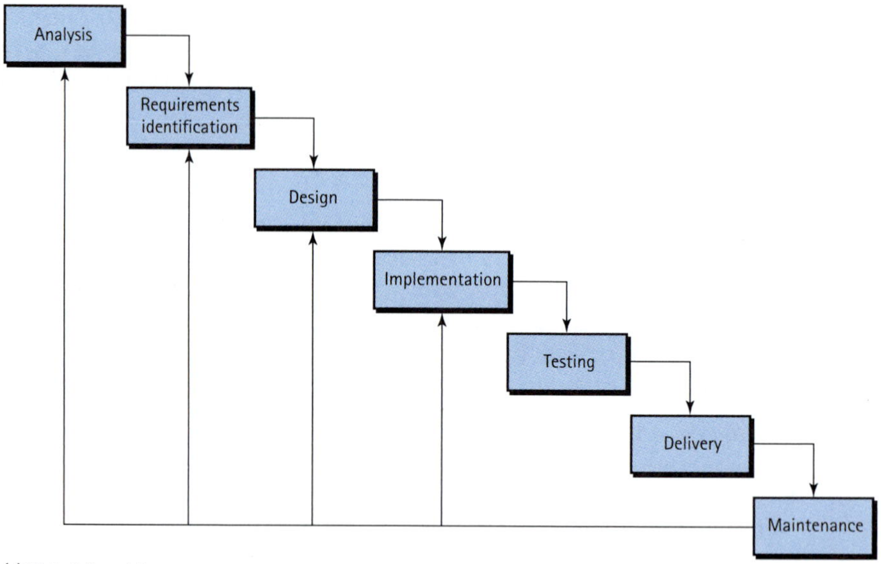

(a) Waterfall model

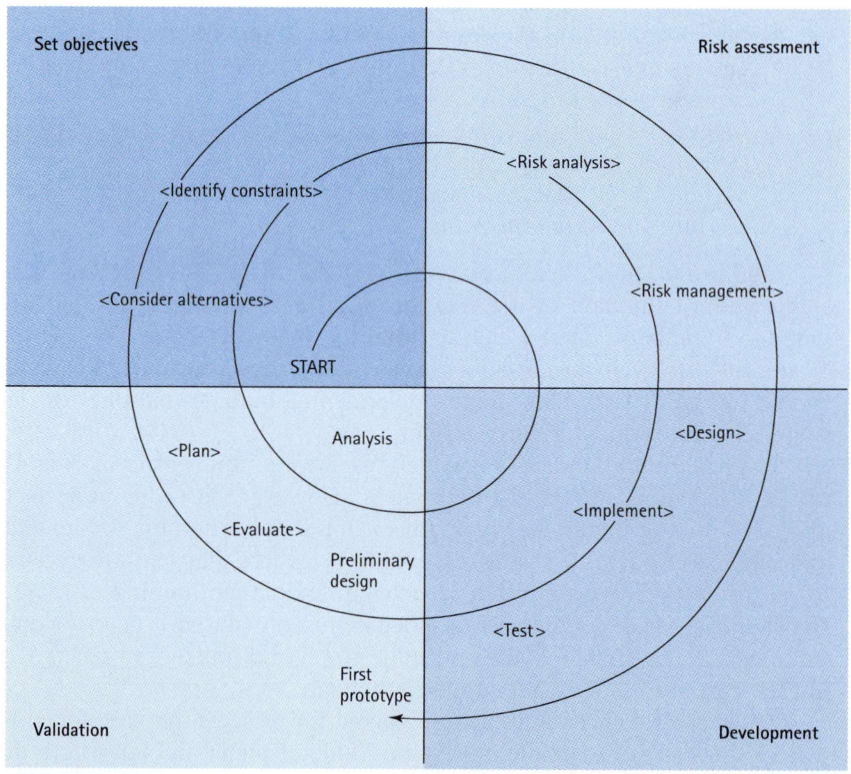

(b) Spiral model

Figure 1.1 *Life-cycle models*

unneeded product, the risk of including unnecessary features, and the risk of creating a confusing interface. Important activities, such as objective-setting, risk assessment, development and validation, are repeated over and over in a spiral manner as the project moves from its original concept to its final form. Unlike the waterfall model, where development blindly proceeds until the testing stage is reached, the spiral model emphasizes continual assessment and adjustment of goals.

Many other models of the software process have been defined. There are models that emphasize prototyping, models for real time systems development, and models that emphasize creative problem solving. In one sense, there are as many models as there are organizations that develop software. Each organization, if they have wise management, pulls ideas from the various standard approaches that best fit with their goals and create their own version of the life cycle, one that works best for them. The top organizations constantly measure how well their approach is working and attempt to continually improve their process. Software development in the real world is not easy and requires good organization, flexibility, and vigilant management.

A Programmer's Toolboxes

What makes our jobs as programmers or software engineers challenging is the tendency of software to grow in size and complexity and to change at every stage of its development. Part of a good software process is the use of tools to manage this size and complexity. Usually a programmer has several toolboxes, each containing tools that help to build and shape a software product.

Hardware One toolbox contains the hardware itself: the computers and their peripheral devices (such as monitors, terminals, storage devices, and printers), on which and for which we develop software.

Software A second toolbox contains various software tools: operating systems to control the computer's resources, text editors to help us enter programs, compilers to translate high-level languages like C++ into something that the computer can execute, interactive debugging programs, test-data generators, and so on. You've used some of these tools already.

Ideaware A third toolbox is filled with the shared body of knowledge that programmers have collected over time. This box contains the algorithms that we use to solve common programming problems as well as data structures for modeling the information processed by our programs. Recall that an algorithm is a step-by-step description of the solution to a problem. How we choose between two algorithms that carry out the same task often depends on the requirements of a particular application. If no relevant requirements exist, the choice may be based on the programmer's own style.

> **Algorithm** A logical sequence of discrete steps that describes a complete solution to a given problem, computable in a finite amount of time

Ideaware contains programming methodologies such as top-down and object-oriented design and software concepts, including information hiding, data encapsulation, and abstraction. It includes aids for creating designs such as CRC (Classes, Responsibilities, and

Collaborations) cards and methods for describing designs such as the UML (Unified Modeling Language). It also contains some tools for measuring, evaluating, and proving the correctness of our programs. We devote most of this book to exploring the contents of this third toolbox.

Some might argue that using these tools takes the creativity out of programming, but we don't believe that to be true. Artists and composers are creative, yet their innovations are grounded in the basic principles of their crafts. Similarly, the most creative programmers build high-quality software through the disciplined use of basic programming tools.

Goals of Quality Software

Quality software entails much more than a program that somehow accomplishes the task at hand. A good program achieves the following goals:

1. It works.
2. It can be modified without excessive time and effort.
3. It is reusable.
4. It is completed on time and within budget.

It's not easy to meet these goals, but they are all important.

Goal 1: Quality Software Works The program must do the task it was designed to perform, and it must do it correctly and completely. Thus the first step in the development process is to determine exactly what the program is required to do. To write a program that works, you first need to have a definition of the program's requirements. For students, the requirements often are included in the instructor's problem description: "Write a program that calculates. . . ." For programmers working on a government contract, the requirements document may be hundreds of pages long.

> **Requirements** A statement of what is to be provided by a computer system or software product
>
> **Software specification** A detailed description of the function, inputs, processing, outputs, and special requirements of a software product; it provides the information needed to design and implement the program

We develop programs that meet the user's requirements using software specifications. The specifications indicate the format of the input and the expected output, details about processing, performance measures (how fast? how big? how accurate?), what to do in case of errors, and so on. The specifications tell exactly *what* the program does, but not *how* it is done. Sometimes your instructor will provide detailed specifications; other times you may have to write them yourself, based on the requirements definition, conversations with your instructor, or guesswork. (We discuss this issue in more detail later in this chapter.)

How do you know when the program is right? A program must be *complete* (it should "do everything" specified) and *correct* (it should "do it right") to meet its requirements. In addition, it should be *usable*. For instance, if the program needs to receive data from a person sitting at a terminal, it must indicate when it expects input. The program's outputs should be readable and understandable to users. Indeed, creating a good user interface is an important subject in software engineering today.

Finally, Goal 1 means that the program should be as *efficient as it needs to be*. We would never deliberately write programs that waste time or space in memory, but not all programs demand great efficiency. When they do, however, we must meet these demands or else the programs will not satisfy the requirements. A space-launch control program, for instance, must execute in "real time"; that is, the software must process commands, perform calculations, and display results in coordination with the activities it is supposed to control. Closer to home, if a desktop-publishing program cannot update the screen as rapidly as the user can type, the program is not as efficient as it needs to be. In such a case, if the software isn't efficient enough, it doesn't meet its requirements; thus, according to our definition, it doesn't work correctly. In Chapter 2, we introduce a way to compare the efficiency of different algorithms.

To summarize, a typical program needs to be

- *complete*: It should "do everything" needed.
- *correct*: It should "do it right."
- *usable*: Its user interface should be "easy to work with."
- *efficient*: It should finish in a "reasonable amount of time" considering the complexity and size of the task.

Goal 2: Quality Software Can Be Modified When does software need to be modified? Changes occur in every phase of its existence.

Software gets changed in the design phase. When your instructor or employer gives you a programming assignment, you begin to think of how to solve the problem. The next time you meet, however, you may be notified of a small change in the program description.

Software gets changed in the coding phase. You make changes in your program as a result of compilation errors. Sometimes you suddenly see a better solution to a part of the problem after the program has been coded, so you make changes.

Software gets changed in the testing phase. If the program crashes or yields wrong results, you must make corrections.

In an academic environment, the life of the software typically ends when a corrected program is turned in to be graded. When software is developed for real-world use, however, most of the changes take place during the "maintenance" phase. Someone may discover an error that wasn't uncovered in testing, someone else may want to include additional functions, a third party may want to change the input format, and a fourth person may want to run the program on another system.

As you see, software changes often and in all phases of its life cycle. Knowing this fact, software engineers try to develop programs that are modified easily. If you think it is a simple matter to change a program, try to make a "small change" in the last program you wrote. It's difficult to remember all the details of a program after some time has passed, isn't it? Modifications to programs often are not even made by the original authors but rather by subsequent maintenance programmers. (Someday you may be the one making the modifications to someone else's program.)

What makes a program easy to modify? First, it should be readable and understandable to humans. Before it can be changed, it must be understood. A well-designed, clearly written, well-documented program is certainly easier for human readers to understand. The number of pages of documentation required for "real-world" programs usually exceeds the number of pages of code. Almost every organization has its own policy for documentation. Reading a well-written program can teach you techniques that help you write good programs. In fact, it's difficult to imagine how anyone could become a good programmer *without* reading good programs.

Second, the program should readily be able to withstand small changes. The key idea is to partition your programs into manageable pieces that work together to solve the problem, yet remain relatively independent. The design methodologies reviewed later in this chapter should help you write programs that meet this goal.

Goal 3: Quality Software Is Reusable It takes time and effort to create quality software. Therefore, it is important to realize as much value from the software as possible.

One way to save time and effort when building a software solution is to reuse programs, classes, functions, and other components from previous projects. By using previously designed and tested code, you arrive at your solution sooner and with less effort. Alternatively, when you create software to solve a problem, it is sometimes possible to structure that software so it can help solve future, related problems. By doing so, you gain more value from the software created.

Creating reusable software does not happen automatically. It requires extra effort during the specification and design phases. To be reusable, software must be well documented and easy to read, so that a programmer can quickly determine whether it can be used for a new project. It usually has a simple interface so that it can easily be plugged into another system. It is also modifiable (Goal 2), in case a small change is needed to adapt it to the new system.

When creating software to fulfill a narrow, specific function, you can sometimes make the software more generally usable with a minimal amount of extra effort. In this way, you increase the chances that you can reuse the software later. For example, if you are creating a routine that sorts a list of integers into increasing order, you might generalize the routine so that it can also sort other types of data. Furthermore, you could design the routine to accept the desired sort order, increasing or decreasing, as a parameter.

One of the main reasons for the rise in popularity of object-oriented approaches is that they lend themselves to reuse. Previous reuse approaches were hindered by inappropriate units of reuse. If the unit of reuse is too small, then the work saved is not worth the effort. If the unit of reuse is too large, then it is difficult to combine it with other system elements. Object-oriented classes, when designed properly, can be very appropriate units of reuse. A class encapsulates both data and actions on the data, making it ideal for reuse.

Goal 4: Quality Software Is Completed on Time and Within Budget You know what happens in school when you turn in your program late. You probably have grieved over an otherwise perfect program that received only half credit—or no credit at all—because you turned it in one day late. "But the network was down five hours last night!" you protest.

Although the consequences of tardiness may seem arbitrary in the academic world, they are significant in the business world. The software for controlling a space launch must be developed and tested before the launch can take place. A patient database system for a new hospital must be installed before the hospital can open. In such cases, the program doesn't meet its requirements if it isn't ready when needed.

"Time is money" may sound trite but failure to meet deadlines is *expensive*. A company generally budgets a certain amount of time and money for the development of a piece of software. As a programmer, you are paid a salary or an hourly wage. If your part of the project is only 80% complete when the deadline arrives, the company must pay you—or another programmer—to finish the work. The extra expenditure in salary is not the only cost, however. Other workers may be waiting to integrate your part of the program into the system for testing. If the program is part of a contract with a customer, monetary penalties may be assessed for missed deadlines. If it is being developed for commercial sales, the company may be beaten to the market by a competitor and eventually forced out of business.

Once you have identified your goals, what can you do to meet them? Where should you start? Software engineers use many tools and techniques. In the next few sections of this chapter, we review some of these techniques to help you understand, design, and code programs.

Specification: Understanding the Problem

No matter which programming design technique you use, the first steps are always the same. Imagine the following all-too-familiar situation. On the third day of class, you are given a 12-page description of Programming Assignment 1, which must be running perfectly and turned in by noon, one week from yesterday. You read the assignment and realize that this program is three times larger than any program you have ever written. What is your first step?

The responses listed here are typical of those given by a class of computer science students in such a situation:

1. Panic 39%
2. Sit down at the computer and begin typing 30%
3. Drop the course 27%
4. Stop and think 4%

Response 1 is a predictable reaction from students who have not learned good programming techniques. Students who adopt Response 3 will find their education progressing rather slowly. Response 2 may seem to be a good idea, especially considering the deadline looming ahead. Resist the temptation, though—the first step is to *think*. Before you can come up with a program solution, you must understand the problem. Read the assignment, and then read it again. Ask questions of your instructor (or manager, or client). Starting early affords you many opportunities to ask questions; starting the night before the program is due leaves you no opportunity at all.

The problem with writing first is that it tends to lock you into the first solution you think of, which may not be the best approach. We have a natural tendency to believe that once we've put something in writing, we have invested too much in the idea to toss it out and start over.

On the other hand, don't agonize about all the possibilities until the day before your deadline. (Chances are that a disk drive, network, or printer will fail that day!) When you think you understand the problem, you should begin writing your design.

Writing Detailed Specifications

Many writers experience a moment of terror when faced with a blank piece of paper—where to begin? As a programmer, however, you don't have to wonder about where to begin. Using the assignment description (your "requirements"), first write a complete definition of the problem, including the details of the expected inputs and outputs, the necessary processing and error handling, and all assumptions about the problem. When you finish this task, you have a *detailed specification*—a formal definition of the problem your program must solve, which tells you exactly what the program should do. In addition, the process of writing the specifications brings to light any holes in the requirements. For instance, are embedded blanks in the input significant or can they be ignored? Do you need to check for errors in the input? On which computer system(s) will your program run? If you get the answers to these questions at this stage, you can design and code your program correctly from the start.

Many software engineers work with user/operational *scenarios* to understand the requirements. In software design, a scenario is a sequence of events for *one* execution of the program. For example, a designer might consider the following scenario when developing the software for a bank's automated teller machine (ATM):

1. The customer inserts a bank card.
2. The ATM reads the account number on the card.
3. The ATM requests a PIN (personal identification number) from the customer.
4. The customer enters 5683.
5. The ATM successfully verifies the account number/PIN combination.
6. The ATM asks the customer to select a transaction type (deposit, show balance, withdrawal, or quit).
7. The customer selects the show balance option.
8. The ATM obtains the current account balance ($1,204.35) and displays it.
9. The ATM asks the customer to select a transaction type (deposit, show balance, withdrawal, or quit).
10. The customer selects quit.
11. The ATM returns the customer's bank card.

Scenarios allow us to get a feel for the behavior expected from the system. Of course, a single scenario cannot show all possible behaviors. For this reason, software engineers typically prepare many different scenarios to gain a full understanding of the system's requirements.

You must know some details to write and run the program. Other details, if not explicitly stated in the program's requirements, may be handled according to the programmer's preference. Assumptions about unstated or ambiguous specifications should always be written explicitly in the program's documentation.

The detailed specification clarifies the problem to be solved. But it does more than that: It also serves as an important piece of written documentation about the program. There are many ways in which specifications may be expressed and a number of different sections that may be included, depending on the nature of the problem. Our recommended program specification includes the following sections:

- Processing requirements
- Sample inputs with expected outputs
- Assumptions

If special processing is needed for unusual or error conditions, it should be specified as well. Sometimes it is helpful to include a section containing definitions of terms used. Likewise, it may prove useful to list any testing requirements so that verifying the program is considered early in the development process.

1.2 Program Design

Remember, the specification of the program tells *what* the program must do, but not *how* it does it. Once you have fully clarified the goals of the program, you can begin to develop and record a strategy for meeting them; in other words, you can begin the design phase of the software life cycle. In this section, we review some ideaware tools that are used for software design, including abstraction, information hiding, stepwise refinement, and visual tools.

Abstraction

The universe is filled with complex systems. We learn about such systems through *models*. A model may be mathematical, like equations describing the motion of satellites around the earth. A physical object such as a model airplane used in wind-tunnel tests is another form of model. In this approach to understanding complex systems, the important concept is that we consider only the essential characteristics of the system; we ignore minor or irrelevant details. For example, although the earth is an oblate ellipsoid, globes (models of the earth) are spheres. The small difference between the earth's equatorial diameter and polar diameter is not important to us in studying the political divisions and physical landmarks on the earth. Similarly, the model airplanes used to study aerodynamics do not include in-flight movies.

An abstraction is a model of a complex system that includes only the essential details. Abstractions are the fundamental way that we manage complexity. Different viewers use different abstractions of a particular system. Thus, while we may see a car as a means to transport us and our friends, the automotive brake engineer may see it as a large mass with a small contact area between it and the road (Figure 1.2).

> **Abstraction** A model of a complex system that includes only the details essential to the perspective of the viewer of the system
>
> **Module** A cohesive system subunit that performs a share of the work

What does abstraction have to do with software development? The programs we write are abstractions. A spreadsheet program that is used by an accountant models the books used to record debits and credits. An educational computer game about wildlife models an ecosystem. Writing software is difficult because both the systems we model and the processes we use to develop the software are complex. One of our major goals is to convince you to use abstractions to manage the complexity of developing software. In nearly every chapter, we make use of abstraction to simplify our work.

Information Hiding

Many design methods are based on decomposing a problem's solution into modules. A module is a cohesive system subunit that performs a share of the work. Decomposing a

Figure 1.2 *An abstraction includes the essential details relative to the perspective of the viewer*

Information hiding The practice of hiding the details of a function or data structure with the goal of controlling access to the details of a module or structure

system into modules helps us manage complexity. Additionally, the modules can form the basis of assignments for different programming teams working separately on a large system. One important feature of any design method is that the details that are specified in lower levels of the program design remain hidden from the higher levels. The programmer sees only the details that are relevant at a particular level of the design. This information hiding makes certain details inaccessible to the programmer at higher levels.

Modules act as an abstraction tool. Because the complexity of its internal structure can be hidden from the rest of the system, the details involved in implementing a module remain isolated from the details of the rest of the system.

Why is hiding the details desirable? Shouldn't the programmer know everything? *No!* In this situation, a certain amount of ignorance truly is advantageous. Information hiding prevents the higher levels of the design from becoming dependent on low-level design details that are more likely to be changed. For example, you can stop a car without knowing whether it has disc brakes or drum brakes. You don't need to know these lower-level details of the car's brake subsystem to stop it.

Furthermore, you don't want to require a complete understanding of the complicated details of low-level routines for the design of higher-level routines. Such a requirement would introduce a greater risk of confusion and error throughout the whole program. For example, it would be disastrous if every time we wanted to stop our car, we had to think, "The brake pedal is a lever with a mechanical advantage of 10.6 coupled to a hydraulic system with a mechanical advantage of 7.3 that presses a semi-metallic pad against a steel disc. The coefficient of friction of the pad/disc contact is...."

Information hiding is not limited to driving cars and programming computers. Try to list *all* the operations and information required to make a peanut butter and jelly sandwich. We normally don't consider the details of planting, growing, and harvesting peanuts, grapes, and wheat as part of making a sandwich. Information hiding lets us deal with only those operations and information needed at a particular level in the solution of a problem.

The concepts of abstraction and information hiding are fundamental principles of software engineering. We will come back to them again and again throughout this book. Besides helping us manage the complexity of a large system, abstraction and information hiding support our quality-related goals of modifiability and reusability. In a well-designed system, most modifications can be localized to just a few modules. Such changes are much easier to make than changes that permeate the entire system. Additionally, a good system design results in the creation of generic modules that can be used in other systems.

To achieve these goals, modules should be good abstractions with strong *cohesion*; that is, each module should have a single purpose or identity and the module should stick together well. A cohesive module can usually be described by a simple sentence. If you have to use several sentences or one very convoluted sentence to describe your module, it is probably *not* cohesive. Each module should also exhibit information hiding so that changes within it do not result in changes in the modules that use it. This independent quality of modules is known as *loose coupling*. If your module depends on the internal details of other modules, it is *not* loosely coupled.

Stepwise Refinement

In addition to concepts such as abstraction and information hiding, software developers need practical approaches to conquer complexity. Stepwise refinement is a widely applicable approach. Many variations of it exist, such as top-down, bottom-up, functional decomposition, and even "round-trip gestalt design." Undoubtedly you have learned a variation of stepwise refinement in your studies, as it is a standard method for organizing and writing essays, term papers, and books. For example, to write a book an author first determines the main theme and the major subthemes. Next, the chapter topics can be identified, followed by section and subsection topics. Outlines can be produced and further refined for each subsection. At some point the author is ready to add detail—to actually begin writing sentences.

In general, with stepwise refinement, a problem is approached in stages. Similar steps are followed during each stage, with the only difference reflecting the level of detail involved. The completion of each stage brings us closer to solving our problem. Let's look at some variations of stepwise refinement:

- *Top-down* With this approach, the problem is first broken into several large parts. Each of these parts is, in turn, divided into sections, the sections are subdivided, and so on. The important feature is that *details are deferred as long as possible* as we move from a general to a specific solution. The outline approach to writing a book involves a form of top-down stepwise refinement.
- *Bottom-up* As you might guess, with this approach the details come first. Bottom-up development is the opposite of the top-down approach. After the detailed components are identified and designed, they are brought together into increasingly higher-level components. This technique could be used, for example, by the author of a cookbook who first writes all the recipes and then decides how to organize them into sections and chapters.

- *Functional decomposition* This program design approach encourages programming in logical action units, called functions. The main module of the design becomes the main program (also called the main function), and subsections develop into functions. This hierarchy of tasks forms the basis for functional decomposition, with the main program or function controlling the processing. The general function of the method is continually divided into subfunctions until the level of detail is considered fine enough to code. Functional decomposition is top-down stepwise refinement with an emphasis on functionality.
- *Round-trip gestalt design* This confusing term is used to define the stepwise refinement approach to object-oriented design suggested by Grady Booch,[1] one of the leaders of the "object" movement. First, the tangible items and events in the problem domain are identified and assigned to candidate classes and objects. Next, the external properties and relationships of these classes and objects are defined. Finally, the internal details are addressed; unless these are trivial, the designer must return to the first step for another round of design. This approach entails top-down stepwise refinement with an emphasis on objects and data.

Good software designers typically use a combination of the stepwise refinement techniques described here.

Visual Tools

Abstraction, information hiding, and stepwise refinement are interrelated methods for controlling complexity during the design of a system. We now look at some tools that can help us visualize our designs. Diagrams are used in many professions. For example, architects use blueprints, investors use market trend graphs, and truck drivers use maps.

Software engineers use different types of diagrams and tables, such as the Unified Modeling Language (UML) and Class, Responsibility, and Collaboration (CRC) cards. The UML is used to specify, visualize, construct, and document the components of a software system. It combines the best practices that have evolved over the past several decades for modeling

---

[1]Grady Booch, *Object Oriented Design with Applications* (Benjamin Cummings, 1991).

systems, and it is particularly well suited to modeling object-oriented designs. UML diagrams represent another form of abstraction. They hide implementation details and allow systems designers to concentrate on only the major design components. UML includes a large variety of interrelated diagram types, each with its own set of icons and connectors. A very powerful development and modeling tool, it is helpful for modeling and documenting designs after they have been developed. See Figure 1.3a.

In contrast, CRC cards are a notational tool that helps us determine our initial designs. CRC cards were first described by Beck and Cunningham, in 1989, as a means to allow object-oriented programmers to identify a set of cooperating classes to solve a problem.

a. A UML Diagram

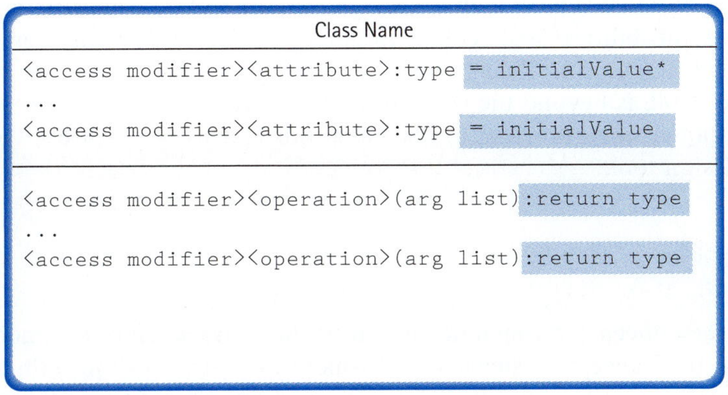

*Shaded areas are optional.

b. A CRC Card

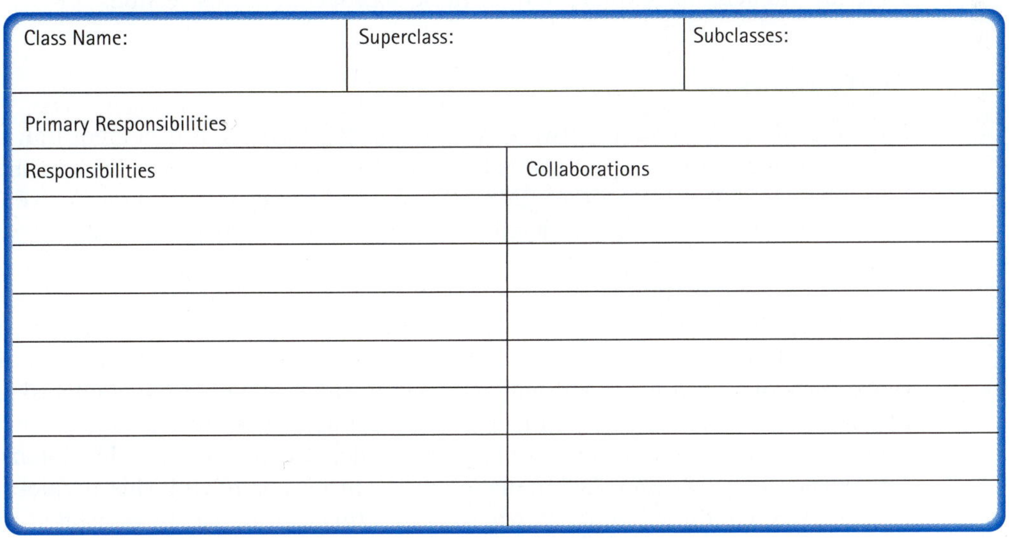

Figure 1.3 *UML Class Diagram and CRC Card*

A programmer uses a physical 4″ × 6″ index card to represent each class that had been identified as part of a problem solution. Figure 1.3b shows a blank CRC card. If the class is of general use, the CRC card may have a place to record the class's primary responsibility. It always contains room for the following information about a class:

1. Class name
2. Responsibilities of the class—usually represented by verbs and implemented by public functions (called methods in object-oriented terminology)
3. Collaborations—other classes or objects that are used in fulfilling the responsibilities

CRC cards are great tools for refining an object-oriented design, especially in a team programming environment. They provide a physical manifestation of the building blocks of a system that allows programmers to walk through user scenarios, identifying and assigning responsibilities and collaborations. We discuss a problem-solving methodology using CRC cards in Chapter 3.

Covering all of UML is beyond the scope of this text. We will however use the UML class diagram as shown in Figure 1.3a to document our classes. We will use CRC cards throughout as a design tool.

1.3 Design Approaches

We have defined the concept of a module, described the characteristics of a good module, and presented the concept of stepwise refinement as a strategy for defining modules. But what should these modules be? How do we define them? One approach is to break the problem into *functional* subproblems (do this, then do this, then do that). Another approach is to divide the problem into the "things" or objects that interact to solve the problem. We explore both of these approaches in this section.

Top-Down Design

One method for designing software is based on the functional decomposition and top-down strategies. First the problem is broken into several large tasks. Each of these tasks is, in turn, divided into sections, the sections are subdivided, and so on. As we said previously, the key feature is that details are deferred as long as possible as we move from a general to a specific solution.

To develop a computer program by this method, we begin with a "big picture" solution to the problem defined in the specification. We then devise a general strategy for solving the problem by dividing it into manageable functional modules. Next, each of the large functional modules is subdivided into several tasks. We do not need to write the top level of the functional design in source code (such as C++); rather, we can write it in English or "pseudocode." (Some software development projects even use special design languages that can be compiled.) This divide-and-conquer activity continues until we reach a level that can be easily translated into lines of code.

Once it has been divided into modules, the problem is simpler to code into a well-structured program. The functional decomposition approach encourages programming in logical units, using functions. The main module of the design becomes the main program (also called the main function), and subsections develop into functions. This *hierarchy of tasks* forms the basis for functional decomposition, with the main program or function controlling the processing.

As an example, let's start the functional design for making a cake.

Make Cake

Get ingredients
Mix cake ingredients
Bake
Cool
Apply icing

The problem now is divided into five logical units, each of which might be further decomposed into more detailed functional modules. Figure 1.4 illustrates the hierarchy of such a functional decomposition.

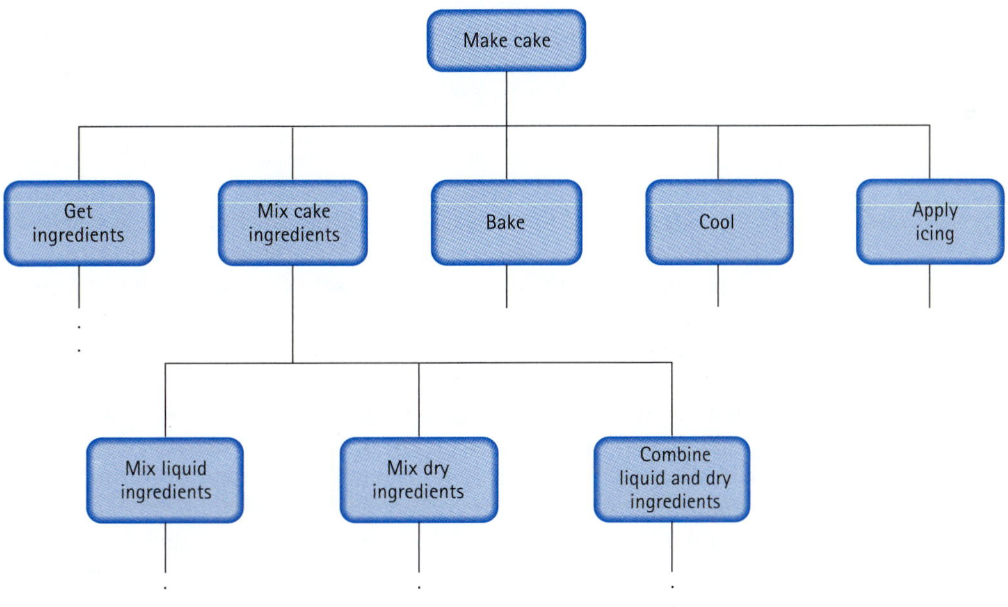

Figure 1.4 *A portion of a functional design for baking a cake*

Object-Oriented Design

In object-oriented design, the first steps are to identify the simplest and most widely used objects and processes in the decomposition and to implement them faithfully. Once you have completed this stage, you often can reuse these objects and processes to implement more complex objects and processes. This *hierarchy of objects* forms the basis for object-oriented design.

Object-oriented design, like top-down design, takes a divide-and-conquer approach. However, instead of decomposing the problem into functional modules, we divide it into entities or things that make sense in the context of the problem being solved. These entities, called *objects*, collaborate and interact to solve the problem. The code that allows these objects to interact is called a *driver program*.

Let's list some of the objects in our baking problem. There are, of course, all of the various ingredients: eggs, milk, flour, butter, and so on. We also need certain pieces of equipment, such as pans, bowls, measuring spoons, and an oven. The baker is another important entity. All of these entities must collaborate to create a cake. For example, a spoon measures individual ingredients and a bowl holds a mixture of ingredients.

Groups of objects with similar properties and behaviors are described by an object class (usually shortened to *class*). Each oven in the world is a unique object. We cannot hope to describe every oven, but we can group oven objects together into a class called oven that has certain properties and behaviors.

Object class (class) The description of a group of objects with similar properties and behaviors; a pattern for creating individual objects

An object class is similar to a C++ `class` (see the sidebar on page 19 on class syntax and the discussion in Chapter 2). C++ types are templates for variables; classes are templates for objects. Like types, object classes have attributes and operations associated with them. For example, an oven class might have an attribute to specify whether it is gas or electric and operations to turn it on or off and to set it to maintain a desired temperature.

With object-oriented design, we determine the classes from the things in the problem as described in the problem statement. We record each object class using a CRC card. From this work, we determine a set of properties (attributes) and a set of responsibilities (operations) to associate with each class. With object-oriented design, the *functionality* of the program is distributed among a set of collaborating objects. Table 1.1 illustrates some of the object classes that participate in baking a cake.

Once we have defined an oven class, we can reuse it in other cooking problems, such as roasting a turkey. Reuse of classes is an important aspect of modern software development. One major goal of this text is to introduce you to a number of classes that are particularly important in the development of software—*abstract data types*. We discuss the concept of an abstract data type in detail in Chapter 2. Throughout the book, we fully develop many abstract data types, and we describe others leaving you to develop them yourself. As these classes are fundamental to computer science, we can often obtain the C++ code for them from a public or private repository or purchase it from vendors who market C++ components. In fact, the C++ language standard includes components in the Standard Template Library (STL). You may wonder why, if they are already available, we spend so much time on their development. Our goal is to teach

Table 1.1 *Example of Object Classes That Participate in Baking a Cake*

Class	Attributes	Responsibilities (Operations)
Oven	Energy source Size Temperature Number of racks	Turn on Turn off Set desired temperature
Bowl	Capacity Current amount	Add to Dump
Egg	Size	Crack Separate (white from yolk)

you how to develop software. As with any skill, you need to practice the fundamentals before you can become a virtuoso.

To summarize, top-down design methods focus on the *process* of transforming the input into the output, resulting in a hierarchy of tasks. Object-oriented design focuses on the *data objects* that are to be transformed, resulting in a hierarchy of objects. Grady Booch puts it this way: "Read the specification of the software you want to build. Underline the verbs if you are after procedural code, the nouns if you aim for an object-oriented program."[2]

We propose that you circle the nouns and underline the verbs. The nouns become objects; the verbs become operations. In a functional design, the verbs are the primary focus; in an object-oriented design, the nouns are the primary focus.

C++ Class Syntax

A C++ class contains both data and functions that operate on the data. A class is declared in two parts: the specification of the class and the implementation of the class functions.

```
class DateType
{
public:
  void  Initialize(int, int, int);
  // Initializes month, day, and year.
  int GetMonth() const;
  // Returns month.
  int GetDay() const;
  // Returns day.
  int GetYear() const;
  // Returns year.
private:
  int month;
```

[2]Grady Booch, "What Is and Isn't Object Oriented Design." *American Programmer*, special issue on object orientation, vol. 2, no. 7–8, Summer 1989.

```
  int day;
  int year;
};
```

A member function is defined like any function with one exception: The name of the class within which the member is declared precedes the member function name with a double colon in between (::). The double colon operator is called the **scope resolution operator**.

```
void DateType::Initialize(int newMonth, int newDay,
  int newYear)
// Post: month is set to newMonth; day is set to
//       newDay; year is set to newYear.
{
  month = newMonth;
  day = newDay;
  year = newYear;
}

int DateType::GetMonth) const
// Post: Class member month is returned.
{
  return month;
}

int DateType::GetDay() const
// Post: Class member day is returned.
{
  return day;
}

int DateType::GetYear() const
// Post: Class member year is returned.
{
  return year;
}
```

If `date` is a variable of type `DateType`, the following statement prints the data fields of `date`.

```
cout << "Month is "  << date.GetMonth() << endl;
     << "Day is " << date.GetDay() << endl;
     << "Year is " << date.GetYear() << endl;
```

1.4 Verification of Software Correctness

At the beginning of this chapter, we discussed some characteristics of good programs. The first of these was that a good program works–it accomplishes its intended function. How do you know when your program meets that goal? The simple answer is, *test it*.

Testing The process of executing a program with data sets designed to discover errors

Debugging The process of removing known errors

Acceptance test The process of testing the system in its real environment with real data

Regression testing Reexecution of program tests after modifications have been made to ensure that the program still works correctly

Program verification The process of determining the degree to which a software product fulfills its specifications

Program validation The process of determining the degree to which software fulfills its intended purpose

Let's look at testing as it relates to the rest of the software development process. As programmers, we first make sure that we understand the requirements. We then come up with a general solution. Next, we design the solution in terms of a computer program, using good design principles. Finally, we implement the solution, using good structured coding, with classes, functions, self-documenting code, and so on.

Once we have the program coded, we compile it repeatedly until no syntax errors appear. Then we run the program, using carefully selected test data. If the program doesn't work, we say that it has a "bug" in it. We try to pinpoint the error and fix it, a process called debugging. Notice the distinction between testing and debugging. Testing is running the program with data sets designed to discover any errors; debugging is removing errors once they are discovered.

When the debugging is completed, the software is put into use. Before final delivery, software is sometimes installed on one or more customer sites so that it can be tested in a real environment with real data. After passing this acceptance test phase, the software can be installed at all customer sites. Is the verification process now finished? Hardly! More than half of the total life-cycle costs and effort generally occur *after* the program becomes operational, in the maintenance phase. Some changes correct errors in the original program; other changes add new capabilities to the software system. In either case, testing must occur after any program modification. This phase is called regression testing.

Testing is useful in revealing the presence of bugs in a program, but it doesn't prove their absence. We can only say for sure that the program worked correctly for the cases we tested. This approach seems somewhat haphazard. How do we know which tests or how many of them to run? Debugging a whole program at once isn't easy. Also, fixing the errors found during such testing can sometimes be a messy task. Too bad we couldn't have detected the errors earlier—while we were designing the program, for instance. They would have been much easier to fix then.

We know how program design can be improved by using a good design methodology. Can we use something similar to improve our program verification activities? Yes, we can. Program verification activities don't need to start when the program is completely coded; they can be incorporated into the entire software development process, from the requirements phase on. Program verification is more than just testing.

In addition to program verification, which involves fulfilling the requirement specifications, the software engineer has another important task—making sure the specified requirements actually solve the underlying problem. Countless times a programmer has finished a large project and delivered the verified software, only to be told, "Well, that's what I asked for but it's not what I need."

The process of determining that software accomplishes its intended task is called program validation. Program verification asks, "Are we doing the job right?"; program validation asks, "Are we doing the right job?"[3]

---

[3]B. W. Boehm, *Software Engineering Economics* (Englewood Cliffs, N.J.: Prentice-Hall, 1981).

Can we really "debug" a program before it has ever been run—or even before it has been written? In this section we review a number of topics related to satisfying the criterion "quality software works." The topics include

- Designing for correctness
- Performing code and design walk-throughs and inspections
- Using debugging methods
- Choosing test goals and data
- Writing test plans
- Structured integration testing

Origin of Bugs

When Sherlock Holmes goes off to solve a case, he doesn't start from scratch every time; he knows from experience all kinds of things that help him find solutions. Suppose Holmes finds a victim in a muddy field. He immediately looks for footprints in the mud, for he can tell from a footprint what kind of shoe made it. The first print he finds matches the shoes of the victim, so he keeps looking. Now he finds another print, and from his vast knowledge of footprints he can tell that it was made by a certain type of boot. He deduces that such a boot would be worn by a particular type of laborer, and from the size and depth of the print he guesses the suspect's height and weight. Now, knowing something about the habits of laborers in this town, he guesses that at 6:30 P.M. the suspect might be found in Clancy's Pub.

In software verification we are often expected to play detective. Given certain clues, we have to find the bugs in programs. If we know what kinds of situations produce program errors, we are more likely to be able to detect and correct problems. We may even be able to step in and prevent many errors entirely, just as Sherlock Holmes sometimes intervenes in time to prevent a crime from taking place.

Let's look at some types of software errors that show up at various points in program development and testing and see how they might be avoided.

Specifications and Design Errors What would happen if, shortly before you were supposed to turn in a major class assignment, you discovered that some details in the professor's program description were incorrect? To make matters worse, you also found out that the corrections were discussed at the beginning of class on the day you got there late, and somehow you never knew about the problem until your tests of the class data set came up with the wrong answers. What do you do now?

Writing a program to the wrong specifications is probably the worst kind of software error. How bad can it be? Let's look at a true story. Some time ago, a computer company contracted to replace a government agency's obsolete system with new hardware and software. A large and complicated program was written, based on specifications and algorithms provided by the customer. The new system was checked out at every point in its development to ensure that its functions matched the requirements in the specifications document. When the system was complete and the new software was executed, users discovered that the results of its calculations did not match those of the old system. A careful comparison

of the two systems showed that the specifications of the new software were erroneous because they were based on algorithms taken from the old system's inaccurate documentation. The new program was "correct" in that it accomplished its specified functions, but the program was useless to the customer because it didn't accomplish its intended functions—it didn't work. The cost of correcting the errors measured in the millions of dollars.

How could correcting the error be so expensive? First, much of the conceptual and design effort, as well as the coding, was wasted. It took a great deal of time to pinpoint which parts of the specification were in error and then to correct this document before the program could be redesigned. Then much of the software development activity (design, coding, and testing) had to be repeated. This case is an extreme one, but it illustrates how critical specifications are to the software process. In general, programmers are more expert in software development techniques than in the "application" areas of their programs, such as banking, city planning, satellite control, or medical research. Thus correct program specifications are crucial to the success of program development.

Most studies indicate that it costs 100 times as much to correct an error discovered after software delivery than it does if the problem is discovered early in the software life cycle. Figure 1.5 shows how fast the costs rise in subsequent phases of software development. The vertical axis represents the relative cost of fixing an error; this cost might be measured in units of hours, hundreds of dollars, or "programmer months" (the amount of work one programmer can do in one month). The horizontal axis represents the stages in the development of a software product. As you can see, an error that would have taken one unit to fix when you first started designing might take 100 units to correct when the product is actually in operation!

Good communication between the programmers (you) and the party who originated the problem (the professor, manager, or customer) can prevent many specification errors. In general, it pays to ask questions when you don't understand something in the program specifications. And the earlier you ask, the better.

A number of questions should come to mind as you first read a programming assignment. What error checking is necessary? What algorithm or data structure should be used

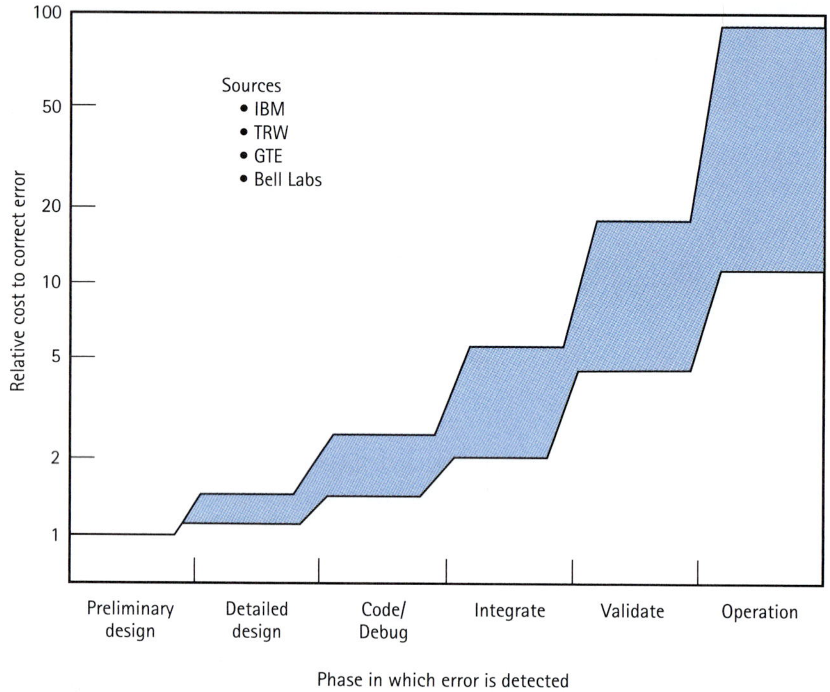

Figure 1.5 *This graph demonstrates the importance of early detection of software errors*

in the solution? What assumptions are reasonable? If you obtain answers to these questions when you first begin working on an assignment, you can incorporate them into your design and implementation of the program. Later in the program's development, unexpected answers to these questions can cost you time and effort. In short, to write a program that is correct, you must understand precisely what your program is supposed to do.

Sometimes specifications change during the design or implementation of a program. In such cases, a good design helps you to pinpoint which sections of the program must be redone. For instance, if a program defines and uses type `StringType` to implement strings, changing the implementation of `StringType` does not require rewriting the entire program. We should be able to see from the design—either functional or object-oriented—that the offending code is restricted to the module where `StringType` is defined. The parts of the program that require changes can usually be located more easily from the design than from the code itself.

Compile-Time Errors In the process of learning your first programming language, you probably made a number of syntax errors. These mistakes resulted in error messages (for example, “TYPE MISMATCH,” “ILLEGAL ASSIGNMENT,” “SEMICOLON EXPECTED,” and so on) when you tried to compile the program. Now that you are more familiar with the programming language, you can save your debugging skills for tracking down really important logical errors. *Try to get the syntax right the first time.* Having your program compile cleanly on the first attempt is not an unreasonable goal. A syntax error wastes computing time and money, as well as programmer time, and it is preventable. Some programmers argue that looking for syntax errors is a waste of their time, that it is faster to let the compiler catch all the typos and syntax errors. Don’t believe them! Sometimes a coding error turns out to be a legal statement, syntactically correct but semantically wrong. This situation may cause very obscure, hard-to-locate errors.

As you progress in your college career or move into a professional computing job, learning a new programming language is often the easiest part of a new software assignment. This does not mean, however, that the language is the least important part. In this book we discuss abstract data types and algorithms that we believe are language independent. That is, they can be implemented in almost any general-purpose programming language. In reality, the success of the implementation depends on a thorough understanding of the features of the programming language. What is considered acceptable programming practice in one language may be inadequate in another, and similar syntactic constructs may be just different enough to cause serious trouble.

For this reason, it is worthwhile to develop an expert knowledge of both the control and data structures and the syntax of the language in which you are programming. In general, if you have a good knowledge of your programming language—and are careful—you can avoid syntax errors. The ones you might miss are relatively easy to locate and correct. Most are flagged by the compiler with an error message. Once you have a “clean” compilation, you can execute your program.

Run-Time Errors Errors that occur during the execution of a program are usually more difficult to detect than syntax errors. Some run-time errors stop execution of the program. When this situation happens, we say that the program “crashed” or “terminated abnormally.”

Run-time errors often occur when the programmer makes too many assumptions. For instance,

```
result = dividend / divisor;
```

is a legitimate assignment statement, if we can assume that `divisor` is never zero. If `divisor` *is* zero, however, a run-time error results.

Sometimes run-time errors occur because the programmer does not fully understand the programming language. For example, in C++ the assignment operator is =, and the equality test operator is ==. Because they look so much alike, they often are miskeyed one for the other. You might think that this would be a syntax error that the compiler would catch, but it is actually a logic error. Technically, an assignment in C++ consists of an expression with two parts: The expression on the right of the assignment operator (=) is evaluated and the result is returned and stored in the place named on the left. The key word here is *returned*; the result of evaluating the right-hand side is the result of the expression. Therefore, if the assignment operator is miskeyed for the equality test operator, or vice versa, the code executes with surprising results.

Let's look at an example. Consider the following two statements:

```
count == count + 1;
if (count = 10)
  .
  .
  .
```

The first statement returns false; count can never be equal to count + 1. The semicolon ends the statement, so nothing happens to the value returned; count has not changed. In the next statement, the expression (count = 10) is evaluated, and 10 is returned and stored in count. Because a nonzero value (10) is returned, the *if* expression always evaluates to true.

Run-time errors also occur because of unanticipated user errors. For instance, if newValue is declared to be of type int, the statement

```
cin  >> newValue;
```

causes a stream failure if the user inputs a nonnumeric character. An invalid filename can cause a stream failure. In some languages, the system reports a run-time error and halts. In C++, the program doesn't halt; the program simply continues with erroneous data. Well-written programs should not stop unexpectedly (crash) or continue with bad data. They should catch such errors and stay in control until the user is ready to quit.

Stream Input and Output

In C++, input and output are considered streams of characters. The keyboard input stream is cin; the screen output stream is cout. Important declarations relating to these streams are supplied in the library file <iostream>. If you plan to use the standard input and output streams, you must include this file in your program. You must also provide for access to the namespace with the *using* directive,

```
#include <iostream>
int main()
{
  using namespace std;

  int intValue;
  float realValue;
```

```
  cout  << "Enter an integer number followed by return."
        << endl;
  cin   >> intValue;
  cout  << "Enter a real number followed by return."
        << endl;
  cin   >> realValue;
  cout  << "You entered "  << intValue  << " and "
        << realValue << endl;
  return 0;
}
```

<< is called the *insertion* operator: The expressions on the right describe what is inserted into the output stream. >> is called the *extraction* operator: Values are extracted from the input stream and stored in the places named on the right. `endl` is a special language feature called a *manipulator*; it terminates the current output line.

If you are reading or writing to a file, you include `<fstream>`. You then have access to the data types `ifstream` (for input) and `ofstream` (for output). Declare variables of these types, use the `open` function to associate each with the external file name, and use the variable names in place of `cin` and `cout`, respectively.

```
#include <fstream>
int main()
{
  using namespace std;

  int intValue;
  float realValue;
  ifstream inData;
  ofstream outData;

  inData.open("input.dat");
  outData.open("output.dat");

  inData   >> intValue;
  inData   >> realValue;
  outData << "The input values are "
          << intValue  << " and "
          << realValue   << endl;
  return 0;
}
```

On input, whether from the keyboard or from a file, the >> operator skips leading whitespace characters (blank, tab, line feed, form feed, carriage return) before extracting the input value. To avoid skipping whitespace characters, you can use the `get` function. You invoke it by giving the name of the input stream, a dot, and then the function name and parameter list:

```
cin.get(inputChar);
```

The `get` function inputs the next character waiting in the input stream, even if it is a white-space character.

Stream Failure

The key to reading data in correctly (from either the keyboard or a file) is to ensure that the order and the form in which the data are keyed are consistent with the order and type of the identifiers on the input statement. If an error occurs while accessing an I/O stream, the stream enters the *fail state*, and any further references to the stream will be ignored. For example, if you misspell the name of the file that is the parameter to the function `open` (`In.dat` instead of `Data.In`, for example), the file input stream will enter the fail state. Alternatively, if you try to input a value when the stream is at the end of the file, the stream will enter the fail state. Your program may continue to execute while the stream remains in the fail state, but all further references to the stream will be ignored.

C++ gives you a way to test the state of a stream: The stream name used in an expression returns a value that is converted to true if the state is good and to false if the stream is in the fail state. For example, the following code segment prints an error message and halts execution if the proper input file is not found:

```
#include <fstream>
#include <iostream>

int main()
{
  using namespace std;
  ifstream inData;

  inData.open("myData.dat");
  if (!inData)
  {
    cout  << "File myData.dat was not found."  << endl;
    return 1;
  }
  .
  .
  .
  return 0;
}
```

By convention, the `main` function returns an exit status of 0 if execution completed normally, whereas it returns a nonzero value (above, we used 1) otherwise.

Robustness The ability of a program to recover following an error; the ability of a program to continue to operate within its environment

The ability of a program to recover when an error occurs is called robustness. If a commercial program is not robust, people do not buy it. Who wants a word processor that crashes if the user says "SAVE" when there is no disk in the drive? We want the program to tell us, "Put your disk in the drive, and press Enter." For some types of software, robustness is a critical requirement. An airplane's automatic pilot system or an intensive care unit's patient-monitoring program cannot afford to just crash. In such situations, a defensive posture produces good results.

In general, you should actively check for error-creating conditions rather than let them abort your program. For instance, it is generally unwise to make too many assumptions about the correctness of input, especially "interactive" input from a keyboard. A better approach is to check explicitly for the correct type and bounds of such input. The programmer can then decide how to handle an error (request new input, print a message, or go on to the next data) rather than leave the decision to the system. Even the decision to quit should be made by a program that controls its own execution. If worse comes to worst, let your program die gracefully.

Of course, not everything that the program inputs must be checked for errors. Sometimes inputs are known to be correct—for instance, input from a file that has been verified. The decision to include error checking must be based upon the requirements of the program.

Some run-time errors do not stop execution but do produce the wrong results. You may have incorrectly implemented an algorithm or used a variable before it was assigned a value. You may have inadvertently swapped two parameters of the same type on a function call or forgotten to designate a function's output data as a reference parameter. (See the Parameter Passing sidebar, page 76.) These "logical" errors are often the hardest to prevent and locate. Later we will talk about debugging techniques to help pinpoint run-time errors. We will also discuss structured testing methods that isolate the part of the program being tested. But knowing that the earlier we find an error, the easier it is to fix, we turn now to ways of catching run-time errors before run time.

Designing for Correctness

It would be nice if there were some tool that would locate the errors in our design or code without our even having to run the program. That sounds unlikely, but consider an analogy from geometry. We wouldn't try to prove the Pythagorean Theorem by proving that it worked on every triangle; that result would merely demonstrate that the theorem works for every triangle we tried. We prove theorems in geometry mathematically. Why can't we do the same for computer programs?

The verification of program correctness, independent of data testing, is an important area of theoretical computer science research. Such research seeks to establish a method for proving programs that is analogous to the method for proving theorems in geometry. The necessary techniques exist, but the proofs are often more complicated than the programs themselves. Therefore a major focus of verification research is the attempt to build automated program provers—verifiable programs that verify other programs. In the meantime, the formal verification techniques can be carried out by hand.[4]

Assertions An assertion is a logical proposition that can be true or false. We can make assertions about the state of the program. For instance, with the assignment statement

```
sum = part + 1 ;      // sum and part are integers.
```

Assertion A logical proposition that can be true or false

Preconditions Assertions that must be true on entry into an operation or function for the postconditions to be guaranteed

we might assert the following: "The value of `sum` is greater than the value of `part`." That assertion might not be very useful or interesting by itself, but let's see what we can do with it. We can demonstrate that the assertion is true by making a logical argument: No matter what value `part` has (negative, zero, or positive), when it is increased by 1, the result is a larger value. Now note what we didn't do. We didn't have to run a program containing this assignment statement to verify that the assertion was correct.

The general concept behind formal program verification is that we can make assertions about what the program is intended to do, based on its specifications, and then prove through a logical argument (rather than through execution of the program) that a design or implementation satisfies the assertions. Thus the process can be broken down into two steps:

1. Correctly assert the intended function of the part of the program to be verified.
2. Prove that the actual design or implementation does what is asserted.

The first step, making assertions, sounds as if it might be useful to us in the process of designing correct programs. After all, we already know that we cannot write correct programs unless we know what they are supposed to do.

Preconditions and Postconditions Let's take the idea of making assertions down a level in the design process. Suppose we want to design a module (a logical chunk of the program) to perform a specific operation. To ensure that this module fits into the program as a whole, we must clarify what happens at its boundaries—that is, what must be true when we enter the module and what must be true when we exit.

To make the task more concrete, picture the design module as it is eventually coded, as a function that is called within a program. To call the function, we must know its exact interface: the name and the parameter list, which indicates its inputs and outputs. But this information isn't enough: We must also know any assumptions that must be true for the operation to function correctly. We call the assertions that must be true on entry into the function preconditions. The preconditions act like a product disclaimer:

---

[4]We do not go into this subject in detail here. For students who are interested in this topic, see David Gries, *The Science of Programming* (New York: Springer-Verlag, 1981).

> **WARNING**
> If you try to execute this operation when the preconditions are not true, the results are not guaranteed.

For instance, when we said that following the execution of

```
sum = part + 1;
```

we can assert that sum is greater than part, we made an assumption—a precondition—that part is not INT_MAX. If this precondition were violated, our assertion would not be true.

> **Postconditions** Assertions that state what results are expected at the exit of an operation or function, assuming that the preconditions are true

We must also know what conditions are true when the operation is complete. The postconditions are assertions that describe the results of the operation. The postconditions do not tell us how these results are accomplished; rather, they merely tell us what the results should be.

Let's consider the preconditions and postconditions for a simple operation, one that deletes the last element from a list and returns its value as an output. (We are using "list" in an intuitive sense here; we formally define it in Chapter 3.) The specification for GetLast is as follows:

GetLast(ListType list, ValueType lastValue)

Function:	Remove the last element in the list and return its value in lastValue.
Precondition:	The list is not empty.
Postconditions:	lastValue is the value of the last element in the list, the last element has been removed, and the list length has been decremented.

What do these preconditions and postconditions have to do with program verification? By making explicit assertions about what is expected at the interfaces between modules, we can avoid making logical errors based on misunderstandings. For instance, from the precondition we know that we must check outside of this operation for the empty condition; this module *assumes* that at least one element is present in the list. The postcondition tells us that when the value of the last list element is retrieved, that element is deleted from the list. This fact is an important one for the list user to know. If we just want to take a peek at the last value without affecting the list, we cannot use GetLast.

Experienced software developers know that misunderstandings about interfaces to someone else's modules are one of the main sources of program problems. We use preconditions and postconditions at the module or function level in this book, because the information they provide helps us to design programs in a truly modular fashion. We can then use the modules we've designed in our programs, confident that we are not introducing errors by making mistakes about assumptions and about what the modules actually do.

Design Review Activities When an individual programmer is designing and implementing a program, he or she can find many software errors with pencil and paper. Deskchecking the design solution is a very common method of manually verifying a program. The programmer writes down essential data (variables, input values, parameters of subprograms, and so on) and walks through the design, marking changes in the data on the paper. Known trouble spots in the design or code should be double-checked. A checklist of typical errors (such as loops that do not terminate, variables that are used before they are initialized, and incorrect order of parameters on function calls) can be used to make the deskcheck more effective. A sample checklist for deskchecking a C++ program appears in Figure 1.6.

Deskchecking Tracing an execution of a design or program on paper

Walk-through A verification method in which a team performs a manual simulation of the program or design

Inspection A verification method in which one member of a team reads the program or design line by line and the other members point out errors

Have you ever been really stuck trying to debug a program and showed it to a classmate or colleague who detected the bug right away? It is generally acknowledged that someone else can detect errors in a program better than the original author can. In an extension of deskchecking, two programmers can trade code listings and check each other's programs. Universities, however, frequently discourage students from examining each other's programs for fear that this exchange will lead to cheating. Thus many students become experienced in writing programs but don't have much opportunity to practice reading them.

Teams of programmers develop most sizable computer programs. Two extensions of deskchecking that are effectively used by programming teams are design or code walk-throughs and inspections. The intention of these formal team activities is to move the responsibility for uncovering bugs from the individual programmer to the group. Because testing is time consuming and errors cost more the later they are discovered, the goal is to identify errors before testing begins.

In a *walk-through*, the team performs a manual simulation of the design or program with sample test inputs, keeping track of the program's data by hand on paper or on a blackboard. Unlike thorough program testing, the walk-through is not intended to simulate all possible test cases. Instead, its purpose is to stimulate discussion about the way the programmer chose to design or implement the program's requirements.

At an *inspection*, a reader (not the program's author) goes through the design or code line by line. Inspection participants point out errors, which are recorded on an inspection report. Some errors are uncovered just by the process of reading aloud. Others may have been noted by team members during their preinspection preparation. As with the walk-through, the chief benefit of the team meeting is the discussion that takes

The Design

1. Does each module in the design have a clear function or purpose?
2. Can large modules be broken down into smaller pieces? (A common rule of thumb is that a C++ function should fit on one page.)
3. Are all the assumptions valid? Are they well documented?
4. Are the preconditions and postconditions accurate assertions about what should be happening in the module they specify?
5. Is the design correct and complete as measured against the program specification? Are there any missing cases? Is there faulty logic?
6. Is the program designed well for understandability and maintainability?

The Code

7. Has the design been clearly and correctly implemented in the programming language? Are features of the programming language used appropriately?
8. Are all output parameters of functions assigned values?
9. Are parameters that return values marked as reference parameters (have `&` to the right of the type if the parameter is not an array)?
10. Are functions coded to be consistent with the interfaces shown in the design?
11. Are the actual parameters on function calls consistent with the parameters declared in the function prototype and definition?
12. Is each data object to be initialized set correctly at the proper time? Is each data object set before its value is used?
13. Do all loops terminate?
14. Is the design free of "magic" numbers? (A "magic" number is one whose meaning is not immediately evident to the reader.)
15. Does each constant, type, variable, and function have a meaningful name? Are comments included with the declarations to clarify the use of the data objects?

Figure 1.6 *Checklist for deskchecking a C++ program*

place among team members. This interaction among programmers, testers, and other team members can uncover many program errors long before the testing stage begins.

At the high-level design stage, the design should be compared to the program requirements to make sure that all required functions have been included and that this program or module correctly "interfaces" with other software in the system. At the low-level design stage, when the design has been filled out with more details, it should be reinspected before it is implemented. When the coding has been completed, the compiled listings should be inspected again. This inspection (or walk-through) ensures that the implementation is consistent with both the requirements and the design. Successful completion of this inspection means that testing of the program can begin.

For over 20 years, the Software Engineering Institute at Carnegie Mellon University has played a major role in supporting research into formalizing the inspection process in large software projects, including sponsoring workshops and conferences. A paper presented at the SEI Software Engineering Process Group (SEPG) Conference reported on a project that was able to reduce the number of product defects by 86.6% by using a two-tiered inspection process of group walk-throughs and formal inspections. The process was applied to packets of requirements, design, or code at every stage of the life cycle. Table 1.2 shows the defects per 1,000 source lines of code (KSLOC) that were found in the various phases of the software life cycle in a maintenance project. This project added 40,000 lines of source code to a software program of half a million lines of code. The formal inspection process was used in all of the phases except testing activities.

Looking back at Figure 1.5, you can see that the cost of fixing an error is relatively cheap until you reach the coding phase. After that stage, the cost of fixing an error increases dramatically. Using the formal inspection process clearly benefited this project.

These design-review activities should be carried out in as nonthreatening a manner as possible. The goal is not to criticize the design or the designer, but rather to remove defects in the product. Sometimes it is difficult to eliminate the natural human emotion of pride from this process, but the best teams adopt a policy of *egoless programming*.

Exception An unusual, generally unpredictable event, detectable by software or hardware, that requires special processing; the event may or may not be erroneous

Exceptions At the design stage, you should plan how to handle exceptions in your program. Exceptions are just what the name implies: exceptional situations. When these situations occur, the flow of control of the program must be altered, usually resulting in a premature end to program execution. Working with exceptions begins at the design phase: What are the unusual situations that the program should recognize? Where in the program can the situations be detected? How should the situations be handled if they arise?

Where—indeed, whether—an exception is detected depends on the language, the software package design, the design of the libraries being used, and the platform (that is, the operating system and hardware). Where an exception *should* be detected depends

Table 1.2 *Defects Found in Different Phases**

Stage	KSLOC
System Design	2
Software Requirements	8
Design	12
Code Inspection	34
Testing Activities	3

*Dennis Beeson, Manager, Naval Air Warfare Center, Weapons Division, F-18 Software Development Team.

on the type of exception, the software package design, and the platform. Where an exception *is* detected should be well documented in the relevant code segments.

An exception *may* be handled in any place in the software hierarchy—from the place in the program module where the exception is first detected through the top level of the program. In C++, as in most programming languages, unhandled built-in exceptions carry the penalty of program termination. Where in an application an exception *should* be handled is a design decision; however, exceptions should be handled at a level that knows what they mean.

An exception need not be fatal. In nonfatal exceptions, the thread of execution may continue. Although the thread of execution may be picked up at any point in the program, the execution should continue from the lowest level that can recover from the exception. When an error occurs, the program may fail unexpectedly. Some of the failure conditions may possibly be anticipated; some may not. All such errors must be detected and managed.

Exceptions can be written in any language. Some languages (such as C++ and Java) provide built-in mechanisms to manage exceptions. All exception mechanisms have three parts:

- Defining the exception
- Generating (raising) the exception
- Handling the exception

C++ gives you a clean way of implementing these three phases: the *try-catch* and *throw* statements. We cover these statements at the end of Chapter 2 after we have introduced some additional C++ constructs.

Program Testing

Eventually, after all the design verification, deskchecking, and inspections have been completed, it is time to execute the code. At last, we are ready to start testing with the *intention of finding any errors that may still remain.*

The testing process is made up of a set of test cases that, taken together, allow us to assert that a program works correctly. We say "assert" rather than "prove" because testing does not generally provide a proof of program correctness.

The goal of each test case is to verify a particular program feature. For instance, we may design several test cases to demonstrate that the program correctly handles various classes of input errors. Alternatively, we may design cases to check the processing when a data structure (such as an array) is empty, or when it contains the maximum number of elements.

Within each test case, we perform a series of component tasks:

- We determine inputs that demonstrate the goal of the test case.
- We determine the expected behavior of the program for the given input. (This task is often the most difficult one. For a math function, we might use a chart of values or a calculator to figure out the expected result. For a function with complex processing, we might use a deskcheck type of simulation or an alternative solution to the same problem.)

- We run the program and observe the resulting behavior.
- We compare the expected behavior and the actual behavior of the program. If they match, the test case is successful. If not, an error exists. In the latter case, we begin debugging.

Unit testing Testing a module or function by itself

Functional domain The set of valid input data for a program or function

For now we are talking about test cases at a module, or function, level. It's much easier to test and debug modules of a program one at a time, rather than trying to get the whole program solution to work all at once. Testing at this level is called unit testing.

How do we know what kinds of unit test cases are appropriate, and how many are needed? Determining the set of test cases that is sufficient to validate a unit of a program is in itself a difficult task. Two approaches to specifying test cases exist: cases based on testing possible data inputs and cases based on testing aspects of the code itself.

Data Coverage In those limited cases where the set of valid inputs, or the functional domain, is extremely small, we can verify a subprogram by testing it against every possible input element. This approach, known as "exhaustive" testing, can prove conclusively that the software meets its specifications. For instance, the functional domain of the following function consists of the values `true` and `false`:

```
void PrintBoolean(bool error)
// Prints the Boolean value on the screen.
{
  if (error)
    cout << "true";
  else
    cout << "false";
  cout << endl;
}
```

It makes sense to apply exhaustive testing to this function, because there are only two possible input values. In most cases, however, the functional domain is very large, so exhaustive testing is almost always impractical or impossible. What is the functional domain of the following function?

```
void PrintInteger(int intValue)
// Prints the integer value intValue on the screen.
{
  cout << intValue;
}
```

It is not practical to test this function by running it with every possible data input; the number of elements in the set of `int` values is clearly too large. In such cases we do not attempt exhaustive testing. Instead, we pick some other measurement as a testing goal.

You can attempt program testing in a haphazard way, entering data randomly until you cause the program to fail. Guessing doesn't hurt (except possibly by wasting time), but it may not help much either. This approach is likely to uncover some bugs in a program, but it is very unlikely to find all of them. Fortunately, strategies for detecting errors in a systematic way have been developed.

One goal-oriented approach is to cover general classes of data. You should test at least one example of each category of inputs, as well as boundaries and other special cases. For instance, in the function `PrintInteger` there are three basic classes of `int` data: negative values, zero, and positive values. You should plan three test cases, one for each class. You could try more than three, of course. For example, you might want to try `INT_MAX` and `INT_MIN`; because the program simply prints the value of its input, however, the additional test cases don't accomplish much.

Other data coverage approaches exist as well. For example, if the input consists of commands, you must test each command. If the input is a fixed-sized array containing a variable number of values, you should test the maximum number of values—that is, the boundary condition. It is also a good idea to try an array in which no values have been stored or one that contains a single element. Testing based on data coverage is called black-box testing. The tester must know the external interface to the module—its inputs and expected outputs—but does not need to consider what is happening inside the module (the inside of the black box). (See Figure 1.7.)

Black-box testing Testing a program or function based on the possible input values, treating the code as a "black box"

Clear- (white-) box testing Testing a program or function based on covering all the statements, branches, or paths of the code

Statement coverage Every statement in the program is executed at least once

Branch A code segment that is not always executed; for example, a *switch* statement has as many branches as there are case labels

Path A combination of branches that might be traversed when a program or function is executed

Path testing A testing technique whereby the tester tries to execute all possible paths in a program or function

Code Coverage A number of testing strategies are based on the concept of code coverage, the execution of statements or groups of statements in the program. This testing approach is called clear- (or white-) box testing. The tester must look inside the module (through the clear box) to see the code that is being tested.

One approach, called statement coverage, requires that every statement in the program be executed at least once. Another approach requires that the test cases cause every branch, or code section, in the program to be executed. A single test case can achieve statement coverage of an *if-then* statement, but it takes two test cases to test both branches of the statement.

A similar type of code-coverage goal is to test program paths. A path is a combination of branches that might be traveled when the program is executed. In path testing, we try to execute all possible program paths in different test cases.

Figure 1.7 *Testing approaches*

The code-coverage approaches are analogous to the ways forest rangers might check out the trails through the woods before the hiking season opens. If the rangers wanted to make sure that all trails were clearly marked and not blocked by fallen trees, they would check each branch of the trails (see Figure 1.8a). Alternatively, if they wanted to classify each of the various trails (which may be interwoven) according to its length and difficulty from start to finish, they would use path testing (see Figure 1.8b).

To create test cases based on code-coverage goals, we select inputs that drive the execution into the various program paths. How can we tell whether a branch or a path is executed? One way to trace execution is to put debugging output statements at the beginning of every branch, indicating that this particular branch was entered. Software projects often use tools that help programmers track program execution automatically.

These strategies lend themselves to measurements of the testing process. We can count the number of paths in a program, for example, and keep track of how many paths have been covered in our test cases. The numbers provide statistics about the current status of testing; for instance, we could say that 75% of the branches of a program have been executed or that 50% of the paths have been tested. When a single programmer is writing a single program, such numbers may be superfluous. In a software development environment with many programmers, however, such statistics are very useful for tracking the progress of testing.

Figure 1.8a *Checking out all the branches*

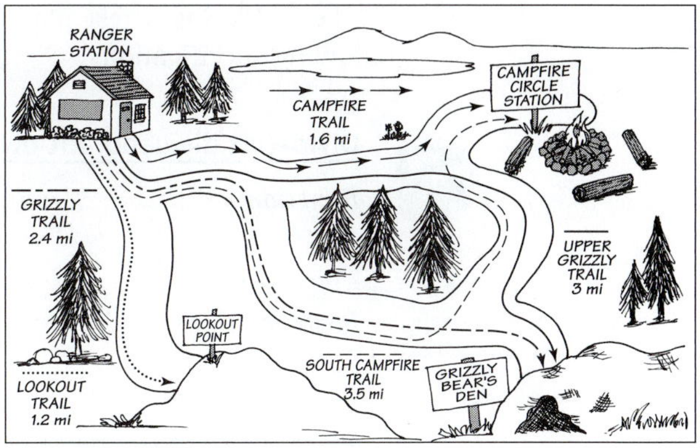

Figure 1.8b *Checking out all the trails*

These measurements can also indicate when a certain level of testing has been completed. Achieving 100% path coverage is often not a feasible goal. A software project might have a lower standard (say, 80% branch coverage) that the programmer who writes the module is required to reach before turning the module over to the project's testing team. Testing in which goals are based on certain measurable factors is called metric-based testing.

Metric-based testing Testing based on measurable factors

Test plan A document showing the test cases planned for a program or module, their purposes, inputs, expected outputs, and criteria for success

Implementing a test plan Running the program with the test cases listed in the test plan

Test Plans Deciding on the goal of the test approach—data coverage, code coverage, or (most often) a mixture of the two—precedes the development of a test plan. Some test plans are very informal—the goal and a list of test cases, written by hand on a piece of paper. Even this type of test plan may be more than you have ever been required to write for a class programming project. Other test plans (particularly those submitted to management or to a customer for approval) are very formal, containing the details of each test case in a standardized format.

Implementing a test plan involves running the program with the input values listed in the plan and observing the results. If the answers are incorrect, the program is debugged and rerun until the observed output always matches the expected output. The process is complete when all test cases listed in the plan give the desired output.

Let's develop a test plan for a function called `Divide`, which was coded from the following specifications:

Divide(int dividend, int divisor, bool& error, float& result)

Function:	Divides one number by another and tests for a divisor of zero.
Preconditions:	None.
Postconditions:	error is true if divisor is 0. result is dividend / divisor, if error is false. result is undefined, if error is true.

Should we use code coverage or data coverage for this test plan? Because the code is so short and straightforward, let's begin with code coverage. A code-coverage test plan is based on an examination of the code itself. Here is the code to be tested:

```
void Divide(int dividend, int divisor, bool& error, float& result)
// Set error to indicate if divisor is zero.
// If no error, set result to dividend / divisor.
{
  if (divisor = 0)
    error = true;
  else
    result = float(dividend) / float(divisor);
}
```

The code consists of one *if* statement with two branches; therefore, we can do complete path testing. There is a case where `divisor` is zero and the true branch is taken and a case where `divisor` is nonzero and the else branch is taken.

Reason for Test Case	Input Values	Expected Output
`divisor` is zero		
(`dividend` can be anything)	`divisor` is 0	`error` is true
	`dividend` is 8	`result` is undefined
`divisor` is nonzero		
(`dividend` can be anything)	`divisor` is 2	`error` is false
	`dividend` is 8	`result` is 4.0

Test driver A program that sets up the testing environment by declaring and assigning initial values to variables, then calls the subprogram to be tested

To implement this test plan, we run the program with the listed input values and compare the results with the expected output. The function is called from a test driver, a program that sets up the parameter values and calls the functions to be tested. A simple test driver is listed below. It is designed to execute both test cases: It assigns the parameter values for Test 1, calls `Divide`, and prints the results; then it repeats the process with new test inputs for Test 2. We run the test and compare the values output from the test driver with the expected values.

```
#include <iostream>

void Divide(int, int, bool&, float&);
// Function to be tested.

void Print(int, int, bool, float);
// Prints results of test case.

int main()
{
  using namespace std;

  bool error;
  float result;
  int dividend = 8;                                    // Test 1
  int divisor = 0;

  Divide(dividend, divisor, error, result);
  cout  << "Test 1: "  << endl;
  Print(dividend, divisor, error, result);
  divisor = 2;                                         // Test 2
  Divide(dividend, divisor, error, result);
  cout  << "Test 2: " << endl;
  Print(dividend, divisor, error, result);
  return 0;
}
```

For Test 1, the expected value for `error` is `true`, and the expected value for `result` is undefined, but the division is carried out anyway! How can that be when `divisor` is zero? If the result of an *if* statement is not what you expect, the first thing to check is the relational operator: Did we use a single = rather than ==? Yes, we did. After fixing this mistake, we run the program again.

For Test 2, the expected value for `error` is `false`, yet the value printed is `true`! Our testing has uncovered another error, so we begin debugging. We discover that the value of `error`, set to `true` in Test 1, was never reset to `false` in Test 2. We leave development of the final correct version of this function as an exercise.

Now let's design a data-coverage test plan for the same function. In a data-coverage plan, we know nothing about the internal working of the function; we know only the interface that is represented in the documentation of the function heading.

```
void Divide(int dividend, int divisor, bool& error, float& result)
// Set error to indicate if divisor is zero.
// If no error, set result to dividend / divisor.
```

There are two input parameters, both of type `int`. A complete data-coverage plan would require that we call the function with all possible values of type `int` for each parameter—clearly overkill. The interface tells us that one thing happens if `divisor` is zero and another thing happens if `divisor` is nonzero. Clearly, we must have at least two test cases: one where `divisor` is zero and one where `divisor` is nonzero. When `divisor` is zero, `error` is set to `true` and nothing else happens, so one test case should verify this result. When `divisor` is nonzero, a division takes place. How many test cases does it take to verify that the division is correct? What are the end cases? There are five possibilities:

- `divisor` and `dividend` are both positive
- `divisor` and `dividend` are both negative
- `divisor` is positive and `dividend` is negative
- `divisor` is negative and `dividend` is positive
- `dividend` is zero

The complete test plan is shown below.

Reason for Test Case	Input Values	Expected Output
`divisor` is zero (`dividend` can be anything)	`divisor` is 0 `dividend` is 8	`error` is true `result` is undefined
`divisor` is nonzero (`dividend` can be anything) combined with `divisor` is positive `dividend` is positive	`divisor` is 2 `dividend` is 8	`error` is false `result` is 4.0
`divisor` is nonzero `divisor` is negative `dividend` is negative	`divisor` is −2 `dividend` is −8	`error` is false `result` is 4.0

(continued)

Reason for Test Case	Input Values	Expected Output
`divisor` is nonzero		
`divisor` is positive	`divisor` is 2	`error` is false
`dividend` is negative	`dividend` is −8	`result` is −4.0
`divisor` is nonzero		
`divisor` is negative	`divisor` is −2	`error` is false
`dividend` is positive	`dividend` is 8	`result` is −4.0
`dividend` is zero		
(`divisor` can be anything)	`divisor` is 2	`error` is false
	`dividend` is 0	`result` is 0.0

In this case the data-coverage test plan is more complex than the code-coverage plan: There are seven cases (two of which are combined) rather than just two. One case covers a zero divisor, and the other six cases check whether the division is working correctly with a nonzero divisor and alternating signs. If we knew that the function uses the built-in division operator, we would not need to check these cases—but we don't. With a data-coverage plan, we cannot see the body of the function.

For program testing to be effective, *it must be planned.* You must design your testing in an organized way, and you must put your design in writing. You should determine the required or desired level of testing, and plan your general strategy and test cases before testing begins. In fact, you should start planning for testing before writing a single line of code.

Planning for Debugging In the previous section we discussed checking the output from our test and debugging when errors were detected. We can debug "on the fly" by adding output statements in suspected trouble spots when problems arise. But in an effort to predict and prevent problems as early as possible, can we also plan our debugging before we ever run the program?

By now you should know that the answer will be yes. When you write your design, you should identify potential trouble spots. You can then insert temporary debugging output statements into your code in places where errors are likely to occur. For example, to trace the program's execution through a complicated sequence of function calls, you might add output statements that indicate when you are entering and leaving each function. The debugging output is even more useful if it also indicates the values of key variables, especially parameters of the function. The following example shows a series of debugging statements that execute at the beginning and end of the function `Divide`:

```
void Divide(int dividend, int divisor, bool& error, float& result)
// Set error to indicate if divisor is zero.
// If no error, set result to dividend / divisor.
{
  using namespace std;
  // For debugging
  cout  << "Function Divide entered."  << endl;
  cout  << "Dividend = "  << dividend << endl;
  cout  << "Divisor = "  << divisor << endl;
  //*************************
  // Rest of code goes here.
  //*************************
  // For debugging
  if (error)
    cout  << "Error = true ";
  else
    cout  << "Error = false ";
  cout  << "and Result = " << result  << endl;
  cout  << "Function Divide terminated."  << endl;
}
```

If hand testing doesn't reveal all the bugs before you run the program, well-placed debugging lines can at least help you locate the rest of the bugs during execution. Note that this output is intended only for debugging; these output lines are meant to be seen only by the tester, not by the user of the program. Of course, it's annoying for debugging output to show up mixed with your application's real output, and it's difficult to debug when the debugging output isn't collected in one place. One way to separate the debugging output from the "real" program output is to declare a separate file to receive these debugging lines, as shown in the following example:

```
#include <fstream>

std::ofstream debugFile;

debugFile  << "This is the debug output from Test 1."  << endl;
```

Usually the debugging output statements are removed from the program, or "commented out," before the program is delivered to the customer or turned in to the professor. (To "comment out" means to turn the statements into comments by preceding them with `//` or enclosing them between `/*` and `*/`.) An advantage of turning the debugging statements into comments is that you can easily and selectively turn them back on for later tests. A disadvantage of this technique is that editing is required throughout the program to change from the testing mode (with debugging) to the operational mode (without debugging).

Another popular technique is to make the debugging output statements dependent on a Boolean flag, which can be turned on or off as desired. For instance, a section of code known to be error-prone may be flagged in various spots for trace output by using the Boolean value `debugFlag`:

```
// Set debugFlag to control debugging mode.
const bool debugFlag = true;
.
.
.
if (debugFlag)
  debugFile  << "Function Divide entered."  << endl;
```

This flag may be turned on or off by assignment, depending on the programmer's needs. Changing to an operational mode (without debugging output) involves merely redefining `debugFlag` as `false` and then recompiling the program. If a flag is used, the debugging statements can be left in the program; only the `if` checks are executed in an operational run of the program. The disadvantage of this technique is that the code for the debugging is always there, making the compiled program larger. If a lot of debugging statements are present, they may waste needed space in a large program. The debugging statements can also clutter up the program, making it more difficult to read. (This situation illustrates another tradeoff we face in developing software.)

Some systems have online debugging programs that provide trace outputs, making the debugging process much simpler. If the system at your school or workplace has a run-time debugger, use it! Any tool that makes the task easier should be welcome, but remember that no tool replaces thinking.

A warning about debugging: Beware the quick fix! Program bugs often travel in swarms, so when you find a bug, don't be too quick to fix it and run your program again. Often as not, fixing one bug generates another. A superficial guess about the cause of a program error usually does not produce a complete solution. In general, time devoted to considering all the ramifications of the changes you are making is time well spent.

If you constantly need to debug, your design process has flaws. Time devoted to considering all the ramifications of the design you are making is time spent best of all.

> **Integration testing** Testing performed to integrate program modules that have already been independently unit tested

Integration Testing In the last two sections we discussed unit testing and planned debugging. In this section we explore many concepts and tools that can help you put your test cases for individual units together for structured testing of your whole program. The goal of this type of testing is to integrate the separately tested pieces, so it is called integration testing.

You can test a large, complicated program in a structured way by using a method very similar to the top-down approach to program design. The central idea is one of divide and conquer: test pieces of the program independently and then use the parts that have been verified as the basis for the next test. The testing can use either a *top-down* or a *bottom-up* approach, or a combination of the two.

Stub A special function that can be used in top-down testing to stand in for a lower-level function

With a top-down approach, we begin testing at the top levels. The purpose of the test is to ensure that the overall logical design works and that the interfaces between modules are correct. At each level of testing, the top-down approach is based on the assumption that the lower-levels work correctly. We implement this assumption by replacing the lower-level subprograms with "placeholder" modules called stubs. A stub may consist of a single trace output statement, indicating that we have reached the function, or a group of debug output statements, showing the current values of the parameters. It may also assign values to output parameters if values are needed by the calling function (the one being tested).

An alternative testing approach is to test from the bottom up. With this approach, we unit test the lowest-level subprograms first. A bottom-up approach can be useful in testing and debugging a critical module, one in which an error would have significant effects on other modules. "Utility" subprograms, such as mathematical functions, can also be tested with test drivers, independently of the programs that eventually call them. In addition, a bottom-up integration testing approach can prove effective in a group-programming environment, where each programmer writes and tests separate modules. The smaller, tested pieces of the program are later verified together in tests of the whole program.

Testing C++ Data Structures

The major topic of this textbook is data structures: what they are, how we use them, and how we implement them using C++. This chapter has provided an overview of software engineering; in Chapter 2 we begin to focus on data and ways to structure it. It seems appropriate to end this section about verification with a look at how we test the data structures we implement in C++.

Throughout this book we implement data structures using C++ classes, so that many different application programs can use the resulting structures. When we first create a class that models a data structure, we do not necessarily have any application programs ready to use it. We need to test the class by itself first, before creating the applications. For this reason, we use a bottom-up testing approach utilizing test drivers.

Every data structure that we implement supports a set of operations. For each structure, we would like to create a test driver that allows us to test the operations in a variety of sequences. How can we write a single test driver that allows us to test numerous operation sequences? The solution is to separate the specific set of operations that we want to test from the test driver program itself. We list the operations, and the necessary parameters, in a text file. The test driver program reads the operations from the text file one line at a time, performs the specified operation by invoking the member function of the data structure being tested, and reports the results to an output file. The test program also reports its general results on the screen.

The testing approach described here allows us to easily change our test cases—we just change the contents of the input file. Testing would be even easier if we could dynamically change the name of the input file, whenever we run the program. We could then run another test case or rerun a previous test case whenever we needed. Therefore, we construct our test driver to read the name of the input file from the

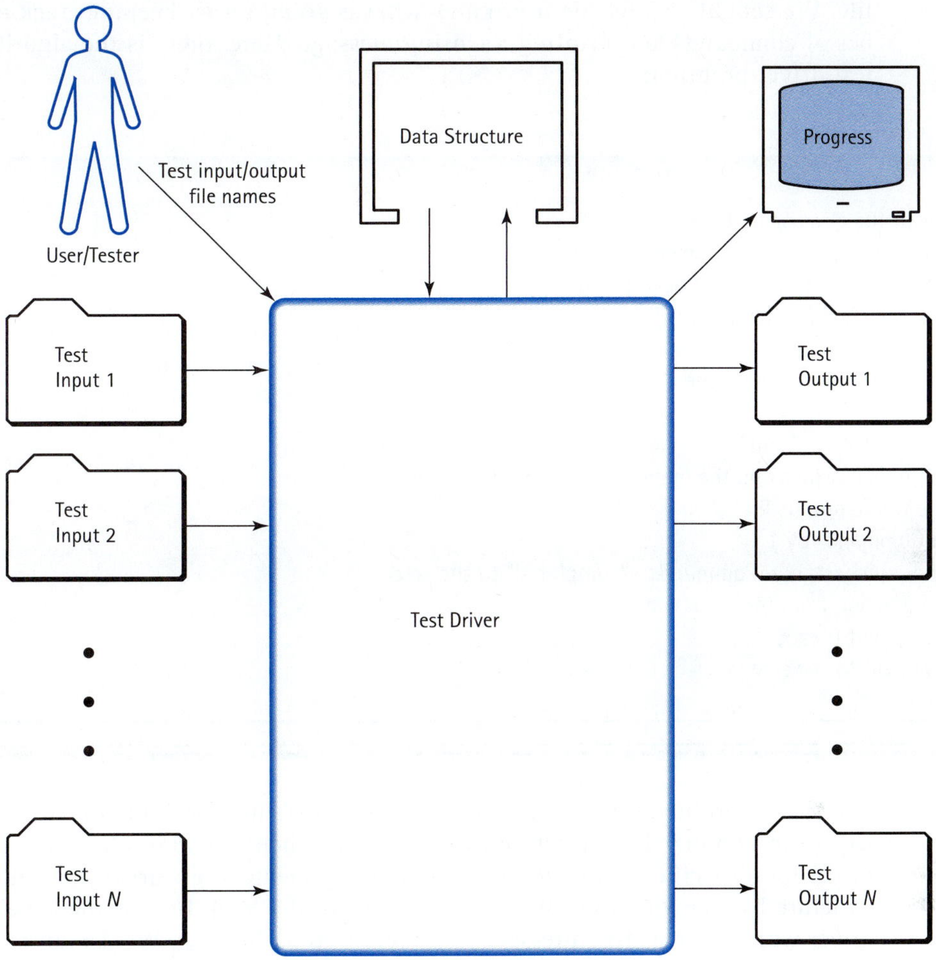

Figure 1.9 *Model of test architecture*

console; we do the same for the output file. Figure 1.9 shows a model of our test architecture.

Our test drivers all follow the same basic algorithm. First, we prompt for and read the file names and prepare the files for input and output. Next, the name of the function to be executed is read from the input file. Because the name of the function drives the flow of control, let's call it `command`. As long as `command` is not "quit," we execute the function with that name, print the results, and read the next function name. We then close the files and quit. Did we forget anything? The output file should have some sort of a label. Let's prompt the user to enter a label for the output file. We should also let the user know what is going on by keeping track of the number of commands and printing a closing message. Here, then, is the algorithm for our test driver program:

```
Declare an instance of the class being tested
Prompt for, read the input file name, and open the file
Prompt for, read the output file name, and open the file
Prompt for and read the label for the output file
Write the label on the output file
Read the next command from the input file
Set numCommands to 0
While the command read is not "quit"
    Execute the command by invoking the member function of the same name
    Print the results to the output file
    Increment numCommands by 1
    Print "Command  number"  numCommands   "completed" to the screen
    Read the next command from the input file
Close the input and output files
Print "Testing completed" to the screen
```

This algorithm provides us with maximum flexibility for minimum extra work when we are testing our data structures. Once we implement the algorithm by creating a test driver for a specific data structure, we can easily create a test driver for a different data structure by changing only the first two steps in the loop. Here is the code for the test driver with the data structure-specific code left to be filled in. We demonstrate how this code can be written in the case study. The statements that must be filled in are shaded.

```
// Test driver
#include <iostream>
#include <fstream>
#include <string>
// #include file containing class to be tested
int main()
{
  using namespace std;
  ifstream inFile;       // File containing operations
  ofstream outFile;      // File containing output
  string inFileName;     // Input file external name
  string outFileName;    // Output file external name
  string outputLabel;
```

```
  string command;        // Operation to be executed
  int numCommands;

  // Declare a variable of the type being tested
  // Prompt for file names, read file names, and prepare files
  cout << "Enter name of input file; press return." << endl;
  cin  >> inFileName;
  inFile.open(inFileName.c_str());

  cout << "Enter name of output file; press return." << endl;
  cin  >> outFileName;
  outFile.open(outFileName.c_str());

  cout << "Enter name of test run; press return." << endl;
  cin  >> outputLabel;
  outFile << outputLabel << endl;

  inFile >> command;
  numCommands = 0;
  while (command != "Quit")
  {

  // The following should be specific to the structure being tested
  // Execute the command by invoking the member function of the
  //  same name
  // Print the results to the output file

    numCommands++;
    cout << "Command number " << numCommands << " completed."
         << endl;
    inFile >> command;
  }

  cout << "Testing completed."  << endl;
  inFile.close();
  outFile.close();
  return 0;
}
```

Note that the test driver gets the test data and calls the member functions to be tested. It also provides written output about the effects of the member function calls, so that the tester can visually check the results. Sometimes test drivers are used to test hundreds or thousands of test cases. In such situations, the test driver should automatically verify whether the test cases were handled successfully. We leave the expansion of this test driver to include automatic test case verification as a programming assignment.

This test driver does not do any error checking to confirm that the inputs are valid. For instance, it doesn't verify that the input command code is really a legal command. Remember that the goal of the test driver is to act as a skeleton of the real program, not to be the real program. Therefore, the test driver does not need to be as robust as the program it simulates.

By now you are probably protesting that these testing approaches are a lot of trouble and that you barely have time to write your programs, let alone "throwaway code" like stubs and drivers. Structured testing methods do require extra work. Test drivers and stubs are software items; they must be written and debugged themselves, even though they are seldom turned in to a professor or delivered to a customer. These programs are part of a class of software development tools that take time to create but are invaluable in simplifying the testing effort.

Such programs are analogous to the scaffolding that a contractor erects around a building. It takes time and money to build the scaffolding, which is not part of the final product; without it, however, the building could not be constructed. In a large program, where verification plays a major role in the software development process, creating these extra tools may be the only way to test the program.

C++ Reading in File Names

The following code segment causes a compile-time error:

```
ifstream inFile;
string fileName;

cout << "Enter the name of the input file" << endl;
cin  >> fileName;
inFile.open(fileName);
```

Why does the error arise? Because C++ recognizes two types of strings. One is a variable of the `string` data type; the other is a limited form of string inherited from the C language. The `open` function expects its argument to be a so-called C string. The code segment shown above passes a `string` variable. Thus it generates a type conflict. To solve this problem, the `string` data type provides a value-returning function named `c_str` that can be applied to a `string` variable to convert it to a C string. Here is the corrected code segment:

```
ifstream inFile;
string fileName;

cout << "Enter the name of the input file" << endl;
cin  >> fileName;
inFile.open(fileName.c_str());
```

Practical Considerations

It is obvious from this chapter that program verification techniques are time consuming and, in a job environment, expensive. It would take a long time to do all of the things discussed in this chapter, and a programmer has only so much time to work on any particular program. Certainly not every program is worthy of such cost and effort. How can you tell how much and what kind of verification effort is necessary?

A program's requirements may provide an indication of the level of verification needed. In the classroom, your professor may specify the verification requirements as part of a programming assignment. For instance, you may be required to turn in a written, implemented test plan. Part of your grade may be determined by the completeness of your plan. In the work environment, the verification requirements are often specified by a customer in the contract for a particular programming job. For

Table 1.3 *Error Rates upon Delivery by Application Domain*[1]

Application Domain	Number Projects	Error Range (Errors/KESLOC)	Normative Error Rate (Errors/ KESLOC)	Notes
Automation	55	2 to 8	5	Factory automation
Banking	30	3 to 10	6	Loan processing, ATM
Command & Control	45	0.5 to 5	1	Command centers
Data Processing	35	2 to 14	8	DB-intensive systems
Environment/Tools	75	5 to 12	8	CASE, compilers, etc.
Military -All	125	0.2 to 3	< 1.0	See subcategories
• Airborne	40	0.2 to 1.3	0.5	Embedded sensors
• Ground	52	0.5 to 4	0.8	Combat center
• Missile	15	0.3 to 1.5	0.5	GNC system
• Space	18	0.2 to 0.8	0.4	Attitude control system
Scientific	35	0.9 to 5	2	Seismic processing
Telecommunications	50	3 to 12	6	Digital switches
Test	35	3 to 15	7	Test equipment devices
Trainers/Simulations	25	2 to 11	6	Virtual reality simulator
Web Business	65	4 to 18	11	Client/server sites
Other	25	2 to 15	7	All others

[1]Source: Donald J. Reifer, Industry Software Cost, Quality and Productivity Benchmarks, STN Vol 7(2), 2004.

instance, a contract with a military customer may specify that formal reviews or inspections of the software product be held at various times during the development process.

A higher level of verification effort may be indicated for sections of a program that are particularly complicated or error-prone. In these cases, it is wise to start the verification process in the early stages of program development so as to avoid costly errors in the design.

A program whose correct execution is critical to human life is obviously a candidate for a high level of verification. For instance, a program that controls the return of astronauts from a space mission would require a higher level of verification than would a program that generates a grocery list. As a more down-to-earth example, consider the potential for disaster if a hospital's patient database system had a bug that caused it to lose information about patients' allergies to medications. A similar error in a database program that manages a Christmas card mailing list, however, would have much less severe consequences.

The error rates over various industries confirms this distinction. The more human-critical, the lower the error rate (Table 1.3).

Case Study

Fraction Class

Write and test a C++ class that represents a fraction.

Logical Level

A fraction is made up of a numerator and a denominator, so our fraction class must have data members for each of these. What operations do we normally apply to fractions? First we must initialize a fraction by storing values into the numerator and the denominator, and we need member functions that return the numerator and the denominator. Another operation would reduce the fraction to its lowest terms. We should also be able to test whether the fraction is equal to zero or greater than 1. If the fraction is greater than or equal to 1 (not a proper fraction), we should have an operation that converts the fraction to a whole number and a fraction. There are binary operations on fractions, but we are asked only to write and test a class that represents a fraction. Binary operations could be added later.

Let's summarize what we have said so far using a CRC card. A CRC card is a 4″ × 6″ or a 5″ × 8″ card on which we record the name of the class, the responsibilities, and the classes with which the class collaborates. CRC cards are used frequently in object-oriented design, and we discuss them in more detail in later chapters. Here we use one to record what we have decided our fraction class must do. We call the actions that the class must perform the *responsibilities of the class.* We use a handwriting font to indicate that CRC cards are a pencil and paper tool. We change to a monospaced font for the operations when we are talking about their implementation.

Class Name: Fraction Type	Superclass:	Subclasses:
Primary Responsibilities: Represents a fraction		
Responsibilities	**Collaborations**	
Initialize (numerator, denominator)	Integers	
Return numerator value	Integers	
Return denominator value	Integers	
Reduce to lowest terms		
Is the fraction zero?		
Is it greater than one?		
Convert to proper fraction		

Before we translate this CRC card into a class definition in C++, let's examine each operation again. Let's change the expressions for the responsibilities into function names. The `Initialize` operation takes two integer values and stores them into the data members of the class. Let's call these data members `num` and `denom`. `getNumerator` and `getDenominator` return the values of the data members. In object-oriented terminology, functions that return the value of an item are usually called "get" appended to the item name.

`Reduce` checks whether the numerator and the denominator have a common factor and, if they do, divides both by the common factor. On second thought, should making sure that the fraction is in reduced form be left to the user of the fraction class? If a fraction is not reduced to its lowest terms, binary arithmetic operations could cause overflow problems; the sizes of the numerator and denominator could become quite large. Let's remove this operation as a member function and make it a precondition for instances of our fraction class. If binary operations are added to the class, it becomes the responsibility of these operations to reduce the resulting fraction to its reduced form.

`IsZero` tests whether the fraction is zero. How do we represent zero as a fraction? The numerator is zero and the denominator is 1, so `IsZero` tests whether the numerator is zero. `IsGreaterThanOrEqualToOne` is too long an identifier. Let's call the operation that tests to see if the numerator is greater than or equal to the denominator `IsNotProper`. `ConvertToProper` returns the whole-number part and leaves the remaining part in the fraction.

We are now ready to write the class definition. We know what each operation should do. What about the preconditions for the operations? All fractions involved must be initialized before the member functions are called and must be in reduced form. `ConvertToProper` should be called only if the fraction is improper.

```
class FractionType
{
public:
  void Initialize(int numerator, int denominator);
  // Function: Initialize the fraction
  // Pre:  Numerator and denominator are in reduced form
  // Post: Fraction is initialized
  int GetNumerator();
  // Function: Returns the value of the numerator
  // Pre:  Fraction has been initialized
  // Post: Numerator is returned
  int GetDenominator();
  // Function: Returns the value of the denominator
  // Pre:  Fraction has been initialized
  // Post: Denominator is returned
  bool IsZero();
  // Function: Determines if fraction is zero
  // Pre:  Fraction has been initialized
  // Post: Returns true if numerator is zero, false otherwise
  bool IsNotProper();
  // Function: Determines if fraction is a proper fraction
  // Pre:  Fraction has been initialized
  // Post: Returns true if fraction is greater than or equal to 1; false
  //       otherwise
  int ConvertToProper();
  // Function: Converts the fraction to a whole number and a
  //  fractional part
  // Pre:  Fraction has been initialized, is in reduced form, and
  //       is not a proper fraction
  // Post: Returns whole number
  //       Remaining fraction is original fraction minus the
  //       whole number; fraction is in reduced form
private:
  int num;
  int denom;
};
```

Application Level (Test Driver)

At this stage, before we write any code for the member functions, we can write our test driver using the algorithm shown in the last section. Let's call the instance of the `FractionType` `fraction`. Here is the portion of the algorithm that we must write:

```
while . . .
    Execute the command by invoking the member function of the same name
    Print the results to the output file
. . .
```

We have six member functions to test. We can set up an *if-then-else* statement comparing the input operation to the member function names. When the name matches, the function is called and the result is written to the output file.

```
if (command is "Initialize")
    Read numerator
    Read denominator
    fraction.Initialize(numerator, denominator)
    Write on outFile "Numerator: ", fraction.GetNumerator()
        "Denominator: ", fraction.GetDenominator()
else if (command is "GetNumerator")
    Write on outFile "Numerator: ", fraction.GetNumerator()
else if (command is "GetDenominator")
    Write on outFile "Denominator: ", fraction.GetDenominator()
else if (command is "IsZero")
    if (fraction.IsZero)
        Write on outFile "Fraction is zero"
    else
        Write on outFile "Fraction is not zero"
else if (command is "IsNotProper")
    if (fraction.IsNotProper())
        Write on outFile "Fraction is improper"
    else
        Write on outFile "Fraction is proper"
else
    Write on outFile " Whole number is ", (fraction.ConvertToProper())
    Write on outFile "Numerator: ", fraction.GetNumerator()
    "Denominator:", fraction.GetDenominator()
```

The file containing the specification of `class FractionType` is in file "`frac.h`". Here are the pieces that must be added to the generalized test driver to test this class:

```
#include "frac.h"          // File containing the class to be tested

FractionType fraction;     // Declaration of FractionType object

while (command != "Quit")
{
  if (command == "Initialize")
  {
```

```
    int numerator, denominator;
    inFile  >> numerator;
    inFile  >> denominator;
    fraction.Initialize(numerator, denominator);
    outFile << "Numerator: "  << fraction.GetNumerator()
      << " Denominator: " << fraction.GetDenominator()
      << endl;
  }
  else if (command == "GetNumerator")
    outFile << "Numerator: "  << fraction.GetNumerator()
      << endl;
  else if (command == "GetDenominator")
    outFile << "Denominator: " << fraction.GetDenominator()
      << endl;
  else if (command == "IsZero")
    if (fraction.IsZero())
      outFile << "Fraction is zero " << endl;
    else
      outFile << "Fraction is not zero " << endl;
  else if (command == "IsNotProper")
    if (fraction.IsNotProper())
      outFile << "Fraction is improper " << endl;
    else
      outFile << "Fraction is proper " << endl;
  else
  {
    outFile << "Whole number is " << fraction.ConvertToProper()
      << endl;
    outFile <<  "Numerator: "  << fraction.GetNumerator()
      <<   " Denominator: " << fraction.GetDenominator()
      << endl;
  }

  :
}
```

Implementation Level

We have the test driver and the specification file containing the class. Now we must write the code for the function definitions and write and implement the test plan. The algorithms for the first five functions are so straightforward that they can be written with no further comment. The fifth function, `ConvertToProper`, must return the whole-number integer. It is extracted by taking the integer result of dividing the denominator into the numerator. The integer remainder becomes the numerator of the remaining fraction, and the denominator remains the same. If the numerator of the remaining fraction is zero, we must set the denominator to 1 to be consistent with the definition of a zero fraction.

```
// Implementation file for class FractionType
#include "frac.h"
void FractionType::Initialize(int numerator, int denominator)
// Function: Initialize the fraction
// Pre:  numerator and denominator are in reduced form
// Post: numerator is stored in num; denominator is stored in
//       denom
{
  num = numerator;
  denom = denominator;
}

int FractionType::GetNumerator()
// Function: Returns the value of the numerator
// Pre:  Fraction has been initialized
// Post: numerator is returned
{
  return num;
}
int FractionType::GetDenominator()
// Function: Returns the value of the denominator
// Pre:  Fraction has been initialized
// Post: denominator is returned
{
  return denom;
}

bool FractionType::IsZero()
// Function: Determines if fraction is zero
// Pre:  Fraction has been initialized
// Post: Returns true if numerator is zero; false otherwise
{
  return (num == 0);
}

bool FractionType::IsNotProper()
// Function: Determines if fraction is a proper fraction
// Pre:  Fraction has been initialized
// Post: Returns true if num is greater than or equal to denom; false
//       otherwise
{
  return (num >= denom);
}

int FractionType::ConvertToProper()
// Function: Converts the fraction to a whole number and a
```

```
//        fractional part
// Pre:   Fraction has been initialized, is in reduced form, and
//        is not a proper fraction
// Post:  Returns num divided by denom
//        num is original num % denom; denom is not changed
{
  int result;
  result = num / denom;
  num = num % denom;
  if (num == 0)
    denom = 1;
  return result;
}
```

Here is the UML diagram for class `FractionType`.

FractionType
-num: int -denom: int
+Initialize (numerator: int, denominator: int): void +GetNumerator(): int +GetDenominator(): int +IsZero(): bool +IsNotProper(): bool +ConvertToProper(): int

The negative sign indicates that the field is private; the plus sign indicates that the field is public. Look back at the CRC card and you see no information about the internal representation of the class. The CRC card is a notational tool used during the design phase. The UML diagram, on the other hand, does display the internal data fields and their types. The UML diagram is documentation for those responsible for maintaining a system.

Test Plan

We have six member functions to test. Two of the six are Boolean functions, so we need two test cases for each. Here, then, is a test plan that has eight cases. Note that we have to initialize the fraction three times: once for a proper fraction, once for an improper fraction, and once for zero.

Here are the input file, the output file, and a screenshot from the run:

Input File

```
Initialize
3
```

Output File

```
Test_Run_for_FractionType
Numerator: 3 Denominator: 4
```

```
4                      Fraction is not zero
IsZero                 Fraction is proper
IsNotProper            Numerator: 3
getNumerator           Denominator: 4
getDenominator         Numerator: 4 Denominator: 3
Initialize             Fraction is improper
4                      Whole number is 1
3                      Numerator: 1 Denominator: 3
IsNotProper            Numerator: 0 Denominator: 1
ConvertToProper        Fraction is zero
Initialize
0
1
IsZero
Quit
```

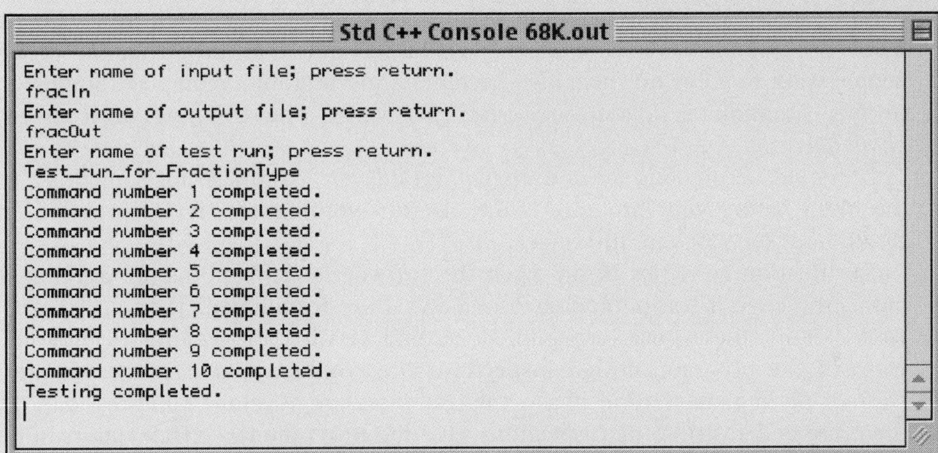

Our test plan has been executed and the right results have been obtained. But we were lucky. All of the commands in the input file were correctly spelled. What would have happened if the command "Initialize" had been "initialize"? The program would have crashed. The misspelled command would have fallen through the sieve and the last `else` branch would have been executed. In this case the code would have tried to print an undefined proper fraction.

This is an example of code that is not *robust*. To make the driver more robust, the names of the commands should be changed to all uppercase or all lowercase before comparing them. In addition, printing the fraction should be an explicit command; the default should always be used for a misspelled command. Remember, if there are N functions to be tested, there must be $N+1$ branches in the driver.

Summary

How are our quality software goals met by the strategies of abstraction and information hiding? When details are hidden at each level, the code becomes simpler and more readable, which makes the program easier to write and modify. Both functional decomposition and object-oriented design processes produce modular units that are also easier to test, debug, and maintain.

One positive side effect of modular design is that modifications tend to be localized in a small set of modules, so the cost of modifications is reduced. Remember that whenever a module is modified, it must be retested to make sure that it still works correctly in the program. By localizing the modules affected by changes to the program, we limit the extent of retesting needed.

We increase reliability by making the design conform to our logical picture and delegating confusing details to lower levels of abstraction. An understanding of the wide range of activities involved in software development—from requirements analysis through maintenance of the resulting program—leads to an appreciation of a disciplined software engineering approach. Everyone knows some programming wizard who can sit down and hack out a program in an evening, working alone, coding without a formal design. But we cannot depend on wizardry to control the design, implementation, verification, and maintenance of large, complex software projects that involve the efforts of many programmers. As computers grow larger and more powerful, the problems that people want to solve on them also become larger and more complex. Some people refer to this situation as a software *crisis*. We'd like you to think of it as a software *challenge*.

It should be obvious by now that program verification is not something you begin the night before your program is due. Design verification and program testing go on throughout the software life cycle.

Verification activities begin when the software specifications are developed. At this point, the overall testing approach and goals are formulated. Then, as program design work begins, these goals are applied. Formal verification techniques may be used for parts of the program, design inspections are conducted, and test cases are planned. During the implementation phase, the test cases are developed and test data to support them are generated. Code inspections give the programmer extra support in debugging the program before it is ever run. When the code has been compiled and is ready to be run, unit (module-level) testing is done, with stubs and drivers used for support. After these units have been completely tested, they are put together in integration tests. Once errors have been found and corrected, some of the earlier tests are rerun to make sure that the corrections have not introduced any new problems. Finally, acceptance tests of the whole system are performed. Figure 1.10 shows how the various types of verification activities fit into the software development life cycle. Throughout the life cycle, one thing remains constant: The earlier in this cycle program errors are detected, the easier (and less costly in time, effort, and money) they are to remove. Program verification is a serious subject; a program that doesn't work isn't worth the disk it's stored on.

Analysis	Make sure that specifications are completely understood. Understand testing requirements.
Specification	Verify the identified requirements. Perform requirements inspections with your client.
Design	Design for correctness (using assertions such as preconditions and postconditions). Perform design inspections. Plan the testing approach.
Code	Understand the programming language well. Perform code inspections. Add debugging output statements to the program. Write the test plan. Construct test drivers and/or stubs.
Test	Unit test according to the test plan. Debug as necessary. Integrate tested modules. Retest after corrections.
Delivery	Execute acceptance tests of the completed product.
Maintenance	Execute regression test whenever the delivered product is changed to add new functionality or to correct detected problems.

Figure 1.10 *Life-cycle verification activities*

Exercises

1. Explain what we mean by "software engineering."
2. Which of these statements is always true?
   a. All of the program requirements must be completely defined before design begins.
   b. All of the program design must be complete before any coding begins.
   c. All of the coding must be complete before any testing can begin.
   d. Different development activities often take place concurrently, overlapping in the software life cycle.
3. Name three computer hardware tools that you have used.
4. Name two software tools that you have used in developing computer programs.
5. Explain what we mean by "ideaware."
6. Explain why software might need to be modified
   a. in the design phase.
   b. in the coding phase.

   c. in the testing phase.
   d. in the maintenance phase.
7. Software quality goal 4 says, "Quality software is completed on time and within budget."
   a. Explain some of the consequences of not meeting this goal for a student preparing a class programming assignment.
   b. Explain some of the consequences of not meeting this goal for a team developing a highly competitive new software product.
   c. Explain some of the consequences of not meeting this goal for a programmer who is developing the user interface (the screen input/output) for a spacecraft launch system.
8. For each of the following, describe at least two different abstractions for different viewers (see Figure 1.1).
   a. A dress
   b. An aspirin
   c. A carrot
   d. A key
   e. A saxophone
   f. A piece of wood
9. Functional decomposition is based on a hierarchy of ________________, and object-oriented design is based on a hierarchy of ________________.
10. What is the difference between an object and an object class? Give some examples.
11. Make a list of potential objects from the description of the automated teller machine scenario given in this chapter.
12. Have you ever written a programming assignment with an error in the specifications? If so, at what point did you catch the error? How damaging was the error to your design and code?
13. Explain why the cost of fixing an error is higher the later in the software cycle that the error is detected.
14. Explain how an expert understanding of your programming language can reduce the amount of time you spend debugging.
15. Give an example of a run-time error that might occur as the result of a programmer making too many assumptions.
16. Define "robustness." How can programmers make their programs more robust by taking a defensive approach?
17. The following program has three separate errors, each of which would cause an infinite loop. As a member of the inspection team, you could save the programmer a lot of testing time by finding the errors during the inspection. Can you help?

```
void Increment(int);
int main()
{
  int count = 1;
  while(count < 10)
  cout  << " The number after "  << count;  /* Function Increment
  Increment(count);                   adds 1 to count */
  cout  << " is " << count << endl;
  return 0;
}
void Increment (int nextNumber)
// Increment the parameter by 1.
{
  nextNumber++;
}
```

18. Is there any way a single programmer (for example, a student working alone on a programming assignment) can benefit from some of the ideas behind the inspection process?
19. When is it appropriate to start planning a program's testing?
    a. During design or even earlier
    b. While coding
    c. As soon as the coding is complete
20. Differentiate between unit testing and integration testing.
21. Explain the advantages and disadvantages of the following debugging techniques:
    a. Inserting output statements that may be turned off by commenting them out
    b. Using a Boolean flag to turn debugging output statements on or off
    c. Using a system debugger
22. Describe a realistic goal-oriented approach to data-coverage testing of the function specified below:

FindElement(list, targetItem, index, found)

Function:	Search list for targetItem.
Preconditions:	Elements of list are in no particular order; list may be empty.
Postconditions:	found is true if targetItem is in list; otherwise, found is false. index is the position of targetItem if found is true.

23. A program is to read in a numeric score (0 to 100) and display an appropriate letter grade (A, B, C, D, or F).
    a. What is the functional domain of this program?
    b. Is exhaustive data coverage possible for this program?
    c. Devise a test plan for this program.
24. Explain how paths and branches relate to code coverage in testing. Can we attempt 100% path coverage?
25. Differentiate between "top-down" and "bottom-up" integration testing.
26. Explain the phrase "life-cycle verification."
27. Write the corrected version of the function `Divide`.
28. Why did we type cast `dividend` and `divisor` in the function `Divide`?
29. The solution to the Case Study did not consider negative fractions.
    a. How should a negative fraction be represented?
    b. Which of the member functions would have to be changed to represent negative fractions? What changes would be involved?
    c. Rewrite the test plan to test for negative fractions.
30. One of the member functions in the Case Study needed an additional test. Which function is it and what should the data be?
31. Name four tools used in software design.
32. Define information hiding.
33. Name four types of step-wise refinement.
34. What is the key feature of top-down design?
35. What characterizes functional decomposition?
36. Name two visual tools used by software developers.
37. In reviews and inspections, what is being reviewed or inspected?
38. Give the basic design of a test driver.
39. Why is exhaustive code coverage testing virtually impossible?
40. Why is exhaustive data coverage testing virtually impossible?

chapter 2

Data Design and Implementation

Goals

After studying this chapter, you should be able to

- Describe an ADT from three perspectives: the logical level, the application level, and the implementation level
- Explain how a specification can be used to record an abstract data type
- Describe the component selector at the logical level, and describe appropriate applications for the C++ built-in types: structs, classes, one-dimensional arrays, and two-dimensional arrays
- Declare a class object
- Implement the member functions of a class
- Manipulate instances of a class (objects)
- Define the three ingredients of an object-oriented programming language: encapsulation, inheritance, and polymorphism
- Distinguish between containment and inheritance
- Use inheritance to derive one class from another class
- Use the C++ exception-handling mechanism
- Access identifiers within a namespace
- Explain the use of Big-O notation to describe the amount of work done by an algorithm

In Chapter 1, we looked at an overview of the design process and reviewed the software engineering principles that, if followed, lead to quality software. The role of testing at all phases of the software life cycle was stressed.

In this chapter, we lay out the logical framework from which we examine data structures. We look at data structures from three points of view: how they are specified, how they are implemented, and how they can be used. In addition, the object-oriented view of data objects is presented. Finally, we examine C++ constructs that can be used to ensure the data structures we construct are correct.

2.1 Different Views of Data

What Do We Mean by Data?

When we talk about the function of a program, we use words such as "add," "read," "multiply," "write," "do," and so on. The function of a program describes what it does in terms of the verbs in the programming language.

The data are the nouns of the programming world: the objects that are manipulated, the information that is processed by a computer program. In a sense, this information is just a collection of bits that can be turned on or off. The computer itself needs to have data in this form. Humans, however, tend to think of information in terms of somewhat larger units such as numbers and lists, so we want at least the human-readable portions of our programs to refer to data in a way that makes sense to us. To separate the computer's view of data from our own view, we use data abstraction to create other views. Whether we use functional decomposition to produce a hierarchy of tasks or object-oriented design to produce a hierarchy of cooperating objects, data abstraction is essential.

Data abstraction The separation of a data type's logical properties from its implementation

Data Abstraction

Many people feel more comfortable with things that they perceive as real than with things that they think of as abstract. As a consequence, "data abstraction" may seem more forbidding than a more concrete entity such as an "integer." But let's take a closer look at that very concrete—and very abstract—integer you've been using since you wrote your earliest programs.

Just what is an integer? Integers are physically represented in different ways on different computers. In the memory of one machine, an integer may be a binary-coded decimal. In a second machine, it may be a sign-and-magnitude binary. And in a third one, it may be represented in one's complement or two's complement notation. Although you may not know what any of these terms mean, that lack of knowledge hasn't stopped you from using integers. (You learn about these terms in an assembly language course, so we do not explain them here.) Figure 2.1 shows several representations of an integer number.

The way that integers are physically represented determines how the computer manipulates them. As a C++ programmer, you rarely get involved at this level; instead,

Binary 10011001

Decimal:	153	–25	–102	–103	99
Representation:	Unsigned	Sign and magnitude	One's complement	Two's complement	Binary-coded decimal

Figure 2.1 *The decimal equivalents of an 8-bit binary number*

you simply use integers. All you need to know is how to declare an `int` type variable and what operations are allowed on integers: assignment, addition, subtraction, multiplication, division, and modulo arithmetic.

Consider the statement

```
distance = rate * time;
```

It's easy to understand the concept behind this statement. The concept of multiplication doesn't depend on whether the operands are, say, integers or real numbers, despite the fact that integer multiplication and floating-point multiplication may be implemented in very different ways on the same computer. Computers would not be so popular if every time we wanted to multiply two numbers we had to get down to the machine-representation level. But that isn't necessary: C++ has surrounded the `int` data type with a nice, neat package and has given you just the information you need to create and manipulate data of this type.

Another word for "surround" is "encapsulate." Think of the capsules surrounding the medicine you get from the pharmacist when you're sick. You don't have to know anything about the chemical composition of the medicine inside to recognize the big blue-and-white capsule as your antibiotic or the little yellow capsule as your decongestant. Data encapsulation means that the physical representation of a program's data is surrounded. The user of the data doesn't see the implementation, but deals with the data only in terms of its logical picture–its abstraction.

> **Data encapsulation** The separation of the representation of data from the applications that use the data at a logical level; a programming language feature that enforces information hiding

If the data are encapsulated, how can the user get to them? Operations must be provided to allow the user to create, access, and change data. Let's look at the operations C++ provides for the encapsulated data type `int`. First, you can create ("construct") variables of type `int` using declarations in your program. Then you can assign values to these integer variables by using the assignment operator or by reading values into them and perform arithmetic operations using +, -, *, /, and %. Figure 2.2 shows how C++ has encapsulated the type `int` in a tidy package.

The point of this discussion is that you have been dealing with a logical data abstraction of "integer" since the very beginning. The advantages of doing so are clear: You can think of the data and the operations in a logical sense and can consider their use without having to worry about implementation details. The lower levels are still there–they're just hidden from you.

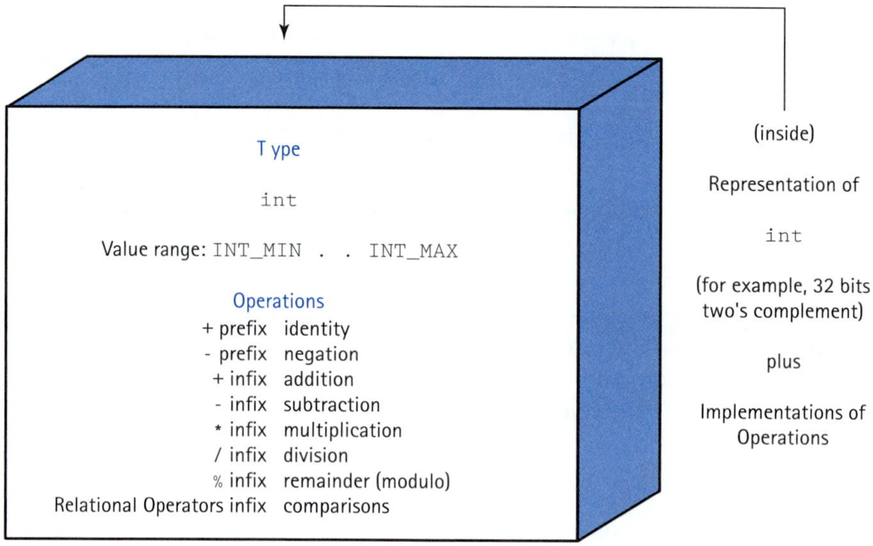

Figure 2.2 *A black box representing an integer*

Remember that the goal in design is to reduce complexity through abstraction. We can extend this goal further: to protect our data abstraction through encapsulation. We refer to the set of all possible values (the *domain*) of an encapsulated data "object," plus the specifications of the operations that are provided to create and manipulate the data, as an abstract data type (ADT for short).

Abstract data type (ADT) A data type whose properties (domain and operations) are specified independently of any particular implementation

Data Structures

A single integer can be very useful if we need a counter, a sum, or an index in a program, but generally we must also deal with data that have lots of parts, such as a list. We describe the logical properties of such a collection of data as an abstract data type; we call the concrete implementation of the data a data structure. When a program's information is made up of component parts, we must consider an appropriate data structure.

Data structure A collection of data elements whose organization is characterized by accessing operations that are used to store and retrieve the individual data elements; the implementation of the composite data members in an abstract data type

Data structures have a few features worth noting. First, they can be "decomposed" into their component elements. Second, the arrangement of the elements is a feature of the structure that affects how each element is accessed. Third, both the arrangement of the elements and the way they are accessed can be encapsulated.

Let's look at a real-life example: a library. A library can be decomposed into its component elements–books. The collection of individual books can be arranged in a number of ways, as shown in Figure 2.3. Obviously, the way the books are physically arranged on the shelves determines how one would go about looking for a specific

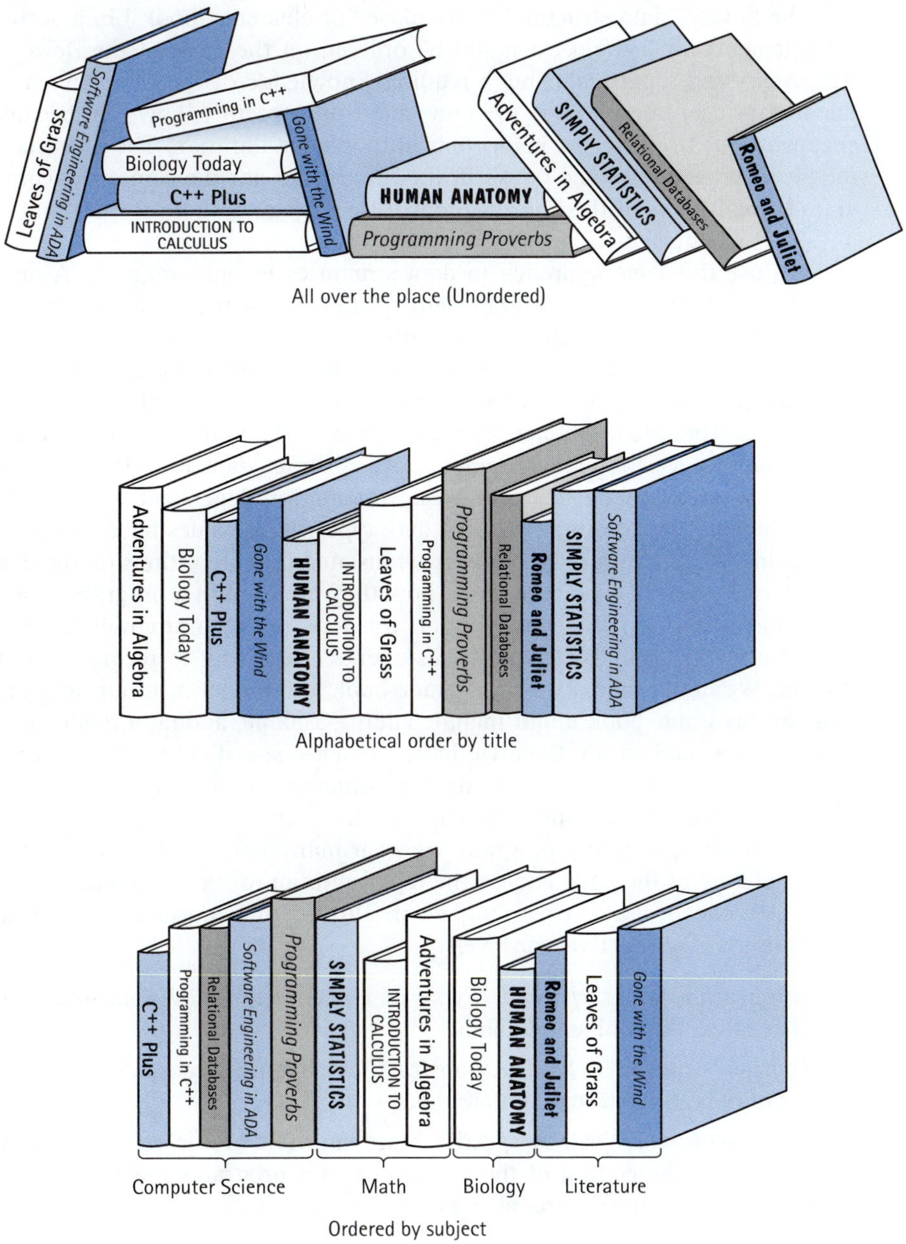

Figure 2.3 *A collection of books ordered in different ways*

volume. The particular library with which we're concerned doesn't let its patrons get their own books, however; if you want a book, you must give your request to the librarian, who retrieves the book for you.

The library "data structure" is composed of elements (books) in a particular physical arrangement; for instance, it might be ordered on the basis of the Dewey decimal system. Accessing a particular book requires knowledge of the arrangement of the books. The library user doesn't have to know about the structure, however, because it has been encapsulated: Users access books only through the librarian. The physical structure and the abstract picture of the books in the library are not the same. The card catalog provides logical views of the library—ordered by subject, author, or title—that differ from its physical arrangement.

We use the same approach to data structures in our programs. A data structure is defined by (1) the logical arrangement of data elements, combined with (2) the set of operations we need to access the elements.

Notice the difference between an abstract data type and a data structure. The former is a high-level description: the logical picture of the data and the operations that manipulate them. The latter is concrete: a collection of data elements and the operations that store and retrieve individual elements. An abstract data type is implementation independent, whereas a data structure is implementation dependent. A data structure is how we implement the data in an abstract data type whose values have component parts. The operations on an abstract data type are translated into algorithms on the data structure.

Another view of data focuses on how they are used in a program to solve a particular problem—that is, their application. If we were writing a program to keep track of student grades, we would need a list of students and a way to record the grades for each student. We might take a by-hand grade book and model it in our program. The operations on the grade book might include adding a name, adding a grade, averaging a student's grades, and so on. Once we have written a specification for our grade book data type, we must choose an appropriate data structure to implement it and design the algorithms to implement the operations on the structure.

In modeling data in a program, we wear many hats. That is, we must determine the logical picture of the data, choose the representation of the data, and develop the operations that encapsulate this arrangement. During this process, we consider data from three different perspectives, or levels:

1. *Application (or user) level:* A way of modeling real-life data in a specific context; also called the problem domain
2. *Logical (or abstract) level:* An abstract view of the data values (the domain) and the set of operations to manipulate them
3. *Implementation level:* A specific representation of the structure to hold the data items, and the coding of the operations in a programming language (if the operations are not already provided by the language)

In our discussion, we refer to the second perspective as the "abstract data type." Because an abstract data type can be a simple type such as an integer or character, as well as a structure that contains component elements, we also use the term "composite data type" to refer to abstract data types that may contain component elements. The third level describes how we actually represent and manipulate the data in memory: the data structure and the algorithms for the operations that manipulate the items on the structure.

Let's see what these different viewpoints mean in terms of our library analogy. At the application level, we focus on entities such as the Library of Congress, the Dimsdale Collection of Rare Books, and the Austin City Library.

At the logical level, we deal with the "what" questions. What is a library? What services (operations) can a library perform? The library may be seen abstractly as "a collection of books" for which the following operations are specified:

- Check out a book
- Check in a book
- Reserve a book that is currently checked out
- Pay a fine for an overdue book
- Pay for a lost book

How the books are organized on the shelves is not important at the logical level, because the patrons don't have direct access to the books. The abstract viewer of library services is not concerned with how the librarian actually organizes the books in the library. Instead, the library user needs to know only the correct way to invoke the desired operation. For instance, here is the user's view of the operation to check in a book: Present the book at the check-in window of the library from which the book was checked out, and receive a fine slip if the book is overdue.

At the implementation level, we deal with the "how" questions. How are the books cataloged? How are they organized on the shelf? How does the librarian process a book when it is checked in? For instance, the implementation information includes the fact that the books are cataloged according to the Dewey decimal system and arranged in four levels of stacks, with 14 rows of shelves on each level. The librarian needs such knowledge to be able to locate a book. This information also includes the details of what happens when each operation takes place. For example, when a book is checked back in, the librarian may use the following algorithm to implement the check-in operation:

CheckInBook

```
Examine due date to see whether the book is late.
if book is late
    Calculate fine.
    Issue fine slip.
Update library records to show that the book has been returned.
Check reserve list to see if someone is waiting for the book.
if book is on reserve list
    Put book on the reserve shelf.
else
    Replace book on the proper shelf, according to the library's shelf arrangement scheme.
```

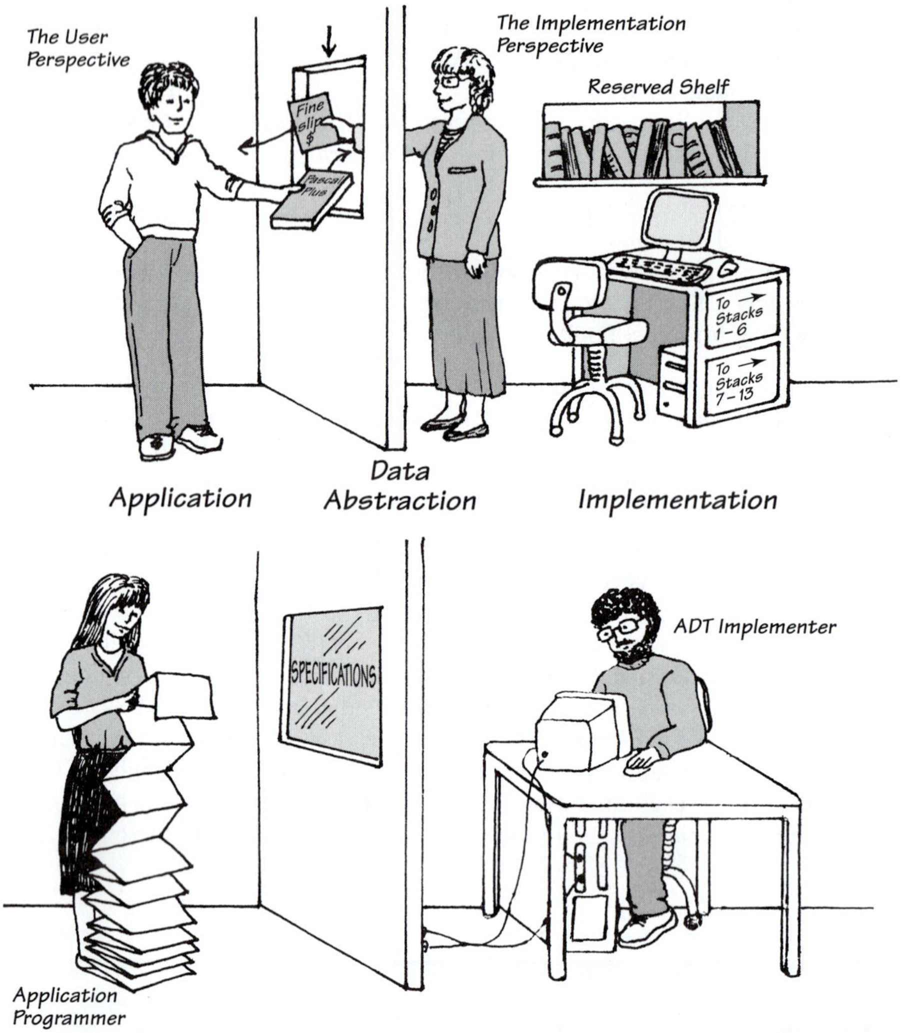

Figure 2.4 *Communication between the application level and implementation level*

All of this activity, of course, is invisible to the library user. The goal of our design approach is to hide the implementation level from the user.

Picture a wall separating the application level from the implementation level, as shown in Figure 2.4. Imagine yourself on one side and another programmer on the other side. How do the two of you, with your separate views of the data, communicate across this wall? Similarly, how do the library user's view and the librarian's view of the library come together? The library user and the librarian communicate through the data abstraction. The abstract view provides the specification of the accessing operations without telling how the operations work. It tells *what* but not *how*. For instance, the abstract view of checking in a book can be summarized in the following specification:

CheckInBook(library, book, fineSlip)

Function:	Check in a book
Preconditions:	book was checked out of this library; book is presented at the check-in desk
Postconditions:	fineSlip is issued if book is overdue; contents of library is the original contents + book

The only communication from the user into the implementation level occurs in terms of input specifications and allowable assumptions–the preconditions of the accessing routines. The only output from the implementation level back to the user is the transformed data structure described by the output specifications, or postconditions, of the routines. The abstract view hides the data structure, but provides windows into it through the specified accessing operations.

When you write a program as a class assignment, you often deal with data at all three levels. In a job situation, however, you may not. Sometimes you may program an application that uses a data type that has been implemented by another programmer. Other times you may develop "utilities" that are called by other programs. In this book we ask you to move back and forth between these levels.

Abstract Data Type Operator Categories

In general, the basic operations that are performed on an abstract data type are classified into four categories: *constructors*, *transformers* (also called *mutators*), *observers*, and *iterators*.

A constructor is an operation that creates a new instance (object) of an abstract data type. It is almost always invoked at the language level by some sort of declaration. Transformers are operations that change the state of one or more of the data values, such as inserting an item into an object, deleting an item from an object, or making an object empty. An operation that takes two objects and merges them into a third object is a binary transformer.[1]

> **Constructor** An operation that creates a new instance of a class
>
> **Transformer** An operation that changes the internal state of an object
>
> **Observer** An operation that allows us to observe the state of an object without changing it
>
> **Iterator** An operation that allows us to process all components in a data structure sequentially.

An observer is an operation that allows us to observe the state of one or more of the data values without changing them. Observers come in several forms: *predicates* that ask if a certain property is true, *accessor* or *selector* functions that return a copy of an item in the object, and *summary* functions that return information about the object

[1]In some of the literature, operations that create new instances are called *primitive constructors*, and transformers are called *nonprimitive constructors*.

as a whole. A Boolean function that returns true if an object is empty and false if it contains any components is an example of a predicate. A function that returns a copy of the last item put into the structure is an example of an accessor function. A function that returns the number of items in the structure is a summary function.

An iterator is an operation that allows us to process all components in a data structure sequentially. Operations that print the items in a list or return successive list items are iterators. Iterators are only defined on structured data types.

In later chapters, we use these ideas to define and implement some useful data types that may be new to you. First, however, let's explore the built-in composite data types C++ provides for us.

2.2 Abstraction and Built-In Types

In the last section, we suggested that a built-in simple type such as `int` or `float` could be viewed as an abstraction whose underlying implementation is defined in terms of machine-level operations. The same perspective applies to built-in composite data types provided in programming languages to build data objects. A composite data type is one in which a name is given to a collection of data items. Composite data types come in two forms: unstructured and structured. An *unstructured* composite type is a collection of components that are not organized with respect to one another. A *structured* data type is an organized collection of components in which the organization determines the method used to access individual data components.

Composite data type A data type that allows a collection of values to be associated with an object of that type

For instance, C++ provides the following composite types: records (structs), classes, and arrays of various dimensions. Classes and structs can have member functions as well as data, but it is the organization of the data we are considering here. Classes and structs are logically unstructured; arrays are structured.

Let's look at each of these types from our three perspectives. First, we examine the abstract view of the structure—how we construct variables of that type and how we access individual components in our programs. Next, from an application perspective, we discuss what kinds of things can be modeled using each structure. These two points of view are important to you as a C++ programmer. Finally, we look at how some of the structures may be implemented—how the "logical" accessing function is turned into a location in memory. For built-in constructs, the abstract view is the syntax of the construct itself, and the implementation level remains hidden within the compiler. So long as you know the syntax, you as a programmer do not need to understand the implementation view of predefined composite data types. As you read through the implementation sections and see the formulas needed to access an element of a composite type, you should appreciate why information hiding and encapsulation are necessary.

Records

The record is not available in all programming languages. FORTRAN, for instance, does not support records; conversely, COBOL, a business-oriented language, uses records extensively. In C++, records are implemented by structs. C++ classes are another implementation of a record. For the purposes of the following discussion, we use the generic term "record," but both structs and classes behave as records.

Logical Level A record is a composite data type made up of a finite collection of not necessarily homogeneous elements called *members* or *fields*. Accessing is done directly through a set of named member or field selectors.

We illustrate the syntax and semantics of the component selector within the context of the following struct declaration:

```
struct CarType
{
  int year;
  char maker[10];
  float price;
};
CarType myCar;
```

The record variable `myCar` is made up of three components. The first, `year`, is of type `int`. The second, `maker`, is an array of characters. The third, `price`, is a `float` number. The names of the components make up the set of member selectors. A picture of `myCar` appears in Figure 2.5.

The syntax of the component selector is the record variable name, followed by a period, followed by the member selector for the component in which you are interested:

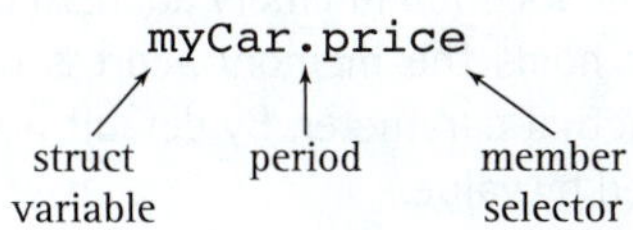

If this expression appears on the right-hand side of an assignment statement, a value is being extracted from that place (for example, `pricePaid = myCar.price`). If it appears on the left-hand side, a value is being stored in that member of the struct (for example, `myCar.price = 20009.33`).

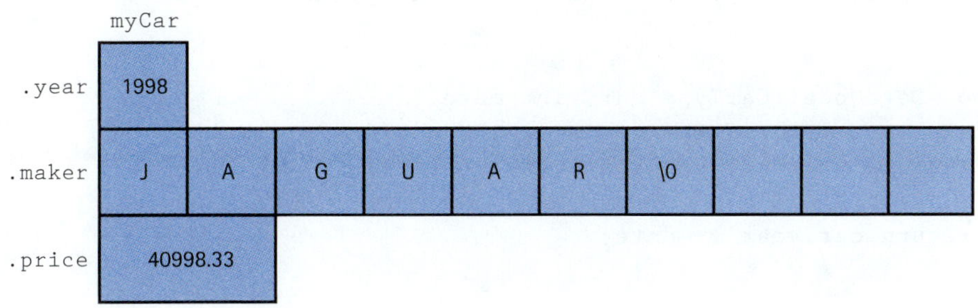

Figure 2.5 *Record* `myCar`

Here `myCar.maker` is an array whose elements are of type `char`. You can access that array member as a whole (for example, `myCar.maker`), or you can access individual characters by using an index.

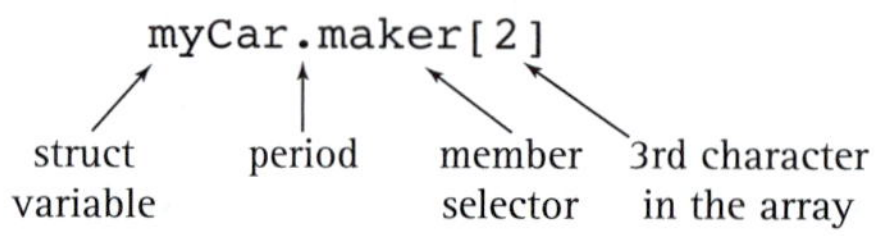

In C++, a struct may be passed as a parameter to a function (either by value or by reference), one struct may be assigned to another struct of the same type, and a struct may be a function return value.

C++ Parameter Passing

C++ supports two types of formal parameters: value parameters and reference parameters. A value parameter is a formal parameter that receives a *copy* of the contents of the corresponding actual parameter (also called *argument*). Because the formal parameter holds a copy of the actual parameter, the actual parameter cannot be changed by the function to which it is a parameter. On the other hand, a reference parameter is a formal parameter that receives the *location* (memory address) of the corresponding actual parameter. Because the formal parameter holds the memory address of the actual parameter, the function can change the contents of the actual parameter. By default in C++, arrays are passed by reference, and nonarray parameters are passed by value.

To specify that a formal nonarray parameter is a reference parameter, append an ampersand (&) to the right of the type name on the formal parameter list. Look at the following examples:

```
void AdjustForInflation(CarType& car, float perCent)
// Increases price by the amount specified in perCent.
{
  car.price = car.price * perCent + car.price;
}

bool LateModel(CarType car, int date)
// Returns true if the car's model year is later than or
//  equal to date; returns false otherwise.
{
  return car.year >= date;
}
```

The function `AdjustForInflation` changes the `price` data member of the formal parameter `car`, so `car` must be a reference parameter. Within the body of the function, `car.price` is the `price` member of the actual parameter. The function `LateModel` examines `car` without changing it, so `car` should be a value parameter. Within the function, `car.year` is a copy of the caller's actual parameter.

Application Level Records (structs) are very useful for modeling objects that have a number of characteristics. This data type allows us to collect various types of data about an object and to refer to the whole object by a single name. We also can refer to the different members of the object by name. You probably have seen many examples of records used in this way to represent objects.

Records are also useful for defining other data structures, allowing programmers to combine information about the structure with the storage of the elements. We make extensive use of records in this way when we develop representations of our own programmer-defined data structures.

Implementation Level Two things must be done to implement a built-in composite data type: (1) memory cells must be reserved for the data, and (2) the *accessing function* must be determined. An accessing function is a rule that tells the compiler and run-time system where an individual element is located within the data structure. Before we examine a concrete example, let's look at memory. The unit of memory that is assigned to hold a value is machine dependent. Figure 2.6 shows several different memory configurations. In practice, memory configuration is a consideration for the compiler writer. To be as general as possible, we will use the generic term *cell* to represent a location in memory rather than "word" or "byte." In the examples that follow, we assume that an integer or character is stored in one cell and a floating-point number in two cells. (This assumption is not accurate in C++, but we use it here to simplify the discussion.)

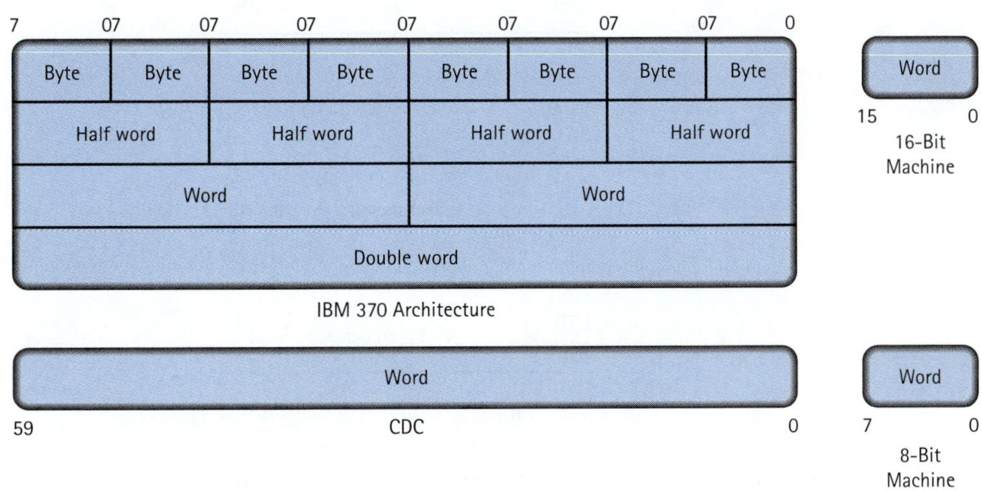

Figure 2.6 *Memory configurations*

The declaration statements in a program tell the compiler how many cells are needed to represent the record. The name of the record then is associated with the characteristics of the record. These characteristics include the following:

- The location in memory of the first cell in the record, called the *base address* of the record
- A table containing the number of memory locations needed for each member of the record

A record occupies a block of consecutive cells in memory.[2] The record's accessing function calculates the location of a particular cell from a named member selector. The basic question is, which cell (or cells) in this consecutive block do you want?

The base address of the record is the address of the first member in the record. To access any member, we need to know how much of the record to skip to get to the desired member. A reference to a record member causes the compiler to examine the characteristics table to determine the member's offset from the beginning of the record. The compiler then can generate the member's address by adding the offset to the base. Figure 2.7 shows such a table for `CarType`. If the base address of `myCar` were 8500, the fields or members of this record would be found at the following addresses:

Address of `myCar.year` = 8500 + 0 = 8500
Address of `myCar.maker` = 8500 + 1 = 8501
Address of `myCar.price` = 8500 + 11 = 8511

We said that the record is a nonstructured data type, yet the component selector depends on the relative positions of the members of the record. This is true: A record is

Member	*Length*	*Offset*
year	1	0
maker	10	1
price	2	11

Address	
8500	year member (length=1)
8501 8502 ⋮ 8509 8510	maker member (length=10)
8511 8512	price member (length=2)

Figure 2.7 *Implementation-level view of* `CarType`

[2]In some machines this statement may not be exactly true, because boundary alignment (full- or half-word) may require that some space in memory be skipped so that the next member starts on an address that is divisible by 2 or 4. See Figure 2.6.

a structured data type if viewed from the implementation perspective. However, from the user's view, it is unstructured. The user accesses the members by name, not by position. For example, if we had defined `CarType` as

```
struct CarType
{
  char make[10];
  float price;
  int year;
};
```

the code that manipulates instances of `CarType` would not change.

One-Dimensional Arrays

Logical Level A one-dimensional array is a structured composite data type made up of a finite, fixed-size collection of ordered homogeneous elements to which direct access is available. *Finite* indicates that a last element is identifiable. *Fixed size* means that the size of the array must be known in advance; it doesn't mean that all slots in the array must contain meaningful values. *Ordered* means that there is a first element, a second element, and so on. (The relative position of the elements is ordered, not necessarily the values stored there.) Because the elements in an array must all be of the same type, they are physically *homogeneous*; that is, they are all of the same data type. In general, it is desirable for the array elements to be logically homogeneous as well—that is, for all the elements to have the same purpose. (If we kept a list of numbers in an array of integers, with the length of the list—an integer—kept in the first array slot, the array elements would be physically, but not logically, homogeneous.)

The component selection mechanism of an array is *direct access*, which means we can access any element directly, without first accessing the preceding elements. The desired element is specified using an index, which gives its relative position in the collection. Later we discuss how C++ uses the index and some characteristics of the array to figure out exactly where in memory to find the element. That's part of the implementation view, and the application programmer using an array doesn't need to be concerned with it. (It's encapsulated.)

Which operations are defined for the array? If the language we were using lacked predefined arrays and we were defining arrays ourselves, we would want to specify at least three operations (shown here as C++ function calls):

```
CreateArray(anArray, numberOfSlots);
// Create array anArray with numberOfSlots locations.

Store(anArray, value, index);
// Store value into anArray at position index.

Retrieve(anArray, value, index);
// Retrieve into value the array element found at position index.
```

Because arrays are predefined data types, the C++ programming language supplies a special way to perform each of these operations. C++'s syntax provides a primitive constructor for creating arrays in memory, with indexes used as a way to directly access an element of an array.

In C++, the declaration of an array serves as a primitive constructor operation. For example, a one-dimensional array can be declared with this statement:

```
int numbers[10];
```

The type of the elements in the array comes first, followed by the name of the array with the number of elements (the array size) in brackets to the right of the name. This declaration defines a linearly ordered collection of 10 integer items. Abstractly, we can picture `numbers` as follows:

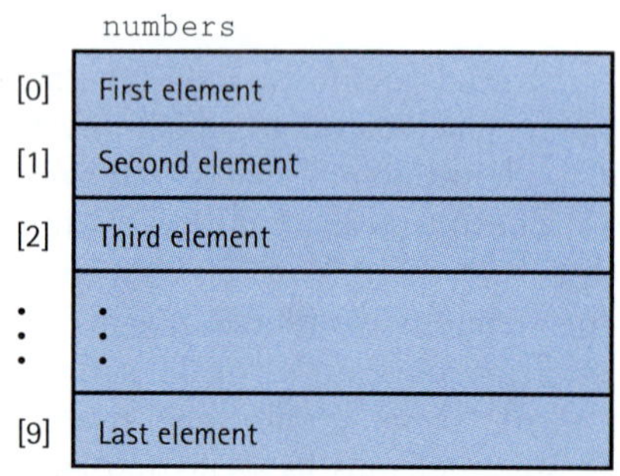

Each element of `numbers` can be accessed directly by its relative position in the array. The syntax of the component selector is described as follows:

array-name[index-expression]

The index expression must be of an integral type (`char`, `short`, `int`, `long`, or an enumeration type). The expression may be as simple as a constant or a variable name, or as complex as a combination of variables, operators, and function calls. Whatever the form of the expression, it must result in an integer value.

In C++, the index range is always 0 through the array size minus 1; in the case of `numbers`, the value must be between 0 and 9. In some other languages, the user may explicitly give the index range.

The semantics (meaning) of the component selector is "Locate the element associated with the index expression in the collection of elements identified by array-name." The component selector can be used in two ways:

1. To specify a place into which a value is to be copied:

   ```
   numbers[2] = 5;
   ```

   or

   ```
   cin >> numbers[2];
   ```

2. To specify a place from which a value is to be retrieved:

```
value = numbers[4];
```

or

```
cout << numbers[4];
```

If the component selector appears on the left-hand side of the assignment statement, it is being used as a transformer: The data structure is changing. If the component selector appears on the right-hand side of the assignment statement, it is being used as an observer: It returns the value stored in a place in the array without changing it. Declaring an array and accessing individual array elements are operations predefined in nearly all high-level programming languages.

In C++, arrays may be passed as parameters (by reference only), but cannot be assigned to one another or serve as the return value type of a function.

C++ One-Dimensional Arrays as Parameters

In C++, arrays can only be *reference* parameters; it is not possible to pass an array by value. Therefore, the ampersand (&) to the right of the type is omitted. When an array is the formal parameter, the base address of the array (the memory address of the first slot in the array) is actually passed to a function. This is true whether the array has one or more dimensions. When declaring a one-dimensional array parameter, the compiler needs to know only that the parameter is an array; it does not need to know its size. If the size of the formal parameter is listed, the compiler ignores it. The code in the function that processes the array is responsible for ensuring that only legitimate array slots are referenced. Therefore, a separate parameter often is passed to the function to specify how many array slots will be processed.

```
int SumValues(int values[], int numberOfValues)
// Returns the sum of values[0] through values[numberOfValues-1].
{
  int sum = 0;

  for (int index = 0; index < numberOfValues; index++)
    sum = sum + values[index];
  return sum;
}
```

If arrays are always passed as reference parameters, how can we protect the actual parameter from inadvertent changes? For example, in `SumValues` the parameter `values` is only to be inspected but not modified. How can we protect it from being changed? We can declare it to be a `const` parameter as follows:

```
int SumValues(const int values[], int numberOfValues)
```

Within the function body, trying to change the contents of `values` now causes a syntax error.

Application Level A one-dimensional array is the natural structure for the storage of lists of like data elements. Examples include grocery lists, price lists, lists of phone numbers, lists of student records, and lists of characters (a string). You have probably used one-dimensional arrays in similar ways in some of your programs.

Implementation Level Of course, when you use an array in a C++ program you do not have to be concerned with all of the implementation details. You have been dealing with an abstraction of the array from the time the construct was introduced, and you will never have to consider all the messy details described in this section.

An array declaration statement tells the compiler how many cells are needed to represent that array. The name of the array then is associated with the characteristics of the array. These characteristics include the following:

- The number of elements (Number)
- The location in memory of the first cell in the array, called the *base address* of the array (Base)
- The number of memory locations needed for each element in the array (SizeOfElement)

The information about the array characteristics is often stored in a table called an *array descriptor* or *dope vector.* When the compiler encounters a reference to an array element, it uses this information to generate code that calculates the element's location in memory at run time.

How are the array characteristics used to calculate the number of cells needed and to develop the accessing functions for the following arrays? As before, we assume for simplicity that an integer or character is stored in one cell and a floating-point number is stored in two cells.

```
int data[10];
float money[6];
char letters[26];
```

These arrays have the following characteristics:

	`data`	`money`	`letters`
Number	10	6	26
Base	unknown	unknown	unknown
SizeOfElement	1	2	1

Let's assume that the C++ compiler assigns memory cells to variables in sequential order. If, when the preceding declarations are encountered, the next memory cell available to be assigned is, say, 100, the memory assignments are as follows. (We have used 100 to make the arithmetic easier.)

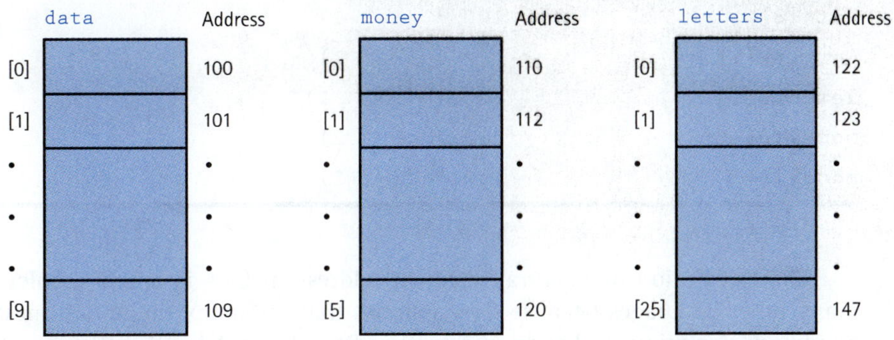

Now we have determined the base address of each array: `data` is 100, `money` is 110, and `letters` is 122. The arrangement of these arrays in memory gives us the following relationships:

Given	The program must access
`data[0]`	100
`data[8]`	108
`letters[1]`	123
`letters[25]`	147
`money[0]`	110
`money[3]`	116

In C++ the accessing function that gives us the position of an element in a one-dimensional array associated with the expression Index is

$$Address(Index) = Base + Offset\ of\ the\ element\ at\ position\ Index$$

How do we calculate the offset? The general formula is

$$Offset = Index * SizeOfElement$$

The whole accessing function becomes

$$Address(Index) = Base + Index * SizeOfElement$$

Let's apply this formula and see if we do get what we claimed we should.

	Base + Index * SizeOfElement	Address
data[0]	100 + (0 * 1)	= 100
data[8]	100 + (8 * 1)	= 108
letters[1]	122 + (1 * 1)	= 123
letters[25]	122 + (25 * 1)	= 147
money[0]	110 + (0 * 2)	= 110
money[3]	110 + (3 * 2)	= 116

The calculation of an array element address in C++ is much simpler than it is in many other languages because C++ assumes that the index range is from 0 through the maximum size minus 1. Languages such as Pascal and Ada allow the user to specify the lower and upper bounds on the index range rather than giving the size. This extra flexibility complicates the indexing process considerably but leaves the abstraction cleaner.

Earlier, we noted that an array is a structured data type. Unlike with a record, whose logical view is unstructured but whose implementation view is structured, both views of an array are structured. The structure is inherent in the logical component selector.

As we mentioned at the beginning of this section, when you use an array in a C++ program you do not have to be concerned with all of these implementation details. The advantages of this approach are very clear: You can think of the data and the operations in a logical sense and can consider their use without having to worry about implementation details. The lower levels are still there—they just remain hidden from you. We strive for this same sort of separation of the abstract and implementation views in the programmer-defined classes discussed in the remainder of this book.

Two-Dimensional Arrays

Logical Level Most of what we have said about the abstract view of a one-dimensional array applies as well to arrays of more than one dimension. A two-dimensional array is a composite data type made up of a finite, fixed-size collection of homogeneous elements ordered in two dimensions. Its component selector is direct access: a pair of indexes specifies the desired element by giving its relative position in each dimension.

A two-dimensional array is a natural way to represent data that is logically viewed as a table with columns and rows. The following example illustrates the syntax for declaring a two-dimensional array in C++.

```
int table[10][6];
```

The abstract picture of this structure is a grid with rows and columns.

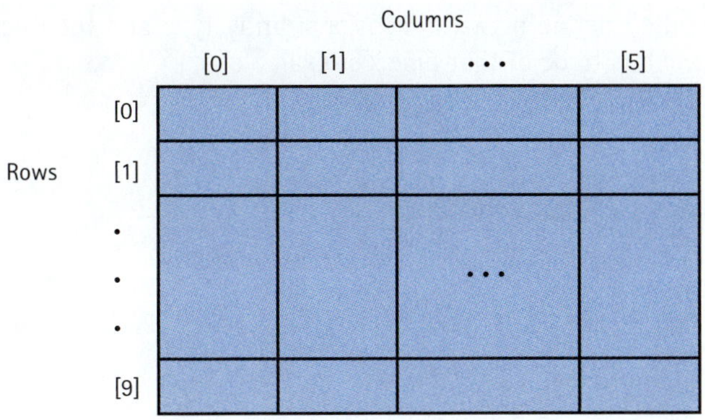

The component selector for the two-dimensional array is as follows:

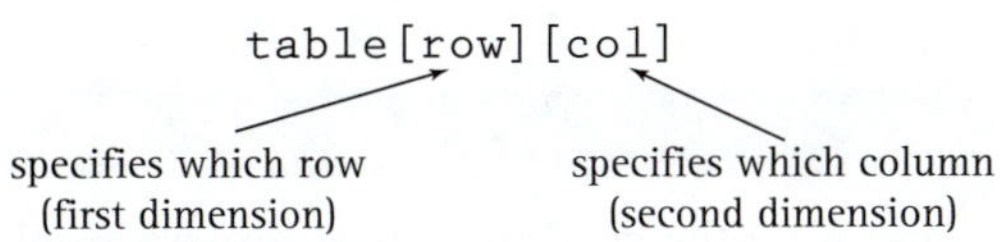

Two-Dimensional Arrays as Parameters

Two-dimensional arrays are stored in row order in C++. That is, all of the elements in one row are stored together, followed by all of the elements in the next row. To access any row other than the first, the compiler must be able to calculate where each row begins; this calculation depends on how many elements are present in each row. The second row begins at the base address plus the number of elements in each row, and each succeeding row begins at the address of the previous row plus the number of elements in each row. The second dimension—the number of columns—tells us how many elements are in each row; therefore the size of the second dimension *must* be included in the declaration of the formal parameter for a two-dimensional array.

```
int ProcessValues(int values[][5])
{
  .
  .
  .
}
```

`ProcessValues` works for an array with any number of rows as long as it has exactly five columns. That is, the size of the second dimension of both the actual and formal array parameters must be identical. To ensure that formal and actual two-dimensional array parameters have the same size, use the *typedef* statement to define a two-dimensional array type and then declare both the actual and the formal parameters to be of that type. For example,

```
const int NUM_ROWS = 5;
const int NUM_COLS = 4;
typedef float TableType[NUM_ROWS][NUM_COLS];

int ProcessValues(TableType table);

TableType mine;
TableType yours;
```

The *typedef* statement associates a two-dimensional `float` array with five rows and four columns with the type name `TableType`; `mine` and `yours` are two such arrays. Any actual parameter for `ProcessValues` should be of type `TableType`. By setting up the types this way, no possible mismatch can occur.

Application Level As mentioned in the previous section, a two-dimensional array is the ideal data structure for modeling data that are logically structured as a table with rows and columns. The first dimension represents rows, and the second dimension represents columns. Each element in the array contains a value, and each dimension represents a relationship. For example, we usually represent a map as a two-dimensional array.

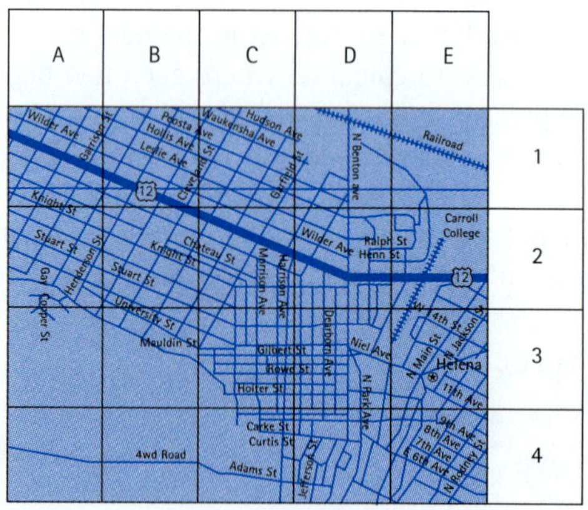

As with the one-dimensional array, the operations available for a two-dimensional array object are so limited (only creation and direct access) that the major application is the implementation of higher-level objects.

Implementation Level The implementation of two-dimensional arrays involves the mapping of two indexes to a particular memory cell. The mapping functions are more complicated than those for one-dimensional arrays. We do not give them here, as you will learn to write these accessing functions in later courses. Our goal is not to teach you to be a compiler writer but rather to give you an appreciation of the value of information hiding and encapsulation.

2.3 Higher-Level Abstraction and the C++ Class Type

In the last section, we examined C++'s built-in data types from the logical view, the application view, and the implementation view. Now we shift our focus to data types that are needed in a program but not provided by the programming language.

The class type is a construct in which the members of the class can be both functions and data; that is, the data members and the code that manipulates them are bound together within the class itself. Because the data are bound together with the operations, we can use one object to build another object; in other words, a data member of an object can be another object.

> **Class** An unstructured type that encapsulates a fixed number of data components with the functions that manipulate them; the predefined operations on an instance of a class are whole assignment and component access
>
> **Client** Software that declares and manipulates objects (instances) of a particular class

When we design an abstract data type, we want to bind the operations of the data type with the data that are being manipulated. The class is the perfect mechanism to implement an abstract data type because it enforces encapsulation. The class acts like the case around a watch that prevents us from accessing the works. The case is provided by the watchmaker, who can easily open it when repairs become necessary.

Classes are written in two parts, the specification and the implementation. The specification, which defines the interface to the class, is like the face and knobs on a watch. The specification describes the *resources* that the class can supply to the program. Resources supplied by a watch might include the value of the current time and operations to set the current time. In a class, the resources include data and operations on the data. The implementation section provides the implementation of the resources defined in the specification; it is like the inside of the watch.

Significant advantages are derived from separating the specification from its implementation. A clear interface is important, particularly when a class is used by other members of a programming team or is part of a software library. Any ambiguity in an interface may result in problems. By separating the specification from its implementation, we are given the opportunity to concentrate our efforts on the design of a class without needing to worry about implementation details.

Another advantage of this separation is that we can change the implementation at any time without affecting the programs that use the class (clients of the class). We can make changes when a better algorithm is discovered or the environment in which the program is run changes. For example, suppose we need to control how text is displayed on screen. Text control operations might include moving the cursor to a particular location and setting text characteristics such as bold, blink, and underline. The algorithms required for controlling these characteristics usually differ from one computer system to another. By defining an interface and encapsulating the algorithms as member functions, we can easily move our program to a different system simply by rewriting the implementation. We do not have to change the rest of the program.

Because the class is such an important construct, we review its syntax and semantics in the next section. Most of you will be familiar with this material. Indeed, we used a class in Chapter 1.

Class Specification

Although the class specification and implementation can reside in the same file, the two parts of a class are usually separated into two files: The specification goes into a header file (`.h` extension), and the implementation goes into a file with the same name but a `.cpp` extension. This physical separation of the two parts of a class reinforces the logical separation.[3]

We describe the syntax and semantics of the class type within the context of defining an abstract data type `Date`.

```
// Declare a class to represent the Date ADT.
// This is file DateType.h.

class DateType
{
public:
  void Initialize(int newMonth, int newDay, int newYear);
  int GetYear() const;     // Returns year
  int GetMonth() const;    // Returns month
  int GetDay() const;      // Returns day
private:
  int  year;
  int  month;
  int  day;
};
```

The data members of the class are `year`, `month`, and `day`. The scope of a class includes the parameters on the member functions, so we must use names other than `month`, `year`, and `day` for our formal parameters. The data members are marked `private`, which means that although they are visible to the human user, they cannot be accessed by client code. Private members can be accessed only by the code in the implementation file.

---

[3]Your system may use extensions different from `.h` and `.cpp` for these files—for example, `.hpp` or `.hxx` (or no extension at all) for header files and `.cxx`, `.c`, or `.C` for implementation files.

The member functions of the class are `Initialize`, `GetYear`, `GetMonth`, and `Get-Day`. They are marked `public`, which means that client code can access these functions. `Initialize` is a constructor operation; it takes values for the year, month, and day and stores these values into the appropriate data members of an object (an instance of the class).[4] `GetYear`, `GetMonth`, and `GetDay` are accessor functions; they are member functions that access the data members of the class. The `const` beside the accessor function names guarantees that these functions do not change any of the data members of the objects to which they are applied.

C++ Scope Rules in C++

The rules of C++ that govern who knows what, where, and when are called *scope rules*. Three main categories of scope exist for an identifier in C++: class scope, local scope, and global scope. Class scope refers to identifiers declared within a class declaration. Local scope is the scope of an identifier declared within a block (statements enclosed within `{}`). Global scope is the scope of an identifier declared outside all functions and classes.

- All identifiers declared within a class are local to the class (class scope).
- The scope of a formal parameter is the same as the scope of a local variable declared in the outermost block of the function body (local scope).
- The scope of a local identifier includes all statements following the declaration of the identifier to the end of the block in which it is declared; it includes any nested blocks unless a local identifier of the same name is declared in a nested block (local scope).
- The name of a function that is not a member of a class has global scope. Once a global function name has been declared, any subsequent function can call it (global scope).
- When a function declares a local identifier with the same name as a global identifier, the local identifier takes precedence (local scope).
- The scope of a global variable or constant extends from its declaration to the end of the file in which it is declared, subject to the condition in the last rule (global scope).
- The scope of an identifier does not include any nested block that contains a locally declared identifier with the same name (local identifiers have name precedence).

Class Implementation

Only the member functions of the class `DateType` can access the data members, so we must associate the class name with the function definitions. We do so by inserting the class name before the function name, separated by the scope resolution operator (`::`). The implementation of the member functions goes into the file `DateType.cpp`. To access the specifications, we must insert the file `DateType.h` by using an `#include` directive.

---

[4]At the implementation level from here on, we use the word *object* to refer to a class object, an instance of a class type.

```
// Define member functions of class DateType.
// This is file DateType.cpp.

#include "DateType.h"  // Gain access to specification of class

void DateType::Initialize
     (int newMonth, int newDay, int newYear)
// Post: year is set to newYear.
//       month is set to newMonth.
//       day is set to newDay.
{
  year = newYear;
  month = newMonth;
  day = newDay;
}

int DateType::GetMonth() const
// Accessor function for data member month.
{
  return month;
}

int DateType::GetYear() const
// Accessor function for data member year.
{
  return year;
}

int DateType::GetDay() const
// Accessor function for data member day.
{
  return day;
}
```

A client of the class `DateType` must have an `#include "DateType.h"` directive for the specification (header) file of the class. Note that system-supplied header files are enclosed in angle brackets (`<iostream>`), whereas user-defined header files are enclosed in double quotes. The client then declares a variable of type `DateType` just as it would any other variable.

```
#include "DateType.h"
DateType today;
DateType anotherDay;
```

Member functions of a class are invoked in the same way that data members of a struct are accessed—with the dot notation. The following code segment initializes two objects of type `DateType` and then prints the dates on the screen:

```
today.Initialize(9, 24, 2003);
anotherDay.Initialize(9, 25, 2003);
cout  << " Today is "  << today.GetMonth()  << "/"  << today.GetDay()
      << "/"  << today.GetYear()  << endl;
cout  << " Another date is "  << anotherDay.GetMonth()  << "/"
      << anotherDay.GetDay()  << "/"  << anotherDay.GetYear()  << endl;
```

Member Functions with Object Parameters

A member function applied to a class object uses the dot notation. What if we want a member function to operate on more than one object—for example, a function that compares the data members of two instances of the class?

Let's expand our class `DateType` with a member function `ComparedTo` that compares two date objects: the instance to which it is applied and its parameter. The function returns `LESS` if the instance comes before the parameter, `EQUAL` if they are the same, and `GREATER` if the instance comes after the parameter. In order to make this work, we must define an enumerated type containing these constants. Here is the enumerated type and the function heading.

The following code compares two instances of the class `DateType`.

```
enum RelationType {LESS, EQUAL, GREATER};
// Prototype of member function in the specification file.

RelationType ComparedTo(DateType someDate);
// Compares self with someDate.
```

To determine which date comes first, we must compare the `year` members of the instance and the parameter. If they are the same, we must compare the `month` members. If both the `year` members and the `month` members are the same, we must compare the `day` members. To access the fields of the instance, we just use their name. To access the fields of the parameter, we prefix the field name with the parameter name and a dot. Here, then, is the code for `comparedTo`.

```
RelationType DateType::ComparedTo(DateType aDate)
// Pre:  Self and aDate have been initialized.
// Post: Function value = LESS, if self comes before aDate.
//                      = EQUAL, if self is the same as aDate.
//                      = GREATER, if self comes after aDate.
{
  if (year < aDate.year)
    return LESS;
```

```
  else if (year > aDate.year)
    return GREATER;
  else if (month < aDate.month)
    return LESS;
  else if (month > aDate.month)
    return GREATER;
  else if (day < aDate.day)
    return LESS;
  else if (day > aDate.day)
    return  GREATER;
  else return EQUAL;
}
```

Self The object to which a member function is applied

In this code, `year` refers to the `year` data member of the object to which the function is applied; `aDate.year` refers to the data member of the object passed as a parameter. The object to which a member function is applied is called self. In the function definition, the data members of self are referenced directly without using dot notation. If an object is passed as a parameter, the parameter name must be attached to the data member being accessed using dot notation. As an example, look at the following client code:

```
switch (today.ComparedTo(anotherDay))
{
  case LESS :
      cout << "today comes before anotherDay";
      break;
  case GREATER :
      cout << "today comes after anotherDay";
      break;
  case EQUAL :
      cout << "today and anotherDay are the same";
      break;
}
```

Now look back at the `ComparedTo` function definition. In that code, `year` in the function refers to the `year` member of `today`, and `aDate.year` in the function refers to the `year` member of `anotherDay`, the actual parameter to the function.

Why do we use `LESS`, `GREATER`, and `EQUAL` when `COMES_BEFORE`, `COMES_AFTER`, and `SAME` would be more meaningful in the context of dates? We use the more general words here, because in other places we use functions of type `RelationType` when comparing numbers and strings.

Difference Between Classes and Structs

In C++, the technical difference between classes and structs is that, without the use of the reserved words `public` and `private`, member functions and data are private by default in classes and public by default in structs. In practice, structs and classes are often used differently. Because the data in a struct is public by default, we can think of a struct as a *passive* data structure. The operations that are performed on a struct are usually global functions to which the struct is passed as a parameter. Although a struct may have member functions, they are seldom defined. In contrast, a class is an *active* data structure where the operations defined on the data members are member functions of the class.

In object-oriented programming, an object is viewed as an active structure with control residing in the object through the use of member functions. For this reason, the C++ class type is used to represent the concept of an object.

2.4 Object-Oriented Programming

In Chapter 1, we said that functional design results in a hierarchy of tasks and that object-oriented design results in a hierarchy of objects. Structured programming is the implementation of a functional design, and object-oriented programming (OOP) is the implementation of an object-oriented design. However, these approaches are not entirely distinct: The implementation of an operation on an object often requires a functional design of the algorithm. In this section, we examine object-oriented programming in more depth.

Concepts

The vocabulary of object-oriented programming has its roots in the programming languages Simula and Smalltalk. It can be very bewildering. Such terms and phrases as "sending a message to," "methods," and "instance variables" are sprinkled throughout the OOP literature. Although this vocabulary can seem daunting, don't panic. There is a straightforward translation between these terms and familiar C++ constructs.

An *object* is a class object or class instance—that is, an instance of a class type. A *method* is a public member function, and an *instance variable* is a private data member. *Sending a message* means calling a public member function. In the rest of this book, we tend to mix object-oriented terms with their C++ counterparts.

There are three basic ingredients in any object-oriented language: encapsulation, inheritance, and polymorphism. We have already discussed encapsulation and how the C++ class construct is designed to encourage encapsulation. In the next two sections we discuss inheritance and polymorphism.

Inheritance Inheritance is a mechanism whereby a hierarchy of classes is constructed such that each descendant class inherits the properties (data and operations) of its ancestor

> **Inheritance** A mechanism used with a hierarchy of classes in which each descendant class inherits the properties (data and operations) of its ancestor class

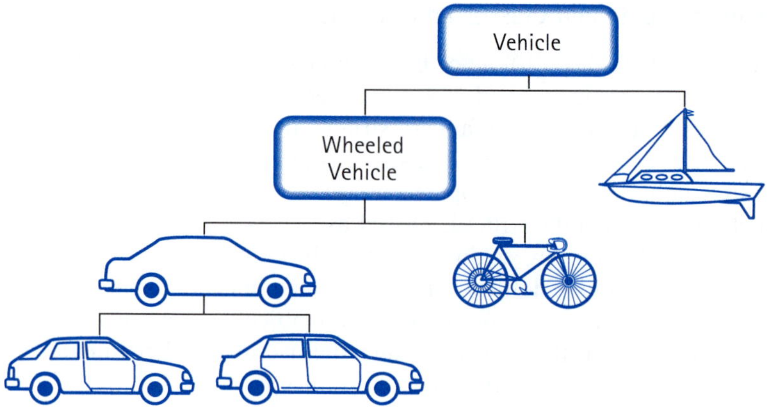

Figure 2.8 *Inheritance hierarchy*

Base class The class being inherited from

Derived class The class that inherits

Polymorphism The ability to determine which of several operations with the same name is appropriate; a combination of static and dynamic binding

Overloading Giving the same name to more than one function or using the same operator symbol for more than one operation; usually associated with static binding

class. In the world at large, it is often possible to arrange concepts into an *inheritance hierarchy*—a hierarchy in which each concept inherits the properties of the concept immediately above it in the hierarchy. For example, we might classify different kinds of vehicles according to the inheritance hierarchy in Figure 2.8. Moving down the hierarchy, each kind of vehicle is both more specialized than its *parent* (and all of its *ancestors*) and more general than its *children* (and all of its *descendants*). A wheeled vehicle inherits properties common to all vehicles (it holds one or more people and carries them from place to place) but has an additional property that makes it more specialized (it has wheels). A car inherits properties common to all wheeled vehicles, but has additional, more specialized properties (four wheels, an engine, a body, and so forth). The inheritance relationship can be viewed as an *is-a relationship*. In this relationship, the objects become more specialized the lower in the hierarchy you go.

Object-oriented languages provide a way for creating inheritance relationships among classes. You can take an existing class (called the base class) and create a new class from it (called the derived class). The derived class inherits all the properties of its base class. In particular, the data and operations defined for the base class are now defined for the derived class. Note the *is-a* relationship—every object of a derived class is also an object of the base class.

Polymorphism Polymorphism is the ability to determine either statically or dynamically which of several methods with the same name (within the class hierarchy) should be invoked. Overloading means giving the same name to several different functions (or using the same operator symbol for different operations). You have already worked with overloaded operators in C++. The arithmetic operators are overloaded because they can be applied to integral values or floating-point values, and the compiler selects the correct operation based on the operand types. The time at which a function name or symbol is associated with code is called binding time (the name is bound to the code). With overloading, the determination of which particular implementation to use occurs statically (at compile time). Determining which implementation to use at compile time is called static binding.

Binding time The time at which a name or symbol is bound to the appropriate code

Static binding The compile-time determination of which implementation of an operation is appropriate

Dynamic binding The run-time determination of which implementation of an operation is appropriate

Composition (containment) A mechanism by which an internal data member of one class is defined to be an object of another class type

Dynamic binding, on the other hand, is the ability to postpone the decision of which operation is appropriate until run time. Many programming languages support overloading; only a few, including C++, support dynamic binding. Polymorphism involves a combination of both static and dynamic binding.

Encapsulation, inheritance, and polymorphism are the three necessary constructs in an object-oriented programming language.

C++ Constructs for OOP

In an object-oriented design of a program, classes typically exhibit one of the following relationships: They are independent of one another, they are related by composition, or they are related by inheritance.

Composition Composition (or containment) is the relationship in which a class contains a data member that is an object of another class type. C++ does not need any special language notation for composition. You simply declare a data member of one class to be of another class type.

For example, we can define a class `PersonType` that has a data member `birthdate` of class `DateType`.

```
#include <string>
class PersonType
{
public:
  void Initialize(string, DateType);
  string GetName() const;
  DateType GetBirthdate() const;
private:
  string name;
  DateType birthdate;
};
```

Deriving One Class from Another Let's use class `PersonType` as a base class and derive class `StudentType` from it with the additional data field `status`.

```
class StudentType : public PersonType
{
public:
  string GetStatus() const;
  void   Initialize(string, DateType, string);
private:
  string status;
};

StudentType student;
```

The colon followed by the words `public` and `PersonType` (a class identifier) says that the new class being defined (`StudentType`) is inheriting the members of class `PersonType`. `PersonType` is called the *base* class or *superclass* and `StudentType` is called the *derived* class or *subclass*.

`student` has three member variables: one of its own (`status`) and two that it inherits from `PersonType` (`name` and `birthdate`). `student` has five member functions: two of its own (`Initialize` and `GetStatus`) and three that it inherits from `PersonType` (`Initialize`, `GetName`, and `GetBirthdate`). Although `student` inherits the private member variables from its base class, it does not have direct access to them. `student` must use the public member functions of `PersonType` to access its inherited member variables.

```
void  StudentType::Initialize
  (string newName, DateType newBirthdate, string newStatus)
{
  status = newStatus;
  PersonType::Initialize(newName, newBirthdate);
}

string StudentType::GetStatus() const
{
  return status;
}
```

Notice that the scope resolution operator (`::`) is used between the type `PersonType` and the member function `Initialize` in the definition of the member function. Because there are now two member functions named `Initialize`, one in `PersonType` and one in `StudentType`, you must indicate the class in which the one you mean is defined. (That's why it's called the scope resolution operator.) If you do not, the compiler assumes you mean the most recently defined one.

The basic C++ rule for passing parameters is that the actual parameter and its corresponding formal parameter must be of an identical type. With inheritance, C++ relaxes this rule somewhat. The type of the actual parameter may be an object of a derived class of the formal parameter.

Remember that inheritance is a logical issue, not an implementation one. A class inherits the behavior of another class and enhances it in some way. Inheritance does *not* mean inheriting access to another class's private variables. Although some languages do allow access to the base class's private members, such access often defeats the concepts of encapsulation and information hiding. With C++, access to the private data members of the base class is not allowed. Neither external client code nor derived class code can directly access the private members of the base class.

Virtual Methods In the previous section we defined two methods with the same name, `Initialize`. The statements

```
person.Initialize("Al", date);
student.Initialize("Al", date, "freshman");
```

are not ambiguous, because the compiler can determine which `Initialize` to use by examining the type of the object to which it is applied. There are times, however, when the compiler cannot make the determination of which member function is intended, and the decision must be made at run time. If the decision is to be left until run time, the word *virtual* must precede the member function heading in the base class definition and a class object passed as a parameter to a virtual function must be a reference parameter. We have more to say about how C++ implements polymorphism when we use it later in the book.

2.5 Constructs for Program Verification

Chapter 1 described methods for verifying software correctness in general. In this section we look at two constructs provided in C++ to help ensure quality software (if we use them!). The first is the exception mechanism, mentioned briefly in Chapter 1. The second is the namespace mechanism, which helps handle the problem of duplicate names appearing in large programs.

Exceptions

Most programs, and student programs in particular, are written under the most optimistic of assumptions: They will compile the first time and execute properly. Such an assumption is far too optimistic for almost any program beyond "Hello world." Programs must deal with all sorts of error conditions and exceptional situations—some caused by hardware problems, some caused by bad input, and some caused by undiscovered bugs.

Aborting the program in the wake of such errors is not an option, as the user would lose all work performed since the last save. At a minimum, a program must warn the user, allow saving, and exit gracefully. In each situation, even if the exception management technique calls for terminating the program, the code detecting the error cannot know how to shut down the program, let alone shut it down gracefully. Transfer of the thread of control and information to a handler that knows how to manage the error situation is essential.

As we said in Chapter 1, working with exceptions begins at the design phase, where the unusual situations and possible error conditions are specified and decisions are made about handling each one. Now let's look at the *try-catch* and *throw* statements, which allow us to alert the system to an exception (*throw* the exception), to detect an exception (*try* code with a possible exception), and to handle an exception (*catch* the exception).

try-catch and throw Statements The code segment in which an exception might occur is enclosed within the *try* clause of a *try-catch* statement. If the exception occurs, the reserved word `throw` is used to alert the system that control should pass to the exception handler. The exception handler is the code segment in the *catch* clause of the associated *try-catch* statement, which takes care of the situation.

The code that may throw an exception is placed in a try block followed immediately by one or more catch blocks. A catch block consists of the keyword `catch` followed by an exception declaration, which is in turn followed by a block of code. If an exception is thrown, execution immediately transfers from the try block to the catch block whose type matches the type of the thrown exception. The exception variable receives the exception of the type that is thrown in the try block. In this way, the thrown exception communicates information about the event to the handler.

```
try
{
  // Code that may raise an exception and/or set some condition
  if (condition)
    throw exception_name; // frequently a string
}
catch (typename variable)
{
  // Code that handles the exception
  //   It may call a cleanup routine and exit if the
  //   program must be terminated
}
// Code to continue processing
//   This will be executed unless the catch block
//   stops the processing.
```

Let's look at a concrete example. You are reading and summing positive values from a file. An exception occurs if a negative value is encountered. If this event happens, you want to write a message to the screen and stop the program.

```
try
{
  infile >> value;
  do
  {
    if (value < 0)
      throw string("Negative value"); // Exception is a string
    sum = sum + value;
  } while (infile);
}
catch (string message)
// Parameter of the catch is type string
{
  // Code that handles the exception
  cout << message << " found in file. Program aborted."
  return 1;
}
// Code to continue processing if exception not thrown
cout << "Sum of values on the file: " << sum;
```

If `value` is less than zero, a string is thrown; `catch` has a string as a parameter. The system recognizes the appropriate handler by the type of the exception and the type of the catch parameter. We will deal with exceptions throughout the rest of the book. As we do, we will show more complex uses of the *try-catch* statement.

Here are the rules we follow in using exceptions within the context of the ADTs we develop:

- The preconditions/postconditions on the functions represent a contract between the client and the ADT that defines the exception(s) and specifies who (client or ADT) is responsible for *detecting* the exception(s).
- The client is always responsible for *handling* the exception.
- The ADT code does not check the preconditions.

When we design an ADT, the software that uses it is called the *client* of the class. In our discussion, we use the terms *client* and *user* interchangeably, thinking of them as the people writing the software that uses the class, rather than the software itself.

Client user of the software

Standard Library Exceptions In C++, the run-time environment (for example, a divide-by-zero error) may implicitly generate exceptions in addition to those being thrown explicitly by the program. The standard C++ libraries provide a predefined hierarchy of error classes in the standard header file, `stdexcept`, including

- `logic_error`
- `domain_error`
- `invalid_argument`
- `length_error`
- `out_of_range`

In addition, the class `runtime_error` provides the following error classes:

- `range_error`
- `overflow_error`
- `underflow_error`

Namespaces

Different code authors tend to use many of the same identifier names (`name`, for example). Because library authors often have the same tendency, some of these names may appear in the library object code. If these libraries are used simultaneously, name clashes may occur, as C++ has a "one definition rule," which specifies that each name in a C++ program should be defined exactly once. The effect of dumping many names into the namespace is called *namespace pollution.*

The solution to namespace pollution involves the use of the namespace mechanism. A namespace is a C++ language technique for grouping a collection of names that logically belong together. This facility allows the enclosing of names in a scope that is similar to a class scope; unlike class scope, however, a namespace can extend over several files and be broken into pieces in a particular file.

Creating a Namespace A namespace is declared with the keyword `namespace` before the block that encloses all of the names to be declared within the space. To access variables and functions within a namespace, place the scope resolution operator (`::`) between the namespace name and the variable or function name. For example, if we define two namespaces with the same function,

```
namespace myNames
{
  void GetData(int&);
};

namespace yourNames
{
  void GetData(int&);
};
```

you can access the functions as follows:

```
myNames::GetData(int& dataValue);    // GetData from myNames
yourNames::GetData(int& dataValue); // GetData from yourNames
```

This mechanism allows identical names to coexist in the same program.

Access to Identifiers in a Namespace Access to names declared in a namespace may always be obtained by explicitly qualifying the name with the name of the namespace with the scope resolution operator (`::`), as shown in the last example. Explicit qualification of names is sufficient to use these names. However, if many names will be used from a particular namespace or if one name is used frequently, then repeated qualification can be awkward. A *using declaration* avoids this repetition for a particular identifier. The *using* declaration creates a local alias for the qualified name within the block in which it is declared, making qualification unnecessary.

For example, by putting the following declaration in the program,

```
using myNames::GetData;
```

the function `GetData` can be used subsequently without qualification. To access `GetData` in the namespace `yourNames`, it would have to be qualified: `yourNames::GetData`.

One other method of access should be familiar: a *using directive*. For example,

```
using namespace myNames;
```

provides access to all identifiers within the namespace `myNames`. You undoubtedly have employed a *using* directive in your program to access `cout` and `cin` defined in the namespace `std` without having to qualify them.

A *using* directive does not bring the names into a given scope; rather, it causes the name-lookup mechanism to consider the additional namespace specified by the directive. The *using* directive is easier to use, but it makes a large number of names visible in this scope and can lead to name clashes.

Rules for Using the Namespace `std` Here are the rules that we follow in the balance of the text in terms of qualifying identifiers from the namespace `std`:

- In function prototypes and/or function definitions, we qualify the identifier in the heading.
- In a function block, if a name is used once, it is qualified. If a name is used more than once, we use a *using* declaration with the name.
- If two or more names are used from a namespace, we use a *using* directive.
- A *using* directive is never used outside a class or a function block.

The goal is to never pollute the global namespace more than is necessary.

2.6 Comparison of Algorithms

There is more than one way to solve most problems. If you were asked for directions to Joe's Diner (see Figure 2.9), you could give either of two equally correct answers:

1. "Go east on the big highway to the Y'all Come Inn, and turn left."
2. "Take the winding country road to Honeysuckle Lodge, and turn right."

The two answers are not the same, but following either route gets the traveler to Joe's Diner. Thus both answers are *functionally correct.*

If the request for directions contained special requirements, one solution might be preferable to the other. For instance, "I'm late for dinner. What's the quickest route to Joe's Diner?" calls for the first answer, whereas "Is there a pretty road that I can take to get to Joe's Diner?" suggests the second. If no special requirements are known, the choice is a matter of personal preference—which road do you like better?

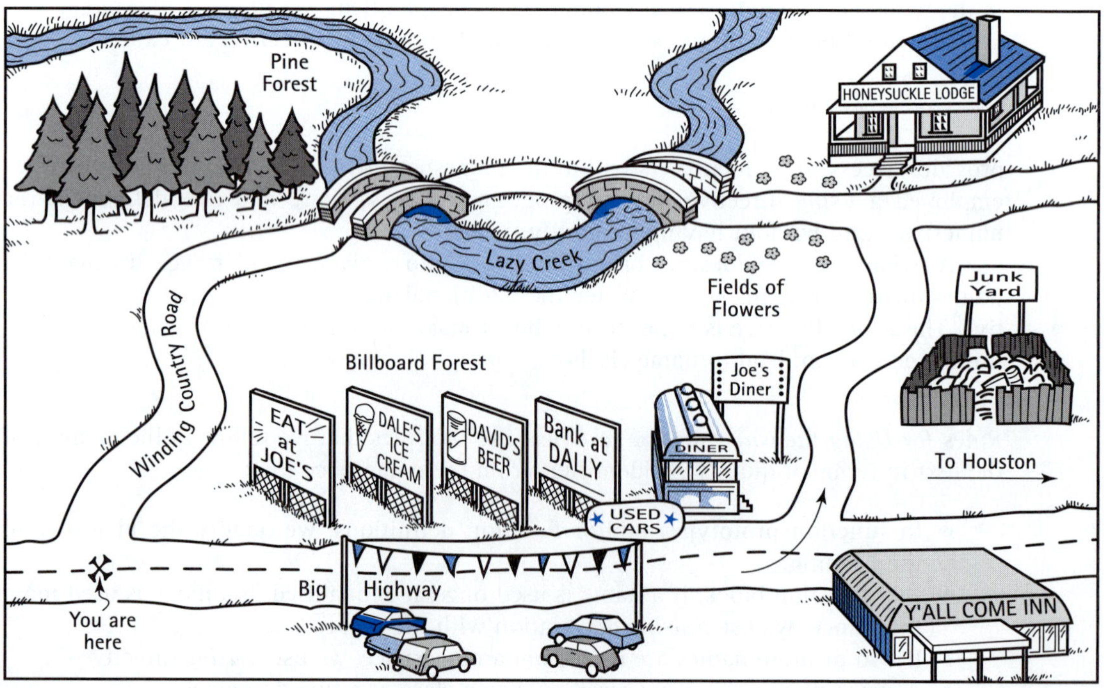

Figure 2.9 *Map to Joe's Diner*

How we choose between two algorithms that perform the same task often depends on the requirements of a particular application. If no relevant requirements exist, the choice may be based on the programmer's own style.

Often the choice between algorithms comes down to a question of efficiency. Which one takes the least amount of computing time? Which one does the job with the least amount of work? We are talking here of the amount of work that the *computer* does. Later we also compare algorithms in terms of how much work the *programmer* does. (One is often minimized at the expense of the other.)

To compare the work done by competing algorithms, we must first define a set of objective measures that can be applied to each algorithm. The *analysis of algorithms* is an important area of theoretical computer science; in advanced courses, students undoubtedly see extensive work in this area. In this book, you learn about a small part of this topic, enough to let you determine which of two algorithms requires less work to accomplish a particular task.

How do programmers measure the work performed by two algorithms? The first solution that comes to mind is simply to code the algorithms and then compare the execution times for running the two programs. The one with the shorter execution time is clearly the better algorithm. *Or is it?* Using this technique, we can determine only that program A is more efficient than program B *on a particular computer.* Execution times are specific to a particular machine. Of course, we could test the algorithms on all possible computers, but we want a more general measure.

A second possibility is to count the number of instructions or statements executed. This measure, however, varies with the programming language used as well as with the individual programmer's style. To standardize this measure somewhat, we could count the number of passes through a critical loop in the algorithm. If each iteration involves a constant amount of work, this measure gives us a meaningful yardstick of efficiency.

Another idea is to isolate a particular operation fundamental to the algorithm and count the number of times that this operation is performed. Suppose, for example, that we are summing the elements in an integer list. To measure the amount of work required, we could count the integer addition operations. For a list of 100 elements, there are 99 addition operations. Note, however, that we do not actually have to count the number of addition operations; it is some *function* of the number of elements (N) in the list. Therefore, we can express the number of addition operations in terms of N: For a list of N elements, $N - 1$ addition operations are carried out. Now we can compare the algorithms for the general case, not just for a specific list size.

If we wanted to compare algorithms for multiplying two real matrices together, we could use a measure that combines the real multiplication and addition operations required for matrix multiplication. This example brings up an interesting consideration: Sometimes an operation so dominates the algorithm that the other operations fade into the background "noise." If we want to buy elephants and goldfish, for example, and we are considering two pet suppliers, we need to compare only the prices of elephants; the cost of the goldfish is trivial in comparison. Similarly, on many computers floating-point multiplication is so much more expensive than addition in terms of computer time that the addition operation is a trivial factor in the efficiency of the whole matrix multiplication algorithm; we might as well count only the multiplication operations and ignore the addition. In analyzing algorithms, we often can find one operation that dominates the algorithm, effectively relegating the others to the "noise" level.

Big-O

We have talked about work as a function of the size of the input to the operation (for instance, the number of elements in the list to be summed). We can express an approximation of this function using a mathematical notation called order of magnitude, or Big-O notation. (This is the letter O, not a zero.) The order of magnitude of a function is identified with the term in the function that increases fastest relative to the size of the problem. For instance, if

Big-O notation (order of magnitude) A notation that expresses computing time (complexity) as the term in a function that increases most rapidly relative to the size of a problem

$$f(N) = N^4 + 100N^2 + 10N + 50$$

then $f(N)$ is of order N^4—or, in Big-O notation, $O(N^4)$. That is, for large values of N, some multiple of N^4 dominates the function for sufficiently large values of N.

Why can we just drop the low-order terms? Remember the elephants and goldfish that we discussed earlier? The price of the elephants was so much greater that we could just ignore the price of the goldfish. Similarly, for large values of N, N^4 is so much larger than 50, $10N$, or even $100N^2$ that we can ignore these other terms. This doesn't mean that the other terms do not contribute to the computing time, but rather that they are not significant in our approximation when *N* is "large."

What is this value *N*? *N* represents the *size* of the problem. Most of the rest of the problems in this book involve data structures—lists, stacks, queues, and trees. Each structure is composed of elements. We develop algorithms to add an element to the structure and to modify or delete an element from the structure. We can describe the work done by these operations in terms of *N*, where *N* is the number of elements in the structure. Yes, we know. We have called the number of elements in a list the *length* of the list. However, mathematicians talk in terms of *N*, so we use *N* for the length when we are comparing algorithms using Big-O notation.

Suppose that we want to write all the elements in a list into a file. How much work is involved? The answer depends on how many elements are in the list. Our algorithm is

```
Open the file
while more elements in list do
    Write the next element
```

If *N* is the number of elements in the list, the "time" required to do this task is

*(N * time-to-write-one-element) + time-to-open-the-file*

This algorithm is O(*N*) because the time required to perform the task is proportional to the number of elements (*N*)—plus a little time to open the file. How can we ignore the open time in determining the Big-O approximation? Assuming that the time necessary to open a file is constant, this part of the algorithm is our goldfish. If the list has only a few elements, the time needed to open the file may seem significant. For large values of *N*, however, writing the elements is an elephant in comparison with opening the file.

The order of magnitude of an algorithm does *not* tell you how long in microseconds the solution takes to run on your computer. Sometimes we need that kind of information. For instance, a word processor's requirements may state that the program must be able to spell-check a 50-page document (on a particular computer) in less than 120 seconds. For such information, we do not use Big-O analysis; we use other measurements. We can compare different implementations of a data structure by coding them and then running a test, recording the time on the computer's clock before and after the test. This kind of "benchmark" test tells us how long the operations take on a particular computer, using a particular compiler. The Big-O analysis, however, allows us to compare algorithms without reference to these factors.

Common Orders of Magnitude

O(1) is called *bounded time.* The amount of work is bounded by a constant and does not depend on the size of the problem. Assigning a value to the *i*th element in an array of *N* elements is O(1), because an element in an array can be accessed directly through its index. Although bounded time is often called constant time, the amount of work is not necessarily constant. Rather, it is *bounded* by a constant.

$O(\log_2 N)$ is called *logarithmic time.* The amount of work depends on the log of the size of the problem. Algorithms that successively cut the amount of data to be processed in half at each step typically fall into this category. Finding a value in a list of ordered elements using the binary search algorithm is $O(\log_2 N)$.

$O(N)$ is called *linear time.* The amount of work is some constant times the size of the problem. Printing all the elements in a list of *N* elements is $O(N)$. Searching for a particular value in a list of unordered elements is also $O(N)$, because you (potentially) must search every element in the list to find it.

$O(N \log_2 N)$ is called (for lack of a better term) *$N \log_2 N$ time.* Algorithms of this type typically involve applying a logarithmic algorithm *N* times. The better sorting algorithms, such as Quicksort, Heapsort, and Mergesort discussed in Chapter 10, have $N \log_2 N$ complexity. That is, these algorithms can transform an unordered list into a sorted list in $O(N \log_2 N)$ time.

$O(N^2)$ is called *quadratic time.* Algorithms of this type typically involve applying a linear algorithm *N* times. Most simple sorting algorithms are $O(N^2)$ algorithms. (See Chapter 10.)

$O(N^3)$ is called *cubic time.* An example of an $O(N^3)$ algorithm is a routine that increments every element in a three-dimensional table of integers.

$O(2^N)$ is called *exponential time.* These algorithms are costly. As you can see in Table 2.1, exponential times increase dramatically in relation to the size of *N*. (Note that the values in the last column grow so quickly that the computation time required for problems of this order may exceed the estimated life span of the universe!)

Example 1: Sum of Consecutive Integers

Throughout this discussion we have been talking about the amount of work the computer must do to execute an algorithm. This determination does not necessarily relate to the size of the algorithm, say, in lines of code. Consider the following two algorithms to initialize to zero every element in an *N*-element array:

Algorithm Init1

```
items[0]  = 0;
items[1]  = 0;
items[2]  = 0;
items[3]  = 0;
          ⋮
items[N - 1]  = 0;
```

Algorithm Init2

```
for (index = 0; index < N; index++)
  items[index] = 0;
```

Both algorithms are $O(N)$, even though they greatly differ in the number of lines of code.

Table 2.1 *Comparison of Rates of Growth*

N	log_2N	$N\ log_2N$	N^2	N^3	2^N
1	0	1	1	1	2
2	1	2	4	8	4
4	2	8	16	64	16
8	3	24	64	512	256
16	4	64	256	4,096	65,536
32	5	160	1,024	32,768	4,294,967,296
64	6	384	4,096	262,114	About one month's worth of instructions on a super-computer
128	7	896	16,384	2,097,152	About 10^{12} times greater than the age of the universe in nanoseconds (for a 6-billion-year estimate)
256	8	2,048	65,536	16,777,216	Don't ask!

Now let's look at two different algorithms that calculate the sum of the integers from 1 to *N*. Algorithm Suml is a simple *for* loop that adds successive integers to keep a running total:

Algorithm Sum1

```
sum = 0;
for (count = 1; count <= n; count++)
  sum = sum + count;
```

That seems simple enough. The second algorithm calculates the sum by using a formula. To understand the formula, consider the following calculation when $N = 9$:

```
  1 +  2 +  3 +  4 +  5 +  6 +  7 +  8 +  9
+ 9 +  8 +  7 +  6 +  5 +  4 +  3 +  2 +  1
---------------------------------------------
 10 + 10 + 10 + 10 + 10 + 10 + 10 + 10 + 10  =  10 * 9 = 90
```

We pair up each number from 1 to *N* with another, such that each pair adds up to $N + 1$. There are *N* such pairs, giving us a total of $(N + 1) * N$. Now, because each number is included twice, we divide the product by 2. Using this formula, we can solve the problem: ((9 + 1) * 9)/2 = 45. Now we have a second algorithm:

Algorithm Sum2

```
sum = ((n + 1) * n) / 2;
```

Both of the algorithms are short pieces of code. Let's compare them using Big-O notation. The work done by Sum1 is a function of the magnitude of *N*; as *N* gets larger, the amount of work grows proportionally. If *N* is 50, Sum1 works 10 times as hard as when *N* is 5. Algorithm Sum1, therefore, is O(*N*).

Sum1 Algorithm

Sum2 Algorithm

To analyze Sum2, consider the cases when *N* = 5 and *N* = 50. They should take the same amount of time. In fact, whatever value we assign to *N*, the algorithm does the same amount of work to solve the problem. Algorithm Sum2, therefore, is O(1).

Is Sum2 always faster? Is it always a better choice than Sum1? That depends. Sum2 might seem to do more "work," because the formula involves multiplication and division, whereas Sum1 calculates a simple running total. In fact, for very small values of *N*, Sum2 actually might do more work than Suml. (Of course, for very large values of *N*, Suml does a proportionally larger amount of work, whereas Sum2 stays the same.) So the choice between the algorithms depends in part on how they are used, for small or large values of *N*.

Another issue is the fact that Sum2 is not as obvious as Suml, and thus it is more difficult for the programmer (a human) to understand. Sometimes a more efficient solution to a problem is more complicated; we may save computer time at the expense of the programmer's time.

What's the verdict? As usual in the design of computer programs, there are tradeoffs. We must look at our program's requirements and then decide which solution is better.

Example 2: Finding a Number in a Phone Book

Suppose you need to look up a friend's number in a phone book. How would you go about finding the number? To keep matters simple, assume that the name you are searching for is in the book—you won't come up empty. Here is a straightforward approach.

Algorithm Lookup1

```
Check the first name in the book
while (have not yet found the name)
   Check the next name in the book
```

Even though this algorithm is inefficient, it is correct and does work.

What is the Big-O efficiency rating of this algorithm? How many steps does it take to find someone's name? Clearly the answers to these questions depend on the size of the phone book and the name that you are searching for. If you are looking for your friend Aaron Aardvark, it probably takes you only one or two steps. If your friend's name is Zina Zyne, you are not so lucky.

The Lookup1 algorithm displays different efficiency ratings under different input conditions. This is not unusual. To handle this situation, analysts define three complexity cases: best case, worst case, and average case. Best case complexity tells us the complexity when we are very lucky; it represents the smallest number of steps that an algorithm can take. In general, best case complexity is not very useful as a complexity measure. Worst case complexity, by contrast, represents the greatest number of steps that an algorithm would require. Average case complexity represents the average number of steps required, considering all possible inputs.

> **Best case complexity** Related to the minimum number of steps required by an algorithm, given an ideal set of input values in terms of efficiency
>
> **Worst case complexity** Related to the maximum number of steps required by an algorithm, given the worst possible set of input values in terms of efficiency
>
> **Average case complexity** Related to the average number of steps required by an algorithm, calculated across all possible sets of input values

Let's evaluate Lookup1 in each of these cases. Following our previous convention we label the size of our phone book N. Our fundamental operation is "checking a name."

- *Best case* The name we are looking for is the first name in the phone book, so it takes us only one step to find the name. The best case Big-O complexity of the algorithm is constant or O(1).

- *Worst case* The name we are looking for is the last name in the phone book, so it takes us N steps to find the name. The worst case Big-O complexity of the algorithm is $O(N)$.
- *Average case* Assuming that each name in the phone book is equally likely to be the name we are searching for, the average number of steps required is $N/2$. Sometimes the name is toward the front of the book, and sometimes it is toward the back of the book. On the average, it is in the middle of the book—thus $N/2$ steps. The average case Big-O complexity of the algorithm is also $O(N)$.

The average case analysis is usually the most difficult. Often, as in this example, it evaluates to the same Big-O efficiency class as the worst case. For our purposes we will typically use worst case analysis.

Let's look at a more efficient algorithm for finding a name in a phone book.

Algorithm Lookup2

```
Set the search area to the entire book
Check the middle name in the search area
while (have not yet found the name)
   if the middle name is greater than the target name
      Set the search area to the first half of the search area
   else
      Set the search area to the second half of the search area
   Check the middle name in the search area
```

With this algorithm we eliminate half of the remaining phone book from consideration each time we check a name. What is the worst case complexity? Another way of asking this is to say, "How many times can you reduce N by half, before you get down to 1?" This is essentially the definition of $\log_2 N$. Thus the worst case complexity of Lookup2 is $O(\log_2 N)$. This is significantly better than the worst case for Lookup1. For example, if each of New York City's 22 million people were listed in your phone book, then in the worst case Lookup1 would take you 22,000,000 steps, but Lookup2 would require only 25 steps.

Note that the successful use of the Lookup2 algorithm depends on the fact that the phone book organizes names in alphabetical order. This is a good example of a situation in which the way the data are structured and organized affects the efficiency of our use of the data.

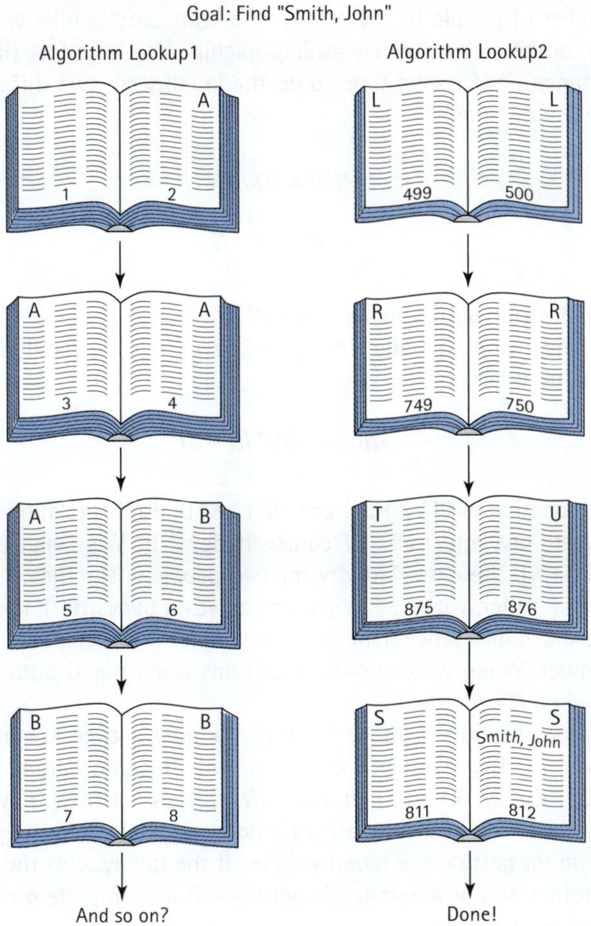

Throughout this text we examine different choices of algorithms and data structures. We compare them using Big-O, but we also examine the program's requirements and the "elegance" of the competing solutions. As programmers, we design software solutions with many factors in mind.

Family Laundry: An Analogy

How long does it take to do a family's weekly laundry? We might describe the answer to this question with the function

$$f(N) = c * N$$

where N represents the number of family members and c is the average number of minutes that each person's laundry takes. We say that this function is $O(N)$ because the total laundry time depends on the number of people in the family. The "constant" c may vary a little for different families—depending on the size of their washing machine and how fast the family members can fold clothes, for instance. That is, the time to do the laundry for two different families might be represented with these functions:

$$f(N) = 100 * N$$

$$g(N) = 90 * N$$

Overall, however, we describe both functions as O(*N*).

Now what happens if Grandma and Grandpa come to visit the family for a week or two? The laundry time function becomes

$$f(N) = 100 * (N + 2)$$

We still say that the function is O(*N*). How can that be? Doesn't the laundry for two extra people take any time to wash, dry, and fold? Of course it does! If *N* is small (the family consists of Mother, Father, and Baby), the extra laundry for two people is significant. But as *N* grows large (the family consists of Mother, Father, 12 kids, and a live-in babysitter), the extra laundry for two people doesn't make much difference. (The family's laundry is the elephant; the guest's laundry is the goldfish.) Remember: When we compare algorithms using Big-O notation, we are concerned with what happens when *N* is "large."

If we are asking the question, "Can we finish the laundry in time to make the 7:05 train?", we want a precise answer. The Big-O analysis doesn't give us this information. Instead, it gives us an approximation. So, if 100 * *N*, 90 * *N*, and 100 * (*N* + 2) are all O(*N*), how can we say which is "better"? We can't—in Big-O terms, they are all roughly equivalent for large values of *N*. Can we find a better algorithm for getting the laundry done? If the family wins the state lottery, they can drop all their dirty clothes at a professional laundry that is a 15-minute drive from their house (30 minutes round trip). Now the function is

$$f(N) = 30$$

This function is O(1). The answer is not dependent on the number of people in the family. If the family switches to a laundry 5 minutes from their house, the function becomes

$$f(N) = 10$$

This function is also O(1). In Big-O terms, the two professional-laundry solutions are equivalent: No matter how many family members or house guests you have, it takes a constant amount of the family's time to do the laundry. (We aren't concerned with the professional laundry's time.)

C++ Character and String Library Functions

C++ provides many character and string-handling facilities in its standard library. Operations available through `<cctype>` include testing to see whether a character is a letter, number, control character, uppercase, or lowercase. Operations available through `<cstring>` include concatenating two strings, comparing two strings, and copying one string into another. See Appendix C for more details.

Case Study

User-Defined Date ADT

We have talked about dates several times so far and have defined a class `DateType` with four responsibilities: `Initialize`, `GetMonth`, `GetYear`, and `GetDay`. We later discussed a responsibility `ComparedTo` that allowed us to compare two date objects. Clearly dates are very useful objects; we use them routinely many times a day. Let's create an abstract data type that includes all of the operations that we might want to apply to dates.

Logical Level

At the logical level, we all know what a date is: It is a day represented by month, day, and year. We know that we need responsibilities to return each of these values. What other functions might we need? As a starting point, let's assume that we will be using a date in an appointment calendar. If we are looking up a date in the appointment calendar, we will need to compare two dates. Good, we know how to do this. We might want to determine the date a certain number of days hence. For example, we might want to write down an appointment two weeks from today.

The `DateType` defined earlier took the date as three integer values and returned each part of the date as an integer. It would be nice to see the month as a string rather than a number. Let's include a function that returns a string representing the month. Do we need a function that prints a date? We have given the user the functions to write a date in any format they wish, so such a function would be redundant.

These observations are summarized in the following CRC card.

Class Name: DateType	Superclass:	Subclasses:
Primary Responsibility: Represent a date		
Responsibilities	Collaborations	
Initialize (month, day, year)		
Return month value as integer		
Return month value as a string	String	
Return day value as integer		
Return year value as integer		
Compare two dates returning LESS, EQUAL, GREATER	RelationType	
Adjust a date (days) returns a date		

Before we present our first ADT specification, a word about notation is in order. Because we want the specification to be as programming-language independent as possible, we use the general word Boolean for the type name of Boolean variables rather than the C++ word `bool`. On the other hand, there is no general word for input and output file types, so we use the C++ `ifstream` and `ofstream`, respectively. We also use the C++ symbol ampersand (&) to indicate reference parameters.

Recall that to distinguish between the logical level and the implementation level, we put logical-level identifiers in handwriting font and implementation-level identifiers in code (monospaced) font. In an ADT specification we use regular paragraph font throughout. In the specifications we also convert the phrases used in the CRC card to operation identifiers. As you may have noticed, the functions that return the value of a field usually begin with "Get." This is standard object-oriented terminology. If there is a function that changes the value of a field, it usually begins with "Set."

Date ADT Specification

Structure: A date

Definitions (provided by user):

RelationType: An enumeration type that consists of LESS, GREATER, EQUAL

Self: The instance to which the function is applied.

Operations:

Initialize(int month, int day, int year)

Function: Initializes date to the values of its parameters.
Precondition: None
Postcondition: Self instance has been defined.

int GetMonth

Function: Returns the month field.
Precondition: Self has been initialized.
Postcondition: Function value = month as an integer.

string GetMonthAsString

Function: Returns the month as a string.
Precondition: Self has been initialized.
Postcondition: Function value = month as a string.

int GetDay

Function: Returns the day.
Precondition: Self has been initialized.
Postcondition: Function value = day.

int GetYear

Function:	Returns the year.
Precondition:	Self has been initialized.
Postcondition:	Function value = year.

RelationType ComparedTo(DateType aDate)

Function:	Determines the ordering of two DateType objects
Precondition:	Self and aDate have been initialized.
Postcondition:	Function value = LESS if self comes before aDate. = GREATER if self comes after aDate. = EQUAL if self and aDate are the same date.

DateType Adjust(int daysAway)

Function:	Returns a date that is daysAway from self.
Precondition:	Self has been initialized.
Postcondition:	Function value = date that is daysAway from self.

Application Level

As we are preparing a class to go into our own library, the test driver is the application level. We can use the same pattern that we used for testing class `FractionType`. Here is the algorithm for the inside of the *while* loop that reads and executes commands. The coding of this algorithm is straightforward, so we do not take up space showing it here.

```
if  (command is "Initialize")
    Prompt for and read month, day, year
    date.Initialize(month, day, year)
    Write on outFile command and date
else if (command is "GetMonth")
    Write on outFile command and GetMonth()
else if (command is "GetMonthAsString")
    Write on outFile command and GetMonthAsString()
else if (command is "GetDay")
    Write on outFile command and GetDay()
else if (command is "GetYear")
    Write on outFile command and GetYear()
else if (command is "ComparedTo")
    Prompt for and read month, day, year
    date2.Initialize(month, day, year)
    Write to outFile command
    switch (date.ComparedTo(date2))
        case LESS :           Write on outFile date, " comes before " , date2
```

case GREATER: Write on outfile date2, " comes before " , date
case EQUAL: Write to outfile date. " and ", date2, " are equal "
else
Prompt for and read days
date2 = date.Adjust(days)
Write on outfile date. " plus ", days, " days is ", date2

Implementation Level

We implemented our previous reduced `DateType` class by having three integer fields: `month`, `day`, and `year`. This is simple and it works. We have already implemented `GetMonth`, `GetDay`, `GetYear`, and `ComparedTo`. This leaves only `GetMonthAsString` and `Adjust`.

GetMonthAsString One obvious way to implement this algorithm is to take the `month` field and create a large *if-then-else* statement that compares the value to the integers beginning with one until it finds a match and then returns the appropriate string. As there are twelve months, the statement would have twelve branches. Another algorithm would be to use a *switch* statement to determine the appropriate string. However, there would be twelve possibilities in the *switch* statement.

A third way of implementing this algorithm would be to have an array of strings indexed from 0 through 12; let's call it `conversionTable`. "January" would be in `conversionTable[1]`, "February" would be in `conversionTable[2]`, etc. Thus, the string for each month is directly indexable by the value in the `month` field. Note, we have a trade-off here. We are giving up one array slot that is never used to save one subtraction every time the method is called. Is this worth it? The answer depends on how many times the method is called. Let's use this technique.

We can code this algorithm directly.

```
static string conversionTable[] =
        {"Error", "January", "February", "March", "April",
         "May", "June", "July", "August", "September",
         "October", "November", "December"};

String DateType::GetMonthAsString()
{
  return conversionTable[month];
}
```

Adjust This algorithm is more complex than the other date algorithms. If the current date plus `daysAway` is still within the same month, there is no problem. If the current date plus `daysAway` is within the next month, then the day must be calculated and the month must be incremented. `daysAway` could, in fact, be several months away or even in the next year (or the next ...).

We can determine whether the current date (self) plus `daysAway` is within the current month by adding `daysAway` to the `day` field and comparing this value (call it `newDay`) to the maximum number of days in the current month. If `newDay` is greater than the number of days in the month, the month must be incremented and `newDay` must be adjusted. This process can be repeated until `newDay` is within the current month. We must not forget to increment the year when the month changes from December to January, and to check for the leap year when the month is February.

We can use the old rhyme "Thirty days hath September, April, June, and November ..." to determine the number of days in each month. We could create either an *if* statement or a *switch* statement to determine the number of days in a particular month. However, we can trade memory for an easier algorithm as we did with `GetMonthAsString`. We can create an `int` array `daysInMonth` indexed from 0 through 12. The contents of the slots 1 through 12 contain the number of days in that month. If the month is February, we must check for a leap year.

Here then is the algorithm.

DateType Adjust(int daysAway)

```
Set newDay to day + daysAway
Set newMonth to month
Set newYear to year
Set finished to false
while NOT finished
    Set daysInThisMonth to daysInMonth[newMonth]
    if newMonth = 2
        if leap year
            Increment daysInThisMonth
        if newDay <= daysInThisMonth
            Set finished to true
        else
            Set newDay to newDay – daysInThisMonth
            Set newMonth to (newMonth MOD 12 )+ 1
            if newMonth = 1
                Increment newYear
returnDate.Initialize(newMonth, newDay, newYear)
return returnDate
```

Most people know that a leap year is a year that is divisible by 4. However, there are some exceptions to this rule. It must not be a multiple of 100. However, when the year is a multiple of 400, it is a leap year anyway.

bool LeapYear

```
return (newYear MOD 4 is 0) AND NOT (newYear MOD 100 is 0) OR
    (newYear MOD 400 is 0)
```

Now we can code function `Adjust`. Let's code the leap year test in line rather than coding a helper function.

```
DateType DateType::Adjust(int daysAway) const
// Pre:  Self has been initialized
// Post: Function value = newDate daysAway from self
{
  int newDay = day + daysAway;
  int newMonth = month;
  int newYear = year;
  bool finished = false;
  int daysInThisMonth;
  DateType returnDate;
  while (! finished)
  {
    daysInThisMonth = daysInMonth[newMonth];
    if (newMonth == 2)
      // test for leap year
      if (((newYear % 4 == 0) && !(newYear % 100 == 0))
         || (newYear % 400 == 0))
        daysInThisMonth++;
    if (newDay <= daysInThisMonth)
      finished = true;
    else
    {
      newDay = newDay - daysInThisMonth;
      newMonth = (newMonth % 12) + 1;
      if (newMonth == 1)
        newYear++;
    }
  }
```

Exceptions Before we can pull all the pieces together, we must look over the functions and see if we should put in any error checking. For example, what happens if the user enters an invalid month, day, or year? Yes, we must be sure that the month is between 1 and 12, and the day is a valid day for that month. But year? Isn't any year ok—silly perhaps, but valid? No, any year before 1583 would be invalid. The Gregorian calendar, our current calendar, was established in 1582 by Pope Gregory XIII. At that time 10 days were dropped from the calendar to make up for small errors that had accumulated through the years. So we must test the year as well to be sure it comes after 1582.

Where are we going to put this test? Class `DateType` could add a precondition to the `Initialize` function that the date is valid, leaving the testing to the application. Alternately, function `Initialize` could check the date and throw an exception if the parameters do not represent a valid date. It is better object-oriented style to put the class in charge of its own fate, so we should add this validity check to the `Initialize` function. Of course, the documentation must warn any application that `Initialize` throws an exception.

Here is the revised function `Initialize` with the augmented documentation.

```
void Initialize(int newMonth, int newDay, int newYear);
// Post: If newMonth, newDay, and newYear represent a
//   valid date, self is initialized to the parameters;
//   otherwise a string exception is thrown, stating the
//   first incorrect parameter.
...
void DateType::Initialize
     (int newMonth, int newDay, int newYear)
// An exception is thrown if newMonth is not between 1 and 12,
// if newDay is not consistent with newMonth, or if newYear is
// before 1583.
{
  if (newMonth < 1 || newMonth > 12)
     throw string("Month is invalid");
  else if (newDay < 1 || newDay > daysInMonth[newMonth])
     throw string("Day is invalid");
  else if (newYear < 1583)
     throw string("Year is invalid");
  year = newYear;
  month = newMonth;
  day = newDay;
}
```

Because class `DateType`'s presentation has spread throughout the chapter, we collect the declarations and implementations here.[5]

```
// File DateType.h contains the declarations and definitions
// for a class that represents the Date ADT
#include <string>
#include <fstream>
using namespace std;
enum RelationType {LESS, EQUAL, GREATER};

class DateType
{
public:
  void Initialize(int newMonth, int newDay, int newYear);
  // Post: If newMonth, newDay, and newYear represent a
  //   valid date, self is initialized to the parameters;
  //   otherwise a string exception is thrown, stating the
  //   first incorrect parameter.
```

[5]In the interest of brevity, we do not repeat the preconditions and postconditions on the member function prototypes unless they have changed from those listed in the Specification of the ADT. The code available on the Web is completely documented.

```
  int GetMonth() const;                    // returns year
  int GetYear() const;                     // returns month
  int GetDay() const;                      // returns day
  string GetMonthAsString() const;         // returns month
                                           //   as a string
  DateType Adjust(int daysAway) const;
  // Returns a date daysAway from self
  RelationType ComparedTo(DateType someDate) const;
private:
  int  year;
  int  month;
  int  day;
};

// File DateType.cpp  contains the implementation of class DateType
#include "DateType.h"
#include <fstream>
#include <iostream>
using namespace std;

// Number of days in each month
static int daysInMonth[] =
   {0, 31, 28, 31, 30, 31, 30, 31, 31, 30, 31, 30, 31};

// Names of the months
static string conversionTable[] =
            {"Error", "January", "February", "March", "April",
             "May", "June", "July", "August", "September",
             "October", "November", "December"};

void DateType::Initialize
     (int newMonth, int newDay, int newYear)
// An exception is thrown if newMonth is not between 1 and
// 12, if newDay is not consistent with newMonth, or if
// newYear is before 1583.
{
  if (newMonth < 1 || newMonth > 12)
    throw string("Month is invalid");
  else if (newDay < 1 || newDay > daysInThisMonth(newMonth)
    throw string("Day is invalid");
  else if (newYear < 1583)
    throw string("Year is invalid");
  year = newYear;
  month = newMonth;
  day = newDay;
}
```

```
int DateType::GetMonth() const
{
  return month;
}

string DateType::GetMonthAsString() const
{
  return conversionTable[month];
}

int DateType::GetYear() const
{
  return year;
}

int DateType::GetDay() const
{
  return day;
}

RelationType DateType::ComparedTo(DateType aDate) const
{
  if (year < aDate.year)
    return LESS;
  else if (year > aDate.year)
    return GREATER;
  else if (month < aDate.month)
    return LESS;
  else if (month > aDate.month)
    return GREATER;
  else if (day < aDate.day)
    return LESS;
  else if (day > aDate.day)
    return  GREATER;
  else return EQUAL;
}

DateType DateType::Adjust(int daysAway) const
{
  int newDay = day + daysAway;
  int newMonth = month;
  int newYear = year;
  bool finished = false;
  int daysInThisMonth;
  DateType returnDate;
  while (! finished)
```

```
  {
    daysInThisMonth = daysInMonth[newMonth];
    if (newMonth == 2)
      if (((newYear % 4 == 0) && !(newYear % 100 == 0))
          || (newYear % 400 == 0))
        daysInThisMonth++;
    if (newDay <= daysInThisMonth)
      finished = true;
    else
    {
      newDay = newDay - daysInThisMonth;
      newMonth = (newMonth % 12) + 1;
      if (newMonth == 1)
      newYear++;
    }
  }

  returnDate.Initialize(newMonth, newDay, newYear);
  return returnDate;
}
```

Test Plan

We have the test driver; now we must create the test plan. There are seven functions in class `DateType`. There are four accessor functions that can be tested with one case each. Function `Initialize` requires six cases: one where the parameters are valid and a minimum of five where the parameters are invalid. Function `ComparedTo` needs seven cases in order to test each branch.

Determining the cases for function `Adjust` is more difficult because the cases are not obvious. Do we need to check to see that each month rolls over correctly as well as several years? No, we can simplify the process by choosing a `daysAway` that will test them all at once, such as 367. Then we need to choose February and three different years, to test the leap year calculation. These observations are summarized in the following test plan:

Operation to Be Tested and Description of Action	Input Values	Expected Output
Initialize		
Valid data	1, 1, 1956	January 1, 1956
Invalid data	0, 1, 1956	Month is invalid
	13, 1, 1956	Month is invalid
	1, 0, 1956	Day is invalid
	1, 32, 1956	Day is invalid
	1, 1, 1492	Year is invalid

ComparedTo	1, 1, 2007 & 2, 1, 2007	LESS
	2, 1, 2007 & 1, 2, 2007	GREATER
	1, 2, 2007 & 1, 3, 2007	LESS
	1, 3, 2007 & 1, 2, 2007	GREATER
	1, 1, 2006 & 1, 1, 2007	LESS
	1, 1, 2007 & 1, 1, 2006	GREATER
	1, 1, 2008 & 1, 1, 2008	EQUAL
Adjust	1, 1, 2006 & 367	January 3, 2007
	2, 27, 2000 & 3	March 1, 2000
	2, 27, 2100 & 3	March 2, 2100
	2, 27, 1964 & 3	March 1, 1964

Here is the output from running the test driver with this data.

```
Initialize: January 1, 1956
Month is invalid
Month is invalid
Day is invalid
Day is invalid
Year is invalid
Initialize: January 1, 2007
ComparedTo
January 1, 2007 comes before February 1, 2007
Initialize: February 1, 2007
ComparedTo
January 2, 2007 comes before February 1, 2007
Initialize: January 2, 2007
ComparedTo
January 2, 2007 comes before January 3, 2007
Initialize: January 3, 2007
ComparedTo
January 2, 2007 comes before January 3, 2007
Initialize: January 1, 2006
ComparedTo
January 1, 2006 comes before January 1, 2007
Initialize: January 1, 2007
ComparedTo
January 1, 2006 comes before January 1, 2007
Initialize: January 1, 2008
ComparedTo
January 1, 2008 and January 1, 2008
```

```
 are equal
Initialize: January 1, 2006
Adjust
January 1, 2006 plus 367 is January 3, 2007
Initialize: February 27, 2000
Adjust
February 27, 2000 plus 3 is March 1, 2000
Initialize: February 27, 2100
Adjust
February 27, 2100 plus 3 is March 2, 2100
Initialize: February 27, 1964
Adjust
February 27, 1964 plus 3 is March 1, 1964
```

Our task is not yet finished. We need to add the UML diagram to the documentation for class `DateType`.

```
DateType
-----------------------------------------------
-month: int
-day: int
-year: int
-----------------------------------------------
+Initialize(month: int, day: int,
            year: int): void
+GetMonth(): int
+GetDay(): int
+GetYear(): int
+GetYearAsString(): string
+ComparedTo(aDate: Datetype): RelationType
+Adjust(daysAway: int): DateType
```

Summary

We have discussed how data can be viewed from multiple perspectives, and we have seen how C++ encapsulates the implementations of its predefined types and allows us to encapsulate our own class implementations.

As we create data structures, using built-in data types such as arrays, structs, and classes to implement them, we see that there are actually many levels of data abstraction. The abstract view of an array might be viewed as the implementation level of the programmer-defined data type List, which uses an array to hold its elements. At the logical level, we do not access the elements of List through their array indexes but rather through a set of accessing operations defined especially for objects of the List type. A data type that is designed to hold other objects is called a *container* or *collection type*. Moving up a level, we might see the abstract view of List as the implementation level of another programmer-defined data type, `ProductInventory`, and so on.

Perspectives on Data

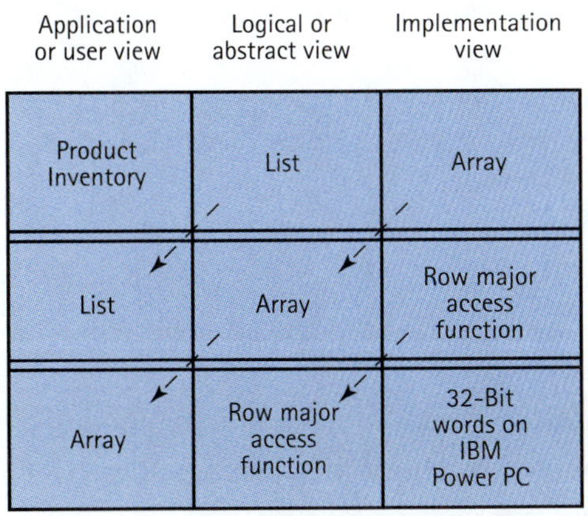

What do we gain by separating these views of the data? First, we reduce complexity at the higher levels of the design, making the program easier to understand. Second, we make the program more easily modifiable: The implementation can be completely changed without affecting the program that uses the data structure. We take advantage of this ability in this text, developing various implementations of the same objects in different chapters. Third, we develop software that is *reusable*: The structure and its accessing operations can be used by other programs, for completely different applications, as long as the correct interfaces are maintained. You saw in Chapter 1 that the design, implementation, and verification of high-quality computer software is a very laborious process. Being able to reuse pieces that are already designed, coded, and tested cuts down on the amount of work required.

In the chapters that follow, we extend these ideas to build other container classes that C++ does not provide: lists, stacks, queues, priority queues, trees, graphs, and sets. We consider these data structures from the logical view: What is our abstract picture of the data, and what accessing operations can we use to create, assign, and manipulate elements in the data structure? We express our logical view as an abstract data type (ADT) and record its description in a data specification.

Next, we take the application view of the data, using an instance of the data type in a short example.

Finally, we change hats and turn to the implementation view of the data type. We consider the C++ type declarations that represent the data structure as well as the design of the functions that implement the specifications of the abstract view. Data structures can be implemented in more than one way, so we often look at alternative representations and methods for comparing them. In some of the chapters, we include a longer Case Study in which instances of the data type are used to solve a problem.

Exercises

1. Explain what we mean by "data abstraction."
2. What is data encapsulation? Explain the programming goal "to protect our data abstraction through encapsulation."
3. Name three perspectives from which we can view data. Using the logical data structure "a list of student academic records," give examples of what each perspective might tell us about the data.
4. Consider the abstract data type GroceryStore.
   a. At the application level, describe GroceryStore.
   b. At the logical level, what grocery store operations might be defined for the customer?
   c. Specify (at the logical level) the operation CheckOut.
   d. Write an algorithm (at the implementation level) for the operation CheckOut.
   e. Explain how parts (c) and (d) represent information hiding.
5. What composite types are predefined in the C++ language?
6. Describe the component selectors for structs and classes at the logical level.
7. Describe the accessing functions for structs and classes at the implementation level.
8. Describe the component selectors for one-dimensional arrays at the logical level.
9. Describe the accessing functions for one-dimensional arrays at the implementation level.
10. a. Declare a one-dimensional array, `name`, that contains 20 characters.
    b. If each character occupies one "cell" in memory, and the base address of `name` is 1000, what is the address of the cell referenced in the following statement?

    ```
    name[9] = 'A';
    ```

Use the following declarations for Exercises 11 and 12:

```
enum MonthType {JAN, FEB, MAR, APR, MAY, JUN, JUL, AUG, SEP,
                OCT, NOV, DEC};
struct WeatherType
{
  int avgHiTemp;
  int avgLoTemp;
  float actualRain;
  float recordRain;
};
```

Assume that an `int` requires one cell in memory, that a `float` number requires two cells, and that the struct members are found in contiguous memory locations with no gaps.

11. a. Declare a one-dimensional array type, `WeatherListType`, of `WeatherType` components, to be indexed by values of type `MonthType`. Declare a variable, `yearlyWeather`, of `WeatherListType`.
    b. Assign the value 1.05 to the actual rainfall member of the July record in `yearlyWeather`.
    c. If the base address of `yearlyWeather` is 200, what is the address of the member that you assigned in part (b)?
12. a. Declare a two-dimensional array, `decadeWeather`, of `WeatherType` components, to be indexed by values of type `MonthType` in the first dimension.
    b. Draw a picture of `decadeWeather`.
    c. Assign the value 26 to the `avgLoTemp` member of the March 2006 entry.
13. a. Define a three-dimensional array at the logical level.
    b. Suggest some applications for three-dimensional arrays.

Use the following declarations for Exercises 14–16.

```
typedef char String[10];
struct StudentRecord
{
  String firstName;
  String lastName;
  int id;
  float gpa;
  int currentHours;
  int totalHours;
};
StudentRecord student;
StudentRecord students[100];
```

Assume that an `int` requires one cell in memory, that a `float` number requires two cells, and that the struct members are found in contiguous memory locations with no gaps.

14. Construct a member-length-offset table for `StudentRecord`.
15. If the base address of `student` is 100, what address does the compiler generate as the target of the following assignment statement?

```
student.gpa = 3.87;
```

16. How much space does the compiler set aside for `students`?

17. Indicate which predefined C++ types would most appropriately model each of the following (more than one may be appropriate for each):
    a. a chessboard
    b. information about a single product in an inventory-control program
    c. a list of famous quotations
    d. the casualty figures (number of deaths per year) for highway accidents in Texas from 1995 to 2005
    e. the casualty figures for highway accidents in each of the states from 1995 to 2005
    f. the casualty figures for highway accidents in each of the states from 1995 to 2005, subdivided by month
    g. an electronic address book (name, address, and phone information for all your friends)
    h. a collection of hourly temperatures for a 24-hour period
18. What C++ construct is used to represent abstract data types?
19. Explain the difference between a C++ struct and class.
20. How is the client prevented from directly accessing the details of an instance of a class?
21. a. The details of a private member can be *seen* by the user of a class. (True or False?)
    b. The details of a private member may be *accessed* by a client program. (True or False?)
22. Why is it good practice to put a class declaration in one file and the implementation in another?
23. Name three ways that classes can relate to each other.
24. Distinguish between composition and inheritance.
25. Distinguish between a base class and a derived class.
26. Does a derived class have access to the private data members of the base class?
27. Does a derived class have access to the public member functions of the base class?
28. a. Write the specification for an ADT SquareMatrix. (A square matrix can be represented by a two-dimensional array with *N* rows and *N* columns.) You may assume a maximum size of 50 rows and columns. Include the following operations:

       `MakeEmpty(n)`, which sets the first `n` rows and columns to zero

       `StoreValue(i, j, value)`, which stores a value into the [i, j] position

       `Add`, which adds two matrices together

       `Subtract`, which subtracts one matrix from another

       `Copy`, which copies one matrix into another

b. Convert your specification to a C++ class declaration.

c. Implement the member functions.

d. Write a test plan for your class.

29. `DateType` keeps only the integer representation of the month, day, and year. When a month is wanted in string form, the string is calculated. An alternate approach would be to add a string field to the date and calculate and store the string representation in the `Initialize` function. Which methods would have to be changed? Would this change make the use of an *if* statement to find the appropriate string more or less attractive? Write the code for this *if* statement.

30. What changes would be necessary if the number of days in the month were carried as a data field in class `DateType` rather than being looked up when necessary? Would this change make the use of a *switch* statement to find the number of days in the month more attractive? Write the code for this `switch` statement.

31. Compare and contrast the implementation of class `DateType` used in the Case Study and the solution proposed in Exercises 29 and 30. These two approaches represent the classic trade-off between space and algorithm complexity. Please comment.

Use the following possible answers for Exercises 32–36.

a. O(1)

b. O(log*N*)

c. O(*N*)

d. O(*N* log*N*)

e. O(*N***N*)

f. O(*N***N***N*)

32. The order of sorting an array of *N* items using one of the better sorting algorithms such as Quicksort.

33. The order of sorting an array of *N* items using one of the slower sorting algorithms such as SelectionSort.

34. The order of an algorithm that decrements every element in a three-dimensional table of *N* rows.

35. The order of an algorithm that increments every element in a two-dimensional table of *N* rows.

36. The order of comparing three items.

37. True or False? O(*N*) is called linear time.

38. True or False? O(*N*) is called log time.

39. True or False? O(*N***N*) is called quadratic time.

40. True or False? O(1) is called constant time.

41. True or False? An algorithm that has complexity O(log*N*) is always faster than one that has O(*N*) complexity.

chapter 3

ADT Unsorted List

Goals

After studying this chapter, you should be able to

- Describe the Abstract Data Type Unsorted List from three perspectives
- Use the Unsorted List operations to implement utility routines to do the following application-level tasks:
  - Print the list of elements
  - Create a list of elements from a file
- Implement the following Unsorted List operations using an array-based implementation
  - Create and destroy a list
  - Determine whether the list is full
  - Put an element into the list
  - Get an element from the list
  - Delete an element from the list
- Write and execute a test plan for an abstract data type
- Declare variables of pointer types
- Access the variables to which pointers point
- Implement the list operations outlined above using a linked implementation
- Compare the two implementations of the ADT Unsorted List in terms of Big-O approximations

In Chapter 2, we defined an abstract data type and showed how all data can be viewed from three perspectives: from the logical perspective, the implementation perspective, and the application perspective. The logical perspective is the abstract view of *what* the ADT does. The implementation perspective offers a picture of *how* the logical operations are carried out. The application perspective shows *why* the ADT behaves as it does—that is, how the behavior can be useful in a real-world problem.

In this chapter, we look at an ADT that should be familiar to all of us: the list. We all know intuitively what a "list" is; in our everyday lives we use lists constantly—grocery lists, lists of things to do, lists of addresses, lists of party guests. Lists are places where we write down things that we want to remember.

3.1 Lists

In computer programs, lists are very useful abstract data types. They are members of a general category of abstract data types called *containers,* whose purpose is to hold other objects. In some languages, the list is a built-in structure. In Lisp, for example, the list is the main data structure provided in the language. In C++, while lists are provided in the Standard Template Library, the techniques for building lists and other abstract data types are so important that we show you how to design and write your own.

Linear relationship Each element except the first has a unique predecessor, and each element except the last has a unique successor

Length The number of items in a list; the length can vary over time

Unsorted list A list in which data items are placed in no particular order; the only relationships between data elements are the list predecessor and successor relationships

Sorted list A list that is sorted by the value in the key; a semantic relationship exists among the keys of the items in the list

Key A member of a record (struct or class) whose value is used to determine the logical and/or physical order of the items in a list

From a theoretical point of view, a list is a homogeneous collection of elements, with a linear relationship between elements. *Linear* means that, at the logical level, each element in the list except the first one has a unique predecessor, and each element except the last one has a unique successor. (At the implementation level, a relationship also exists between the elements, but the physical relationship may not be the same as the logical one.) The number of items in the list, which we call the length of the list, is a property of a list. That is, every list has a length.

Lists can be unsorted—their elements may be placed into the list in no particular order—or they can be sorted in a variety of ways. For instance, a list of numbers can be sorted by value, a list of strings can be sorted alphabetically, and a list of grades can be sorted numerically. When the elements in a sorted list are of composite types, their logical (and often physical) order is determined by one of the members of the structure, called the key member. For example, a list of students on the honor roll can be sorted alphabetically by name or numerically by student identification number. In the first case, the name is the key; in the second case, the identification number is the key. Such sorted lists are also called *key-sorted lists.*

If a list cannot contain items with duplicate keys, it is said to have *unique* keys. This chapter deals with unsorted lists. In Chapter 4, we examine lists of elements with unique keys, sorted from smallest to largest key value.

3.2 Abstract Data Type Unsorted List

Logical Level

Programmers can provide many different operations for lists. For different applications we can imagine all kinds of things users might need to do to a list of elements. In this chapter we formally define a list and develop a set of general-purpose operations for creating and manipulating lists. By doing so, we build an abstract data type.

In the next section we design the specifications for a List ADT where the items in the list are unsorted; that is, no semantic relationship exists between an item and its predecessor or successor. Items simply appear next to one another in the list.

Abstract Data Type Operations

The first step in designing any abstract data type is to stand back and consider what a user of the data type would want it to provide. Recall that there are four kinds of operations: constructors, transformers, observers, and iterators. We begin by reviewing each type and consider each kind of operation with respect to the List ADT. We use a handwriting font for operation names at the logical level and change to a monospaced font when we refer to specific implementation.

Constructors A constructor creates an instance of the data type. It is usually implemented with a language-level declaration.

Transformers (also called mutators) Transformers are operations that change the structure in some way: They may make the structure empty, put an item into the structure, or remove a specific item from the structure. For our Unsorted List ADT, let's call these transformers MakeEmpty, PutItem, and DeleteItem.

MakeEmpty needs only the list, no other parameters. As we implement our operations as member functions, the list is the object to which the function is applied. PutItem and DeleteItem need an additional parameter: the item to be inserted or removed. For this Unsorted List ADT, let's assume that the item to be inserted is *not* currently in the list and the item to be deleted *is* in the list.

A transformer that takes two lists and creates a third list by appending one list to the other would be a *binary transformer*.

Observers Observers come in several forms. They ask true/false questions about the data type (Is the structure empty?), select or access a particular item (Give me a copy of the last item.), or return a property of the structure (How many items are in the structure?). The Unsorted List ADT needs at least two observers: IsFull and GetLength. IsFull returns true if the list is full; GetLength tells us how many items appear in the list. Another useful observer searches the list for an item with a particular key and returns a copy of the associated information if it is found; let's call it GetItem.

If an abstract data type places limits on the component type, we could define other observers. For example, if we know that our abstract data type is a list of numerical values, we could define statistical observers such as `Minimum`, `Maximum`, and `Average`. Here, we are interested in generality; we know nothing about the type of the items on the list, so we use only general observers in our ADT.

In most of our discussions of error checking to date, we have put the responsibility of checking for error conditions on the user through the use of preconditions that prohibit the operation's call if these error conditions exist. In making the client responsible for checking for error conditions, however, we must make sure that the ADT gives the user the tools with which to check for the conditions. In another approach, we could keep an error variable in our list, have each operation record whether an error occurs, and provide operations that test this variable. The operations that check whether an error has occurred would be observers. However, in the Unsorted List ADT we are specifying, let's have the user prevent error conditions by obeying the preconditions of the ADT operations.

Iterators Iterators are used with composite types to allow the user to process an entire structure, component by component. To give the user access to each item in sequence, we provide two operations: one to initialize the iteration process (analogous to Reset or Open with a file) and one to return a copy of the "next component" each time it is called. The user can then set up a loop that processes each component. Let's call these operations `ResetList` and `GetNextItem`. Note that `ResetList` is not an iterator itself, but rather an auxiliary operation that supports the iteration. Another type of iterator takes an operation and applies it to every element in the list.

C++ Declarations and Definitions

In general programming terminology, a *declaration* associates an identifier with a data object, an action (such as a function), or a data type. C++ terminology distinguishes between a declaration and a definition. A declaration becomes a *definition* when it binds storage to the identifier. Hence, all definitions are declarations, but not all declarations are definitions. For example, a function prototype is a declaration, but a function heading with a body is a function definition. On the other hand, declarations such as `typedef` can never be definitions, because they are not bound to storage. Because of the way that C++ treats classes, their specification is also a definition. Because the ISO/ANSI C++ standard uses the term "definition" rather than "declaration" when referring to a class, we do the same here.

Generic Data Types

A generic data type is one for which the operations are defined but the types of the items being manipulated are not. Some programming languages have a built-in mechanism for defining generic data types; others lack this feature. Although C++ does have such a mechanism (called a template), we postpone its description until Chapter 6. Here we present a simple, general-purpose way of simulating

Generic data type A type for which the operations are defined but the types of the items being manipulated are not

generics that works in any programming language. We let the user define the type of the items on the list in a class named ItemType and have our Unsorted List ADT include the class definition.

Two of the list operations (DeleteItem and GetItem) will involve the comparison of the keys of two list components (as does PutItem if the list is sorted by key value). We could require the user to name the key data member "key" and compare the key data members using the C++ relational operators. However, this approach isn't a very satisfactory solution for two reasons: "key" is not always a meaningful identifier in an application program, and the keys would be limited to values of simple types. C++ does have a way to change the meaning of the relational operators (called *overloading* them), but for now we present a general solution rather than a language-dependent one.

We let the user define a member function ComparedTo in the class ItemType. This function compares two items and returns LESS, GREATER, or EQUAL depending on whether the key of one item comes before the key of the other item, the first key comes after it, or the keys of the two items are equal, respectively. If the keys are of a simple type such as an identification number, ComparedTo would be implemented using the relational operators. If the keys are strings, function ComparedTo would use the string-comparison operators supplied in <string>. If the keys are people's names, both the last name and the first name would be compared. Therefore, our specification assumes that ComparedTo is a member of ItemType.

Our ADT needs one more piece of information from the client: the maximum number of items on the list. As this information varies from application to application, it is logical for the client to provide it.

Let's summarize our observations in two CRC cards: one for ItemType and the other for UnsortedType. Note that UnsortedType collaborates with ItemType.

Class Name: ItemType	Superclass:	Subclasses:

Responsibilities	Collaborations
Provide	
MAX_ITEMS	
enum RelationType (LESS, GREATER, EQUAL)	
ComparedTo (item) returns RelationType	
. . .	

Class Name: UnsortedType	Superclass:	Subclasses:

Responsibilities	Collaborations
MakeEmpty	
IsFull returns Boolean	
GetLength returns integer	
GetItem (item, found) returns item	ItemType
PutItem (item)	ItemType
DeleteItem (item)	ItemType
ResetList	
GetNextItem returns item	ItemType
. . .	

Now we can formalize the specification for the Unsorted List ADT.

Unsorted List ADT Specification

Structure:

The list elements are of ItemType. The list has a special property called the *current position*—the position of the last element accessed by **GetNextItem** during an iteration through the list. Only **ResetList** and **GetNextItem** affect the current position.

Definitions (provided by user):

MAX_ITEMS: A constant specifying the maximum number of items to be on the list.

ItemType: Class encapsulating the type of the items in the list

RelationType: An enumeration type that consists of LESS, GREATER, EQUAL

Member function of ItemType that must be included:

RelationType ComparedTo(ItemType item)

Function: Determines the ordering of two ItemType objects based on their keys.

Precondition: Self and item have their key members initialized.

Postcondition:

Function value = LESS if the key of self is less than the key of item.
= GREATER if the key of self is greater than the key of item.
= EQUAL if the keys are equal.

Operations (provided by Unsorted List ADT)

MakeEmpty

Function: Initializes list to empty state.

Preconditions: None

Postcondition: List is empty.

Boolean IsFull

Function: Determines whether list is full.

Precondition: List has been initialized.

Postcondition: Function value = (list is full)

int GetLength

Function: Determines the number of elements in list.

Precondition: List has been initialized.

Postcondition: Function value = number of elements in list

ItemType GetItem (ItemType item , Boolean& found)

Function: Get list element whose key matches item's key (if present).

Preconditions: List has been initialized.
Key member of item is initialized.

Postconditions: If there is an element someItem whose key matches item's key, then found = true and copy of someItem is returned; otherwise found = false and item is returned.
List is unchanged.

PutItem (ItemType item)

Function: Puts item to list.

Preconditions: List has been initialized.
List is not full.
item is not in list.

Postcondition: item is in list.

DeleteItem (ItemType item)

Function:	Deletes the element whose key matches item's key.
Preconditions:	List has been initialized.
	Key member of item is initialized.
	One and only one element in list has a key matching item's key.
Postcondition:	No element in list has a key matching item's key.

ResetList

Function:	Initializes current position for an iteration through the list.
Precondition:	List has been initialized.
Postcondition:	Current position is prior to list.

ItemType GetNextItem ()

Function:	Gets the next element in list.
Preconditions:	List has been initialized.
	Current position is defined.
	Element at current position is not last in list.
Postconditions:	Current position is updated to next position.
	Returns a copy of element at current position.

Because we do not know the makeup of the key member in the `ItemType`, we must pass an entire object of `ItemType` as the parameter to both `GetItem` and `DeleteItem`. Notice that the preconditions for both operations state that the key member of the parameter `item` is initialized. `GetItem` fills in the rest of the members of `item` if a list component with the same key is found, and `DeleteItem` removes from the list the component whose key matches that of `item`.

The specifications of the operations are somewhat arbitrary. For instance, we specified in the preconditions of `DeleteItem` that the element to delete must exist in the list and must be unique. We could also specify an operation that does not require the element to be in the list and leaves the list unchanged if the item is not present. This decision is a design choice. If we were designing a specification for a specific application, then the design choice would be based on the requirements of the problem. In this case, we made an arbitrary decision. In the exercises, you are asked to examine the effects of different design choices.

The operations defined in this specification are a sufficient set to create and maintain an unsorted list of elements. Notice that no operation depends on the type of the items in the structure. This data independence makes the Unsorted List ADT truly abstract. Each program that uses the Unsorted List ADT defines `ItemType` within the context of the application and provides a comparison member function defined on two items of type `ItemType`.

Application Level

The set of operations provided for the Unsorted List ADT may seem rather small and primitive. In fact, this set of operations gives you the tools to create other special-purpose routines that require a knowledge of `ItemType`. For instance, we have not included a print operation. Why? Because to write a print routine, we must know what the data members look like. The user (who does know what the data members look like) can use the `GetLength`, `ResetList`, and `GetNextItem` operations to iterate through the list, printing each data member in turn. In the code that follows, we assume that the user has defined a member function for `ItemType` that prints the data members of one item. We also assume that the Unsorted List ADT is itself implemented as a class with the operations as member functions.

```
void PrintList(std::ofstream& dataFile, UnsortedType list)
// Pre:  list has been initialized.
//       dataFile is open for writing.
// Post: Each component in list has been written to dataFile.
//       dataFile is still open.
{
  int length;
  ItemType item;

  list.ResetList();
  length = list.GetLength();
  for (int counter = 1; counter <= length; counter++)
  {
    item = list.GetNextItem();
    item.Print(dataFile);
  }
}
```

Note that we defined a local variable `length`, stored the result of `list.GetLength()` in it, and used the local variable in the loop. We did so for efficiency reasons: The function is called only once, saving the overhead of extra function calls.

Another operation that depends on the application reads data (of type `ItemType`) from a file and creates a list containing these elements. Without knowing how the list is implemented, the user can write a function `CreateListFromFile`, using the operations specified in the Unsorted List ADT. We assume a function `GetData`, which accesses the individual data members from the file and returns them in `item`.

```
void CreateListFromFile(std::ifstream& dataFile, UnsortedType& list)
// Pre:  dataFile exists and is open.
// Post: list contains items from dataFile.
//       dataFile is in the fail state due to end-of-file.
```

```
//        Items read after the list becomes full are discarded.
{
  ItemType item;

  list.MakeEmpty();
  GetData(dataFile, item); // Reads one item from dataFile.
  while (dataFile)
  {
    if (!list.IsFull())
      list.PutItem(item);
    GetData(dataFile, item);
  }
}
```

In these two functions we have made calls to the list operations specified for the Unsorted List ADT, creating and printing a list *without knowing how the list is implemented.* At an application level, these tasks are logical operations on a list. At a lower level, these operations are implemented as C++ functions that manipulate an array or other data-storing medium holding the list's elements. Multiple functionally correct ways are available to implement an abstract data type. Between the user picture and the eventual representation in the computer's memory, intermediate levels of abstraction and design decisions are possible. For instance, how is the logical order of the list elements reflected in their physical ordering? We address questions like this as we now turn to the implementation level of our ADT.

Implementation Level

The logical order of the list elements may or may not mirror the way that we actually store the data. If we implement a list in an array, the components are arranged so that the predecessor and the successor of a component are physically before and after it. Later in this chapter, we introduce a way of implementing a list in which the components are sorted logically rather than physically. However, the way that the list elements are physically arranged certainly affects the way that we access the elements of the list. This arrangement may have implications for how efficient the list operations are. For instance, there is nothing in the specification of the Unsorted List ADT that requires us to implement the list with the elements stored in random order. If we stored the elements in an array, completely sorted, we could still implement all the Unsorted List operations. Does it make a difference if the items are stored unsorted or sorted? We answer the question in Chapter 4.

There are two ways to implement a list that preserves the order of the list items; that is, that stores the elements physically in such a way that, from one list element, we can access its logical successor directly. We look at both in this chapter. The first is a *sequential array-based* list representation. The distinguishing feature of this implemen-

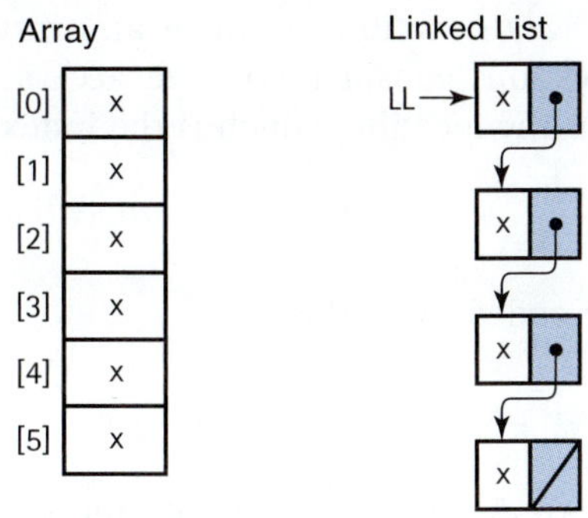

Figure 3.1 *Comparison of Array and Linked Structure*

tation is that the elements are stored sequentially, in adjacent slots in an array. The order of the elements is implicit in their placement in the array.

The second approach is a *linked-list* representation. In a linked implementation, the data elements are not constrained to be stored in physically contiguous, sequential order; rather, the individual elements are stored "somewhere in memory," and their order is maintained by explicit links between them. Figure 3.1 shows the difference between an array and a linked list.

Before we go on, let's establish a design terminology that we can use in our algorithms, independent of the eventual list implementation.

List Design Terminology Assuming that `location` "accesses" a particular list element,

Node(location) refers to all data at `location`, including implementation-specific data.
Info(location) refers to the user's data at `location`.
Info(last) refers to the user's data at the last location in the list.
Next(location) gives the location of the node following Node(location).

What, then, is `location`? For an array-based implementation, `location` is an index, because we access array slots through their indexes. For example, the design statement

Print element Info(location)

means "Print the user's data in the array slot at index `location`"; eventually it might be coded in C++ as

```
list.info[location].Print(dataFile);
```

When we look at a linked implementation later in the chapter, the translation is quite different but the algorithms remain the same. That is, our code implementing the operations changes, but the algorithms do not. Thus, using this design notation, we define implementation-independent algorithms for our Unsorted List ADT.

But what does Next(location) mean in an array-based sequential implementation? To answer this question, consider how we access the next list element stored in an array: We increment the location, which is the index. The design statement

Set location to Next(location)

might, therefore, be coded in C++ as

```
location++; // location is an array index.
```

We have not introduced this list design terminology just to force you to learn the syntax of another computer "language." Rather, we want to encourage you to think of the list, and the parts of the list elements, as *abstractions*. We have intentionally made the design notation similar to the syntax of function calls to emphasize that, at the design stage, the implementation details can be hidden. A lower level of detail is encapsulated in the "functions" Node, Info, and Next. Using this design terminology, we hope to record algorithms that can be coded for both array-based and linked implementations.

Data Structure In our implementation, the elements of a list are stored in an array of class objects.

```
ItemType info[MAX_ITEMS];
```

We need a `length` data member to keep track of both the number of items we have stored in the array and the location where the last item was stored. Because the list items are unsorted, we place the first item put into the list into the first slot, the second item into the second slot, and so forth. Because our language is C++, we must remember that the first slot is indexed by 0, the second slot by 1, and the last slot by `MAX_ITEMS - 1`. Now we know where the list begins—in the first array slot. Where does the list end? The *array* ends at the slot with index `MAX_ITEMS - 1`, but the *list* ends in the slot with index `length - 1`.

Is there any other information about the list that we must include? Both operations `ResetList` and `GetNextItem` refer to a "current position." What is this current position? It is the index of the last element accessed in an iteration through the list. Let's call it `currentPos`. `ResetList` initializes `currentPos` to `-1`. `GetNextItem` increments `currentPos` and returns the value in `info[currentPos]`. The ADT specification states that only `ResetList` and `GetNextItem` affect the current position. Figure 3.2 illustrates the data members of our class `UnsortedType`.

```
#include "ItemType.h"
// File ItemType.h must be provided by the user of this class.
//  ItemType.h must contain the following definitions:
//  MAX_ITEMS:     the maximum number of items on the list
//  ItemType:      the definition of the objects on the list
//  RelationType:  {LESS, GREATER, EQUAL}
```

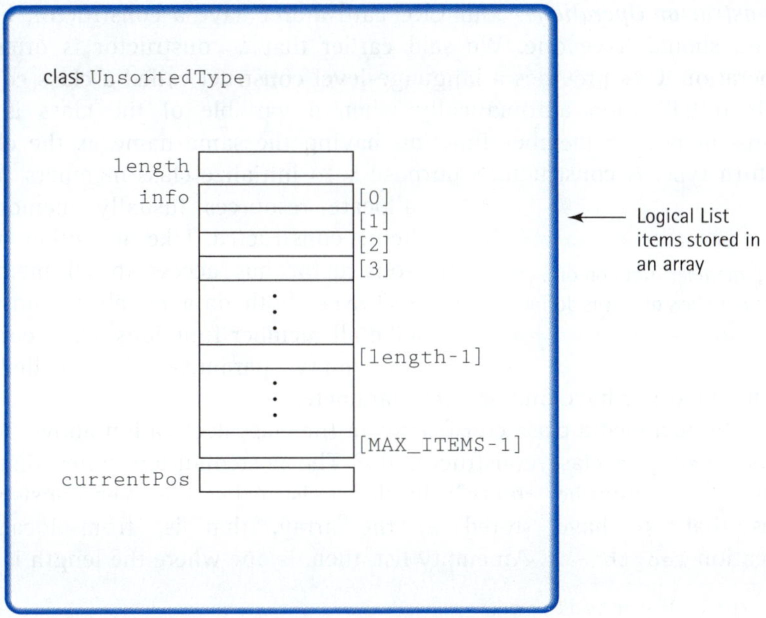

Figure 3.2 *Data members of class UnsortedType*

```
//  Member function ComparedTo(ItemType item) which returns
//       LESS, if self "comes before" item
//       GREATER, if self "comes after" item
//       EQUAL, if self and item are the same

class UnsortedType
{
public:
  UnsortedType();
  void MakeEmpty();
  bool IsFull() const;
  int GetLength() const;
  ItemType GetItem(ItemType item, bool& found);
  void PutItem(ItemType item);
  void DeleteItem(ItemType item);
  void ResetList();
  ItemType GetNextItem();
private:
  int length;
  ItemType info[MAX_ITEMS];
  int currentPos;
};
```

Now let's look at the operations that we have specified for the Unsorted List ADT.

Constructor Operations Our CRC card didn't have a constructor, but we know that a class should have one. We said earlier that a constructor is often a language-level operation. C++ provides a language-level construct called a **class constructor** that does this initialization automatically when a variable of the class is declared. A class constructor is a member function having the same name as the class but having no return type. A constructor's purpose is to initialize class members, and if necessary, to allocate resources (usually memory) for the object being constructed. Like any other member function, a constructor has access to all members, `public` and `private`, both data members and function members. Like all member functions, class constructors can have an empty parameter list (called a *default* class constructor) or have one or more parameters.

Class constructor A special member function of a class that is implicitly invoked when a class object is defined

We included a class constructor in the class declaration above. Now, what must the `UnsortedType` class constructor do? The postcondition states that the list is empty. Any array cannot be "empty"; the slots exist. A list, however, consists of only those values that we have stored in the array, that is, from location zero through location `length - 1`. An empty list, then, is one where the length is 0.

```
UnsortedType::UnsortedType()
{
  length = 0;
}
```

Notice that we do *not* have to do anything to the array that holds the list items to make a list empty. If `length` is zero, the list is empty. If `length` is not zero, we must have stored items in the array through the `length - 1` position, covering up what was there. What is present in the array from the `length` position to the end is of no interest to us. *This distinction is very important: The list is between positions 0 and* `length - 1`*; the array is between positions 0 and* `MAX_ITEMS - 1`*.*

C++ Rules for Using Class Constructors

C++ has intricate rules governing the use of constructors. The following guidelines are especially pertinent:

1. A constructor cannot return a function value, so the function is declared without a return value type. Although not necessary, *return* statements with no expressions are allowed at the end of a constructor. Thus `return;` is legal in a constructor, but `return 0;` is not.
2. Like any other member function, a constructor may be overloaded. Hence, a class may provide several constructors. When a class object is declared, the compiler chooses the appropriate constructor based on the number and data types of the parameters to the constructor, just as in any other call to overloaded functions.
3. Arguments to a constructor are passed by placing the argument list immediately after the name of the class object being declared:

```
SomeType myObject(argument1, argument2);
```

4. If a class object is declared without a parameter list, as in the statement

```
SomeType myObject;
```

then the effect depends on the constructors (if any) provided by the class. If the class has no constructors, the compiler generates a default constructor that does nothing. If the class does have constructors, then the default (parameterless) constructor is invoked if there is one. If the class has constructors but no default constructor, a syntax error occurs.

5. If a class has at least one constructor, and an array of class objects is declared as in the statement

```
SomeType myObject[5];
```

then one of the constructors must be the default (parameterless) constructor. This constructor is invoked for each element in the array.

Observer Operations The observer function `IsFull` checks whether `length` is equal to `MAX_ITEMS`.

```
bool UnsortedType::IsFull() const
{
  return (length == MAX_ITEMS);
}
```

The body of the observer member function `GetLength` is also just one statement.

```
int UnsortedType::GetLength() const
{
  return length;
}
```

So far we have not used our special design terminology. The algorithms have all been one (obvious) statement long. The next operation, `GetItem`, is more complex. The `GetItem` operation allows the list user to access the list item with a specified key, if that element exists in the list. `item` (with the key initialized) is input to this operation; `item` and a flag (`found`) are returned. If the key of `item` matches a key in the list, then `found` is true and a copy of the item with the matching key is returned. Otherwise, `found` is false and `item` is the input value returned. Notice that `item` is used for both input to and output from the function. Conceptually, the key member is input; the other data members are output because the function fills them in.

To retrieve an element, we must first find it. Because the items are unsorted, we must use a linear search. We begin at the first component in the list and loop until either we find an item with the same key or there are no more items to examine. Recognizing a match is easy: `item.ComparedTo(info[location])` returns `EQUAL`. But how do we know when to stop searching? If we have examined the last element, we can stop. Thus, in our design terminology, we continue looking as long as we have not examined Info(last). Our looping statement is a *while* statement with the expression (moreToSearch AND NOT found). The body of the loop is a *switch* statement based on the results of function `ComparedTo`. We summarize these observations in the following algorithm:

```
GetItem
Initialize location to position of first item
Set found to false
Set moreToSearch to (have not examined Info(last))
while moreToSearch AND NOT found
    switch (item.ComparedTo(Info(location)))
        case LESS    :
        case GREATER : Set location to Next(location)
                       Set moreToSearch to (have not examined Info(last))
        case EQUAL   : Set found to true
                       Set item to Info(location)
return item
```

Before we code this algorithm, let's look at the cases where we find the item in the list and where we examine Info(last) without finding it. We represent these cases in Figure 3.3 in an honor roll list. First, we retrieve Sarah. Sarah is in the list, so `moreToSearch` is `true`, `found` is `true`, and `location` is `1`. That's as it should be (see Figure 3.3a). Next, we retrieve Susan. Susan is not in the list, so `moreToSearch` is `false`, `found` is `false`, and `location` is equal to `length` (see Figure 3.3b).

Now we are ready to code the algorithm, replacing the general design notation with the equivalent array notation. The substitutions are straightforward except for initializing `location` and determining whether we have examined Info(last). To initialize `location` in an array-based implementation in C++, we set it to 0. We know we have not examined Info(last) as long as `location` is less than `length`. Be careful: Because C++ indexes arrays starting with 0, the last item in the list is found at index `length - 1`. Here is the coded algorithm:

```
ItemType UnsortedType::GetItem(ItemType item, bool& found)
// Pre:  Key member(s) of item is initialized.
// Post: If found, item's key matches an element's key in the
//       list and a copy of that element is returned;
//       otherwise, item is returned.
```

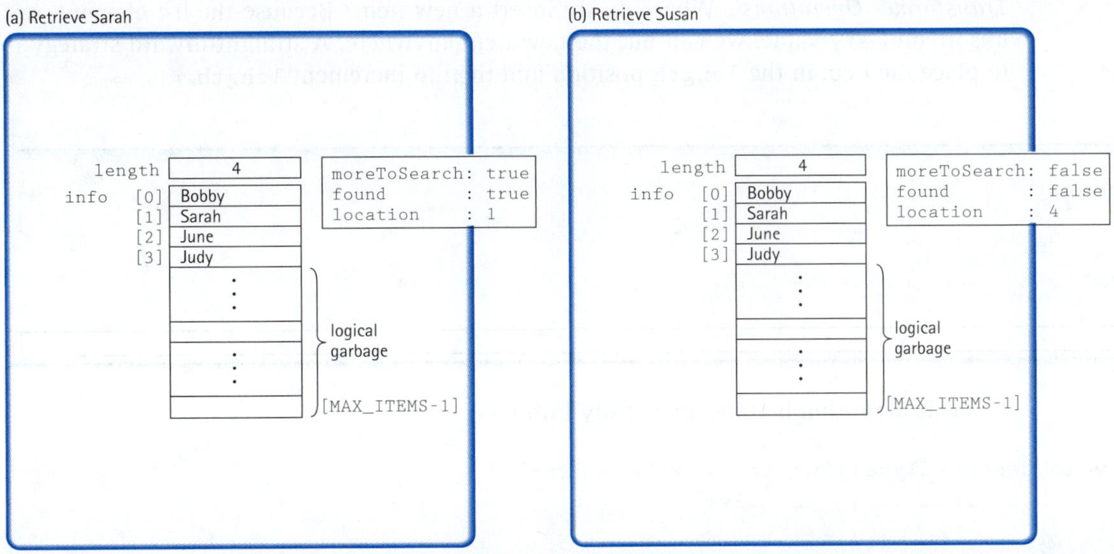

Figure 3.3 *Retrieving an item in an unsorted list*

```
{
  bool moreToSearch;
  int location = 0;
  found = false;

  moreToSearch = (location < length);

  while (moreToSearch && !found)
  {
    switch (item.ComparedTo(info[location]))
    {
      case LESS    :
      case GREATER : location++;
                     moreToSearch = (location < length);
                     break;
      case EQUAL   : found = true;
                     item = info[location];
                     break;
    }
  }
  return item;
}
```

Note that a *copy* of the list element is returned. The caller cannot access directly any data in the list.

Transformer Operations Where do we insert a new item? Because the list elements are unsorted by key value, we can put the new item anywhere. A straightforward strategy is to place the item in the `length` position and then to increment `length`.

PutItem

Set Info(length) to item
Increment length

This algorithm is translated easily into C++.

```
void UnsortedType::PutItem(ItemType item)
// Post: item is in the list.
{
  info[length] = item;
  length++;
}
```

The `DeleteItem` function takes an item with the key member indicating which item to delete. This operation clearly has two parts: finding the item to delete and removing it. We can use the `GetItem` algorithm to search the list: When `ComparedTo` returns `GREATER` or `LESS`, we increment `location`; when it returns `EQUAL`, we exit the loop and remove the element.

How do we "remove the element from the list"? Let's look at the example in Figure 3.4. Removing Judy from the list is easy, for hers is the last element in the list (see Figures 3.4a and 3.4b). If Bobby is deleted from the list, however, we need to move up all the elements that follow to fill in the space—or do we? If the list is sorted by value, we would have to move all elements up, as shown in Figure 3.4c. Because the list is unsorted, however, we can just swap the item in the `length - 1` position with the item being deleted (see Figure 3.4d). In an array-based implementation, we do not actually remove the element; instead, we cover it up with the element that previously followed it (if the list is sorted) or the element in the last position (if the list is unsorted). Finally, we decrement `length`.

Because the preconditions for `DeleteItem` state that an item with the same key is definitely present in the list, we do not need to test for the end of the list. This choice simplifies the algorithm so much that we give the code with no further discussion.

```
void UnsortedType::DeleteItem(ItemType item)
// Pre:  item's key has been initialized.
//       An element in the list has a key that matches item's.
// Post: No element in the list has a key that matches item's.
{
  int location = 0;
```

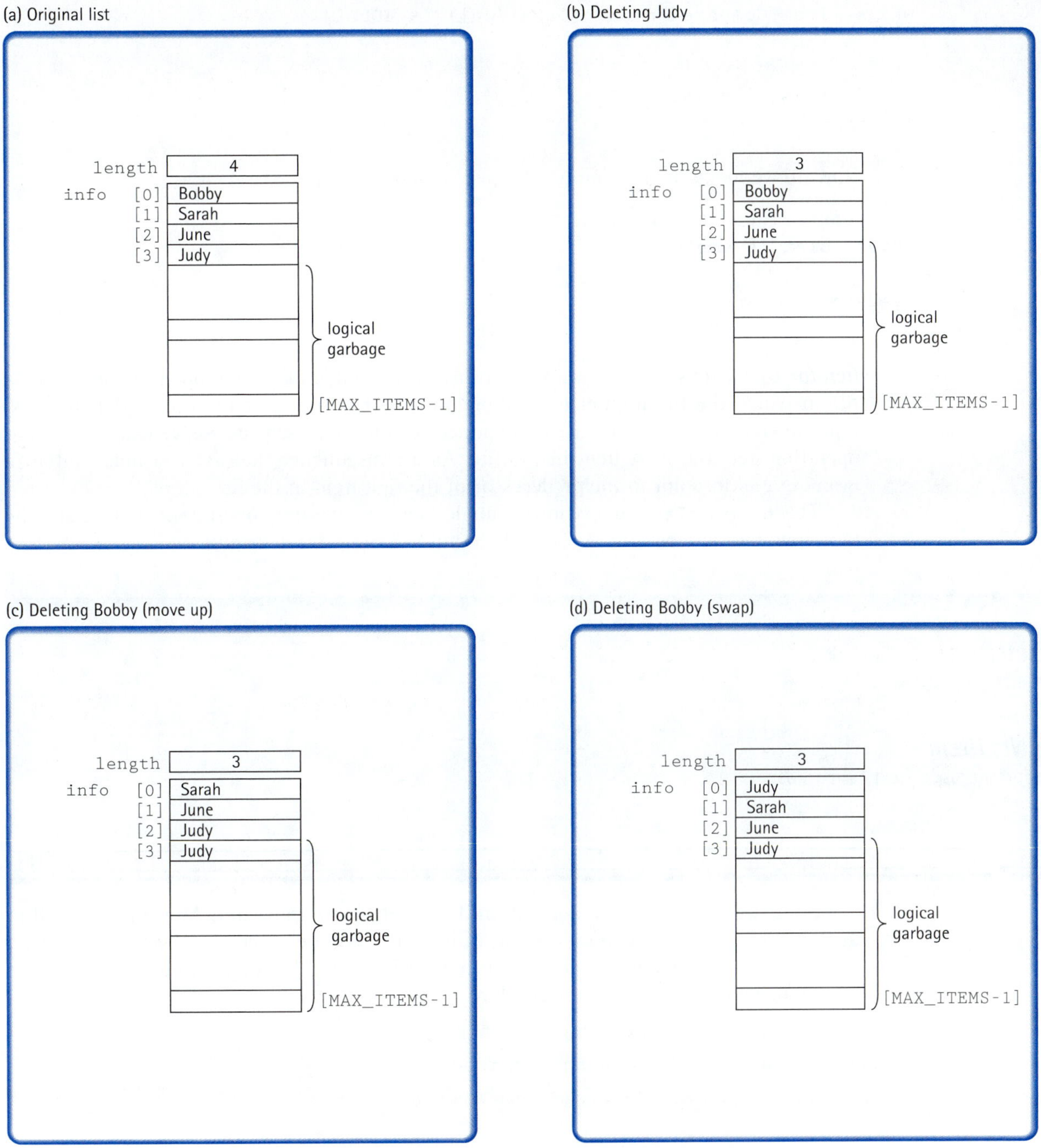

Figure 3.4 *Deleting an item in an unsorted list*

```
  while (item.ComparedTo(info[location]) != EQUAL)
    location++;

  info[location] = info[length - 1];
  length--;
}
```

How do we make the list empty? We just set length to 0.

```
void UnsortedType::MakeEmpty()
// Post: List is empty.
{
   length = 0;
}
```

Iterator Operations The `ResetList` function is analogous to the open operation for a file in which the file pointer is positioned at the beginning of the file so that the first input operation accesses the first component of the file. Each successive call to an input operation gets the next item in the file. As a consequence, `ResetList` must initialize `currentPos` to point to the predecessor of the first item in the list.

The `GetNextItem` operation is analogous to an input operation; it accesses the next item by incrementing `currentPos` and returning Info(currentPos).

ResetList

Initialize currentPos

GetNextItem

Set currentPos to Next(currentPos)
return Info(currentPos)

`currentPos` remains undefined until `ResetList` initializes it. After the first call to `GetNextItem`, `currentPos` is the location of the last item accessed by `GetNextItem`. Therefore, to implement this algorithm in an array-based list in C++, `currentPos` must be initialized to `-1`. These operations are coded as follows:

```
void UnsortedType::ResetList()
// Post: currentPos has been initialized.
{
  currentPos = -1;
}
```

What would happen if a transformer operation is executed between calls to GetNext-Item? The iteration would be invalid. We should add a precondition to prevent this from happening.

```
ItemType UnsortedType::GetNextItem()
// Pre:  ResetList was called to initialized iteration.
//       No transformer has been executed since last call.
//       currentPos is defined.
// Post: item is current item.
//       Current position has been updated.
{
  currentPos++;
  return info[currentPos];
}
```

ResetList and GetNextItem are designed to be used in a loop in the client program that iterates through all items in the list. The precondition in the specifications for GetNextItem protects against trying to access an array element that is not present in the list. This precondition requires that, before a call to GetNextItem, the element at the current position not be the last item in the list. Notice that this precondition places the responsibility for accessing only defined items on the client rather than on GetNextItem.

Here are the complete specification and implementation files for the array-based version of class UnsortedType with reduced documentation.

```
// File "UnsortedType.h" contains the specification for the
// class UnsortedType.
#include "ItemType.h"
// File ItemType.h must be provided by the user of this class.
//  ItemType.h must contain the following definitions:
//  MAX_ITEMS:     the maximum number of items on the list
//  ItemType:      the definition of the objects on the list
//  RelationType:  {LESS, GREATER, EQUAL}
//  Member function ComparedTo(ItemType item) which returns
//       LESS, if self "comes before" item
//       GREATER, if self "comes after" item
//       EQUAL, if self and item are the same

class UnsortedType
{
public:
  UnsortedType();
  void MakeEmpty();
```

```
  bool IsFull() const;
  int GetLength() const;
  ItemType GetItem(ItemType item, bool& found);
  void PutItem(ItemType item);
  void DeleteItem(ItemType item);
  void ResetList();
  ItemType GetNextItem();
private:
  int length;
  ItemType info[MAX_ITEMS];
  int currentPos;
};

// Implementation file for Unsorted.h

#include "unsorted.h"
UnsortedType::UnsortedType()
{
  length = 0;
}
bool UnsortedType::IsFull() const
{
  return (length == MAX_ITEMS);
}
int UnsortedType::GetLength() const
{
  return length;
}
ItemType UnsortedType::GetItem(ItemType item, bool& found)
// Pre:  Key member(s) of item is initialized.
// Post: If found, item's key matches an element's key in the
//       list and a copy of that element has been returned;
//       otherwise, item is returned.
{
  bool moreToSearch;
  int location = 0;
  found = false;

  moreToSearch = (location < length);
```

```
  while (moreToSearch && !found)
  {
    switch (item.ComparedTo(info[location]))
    {
      case LESS    :
      case GREATER : location++;
                     moreToSearch = (location < length);
                     break;
      case EQUAL   : found = true;
                     item = info[location];
                     break;
    }
  }
  return item;
}
void UnsortedType::MakeEmpty()
// Post: list is empty.
{
  length = 0;
}
void UnsortedType::PutItem(ItemType item)
// Post: item is in the list.
{
  info[length] = item;
  length++;
}
void UnsortedType::DeleteItem(ItemType item)
// Pre:  item's key has been initialized.
//       An element in the list has a key that matches item's.
// Post: No element in the list has a key that matches item's.
{
  int location = 0;

  while (item.ComparedTo(info[location]) != EQUAL)
    location++;

  info[location] = info[length - 1];
  length--;
}
```

```
void UnsortedType::ResetList()
// Post: currentPos has been initialized.
{
  currentPos = -1;
}
ItemType UnsortedType::GetNextItem()
// Pre:  ResetList was called to initialized iteration.
//       No transformer has been executed since last call.
//       currentPos is defined.
// Post: item is current item.
//       Current position has been updated.
{
  currentPos++;
  return info[currentPos];
}
```

Notes on the Array-Based List Implementation In several of our list operations, we have declared the local variable `location`, which contains the array index of the list item being processed. The values of array indexes are never revealed outside of the list operations; this information remains internal to the implementation of the Unsorted List ADT. If the list user wants an item in the list, the `GetItem` operation does not give the user the index of the item; instead, it returns a copy of the item. If the user wants to change the values of data members in an item, those changes are not reflected in the list unless the user deletes the original values and inserts the modified version. The list user can never see or manipulate the physical structure in which the list is stored. These details of the list implementation are encapsulated by the ADT.

Test Plan The class `UnsortedType` has a constructor and seven other member functions: `PutItem` and `DeleteItem` (transformers); `IsFull`, `GetLength`, and `GetItem` (observers); and `ResetList` and `GetNextItem` (iterators). Because our operations are independent of the type of the objects on the list, we can define `ItemType` to be `int` and know that if our operations work with these data, they work with any other `ItemType`. Here, then, is the definition of `ItemType` that we use in our test plan. We set the maximum number of items to 5. We include a member function to print an item of the class `ItemType` to an `ofstream` object (a file). We need this function in the driver program to see the value in a list item.

```
// The following declarations and definitions go into file ItemType.h.
#include <fstream>

const int MAX_ITEMS = 5;
enum RelationType  {LESS, GREATER, EQUAL};

class ItemType
{
```

```
public:
  ItemType();
  RelationType ComparedTo(ItemType) const;
  void Print(std::ofstream&) const;
  void Initialize(int number);
private:
  int value;
};

// The following definitions go into file ItemType.cpp.
#include <fstream>
#include "ItemType.h"
ItemType::ItemType()
{
  value = 0;
}

RelationType ItemType::ComparedTo(ItemType otherItem) const
{
  if (value < otherItem.value)
    return LESS;
  else if (value > otherItem.value)
    return GREATER;
  else return EQUAL;
}

void ItemType::Initialize(int number)
{
  value = number;
}

void ItemType::Print(std::ofstream& out) const
// Pre:  out has been opened.
// Post: value has been sent to the stream out.
{
  out << value << " ";
}
```

The preconditions and postconditions in our specification determine the tests necessary for a black-box testing strategy. The code of the functions determines a clear-box testing strategy. To test the ADT Unsorted List implementation, we use a combination of the two strategies. Because a precondition on all other operations is that the list has been initialized, we test the constructor by checking whether the list is empty initially (a call to `GetLength` returns 0).

`GetLength`, `PutItem`, and `DeleteItem` must be tested together. That is, we insert several items and check the length; we delete several items and check the length. How do we know that `PutItem` and `DeleteItem` work correctly? We write an auxiliary function `PrintList` that uses `GetLength`, `ResetList`, and `GetNextItem` to iterate through the list, printing out the values. We call `PrintList` to check the status of the list after a series of insertions and deletions. To test the `IsFull` operation, we insert four items and print the result of the test, and then insert the fifth item and print the result of the test. To test `GetItem`, we search for items that we know are present in the list and for items that we know are not found in the list.

How do we choose the values used in our test plan? We look at the end cases. What are the end cases in a list? The item is in the first position in the list, the item is in the last position in the list, and the item is the only one in the list. We must be sure that `DeleteItem` can correctly delete items in these positions. We must also confirm that `GetItem` can find items in these same positions and correctly determine that values that are less than the one in the first position or greater than the one in the last position are not found. Notice that this test plan involves a black-box strategy. That is, we look at the list as described in the interface, not the code.

These observations are summarized in the following test plan. The tests are shown in the order in which they should be performed.

Operation to Be Tested and Description of Action	Input Values	Expected Output
Constructor		
print `GetLength`		0
`PutItem`		
Put four items and print	5, 7, 6, 9	5 7 6 9
Put item and print	1	5 7 6 9 1
`GetItem`		
Get 4 and print whether found		Item is not found
Get 5 and print whether found		Item is found
Get 9 and print whether found		Item is found
Get 10 and print whether found		Item is not found
`IsFull`		
Invoke (list is full)		List is full
Delete 5 and invoke		List is not full
`DeleteItem`		
Delete 1 and print		7 6 9
Delete 6 and print		7 9

What about testing `GetLength`, `ResetList`, and `GetNextItem`? They do not appear explicitly in the test plan, but they are tested each time we call the auxiliary function `PrintList` to print the contents of the list.

Here are the UML diagrams for `ItemType`, used in testing, and `UnsortedType`. These diagrams become part of the documentation for class `UnsortedType`. When a class contains an instance of another class, such as the array of class `ItemType` contained in the `UnsortedType`, we draw a solid diamond at the end of the line next to the containing class. An ampersand (&) following the parameter type on a method (function) heading indicates that the parameter is a reference parameter.

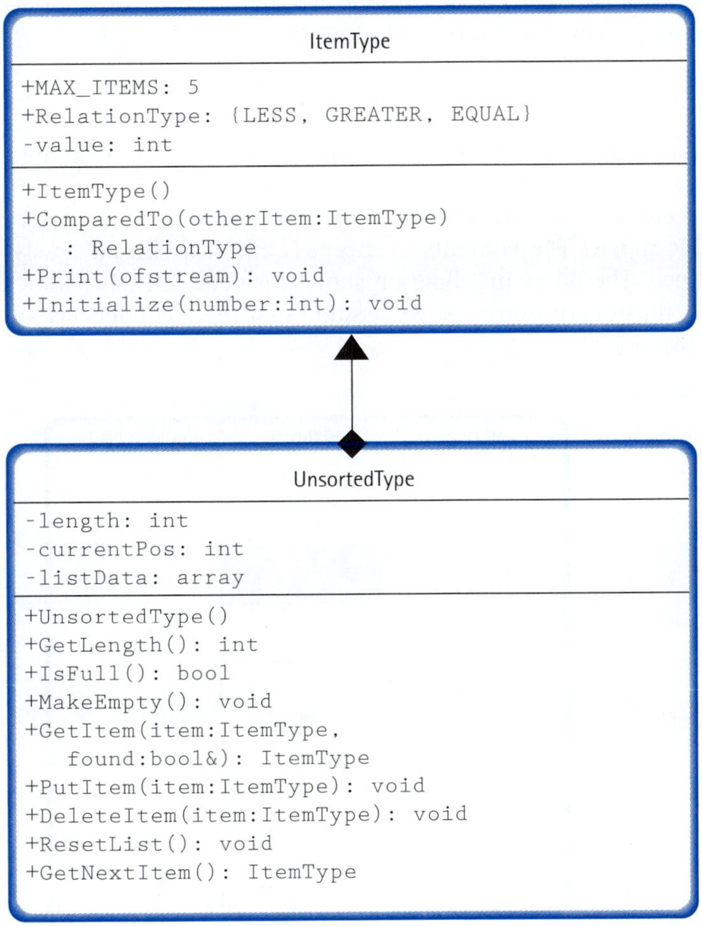

On the Web, the file `listType.in` contains the input to `listDr.cpp` (the test driver) that reflects this test plan; `listType.out` and `listTest.screen` contain the output.

3.3 Pointer Types

Logical Level

Pointers are simple—not composite—types, but they allow us to *create* composite types at run time. We describe the creation process, accessing function, and use of pointers in this chapter.

A pointer variable does not contain a data value in the ordinary sense; rather, it contains the *memory address* of another variable. To declare a pointer that can point to an integer value, you use the following syntax:

```
int* intPointer;
```

The asterisk (*) as a postfix symbol on the type says that the variable being defined is a pointer to an object of that type: `intPointer` can point to a place in memory that can contain a value of type `int`. (Alternatively, the asterisk may serve as a prefix symbol on the variable name.) The contents of `intPointer`, as with all newly defined variables, are undefined. The following diagram shows memory after this statement has been executed. (For illustrative purposes, we assume that the compiler has allocated location 10 to `intPointer`.)

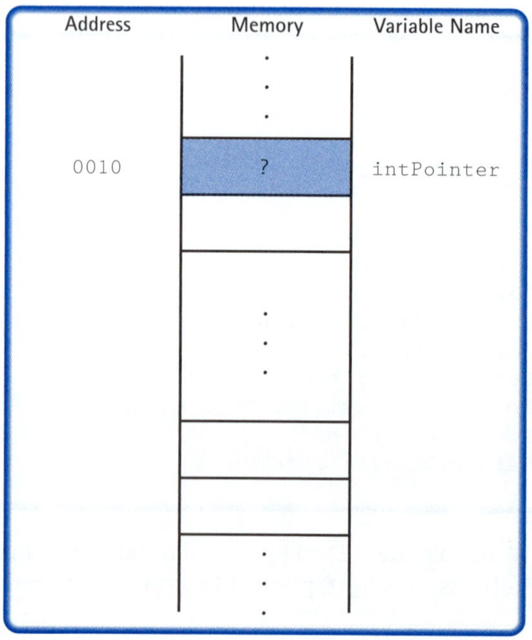

How do we get `intPointer` something to point to? One way is to use the prefix `&` operator, which is called the *address-of* operator. Given the declarations

```
int alpha;
int* intPointer;
```

the assignment statement

```
intPointer = &alpha;
```

takes the address of `alpha` and stores it into `intPointer`. If `alpha` is at address 33, memory looks like this:

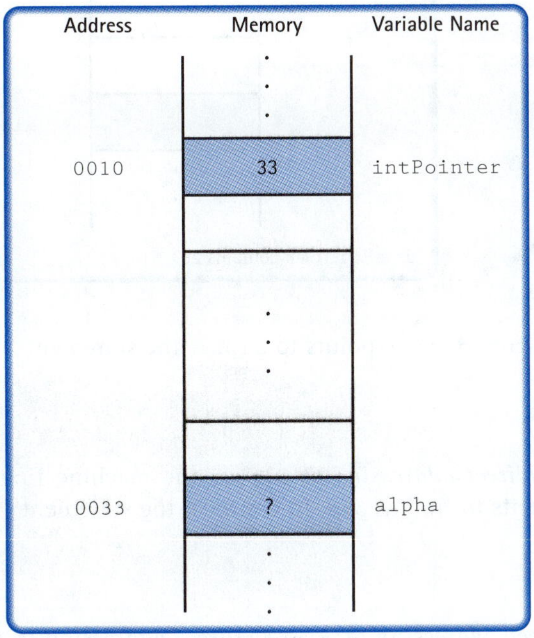

We have a pointer, and we have a place to which the pointer points, but how do we access that place? An asterisk (*) as a prefix to the pointer name accesses the place to which the pointer points. The asterisk is called the dereference operator. Let's store 25 in the place to which `intPointer` points.

Dereference operator An operator that, when applied to a pointer variable, denotes the variable to which the pointer points

```
*intPointer = 25;
```

Memory now looks like this:

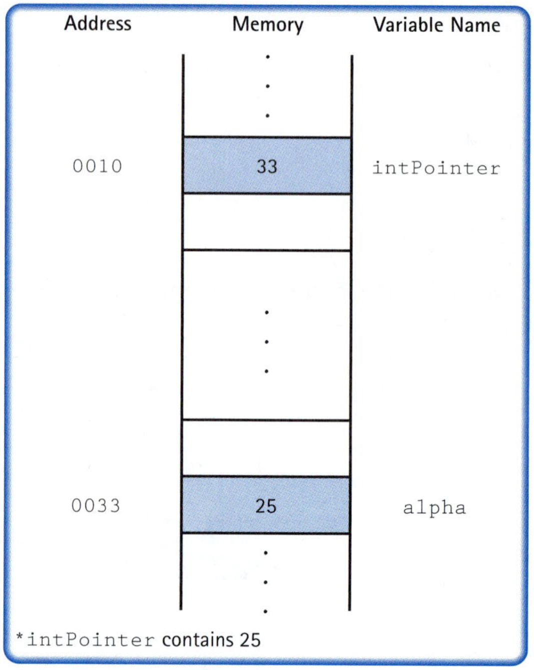

Because `intPointer` points to `alpha`, the statement

```
*intPointer = 25;
```

represents *indirect addressing* of `alpha`; the machine first accesses `intPointer`, then uses its contents to find `alpha`. In contrast, the statement

```
alpha = 10;
```

involves *direct addressing* of `alpha`. Direct addressing is analogous to opening a post office box (P.O. Box 15, for example) and finding a package, whereas indirect addressing is analogous to opening P.O. Box 15 and finding a note telling you that your package is sitting in P.O. Box 23.

Dynamic allocation Allocation of memory space for a variable at run time (as opposed to static allocation at compile time)

A second method for getting `intPointer` something to point to is called dynamic allocation. In the previous example, the memory space for both `intPointer` and `alpha` was allocated *statically* (at compile time). Alternatively, our programs can allocate memory *dynamically* (at run time).

To achieve dynamic allocation of a variable, we use the C++ operator `new`, followed by the name of a data type:

```
intPointer = new int;
```

At run time, the `new` operator allocates a variable capable of holding an `int` value and returns its memory address, which is then stored into `intPointer`. If the `new` operator returns the address 90 as a result of executing the preceding statement, memory looks like this:

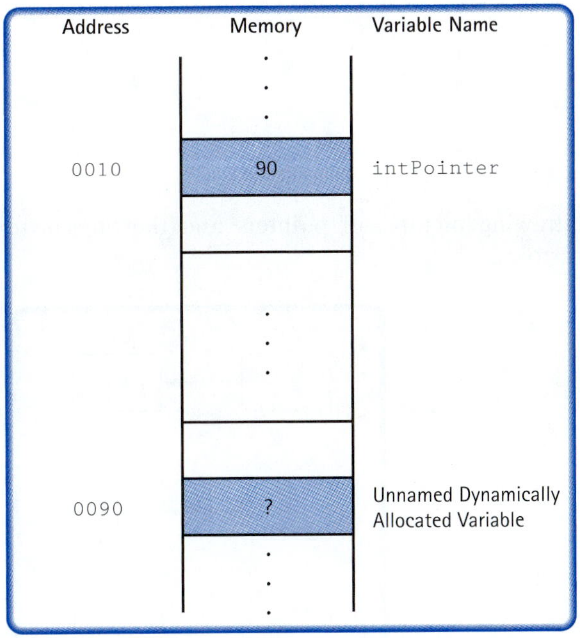

Variables created by `new` reside on the free store (or heap), a region of memory set aside for dynamic allocation. A dynamically allocated variable has no name and cannot be directly addressed. It must be indirectly addressed through the pointer returned by `new`.

> **Free store (heap)** A pool of memory locations reserved for dynamic allocation of data

Sometimes we want a pointer to point to nothing. By definition in C++, a pointer value of `0` is called the *null pointer*; it points to nothing. To help distinguish the null pointer from the integer value 0, `<cstddef>` contains the definition of a named constant `NULL` that we use instead of referring directly to 0. Let's look at a few more examples.

```
bool*  truth = NULL;
float*  money = NULL;
```

When drawing pictures of pointers, we use a diagonal line from the upper right to the lower left to indicate that the value is NULL.

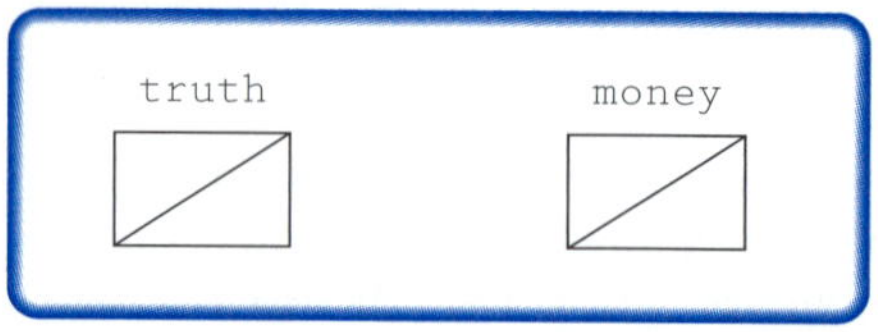

Let's examine memory after a few more pointer manipulations.

```
truth = new bool;
*truth = true;
money = new float;
*money = 33.46;
float* myMoney = new float;
```

When drawing pictures of pointers and the objects to which they point, we use boxes and arrows.

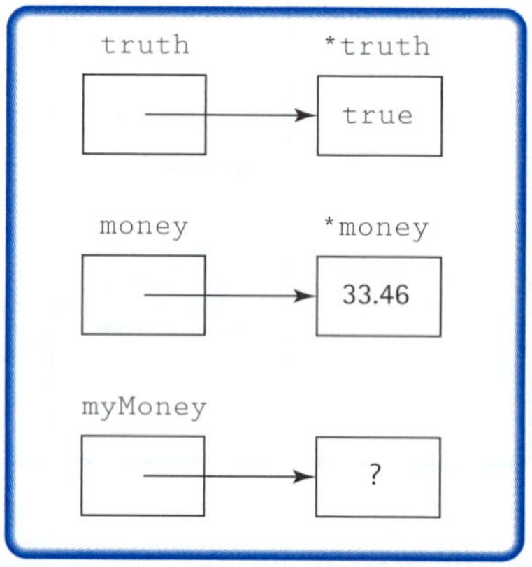

Any operation that can be applied to a constant or a variable of type `int` can be applied to `*intPointer`. Any operation that can be applied to a constant or a variable of type `float` can be applied to `*money`. Any operation that can be applied to a constant or a variable of type `bool` can be applied to `*truth`. For example, we can read a value into `*myMoney` with the following statement:

```
std::cin >> *myMoney;
```

If the current value in the input stream is 99.86, then `*myMoney` contains 99.86 after the execution of the preceding statement.

Pointer variables can be compared for equality and assigned to one another as long as they point to variables of the same data type. Consider the following two statements:

```
*myMoney = *money;
myMoney = money;
```

The first statement copies the value in the place pointed to by `money` into the place pointed to by `myMoney`.

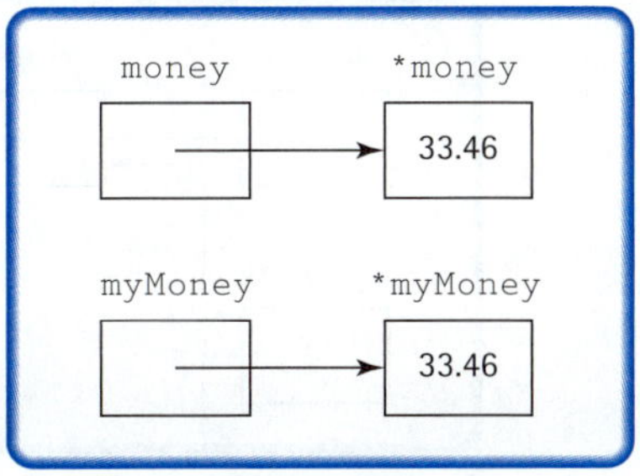

The second statement copies the value in `money` into `myMoney`, giving the following configuration:

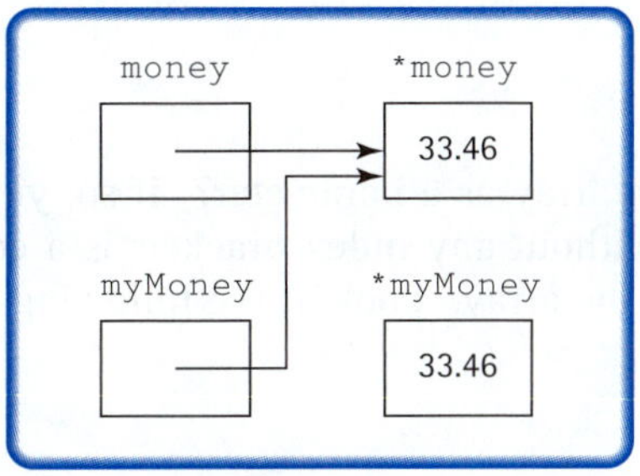

At this point, the location that holds the second copy of 33.46 cannot be accessed; no pointer points to it. This situation is called a memory leak, and the memory cells that can no longer be accessed are called garbage. Some programming languages, such as Java, provide garbage collection; that is, the run-time support system periodically goes through memory and reclaims the memory locations for which no access path exists.

> **Memory leak** The loss of available memory space that occurs when memory is allocated dynamically but never deallocated
>
> **Garbage** Memory locations that can no longer be accessed

To avoid memory leaks, C++ provides the operator `delete`, which returns to the free store a memory location allocated previously by the `new` operator. This memory may then be allocated again if necessary. The following code segment prevents our memory leak:

```
delete myMoney;
myMoney = money;
```

The location originally pointed to by `myMoney` is no longer allocated. Note that `delete` does not delete the pointer variable, but rather the variable to which the pointer points.

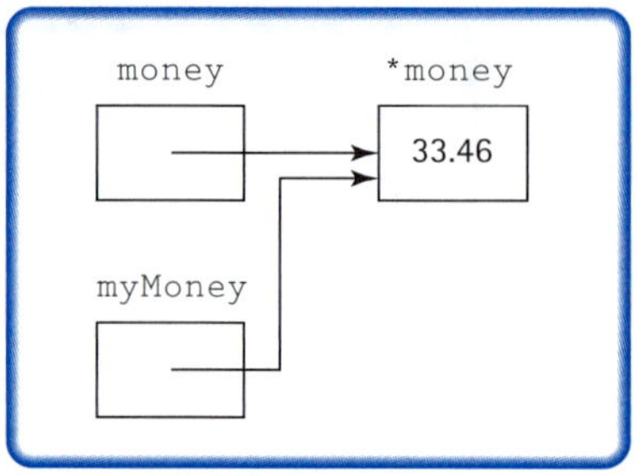

Notice the difference between assigning one pointer to another (`myMoney = money`) and assigning the pointed-to locations (`*myMoney = *money`). *Always be careful to distinguish between the pointer and the object to which it points!*

Application Level

Have you passed an array as a parameter? If so, you have used a *pointer constant*. The name of an array without any index brackets is a constant pointer expression–namely, the base address of the array. Look at the following code segment:

```
char alpha[20];
char* alphaPtr;
char* letterPtr;
void Process(char[]);
.
.
alphaPtr = alpha;
letterPtr = &alpha[0];
Process(alpha);
```

Here `alphaPtr` is assigned the constant pointer expression `alpha`; `letterPtr` is assigned the address of the first position in the array `alpha`. `alphaPtr` and `letterPtr` both contain the address of the first position in the array `alpha`. When the prototype for the function `Process` says that it takes a `char` array as a parameter, it means that it expects a pointer expression (the base address of the array) as an actual parameter. The calling statement, therefore, sends the name of the array without any index brackets to the function.

Pointers can be used with other composite types as well.

```
struct MoneyType
{
  int dollars;
  int cents;
};

MoneyType* moneyPtr = new MoneyType;
moneyPtr->dollars = 3245;
moneyPtr->cents = 33;
```

The arrow operator (`->`) provides a shortcut for dereferencing a pointer and accessing a struct or class member. That is, `moneyPtr->cents` is shorthand for `(*moneyPtr).cents`. (The dereferencing operator has lower precedence than the dot operator, so the parentheses are necessary.)

In the next section we will use the idea of a pointer pointing to a variable of a composite type in which one of the data members is a pointer to another variable of the same composite type. Using this technique, we can build *linked structures*. One named pointer acts as the *external pointer* to the structure, and the structure is chained together by having a data member in each variable in the chain act as a pointer to the next one in the chain. The last variable in the chain has `NULL` in its pointer member.

Implementation Level

A pointer variable simply contains a memory address. The operating system controls memory allocation and grants memory to your program on request.

3.4 Implementing Class `UnsortedType` as a Linked Structure

For our first implementation we used an array. An array's components are accessed by their position in the structure. Arrays, the first organizational structure a student usually learns, are used to implement other structures as we showed earlier in this chapter. They are available as a basic language construct in most high-level programming languages.

As we also said earlier, a linked structure is a collection of separate elements, with each element linked to the one that follows it in the list. We can think of a linked list as a chain of elements. The linked list is a versatile, powerful, basic implementation structure, and like the array, it is one of the primary building blocks for the more complicated structures. Teaching you how to work with links and linked lists is one of the important goals of this textbook. Not only can links be used to implement the more complicated classic structures, but they can also be used to create your own structures.

Now, let's see how we might use the concept of dynamic storage allocation to implement a linked list.

Linked Structures

As we look at implementing a linked structure, let's use the `PutItem` function of the `UnsortedType` as our example. We can modify function `PutItem` to allocate space for each new element dynamically.

PutItem

Allocate space for new item
Put new item into the allocated space
Put the allocated space into the list

Implementing the first part of this operation is simple. We use the built-in C++ operator `new` to allocate space dynamically:

```
// Allocate space for new item.
itemPtr = new ItemType;
```

The `new` operator allocates a block of memory big enough to hold a value of type `ItemType` (the type of data contained in the list) and returns the block's address, which is copied into the variable `itemPtr`. Let's say for the moment that `itemPtr` has been declared to be of type `ItemType*`. Now we can use the dereference operator (`*`) to put `newItem` into the space that was allocated: `*itemPtr = newItem`. The situation at this point is pictured in Figure 3.5, with `newItem` being 'E'.

The third part of the `PutItem` operation is to "put the allocated space into the list." How do we do this? Let's think for a minute what happens after we have inserted a few

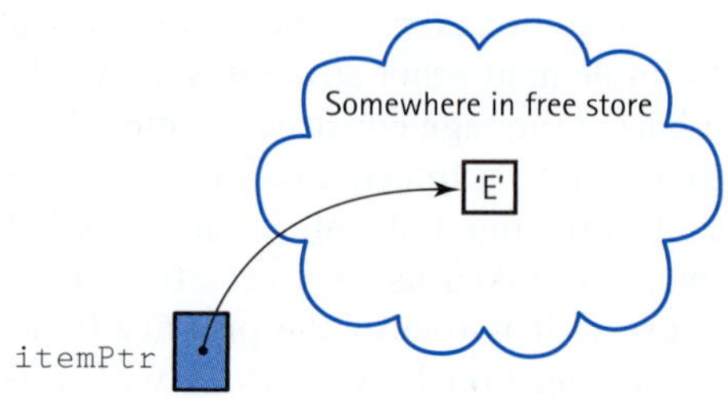

Figure 3.5 *Putting new element into the allocated space*

Figure 3.6 *After four calls to* `PutItem`

characters. Space is allocated for each new element, and each character is put into the space. Figure 3.6 shows the results of calling `PutItem` to add the characters 'D', 'A', 'L', and 'E' to the list.

Whoops—we see our data in the dynamically allocated space, but it's not a list! There's no order. Even worse, because we haven't returned the pointers to the dynamically allocated space from function `PutItem`, we have no way to access any of the elements any more. Clearly, the third part of the `PutItem` operation needs to do something to fix this situation. Where can we store the pointers to our data?

One possibility that comes to mind is to declare the list as an array of pointers and to put the pointer to each new item into this array, as shown in Figure 3.7. This solution would keep track of the pointers to all the elements in the correct order, but it wouldn't solve our original problem: we still need to declare an array of a particular size. Where else could we put the pointers? It would be nice if we could just chain all the elements together somehow, as shown in Figure 3.8. We call each element in this "linked" list a **node**.

This solution looks promising. Let's see how we might use this idea to implement the list. First we insert the character 'D'. `PutItem` uses operator `new` to allocate space

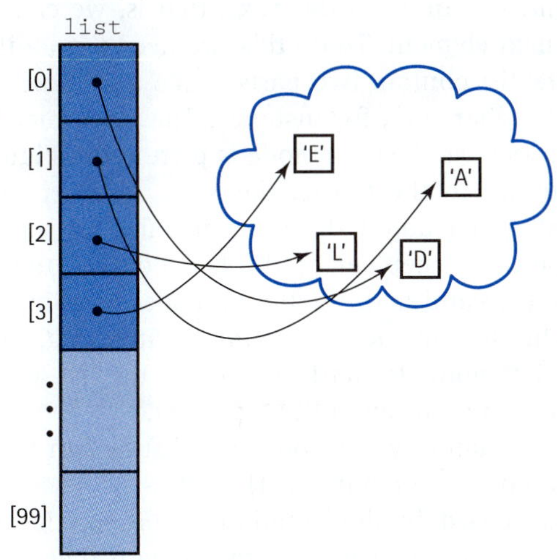

Figure 3.7 *One way to keep track of the pointers*

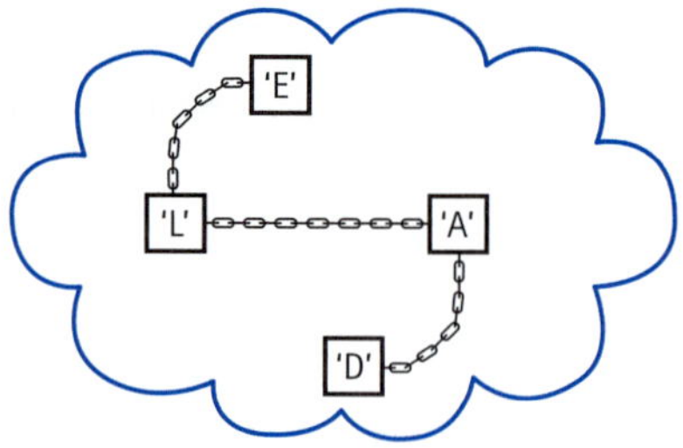

Figure 3.8 *Chaining the list elements together*

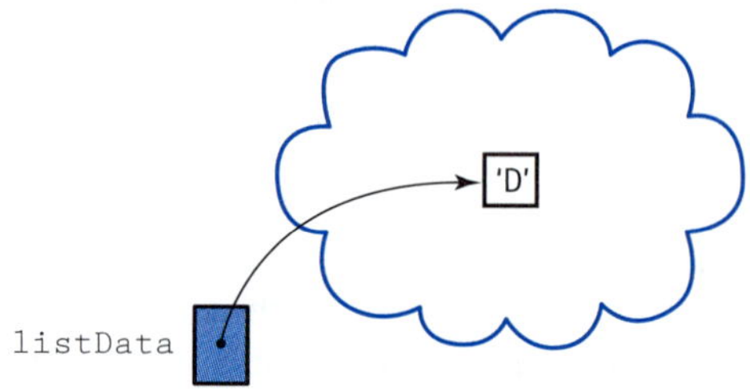

Figure 3.9 *Putting in the first element*

for the new node, and puts 'D' into the space. There's now one element in the list. We don't want to lose the pointer to this element, so we need a data member in our list class in which to store the pointer to the top of the list (`listData`). Figure 3.9 illustrates the first `PutItem` operation.

Now we call `PutItem` to add the character 'A' to the list. `PutItem` applies `new` to allocate space for the new element and puts 'A' into the space. Next we want to chain 'A' to 'D', the old top list element. We can establish a link between the two elements by letting one element "point" to the next; that is, we can store into each list element the address of the next element. To do this, we need to modify the list node type. Let's make each node in the list contain two parts: `info` and `next`. The `info` member contains the list user's data—a character, for instance. The `next` member contains the address of the next element in the list. A single node is pictured in Figure 3.10.

As you can see in the figure, the `next` member of each node points to the next node in the list. What about the `next` member of the last node? We cannot leave it unassigned. The `next` member of the last node in the list must contain some special value that is not a valid address. `NULL`, a special pointer constant available in `<cstddef>`, says, "This pointer doesn't point to anything." We can put `NULL` in the `next` member of the last node, to mark the end of the list. Graphically, we use a slash across the `next` member to represent a `NULL` pointer.

Earlier in the chapter we introduced a list design terminology that incorporated the abstraction of a node (see Figure 3.11).

In the array-based implementation `location` is an index; in our pointer-based implementation it must be a pointer to a record that contains both the user's information and a pointer to the next node on the list.

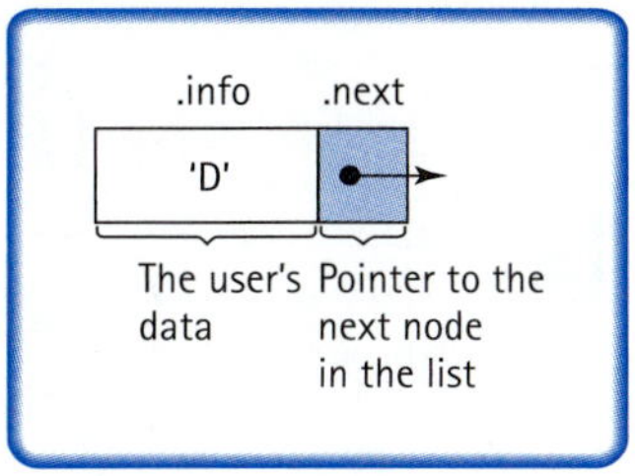

Figure 3.10 *A single node*

Now let's return to our `PutItem` algorithm. We have allocated a node to contain the new element 'A' using operator `new` (Figure 3.12a). Let's revert to our design terminology, and call the pointer `location`.

```
Set location to address of a new node of type ItemType   // Allocate space for new item
```

Then the new value, 'A' is put into the node (Figure 3.12b):

```
Set Info(location) to newItem          // Put new item into the allocated space
```

Now we are ready to link the new node to the list. Where should we link it? Should the new node come before or after the node containing 'D'? In the array-based

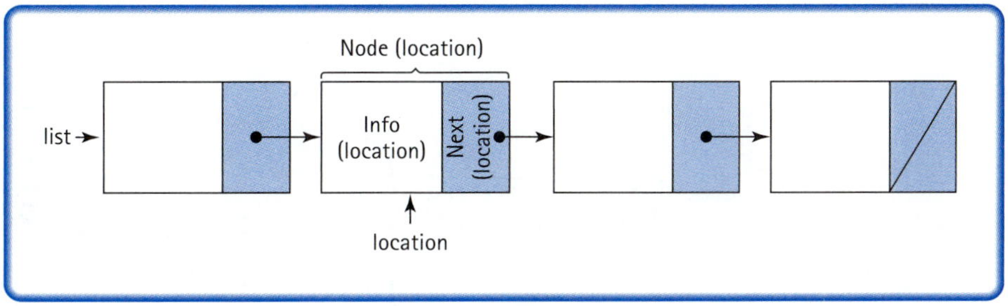

Figure 3.11 *Node terminology*

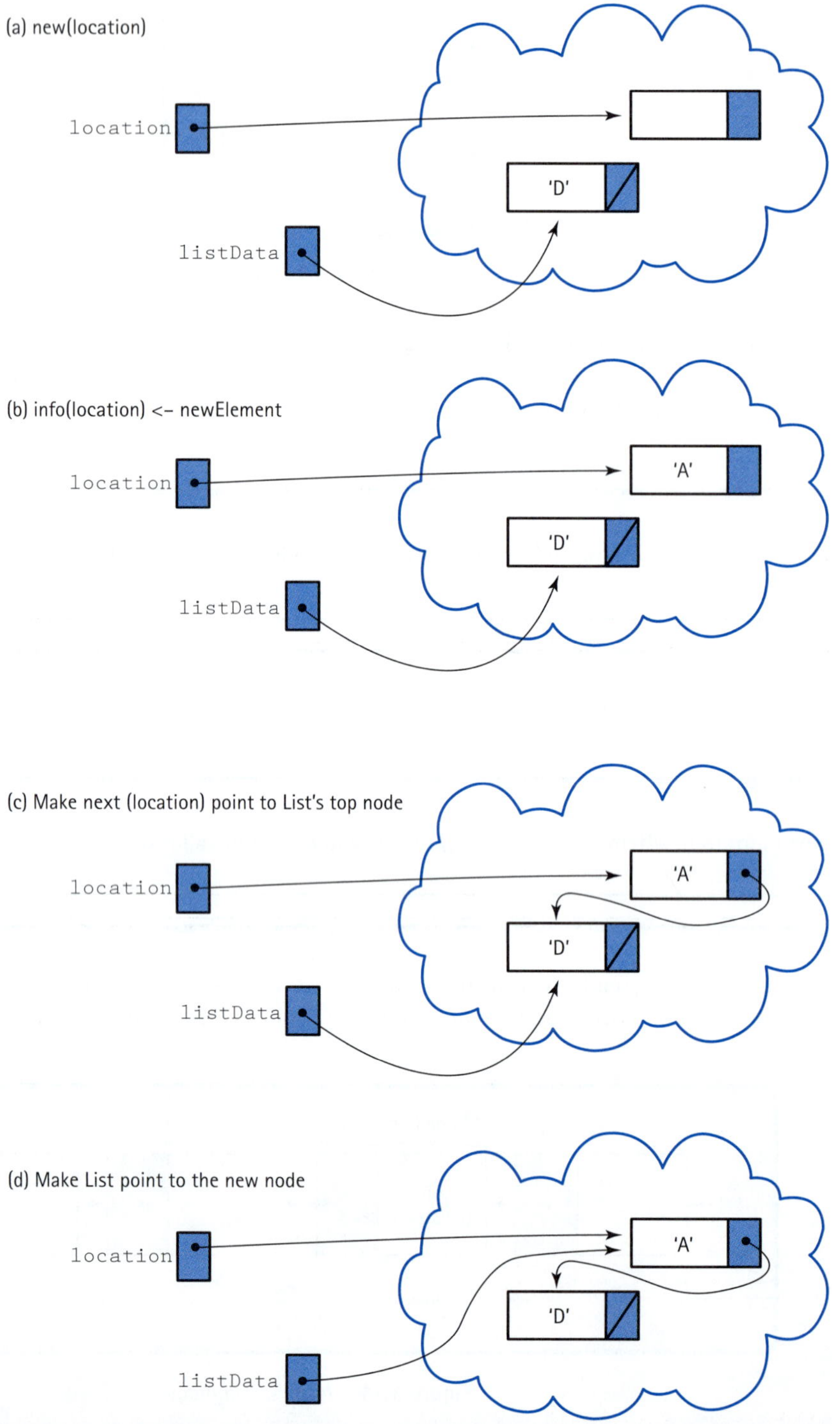

Figure 3.12 *The second `PutItem` operation*

implementation, we put the new item at the end because that was the easiest place to put it. What is the analogous place in the linked implementation? At the beginning of the list. Because the list is unsorted, we can put the new item wherever we choose, and we choose the easiest place: at the front of the list.

Linking the new node to the (previous) first node in the list is a two-step process:

```
Make Next(location) point to the stack's top node     // (Figure 3.12c)
Make listData point to the new node                   // (Figure 3.12d)
```

Note that the order of these tasks is critical. If we changed the `listData` pointer before making Next(`location`) point to the beginning of the list, we would have lost access to the list nodes! (See Figure 3.13.) This situation is generally true when we are dealing with a linked structure: you must be very careful to change the pointers in the correct order, so that you do not lose access to any of the data.

Before we code this algorithm, let's see how the list data are declared. Remember that from the `UnsortedType` user's point of view, nothing has changed; the prototype for member function `PutItem` is the same as it was for the array-based implementation.

```
void PutItem(ItemType newItem);
```

`ItemType` is still the type of data that the user wants to put in the list. Class `UnsortedType`, however, needs new definitions. It no longer is a class with an array member to hold the items; its member is `listData`, the pointer to a single node, the top of the list. The node to which `listData` points has two parts, `info` and `next`, which suggests a C++ struct or class representation. We choose to make `NodeType` a struct rather than a

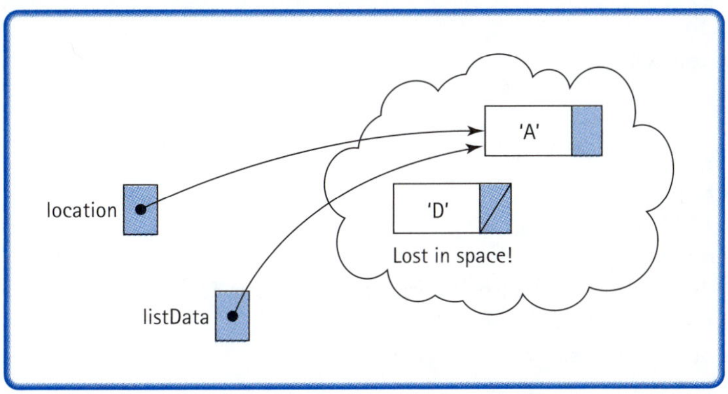

Figure 3.13 *Be careful when you change pointers*

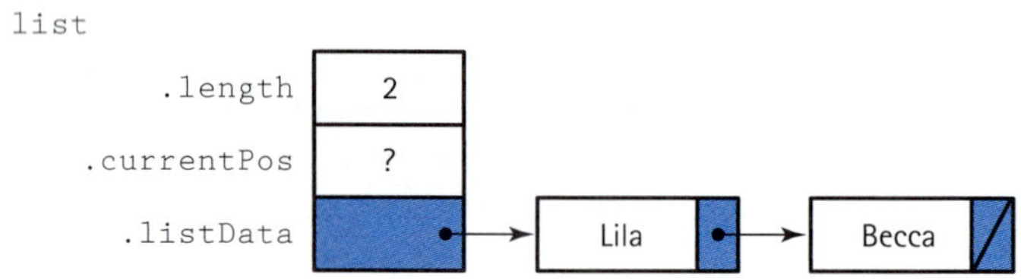

Figure 3.14 *Honor roll list with two items (`ResetList` has not been called)*

class, because the nodes in the structure are passive. They are acted upon by the member functions of `UnsortedType`.

We complete the coding of `PutItem` within the context of class `UnsortedType`.

Class `UnsortedType`

In order to implement the Unsorted List ADT, we need to record two pieces of information about the structure in addition to the list of items. The `GetLength` operation returns the number of items in the list. In the array-based implementation, the `length` member defines the extent of the list within the array. *Therefore, the `length` member must be present.* In a link-based list we have a choice: we can keep a `length` member or we can count the number of elements each time the `GetLength` operation is called. Keeping a `length` member requires an addition operation each time `PutItem` is called and a subtraction operation each time `DeleteItem` is called. Which is better? We cannot determine in the abstract; it depends on the relative frequency of use of the `GetLength`, `PutItem`, and `DeleteItem` operations. Here, let's explicitly keep track of the length of the list by including a `length` member in the `UnsortedType` class.

`ResetList` and `GetNextItem` require that we keep track of the current position during an iteration, so we need a `currentPos` member. In the array-based implementation, `currentPos` is an array index. What is the logical equivalent within a linked list? A *pointer*. Figure 3.14 pictures this structure.

```
struct NodeType;

class UnsortedType
{
public:
  UnsortedType();
  void MakeEmpty();
  bool IsFull() const;
  int GetLength() const;
  ItemType GetItem(ItemType item, bool& found);
  void PutItem(ItemType item);
  void DeleteItem(ItemType item);
  void ResetList();
  ItemType GetNextItem();
```

```
private:
  NodeType* listData;
  int length;
  NodeType* current Pos;
};
```

The function headings (prototypes) that complete the specification are identical to those for the array-based implementation. Remember that the specification of the class is the interface that the user sees. The interface documentation tells the user what the operations do and this doesn't change with the implementation. However, in the linked implementation, our private data fields are different: `currentPos` and `listData` are pointers to nodes.

`NodeType` is a struct containing the user's data, as well as a pointer to the next node. We alert the compiler that we are going to use a pointer to `NodeType` before we have defined `NodeType` by using the statement

```
struct NodeType;
```

before the class.

This statement, called a *forward declaration*, is analogous to a function prototype: the compiler is told the nature of an identifier before the identifier is fully defined. The definition of `NodeType` (shown below) comes later in either the header file or the implementation file.

```
struct NodeType
{
  ItemType info;
  NodeType* next;
};
```

Let's complete the implementation of `PutItem` before we look at the other operations.

Function `PutItem`

Here are the pieces of the detailed algorithm collected together.

PutItem

Set location to address of a new node of type ItemType
Set Info(location) to item
Make Next(location) point to the list's top node
Make listData point to the new node

Table 3.1 *Comparing Node Design Notation to C++ Code*

Design Notation	C++ Code
Node(location)	`*location`
Info(location)	`location->info`
Next(location)	`location->next`
Set location to Next(location)	`location = location->next`
Set Info(location) to value	`location->info = value`

Table 3.1 summarizes the relationship between the design and the code terminology. Using this table, we can code function `PutItem`.

We use a local variable, `location`, of type `NodeType*`. The first two tasks are simple:

```
// Allocate space for new item.
location = new NodeType;

// Put new item into the allocated space.
location->info = newItem;
```

`location` is a pointer to a node containing an `info` member and a `next` member. `*location` is the way that we reference this node; it is a struct with two members. Because `*location` is a struct, we can access its members in the usual way—by adding a period, followed by the desired member name. So `(*location).info` refers to the `info` member of the struct on the free store pointed to by `location`. The parentheses are necessary because the dot operator has higher precedence than the dereferencing operator (`*`). Because we so often want to access the members of the struct or class to which a pointer points, C++ provides the `->` operator, which both dereferences the pointer and accesses a member. So the expression `(*location).info` is equivalent to `location->info`. The shaded area in

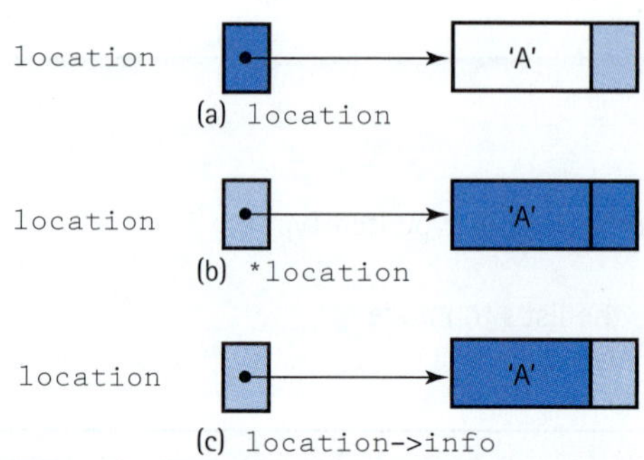

Figure 3.15 *Pointer dereferencing and member selection*

Figure 3.15(a) corresponds to `location`, the shaded area in (b) corresponds to `*location`, and the shaded area in (c) corresponds to `location->info`.

`location->info` is the same type as the user's data, so we can assign `newItem` to it. So far, so good.

Now for the linking task:

```
Make Next(location) point to the list's first node      // [Figure 3.12(c)]
Make listData point to the new node                     // [Figure 3.12(d)]
```

Next(`location`) is the `next` member of the node pointed to by `location`. We can access it just as we accessed the `info` member: `location->next`. What can we put into this field? It is declared as a pointer, so we can assign it another value of the same pointer type. We want to make this member point to the list's top node. Because we have a pointer to the list's first node (`listData`), this assignment is simple.

```
location->next = listData;
```

Finally, we need to complete the linking by making `listData` point to the new node. `listData` is declared as a pointer, so we can assign another value of the same pointer type to it. Because we have a pointer to the new node (the local variable `location`), this assignment can be made:

```
listData = location;
```

Here is the complete function `PutItem`.

```
void UnsortedType::PutItem(ItemType item)
// item is in the list; length has been incremented.
{
  NodeType* location;           // Declare a pointer to a node

  location = new NodeType;      // Get a new node
  location->info = item;        // Store the item in the node
  location->next = listData;    // Store address of first node
                                //   in next field of new node
  listData = location;          // Store address of new node
                                //   into external pointer

  length++;                     // Increment length of the list
}
```

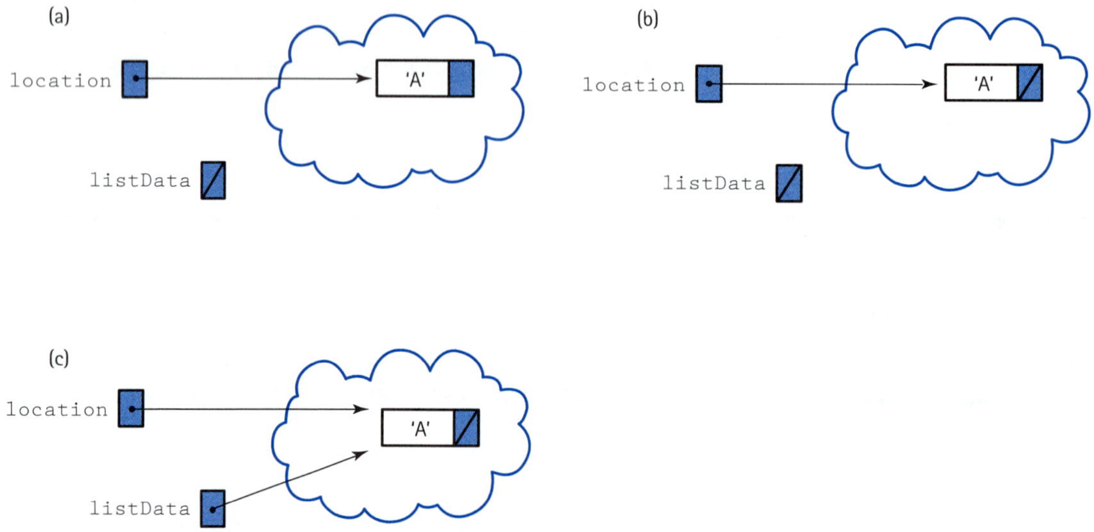

Figure 3.16 *Putting an item into an empty list*

You have seen how this algorithm works on a list that contains at least one value. What happens if this function is called when the list is empty? Space is allocated for the new element and the element is put into the space (Figure 3.16a). Does the function correctly link the new node to the top of an empty list? Let's see. The `next` member of the new node is assigned the value of `listData`. What is this value when the list is empty? It is `NULL`, which is exactly what we want to put into the `next` member of the last node of a linked list (Figure 3.16b). Then `listData` is reset to point to the new node (Figure 3.16c). So this function works for an empty list, as well as for a list that contains at least one element.

From the List ADT implementor's perspective, the algorithms for the rest of the list operations are very similar to the ones developed for the sequential (array-based) implementation.

Constructor

To initialize an empty list we merely set `listData` (the external pointer to the linked list) to `NULL` and set `length` to 0. Here is the class constructor to implement this operation:

```
UnsortedType::UnsortedType()  // Class constructor
{
  length = 0;
  listData = NULL;
}
```

Observer Operations

What about function IsFull? Using dynamically allocated nodes rather than an array, we no longer have an explicit limit on the list size. We can continue to get more nodes until we run out of memory on the free store. The ISO C++ Standard provides that the new operator in C++ throws a bad_alloc exception when there is no more space to allocate. The bad_alloc exception is defined in the <new> header. The exception needs to be handled because an unhandled exception carries the sentence of death for the program.

```
bool UnsortedType::IsFull() const
// Returns true if there is no room for another ItemType
//  on the free store; false otherwise.
{
  NodeType* location;
  try
  {
    location = new NodeType;
    delete location;
    return false;
  }
  catch(std::bad_alloc exception)
  {
    return true;
  }
}
```

As in the array-based implementation, the GetLength operation just returns the length data member.

```
int UnsortedType::GetLength() const
// Post: Number of items in the list is returned.
{
  return length;
}
```

Function MakeEmpty

The MakeEmpty operation for a linked list is more complicated than its sequential list counterpart, because the dynamically allocated space used by the elements must be freed, one node at a time. Data member listData is deallocated when the list goes out of scope, but the nodes pointed to by listData do not. We must loop through the list returning the nodes to the free store with the delete operator. The easiest approach is just to unlink each successive node in the list and free it. How do we know when there are "more nodes in the list"? As long as listData is not NULL, the list is not empty. So the resulting condition on the loop is while(listData != NULL). We must also set length to zero.

```
void UnsortedType::MakeEmpty()
// Post: List is empty; all items have been deallocated.
{
  NodeType* tempPtr;

  while (listData != NULL)
  {
    tempPtr = listData;
    listData = listData->next;
    delete tempPtr;
  }
  length = 0;
}
```

Function `GetItem`

The algorithm for the linked implementation is the same as the one for the array-based implementation. Given the parameter `item`, we traverse the list looking for a location where `item.ComparedTo(`Info(location)`)` returns `EQUAL`. The difference is in how we traverse the list and how we access Info(location) to send it as a parameter to `ComparedTo`.

When we coded the array-based function, we directly substituted the index notation for the list notation. Can we directly substitute the pointer notation for the list notation in the linked list? Let's try it and see. The algorithm follows; the substitutions are marked in boldface for emphasis.

GetItem

```
Initialize location to listData
Set found to false
Set moreToSearch to (location != NULL)
while moreToSearch AND NOT found
    switch (item.ComparedTo(location -> info))
        case LESS     :
        case GREATER  : Set location to location -> next
                        Set moreToSearch to (location != NULL)
        case EQUAL    : Set found to true
                        Set item to location -> info
return item
```

Let's look at this algorithm and be sure that the substitutions do what we want by examining the value of `location` at the end. There are two cases:

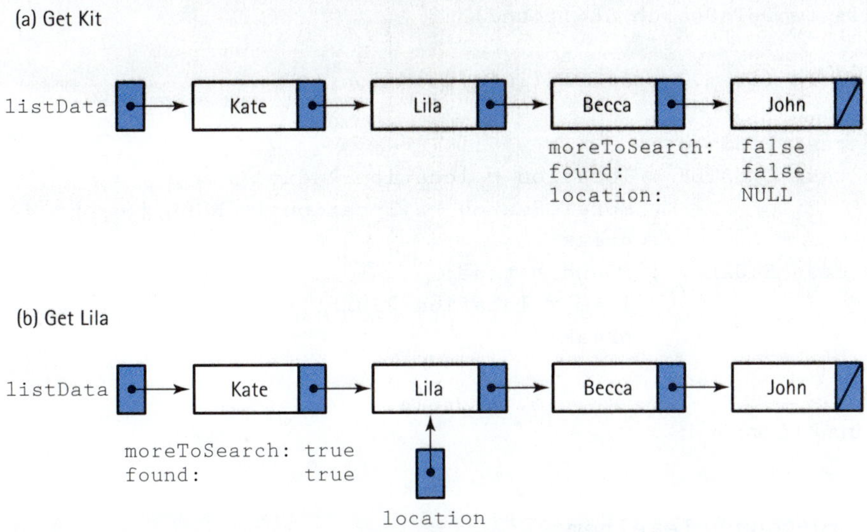

Figure 3.17 *Retrieving an item in an unsorted linked list*

1. *location = NULL*. If we reach the end of the list without finding an item whose key is equal to `item`'s key, then the item is not in the list. `location` correctly has the null pointer value (see Figure 3.17a).
2. *item.ComparedTo(location->info) = EQUAL*. In this case, we have found the element within the list and have copied it into `item` (see Figure 3.17b).

We can now code this algorithm being reasonably confident that it is correct.

```
ItemType UnsortedType::GetItem(ItemType item, bool& found)
// Pre:  Key member(s) of item is initialized.
// Post: If found, item's key matches an element's key in the
//       list and a copy of that element is returned;
//       otherwise, item is returned.
{
  bool moreToSearch;
  NodeType* location;

  location = listData;
  found = false;
  moreToSearch = (location != NULL);
```

```
  while (moreToSearch && !found)
  {
    switch (item.ComparedTo(info[location]))
    {
      case LESS    :
      case GREATER : location = location->next;
                     moreToSearch = (location != NULL);
                     break;
      case EQUAL   : found = true;
                     item = location->info;
                     break;
    }
  }
  return item;
}
```

Function `DeleteItem`

In order to delete an item, we must first find it. In Figure 3.18, we see that `location` is left pointing to the node that contains the item for which we are searching, the one to be removed. In order to remove it, we must change the pointer in the *previous* node. That is, the `next` data member of the previous node must be changed to the `next` data member of the one being deleted.

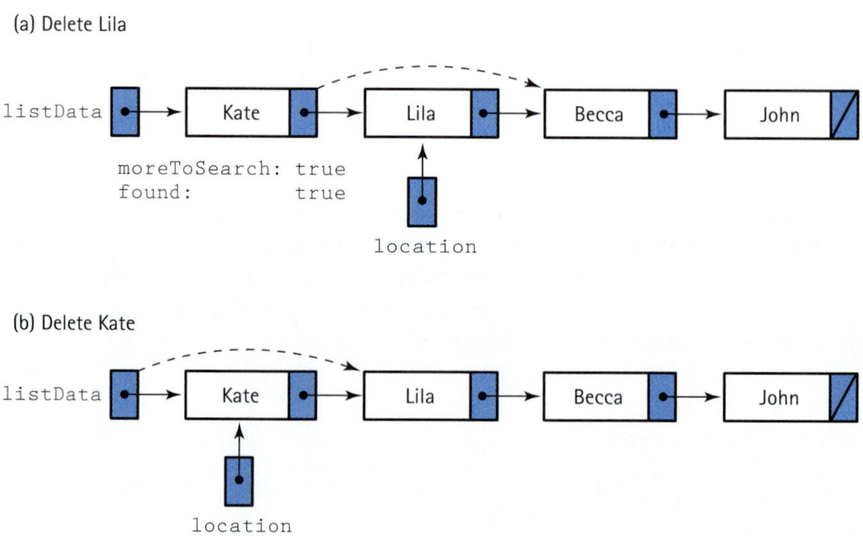

Figure 3.18 *Deleting an interior node and deleting the first node*

location now points to a node no longer needed, so we must deallocate it using the delete operator.

Because we know from the specifications that the item to be deleted is in the list, we can change our search algorithm slightly. Rather than compare the item for which we are searching with the information in Info(location), we compare it with Info(location->next). When we find a match, we have pointers to both the previous node (location) and the one containing the item to be deleted (location->next). Note that removing the first node must be a special case because the external pointer to the list (listData) must be changed. Is removing the last node a special case? No. The next data member of the node being deleted is NULL and it is stored into the next data member of Node(location), where it belongs.

```
void UnsortedType::DeleteItem(ItemType item)
// Pre:  item's key has been initialized.
//       An element in the list has a key that matches item's.
// Post: No element in the list has a key that matches item's.
{
  NodeType* location = listData;
  NodeType* tempLocation;

  // Locate node to be deleted.
  if (item == listData->info)
  {
    tempLocation = location;      // Save pointer to node
    listData = listData->next;    // Delete first node.
  }
  else
  {
    while (!(item==(location->next)->info))
      location = location->next;

      // Delete node at location->next
      tempLocation = location->next;
      location->next = (location->next)->next;
  }
  delete tempLocation;      // Return node
  length--;
}
```

Note that we had to save the pointer to the node being deleted in order to return the node to available space.

Functions `ResetList` and `GetNextItem`

The Unsorted List ADT specification defines the "current position" to mean the location of the last item accessed during an iteration through the list. In the array-based implementation, `ResetList` initialized `currentPos` to -1, and `GetNextItem` incremented `currentPos` and returned `info[currentPos]`. For `currentPos`, we used the special value -1 to mean "prior to the first item in the list." In the linked implementation, what special pointer value can we use for "prior to the first item in the list"? We can use the special pointer value `NULL`. Therefore `ResetList` sets the `currentPos` member to `NULL`, and `GetNextItem` sets `currentPos` either to `listData` (in case `currentPos` was `NULL`) or to `currentPos->next` (in case it was not `NULL`) before returning `currentPos->info`.

```
void UnsortedType::ResetList()
// Post: Current position has been initialized.
{
  currentPos = NULL;
}

ItemType UnsortedType::GetNextItem()
// Pre:   No transformer has been executed since last call.
// Post:  A copy of the next item in the list is returned.
//        When the end of the list is reached, currentPos
//        is reset to begin again.
{
  if (currentPos == NULL)
    currentPos = listData;
  else
    currentPos = currentPos->next;
  return currentPos->info;
}
```

Recall from the specifications that the body of `GetNextItem` is not required to check for running off the end of the list. That is the responsibility of the caller. A precondition of `GetNextItem` is that the item at the current position is not the last in the list. However, when working with linked lists an error can cause the program to crash with no warning. So we changed the post condition to show that if the last item has been accessed the list begins again.

Here is the implementation file for the linked version of class `UnsortedType`.

```
// This file contains the linked implementation of class
// UnsortedType.
```

```
#include "UnsortedType.h"

UnsortedType::UnsortedType()  // Class constructor
{
  length = 0;
  listData = NULL;
}
bool UnsortedType::IsFull() const
// Returns true if there is no room for another ItemType
//  on the free store; false otherwise.
{
  NodeType* location;
  try
  {
    location = new NodeType;
    delete location;
    return false;
  }
  catch(std::bad_alloc exception)
  {
    return true;
  }
}

int UnsortedType::GetLength() const
// Post: Number of items in the list is returned.
{
  return length;
}

void UnsortedType::MakeEmpty()
// Post: List is empty; all items have been deallocated.
{
NodeType* tempPtr;

  while (listData != NULL)
  {
    tempPtr = listData;
    listData = listData->next;
    delete tempPtr;
  }
  length = 0;
}
```

```
void UnsortedType::PutItem(ItemType item)
// item is in the list; length has been incremented.
{
  NodeType* location;             // Declare a pointer to a node

  location = new NodeType;        // Get a new node
  location->info = item;          // Store the item in the node
  location->next = listData;      // Store address of first node in
//   next field of new node
  listData = location;            // Store address of new node into
//   external pointer
  length++;   // Increment length of the list
}
ItemType UnsortedType::GetItem(ItemType item, bool& found)
// Pre:  Key member(s) of item is initialized.
// Post: If found, item's key matches an element's key in the
//       list and a copy of that element has been returned;
//       otherwise, item is returned.
{
  bool moreToSearch;
  NodeType<ItemType>* location;

  location = listData;
  found = false;
  moreToSearch = (location != NULL);

  while (moreToSearch && !found)
  {
    switch (item.ComparedTo(info[location]))
    {
      case LESS    :
      case GREATER : location = location->next;
                     moreToSearch = (location != NULL);
                     break;
      case EQUAL   : found = true;
                     item = location->info;
                     break;
    }
  }
  return item;
}
```

```
void UnsortedType::DeleteItem(ItemType item)
// Pre:  item's key has been initialized.
//       An element in the list has a key that matches item's.
// Post: No element in the list has a key that matches item's.
{
  NodeType<ItemType>* location = listData;
  NodeType<ItemType>* tempLocation;

  // Locate node to be deleted.
  if (item == listData->info)
  {
    tempLocation = location;
    listData = listData->next;          // Delete first node.
  }
  else
  {
    while (!(item==(location->next)->info))
      location = location->next;

    // Delete node at location->next
    tempLocation = location->next;
    location->next = (location->next)->next;
  }
  delete tempLocation;
  length--;
}

void UnsortedType::ResetList()
// Post: Current position has been initialized.
{
  currentPos = NULL;
}

ItemType UnsortedType::GetNextItem()
// Post:  A copy of the next item in the list is returned.
//        When the end of the list is reached, currentPos
//        is reset to begin again.
{
  if (currentPos == NULL)
    currentPos = listData;
  else
    currentPos = currentPos->next;
  return currentPos->info;
}
```

Here are the UML diagrams for the linked class `UnsortedList`.

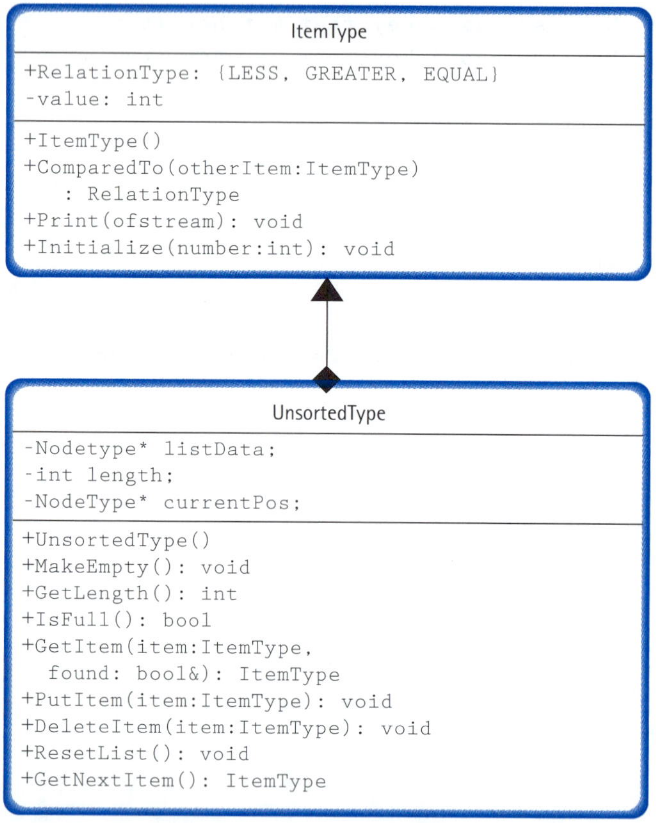

Note that the CRC card for the `UnsortedType` does not change because it contains no implementation information. However, the UML diagram used for maintenance documentation does change. It shows the data fields. Note also that the UML diagram for `ItemType` no longer contains a reference to `MAX_ITEMS`. The test plan developed for the array-based version is equally valid for the linked version.

Lifetime of a Variable

The *lifetime* of a variable is the time during program execution when the variable has storage assigned to it.

- The lifetime of a global variable is the entire execution of the program.
- The lifetime of a local variable is the execution of the block in which it is declared.
- The lifetime of a dynamically allocated variable is from the time it is allocated until the time it is deallocated.

There are times when it is useful for a local variable to retain its value, so C++ lets the user extend the lifetime of a local variable to the entire run of the program. To do this, you preface the data type identifier with the reserved word `static` when the variable is defined. The default storage class is automatic in which storage is allocated on entry and deallocated on exit from a block.

Class Destructors

We pointed out when we were designing the `MakeEmpty` function in the linked implementation, that `listData` is deallocated when the list goes out of scope, but not the nodes that `listData` points to. Therefore, we must include a class `destructor`. A class destructor is a member function named the same as a class constructor except that the destructor has a tilde (~) in front of the type name. A destructor is implicitly invoked when a class object goes out of scope—for example, when control leaves the block in which an object is declared. We include the following prototype of the destructor in the `public` part of the class definition:

```
~UnsortedType();    // Destructor.
```

and implement the function as follows:

```
UnsortedType::~UnsortedType()
// Post: List is empty; all items have been deallocated.
{
  NodeType* tempPtr;

  while (listData != NULL)
  {
    tempPtr = listData;
    listData = listData->next;
    delete tempPtr;
  }
}
```

See how this class destructor differs from an operation that makes a list empty? The class destructor releases the space that was allocated to the array but does not set `length` to 0. Making a structure empty is a logical operation defined in an ADT specification, but a class destructor is an implementation-level operation. Implementations that do not use dynamically allocated space usually do not need destructors. However, *implementations that use dynamically allocated space almost always need a destructor.*

3.5 Comparing Unsorted List Implementations

Now let's compare the sequential and linked implementations of the Unsorted List ADT. In order to determine the Big-O notation for the complexity of these functions, we must first determine the size factor. Here we are considering algorithms to manipulate items in a list. Therefore the size factor is the number of items on the list: `length`.

We look at two different factors: the amount of memory required to store the structure and the amount of work the solution does. An array variable of the maximum list size takes the same amount of memory, no matter how many array slots are actually used, because we need to reserve space for the maximum possible (`MAX_ITEMS`). The linked implementation using dynamically allocated storage space requires only enough space for the number of elements actually in the list at run time. However, each node element is larger, because we must store the link (the `next` member) as well as the user's data.

We can use Big-O notation to compare the efficiency of the two implementations. Most of the operations are nearly identical in the two implementations. The class constructor, `IsFull`, `Reset`, and `GetNextItem` functions in both implementations clearly have O(1) complexity because they are not dependent on the number of items in the list. `MakeEmpty` is an O(1) operation for a sequential list but becomes an O(N) operation for a linked list in dynamic storage. The sequential implementation merely marks the list as empty, while the linked implementation must actually access each list element to free its dynamically allocated space.

`GetLength` is always O(1) in an array-based implementation, but we have a choice in the linked version. We chose to make it O(1) by keeping a counter of the number of elements we insert and delete. If we had chosen to implement `GetLength` by counting the number of elements each time the function is called, the operation would be O(N). The moral here is that you must know how `GetLength` is implemented in a linked implementation in order to specify its Big-O measure.

The `GetItem` operations are virtually identical for the two implementations. Beginning at the first element, the algorithms examine one element after another until the correct element is found. Because they must potentially search through all the elements in a list, the loops in both implementations are O(N).

Because the list is unsorted, we can choose to put the new item into a directly accessible place: the last position in the array-based implementation or the front in the linked version. Therefore, the complexity of `PutItem` is the same in both implementations: O(1). In both implementations, `DeleteItem` has O(N) because the list must be searched for the item to delete, even though the actual removal is O(1) in the linked version and O(N) in the array-based version.

Table 3.2 summarizes these complexities. We have replaced `length` with N, the generic name for the size factor. For those operations that require an initial search, we break the Big-O into two parts: the search and what is done following the search.

Table 3.2 *Big-O Comparison of Sorted List Operations*

	Array Implementation	Linked Implementation
Class constructor	O(1)	O(1)
`MakeEmpty`	O(1)	O(*N*)
`IsFull`	O(1)	O(1)
`GetLength`	O(1)	O(1)
`ResetList`	O(1)	O(1)
`GetNextItem`	O(1)	O(1)
`GetItem`	O(*N*)	O(*N*)
`PutItem`		
Find	O(1)	O(1)
Insert	O(1)	O(1)
Combined	O(1)	O(1)
`DeleteItem`		
Find	O(*N*)	O(*N*)
Delete	O(1)	O(1)
Combined	O(*N*)	O(*N*)

Case Study

Creating a Deck of Playing Cards

As an avid card player, you planned to write programs to play Poker and Solitaire. As a prelude you begin by developing a set of ADTs that will allow you to simulate a deck of 52 playing cards, consisting of the four suits (hearts, clubs, diamonds, spades) with 13 values (Ace through King) in each suit. Once you have these working, you can use them in other programs.

Logical Level What do we need to write ADTs for? Let's start with cards and decks. A card is represented by a suit and a rank. Do we need separate classes to represent suits and rank, or can we just use strings and integers or perhaps enums? Before deciding on the representation, let's consider what we might want to do with an individual card. We need to return its properties (rank and suit). We should also convert the card to a string for printing. There are no transformers necessary for a card. A card doesn't change; it is immutable. Integers between 1 and 13 are an obvious choice to represent a card's rank. There is no such obvious choice for suit, but an enumerated type CLUB, DIAMOND, HEART, and SPADE would be sufficient to represent the suits. Thus suit and rank do not need to be classes themselves.

Now let's turn our observations into responsibilities for a card. We should provide a constructor that takes a rank and a suit. An empty card makes no sense, but we should provide a default constructor. Let's set it to the Ace of Clubs. We need observers for both of the data members. Will we need to compare cards? Yes; we should support a comparison operator. Finally, we need an operation that returns the card as a string. Here is the CRC card for Card:

Class Name: CardType	Superclass: None	Subclasses: None
Responsibilities	**Collaborations**	
Initialize Card()		
Initialize Card(int, Suits)		
GetRank returns int		
GetSuit returns Suits		
CompareTo returns RelationType		
ToString returns string		

Card ADT Specification

Structure: A playing card

Definitions:

RelationType: An enumeration type that consists of LESS, GREATER, EQUAL

Suits: An enumeration type that consists of CLUB, DIAMOND, HEART, SPADE

Self: The instance to which the function is applied.

Operations:

Initialize(int, Suits)

Function: Initializes card to the values of its parameters.

Precondition: None

Postcondition: Self instance has been defined.

Initialize

Function: Initializes card to the default values.

Precondition: None

Postcondition: Self instance has been defined.

int GetRank

Function:	Returns the rank field.
Preconditions:	Self has been initialized.
Postconditions:	Function value is rank as an integer.

Suits GetSuit

Function:	Returns the suit as an enumerated type
Precondition:	Self has been initialized.
Postcondition:	Function value is a suit.

string ToString

Function:	Returns card as a string.
Precondition:	Self has been initialized.
Postcondition:	Function value is card as a string.

RelationType ComparedTo(Card aCard)

Function:	Determines the ordering of two Card objects
Precondition:	Self and aCard have been initialized.
Postcondition:	Function value = LESS if self comes before aCard. = GREATER if self comes after aCard. = EQUAL if self and aCard are the same.

Implementation Level As in the case of the ADT DateType, the application level for the ADT Card is the testing of the class. The ADT Card will go into our library until we are ready to use it. We are now ready to code the class. Here is the specification file for class `Card`.

```
// Specification file for class Card,
// which represents a playing card.
#include <string>
using namespace std;
enum Suits {CLUB, DIAMOND, HEART, SPADE};
enum RelationType {LESS, EQUAL, GREATER};
class Card
{
public:
  // Constructors
  Card();
  Card(int initRank, Suits initSuit);
  // Observers
  int GetRank() const;
  Suits GetSuit() const;
  string ToString() const;
  // Relational operators
```

```
  RelationType ComparedTo
    (const Card& aCard) const;
private:
  int rank;
  Suits suit;
 };
```

The only complicated operations are `ToString` and `ComparedTo`. `ToString` can use a 4-element array of strings indexed by the suit to provide the written form of the suit. We can use a 13-array of strings indexed by the rank to provide the written form of the rank. To determine if two cards are equal is straightforward, but the less than and greater than are ambiguous. The ordering of a new deck has the Ace as the lowest value in a suit. In many card games, the Ace is considered higher than any other card in the suit. So, which do we mean? Here we assume the Bridge and Poker ordering: The Ace is the highest value in the suit. We have to compare the suit and if they are equal, we compare the value with the Ace as a special case.

ComparedTo(aCard)

```
if suit < aCard.suit
    return LESS
else if suit > aCard.suit
    return GREATER
else if rank = aCard.rank
    return EQUAL
else if rank = Ace
    return GREATER
else if aCard.rank = Ace
    return LESS
else if rank < aCard.rank
    return LESS
else if rank > aCard.rank
    return GREATER
else
    return EQUAL
```

ToString

```
Create a 4-slot string array (convertSuit)
Store name of suit in each slot
Create a 13-slot string array (convertRank)
Store name of rank in each slot
Set printString to convertRank[rank-1]+ " of " + convertSuit[suit] ;
return printString
```

Now we can code the implementation file for class `Card`.

```
// Implementation file for class Card
#include "card.h"

Card::Card()
{
  rank = 1;
  suit = CLUB;
}

Card::Card(int initRank, Suits initSuit)
{
  rank = initRank;
  suit = initSuit;
}

int Card::GetRank() const
{ return rank; }

Suits Card::GetSuit() const
{ return suit; }

RelationType Card::ComparedTo(const Card& someCard) const
// Returns relative position of self to someCard.
{
  if (suit < someCard.suit)
    return LESS;
  else if (suit > someCard.suit)
    return GREATER;
  else if (rank == someCard.rank)
    return EQUAL;
  else if (rank == 1)
    return GREATER;
  else if (someCard.rank == 1)
    return LESS;
  else if (rank < someCard.rank)
    return LESS;
  else if (rank > someCard.rank)
    return GREATER;
  else
    return EQUAL;
}
```

```
string Card::ToString() const
{
  string convertRank[13] = {"Ace", "Two", "Three", "Four",
    "Five", "Six", "Seven", "Eight", "Nine", "Ten", "Jack", "Queen",
    "King"};
  string convertSuit[4] = {"Clubs", "Diamonds", "Hearts",
    "Spades"};
  string printString = convertRank[rank-1]+ " of " + convertSuit[suit] ;
  return printString;
}
```

Logical Level We go back to the logical level to determine the responsibilities for our ADT deck. The default constructor can set the deck to empty. An operation, GenerateDeck, can build a full deck of cards in order. We need the ability to shuffle the deck, to examine a card, to insert a card, and to ask whether the deck is empty. It's also helpful to know how many cards are left in the deck. Except for a shuffle operation, it sounds like the operations for our List ADT: `UnsortedType`. We can create a descendent class of `UnsortedType`, which has GenerateDeck and a shuffle operation.

Here is a CRC card that outlines those responsibilities:

Class Name: Deck	Superclass: UnsortedType	Subclasses: none
Responsibilities	**Collaborations**	
Create Deck		
GenerateDeck	Card	
Shuffle deck	Card	

Here is the specification for the ADT Deck.

Deck ADT Specification

Structure: A collection of 52 playing cards

Operations:

Initialize

Function: Initializes list of cards to the empty list.

Precondition: None

Postcondition: Self instance is empty.

GenerateDeck

Function: Initializes list of cards to bridge order.

Precondition: None

Postcondition: Self instance is in poker (bridge) order.

Shuffle

Function: Randomizes the order of the cards in the list.
Preconditions: Self has been initialized.
Postconditions: Self instance is in pseudorandom order.

Implementation Level We are now ready to move to the implementation level to finish coding ADT deck.

```
// Specification file for class Deck, which represents
// a deck of 52 playing cards.
// class Deck is derived from class UnsortedType, and
// uses the list to contain the playing cards.
#include "unsorted.h"

class Deck : public UnsortedType
{
public:
  // Constructor
  Deck();     // Sets deck to empty
  // Transformers
  void GenerateDeck();
  // Generates deck in bridge (poker) order
  void Shuffle();
  // Reorders the cards
};
```

The only operation that requires much thought is GenerateDeck. We can use PutItem to insert the cards into the `deck`. But how do we generate the cards in order? A nested `for` loop, counting through `Suits` in the outer loop and rank in the inner loop accomplishes this task. What about shuffle? How does a person do it by hand? He or she divides the deck into two nearly equal parts, and then merges the two parts back together. This process can be implemented directly. We can use a random number generator to determine the relative sizes of the two halves, but we don't want the split to be too unbalanced. Let's keep it between 23 and 30. We then copy the cards from the deck into the first half (deckA) and then copy the remaining cards into the second half (deckB). We then reinitialize the deck and merge the two halves together. Because this is so complicated, let's write the pseudocode first.

Shuffle

Split deck
Merge decks

Split deck

```
Set split size to between 23 and 30
For counter going from 1 to splitSize
    Get card from deck
    Put card into deckA
For counter going from splitSize to deck size (i.e., 52)
    Get card from deck
    Put card into deckB
```

We said we could use a random number generator to determine the size of the split. Where do we get a random-number generator? You can find the formula in a statistics book and code it yourself. However, there is an easier way. C++ compilers have one available in the standard library—the `rand` function.

```
#include <stdlib.h>
   .
   .
   .
randomInt = rand();
```

`rand` returns a random integer in the range of 0 through `RAND_MAX`, a constant defined in `<stdlib.h>`. (`RAND_MAX` is typically the same as `INT_MAX`.) To convert the number to between 1 and 52, we take the random number MOD 52 plus 1. A random number generator has a seed that must be set before it can be executed. `rand` comes with a default seed, but we should set it ourselves by using function `srand`. Using the machine's clock is a good way to choose the seed. We can access the clock by using function `time(NULL)` in `<time.h>`.

Merge decks

```
Set deck to empty
Set lengthA to deckA.length
Set lengthB to deckB.length
if lengthA < = lengthB
    for counter going from 1 to lengthA
        Get card from deckA
        Put card in deck
        Get card from deckB
        Put card in deck
    for counter going from lengthB + 1 to deck size
        Get card from deckB
        Put card in deck
```

```
else
    for counter going from 1 to lengthB
        Get card from deckA
        Put card in deck
        Get card from deckB
        Put card in deck
    for counter going from lengthA + 1 to deck size
        Get card from deckA
        Put card in deck
```

There is a lot of duplicated code here. We can reduce it by making Merge a helper function that takes two decks as parameters. The first parameter is always the shorter one. Here is the revised algorithm.

Merge (shorterDeck, longerDeck) returns deck

```
for counter going from 1 to shortDeck length
    Get card from shorterDeck
    Put card in deck
    Get card from longerDeck
    Put card in deck
for counter going from longerDeck length + 1 to deck size
    Get card from longerDeck
    Put card in deck
return deck
```

```
// Implementation file for class Deck, which
// represents a collection of 52 bridge cards.
#include <iostream>
#include "Deck.h"
#include <cstdlib>
#include <time.h>

Deck::Deck()
// The UnsortedType constructor is called.
{}

void Deck::GenerateDeck()
// Generates deck in bridge (poker) order
```

```
{
  MakeEmpty();
  for(Suits suit = CLUB; suit <= SPADE; suit = Suits(suit+1))
    for(int value = 1; value <= 13; value++)
       PutItem(Card(value, suit));
}

Deck Merge(Deck shorterDeck, Deck longerDeck)
// Merges two decks, one card at a time, until first
// deck is empty.  Rest of second deck is appended.
{
  Deck deck;
  Card card;
  int counter;
  shorterDeck.ResetList();
  longerDeck.ResetList();
  for (counter = 1; counter <= shorterDeck.GetLength();
    counter++)
  {
    card = shorterDeck.GetNextItem();
    deck.PutItem(card);
    card = longerDeck.GetNextItem();
    deck.PutItem(card);
  }
  int remaining = longerDeck.GetLength() - shorterDeck.GetLength();
  for (counter = 1; counter <= remaining; counter++)
  {
    card =longerDeck.GetNextItem();
    deck.PutItem(card);
  }
  return deck;
}

void Deck::Shuffle()
// Spilts deck into two parts, using random number generator
// to determine size of parts.  Parts are merged one card
// at a time, using helper function Merge.
{
  srand(time(NULL));
  Deck deckA;
  Deck deckB;
  Card card;
  ResetList();
  int splitSize;
  int counter;
  splitSize = ((rand() % 8 + 1) + 22;
```

```
  for (counter = 1; counter <= splitSize; counter++)
  {
    card = GetNextItem();
    deckA.PutItem(card);
  }

  for (counter = splitSize+1; counter <= GetLength();
    counter ++)
  {
    card = GetNextItem();
    deckB.PutItem(card);
  }

  MakeEmpty();
  if (splitSize < (52 - splitSize))
    *this = Merge(deckA, deckB);
  else
    *this = Merge(deckB, deckA);
}
```

Testing A proper driver for these classes should exercise them as much as possible. Here we are limited by space to some basic tests. We create a deck and print it out to check the default constructor. Then we apply `GenerateDeck` and print the results. We shuffle the deck and print it. Actually, we should shuffle seven times and print the results. Why seven times? In the 1980s mathematicians Persi Diaconis and Dave Bayer determined that seven shuffles are enough to ensure randomization. In 2000, Trefethen argued that six shuffles were enough. We have erred on the safe side and chosen to shuffle the deck seven times.

Here is the driver that implements these tests. Note that we made use of a helper function `PrintDeck`.

```
// Test driver for class Deck
#include <iostream>
#include "Deck.h"
int main ()
{
  void PrintDeck(Deck deck);

  Deck deck;
  Card card;
  cout << "Deck after default constructor" << endl;
  PrintDeck(deck);
  deck.GenerateDeck();
  cout << "Deck after GenerateDeck" << endl;
  PrintDeck(deck);
  for (int count = 1; count <=10; count++)
```

```
    deck.Shuffle();
  cout << "Deck after ten shuffles" << endl;
  PrintDeck(deck);
  return 0;
}

void PrintDeck(Deck deck)
{
  if (deck.GetLength() == 0)
     cout << "Deck is empty." << endl;
  else
  {
    deck.ResetList();
    Card card;
    for (int counter = 1; counter <= deck.GetLength(); counter++)
    {
      card = deck.GetNextItem();
      cout << card.ToString() << endl;
    }
  }
  cout << endl;
}
```

Before we can run this driver, we need to make the connection between `Card` and `ItemType`, which `UnsortedType` requires. Recall that `UnsortedType` includes a file `ItemType.h`, which defines the items to be on the list. We must include a `typedef` statement in `Card` that equates it to `ItemType` and include a maximum list size, which in this case, is 52.

Here is the output, shown in two columns to save space.

```
Deck after default constructor
Deck is empty.

Deck after GenerateDeck
Ace of Clubs
Two of Clubs
Three of Clubs
Four of Clubs
Five of Clubs
Six of Clubs
Seven of Clubs
Eight of Clubs
Nine of Clubs
Ten of Clubs
Jack of Clubs
Queen of Clubs
King of Clubs
Ace of Diamonds
Two of Diamonds
Three of Diamonds
Four of Diamonds
Five of Diamonds
Six of Diamonds
Seven of Diamonds
Eight of Diamonds
Nine of Diamonds
Ten of Diamonds
Jack of Diamonds
Queen of Diamonds
King of Diamonds
Ace of Hearts
Two of Hearts
```

```
Three of Hearts
Four of Hearts
Five of Hearts
Six of Hearts
Seven of Hearts
Eight of Hearts
Nine of Hearts
Ten of Hearts
Jack of Hearts
Queen of Hearts
King of Hearts
Ace of Spades
Two of Spades
Three of Spades
Four of Spades
Five of Spades
Six of Spades
Seven of Spades
Eight of Spades
Nine of Spades
Ten of Spades
Jack of Spades
Queen of Spades
King of Spades


Deck after ten shuffles
Seven of Diamonds
Ace of Spades
Three of Spades
Ten of Diamonds
Two of Hearts
Ace of Hearts
King of Diamonds
Seven of Spades
Queen of Clubs
King of Spades
Three of Diamonds
Queen of Spades
Nine of Diamonds
Jack of Spades
King of Hearts
Nine of Hearts
Four of Clubs
Jack of Diamonds
Six of Diamonds
Eight of Spades
Five of Diamonds
Six of Hearts
Four of Diamonds
Six of Spades
Two of Spades
Five of Spades
Two of Diamonds
Four of Spades
Ten of Clubs
Eight of Diamonds
Ace of Diamonds
King of Clubs
Six of Clubs
Eight of Clubs
Jack of Clubs
Nine of Spades
Two of Clubs
Queen of Hearts
Nine of Clubs
Jack of Hearts
Ten of Spades
Ten of Hearts
Five of Clubs
Seven of Clubs
Three of Clubs
Eight of Hearts
Ace of Clubs
Seven of Hearts
Queen of Diamonds
Five of Hearts
Four of Hearts
Three of Hearts
```

Here is the UML diagram for our deck of playing cards.

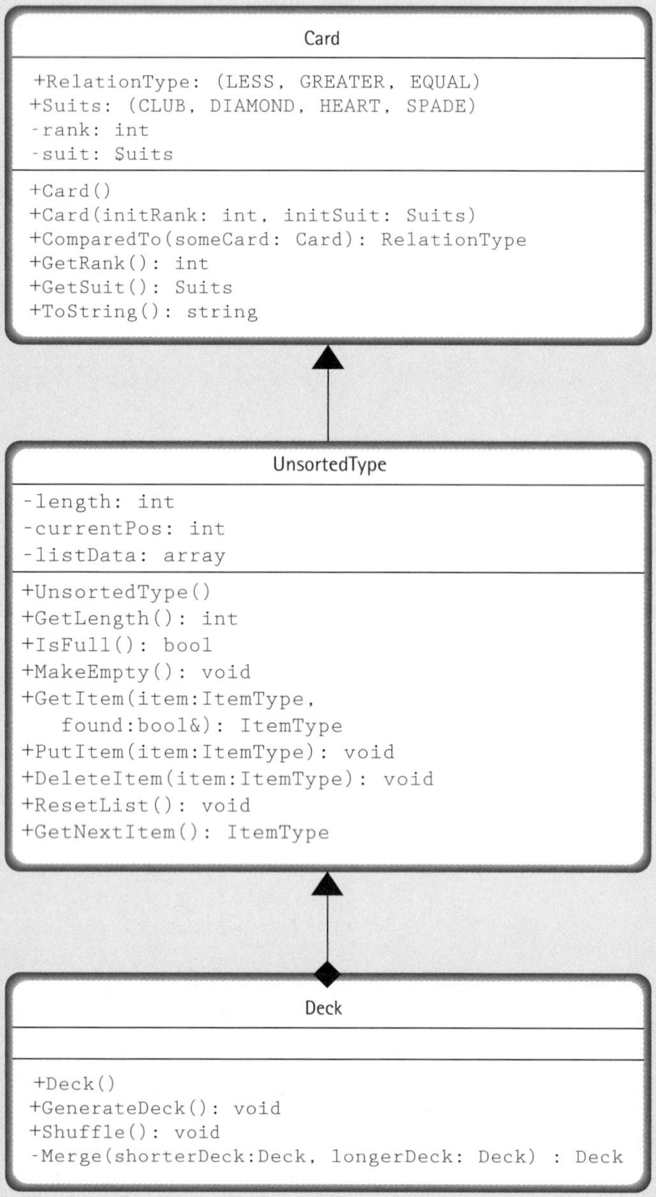

Summary

In this chapter, we created an abstract data type that represents a list. The Unsorted List ADT assumes that the list elements are not sorted by key. We have viewed it from three perspectives: the logical level, the application level, and the implementation level.

We have presented two quite different implementations of the class that encapsulates the Unsorted List ADT. The first is an array-based implementation in which the items in the list are stored in an array; the second is a linked-list implementation in which the items are stored in nodes that are linked together. We examined the C++ pointer data type, which allows the nodes in a linked list to be chained.

In order to make the software as reusable as possible, the specification of each ADT states that the user of the ADT must prepare a class that defines the objects to be in each container class. A member function `ComparedTo` that compares two objects of this class must be included in the definition. This function returns one of the constants in `RelationType`: `LESS`, `EQUAL`, `GREATER`. By requiring the user to provide this information about the objects on the list, the code of the ADTs is very general.

The operations on the two ADTs were compared using Big-O notation. Insertion into an unsorted list has O(1) in both implementations. Deletions from both have $O(N)$. Searching in the unsorted list has $O(N)$; searching in a sorted list has order $O(\log_2 N)$ if a binary search is used.

The Case Study simulated a deck of playing cards. Comparing one card with another demonstrated the use of abstraction in the `RelationType` enumerated type. The deck was implemented using a derived class of `UnsortedType`, demonstrating the value of inheritance.

Figure 3.19 shows the relationships among the three views of the list data in the Case Study.

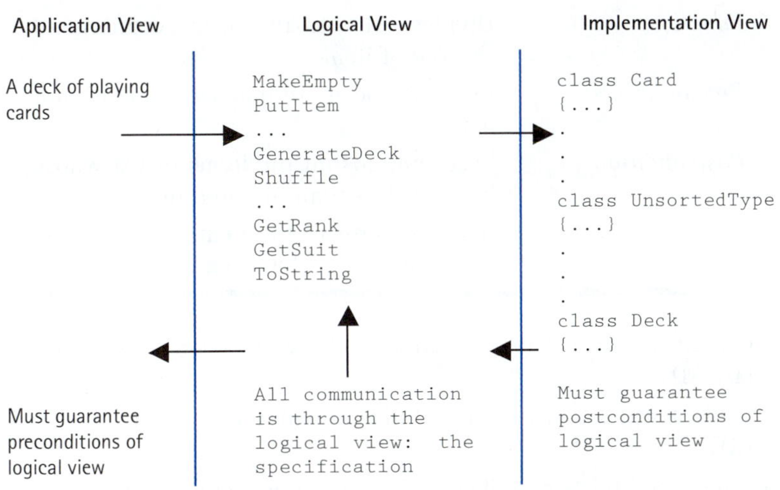

Figure 3.19 *Relationships among the views of data*

Exercises

1. The Unsorted List ADT is to be extended with a Boolean member function, `IsThere`, which takes as a parameter an item of type `ItemType` and determines whether there is an element with this key in the list.
   a. Write the specifications for this function.
   b. Write the prototype for this function.
   c. Write the function definition using an array-based implementation.
   d. Write the function definition using a linked implementation.
   e. Describe this function in terms of Big-O.
2. Rather than enhancing the Unsorted List ADTs by adding a member function `IsThere`, you decide to write a client function to do the same task.
   a. Write the specifications for this function.
   b. Write the function definition.
   c. Write a paragraph comparing the client function and the member function (Exercise 1) for the same task.
   d. Describe this function in terms of Big-O.
3. An Unsorted Type ADT is to be extended by the addition of function `SplitLists`, which has the following specifications:

SplitLists(UnsortedType list, ItemType item, UnsortedType& list1, UnsortedType& list2)

Function:	Divides list into two lists according to the key of item.
Preconditions:	list has been initialized and is not empty.
Postconditions:	list1 contains all the items of list whose keys are less than or equal to item's key; list2 contains all the items of list whose keys are greater than item's key.

   a. Implement `SplitLists` as an array-based member function of the Unsorted List ADT.
   b. Implement `SplitLists` as a linked member function of the Unsorted List ADT.
4. Implement SplitLists described in Exercise 3 as a client function.
5. The specifications for the Unsorted List ADT state that the item to be deleted is in the list.

a. Rewrite the specification for `DeleteItem` so that the list is unchanged if the item to be deleted is not in the list.

b. Implement `DeleteItem` as specified in (a) using an array-based implementation.

c. Rewrite the specification for `DeleteItem` so that all copies of the item to be deleted are removed if they exist.

d. Implement `DeleteItem` as specified in (c) using an array-based implementation.

6. Redo Exercise 5(b) and 5(d), using a linked implementation.

7. a. Explain the difference between an array-based and a linked representation of a list.

   b. Give an example of a problem for which an array-based list would be the better solution.

   c. Give an example of a problem for which a linked list would be the better solution.

8. True or False? If you answer False, correct the statement.

   a. An array is a random-access structure.

   b. A sequential list is a random-access structure.

   c. A linked list is a random-access structure.

   d. A sequential list is always stored in a statically allocated structure.

Use the linked list pictured below for Exercises 9 through 12.

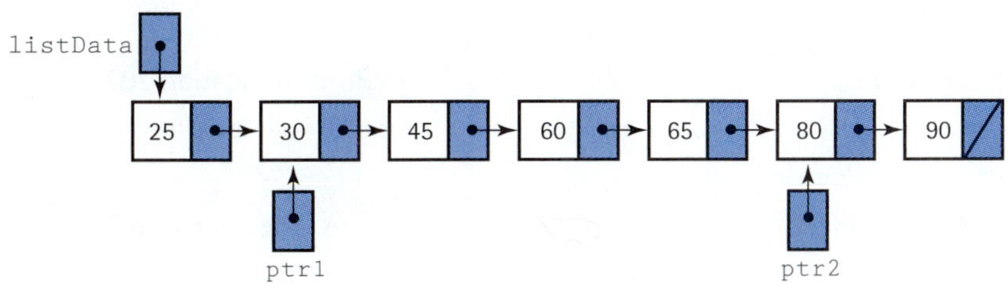

9. Give the values of the following expressions:

   a. `ptr1->info`

   b. `ptr2->next->info`

   c. `listData->next->next->info`

10. Are the following expressions true or false?

    a. `listdata->next == ptr1`

    b. `ptr1->next->info == 60`

    c. `ptr2->next == NULL`

    d. `listData->info == 25`

11. Decide whether the *syntax* of each of the following statements is valid or invalid. If it is valid, mark it OK; if it is invalid, explain what is wrong.
    a. `listData->next = ptr1->next;`
    b. `listData->next = *(ptr2->next);`
    c. `*listData = ptr2;`
    d. `ptr2 = ptr1->next->info;`
    e. `ptr1->info = ptr2->info;`
    f. `ptr2 = ptr2->next->next;`
12. Write *one* statement to do each of the following:
    a. Make `listData` point to the node containing 45.
    b. Make `ptr2` point to the last node in the list.
    c. Make `listData` point to an empty list.
    d. Set the `info` member of the node containing 45 to 60.

If memory locations are allocated as shown in the second column of the following table, what is printed by the statements in the first column? Fill in the last column in the following table for Exercises 13 through 18. The exercise number is in the first column in comments.

Statements	Memory Allocated	What Is Printed?
`int value;`	value is assigned to location 200	
`value = 500;`		
`char* charPtr;`	charPtr is at location 202	
`char string[10] = "Good luck";`	string[0] is at location 300	
`charPtr = string;`		
`cout << &value;      // Exercise 13`	& means "the address of"	
`cout << value;       // Exercise 14`		
`cout << &charPtr;    // Exercise 15`	& means "the address of"	
`cout << charPtr;     // Exercise 16`		
`cout << *charPtr;    // Exercise 17`		
`cout << string[2];   // Exercise 18`		

13. An Unsorted List ADT is to be extended by the addition of a member function `Head`, which has the following precondition and postcondition:

    Precondition: list has been initialized and is not empty.

    Postcondition: return value is the last item inserted in the list.

a. Will this addition be easy to implement in the array-based class `UnsortedType`? Explain.

b. Will this addition be easy to implement in the linked class `UnsortedType`? Explain.

14. An Unsorted List ADT is to be extended by the addition of function `Tail`, which has the following precondition and postcondition:

Precondition: list has been initialized and is not empty.

Postcondition: return value is a new list with the last item inserted in the list removed.

a. Will this addition be easy to implement in the array-based class `UnsortedType`? Explain.

b. Will this addition be easy to implement in the linked implementation of class `UnsortedType`? Explain.

15. `DeleteItem` does not maintain the order of insertions because the algorithm swaps the last item into the position of the one being deleted and then decrements `length`. Would there be any advantage to having `DeleteItem` maintain the insertion order? Justify your answer.

16. Give a Big-O estimate of the run time for the functions you wrote in Exercises 5 and 6.

17. a. Change the specifications for the array-based Unsorted List ADT so that `PutItem` throws an exception if the list is full.

b. Implement the revised specifications in (a).

18. Based on the following declarations, tell whether each statement below is syntactically legal (yes) or illegal (no).

```
int* p;
int* q;
int* r;
int a;
int b;
int c;
```

	Yes/no		Yes/no		Yes/no
a. `p = new int;`	____	f. `r = NULL;`	____	k. `delete r;`	____
b. `q* = new int;`	____	g. `c = *p;`	____	l. `a = new p;`	____
c. `a = new int;`	____	h. `p = *a;`	____	m. `q* = NULL;`	____
d. `p = r;`	____	i. `delete b;`	____	n. `*p = a;`	____
e. `q = b;`	____	j. `q = &c;`	____	o. `c = NULL;`	____

19. The following program has careless errors on several lines. Find and correct the errors and show the output where requested.

```
#include <iostream>
int main ()
{
  int* ptr;
  int* temp;
  int x;

  ptr = new int;
  *ptr = 4;
  *temp = *ptr;
  cout  << ptr  << temp;
  x = 9;
  *temp = x;
  cout  << *ptr  << *temp;
  ptr = new int;
  ptr = 5;
  cout  << *ptr  << *temp; // output:__________________
  return 0;
}
```

Exercises 20 through 28 refer to blanks in the following code segment.

```
Class UnsortedType
{
public:
  //all the prototypes go here.
private:
  int length;
  NodeType* listData;
};
void UnsortedType::DeleteItem(ItemType item)
// Pre:  Item is in list
{
  NodeType* tempPtr;        // pointer delete
  NodeType* predLoc;        // trailing pointer
  NodeType* location;       // traveling pointer
  bool found = false;

  location = listData;
  predLoc = ______________;                      // 20
  length--;
```

```
    // Find node to delete.
    while (____________)                                // 21
    {
      switch (__________________)                       // 22
      {
        case GREATER: ;
         case LESS    : predLoc = location;
                        location = ___________;         // 23
                        break;
         case EQUAL   : found = ___________;            // 24
                    break;
      }
    }
    // delete location
    tempPtr = _____________;                            // 25
    if (____________)                                   // 26
      ____________ = location->next;                    // 27
    else
      predLoc->next = _____________;                    // 28
    delete tempPtr;
  }
```

20. Read the code segment above and fill in blank #20.
    a. NULL
    b. True
    c. false
    d. listData
    e. answer not shown
21. Read the code segment above and fill in blank #21.
    a. true
    b. !found
    c. false
    d. moreToSearch
    e. answer not shown
22. Read the code segment above and fill in blank #22.
    a. item.ComparedTo(listData->info)
    b. item.ComparedTo(location->next)
    c. item.ComparedTo(location->info)

d. item.ComparedTo(location)

e. answer not shown

23. Read the code segment above and fill in blank #23.

a. item

b. *location.next

c. (*location).next

d. predLoc

e. answer not shown

24. Read the code segment above and fill in blank #24.

a. false

b. true

c. predLoc == NULL

d. location != NULL

e. answer not shown

25. Read the code segment above and fill in blank #25.

a. preLoc

b. location

c. predLoc->next

d. location->next

e. answer not shown

26. Read the code segment above and fill in blank #26.

a. predLoc == NULL

b. location == NULL

c. predLoc == location

d. predLoc->next == NULL

e. answer not shown

27. Read the code segment above and fill in blank #27.

a. predLoc

b. location

c. location->next

d. listData

e. answer not shown

28. Read the code segment above and fill in blank #28.
   a. listData
   b. predLoc->next
   c. location->next
   d. newNode->next
   e. answer not shown

chapter 4

ADT Sorted List

Goals

After studying this chapter, you should be able to

- Describe the Abstract Data Type Sorted List from three perspectives
- Implement the following Sorted List operations using an array-based implementation
  - Create and destroy a list
  - Determine whether the list is full
  - Put an element into the list
  - Get an element from the list
  - Delete an element from the list
- Create an array in dynamically allocated storage
- Implement the list operations outlined above using a linked implementation
- Implement the binary search algorithm
- Compare the two implementations of the ADT Sorted List in terms of Big-O approximations
- Compare the implementations of the Unsorted List ADT and the Sorted List ADT in terms of Big-O Analysis
- Distinguish between bounded and unbounded ADTs at the logical and implementation levels
- Identify and apply the phases of the object-oriented methodology

4.1 Abstract Data Type Sorted List

In the last chapter, we said that a list is a linear sequence of items; from any item (except the last) you can access the next one. We looked at the specifications and implementation for the operations that manipulate a list and guarantee this property.

In this chapter, we add an additional property: The key member of any item (except the first) comes before the key member of the next one. We call a list with this property a *sorted list*.

Logical Level

When we defined the specifications for the Unsorted List ADT, we commented that there was nothing in the specifications to prevent the list from being stored and maintained in sorted order. Now, we have to change the specifications to guarantee that the list is sorted. We must add preconditions to those operations for which order is relevant. The observer functions do not change the state of the list, so we do not have to change them. The algorithm for `GetItem` can be improved but still works on a sorted list. The algorithms for `ResetList` and `GetNextItem` are not changed by the additional property. What then must be changed? `PutItem` and `DeleteItem`. Notice that these comments apply to the ADT at the logical level, so are in handwriting font. The changed specifications are shaded.

Sorted List ADT Specification

Structure:

The list elements are of ItemType. The list has a special property called the *current position*—the position of the last element accessed by **GetNextItem** during an iteration through the list. Only **ResetList** and **GetNextItem** affect the current position.

Definitions (provided by user in class ItemType):

MAX_ITEMS: A constant specifying the maximum number of items in the list

RelationType: An enumeration type that consists of LESS, GREATER, EQUAL

Member function of ItemType that must be included:

RelationType ComparedTo(ItemType item)

Function: Determines the ordering of two ItemType objects based on their keys.

Precondition: Self and item have their key members initialized.

Postcondition:

Function value = LESS if the key of self is less than the key of item.
= GREATER if the key of self is greater than the key of item.
= EQUAL if the keys are equal.

Operations (provided by Sorted List ADT)

MakeEmpty

Function: Initializes list to empty state.

Preconditions: None

Postcondition: List is empty.

Boolean IsFull

Function: Determines whether list is full.

Precondition: List has been initialized.

Postcondition: Function value = (list is full)

int GetLength

Function: Determines the number of elements in list.

Precondition: List has been initialized.

Postcondition: Function value = number of elements in list

GetItem (ItemType item, Boolean& found)

Function: Retrieves list element whose key matches item's key (if present).

Preconditions: List has been initialized.
Key member of item is initialized.

Postconditions: If there is an element someItem whose key matches item's key, then found = true and item is returned; otherwise found = false and original item is returned.
List is unchanged.

PutItem (ItemType item)

Function: Adds item to list.

Preconditions: List has been initialized.
List is not full.
item is not in list.
List is sorted by key member using function ComparedTo.

Postconditions: item is in list.
List is still sorted.

DeleteItem (ItemType item)

Function:	Deletes the element whose key matches item's key.
Preconditions:	List has been initialized.
	Key member of item is initialized.
	List is sorted by key member using function ComparedTo.
	One and only one element in list has a key matching item's key.
Postconditions:	No element in list has key matching item's key.
	List is still sorted.

ResetList

Function:	Initializes current position for an iteration through the list.
Precondition:	List has been initialized.
Postcondition:	Current position is prior to list.

GetNextItem (ItemType)

Function:	Gets the next element in list.
Preconditions:	List has been initialized.
	Current position is defined.
	Element at current position is not last in list.
Postconditions:	Current position is updated to next position.
	Returns a copy of element at current position.

Application Level

The application level for the Sorted List ADT is the same as that for the Unsorted List ADT. As far as the user is concerned, the interfaces are the same. The only difference is that when `GetNextItem` is called in the Sorted List ADT, the element returned is the next one in order by key. If the user wants that property, the client code includes the file containing the class `SortedType` rather than `UnsortedType`.

Implementation Level

`PutItem` Function To add an element to a sorted list, we must first find the place where the new element belongs, which depends on the value of its key. Let's use an example to illustrate the insertion operation. Suppose that Becca has made the honor roll. To add the element Becca to the sorted list pictured in Figure 4.1a while maintaining the alphabetic ordering, we must accomplish three tasks:

1. Find the place where the new element belongs.
2. Create space for the new element.
3. Put the new element in the list.

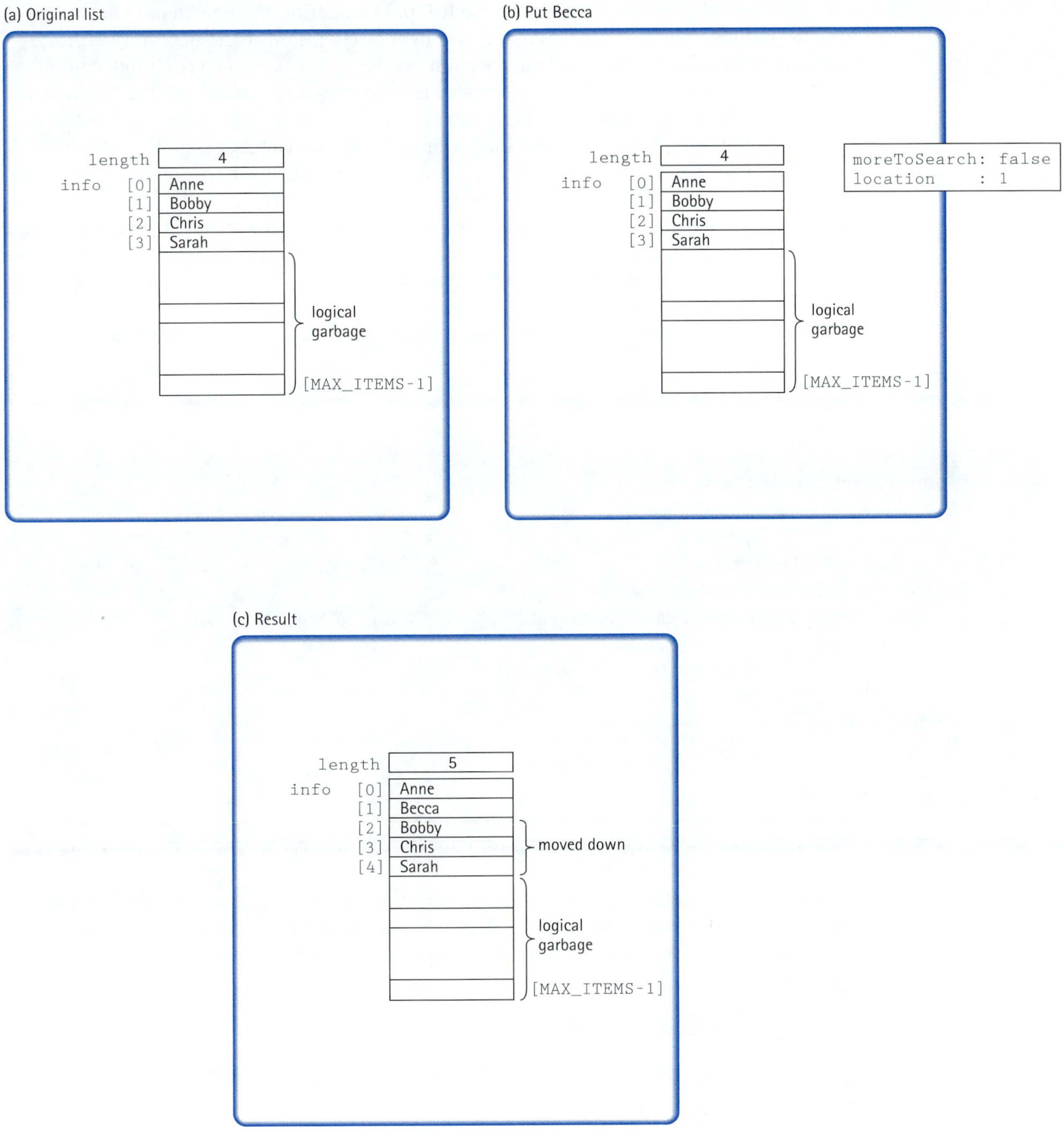

Figure 4.1 *Putting an item into a sorted list*

The first task involves traversing the list and comparing the new item to each item in the list until we find an item where the new item is less (in this case, Becca). We set `moreToSearch` to `false` when we reach a point where `item.ComparedTo(`Info(location)`)` is `LESS`. At this point, `location` indicates where the new item should go (see Figure 4.1b). If we don't find a place where `item.ComparedTo(`Info(location)`)` is `LESS`, then the item should be put at the end of the list. In this case, `location` equals `length`.

Now that we know where the element belongs, we need to create space for it. Because the list is sorted, Becca must be put into the list at Info(location). Of course, this position may already be occupied. To "create space for the new element," we must move down all list elements that follow it, from `location` through `length - 1`. Then, we just assign `item` to Info(location) and increment `length`. Figure 4.1c shows the resulting list.

Let's summarize these observations in algorithm form before we write the code:

PutItem

```
Initialize location to position of first item
Set moreToSearch to (have not examined Info(last))
while moreToSearch
    switch (item.ComparedTo(Info(location)))
        case LESS     : Set moreToSearch to false
        case EQUAL    : // Cannot happen because item is not in list.
        case GREATER : Set location to Next(location)
                       Set moreToSearch to (have not examined Info(last))
for index going from length DOWNTO location + 1
    Set Info(index ) to Info(index – 1)
Set Info(location) to item
Increment length
```

Recall that the preconditions on `PutItem` state that the `item` is not already present in the list, so we do not need to have `EQUAL` as a label in the *switch* statement. Translating the list notation into the array-based implementation gives us the following function:

```
void SortedType::PutItem(ItemType item)
{
  bool moreToSearch;
  int location = 0;

  moreToSearch = (location < length);
```

```
    while (moreToSearch)
    {
      switch (item.ComparedTo(info[location]))
      {
        case LESS    : moreToSearch = false;
                       break;
        case GREATER : location++;
                       moreToSearch = (location < length);
                       break;
      }
    }
    for (int index = length; index > location; index--)
      info[index] = info[index - 1];
    info[location] = item;
    length++;
}
```

Does this function work if the new element belongs at the beginning or the end of the list? Draw a picture to confirm for yourself how the function works in each case.

`DeleteItem` Function When discussing the function `DeleteItem` for the Unsorted List ADT, we commented that if the list was sorted, we would have to move the elements up one position to cover the one being removed. Moving the elements up one position is the mirror image of moving the elements down one position. The loop control for finding the item to delete is the same as for the unsorted version.

```
Initialize location to position of first item
Set found to false
while NOT found
    switch (item.ComparedTo(Info(location)))
        case GREATER : Set location to Next(location)
        case LESS    : // Cannot happen because list is sorted.
        case EQUAL   : Set found to true
for index going from location + 1 TO length – 1
    Set Info(index – 1) to Info(index)
Decrement length
```

Examine this algorithm carefully and convince yourself that it is correct. Try cases where you are deleting the first item and the last one.

```
void SortedType::DeleteItem(ItemType item)
{
  int location = 0;

  while (item.ComparedTo(info[location]) != EQUAL)
    location++;
  for (int index = location + 1; index < length; index++)
    info[index - 1] = info[index];
  length--;
}
```

Improving the `GetItem` Function If the list is not sorted, the only way to search for a value is to start at the beginning and look at each item in the list, comparing the key member of the item for which we are searching to the key member of each item in the list in turn. We used this algorithm in the `GetItem` operation in the Unsorted List ADT.

If the list is sorted by key value, there are two ways to improve the searching algorithm. The first way is to stop when we pass the place where the item would be found if it were present. Look at Figure 4.2a. If you are searching for Chris, a comparison with Judy would show that Chris is `LESS`. Thus you have passed the place where Chris would be found if it were present. At this point you can stop and return `found` as `false`. Figure 4.2b shows what happens when you are searching for Susy: `location` is equal to `4`, `moreToSearch` is `false`, and `found` is `false`.

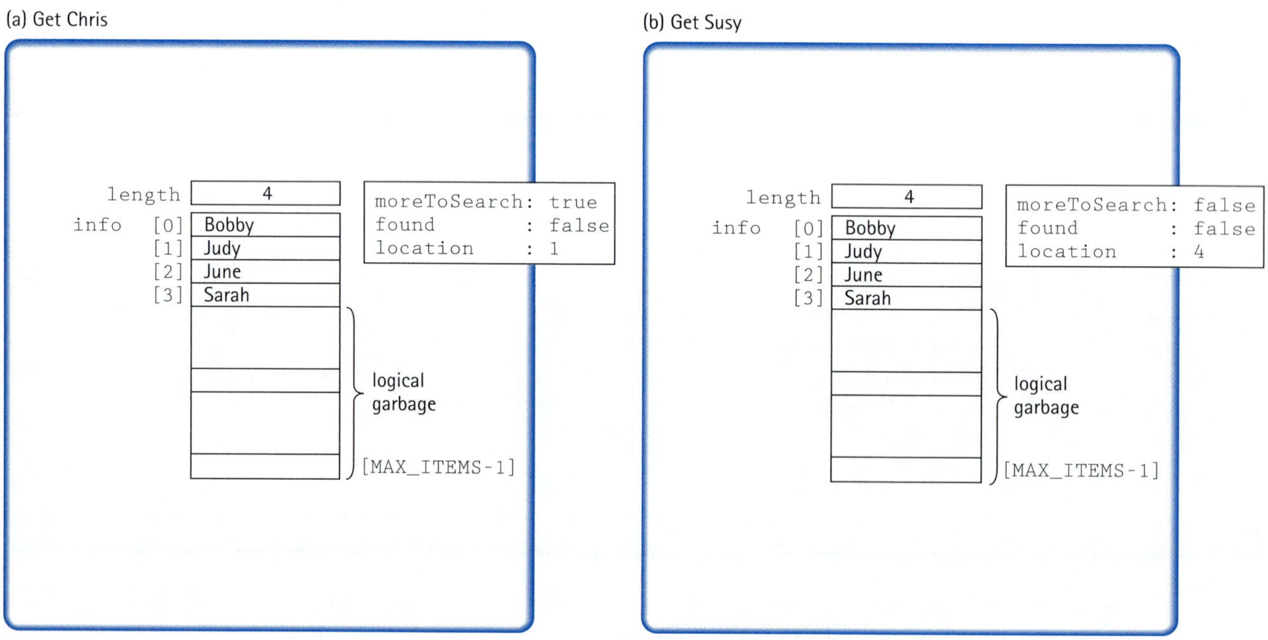

Figure 4.2 *Getting an item from a sorted list*

If the item we seeking appears in the list, the search is the same for both the unsorted list and the sorted list. When the item is *not* there, however, the new algorithm is better. We do not have to search all of the items to confirm that the one we want is not present. When the list is sorted, however, we can improve the algorithm even more.

Binary Search Algorithm We mentioned this algorithm in Chapter 1. Let's work through it carefully; it is a very important algorithm. Think of how you might go about finding a name in a phone book, and you can get an idea of a faster way to search. Let's look for the name "David." We open the phone book to the middle and see that the names there begin with M. M is larger than D, so we search the first half of the phone book, the section that contains A to M. We turn to the middle of the first half and see that the names there begin with G. G is larger than D, so we search the first half of this section, from A to G. We turn to the middle page of this section, and find that the names there begin with C. C is smaller than D, so we search the second half of this section—that is, from D to G—and so on, until we reach the single page that contains "David." Figure 4.3 illustrates this algorithm.

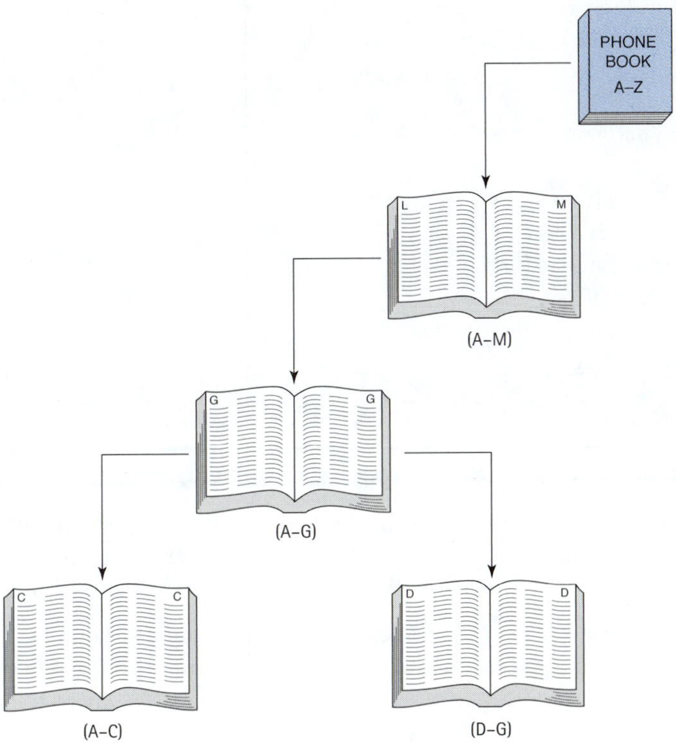

Figure 4.3 *A binary search of the phone book*

We begin our search with the whole list to examine; that is, our current search area goes from `info[0]` through `info[length - 1]`. In each iteration, we split the current search area in half at the midpoint; if the item is not found there, we search the appropriate half. The part of the list being searched at any time is the *current search area*. For instance, in the first iteration of the loop, if a comparison shows that the item comes before the element at the midpoint, the new current search area goes from index 0 through the midpoint – 1. If the item comes after the element at the midpoint, the new current search area goes from the midpoint + 1 through index `length - 1`. Either way, the current search area has been split in half. We can keep track of the boundaries of the current search area with a pair of indexes, `first` and `last`. In each iteration of the loop, if an element with the same key as `item` is not found, one of these indexes is reset to shrink the size of the current search area.

How do we know when to quit searching? Two terminating conditions are possible: `item` is not in the list and `item` has been found. The first terminating condition occurs when there's no more to search in the current search area. The second terminating condition occurs when `item` has been found.

```
Set first to 0
Set last to length – 1
Set found to false
Set moreToSearch to (first <= last)
while moreToSearch AND NOT found
    Set midPoint to (first + last) / 2
    switch (item.ComparedTo(Info[midPoint]))
        case LESS     : Set last to midPoint – 1
                        Set moreToSearch to (first <= last)
        case GREATER  : Set first to midPoint + 1
                        Set moreToSearch to (first <= last)
        case EQUAL    : Set found to true
return item
```

Notice that when we look in the lower half or upper half of the search area, we can ignore the midpoint because we know it is not there. Therefore, `last` is set to `midPoint - 1`, or `first` is set to `midPoint + 1`. The coded version of our algorithm follows:

```
ItemType SortedType::GetItem(ItemType item, bool& found)
{
  int midPoint;
  int first = 0;
  int last = length - 1;
```

```
  bool moreToSearch = first <= last;
  found = false;
  while (moreToSearch && !found)
  {
    midPoint = (first + last) / 2;
    switch (item.ComparedTo(info[midPoint]))
    {
      case LESS    : last = midPoint - 1;
                     moreToSearch = first <= last;
                     break;
      case GREATER : first = midPoint + 1;
                     moreToSearch = first <= last;
                     break;
      case EQUAL   : found = true;
                     item = info[midPoint];
                     break;
    }
  }
  return item;
}
```

Let's do a walk-through of the binary search algorithm. We are searching for the item "bat." Figure 4.4a shows the values of `first`, `last`, and `midPoint` during the first

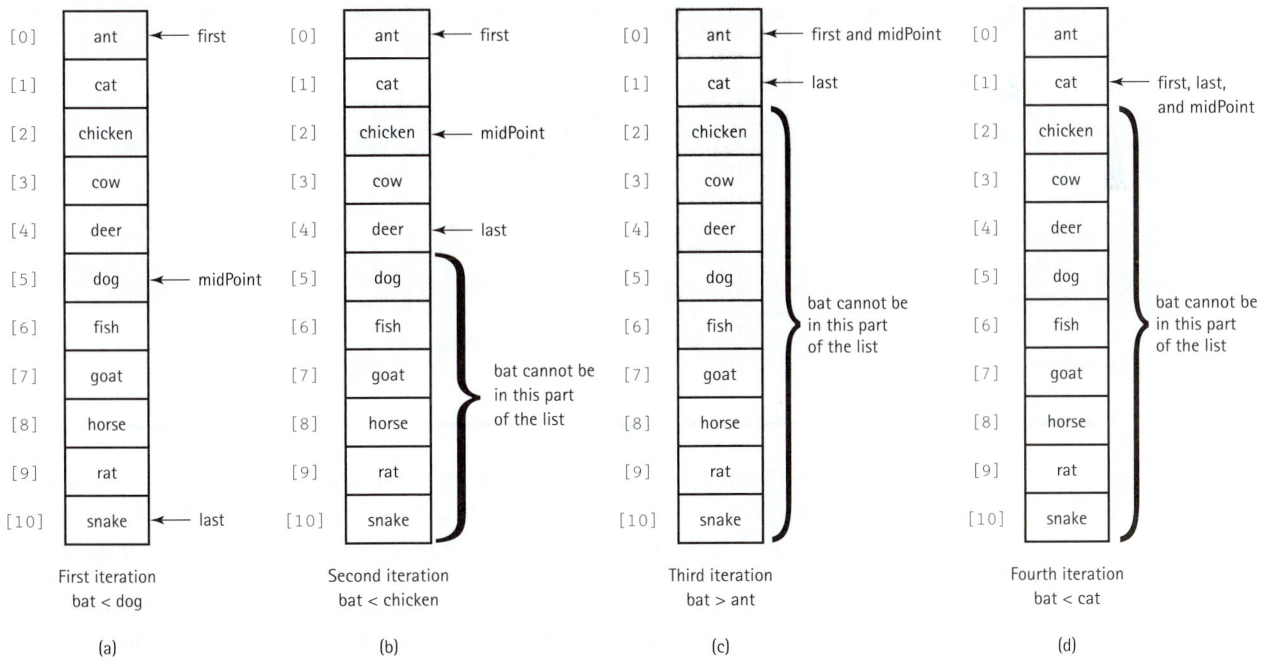

Figure 4.4 *Trace of the binary search algorithm*

iteration. In this iteration, "bat" is compared with "dog," the value in `info[midpoint]`. Because "bat" is less than (comes before) "dog," `last` becomes `midPoint - 1` and `first` stays the same. Figure 4.4b shows the situation during the second iteration. This time, "bat" is compared with "chicken," the value in `info[midpoint]`. Because "bat" is less than (comes before) "chicken," `last` becomes `midPoint - 1` and `first` again stays the same.

In the third iteration (Figure 4.4c), `midPoint` and `first` are both 0. The item "bat" is compared with "ant," the item in `info[midpoint]`. Because "bat" is greater than (comes after) "ant," `first` becomes `midPoint + 1`. In the fourth iteration (Figure 4.4d), `first`, `last`, and `midPoint` are all the same. Again, "bat" is compared with the item in `info[middle]`. Because "bat" is less than "cat," `last` becomes `midPoint - 1`. Now that `last` is less than `first`, the process stops; `found` is `false`.

The binary search is the most complex algorithm that we have examined so far. Table 4.1 shows `first`, `last`, `midPoint`, and `info[midpoint]` for searches of the items "fish," "snake," and "zebra," using the same data as in the previous example. Examine the results in Table 4.1 carefully.

Table 4.1 *Iteration Trace of the Binary Search Algorithm*

Iteration	first	last	midPoint	info[midPoint]	Terminating Condition
item: fish					
First	0	10	5	dog	
Second	6	10	8	horse	
Third	6	7	6	fish	found is true
item: snake					
First	0	10	5	dog	
Second	6	10	8	horse	
Third	9	10	9	rat	
Fourth	10	10	10	snake	found is true
item: zebra					
First	0	10	5	dog	
Second	6	10	8	horse	
Third	9	10	9	rat	
Fourth	10	10	10	snake	
Fifth	11	10			last < first

Notice that the loop never executes more than four times. It never executes more than four times in a list of 11 components because the list is cut in half each time through the loop. Table 4.2 compares a linear search and a binary search in terms of the average number of iterations needed to find an item.

If the binary search is so much faster, why not use it all the time? It is certainly faster in terms of the number of times through the loop, but more computations are executed

Table 4.2 *Comparison of Linear and Binary Search*

	Average Number of Iterations	
Length	Linear Search	Binary Search
10	5.5	2.9
100	50.5	5.8
1,000	500.5	9.0
10,000	5000.5	12.4

within the binary search loop than in the other search algorithms. If the number of components in the list is small (say, less than 20), the linear search algorithms are faster because they perform less work at each iteration. As the number of components in the list increases, however, the binary search algorithm becomes relatively more efficient. Always remember that the binary search requires the list to be sorted and sorting takes time.

Here is the implementation file for class `SortedType` with reduced documentation. As the specification file is the same as the one for the unsorted list, we do not repeat it.

```
// Implementation file for sorted.h

#include "sorted.h"
SortedType::SortedType()
{
  length = 0;
}

void SortedType::MakeEmpty()
{
  length = 0;
}

bool SortedType::IsFull() const
{
  return (length == MAX_ITEMS);
}

int SortedType::GetLength() const
{
  return length;
}
```

```
ItemType SortedType::GetItem(ItemType item, bool& found)
{
  // Binary search algorithm is used.
  int midPoint;
  int first = 0;
  int last = length - 1;

  bool moreToSearch = first <= last;
  found = false;
   while (moreToSearch && !found)
  {
    midPoint = ( first + last) / 2;
    switch (item.ComparedTo(info[midPoint]))
    {
      case LESS    : last = midPoint - 1;
                     moreToSearch = first <= last;
                     break;
      case GREATER : first = midPoint + 1;
                     moreToSearch = first <= last;
                     break;
      case EQUAL   : found = true;
                     item = info[midPoint];
                     break;
    }
  }
  return item;
}

void SortedType::DeleteItem(ItemType item)
{
  int location = 0;

  while (item.ComparedTo(info[location]) != EQUAL)
    location++;
  for (int index = location + 1; index < length; index++)
    info[index - 1] = info[index];
  length--;
}

void SortedType::PutItem(ItemType item)
```

```
{
  bool moreToSearch;
  int location = 0;

  moreToSearch = (location < length);
  while (moreToSearch)
  {
    switch (item.ComparedTo(info[location]))
    {
      case LESS    : moreToSearch = false;
                     break;
      case GREATER : location++;
                     moreToSearch = (location < length);
                     break;
    }
  }
  for (int index = length; index > location; index--)
    info[index] = info[index - 1];
  info[location] = item;
  length++;
}

void SortedType::ResetList()
// Post: currentPos has been initialized.
{
  currentPos = -1;
}

ItemType SortedType::GetNextItem()
// Post: item is current item.
//       Current position has been updated.
{
  currentPos++;
  return info[currentPos];
}
```

Test Plan We can use the same test plan that we employed with the unsorted list with the expected outputs changed to reflect the ordering. We need to modify the items to be deleted to reflect where the items fall in the list; that is, we need to delete one from each end as well as from in the middle.

Operation to Be Tested and Description of Action	Input Values	Expected Output
Constructor		
print `getLength`		0
`PutItem`		
Put four items and print	5, 7, 6, 9	5 6 7 9
Put item and print	1	1 5 6 7 9
`GetItem`		
Get 4 and print whether found		Item is not found
Get 1 and print whether found		Item is found
Get 9 and print whether found		Item is found
Get 10 and print whether found		Item is not found
`IsFull`		
Invoke (list is full)		List is full
Delete 5 and invoke		List is not full
`DeleteItem`		
Delete 1 and print		7 6 9
Delete 6 and print		7 9
Delete 9 and print		7

File `SlistType.in` contains the input to `listDr.cpp` (the test driver) that reflects this test plan; `SlistType.out` and `SlistTest.screen` contain the output. The UML diagram for `SortedType` is identical to that for the `UnsortedType`, except for the name of the class.

SortedType

`-length: int`
`-currentPos: int`
`-listData: array`

`+SortedType()`
`+MakeEmpty(): void`
`+GetLength(): int`
`+IsFull(): bool`
`+RetrieveItem(item:ItemType,`
`  found: bool&): ItemType`
`+PutItem(item:ItemType): void`
`+DeleteItem(item:ItemType): void`
`+ResetList(): void`
`+GetNextItem(): ItemType`

4.2 Dynamically Allocated Arrays

Wouldn't it be nice if we could find a technique for the client to be able to specify the maximum number of items on the list at run time? And of course, we wouldn't be asking if C++ didn't provide a way. We can let the maximum number of items be a parameter to a class constructor. But the implementation structure is an array, and doesn't the compiler need to know at compile time what the size of an array is to be? Yes, it does if the array is in static storage, but memory for the array can be allocated at run time *if we let it be in dynamic storage (the free store or heap)*. This change requires the following changes in the class definition:

```
{
public:
  SortedType(int max);      // max is maximum list size
  SortedType();             // Default size is 500
  // Rest of the prototypes go here.
private:
  int length;
  int maxList;              // Maximum number of list items
  ItemType* info;           // Pointer to dynamically allocated memory
  int currentPos;
};
```

When declaring a class object, the client can specify the maximum number of list items by using the parameterized constructor:

```
SortedType myList(100);
// List of at most 100 items.
```

Or the client can accept the default size of 500 by using the default constructor:

```
SortedType yourList;
```

Within the function definition for each constructor, the idea is to use the `new` operator to allocate an array of exactly the desired size. Earlier we saw that the expression `new SomeType` allocates a single variable of type `SomeType` on the free store and returns a pointer to it. To allocate an array, you attach to the data type name the array size in brackets: `new AnotherType[size]`. In this case, the `new` operator returns the base address of the newly allocated array. Here are the implementations of the `SortedType` constructors:

```
SortedType::SortedType(int max)
{
  maxList = max;
  length = 0;
  info = new ItemType[maxList];
}
SortedType::SortedType()
{
  maxList = 500;
  length = 0;
  info = new ItemType[maxList];
}
```

Notice that `info` is now a pointer variable, not an array name. It points to the first element of a dynamically allocated array. However, a basic fact in C++ is that you can attach an index expression to any pointer—not only an array name—as long as the pointer points to an array. Therefore `info` can be indexed exactly as it was when it was defined as an array of type `ItemType` (see Figure 4.5). Thus, only one member function needs to be changed: `IsFull`.

```
bool SortedType::IsFull()
{
  return (lenth == maxList);
}
```

We do need to use a class destructor. When the list goes out of scope, the memory allocated to `top`, `maxList`, and `items` is deallocated, but the array that `items` points to is not. To deallocate an array, insert brackets between the word `delete` and the name of the pointer.

```
SortedType::~SortedType()
{
  delete [] info;
}
```

Before we leave this `SortedType` implementation, let's ask if it's necessary to provide both a parameterized constructor and a default constructor. Isn't the parameterized constructor good enough? In most cases, yes. However, the user may want to declare an array of list objects, in which case the parameterized constructor cannot be used. (Remember the rule: If a class has any constructors at all and an array of class objects is declared, one of the constructors must be the default constructor, and it is invoked for

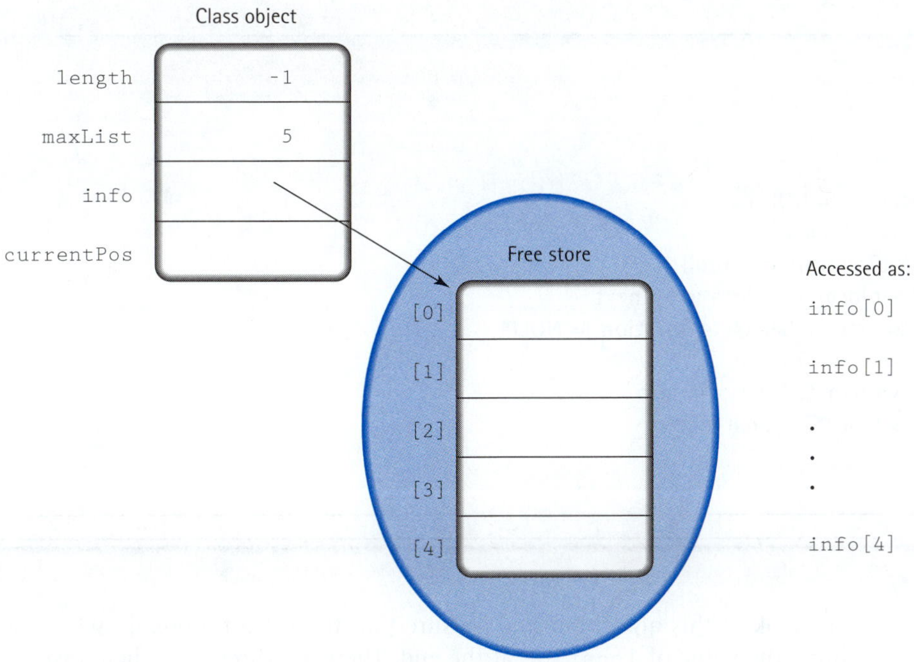

Figure 4.5 *A list in which the array is in dynamic storage*

each element in the array.) Therefore, it's wisest to include a default constructor in the SortedType class to allow client code like this:

```
SortedType SortedGroup[10];
// 10 sorted lists, each of size 500.
```

4.3 Implementing the Sorted List as a Linked Structure

When writing the array-based implementation of the Sorted List ADT, we found that we had to change only PutItem and DeleteItem from the Unsorted List versions, but that GetItem could be made more efficient. Because both PutItem and DeleteItem must search the list, let's look at GetItem first.

Function GetItem

For the unsorted version, we took the array-based algorithm and changed the array notation to linked notation. Let's try that approach again.

```
GetItem
Set location to listData
Set found to false
Set moreToSearch to (location != NULL)
while moreToSearch AND NOT found
    switch (item.ComparedTo(location->info))
        case GREATER : Set location to location->next
                       Set moreToSearch to (location != NULL)
        case EQUAL   : Set found to true
                       Set item to location->info
        case LESS    : Set moreToSearch to false
return item
```

Let's look at this algorithm and be sure that the substitutions do what we want by examining the value of `location` at the end. There are three cases here instead of two:

1. *`location` = `NULL`*. If we reach the end of the list without finding an item whose key is equal to `item`'s key, then the item is not in the list. `location` correctly has the value `NULL` (see Figure 4.6a, assuming the people's names are in alphabetical order).
2. *`item.ComparedTo(location->info)` = `EQUAL`*. In this case, we have found the element within the list and have copied it into `item` (see Figure 4.6b, assuming the people's names are in alphabetical order).

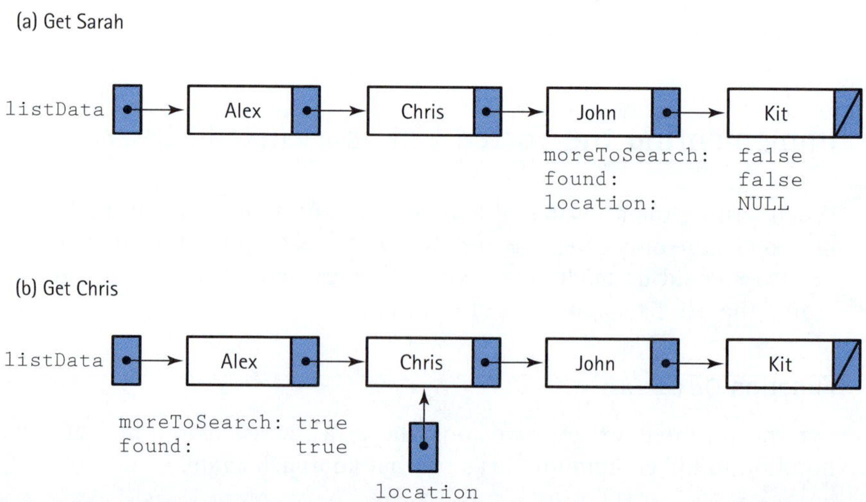

Figure 4.6 *Getting an item in a sorted linked list*

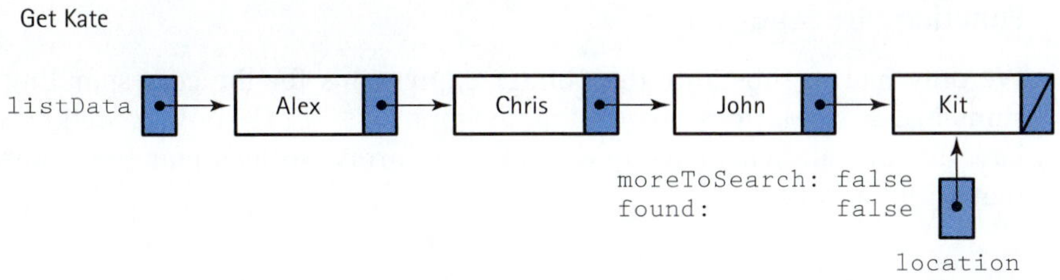

Figure 4.7 *Getting an item that is not there*

3. *item.ComparedTo(location->info) = LESS*. In this case, we have passed the location where the item belongs, so it isn't in the list (see Figure 4.7).

Having looked at all three cases, we can again code this algorithm, being reasonably confident that it is correct. We use the relational operators here as well.

```
ItemType SortedType::GetItem(ItemType item,
     bool& found)
{
  bool moreToSearch;
  NodeType* location;

  location = listData;
  found = false;
  moreToSearch = (location != NULL);

  while (moreToSearch && !found)
  {
    if (location->info < item)
    {
      location = location->next;
      moreToSearch = (location != NULL);
    }
    else if (item == location->info)
    {
      found = true;
      item = location->info;
    }
    else
      moreToSearch = false;
  }
  return item;
}
```

Function `PutItem`

We only had to substitute the pointer expressions for the corresponding index expressions in `GetItem`. Does this technique work for `PutItem`? Well, we know that we don't have to shift any elements as we did in an array, so let's make the substitutions up to that point and see.

```
PutItem
Set location to listData
Set moreToSearch to (location != NULL)
while moreToSearch
    switch (item.ComparedTo(location->info))
        case GREATER : Set location to location->next
                       Set moreToSearch to (location != NULL)
        case LESS    : Set moreToSearch to false
⋮
```

When we exit the loop, `location` is pointing to the location where `item` goes. That's correct. (See Figure 4.7.) We just need to get a new node, put `item` into the `info` member, put `location` into the `next` member, and put the address of the new node in the `next` member of the node before it (the node containing John). *Oops! We don't have a pointer to the node before it.* We must keep track of the previous pointer as well as the current pointer. When a similar problem arose with `DeleteItem` in the unsorted version, we compared one item ahead (`(location->next)->info`). Can we do that here? No. We could use that technique because we knew that the item for which we were searching was present in the list. Here we know that the item for which we are searching is *not* in the list. If the new item was supposed to go at the end of the list, this algorithm would crash because `location->next` would be `NULL`. (See Figure 4.8.)

We could change the way of determining `moreToSearch`, but an easier method for handling this situation exists. We use two pointers to search the list, with one pointer always trailing one node behind. We call the previous pointer `predLoc` and let it trail

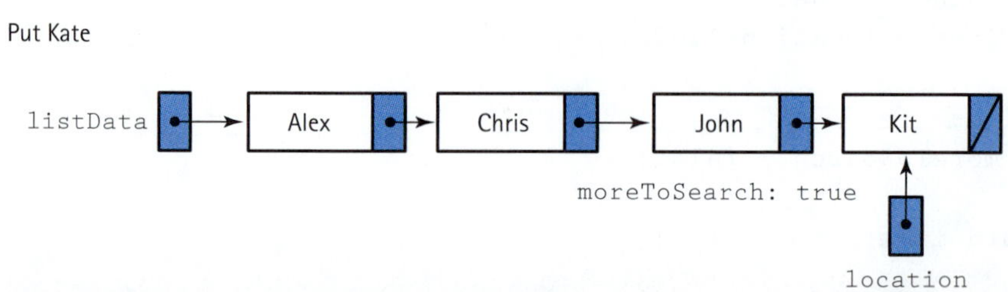

Figure 4.8 *Putting at the end of the list*

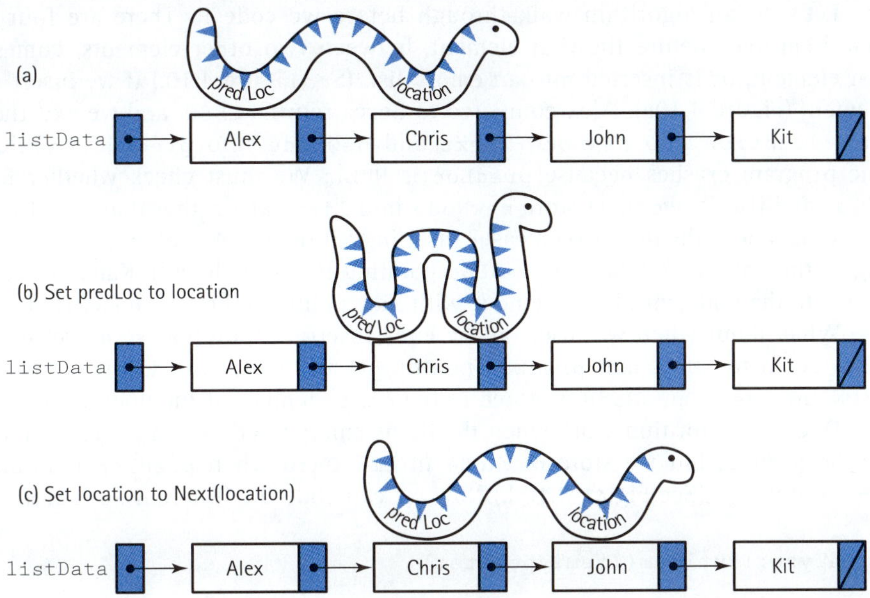

Figure 4.9 *The inchworm effect*

one node behind `location`. When `ComparedTo` returns `GREATER`, we advance both pointers. As Figure 4.9 shows, the process resembles the movement of an inchworm. `predLoc` (the tail of the inchworm) catches up with `location` (the head), and then `location` advances. Because no node precedes the first one, we initialize `predLoc` to `NULL`. Now let's summarize these thoughts in an algorithm:

PutItem(item) Revised

```
Set location to listData
Set predLoc to NULL
Set moreToSearch to (location != NULL)
while moreToSearch
    switch (item.ComparedTo(location->info))
        case GREATER : Set predLoc to location
                       Set location to location->next
                       Set moreToSearch to (location != NULL)
        case LESS    : Set moreToSearch to false
Set newNode to the address of a newly allocated node
Set newNode->info to item
Set newNode->next to location
Set predLoc->next to newNode
Increment length
```

Let's do an algorithm walk-through before we code it. There are four cases: the new item goes before the first element, between two other elements, comes after the last element, or is inserted into an empty list. (See Figure 4.10.) If we insert at the first element (Figure 4.10a), Alex compared to Becca returns `LESS`, and we exit the loop. We store `location` into `newNode->next` and `newNode` into `predLoc->next`. Whoops! The program crashes because `predLoc` is `NULL`. We must check whether `predLoc` is `NULL`, and if it is, we must store `newNode` into `listData` rather than `predLoc->next`.

What about the in-between case? Inserting Kit (Figure 4.10b) leaves `location` pointing to the node with Lila and `predLoc` pointing to the node with Kate. `newNode->next` points to the node with Lila; the node with Kate points to the new node. That's fine.

What about when we insert at the end? Inserting Kate (Figure 4.10c) leaves `location` equal to `NULL`, and `predLoc` pointing to the node with Chris. `NULL` is stored in `newNode->next`; `newNode` is stored in the `next` member of the node containing Chris.

Does the algorithm work when the list is empty? Let's see. `location` and `predLoc` are both `NULL`, but we store `newNode` in `listData` when `predLoc` is `NULL`, so there isn't a problem. (See Figure 4.10d.) Now we can code the function `PutItem`.

```
void SortedType::PutItem(ItemType item)
{
  NodeType* newNode;  // Pointer to node being inserted.
  NodeType* predLoc;  // Trailing pointer.
  NodeType* location; // Traveling pointer.
  bool moreToSearch;
  location = listData;
  predLoc = NULL;
  moreToSearch = (location != NULL);

  // Find insertion point.
  while (moreToSearch)
  {
    if (location->info < item)
    {
      predLoc = location;
      location = location->next;
      moreToSearch = (location != NULL);
    }
    else
      moreToSearch = false;
  }

  // Prepare node for insertion.
  newNode = new NodeType;
```

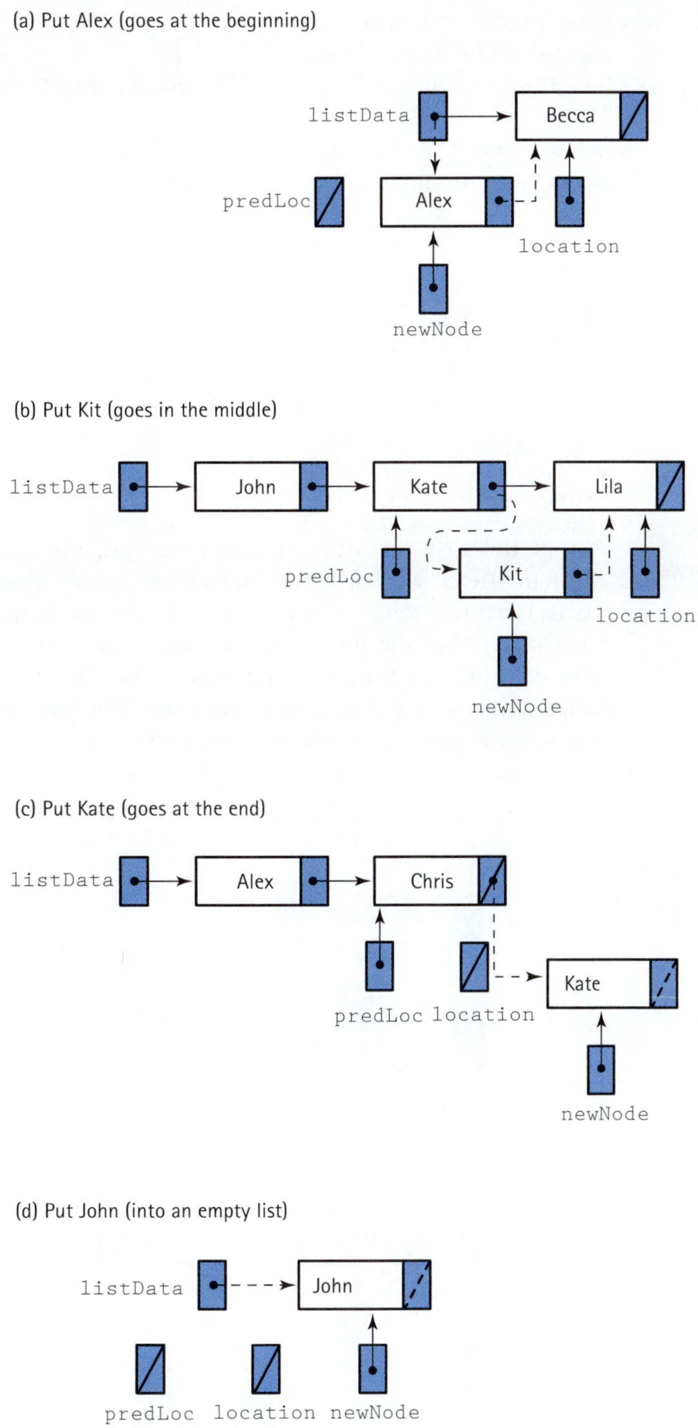

Figure 4.10 *Four insertion cases*

```
    newNode->info = item;
    // Insert node into list.
    if (predLoc == NULL)          // Insert as first.
    {
      newNode->next = listData;
      listData = newNode;
    }
    else
    {
      newNode->next = location;
      predLoc->next = newNode;
    }
    length++;
  }
```

Function DeleteItem

As in the case of GetItem and PutItem, the DeleteItem algorithm begins with a search. Here we exit the searching loop when item.ComparedTo(location->info) returns EQUAL. Once we have found the item, we delete it. Because our precondition states that the item to be deleted is present in the list, we have a choice. We can use the unsorted list algorithm exactly as it is or we can write an algorithm that is the mirror image of the insertion. We leave the coding of the new algorithm to you as an exercise. Figure 4.11 illustrates the four cases that occur.

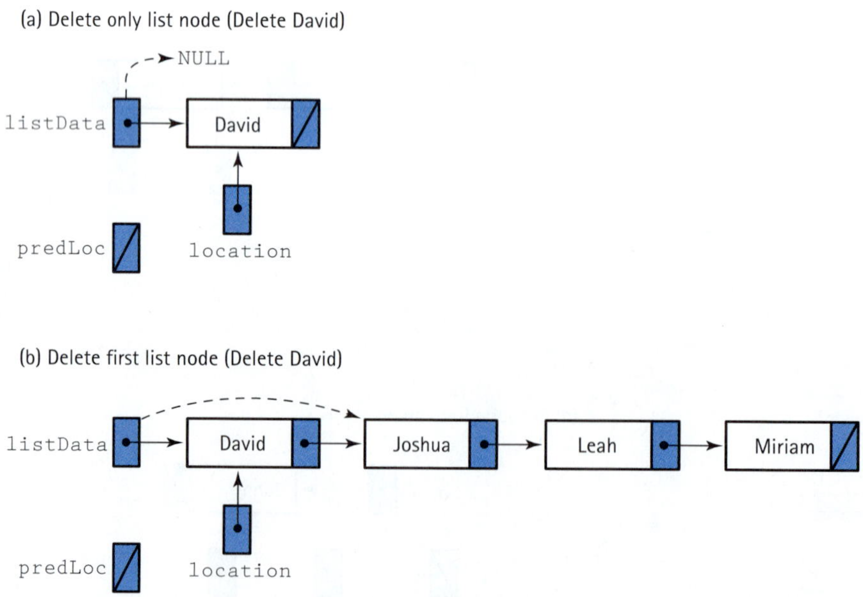

Figure 4.11 *Deleting from a linked list*

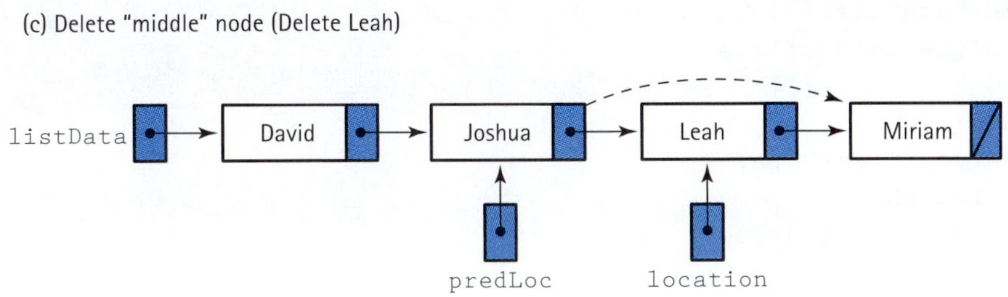

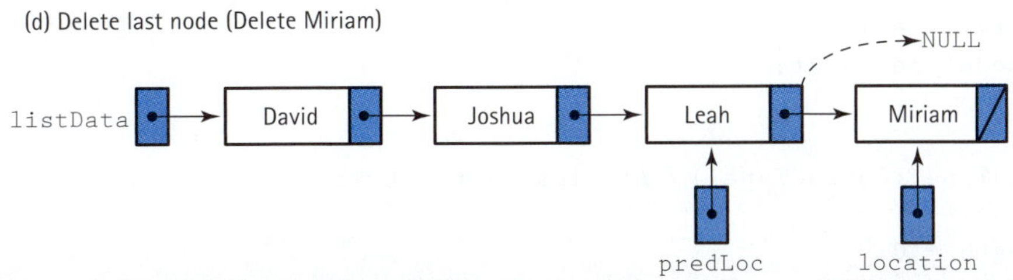

Figure 4.11 *(continued)*

Code

Here are the specification and implementation files for the linked version of class `SortedType`, with reduced documentation. Note that we have included a destructor.

```
#include "ItemType.h"
// Header file for Sorted List ADT.
struct NodeType;

class SortedType
{
public:
  SortedType();      // Class constructor
  ~SortedType();     // Class destructor

  bool IsFull() const;
  int  GetLength() const;
  void MakeEmpty();
  ItemType GetItem(ItemType item, bool& found);
  void PutItem(ItemType item);
  void DeleteItem(ItemType item);
```

```
  void ResetList();
  ItemType GetNextItem();

private:
  NodeType* listData;
  int length;
  NodeType* currentPos;
};
struct NodeType
{
    ItemType info;
    NodeType* next;
};

SortedType::SortedType()  // Class constructor
{
  length = 0;
  listData = NULL;
}

bool SortedType::IsFull() const
{
  NodeType* location;
  try
  {
    location = new NodeType;
    delete location;
    return false;
  }
  catch(bad_alloc exception)
  {
    return true;
  }
}

int SortedType::GetLength() const
{
  return length;
}

void SortedType::MakeEmpty()
{
  NodeType* tempPtr;
```

```
  while (listData != NULL)
  {
    tempPtr = listData;
    listData = listData->next;
    delete tempPtr;
  }
  length = 0;
}

ItemType SortedType::GetItem(ItemType item, bool& found)
{
  bool moreToSearch;
  NodeType* location;

  location = listData;
  found = false;
  moreToSearch = (location != NULL);

  while (moreToSearch && !found)
  {
    switch(item.ComparedTo(loction->info)
    {
      case GREATER: location = location->next;
                    moreToSearch = (location != NULL);
                    break;
      case EQUAL:   found = true;
                    item = location->info;
                    break;
      case LESS:    moreToSearch = false;
                    break;
    }
  }
  return item;
}

void SortedType::PutItem(ItemType item)
{
  NodeType* newNode;       // pointer to node being inserted
  NodeType* predLoc;       // trailing pointer
  NodeType* location;      // traveling pointer
  bool moreToSearch;

  location = listData;
  predLoc = NULL;
  moreToSearch = (location != NULL);
```

```
  // Find insertion point.
  while (moreToSearch)
  {
    switch(item.ComparedTo(location->info))
    {
      case GREATER: predLoc = location;
                    location = location->next;
                    moreToSearch = (location != NULL);
                    break;
      case LESS:    moreToSearch = false;
                    break;
    }
  }

  // Prepare node for insertion.
  newNode = new NodeType;
  newNode->info = item;

  // Insert node into list.
  if (predLoc == NULL)          // Insert as first.
  {
    newNode->next = listData;
    listData = newNode;
  }
  else
  {
    newNode->next = location;
    predLoc->next = newNode;
  }
  length++;
}

void SortedType::DeleteItem(ItemType item)
{
  NodeType* location = listData;
  NodeType* tempLocation;

  // Locate node to be deleted.
  if (item.ComparedTo(listData->info) == EQUAL)
  {
    tempLocation = location;
    listData = listData->next;    // Delete first node.
  }
  else
  {
    while ((item.ComparedTo(location->next)->info) != EQUAL)
```

```
    location = location->next;

   // Delete node at location->next
   tempLocation = location->next;
   location->next = (location->next)->next;
  }
  delete tempLocation;
  length--;
}

void SortedType::ResetList()
{
  currentPos = NULL;
}

ItemType SortedType::GetNextItem()
{
  ItemType item;
  if (currentPos == NULL)
    currentPos = listData;
  item = currentPos->info;
  currentPos = currentPos->next;
  return item;
}

SortedType::~SortedType()
{
  NodeType* tempPtr;

  while (listData != NULL)
  {
    tempPtr = listData;
    listData = listData->next;
    delete tempPtr;
  }
}
```

Comparing Sorted List Implementations

Methods applied to a dynamically allocated array behave exactly the same as those applied to a statically allocated array so we group them together in the following discussion.

We developed three algorithms for `GetItem` in an array-based list: a sequential search, a sequential search with an exit when the place is passed where the item would be if present, and a binary search. The first two have order $O(N)$. What about the binary search algorithm? We showed a table comparing the number of items searched in a linear search versus a binary search for certain sizes of lists. How do we describe this algorithm using Big-O notation? To figure this out, let's see how many times we can split a list of N items in half. Assuming that we don't find the item we are looking for at one of the earlier midpoints, we have to divide the list $\log_2 N$ times at the most, before we run out of elements to split. In case you aren't familiar with logs,

$$2^{\log_2 N} = N$$

That is, if $N = 1024$, $\log_2 N = 10 (2^{10} = 1024)$. How does that apply to our searching algorithms? The sequential search is $O(N)$; in the worst case, we would have to search all 1024 elements of the list. The binary search is $O(\log_2 N)$; in the worst case we would have to make $\log_2 N + 1$, or 11, search comparisons. A heuristic (a rule of thumb) tells us that a problem that is solved by successively splitting it in half is an $O(\log_2 N)$ algorithm. Figure 4.12 illustrates the relative growth of the sequential and binary searches, measured in number of comparisons.

The first two searches can be implemented in a linked list but a binary search cannot. (How do you get directly to the middle of a linked list?) Therefore, the array-based algorithm for searching a list is faster than the linked version if the binary search algorithm is used.

In both sorted list implementations, the `PutItem` function uses a sequential search to find the insertion position; therefore, the search parts of the algorithms have $O(N)$ complexity. The array-based list must also move down all the elements that follow the insertion position to make room for the new element. The number of elements to be moved ranges from 0, when we insert at the end of the list, to `length`, when we insert at the beginning of the list. So the insertion part of the algorithm also has $O(N)$ complexity for the array-based list. Because $O(N) + O(N) = O(N)$, the sequential list's `PutItem` operation has $O(N)$. Even if we used the binary search to find where the item belongs ($O(\log_2 N)$), the items would have to be moved to make room for the new one ($O(N)$). $O(\log_2 N) + O(N)$ is $O(N)$.

The insertion part of the algorithm for the linked list representation simply requires the reassignment of a couple of pointers. This makes the insertion task $O(1)$ for a linked list, which is one of the main advantages of linking. However, adding the insertion task to the search task gives us $O(N) + O(1) = O(N)$—the same Big-O approximation as for the sequential list! Doesn't the linking offer any advantage in efficiency? Perhaps. But

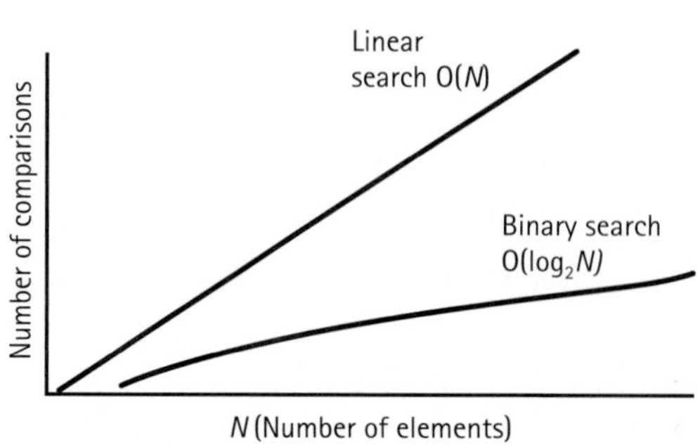

Figure 4.12 *Comparison of linear and binary searches*

remember that the Big-O evaluations are only rough approximations of the amount of work that an algorithm does.

The `DeleteItem` function is similar to `PutItem`. In both implementations, the search task is performed, an $O(N)$ operation. Then the sequential list's delete operation "deletes" the element by moving up all the subsequent elements in the list, which adds $O(N)$. The whole function is $O(N) + O(N)$, or $O(N)$. The linked list deletes the element by unlinking it from the list, which adds $O(1)$ to the search task. The whole function is $O(N) + O(1)$, or $O(N)$. Thus both `DeleteItem` operations are $O(N)$; for large values of N, they are roughly equivalent.

The fact that two operations have the same Big-O measure does not mean that they take the same amount of time to execute, however. The sequential implementation requires, on average, a great deal of data movement for both `PutItem` and `DeleteItem`. Does all this data movement really make any difference? It doesn't matter too much in textbook examples; the lists are very small. If there are 1000 items in a list, however, the data movement starts to add up.

Table 4.3 summarizes the Big-O comparison of the sorted list operations for sequential and linked implementations.

Table 4.3 *Big-O Comparison of Sorted List Operations*

	Array Implementation	Linked Implementation
class constructor	$O(1)$	$O(1)$
MakeEmpty	**$O(1)$**	**$O(N)$**
IsFull	$O(1)$	$O(1)$
GetLength	$O(1)$	$O(1)$
ResetList	$O(1)$	$O(1)$
GetNextItem	$O(1)$	$O(1)$
GetItem	$O(N)$*	$O(N)$
PutItem		
Find	$O(N)$*	$O(N)$
Put	**$O(N)$**	**$O(1)$**
Combined	$O(N)$	$O(N)$
DeleteItem		
Find	$O(N)$*	$O(N)$
Delete	**$O(N)$**	**$O(1)$**
Combined	$O(N)$	$O(N)$

*$O(\log_2 N)$ if a binary search is used.

4.4 Comparison of Unsorted and Sorted List ADT Algorithms

Table 4.4 shows both implementations for both the Unsorted List ADT and the Sorted List ADT.

The big difference in the complexity between the Unsorted List and the Sorted List lies in the insertion algorithm. The Unsorted List is O(1) and the Sorted List is O(N). The array-based and linked insertion into a sorted list are both O(N), but the array-based version is actually O($2N$); we just throw away the constant. Does that mean we should ignore the differences in constants? No; if two algorithms have the same complexity, then you can look at the constants.

Think of the common orders of complexity as being bins into which we sort algorithms (Figure 4.13). For small values of the size factor, an algorithm in one bin may actually be faster than the equivalent algorithm in the next-more-efficient bin. As the size factor increases, the differences among algorithms in the different bins gets larger. When choosing between algorithms within the same bin, you look at the constants to determine which to use.

Table 4.4 *Big-O Comparison of List Operations in Each Implementation*

Function	Unsorted List ADT		Sorted List ADT	
	Array-based	Linked	Array-based	Linked
Class constructor	O(1)	O(1)	O(1)	O(1)
MakeEmpty	O(1)	O(N)	O(1)	O(N)
IsFull	O(1)	O(1)	O(1)	O(1)
GetLength	O(1)	O(1)	O(1)	O(1)
ResetList	O(1)	O(1)	O(1)	O(1)
GetNextItem	O(1)	O(1)	O(1)	O(1)
GetItem	O(N)	O(N)	linear search O(N) binary search O($\log_2 N$)	O(N)
PutItem				
Find	O(1)	O(1)	O(N)	O(N)
Put	O(1)	O(1)	O(N)	O(1)
Combined	O(1)	O(1)	O(N)	O(N)
DeleteItem				
Find	O(N)	O(N)	O(N)	O(N)
Delete	O(1)	O(1)	O(N)	O(1)
Combined	O(N)	O(N)	O(N)	O(N)

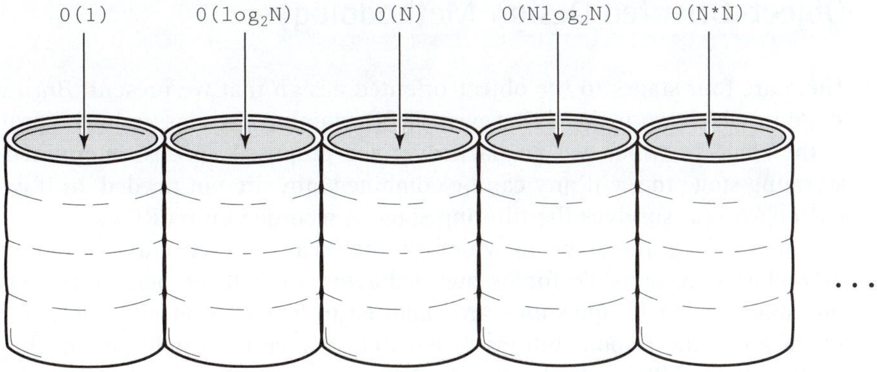

Figure 4.13 *Complexity bins*

4.5 Bounded and Unbounded ADTs

A bounded ADT is one where there is a logical limit on the number of items to be stored in the structure. An unbounded ADT is one where there is no logical limit. We tend to think of array-based structures as being bounded and linked structures as being unbounded. However, this is an implementation interpretation, not a logical one.

Bounded ADT An ADT for which there is a logical limit on the number of items in the structure

Unbounded ADT An ADT for which there is no logical limit on the number of items in the structure

For example, a client may have a reason for knowing that the maximum number of items on a list will never exceed a certain value, that the list is logically bounded. If an attempt to add an additional item is made, the client wants to be notified by having an exception thrown.

Thus far, we have implemented our list ADTs as physically bounded (array-based) or physically unbounded (linked) without regard to the logical issue. We could make an array-based implementation unbounded by having the class increase the size of the array when the array is full and copying the current array elements into the new array. This is easy to do if the array is dynamically allocated. We could make a linked implementation bounded by requiring the client to provide MAX_ITEMS and comparing the length to it before an item is added.

The moral here is that the documentation for an ADT must state whether the implementation is bounded or unbounded. If bounded, the client must have the facility, probably through a constructor, to set the size of the structure, and an exception must be thrown if an attempt to go beyond that size is made. If unbounded, the documentation must state that `IsFull` returns true only if the program runs out of memory. The client then makes a choice of which implementation to use based on whether the ADT is logically bounded or unbounded.

4.6 Object-Oriented Design Methodology

There are four stages to the object-oriented design that we present. *Brainstorming* is the stage in which we make a first pass at determining the classes in the problem. *Filtering* is the stage in which we go back over the proposed classes determined in the brainstorming stage to see if any can be combined, any are not needed, or if any are missing. Each class that survives the filtering stage is recorded on a CRC card.

Scenarios is the stage in which the behavior of each class is determined. Because each class is responsible for its own behavior, we call the behaviors *responsibilities*. In this stage, "what if" questions are explored to be sure that all situations are examined. When all of the responsibilities of each class have been determined, they are recorded on the class's CRC card, along with the names of any other classes with which it must collaborate (interact) to complete its responsibility.

In *Responsibility Algorithms*, the last stage, we write the algorithms for each of the responsibilities outlined on the CRC cards. Now you can see where the term CRC comes from: Class, Responsibility, and Collaboration.

Although these techniques are designed to be applied in groups, we can apply them to our own individual thought processes as well, so let's look at each of these stages in a little more detail.

Brainstorming

Just exactly what is *brainstorming*? The dictionary defines it as a group problem-solving technique that involves the spontaneous contribution of ideas from all members of the group.[1] Brainstorming brings to mind a movie or TV show where a group of bright young people toss around ideas about an advertising slogan for the latest revolutionary product. This picture seems at odds with the traditional picture of a computer analyst working alone in a closed, windowless office for days who finally jumps up shouting "Ah ha!" As computers have become more powerful, the problems that can be solved have become more and more complex, and the picture of the genius locked in a windowless room has become obsolete. Solutions to complex problems need new and innovative solutions based on collective "Ah ha!"s.

Belin and Simone list four principles of successful brainstorming.[2] First and foremost, all ideas are potential good ideas. It is imperative that the members of the group don't censor their own ideas or make judgments out of hand on other's ideas. The next principle relates to pace: Think fast and furiously first, and ponder later. The faster the pace at first, the better the creative juices flow. Thirdly, give every voice a turn. To slow down those predisposed to hog the conversation and spur those reluctant to talk, use a rotation. Continue the pattern until team members are truly forced to "pass" because they are out of ideas. Lastly, a little humor can be a powerful force. Humor helps convert a random group into a cohesive team.

---

[1] *Webster's New Collegiate Dictionary.*

[2] Belin, D. and Simone S. S. *The CRC Card Book.* Addison-Wesley. 1997.

In the context of object-oriented problem solving, brainstorming is a group activity designed to produce a list of candidate classes to be used to solve a particular problem. Belin and Simone point out that although each project is different and each team has a different personality, the following four steps are a good general approach.

Step 1 is to review brainstorming principles at the beginning of the meeting to remind everyone that this is a group activity and personal style should be put aside.

Step 2 is to state specific session objectives such as: "Today we want to come up with a list of candidate classes for the student project." or "Today we want to determine the classes that are active during the registration phase."

Step 3 is to use a round-robin technique to allow the group to proceed at an even tempo but give people enough time to think. Each person should contribute a possible object class to the list. A facilitator should keep the discussion on target, and a scribe should take notes. The brainstorming stops when each person in the group has to "pass" because he or she cannot think of another class to suggest.

Step 4 of Belin and Simone's process is to discuss the classes and select the ones that belong in the final list. We prefer to think of this stage as separate from brainstorming and discuss it in the next section.

Just as the people brainstorming for an advertising slogan know something of the product before the session, brainstorming for classes requires that the participants know something about the problem. Each participant should be familiar with the requirements document and any correspondence relating to the technical aspects of the project. If there seem to be ambiguities, participants should conduct interviews to clarify these points before the brainstorming sessions. Each team member should enter the brainstorming sessions with a clear understanding of the problem to be solved. No doubt during the preparation, each team member will have generated his/her own preliminary list of classes.

Filtering

The brainstorming session produces a tentative list of classes. The next phase is to take the tentative list of classes and determine which are the core classes in the problem solution. There may be two classes on the list that are actually the same thing. These duplicate classes usually arise because people within different parts of an organization use different names for the same concept or entity. There may be two classes in the list that have many common attributes and behaviors. The common parts should be gathered together into a super class with the two classes deriving the common properties and adding the properties that are different.

There may be classes that really don't belong in the problem solution. For example, if we are simulating a calculator, we might list the user as a possible class. However, the user is not within the simulation as a class; the user is an entity outside the problem that provides input to the simulation. Another possible class might be the *on* button. However, a little thought shows that the *on* button is not part of the simulation; it is what starts the simulation program running.

As the filtering is complete, CRC cards should be written for each of the classes that have survived to this stage.

Scenarios

The goal of this phase is to assign responsibilities to each class. What are responsibilities? They are the tasks that each class must perform. Responsibilities are eventually implemented as subprograms. At this stage we are interested only in *what* the tasks are, not in how they might be carried out.

There are two types of responsibilities: what a class must know about itself (knowledge) and what a class must be able to do (behavior). A class *encapsulates* its data (knowledge); objects in one class cannot directly access data in another class. Encapsulation is a key to abstraction. However, each class has the responsibility of making data (knowledge) available to other classes that need it. Therefore, each class has responsibility for knowing the things about itself that others need to know.

For example, a student class should "know" or "get" its name and address. Although the responsibilities for this knowledge might be called *get name* and *get address*, whether the address is kept in the student class or whether the student class must ask some other class to access the address is irrelevant at this stage. The important fact is that the student class is able to access and return (get) its own address.

The responsibilities for behavior look more like the tasks we described in top-down design. For example, a responsibility might be for the student class to calculate its GPA (grade point average). In top-down design, we would say that a task is to calculate the GPA given the data. In object-oriented design, we say that the student class is responsible for calculating its own GPA. The distinction is both subtle and profound. The final code for the calculation may look the same, but it is executed in different ways. In an imperative program, the program calls the subprogram that calculates the GPA, passing the student object as a parameter. In an object-oriented program, a message is sent to the object of the class to calculate its GPA. There are no parameters because the object to which the message is sent knows its own data.

> **Scenario** A sequence of steps that describes an interaction between a client and an application or program

How do we go about determining the responsibilities? The name for this phase gives a clue as to how to go about assigning responsibilities to classes. For our purposes, a **scenario** is a sequence of steps that describes an interaction between a client (user) and an application or program.

Here is how the process works. The team uses play acting to test different scenarios. Each member of the team plays the role of one of the classes. Scenarios are "what if" scripts that allow participants to act out different situations. When a class has been sent a message, the actor holds up the CRC card and responds to the message sending messages to others as needed. As the scripts are being acted out, missing responsibilities are unearthed and unneeded responsibilities are detected. Sometimes the need for new classes surfaces. Although waving cards in the air when "you" are active may be a little embarrassing at first, team members quickly get into the spirit of the action, when they see how effective the technique is. (See Figure 4.14.)

The output from this phase is a set of CRC cards representing the core classes in the problem solution. The responsibilities for each class are listed on the card, along with the classes with which a responsibility must collaborate.

Figure 4.14 *A scenario walk-through in progress*

The formal methodology that incorporates UML diagrams calls a collection of scenarios related to a common goal a use case. A use case diagram is now part of UML. In this text, we prefer to keep our discussion of scenarios informal.

Use case A collection of scenarios related to a common goal

Responsibility Algorithms

Eventually, the algorithms must be written for the responsibilities. Because of the process of focusing on data rather than actions in the object-oriented view of design, the algorithms for carrying out responsibilities tend to be fairly short. For example, the knowledge responsibilities usually just return the contents of one of an object's variables, or send a message to another object to retrieve it. Action responsibilities are a little more complicated, often involving calculations. Thus, the top-down method of designing an algorithm is usually appropriate for designing many responsibility algorithms.

Final Word

To summarize, top-down design methods focus on the *process* of transforming the input into the output, resulting in a hierarchy of tasks. Object-oriented design focuses on the *data objects* that are to be transformed, resulting in a hierarchy of objects. The nouns in the problem description become objects; the verbs become operations. In a top-down design, the verbs are the primary focus; in an object-oriented design, the nouns are the primary focus.

The methodology that we have described makes use of the CRC card. This card is simply a notational device to help you organize your classes; its use is not a methodology.

Case Study

Evaluating Card Hands

Problem In the last chapter we developed classes `Card`, which represented a playing card, and `Deck`, which represented a collection of 52 playing cards. Now we are ready to take the next step. Many card games such as Spades, Hearts, Bridge, and Poker all have one thing in common: They require a random subset of a deck of cards, called a *hand.* The different games examine a hand and evaluate it in some way.

Our current task is first to divide the deck into hands. When this is complete, we will evaluate hands for Texas Holdem, a five-card Poker game.

Brainstorming First we look carefully at the problem statement and determine possible objects. The nouns in the description form the first pass.

card
collection
games
Spades
Hearts
Bridge
Poker
subset
hand
hands
Texas Holdem

The first two are already represented by classes. The next five represent games and are not relevant at this stage. Subset is a description of from where the cards come. Texas Holdem is a specific game for which we should evaluate a hand. So we are left with only two objects: a hand and a collection of hands.

How can we characterize a hand? It is a list of cards. The operations should include all the standard list operations: initialization, insertion, deletion, and printing. That sounds just like a deck without the generate and shuffle operations. Are a deck and a hand actually the same thing? Can a hand be a derived class of deck with an evaluate responsibility? Yes, we could view a hand that way. However, in most games, one hand is better than another. That is, you can compare one hand with another. In Bridge, you assign a value called high card points, which sums 4 * number of Aces, 3 * number of Kings, 2 * number of Queens, and 1 * number of Jacks. The hand with more high card points is better than one with less. In Poker, you value your hand according to a set of rules involving rank and suit that we discuss later. If the cards are in order, the evaluation may be easier. Thus we should do what we did with class `Deck`, we make ADT Hand a derived class of class `SortedType`.

We are not evaluating a hand at this time; we are just looking ahead to make future processing easier. Each game that uses Hand must derive a subclass that evaluates the hand according to the rules of the particular game.

Class Name: Hand	Superclass: None	Subclasses: None
Responsibilities	**Collaborations**	
Initialize Hand()		

Wait a minute. We are inserting an unnecessary layer. Hand has no responsibilities that are not present in `SortedType`. Thus, a hand can be directly represented by class `SortedType`. We do need a responsibility, which takes a deck and divides it into hands. But how do we represent a collection of hands? Should we just give each a name? No. The number of hands and the number of cards in each varies among games. The best structure would be an array of hands. The procedure that does the dealing needs to know the number of cards in each hand and the number of hands.

What interface do we give to the user? Should the user declare the array of hands and pass it as an argument to a procedure that deals the hands? Or would it be better to encapsulate the hands into a class, which then returns a hand as requested? The first is a top-down approach; the second is an object-oriented approach. We choose the second. Here is the CRC card for ADT Hands.

Class Name: Hands	Superclass: None	Subclasses: None
Responsibilities	**Collaborations**	
Initialize Hands (numPlayers)		
Deal(numCards)	Deck	
GetHand(which) returns SortedType	SortedType	

Hands ADT Specification

Structure: An array of hands (a sorted list of cards)

Operations:

Initialize(int numPlayers)

Function: Creates an array of numPlayers of sortedLists.

Precondition: None

Postcondition: Self instance is empty.

Deal(int numCards)

Function: Deal numCards to numPlayers.

Precondition: numCards * numPlayers <= 52

Postcondition: Self instance is an array of numPlayers, each with a sorted list of numCards (a hand)

SortedType GetHand(int which)

Function: Returns hand of which player.

Preconditions: Self has been initialized. which is between 1 and numPlayers

Postcondition: Self instance has not been changed.

Implementation Level The beauty of having a specification that includes the pre and postconditions is that the class specification can be written directly from the specifications. Because the array size differs at run time, we must dynamically allocate and deallocate the array.

```
// Specification file for class Hands, which
// represents a collection of hands (sorted list
// of cards)

#include "deck.h"
#include "sortedType.h"
using namespace std;
class Hands
{
public:
  Hands();
  Hands(int players);
  ~Hands();
  void Deal(int numCards);
  SortedType GetHand(int which);
```

```
private:
  int numPlayers;
  SortedType* hands;
  Deck deck;
};
```

Responsibility Deal is the only one that is slightly complicated. There are at least two ways to deal numCards to numPlayers. We can deal numCards to each player or deal one card to each player numCards times. Does it matter? Probably not, but the second choice would seem to randomize the cards one more time. Of course, random is random, but since we are dealing with pseudorandomness, let's use the second option. We must declare, generate, and shuffle a deck of cards. Let's generate the deck in the constructor, but shuffle the deck before we deal the hands. We must not forget to set the hands to empty before dealing.

Deal (int numCards)

Shuffle deck
Set each hand to empty
Deal Cards

```
// Implementation file for class Hands
#include "hands.h"
#include <iostream>
using namespace std;

Hands::Hands()
{
  SortedType();
}

Hands::Hands(int players)
{
  numPlayers = players;
  hands = new SortedType[numPlayers];
  deck.GenerateDeck();
}

Hands::~Hands()
{
  delete [] hands;
}
```

```
void Hands::Deal(int numCards)
{
  deck.ResetList();
  for (int i = 0; i < 7; i++)
    deck.Shuffle();
  Card card;
  deck.ResetList();
  for (int i = 0; i < numPlayers; i++)
    hands[i].MakeEmpty();

  for (int cards = 0; cards < numCards; cards++)
    for (int players = 0; players < numPlayers; players++)
    {
      card = deck.GetNextItem();
      hands[players].PutItem(card);
    }
}

SortedType Hands::GetHand(int which)
{  return hands[which-1]; }
```

The test driver for this part of the assignment can be modeled on the test driver for class `Deck`. We create a helper function `PrintHand`, which prints the cards in a hand. First we print all the hands to see if they are created correctly, then we call GetHand(2) to see if hand two is repeated.

```
// Test driver for class Hands
#include <iostream>
#include "Hands.h"
using namespace std;

void PrintHand(SortedType&);

int main ()
{
  SortedType hand;
  Hands hands(4);
  hands.Deal(5);
  for (int player = 1; player <= 4; player++)
  {
    cout << "Hand: " << player << endl;
    hand = hands.GetHand(player);
    PrintHand(hand);
  }
```

```
  hand = hands.GetHand(2);
  cout << "Hand 2: " << endl;
  PrintHand(hand);
  return 0;
}

void PrintHand(SortedType& hand)
{
  if (hand.GetLength() == 0)
     cout << "Hand is empty." << endl;
  else
  {
    hand.ResetList();
    Card card;
    for (int counter = 1; counter <= hand.GetLength(); counter++)
    {
      card = hand.GetNextItem();
      cout << card.ToString() << endl;
    }
  }
  cout << endl;
}
```

When we try to run this simple program, we get the following error:

```
error: multiple definition of 'enum Suits'
error: multiple definition of 'enum RelationType'
```

How can that be? There is only one copy of each in `Card`. *But* `Card` is included in both `SortedType` and `UnsortedType`. So the preprocessor thinks `RelationType` and `Suits` are defined more than once. This happens often, so we put their definitions in a separate file to be included in other files. Let's call the file "enums.h".

```
#ifndef ENUMS
#define ENUMS
enum RelationType {LESS, EQUAL, GREATER};
enum Suits {CLUB, DIAMOND, HEART, SPADE};
#endif
```

The lines beginning with "#" are directives to the preprocessor. `ENUMS` (or any identifier you wish to use) is a preprocessor identifier, not a C++ program identifier. In effect, these directives say:

If the preprocessor identifier `ENUMS` has not already been defined, then

1. define `ENUMS` as an identifier known to the preprocessor, and
2. let the declaration pass through to the compiler.

If a subsequent `#include "enums.h"` is encountered, the test `#ifndef ENUMS` will fail. The declaration will not pass through to the compiler a second time.

We run the test again and get a build error. The builder thinks there are two copies of `Card`. Well, yes there are. `Card` itself is included in both `SortedType` and `UnsortedType`. We must put the `#ifndef` around the definition of `Card`. Rather than creating file "enum.h," we can just leave the declarations in `Card`.

```
Hand: 1
Three of Clubs
Four of Clubs
Eight of Hearts
Seven of Spades
Eight of Spades

Hand: 2
Five of Clubs
Six of Clubs
Four of Spades
Nine of Spades
Ten of Spades

Hand: 3
Ten of Clubs
King of Hearts
Two of Spades
Three of Spades
Ace of Spades

Hand: 4
Nine of Clubs
Four of Diamonds
King of Diamonds
Jack of Spades
King of Spades

Hand 2:
Five of Clubs
Six of Clubs
Four of Spades
Nine of Spades
Ten of Spades
```

Logical Level Now we have to evaluate a hand. Our test case is Texas Holdem. Hands are rated, from best to worst, as follows:

Royal Flush

Ranks from 10 through Ace; all of the same suit.

Straight Flush

Rank in sequence; all cards of the same suit.

4 of a Kind

Four cards with the same rank.

Full House (or Boat)

Three cards of one rank and two cards of a second rank.

Flush

All cards of the same suit.

Straight

All cards with ranks in sequence.

3 of a Kind

Three cards with the same rank.

2 Pair

Two sets of cards of the same rank.

1 Pair

Two cards of the same rank.

High Card

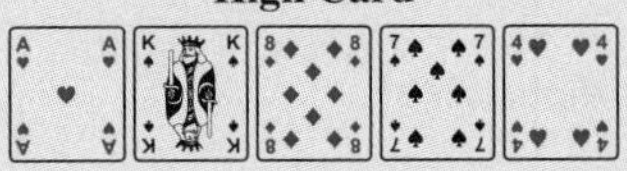

Highest rank in hand.

We need an enumerated type to represent these possibilities. How about

```
enum  HandIs {ROYAL, STRAIGHT_FLUSH, FOUR, FULL_HOUSE, FLUSH,
              STRAIGHT, THREE, TWO_PAIR, ONE_PAIR, HIGH_CARD};
```

The *Evaluate* responsibility will return a value of *HandIs*. We can approach the algorithm in two ways: We can check each hand in sequence against all the ten criteria. However, a little thought shows that three (Royal Flush, Straight Flush, and Flush) are concerned first with suit and then with rank, while the others relate only to rank. So we need a helper responsibility *SameSuit* that returns true if all of the cards are of the same suit. We apply this responsibility first. If it returns true, we check for the kind of flush. Thus, we also need a helper responsibility *IsStraight* that returns true if the ranks are in order.

HandIs CheckSuits

```
if SameSuit
    if IsStraight
        if first rank is Ten
            return ROYAL
        else
            return STRAIGHT_FLUSH
    else
        return FLUSH
```

SameSuit needs a loop to check to see if all are of the same suit. The loop ends either when we have seen all of the hand or when we find two cards with differing suits. We can use a Boolean variable *stillPossible* that is true until we find differing suits or we have compared all the cards. At the end of the loop, if *comparisons* equals *limit*, we have compared all the cards and they match.

Boolean SameSuit

```
hand.ResetList()
Set stillPossible to true
Set limit to hand.GetLength()
Set card1 to hand.GetNextItem()
Set card2 to hand.GetNextItem()
Set comparisons to 1
while stillPossible
    if card1.GetSuit() equals card2.GetSuit()
        if comparisons < limit                    // Compared them all?
            Set card1 to card2
            Set card2 to hand.GetNextItem()
            Increment comparisons
        else Set stillPossible to false
    else Set stillPossible to false
if comparisons equals limit
    return true
else return false
```

We can have a similar algorithm to determine if there is a Straight. Each rank must be the previous rank incremented by one. Again we can use a Boolean variable *stillPossible* that is true until we find a card out of order or we have looked at all the cards.

Boolean IsStraight

```
hand.ResetList()
Set stillPossible to true
Set limit to hand.GetLengt()
Set card1 to hand.GetNextItem()
Set card2 to hand.GetNextItem()
Set comparisons to 1
while stillPossible
    if card1.GetRank()+1 equals card2.GetRank()
        if comparisons < limit                    // Compared them all?
            Set card1 to card2
            Set card2 to hand.GetNextItem()
            Increment comparisons
        else Set stillPossible to false
    else
        Set stillPossible to false
if comparisons equals limit
    return true
else
    return false
```

Can we do something like this strategy with the ranks? Yes, with the exception of a regular Straight and high card, the others all contain at least one pair. We already have a helper responsibility *IsStraight* and high card is the case where none of the others fit.

Let's go back to our four hands and evaluate them. Hand 1 is ONE_PAIR; Hand 2 is HIGH_CARD; Hand 3 is HIGH_CARD; and Hand 4 is ONE_PAIR. We had to examine each card to find the pairs. However, an auxiliary data structure can help us. We declare an array of 14 integers. We ignore [0]. Each slot can be a counter for the number of times that rank has been seen. Once this array has been built, a quick scan gives us the rest of the evaluations. Any cell that has a 2 represents a pair; any cell that has a 3 represents a three of a kind; any cell that has a 4 represents a four of a kind.

HandIs CheckRanks

```
Build Counter
Set index to 1
Set onePair to 0
Set threeKind to 0
Set fourKind to 0
while index < 14
    if counter[index] is < 2
        index++
    else
        if counter[index] is 2
            onePair++
            index++
        else
            if counter[index] is 3
                threeKind++
                index++
            else
                if counter[index] is 4
                    four Kind++;
                    Set index to 14
HandIs EvaluateRanks
```

Build Counter

```
for i going from 1 to length of hand
    Set counter[i] to 0
hand.ResetList()
for i going from 1 to length of hand
    Set increment to hand.GetNextItem().GetRank()
    Set counter[increment] to counter[increment] + 1
```

HandIs EvaluateRank

```
if (onePair is 1 and threeKind is 1)
    return FULL_HOUSE
else if (onePair is 2)
    return TWO_PAIR
else if (threeKind is 1)
    return THREE
else if (fourKind is 1)
    return FOUR
else if (onePair is 1)
    return ONE_PAIR
else if (IsStraight)
    return STRAIGHT
else return HIGH_CARD
```

Now we have the algorithm for the Evaluate responsibility. We need to encapsulate it into a class with a ToString responsibility. Note that Evaluation needs no private data.

Evaluation ADT Specification

Operations:

HandIs Evaluate(SortedType hand)

Function: Evaluate a hand using rules of Texas Holdem poker.

Precondition: None

Postcondition: Returns result of applying rules to hand

string ToString(HandIs evaluation)

Function: Returns evaluation as a string

Preconditions: Evaluation has been defined.

Postconditions: Self instance has not been changed.

Implementation Level The specification of the header file is straightforward. The complexity is when we try to code the Evaluate responsibility.

```
// Specification for class Evaluation

#include <string>
using namespace std;
#include "sorted.h"
```

```
enum  HandIs {ROYAL, STRAIGHT_FLUSH, FOUR, FULL_HOUSE, FLUSH,
              STRAIGHT, THREE, TWO_PAIR, ONE_PAIR, HIGH_CARD};
class Evaluation
{
public:
  HandIs Evaluate(SortedType hand);
  string ToString(HandIs eval) const;
};
```

As we begin coding these algorithms, we realize that there is a large omission: We need to put all the checks together into one function. That is, CheckSuits and CheckRanks must be combined to send back the evaluation. This can be tricky. Both of these modules send back a HandIs variable. Our CheckSuits module sends back the correct evaluation *if the cards are all of the same suit.* The return variable is undefined if they are not all the same suit. There is no way to test a variable to determine if it is undefined. Thus, we need to make CheckSuits a Boolean function with an IsHand parameter. Here is the main evaluation module. We have added the hand as a parameter.

HandIs Evaluation

```
HandIs eval
if CheckSuits(eval, hand)
    return eval
else
    return checkRanks(hand)
```

```
// Implementation file for class Evaluation
#include "Evaluation.h"
#include <iostream>

int counter[14];

bool SameSuits(SortedType hand)
{
  hand.ResetList();
  bool stillPossible = true;
  int limit = hand.GetLength();
  Card card1 = hand.GetNextItem();
  Card card2 = hand.GetNextItem();
  int comparisons = 1;
  while (stillPossible)
  {
    if (card1.GetSuit() == card2.GetSuit())
```

```
    {
      if (comparisons < limit)
      {
        card1 = card2;
        card2 = hand.GetNextItem();
        comparisons++;
      }
      else stillPossible = false;
    }
    else stillPossible = false;
  }
  if (comparisons ==  limit)
    return true;
  else return false;
}

bool IsStraight(SortedType hand)
{
  hand.ResetList();
  bool stillPossible = true;
  int limit = hand.GetLength();
  Card card1 = hand.GetNextItem();
  Card card2 = hand.GetNextItem();
  int comparisons = 1;
  while (stillPossible)
  {
    if (card1.GetRank() +1  == card2.GetRank())
    {
      if (comparisons < limit)
      {
        card1 = card2;
        card2 = hand.GetNextItem();
        comparisons++;
      }
     else
      stillPossible = false;
    }
    else stillPossible = false;
  }

  if (comparisons == limit)
      return true;
  else return false;
}
```

During the coding phase, we removed duplication by evaluating *IsStraight* and *SameSuits* at the beginning of the function and saving the results. This allowed us to move the check for the regular Straight to this function. We also folded module EvaluateHands into the CheckRanks module.

```
bool CheckSuits(HandIs& eval, SortedType hand)
{
  bool found = false;

  bool isStraight = IsStraight(hand);
  bool sameSuits = SameSuits(hand);
  hand.ResetList();
  int first = hand.GetNextItem().GetRank();
  if (sameSuits)
  {
    found =  true;
    if (isStraight)
    {
      if (first == 10)
        eval = ROYAL;
      else
        eval = STRAIGHT_FLUSH;
    }
    else
      eval = FLUSH;
  }
  else if (isStraight)
  {
    eval = STRAIGHT;
    found = true;
  }
  return found;
}

void BuildCounter(SortedType hand)
{
  for (int index = 0; index <= 14; index++)
    counter[index] = 0;
  hand.ResetList();
  int limit =  hand.GetLength();
  for (int index = 1; index <= limit; index++)
  {
    int increment = hand.GetNextItem().GetRank();
    counter[increment] = counter[increment]+ 1;
  }
}

HandIs CheckRanks(SortedType hand)
{
```

```
  HandIs eval;
  BuildCounter(hand);
  int index = 1;
  int onePair = 0;
  int threeKind = 0;
  int fourKind = 0;
  while (index < 14)
  {
    if (counter[index] < 2)
      index++;
    else
      if (counter[index] == 2)
      {
        onePair++;
        index++;
      }
      else
        if (counter[index] == 3)
        {
          threeKind++;
          index++;
        }
      else
        if (counter[index] == 4)
        {
          fourKind++;
          index = 14;
        }
  }
  if (onePair == 1 &&  threeKind == 1)
       eval = FULL_HOUSE;
    else if (onePair == 2)
      eval = TWO_PAIR;
    else if (threeKind == 1)
      eval = THREE;
    else if (onePair == 1)
      eval = ONE_PAIR;
    else if (fourKind == 1)
      eval = FOUR;
      else eval = HIGH_CARD;

  return eval;
}
```

```
HandIs Evaluation::Evaluate(SortedType hand)
{
  HandIs eval;
  if (CheckSuits(eval, hand))
    return eval;
  else
    return CheckRanks(hand);
}

string Evaluation::ToString(HandIs eval) const
{
  string convertEval[] = {"ROYAL", "STRAIGHT_FLUSH", "FOUR", "FULL_HOUSE",
                          "FLUSH", "STRAIGHT", "THREE", "TWO_PAIR",
                          "ONE_PAIR", "HIGH_CARD"};

  return convertEval[eval];
}
```

We have a clean run, but testing this code with all the branching looks very daunting. Well it would be if we had to randomly generate the hands. We would have to run a *very* long time to generate the ten combinations. What we can do is have the test driver generate known hands. Here is the test driver and the results of evaluating ten such hands.

```
// Test driver for class Evaluation
#include <iostream>
#include "Hands.h"
#include "Evaluation.h"
using namespace std;

void PrintHand(SortedType&);

int main ()
{
  int rank;
  int suit;
  Card card;
  SortedType hand;
  cout << "Type in hand as rank/suit pairs" << endl;
  for (int count = 1; count <=5; count++)
  {
    cin >> rank >> suit;
    hand.PutItem(Card(rank, Suits(suit)));
  }
  PrintHand(hand);
  Evaluation evaluation();
```

```
  HandIs eval;
  eval = evaluation.Evaluate();
  cout << evaluation.ToString(eval) << endl;
  return 0;
}

void PrintHand(SortedType& hand)
{
  if (hand.GetLength() == 0)
     cout << "Hand is empty." << endl;
  else
  {
    hand.ResetList();
    Card card;
    for (int counter = 1; counter <= hand.GetLength(); counter++)
    {
      card = hand.GetNextItem();
      cout << card.ToString() << endl;
    }
  }
  cout << endl;
}
```

```
Type in hand as rank/suit pairs
9 0 4 1 13 1 12 3 13 3
Nine of Clubs
Four of Diamonds
King of Diamonds
Queen of Spades
King of Spades

ONE_PAIR

Type in hand as rank/suit pairs
9 0 10 0 11 00 12 0 13 0
Nine of Clubs
Ten of Clubs
Jack of Clubs
Queen of Clubs
King of Clubs

STRAIGHT_FLUSH

Type in hand as rank/suit pairs
10 0 11 0 12 0 13 0 14 0
Ten of Clubs
Jack of Clubs
Queen of Clubs
King of Clubs
Ace of Clubs

ROYAL

Type in hand as rank/suit pairs
9 0 10 0 11 1 12 2 13 3
Nine of Clubs
Ten of Clubs
Jack of Diamonds
Queen of Hearts
King of Spades

STRAIGHT

Type in hand as rank/suit pairs
9 0 9 2 10 2 10 3 13 3
Nine of Clubs
Nine of Hearts
```

```
Ten of Hearts
Ten of Spades
King of Spades

TWO_PAIR

Type in hand as rank/suit pairs
9 0 9 1 10 1 10 2 10 3
Nine of Clubs
Nine of Diamonds
Ten of Diamonds
Ten of Hearts
Ten of Spades

FULL_HOUSE

Type in hand as rank/suit pairs
9 0 4 0 6 0 12 0 14 0
Four of Clubs
Six of Clubs
Nine of Clubs
Queen of Clubs
Ace of Clubs

FLUSH

Type in hand as rank/suit pairs
9 0 9 1 9 2 9 3 13 3
Nine of Clubs
Nine of Diamonds
Nine of Hearts
Nine of Spades
King of Spades

FOUR

Type in hand as rank/suit pairs
9 0 9 1 9 2 10 3 13 3
Nine of Clubs
Nine of Diamonds
Nine of Hearts
Ten of Spades
King of Spades

THREE

Type in hand as rank/suit pairs
5 0 6 0 4 3 9 3 10 3
Five of Clubs
Six of Clubs
Four of Spades
Nine of Spades
Ten of Spades

HIGH_CARD
```

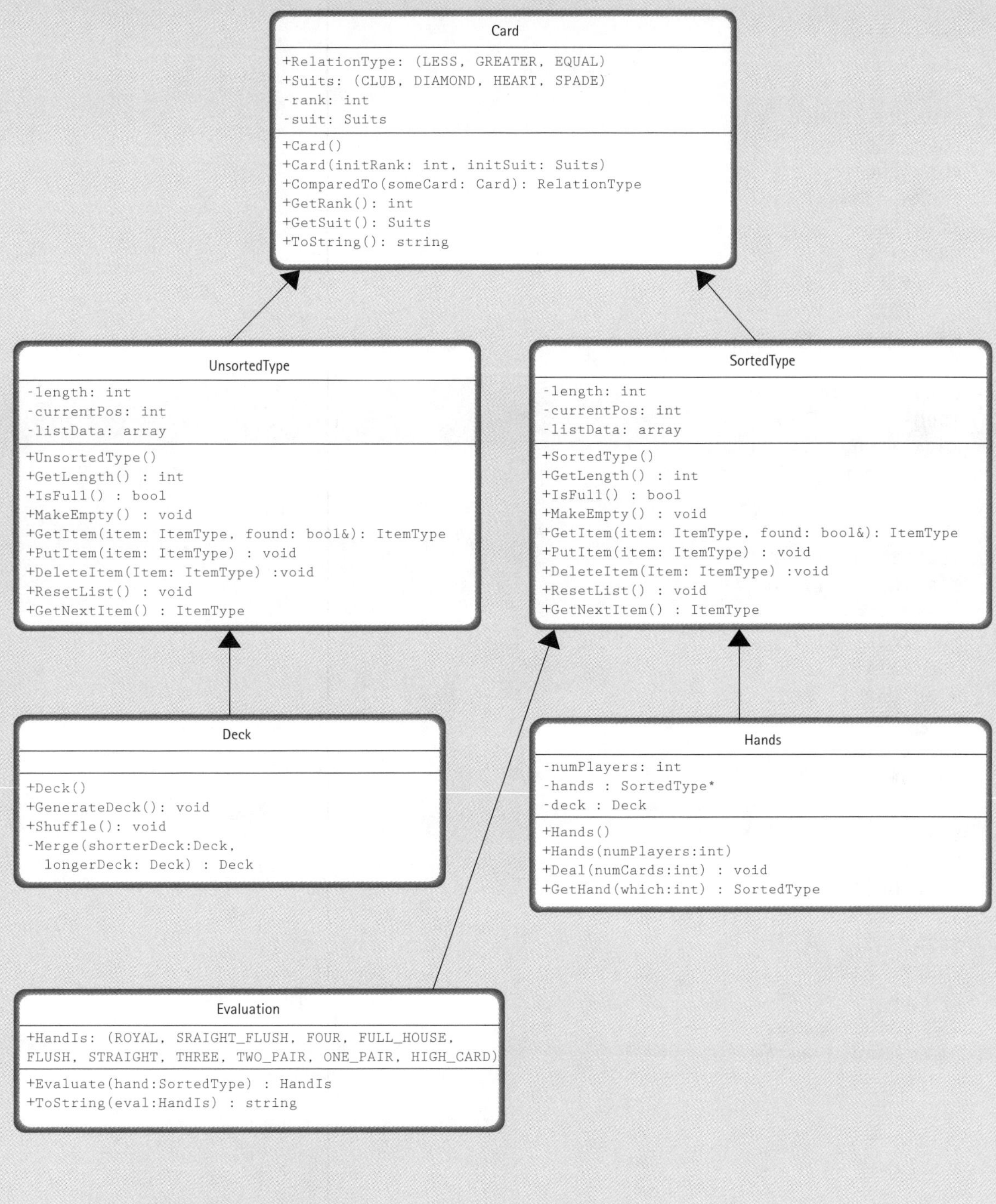
Card
+RelationType: (LESS, GREATER, EQUAL)
+Suits: (CLUB, DIAMOND, HEART, SPADE)
-rank: int
-suit: Suits
+Card()
+Card(initRank: int, initSuit: Suits)
+ComparedTo(someCard: Card): RelationType
+GetRank(): int
+GetSuit(): Suits
+ToString(): string
UnsortedType
-length: int
-currentPos: int
-listData: array
+UnsortedType()
+GetLength() : int
+IsFull() : bool
+MakeEmpty() : void
+GetItem(item: ItemType, found: bool&): ItemType
+PutItem(item: ItemType) : void
+DeleteItem(Item: ItemType) :void
+ResetList() : void
+GetNextItem() : ItemType
SortedType
-length: int
-currentPos: int
-listData: array
+SortedType()
+GetLength() : int
+IsFull() : bool
+MakeEmpty() : void
+GetItem(item: ItemType, found: bool&): ItemType
+PutItem(item: ItemType) : void
+DeleteItem(Item: ItemType) :void
+ResetList() : void
+GetNextItem() : ItemType
Deck
+Deck()
+GenerateDeck(): void
+Shuffle(): void
-Merge(shorterDeck:Deck,
longerDeck: Deck) : Deck
Hands
-numPlayers: int
-hands : SortedType*
-deck : Deck
+Hands()
+Hands(numPlayers:int)
+Deal(numCards:int) : void
+GetHand(which:int) : SortedType
Evaluation
+HandIs: (ROYAL, SRAIGHT_FLUSH, FOUR, FULL_HOUSE,
FLUSH, STRAIGHT, THREE, TWO_PAIR, ONE_PAIR, HIGH_CARD)
+Evaluate(hand:SortedType) : HandIs
+ToString(eval:HandIs) : string

Here is the distribution of results over three different runs of 100, 1,000, and 10,000 hands.

```
Enter limit
100
ROYAL:  0
STRAIGHT_FLUSH:  1
FOUR:  0
FULL_HOUSE:  1
FLUSH:  8
STRAIGHT:  1
THREE:  1
TWO_PAIR:  16
ONE_PAIR:  138
HIGH_CARD:  834

Enter limit
1000
ROYAL:  0
STRAIGHT_FLUSH:  6
FOUR:  2
FULL_HOUSE:  4
FLUSH:  45
STRAIGHT:  17
THREE:  67
TWO_PAIR:  158
ONE_PAIR:  1663
HIGH_CARD:  8038

Enter limit
10000
ROYAL:  0
STRAIGHT_FLUSH:  62
FOUR:  0
FULL_HOUSE:  62
FLUSH:  572
STRAIGHT:  94
THREE:  241
TWO_PAIR:  1277
ONE_PAIR:  14952
HIGH_CARD:  82740
```

Summary

In this chapter, we have created two implementations—array based and linked—of the abstract data type that represents sorted lists. The Sorted List ADT assumes that the list elements are sorted by key. We have viewed this ADT from three perspectives: the logical level, the application level, and the implementation level.

A four-stage object-oriented design methodology was described. Brainstorming is the process of coming up with a possible set of object classes in the problem solution. Filtering is the process of reexamining the tentative classes, eliminating those that are not appropriate, combining some classes, and creating additional classes if necessary. Scenarios is the part of the process in which you examine the responsibilities of each proposed class and role play to see if all situations are covered. Responsibility algorithms is the phase where algorithms are derived to carry out the responsibilities. CRC cards are used as a visual means of recording classes and their responsibilities. In contrast, UML diagrams are used to document a class and show the data fields and their types.

The extended Case Study uses this methodology and the Sorted List ADT.

Exercises

1. The Sorted List ADT is to be extended with a Boolean member function, `IsThere`, which takes as a parameter an item of type `ItemType` and determines whether there is an element with this key in the list.
   a. Write the specifications for this function.
   b. Write the prototype for this function.
   c. Write the array-based function definition using the binary search algorithm.
   d. Describe this function in terms of Big-O.
2. Redo Exercise 1(c) using a linked implementation.
3. Rather than enhancing the Sorted List ADTs by adding a member function `IsThere`, you decide to write a client function to do the same task.
   a. Write the specifications for this function.
   b. Write the function definition.
   c. Were you able to use the binary search algorithm? Explain your answer.
   d. Describe this function in terms of Big-O.
   e. Write a paragraph comparing the client function and the member function for the same task.
4. Write a client function that merges two instances of the Sorted List ADT using the following specification.

MergeLists(SortedType list1, SortedType list2, SortedType& result)

Function:	Merge two sorted lists into a third sorted list.

Preconditions:	list1 and list2 have been initialized and are sorted by key using function ComparedTo. list1 and list2 do not have any keys in common.
Postconditions:	result is a sorted list that contains all of the items from list1 and list2.

a. Write the prototype for `MergeLists`.

b. Write the function definition, using an array-based implementation.

c. Write the function definition, using a linked implementation.

d. Describe the algorithm in terms of Big-O.

5. Rewrite Exercise 4, making `MergeLists` an array-based member function of the Sorted List ADT.

6. Rewrite Exercise 5, making `MergeLists` a linked member function of the Sorted List ADT.

7. The specifications for the Sorted List ADT state that the item to be deleted is in the list.

   a. Rewrite the specification for `DeleteItem` so that the list is unchanged if the item to be deleted is not in the list.

   b. Implement `DeleteItem` as specified in (a) using an array-based implementation.

   c. Implement `DeleteItem` as specified in (a) using a linked implementation.

   d. Rewrite the specification for `DeleteItem` so that all copies of the item to be deleted are removed if they exist.

   e. Implement `DeleteItem` as specified in (d) using an array-based implementation.

   f. Implement `DeleteItem` as specified in (d) using a linked implementation.

8. A Sorted List ADT is to be extended by the addition of function `SplitLists`, which has the following specifications:

SplitLists(SortedType list, ItemType item, SortedType& list1, SortedType& list2)

Function:	Divides list into two lists according to the key of item.
Preconditions:	list has been initialized and is not empty.

Postconditions: list1 contains all the items of list whose keys are less than or equal to item's key;
list2 contains all the items of list whose keys are greater than item's key.

a. Implement `SplitLists` as a member function of the array-based Sorted List ADT.

b. Implement `SplitLists` as a member function of the linked Sorted List ADT.

c. Compare the algorithms used in (a) and (b).

d. Implement `SplitLists` as a client function of the array-based Sorted List ADT.

e. Implement `SplitLists` as a client function of the linked Sorted List ADT.

9. A Sorted List ADT is to be extended by the addition of a member function `Head`, which has the following precondition and postcondition:

   Precondition: list has been initialized and is not empty.

   Postcondition: return value is the last item inserted in the list.

   a. Will this addition be easy to implement in the array-based `SortedType`? Explain.

   b. Will this addition be easy to implement in linked `SortedType`? Explain.

10. A List ADT is to be extended by the addition of function `Tail`, which has the following precondition and postcondition:

    Precondition: list has been initialized and is not empty.

    Postcondition: return value is a new list without the most recently inserted item.

    a. Will this addition be easy to implement in the array-based `SortedType`? Explain.

    b. Will this addition be easy to implement in linked `SortedType`? Explain.

11. a. Change the specifications for the Sorted List ADT so that `PutItem` throws an exception if the list is full.

    b. Implement the revised specifications in (a) using an array-based implementation.

    c. Implement the revised specifications in (a) using a linked implementation.

12. Write a class based on class `UnsortedType` as a bounded linked implementation. Provide a parameterized constructor that takes the maximum number of items as a parameter. If function `PutItem` is called when the list if full, throw an exception.

13. Write a class based on class `SortedType` as a bounded linked implementation. Provide a parameterized constructor that takes the maximum number of items as a parameter. If function `PutItem` is called when the list if full, throw an exception.

14. Write a class based on class `UnsortedType` as an unbounded array-based implementation. If the dynamically allocated array is full, create an array double the size and move the elements into it.

15. Write a class based on class `SortedType` as an unbounded array-based implementation. If the dynamically allocated array is full, create an array double the size and move the elements into it.
16. What are the major steps in performing object-oriented design?
17. In the object-oriented design of an airline passenger reservation program, suppose that "airplane" has been identified as one object and "airplane seat" has been identified as another object. Focusing specifically on the airplane object, how does it relate to the airplane seat object?
18. The OOP phrase "instance variable" is equivalent to what C++ construct?
19. The OOP phrase "message passing" is equivalent to what C++ construct?
20. Define responsibility and distinguish between an action responsibility and a knowledge responsibility.
21. What are the three ways that two classes can relate to one another?
22. How can you avoid including a header file multiple times?

chapter 5

ADTs Stack and Queue

Goals

After studying this chapter, you should be able to

- Describe a stack and its operations at a logical level
- Demonstrate the effect of stack operations using a particular implementation of a stack
- Implement the Stack ADT, in two array-based implementations and a linked implementation
- Describe the structure of a queue and its operations at a logical level
- Demonstrate the effect of queue operations using a particular implementation of a queue
- Implement the Queue ADT, using both an array-based implementation and a linked implementation
- Use inheritance to create a Counted Queue ADT

In Chapter 2, we looked at the built-in structures in C++ from the logical view, the application view, and the implementation view. We saw that at the language level, the logical view is the syntax of the construct itself, and the implementation view is hidden within the compiler. In Chapters 3 and 4, we defined the ADTs Unsorted List and Sorted List. For these user-defined ADTs, the logical view is the class definition where the documentation on the prototypes of the member functions becomes the interface between the client program and the ADT. In this chapter we expand your toolkit of ADTs to include two important new ones: the stack and the queue.

5.1 Stacks

Logical Level

Consider the items pictured in Figure 5.1. Although the objects are all different, each illustrates the same concept—a stack. At the logical level, a stack is an ordered group of homogeneous items or elements. The removal of existing items and the addition of new items can take place only at the top of the stack. For instance, if your favorite blue shirt is underneath a faded, old, red one in a stack of shirts, you must first remove the red shirt (the top item) from the stack. Only then can you remove the desired blue shirt, which is now the top item in the stack. The red shirt may then be replaced on the top of the stack or thrown away.

> **Stack** An abstract data type in which elements are added and removed from only one end; a "last in, first out" (LIFO) structure

The stack may be considered an "ordered" group of items because elements occur in a particular sequence organized according to how long they've been in the stack. The items that have been present in the stack the longest are at the bottom; the most recent are at the top. At any time, given any two elements in a stack, one is higher than the other. (For instance, the red shirt was higher in the stack than the blue shirt.)

Because items are added and removed only from the top of the stack, the last element to be added is the first to be removed. A handy mnemonic can help you remember this rule of stack behavior: A stack is a LIFO (Last In, First Out) structure.

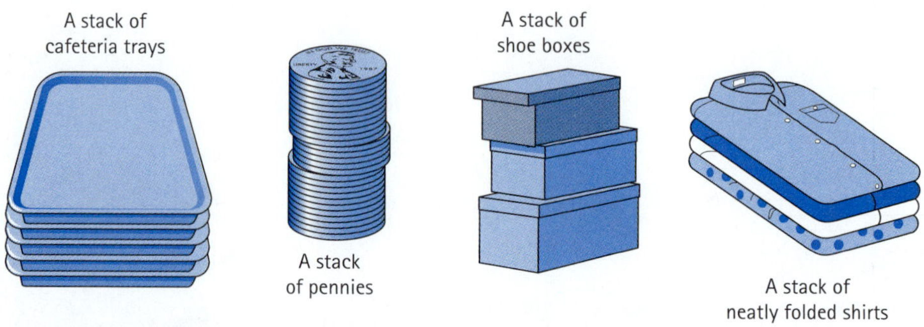

Figure 5.1 *Real-life stacks*

The accessing protocol for a stack is summarized as follows: Both to retrieve elements and to store new elements, access only the top of the stack.

Operations on Stacks The logical picture of the structure provides only half of the definition of an abstract data type. The other half consists of a set of operations that allows the user to access and manipulate the elements stored in the structure. Given the logical view of a stack, what kinds of operations do we need to use a stack?

The operation that adds an element to the top of a stack is usually called Push, and the operation that removes the top element from the stack is referred to as Pop. Because we may need to examine the item at the top of the stack we can have Pop return the top element or we can use a separate operation Top to return a copy of the top element without removing it. We must be able to tell whether a stack contains any elements before we pop it, so we need a Boolean operation IsEmpty. As a logical data structure, a stack is never conceptually "full," but for a particular implementation you may need to test whether a stack is full before pushing. We call this Boolean operation IsFull. Figure 5.2 shows how a stack, envisioned as a stack of building blocks, is modified by several Push and Pop operations.

We now have a logical picture of a stack and are almost ready to use it in a program. The part of the program that uses the stack, of course, won't care how the stack is actually implemented—we want the implementation level to be hidden, or encapsulated. The accessing operations such as Push, Pop, and Top serve as windows into the stack encapsulation, through which the stack's data are passed. The interfaces to the accessing operations are described in the following specification for the Stack ADT.

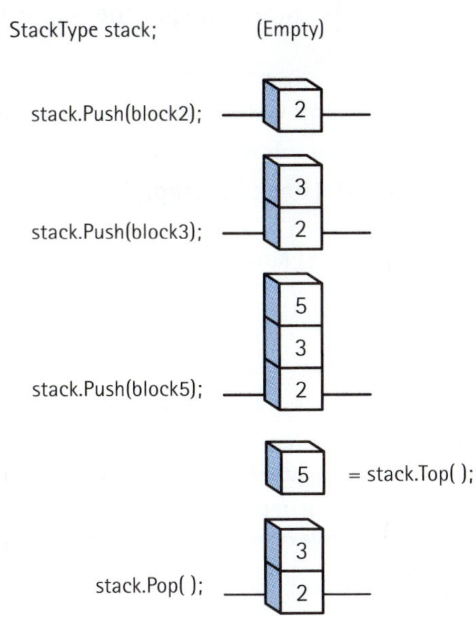

Figure 5.2 *The effects of Push and Pop operations*

Stack ADT Specification

Structure: Elements are added to and removed from the top of the stack.

Definitions (provided by users in class `ItemType`):

MAX_ITEMS: Maximum number of items that might be on the stack.

Operations (provided by the ADT):

Boolean IsEmpty

Function: Determines whether the stack is empty.

Precondition: Stack has been initialized.

Postcondition: Function value = (stack is empty).

Boolean IsFull

Function: Determines whether the stack is full.

Precondition: Stack has been initialized.

Postcondition: Function value = (stack is full).

Push(ItemType newItem)

Function: Adds newItem to the top of the stack.

Precondition: Stack has been initialized.

Postconditions: If (stack is full), exception FullStack is thrown, else newItem is at the top of the stack.

Pop

Function: Removes top item from the stack.

Precondition: Stack has been initialized.

Postconditions: If (stack is empty), exception EmptyStack is thrown, else top element has been removed from stack.

ItemType Top

Function: Returns a copy of the top item on the stack.

Precondition: Stack has been initialized.

Postconditions: If (stack is empty), exception EmptyStack is thrown, else a copy of the top element is returned.

This stack specification has a `Pop` that removes the top item but does not return it. Thus a `Top/Pop` combination must be used to examine and remove the item. An alternative design is to have the `Pop` operation return the top item. In this case, if you wish to examine but not remove an item, you must use a `Pop/Push` pair. In the Case Study at the end of the chapter, the second alternative is more appropriate.

Application Level

Now let's look at an example of how we might use the stack operations in a program. Stacks are very useful ADTs that are often used in situations where we must process nested components.

For example, programming language systems typically use a stack to keep track of operation calls. The main program calls operation A, which in turn calls operation B, which in turn calls operation C. When C finishes, control returns to B; when B finishes, control returns to A; and so on. The call-and-return sequence is essentially a LIFO sequence, so a stack is the perfect structure for tracking it. When an exception is thrown, this sequence of operation calls is followed while looking for an appropriate *catch* statement.

Compilers often use stacks to perform syntax analysis of language statements. The definition of a programming language usually consists of nested components—for example, *for* loops can contain *if-then* statements that contain *while* loops that contain *for* loops. As a compiler works through such nested constructs, it "saves" information about what it is currently working on in a stack. When it finishes its work on the innermost construct, the compiler can "retrieve" its previous status from the stack, and pick up where it left off. Similarly, an operating system sometimes saves information about the currently executing process on a stack, so that it can work on a higher-priority interrupting process. If that process becomes interrupted by an even higher-priority process, its information can also be pushed onto the process stack. When the operating system finishes its work on the highest-priority process, it pops the information about the most recently stacked process, and continues working on it.

Let's look at a simpler problem related to nested components—the problem of determining whether a set of parentheses is "well formed." For this classic problem, a stack is an appropriate data structure. The general problem can be stated as follows: Determine whether a set of paired symbols is used appropriately. The specific problem is: Given a set of different types of paired symbols, determine whether the opening and closing versions of each type are paired correctly. For our example, we consider parenthesis pairs (), [], and {}.[1] Any number of other characters may appear in the input, but a closing

---

[1]An overzealous copyeditor once changed parenthesized expressions in a Pascal program from plain parentheses to alternating parentheses and square brackets. Fortunately, when all of the programs were tested, this change was caught.

Well-Formed Expressions	Ill-Formed Expressions
(xx (xx ( )) xx)	(xx (xx ( )) xxx) xxx)
[ ] ( ) { }	] [
([ ] { xxx } xxx ( ) xxx)	(xx [xxx) xx]
([{ [((([{ x }]) x)] } x])	([{ [((([{ x }]) x)] } x })
xxxxxxxxxxxxxxxxxxxxxxxxxx	xxxxxxxxxxxxxxxxxxxxxxx {

Figure 5.3 *Well-formed and ill-formed expressions*

parenthesis symbol must match the last unmatched opening parenthesis symbol and all parenthesis symbols must be matched when the input is finished. Figure 5.3 shows examples of both well-formed and ill-formed expressions.

The program reads an expression character by character. For each character, it does one of three tasks, depending on whether the character is an opening special symbol, a closing special symbol, or not a special symbol. If the character is not a special symbol, it is discarded and another character is read. If the character is an opening special symbol, it is saved on the stack. If the character is a closing special symbol, it must be checked against the last opening special symbol, which is on the top of the stack. If they match, the character and the last opening special symbol are discarded and the program processes the next character. If the closing special symbol does not match the top of the stack or if the stack is empty, then the expression is ill formed. When the program has processed all of the characters, the stack should be empty—otherwise, extra opening special symbols are present.

Now we are ready to write the main algorithm, where `stack` is an instance of `StackType` and `symbol` is the character being examined.

Main Algorithm

```
Set balanced to true
Set symbol to the first character in current expression
while (there are still more characters AND expression is still balanced)
    Process symbol
    Set symbol to next character in current expression
if (balanced)
    Write "Expression is well formed."
else
    Write "Expression is not well formed."
```

The algorithm follows this basic pattern:

```
Get the first piece of information
while not finished processing information
    Handle the current information
    Get the next piece of information
```

It uses this processing pattern for both the lines of expressions (if there is more than one) and the characters within each line. Your programming proficiency will increase as you recognize such patterns and "reuse" them when appropriate.

The only part of the algorithm that may require expansion before moving on to the coding stage is the "Process symbol" command. Earlier, we described how to handle each type of character. Here are those steps in algorithmic form:

Process Symbol

```
if (symbol is an opening symbol)
    Push symbol onto the stack
else if (symbol is a closing symbol)
    if the stack is empty
        Set balanced to false
    else
        Set openSymbol to the character at the top of the stack
        Pop the stack
        Set balanced to (symbol matches openSymbol)
```

matches

```
symbol is ')' and openSymbol is '(' OR
symbol is '}' and openSymbol is '{' OR
symbol is ']' and openSymbol is '['
```

We are now ready to code this algorithm as the program `Balanced`. We make use of `stack` of the class `StackType`. We could code a class `SymbolType` with member functions `IsOpen`, `IsClosed`, and `Matches` and one data item of type `char`. However, because a symbol is just a built-in data type, a procedural solution is simpler.

```
#include "StackType.h"
#include <iostream>
bool IsOpen(char symbol);
bool IsClosed(char symbol);
bool Matches(char symbol, char openSymbol);

int main()
{
  using namespace std;
  char symbol;
  StackType stack;
  bool balanced = true;
  char openSymbol;

  cout << "Enter an expression and press return." << endl;
  cin.get(symbol);
  while (symbol != '\n' && balanced)
  {
    if (IsOpen(symbol))
      stack.Push(symbol);
    else if (IsClosed(symbol))
    {
      if (stack.IsEmpty())
        balanced = false;
      else
      {
        openSymbol = stack.Top();
        stack.Pop();
        balanced = Matches(symbol, openSymbol);
      }
    }
    cin.get(symbol);
  }
  if (balanced)
    cout << "Expression is well formed." << endl;
  else
    cout << "Expression is not well formed."  << endl;
  return 0;
}
```

```
bool IsOpen(char symbol)
{
  if ((symbol == '(') || (symbol == '{') || (symbol == '['))
    return true;
  else
    return false;
}

bool IsClosed(char symbol)
{
  if ((symbol == ')') || (symbol == '}') || (symbol == ']'))
    return true;
  else
    return false;
}

bool Matches(char symbol, char openSymbol)
{
  return  (((openSymbol == '(') && symbol == ')')
        || ((openSymbol == '{') && symbol == '}')
        || ((openSymbol == '[') && symbol == ']'));
}
```

In this expression checker, we have acted as stack users. We have written an interesting stack application, without even considering how the stack is implemented. The stack user doesn't need to know the implementation! The details of the implementation remain hidden inside the `StackType` class. As users, however, we did not adhere to the specifications carefully. We should have included `Push`, `Pop`, and `Top` with a *try/catch* statement. We leave this correction as an exercise.

Implementation Level

Next, we consider the implementation of our Stack ADT. After all, our functions `Push`, `Pop`, and `Top` are not magically available to the C++ programmer. We need to write these routines to include them in a program.

Because all elements of a stack are of the same type, an array seems like a reasonable structure to hold them. We can put elements into sequential slots in the array, placing the first element pushed into the first array position, the second element pushed into the second array position, and so on. The floating "high-water" mark is the top element in the stack. Why, this approach sounds just like our Unsorted List ADT implementation! Here `info[length - 1]` is the top of the stack.

Be careful: We are not saying that a stack is an unsorted list. A stack and an unsorted list are two entirely different abstract data types. We are saying, however, that we can use the same *implementation strategy* for both.

Definition of the Stack Class We implement our Stack ADT as a C++ class. Just as we did for the various versions of the List ADT, we require the user to provide us with a class called `ItemType`, which defines the items on the stack. However, we do not need a comparison function because none of the operations requires comparing two items on the stack.

Which data members does our Stack ADT need? We need the stack items themselves and a variable indicating the top of the stack (which behaves in the same way as `length` in the List ADT). What about error conditions? Our specifications leave error checking to the user (client) by having the ADT throw an exception when a push operation is attempted but the stack is full or when a pop or top operation is attempted but the stack is empty. We include two exception classes, `FullStack` and `EmptyStack`, in the following specification file, `StackType.h`.

```
#include ItemType.h
// ItemType.h must be provided by the user of this class.
// This file must contain the following definitions:
//   MAX_ITEMS:     the maximum number of items on the stack.
//   ItemType:      the definition of the objects on the stack.


class FullStack
// Exception class used by Push when stack is full.
{};

class EmptyStack
// Exception class used by Pop and Top when stack is empty.
{};
```

```
class StackType
{
public:
  StackType();
  bool IsEmpty() const;
  bool IsFull() const;
  void Push(ItemType item);
  void Pop();
  ItemType Top() const;
private:
  int top;
  ItemType items[MAX_ITEMS];
};
```

Definitions of Stack Operations In the List ADT, `length` indicated how many items were present on the list. In the Stack ADT, `top` indicates which element is on top. Thus our analogy to the List ADT is off by one. The class constructor sets `top` to -1 rather than 0. `IsEmpty` should compare `top` with -1, and `IsFull` should compare `top` with `MAX_ITEMS -1`.

```
StackType::StackType()
{
  top = -1;
}

bool StackType::IsEmpty() const
{
  return (top == -1);
}

bool StackType::IsFull() const
{
  return (top == MAX_ITEMS-1);
}
```

Now we must write the algorithm to `Push` an item on the top of the stack, `Pop` an item from the top of the stack, and return a copy of the top item. `Push` must increment `top` and store the new item into `items[top]`. If the stack is already full when we invoke `Push`, the resulting condition is called stack overflow. We can handle error checking for overflow conditions in a number of ways. Our specification states that overflow causes an exception to be thrown; thus the client is responsible for handling overflow by enclosing the operation within a *try/catch* statement. Alternatively, we could pass an error flag as a parameter, which `Push` sets to true if overflow occurs.

> **Stack overflow** The condition resulting from trying to push an element onto a full stack

Push
if stack is full
  throw an exception FullStack
else
  Increment top
  Set items[top] to newItem

```
void StackType::Push(ItemType newItem)
{
  if (IsFull())
    throw FullStack();
  top++;
  items[top] = newItem;
}
```

The constructor for the exception class is called in the `throw` statement, because C++ requires us to throw an *object* of an exception type. Because the documentation states that the functions `Push`, `Pop`, and `Top` can throw exceptions, calls to them must be enclosed within a *try* block. The following example shows what the client code might do with the exception:

```
try
{
  // Code
  stack.Push(item);
  stack.Pop();
  // More code
}
catch (FullStack exceptionObject)
{
  cerr << "FullStack exception thrown"   << endl;
}
catch (EmptyStack exceptionObject)
{
  cerr << "EmptyStack exception thrown"  << endl;
}
```

In this case, the `FullStack` or `EmptyStack` object that is thrown is not accessed. If the exception class has member functions, they could be applied to `exceptionObject`.

If the exception is so severe that the program should halt, the exit function can be used.

```
catch (EmptyStack exceptionObject)
{
  cerr << "EmptyStack exception thrown"  << endl
     << "Exiting with error code 2" << endl;
  exit(2);
}
```

The Error Stream cerr

You already know about cin and cout, which are defined in the <iostream> header file. A third stream defined in <iostream>, cerr, is called the error output stream. As its name suggests, cerr is intended specifically for error messages.

Use of exit(n)

Calling exit(n), which is available in <cstdlib>, anywhere in a program cleans up and then terminates the program. We cannot use return to terminate a program in any function other than main. Using return in a function returns to the caller, which would not end the program. In main, exit(n) has the same effect as return n.

Pop is essentially the reverse of Push: We decrement top. If the stack is empty when we invoke Pop or Top, a stack underflow results. As with the Push function, the specifications for the operations say to throw an exception in this event.

Stack underflow The condition resulting from trying to pop an empty stack

Here is the code for Pop and Top:

```
void StackType::Pop()
{
  if(IsEmpty())
    throw EmptyStack();
  top--;
}

ItemType StackType::Top() const
{
```

```
    if (IsEmpty())
      throw EmptyStack();
    return items[top];
  }
```

Figure 5.4 shows the result of pushing and popping where the stack items are characters.

Test Plan The test plan for the Stack ADT closely resembles the test plan for the List ADT. Because we are testing the implementation of an abstract data type that we have just written, we use a clear-box strategy, checking each operation. Unlike with the List ADT, however, we do not have an iterator that allows us to cycle through the items and print them. Instead, we must use a combination of calls to `Top` and `Pop` to print what is in the stack, destroying it in the process.

Because the type of data stored in the stack has no effect on the operations that manipulate the stack, we can define `ItemType` to represent `int` values and set `MAX_ITEMS` to 5, knowing that the code will work the same way whether `MAX_ITEMS` is 5 or 1,000.

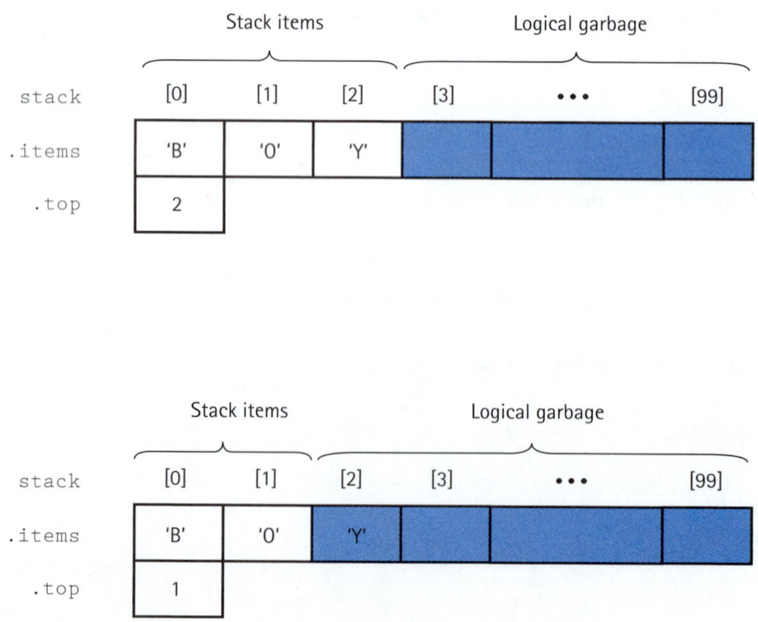

Figure 5.4 *The effect of a `Pop` following a series of `Pushes`*

Operation to Be Tested and Description of Action	Input Values	Expected Output or Program Behavior
Class constructor		
Apply `IsEmpty` immediately		Stack is empty
`Push`, `Pop`, and `Top`		
Push 4 items,		
top, pop, and print	5, 7, 6, 9	9, 6, 7, 5
Push with duplicates		
and pop, top, and print	2, 3, 3, 4	4, 3, 3, 2
`Push`, `Pop`, and `Top`		
interlace operations		
Push	5	
Pop		
Push	3	
Push	7	
Pop		
Top and print		3
`IsEmpty`		
Invoke when empty		Stack is empty
Push and invoke		Stack is not empty
Pop and invoke		Stack is empty
`IsFull`		
Push 4 items and invoke	1, 2, 3, 4	Stack is not full
Push another item and invoke	5	Stack is full
throw `FullStack`		Caught by driver
Push 5 items then	1, 2, 3, 4, 5	
Push another item	6	
throw `EmptyStack`		Caught by driver
When stack is empty,		
Attempt to pop		
Attempt to top		

On the Web, the program `StackDr.cpp` is the test driver, the input file is `StackType.in`, and the output files are `StackType.out` and `StackType.screen`. Examine `StackDr.cpp` to see how the *try/catch* statement is used.

Alternate Array-Based Implementation

In the last chapter, we introduced a way to implement an array-based list using an array, the storage for which is allocated at run time. We can use the same technique to implement a stack in a dynamically allocated array. We can let the maximum number of items be a parameter to a class constructor. This change requires the following changes in the class definition:

```
class StackType
{
public:
  StackType(int max);  // max is stack size.
  StackType();         // Default size is 500.
  // Rest of the prototypes go here.
private:
  int top;
  int maxStack;        // Maximum number of stack items.
  ItemType* items;     // Pointer to dynamically allocated memory.
};
```

When declaring a class object, the client can specify the maximum number of stack items by using the parameterized constructor:

```
StackType myStack(100);
// Integer stack of at most 100 items.
```

Or the client can accept the default size of 500 by using the default constructor:

```
StackType aStack;
```

Earlier we saw that to allocate an array, you attach to the data type name the array size in brackets: `new AnotherType[size]`. In this case, the `new` operator returns the base address of the newly allocated array. Here are the implementations of the `StackType` constructors:

```
StackType::StackType(int max)
{
  maxStack = max;
  top = -1;
  items = new ItemType[maxStack];
}
StackType::StackType()
{
  maxStack = 500;
  top = -1;
  items = new ItemType[maxStack];
}
```

Notice that `items` is now a pointer variable, not an array name. It points to the first element of a dynamically allocated array. `items` can be indexed exactly as it was when it was defined as an array of type `ItemType`. Thus, only one member function needs to be changed: `IsFull`. In the previous implementation, the size of the array was set as a constant; here, it is a class data member.

```
bool StackType::IsFull()
{
  return (top == maxStack-1);
}
```

We mustn't forget that we need a class destructor. We include the following prototype of the destructor in the `public` part of the class definition:

```
~StackType(); // Destructor.
```

and implement the function as follows:

```
StackType::~StackType()
{
  delete [] items;
}
```

5.2 Implementing a Stack as a Linked Structure

For the Unsorted List ADT, we put the next element at the end of the list in the array-based implementation and at the first of the list in the linked version. We did this because it gave us immediate access to the insertion point. Push in the array-based version puts the new element in the end. Should the linked version put the new element at the first? Yes, because it gives us immediate access to the insertion point, which in turn gives us immediate access to the last item inserted.

The specification for the Stack does not say that it is logically bounded, so we make this implementation bounded only by memory. Here is the header file for our linked class `StackType`.

```
// Header file for Stack ADT.
typedef char ItemType;
struct NodeType;

class StackType
{
public:
  StackType();
  ~StackType();
  void Push(ItemType);
  void Pop();
  ItemType Top();
  bool IsEmpty() const;
  bool IsFull() const;
private:
  NodeType* topPtr;
...
```

Function `Push`

We can just "borrow" the `InsertItem` code from class `UnsortedType`. However, the Stack ADT specification requires that we throw an exception if the stack is full. Thus, we must put the code within an *if-else* statement.

```
void StackType::Push(ItemType newItem)
// Adds newItem to the top of the stack.
// Stack is bounded by size of memory.
// Pre:  Stack has been initialized.
```

```
// Post: If stack is full, FullStack exception is thrown;
//       else newItem is at the top of the stack.

{
  if (IsFull())
    throw FullStack();
  else
  {
    NodeType* location;
    location = new NodeType;
    location->info = newItem;
    location->next = topPtr;
    topPtr = location;
  }
}
```

Function Pop

Now let's look at the Pop operation. The algorithm for Pop is

Pop

```
Set item to Info(top node)    // Access the information in the top node
Unlink the top node from the stack
Deallocate the old top node
```

```
void StackType::Pop()
// Removes top item from Stack and returns it in item.
// Pre:  Stack has been initialized.
// Post: If stack is empty, EmptyStack exception is thrown;
//       else top element has been removed.
{
  if (IsEmpty())
    throw EmptyStack();
  else
  {
    NodeType* tempPtr;
```

```
        tempPtr = topPtr;
        topPtr = topPtr->next;
        delete tempPtr;
    }
}
```

Let's walk through this function, using the stack in Figure 5.5. We save a pointer to the first node, so that we can access it later to delete it (Figure 5.5a). Then the external pointer to the stack is advanced to jump over the first node, making the second node

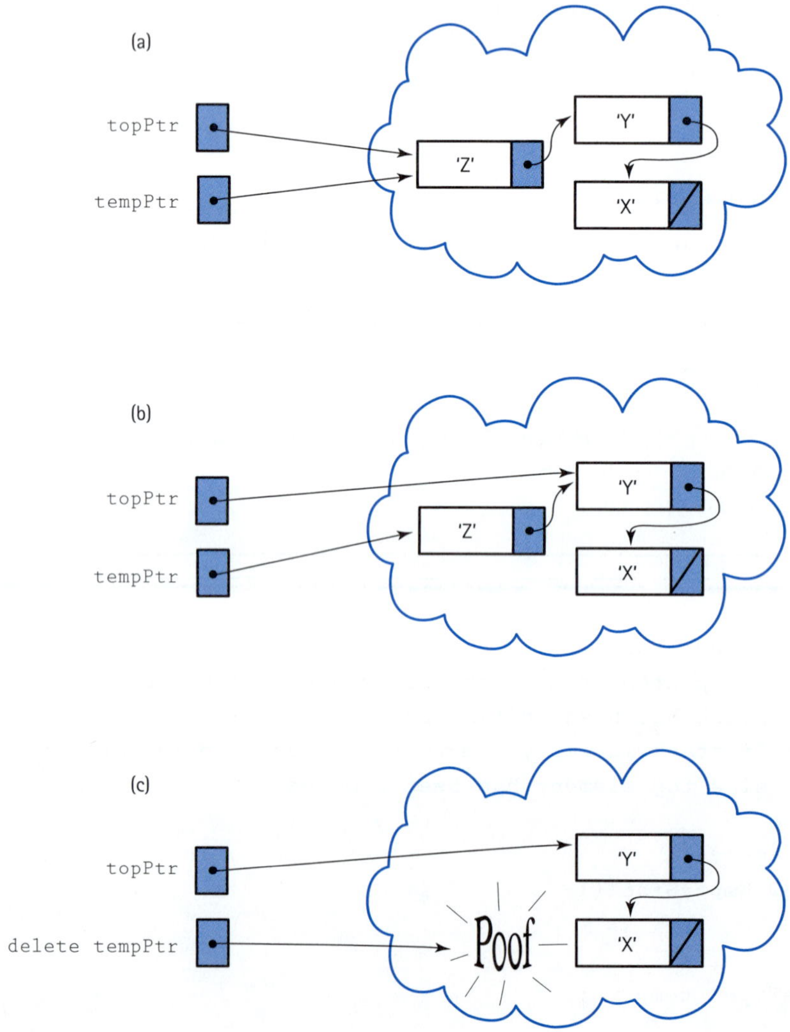

Figure 5.5 *Popping the stack*

the new top item. How do we know the address of the second node? We get it from the `next` member of the first node (`topPtr->next`). This value is assigned to `topPtr` to complete the unlinking task (Figure 5.5b). Finally, we free the space occupied by the old top node by using the `delete` operator, giving it the address we saved in `tempPtr` (Figure 5.5c).

Does this function work if there is only one node in the stack when `Pop` is called? Let's see. We unlink the first/last node from the stack. We save a pointer to the node, as before, and then try to assign `topPtr->next` to `topPtr` (Figure 5.6). What is the value of `topPtr->next`? Because this is the last node in the list, its `next` member should contain `NULL`. This value is assigned to `topPtr`, which is exactly what we want, because a `NULL` stack pointer means that the stack is empty. So the function works for a stack of one element.

What happens if `Pop` does not check for the empty stack? If `topPtr` contains `NULL`, then the assignment statement

```
topPtr = topPtr->next;
```

results in a run-time error. On some systems you get the message ATTEMPT TO DEREFERENCE NULL POINTER; on other systems the screen freezes. But this is not our problem because the code does check for the empty stack before continuing with the operation.

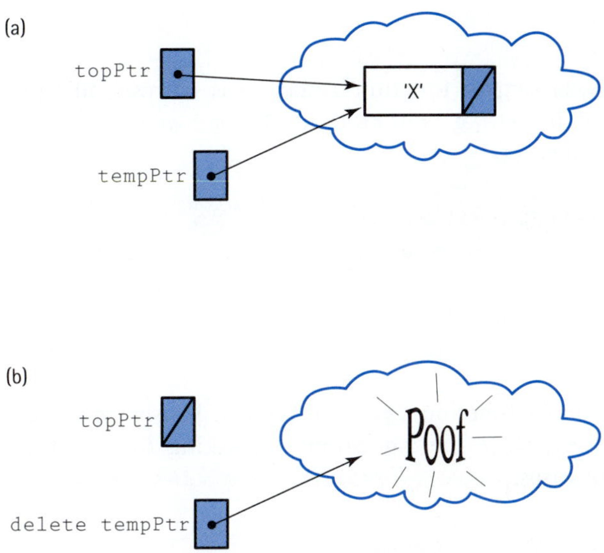

Figure 5.6 *Popping the last element on the stack*

Function `Top`

A glance at any of the previous figures shows that the information in the top of the stack is in the info field of the first node.

```
ItemType StackType::Top()
// Returns a copy of the top item in the stack.
// Pre:  Stack has been initialized.
// Post: If stack is empty, EmptyStack exception is thrown;
//       else a copy of the top element is returned.
{
  if (IsEmpty())
    throw EmptyStack();
  else
    return topPtr->info;
}
```

Other Stack Functions

In the explanation of pushing the first element, it was noted that an empty stack is indicated by a `NULL` pointer. This fact has implications for the other stack operations. To initialize a stack to the empty state, we merely need to set `topPtr` to `NULL`:

```
StackType::StackType()     // Class constructor.
{
  topPtr = NULL;
}
```

That was simple; function `IsEmpty` is correspondingly simple. If we initialize an empty stack by setting `topPtr` to `NULL`, then we can detect an empty stack by checking for a `NULL` pointer.

```
bool StackType::IsEmpty() const
// Returns true if there are no elements on the stack; false otherwise.
{
  return (topPtr == NULL);
}
```

What about function `IsFull`? We can just borrow the code from one of the other linked classes, since the algorithms for asking for and finding if a node exists is the same in all cases.

```
bool StackType::IsFull() const
// Returns true if there is no room for another ItemType
//  on the free store; false otherwise.
{
```

```
  NodeType* location;
  try
  {
    location = new NodeType;
    delete location;
    return false;
  }
  catch(std::bad_alloc exception)
  {
    return true;
  }
}
```

Our class definition also provides a class destructor. Do we need one? Yes, we do. Remember that any class that uses dynamic data needs a destructor.

```
StackType::~StackType()
// Post: stack is empty; all items have been deallocated.
{
  NodeType* tempPtr;

  while (topPtr != NULL)
  {
    tempPtr = topPtr;
    topPtr = topPtr->next;
    delete tempPtr;
  }
}
```

The linked implementation of the Stack ADT can be tested using the same test plan that was written for the array-based version.

Comparing Stack Implementations

We have looked at three different implementations of the Stack ADT. The first two were similar because they used an array to store the items; one used a static array and one used a dynamically allocated array. The third implementation is very different, using dynamic allocation for each item in the stack. We can compare these implementations in terms of storage requirements and efficiency of the algorithms. An array variable of the maximum stack size takes the same amount of memory, no matter how many array slots are actually used; we need to reserve space for the maximum possible. This is true no matter how space for the array is allocated. The linked implementation using dynamically allocated storage only requires space for the number of elements actually on the stack at run time. Note, however, that the elements are larger because we must store the link as well as the user's data.

We compare the relative "efficiency" of the three implementations in terms of Big-O notation. In all three implementations, the class constructor, `IsFull`, and `IsEmpty` clearly have O(1). They always take a constant amount of work. What about `Push`, `Top`, and `Pop`? Does the number of elements in the stack affect the amount of work done by these operations? No, it does not. In all three implementations, we directly access the top of the stack, so these operations also take a constant amount of work. They too have O(1) complexity.

The class destructors do differ from one implementation to the other. The array-based implementation in static storage did not need a destructor, but the array-based implementation in dynamic storage did need one. The destructor for the dynamically allocated array returns a single block of storage; the size of the block of cells does not change the amount of work. The complexity is therefore O(1). The linked implementation must process every node in the stack, in order to free the node space. This operation, therefore, has O(*N*) complexity, where *N* is the number of nodes in the stack.

Overall the three stack implementations are roughly equivalent in terms of the amount of work they do, only differing in one of the five operations and the class destructor. Note that if the difference had been in the `Push`, `Top`, or `Pop` operation, rather than the less frequently called destructor it would be more significant. Table 5.1 summarizes the Big-O comparison of the stack operations. The operation that differs between the three implementations is in boldface.

Table 5.1 *Big-O Comparison of Stack Operations*

	Static Array Implementation	Dynamic Array Implementation	Linked Implementation
class constructor	O(1)	O(1)	O(1)
IsFull	O(1)	O(1)	O(1)
IsEmpty	O(1)	O(1)	O(1)
Push	O(1)	O(1)	O(1)
Pop	O(1)	O(1)	O(1)
destructor	**NA**	**O(1)**	**O(*N*)**

So which is better? The answer, as usual, is: it depends on the situation. The linked implementation certainly gives more flexibility, and in applications where the number of stack items can vary greatly, it wastes less space when the stack is small. In situations where the stack size is totally unpredictable, the linked implementation is preferable, because size is largely irrelevant. Why then would we ever want to use an array-based implementation? Because it is short, simple, and efficient. If pushing and popping occur frequently, the array-based implementation executes faster because it does not incur the run-time overhead of the `new` and `delete` operations. When `maxStack` (`MAX_ITEMS` in the ADT specification) is small and we can be sure that we do not need to exceed the declared stack size, the array-based implementation is a good choice. Also, if you are programming in a language that does not support dynamic storage allocation, an array implementation may be the only good choice.

5.3 Queues

Logical Level

A stack is an abstract data structure with the special property that elements are always added to and removed from the top. We know from experience that many collections of data elements operate in the reverse manner: Items are added at one end and removed from the other. This structure, called a FIFO (First In, First Out) queue, has many uses in computer programs. We consider the FIFO queue data structure at three levels: logical, implementation, and application. In the rest of this chapter, "queue" refers to a FIFO queue. (Chapter 9 discusses another queue-type abstract data type, the priority queue. The accessing protocol of a priority queue differs from that of a FIFO queue.)

> **Queue** An abstract data type in which elements are added to the rear and removed from the front; a "first in, first out" (FIFO) structure

A queue (pronounced like the letter Q) is an ordered, homogeneous group of elements in which new elements are added at one end (the "rear") and elements are removed from the other end (the "front"). As an example of a queue, consider a line of students waiting to pay for their textbooks at a university bookstore (see Figure 5.7). In theory, if not in practice, each new student gets in line at the rear. When the cashier is ready to help a new customer, the student at the front of the line is served.

Figure 5.7 *A FIFO queue*

To add elements to a queue, we access the rear of the queue; to remove elements, we access the front of the queue. The middle elements are logically inaccessible, even if we physically store the queue elements in a random-access structure such as an array. It is convenient to picture the queue as a linear structure with the front at one end and the rear at the other end. However, we must stress that the "ends" of the queue are abstractions; they may or may not correspond to any physical characteristics of the queue's implementation. The essential property of the queue is its FIFO access.

Like a stack, a queue is a holding structure for data that we use later. We put a data item onto the queue; when we need it later, we remove it from the queue. If we want to change the value of an element, we must take that element off the queue, change its value, and then return it to the queue. We do not directly manipulate the values of items that are currently in the queue.

Operations on Queues The bookstore example suggests two operations that we can apply to a queue. First, new elements can be added to the rear of the queue, an operation that we call Enqueue. We can also remove elements from the front of the queue, an operation that we call Dequeue. Unlike the stack operations Push and Pop, the adding and removing operations on a queue do not have standard names. Enqueue is sometimes called Enq, Enqueue, Add, and Insert; Dequeue is also called Deq, Deque, Remove, and Serve.

Another useful queue operation is checking whether the queue is empty. The IsEmpty function returns true if the queue is empty and false otherwise. We can apply Dequeue only when the queue is not empty. Theoretically, we can always apply Enqueue, because in principle a queue has no limit on its size. We know from our experience with stacks, however, that certain implementations (an array representation, for instance) require that we test whether the structure is full before we add another element. This real-world consideration applies to queues as well, so we define an IsFull operation. We also need an operation to restore a queue to an empty state, which we call MakeEmpty. Figure 5.8 shows how a series of these operations would affect a queue.

We have briefly described a set of accessing operations for a queue. Before we talk about this structure's use and implementation, let's define the specification for the Queue ADT.

We continue to leave the statements in the specifications defining what the user must provide. However, as we are using C++, we assume that this information might be provided when a class object is declared (in the form of a constructor parameter or an included class).

Queue ADT Specification

Structure: Elements are added to the rear and removed from the front of the queue.

Definitions (provided by user in class ItemType):

MAX_ITEMS: Maximum number of items that might be on the queue.

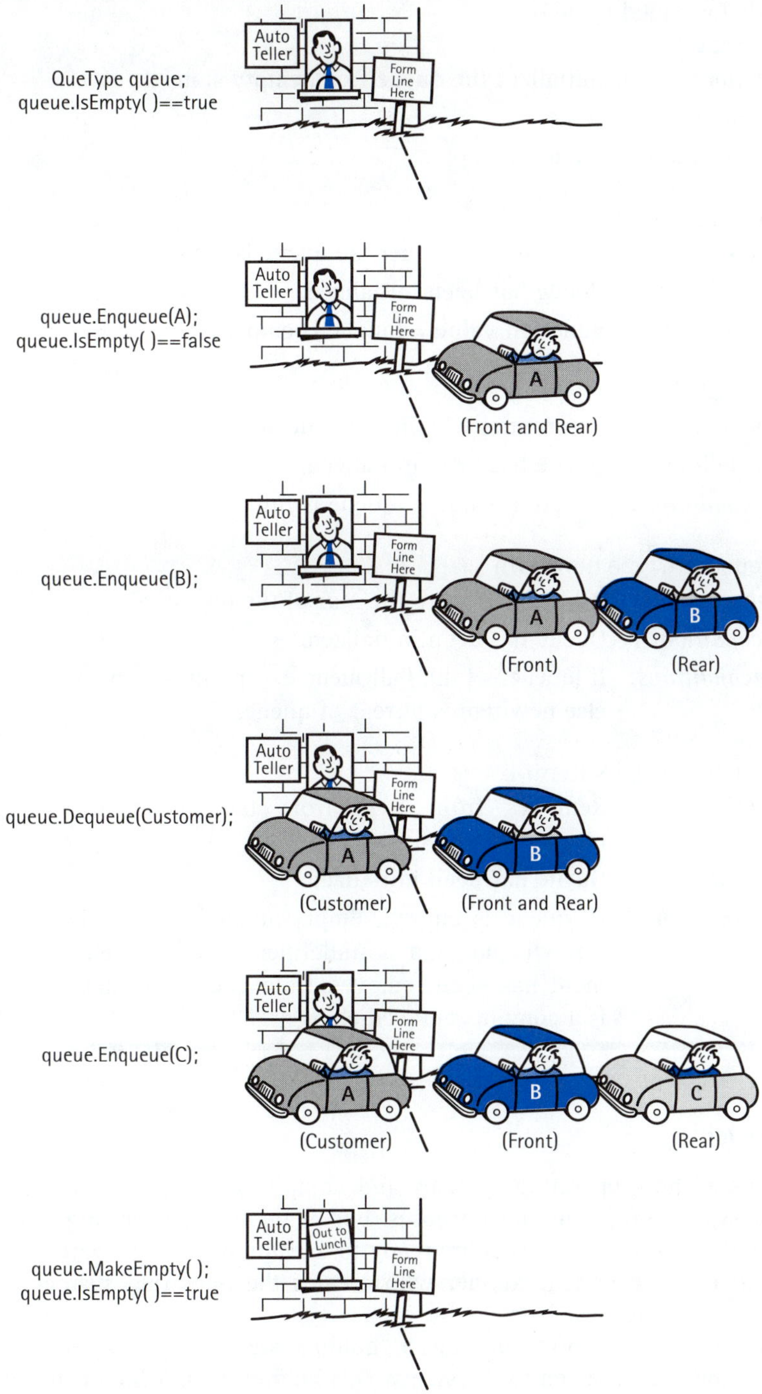

Figure 5.8 *The effects of queue operations*

Operations (provided by ADT):

MakeEmpty

Function: Initializes the queue to an empty state.

Precondition: None.

Postcondition: Queue is empty.

Boolean IsEmpty

Function: Determines whether the queue is empty.

Precondition: Queue has been initialized.

Postcondition: Function value = (queue is empty).

Boolean IsFull

Function: Determines whether the queue is full.

Precondition: Queue has been initialized.

Postcondition: Function value = (queue is full).

Enqueue(ItemType newItem)

Function: Adds newItem to the rear of the queue.

Precondition: Queue has been initialized.

Postconditions: If (queue is full), FullQueue exception is thrown, else newItem is at rear of queue.

Dequeue(ItemType& item)

Function: Removes front item from the queue and returns it in item.

Precondition: Queue has been initialized.

Postconditions: If (queue is empty), EmptyQueue exception is thrown and item is undefined, else front element has been removed from queue and item is a copy of removed element.

Application Level

We have discussed how operating systems and compilers can use stacks. Queues are often used for system programming purposes. For example, an operating system often maintains a FIFO list of processes that are ready to execute or that are waiting for a particular event to occur. The programmer who creates the operating system can use a Queue ADT to implement these lists.

Computer systems must often provide a "holding area" for messages between two processes, two programs, or even two systems. This holding area, which is usually called a "buffer," is often implemented as a FIFO queue. For example, if a large number of mail messages arrive at a mail server at about the same time, the messages are held in a buffer until the mail server can begin processing them. It processes the messages in the order they arrived—that is, first in, first out order. (Some mail servers may handle the messages based on a priority system; in such a case, the priority queue described in Chapter 9 would be a more appropriate ADT.)

To demonstrate the use of queues, we first look at a simple problem: identifying palindromes. A palindrome is a string that reads the same forward as backward. While we are not sure of their general usefulness, identifying these strings provides us with a good example for the use of both queues and stacks. Besides, palindromes can be entertaining. Some famous palindromes are:

- A tribute to Teddy Roosevelt, who orchestrated the creation of the Panama Canal: "A man, a plan, a canal—Panama!"
- Allegedly muttered by Napoleon Bonaparte upon his exile to the island of Elba (although this is difficult to believe given that Napoleon mostly spoke French!): "Able was I ere, I saw Elba."
- Overheard in a Chinese restaurant: "Won ton? Not now!"
- Possibly the world's first palindrome: "Madam, I'm Adam."
- Followed immediately by one of the world's shortest palindromes: "Eve."

As you can see, the rules for what constitutes a palindrome are somewhat lenient. Typically, we do not worry about punctuation, spaces, or matching the case of letters. Two obvious algorithms exist for determining whether a string is a palindrome. The first algorithm starts at both ends, moving inward as you compare the characters. Three cases are possible:

1. There are two characters that do not match.
2. The characters all match, including the two middle characters.
3. The number of characters is odd and the characters on the right and left of the middle character match.

The second algorithm copies the string in reverse order and matches the two copies character by character. As we already have a structure that returns a string in reverse order, let's use the second algorithm.

The characters are read character by character and stored into a queue and a stack. When all of the characters in the line have been processed, the program repeatedly pops a letter from the stack, and dequeues a letter from the queue. As long as these letters match each other, the entire way through this process, we have a palindrome. Can you see why? Because the queue is a first in, first out list, the letters are returned from the queue in the same order they appear in the string. The letters taken from the stack, however, are returned in the opposite order from how they appear in the string. Thus this algorithm compares the letters from the forward view of the string to the letters from the backward view of the string.

Now we are ready to write the main algorithm assuming an instance of a Stack ADT and an instance of the Queue ADT. The basic flow of the algorithm is to continuously read and handle characters until we reach the end of the line.

Main Algorithm

```
Set character to the first character in string
while (character != '\n')
    Push the character onto the stack
    Enqueue the character
    Set character to next character
Set palindrome to true
while (palindrome AND ! queue.IsEmpty())
    Set stackChar to the top of the stack
    Pop the stack
    Set queChar to the front of the queue
    if (stackChar != queChar)
        Set palindrome to false
if (palindrome)
    Write "String is a palindrome."
else
    Write "String is not a palindrome."
```

All of the statements in the algorithm can be coded immediately, using `StackType` and `QueType` objects. The program is found in the file `palindrome.cpp`.

```
#include "QueType.h"
#include "StackType.h"
#include <iostream>

int main()
{
  using namespace std;
  bool palindrome = true;
  char character;
  StackType stack(40);
  QueType queue(40);
  char stackChar;
  char queChar;
  cout << "Enter a string; press return." << endl;
  cin.get(character);
  while (character != '\n')
  {
    stack.Push(character);
```

```
    queue.Enqueue(character);
    cin.get(character);
  }

  while (palindrome && !queue.IsEmpty())
  {
    stackChar = stack.Top();
    stack.Pop();
    queue.Dequeue(queChar);

    if (stackChar != queChar)
      palindrome = false;
  }

  if (palindrome)
    cout << "String is a palindrome" << endl;
  else
    cout << "String is not a palindrome" << endl;
  return 0;
}
```

The two screenshots illustrate the correctness and the limitations of this algorithm. Uppercase and lowercase letters are not considered to be the same. Does this algorithm have other problems? You are asked to examine this question and improve this algorithm in the exercises.

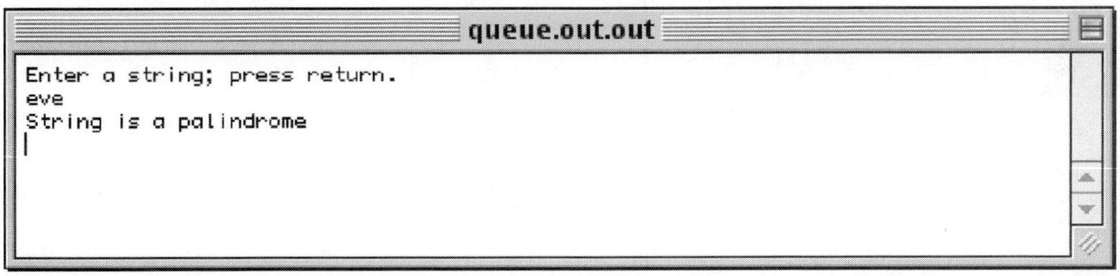

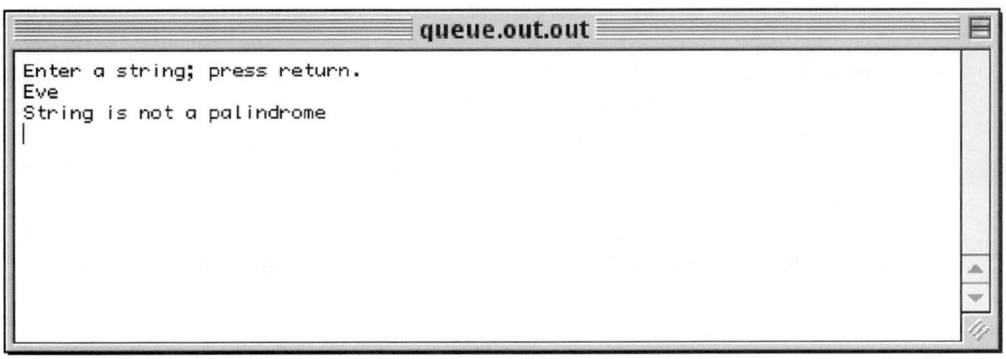

Implementation Level

Now that we've had the opportunity to be queue users, let's look at how we might implement a queue in C++. Like a stack, a queue can be stored in a static array with its size fixed at compile time or in a dynamically allocated array with its size determined at run time. We look at the dynamic implementation here.

Definition of the Queue Class To concentrate on the ADT Queue itself, we implement it as a queue of `char` items. Let's make the array dynamically allocated. As with the stack class, we do not need a comparison function because none of the operations requires comparing items on the queue.

Which data members does our Queue ADT need? We need the items themselves, but at this stage we do not know what else we need. We allow the user to determine the maximum size by using a parameterized constructor. Note also that we implement a `MakeEmpty` function as well as a class constructor.

```
typedef char ItemType;
class QueType
{
public:
  QueType(int max); // max is the size of the queue.
  QueType();        // Default size of 500.
  ~QueType();
  void MakeEmpty();
  bool IsEmpty() const;
  bool IsFull() const;
  void Enqueue(ItemType item);
  void Dequeue(ItemType& item);
private:
  ItemType* items;
  int maxQue;
  // Whatever else we need.
};
```

Implementations of Queue Operations The first question to consider is how we order the items in the array. In implementing the stack, we began by inserting an element into the first array position and then let the top float with subsequent `Push` and `Pop` operations. The bottom of the stack, however, remained fixed at the first slot in the array. Can we use a similar solution for a queue, keeping the front of the queue fixed in the first array slot and letting the rear move down as we add new elements?

Let's see what happens after a few `Enqueue` and `Dequeue` operations if we insert the first element into the first array position, the second element into the second position, and so on. After four calls to `Enqueue` with parameters 'A', 'B', 'C', and 'D', the queue would look like this:

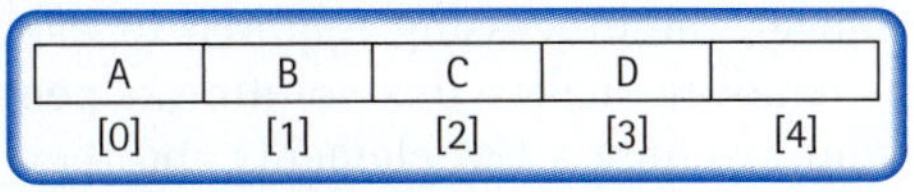

Recall that the front of the queue is fixed at the first slot in the array, whereas the rear of the queue moves down with each `Enqueue`. Now we `Dequeue` the front element in the queue:

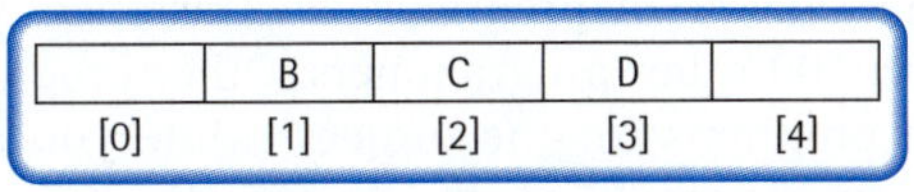

This operation deletes the element in the first array slot and leaves a hole. To keep the front of the queue fixed at the top of the array, we need to move every element in the queue up one slot:

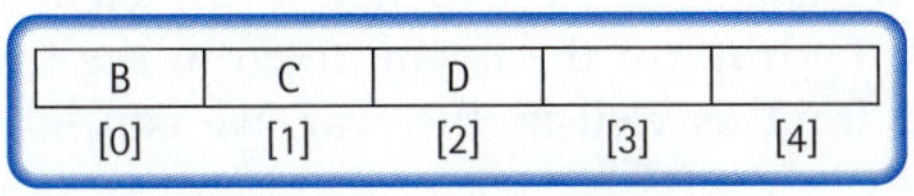

Let's summarize the queue operations corresponding to this queue design. The `Enqueue` operation would be the same as `Push`. The `Dequeue` operation would be more complicated than `Pop`, because all remaining elements of the queue would have to be shifted up in the array, so as to move the new front of the queue up to the first array slot. The class constructor, `MakeEmpty`, `IsEmpty`, and `IsFull` operations could be the same as the equivalent stack operations.

Before going any further, we want to stress that this design would work. It may not be the best design for a queue, but it could be implemented successfully. Multiple *functionally correct* ways to implement the same abstract data structure exist. One design may not be as good as another (because it uses more space in memory or takes longer to execute), yet may still be correct. Although we don't advocate the use of poor designs for programs or data structures, the first requirement must always be program correctness.

Now let's evaluate this particular design. Its strengths are its simplicity and ease of coding; it is almost exactly like the stack implementation. Although the queue is accessed from both ends rather than just one end (as in the stack), we have to keep track of only the rear, because the front remains fixed. Only the `Dequeue` operation is more complicated. What is the weakness of the design? The need to move all of the elements up every time we remove an element from the queue increases the amount of work needed to dequeue items.

How serious is this weakness? To make this judgment, we must know something about how the queue will be used. If this queue is used for storing large numbers of elements at one time, or if the elements in the queue are large (class objects with many data members, for instance), the processing required to move up all elements after the front element has been removed makes this solution a poor one. On the other hand, if the queue generally contains only a few elements and they are small (integers, for instance), the data movement may not require much processing. Furthermore, we need to consider whether performance—how fast the program executes—is important to the application that uses the queue. Thus the complete evaluation of the design depends on the client program's requirements.

In the real programming world, of course, you don't always know the exact uses or complete requirements of programs. For instance, you may be working on a very large project with 100 other programmers. Other programmers may be writing the specific application programs for the project, while you are producing some utility programs that are used by all of the different applications. If you don't know the requirements of the various users of your package of queue operations, you must design general-purpose utilities. In this situation, the design described here is not the best option.

Another Queue Design The need to move the elements in the array arose from our decision to keep the front of the queue fixed in the first array slot. If we keep track of the index of the front as well as the rear, we can let both ends of the queue float in the array.

Figure 5.9 shows how several `Enqueue` and `Dequeue` operations would affect the queue. (For simplicity, the figure shows only the elements in the queue. The other slots

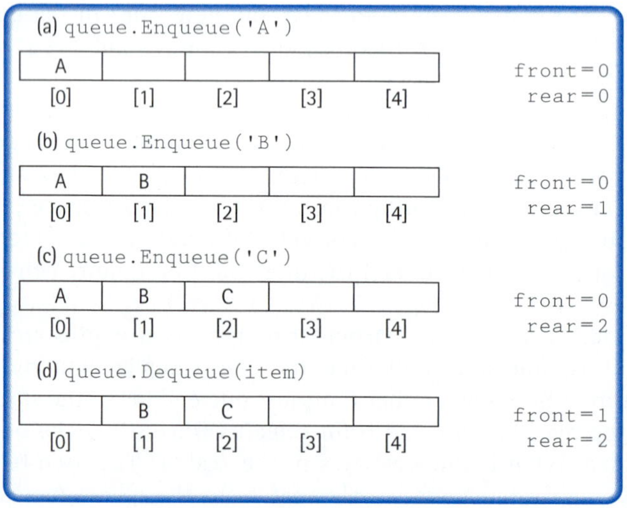

Figure 5.9 *The effect of* `Enqueue` *and* `Dequeue`

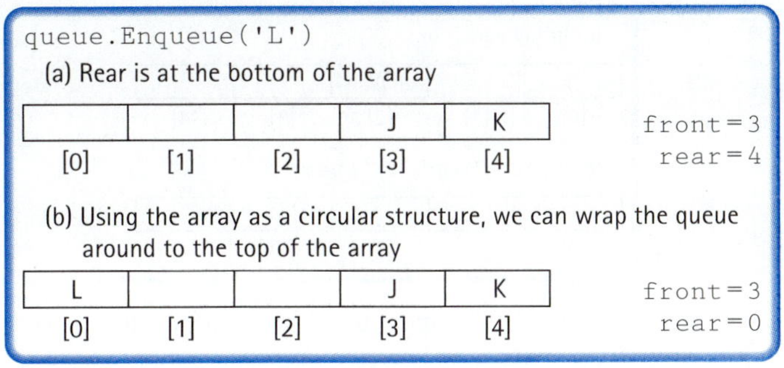

Figure 5.10 *Wrapping the queue elements around*

contain logical garbage, including dequeued values.) The `Enqueue` operations have the same effect as before; they add elements to subsequent slots in the array and increment the index of the rear indicator. The `Dequeue` operation is simpler, however. Instead of moving elements up to the beginning of the array, it merely increments the front indicator to the next slot.

Letting the queue elements float in the array creates a new problem when the rear indicator reaches the end of the array. In our first design, this situation told us that the queue was full. Now, however, the rear of the queue might potentially reach the end of the (physical) array when the (logical) queue is not yet full (Figure 5.10a).

Because space may still be available at the beginning of the array, the obvious solution is to let the queue elements "wrap around" the end of the array. In other words, we can treat the array as a circular structure, in which the last slot is followed by the first slot (Figure 5.10b). To get the next position for the rear indicator, for instance, we can use an *if* statement:

```
if (rear == maxQue - 1)
  rear = 0;
else
  rear = rear + 1
```

We can also reset `rear` by using the remainder (%) operator:

```
rear = (rear + 1) % maxQue;
```

This solution leads us to a new problem: How do we know whether a queue is empty or full? In Figure 5.11, we remove the last element, leaving the queue empty. In Figure 5.12, we add an element to the last free slot in the queue, leaving the queue full. The values of `front` and `rear`, however, are identical in the two situations. We cannot distinguish between a full queue and an empty queue.

The first solution that comes to mind is to add another data member to our queue class, in addition to `front` and `rear`—a count of the elements in the queue. When the

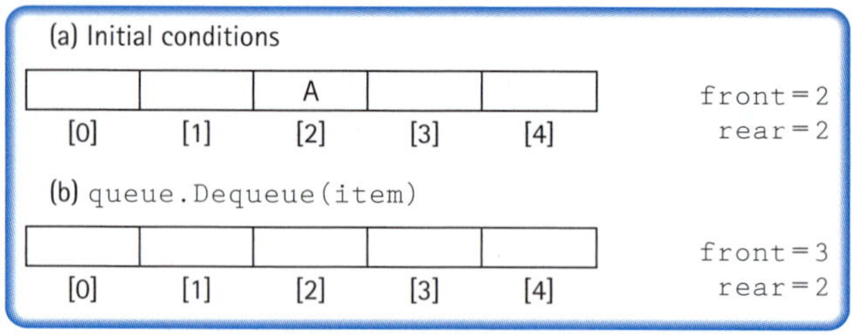

Figure 5.11 *An empty queue*

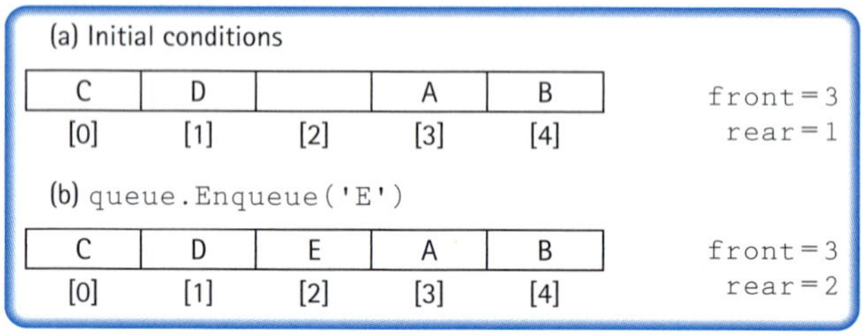

Figure 5.12 *A full queue*

count member is 0, the queue is empty; when the count is equal to the maximum number of array slots, the queue is full. Note that keeping this count adds work to the `Enqueue` and `Dequeue` routines. If the queue user frequently needed to know the number of elements in the queue, however, this solution would certainly be a good one. We leave the development of this solution as an exercise.

Another common, but less intuitive approach is to let `front` indicate the index of the array slot *preceding* the front element in the queue, rather than the index of the front element itself. (The reason for this choice may not be clear immediately, but keep reading.) If `rear` still indicates the index of the rear element in the queue, the queue is empty when `front` is equal to `rear`. To dequeue an element, we increment `front` to indicate the true location of the front queue element, and assign the value in that array slot to `item`. (Updating `front` precedes assigning the value in this design, because `front` does not point to the actual front element at the beginning of `Dequeue`.) After this `Dequeue` operation, `IsEmpty` finds that `front` is equal to `rear`, indicating that the queue is empty (see Figure 5.13).

An additional convention that we must establish to implement this scheme is that the slot indicated by `front` (the slot preceding the true front element) is reserved. It cannot contain a queue element. Thus, if there are 100 array positions, the maximum size of the queue is 99 elements. To test for a full queue, we check whether the next space available (after `rear`) is the special reserved slot indicated by `front` (see Figure 5.14).

To enqueue an element, we must first increment `rear` so that it contains the index of the next free slot in the array. We can then insert the new element into this space.

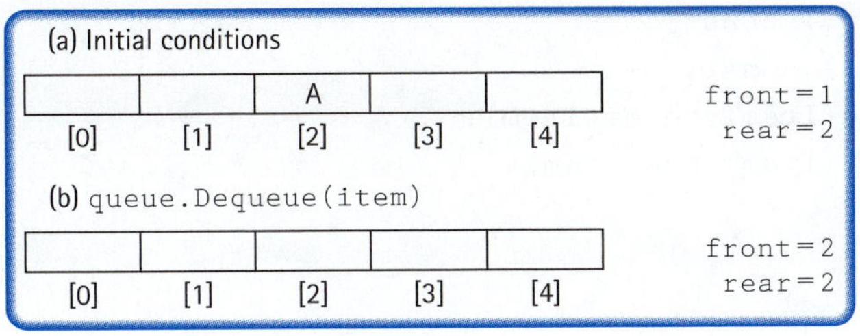

Figure 5.13 *Testing for an empty queue*

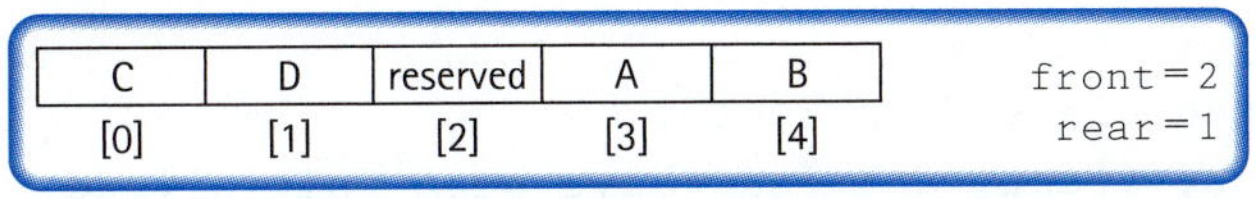

Figure 5.14 *Testing for a full queue*

Using this scheme, how do we initialize a queue to its empty state? We want `front` to indicate the array index that precedes the front of the queue, so that when we first call `Enqueue` the front of the queue is in the first slot of the array. Which position precedes the first array slot? Because the array is circular, the first slot is preceded by the last slot. As a consequence, we initialize `front` to `maxQue - 1`. Because our test for an empty queue is checking whether `front` is equal to `rear`, we initialize `rear` to `front`, or `maxQue - 1`.

Now we see that we must add two data members to the `QueType` class: `front` and `rear`. The header file follows. Through the parameterized constructor, we let the user determine the maximum size of the queue when a class object is declared. Because our implementation takes one more array slot, we must increment `max` (the parameter to the constructor) before we save it in `maxQue`. (This implementation is called a circular or ring queue.)

```
class FullQueue
{};
class EmptyQueue
{};

typedef char ItemType;
class QueType
{
public:
  QueType(int max);
  QueType();
  ~QueType();
  void MakeEmpty();
```

```
  bool IsEmpty() const;
  bool IsFull() const;
  void Enqueue(ItemType newItem);
  void Dequeue(ItemType& item);
private:
  int front;
  int rear;
  ItemType* items;
  int maxQue;
};
QueType::QueType(int max)
// Parameterized class constructor.
// Post: maxQue, front, and rear have been initialized.
//       The array to hold the queue elements has been dynamically
//       allocated.
{
  maxQue = max + 1;
  front = maxQue - 1;
  rear = maxQue - 1;
  items = new ItemType[maxQue];
}
QueType::QueType()      // Default class constructor.
// Post: maxQue, front, and rear have been initialized.
//       The array to hold the queue elements has been dynamically
//       allocated.
{
  maxQue = 501;
  front = maxQue - 1;
  rear = maxQue - 1;
  items = new ItemType[maxQue];
}
QueType::~QueType()     // Class destructor.
{
  delete [] items;
}
void QueType::MakeEmpty()
// Post: front and rear have been reset to the empty state.
{
  front = maxQue - 1;
  rear = maxQue - 1;
}
```

```
bool QueType::IsEmpty() const
// Returns true if the queue is empty; false otherwise.
{
  return (rear == front);
}

bool QueType::IsFull() const
// Returns true if the queue is full; false otherwise.
{
  return ((rear + 1) % maxQue == front);
}

void QueType::Enqueue(ItemType newItem)
// Post: If (queue is not full) newItem is at the rear of the queue;
//       otherwise, a FullQueue exception is thrown.
{
  if (IsFull())
    throw FullQueue();
  else
  {
    rear = (rear +1) % maxQue;
    items[rear] = newItem;
  }
}

void QueType::Dequeue(ItemType& item)
// Post: If (queue is not empty) the front of the queue has been
//       removed and a copy returned in item;
//       otherwise, an EmptyQueue exception is thrown.
{
  if (IsEmpty())
    throw EmptyQueue();
  else
  {
    front = (front + 1) % maxQue;
    item = items[front];
  }
}
```

Note that `Dequeue`, like the stack `Pop` operation, does not actually remove the value of the item from the array. The dequeued value still physically exists in the array. It no longer exists in the queue, however, and cannot be accessed because of the change in `front`. That is, the dequeued data element exists in the implementation but not in the abstraction.

Test Plan To make sure that you have tested all the necessary cases, make a test plan, listing the various queue operations and what tests are needed for each, as we did for stacks. (For example, to test the function IsEmpty, you must call it at least twice—once when the queue is empty and once when it is not.)

We want to Enqueue elements until the queue is full and then call the functions IsEmpty and IsFull to see whether they correctly judge the state of the queue. We can then Dequeue all elements in the queue, printing them out as we go, to confirm that they are correctly removed. At that point, we can call the queue status functions again to see whether the empty condition is detected correctly. We also want to test the "tricky" part of the array-based algorithm: Enqueue until the queue is full, Dequeue an element, then Enqueue again, forcing the operation to circle back to the beginning of the array.

On the Web, the test driver is located in QueDr.cpp, the input file is QueType.in, and the output files are QueType.out and QueType.screen.

Comparing Array Implementations The circular array solution is not nearly as simple or intuitive as our first queue design. What did we gain by adding some amount of complexity to our design? By using a more efficient Dequeue algorithm, we achieved better performance. To find out how much better, let's analyze the first design. Because the amount of work needed to move all of the remaining elements is proportional to the number of elements, this version of Dequeue is an $O(N)$ operation. The second array-based queue design simply requires Dequeue to change the values of the front indicator and to put the value into item to be returned. The amount of work never exceeds some fixed constant, no matter how many elements are in the queue, so the algorithm has $O(1)$ complexity.

The other operations all have $O(1)$ complexity. No matter how many items are in the queue, they do (essentially) a constant amount of work.

Counted Queue

Our Queue ADT did not have an operation that determined the number of items on the queue. Let's define a new class called CountedQueType that is derived from the class QueType and has a data member length that records the number of items on the queue.

```
typedef char ItemType;
class CountedQueType : public QueType
{
public:
  CountedQueType(int max);
  void Enqueue(ItemType newItem);
  void Dequeue(ItemType& item);
  int GetLength() const;
  // Returns the number of items on the queue.
private:
  int length;
};
  :
```

Although we used inheritance in the Case Study in the last chapter, we review it in more detail here. The line

```
class CountedQueType : public QueType
```

states that `CountedQueType` is derived from `QueType`; that is, `CountedQueType` is the derived class and `QueType` is the base class. The reserved word `public` declares `QueType` to be a *public base class* of `CountedQueType`. As a result, all public members of `QueType` are also public members of `CountedQueType`. In other words, `QueType`'s member functions `Enqueue`, `Dequeue`, `IsEmpty`, and `IsFull` can also be invoked for objects of type `CountedQueType`. The public part of the class `CountedQueType` further specializes the base class by redefining the inherited functions `Enqueue` and `Dequeue` and by adding the data member `length`, an operation that returns the value of `length`, and its own class constructor.

Every object of type `CountedQueType` has an object of type `QueType` as a subobject. That is, an object of type `CountedQueType` is an object of type `QueType` and more. Figure 5.15 shows a *class interface diagram* for the `CountedQueType` class. The public interface, shown as ovals at the side of the large circles, consists of the operations available to the client code. The private data items shown in the interior are inaccessible to clients. A dashed line between ovals indicates that the two operations are the same. For example, `IsEmpty` applied to an object of `CountedQueType` is the `IsEmpty` member function defined in type `QueType`. However, `Enqueue` applied to an object of type `CountedQueType` is not the `Enqueue` defined in `QueType`, but rather the one defined in `CountedQueType`.

C++ uses the terms *base class* and *derived class*; the corresponding terms *superclass* and *subclass* are also used in the literature. The use of "superclass" and "subclass" can prove confusing, however, because the prefix *sub* usually implies something smaller than the original (for example, a subset of a mathematical set). In reality, a subclass is often "bigger" than its superclass—that is, it includes more data and/or functions.

Implementation of the Derived Class The implementation of the `CountedQueType` class needs to deal with only the new features that differ from those in `QueType`. Specifically, we must write the code to override the `Enqueue` and `Dequeue` functions, and we must write the `GetLength` function and the class constructor. The new `Enqueue` and `Dequeue` functions just need to increment or decrement the `length` data member and call the `QueType` functions of the same name. `GetLength` simply returns the value of `length`. The class constructor sets `length` to zero and can use the `QueType` class constructor to initialize the rest of the class data members. Because `Enqueue` and `Dequeue` can throw exceptions, the calls to them must be enclosed within a *try/catch* statement. We just forward the exceptions to the client's level. Here is the code. A discussion of the syntactic details follows.

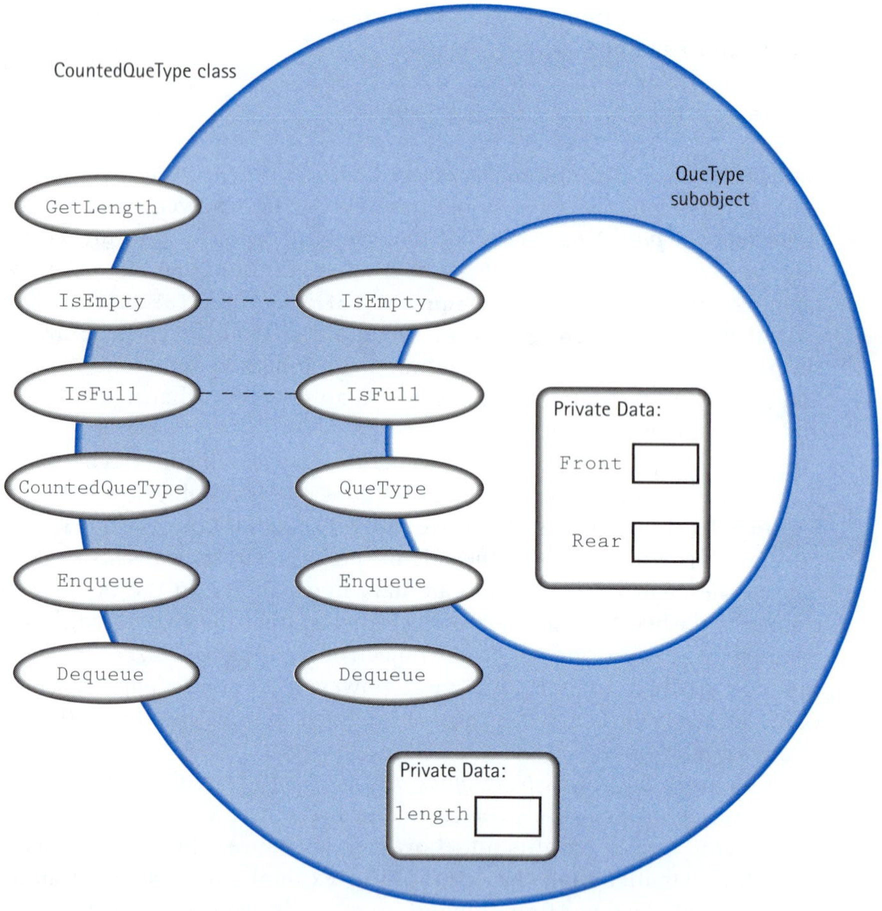

Figure 5.15 *Class interface diagram for `CountedQueType` class*

```
#include "CountedQueType.h"

void CountedQueType::Enqueue(ItemType newItem)
{
  try
  {
    QueType::Enqueue(newItem);
    length++;
  }
  catch(FullQueue)
  {
    throw FullQueue();
  }
}
```

```
void CountedQueType::Dequeue(ItemType& item)
{
  try
  {
    QueType::Dequeue(item);
    length--;
  }
  catch(EmptyQueue)
  {
    throw EmptyQueue();
  }
}

int CountedQueType::GetLength() const
{
  return length;
}

CountedQueType::CountedQueType(int max) : QueType(max)
{
  length = 0;
}
```

Note two points of syntax here. For `Enqueue` to invoke the `Enqueue` defined in `QueType`, the name of the class must precede the function name, with the scope resolution operator (`::`) appearing in between the two names. The same is true for `Dequeue`. In the class constructor, `length` is set to zero, but how are `front` and `rear` set? The colon followed by `QueType(max)` after the parameter list of the derived-class constructor causes the invocation of the base-class constructor. This construct (colon followed by a call to the base-class constructor) is known as a *constructor initializer.*

A class such as `QueType` can be used as-is in many different contexts or can be adapted to a particular context by using inheritance. Inheritance allows us to create *extensible* data abstractions—a derived class typically extends the base class by including additional private data or public operations or both.

The items on an instance of a `CountedQueType` are characters because we extended the `QueType` that we examined earlier.

Application of the `CountedQueType` Class FIFO queues are often used as "waiting lines." Such waiting lines are common on multiuser computer systems and networked systems of workstations. If you use a multiuser or networked computer system, you probably share a printer with other users. When you request a printout of a file, your request is added to a print queue. When your request reaches the front of the print queue, your file is printed. The print queue ensures that only one person at a time has access to the printer and that this access is doled out on a first come, first served basis. Similarly, queues are used to schedule use of other shared resources such as disks and tapes.

Another application area in which queues figure prominently as data structures is the computer simulation of real-world situations. For instance, consider a bank that plans to install drive-up teller windows. The bank should hire enough tellers to service each car within a "reasonable" wait time, but not too many tellers for the number of customers. It may want to run a computer simulation of typical customer transactions, using objects to represent real-world physical objects such as tellers, cars, and a clock. The queue is used to represent the waiting customers.

Queuing simulations usually involve servers (the bank tellers), the items in the queue (people, cars, or whatever is waiting to be served), and the amount of time each item in the queue requires. By varying these parameters and keeping track of the average queue lengths, management can determine how many servers must be employed to keep the customers happy. Therefore, in simulations using queues, the number of items in each queue is important information. Of course, the client program can calculate this information by dequeuing, counting, and enqueuing again, but a derived counted queue is a better choice.

Inheritance and Accessibility Inheritance is a logical issue, not an implementation issue. A class inherits the behavior of another class and enhances it in some way. Inheritance does *not* mean inheriting access to another class's private variables. Although some languages do allow access to the base class's private members, such access often defeats the purpose of encapsulation and information hiding. C++ does not allow access to the private data members of the base class. Neither external client code nor derived class code can directly access the private members of the base class.

5.4 Implementing a Queue as a Linked Structure

Function `Enqueue`

In the array-based implementation of a queue, we decided to keep track of two indexes that pointed to the front and rear boundaries of the data in the queue. In a linked representation, we can use two pointers, `front` and `rear`, to mark the front and the rear of the queue. (See Figure 5.16. By now you realize that dynamically allocated nodes in

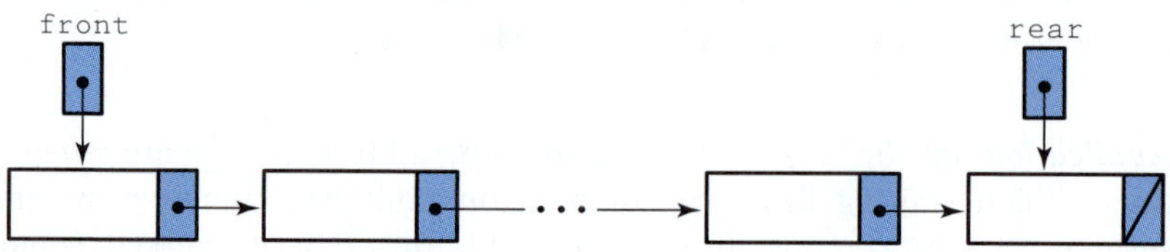

Figure 5.16 *A linked queue representation*

linked structures exist "somewhere on the free store," rather than in adjacent locations like array slots, but we will show the nodes arranged linearly for clarity.)

We can `Dequeue` elements from the queue using an algorithm similar to our stack `Pop` algorithm, with `front` pointing to the first node in the queue. Because we add new elements to the queue by inserting after the last node, however, we need a new `Enqueue` algorithm (see Figure 5.17).

Enqueue
Get a node for the new item
Insert the new node at the rear of the queue
Update pointer to the rear of the queue

The first of these tasks is familiar from the stack `Push` operation. We get the space using C++'s `new` operator and then store the new item into the node's `info` member. The new node is inserted at the rear end of the queue, so we also need to set the node's `next` member to `NULL`.

```
// Get a node for the new item.
Set newNode to the address of a newly allocated node
Set Info(newNode) to newItem
Set Next(newNode) to NULL
```

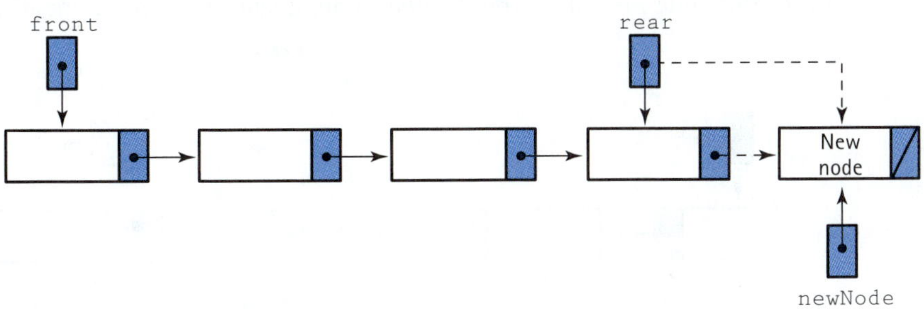

Figure 5.17 *The `Enqueue` operation*

The second part of the `Enqueue` algorithm involves updating the `next` member of Node(`rear`) to make it point to the new node. This task is simple:

```
// Insert the new node at the rear of the queue.
Set Next(rear) to newNode
```

What happens if the queue is empty, when we `Enqueue` the first element? In this case, no Node(`rear`) exists; we must set `front` to point to the new node. We modify the algorithm to take this condition into account:

```
// Insert the new node at the rear of the queue.
if the queue is empty
    Set front to newNode
else
    Set Next(rear) to newNode
```

The last task in the `Enqueue` algorithm, updating the `rear` pointer, simply involves the assignment `rear = newNode`. Does this approach work if this node is the first one in the queue? Yes—we want `rear` to always point to the rear node following a call to `Enqueue`, regardless of how many items are in the queue.

Note the relative positions of `front` and `rear`. Had they been reversed (as in Figure 5.18), we could have used our stack `Push` algorithm for the `Enqueue` operation. But how could we `Dequeue`? To delete the last node of the linked queue, we need to reset `front` to point to the node preceding the deleted node. Because our pointers all go forward, we

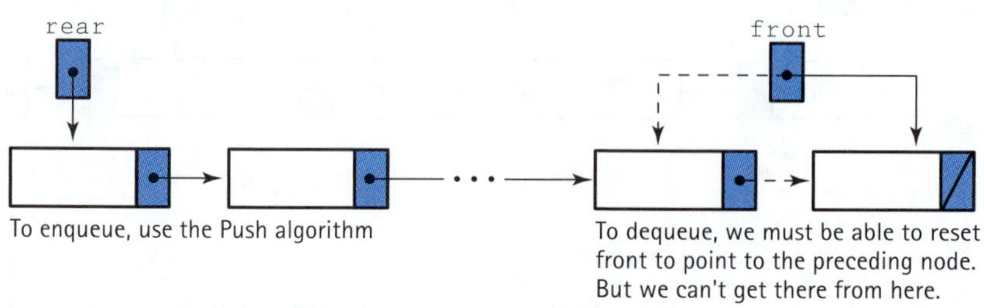

Figure 5.18 *A bad queue design*

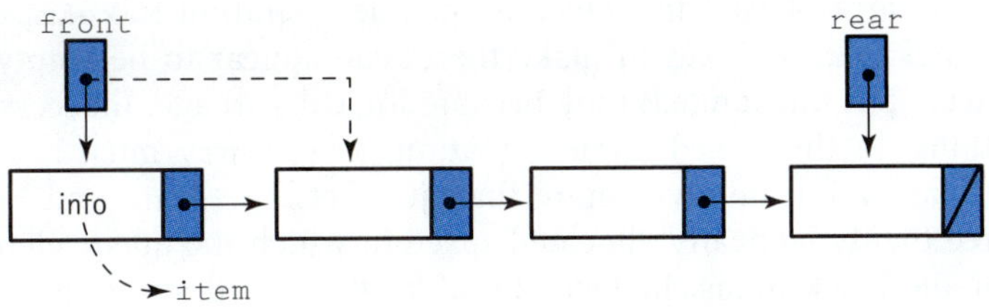

Figure 5.19 *The* `Dequeue` *operation*

can't get back to the preceding node. To accomplish this task, we would have to either traverse the whole list (an O(*N*) solution—very inefficient, especially if the queue is long) or keep a list with pointers in both directions. This kind of a *doubly linked* structure is not necessary if we set up our queue pointers correctly in the first place.

Function `Dequeue`

In writing the `Enqueue` algorithm, we noticed that inserting into an empty queue is a special case because we need to make `front` point to the new node. Similarly, in our `Dequeue` algorithm, we need to allow for the case of deleting the last node in the queue, leaving the queue empty. If `front` is `NULL` after we delete the front node, we know that the queue is now empty. In this case, we need to set `rear` to `NULL` as well. Figure 5.19 illustrates the algorithm for removing the front element from a linked queue. This algorithm assumes that the test for an empty queue was performed as specified, so we know that the queue contains at least one node. (We can make this assumption because an exception is thrown if it isn't true.) As with `Pop`, we need to keep a local pointer to the node being removed, allowing us to access it for the `delete` operation after the `front` pointer change.

```
Dequeue
Set tempPtr to front          // Save it for deallocating
Set item to Info(front)
Set front to Next(front)
if queue is now empty
    Set rear to NULL
Deallocate Node(tempPtr)
```

How do we know when the queue is empty? Both `front` and `rear` should then be `NULL` pointers. This fact makes the class constructor and `IsEmpty` extremely simple. What about the function `IsFull`? We can use the same `IsFull` we wrote for the Stack ADT.

In the array-based implementation, the operation `MakeEmpty` merely changed the `front` and `rear` indexes to make the queue appear to be empty. The data slots in the array were left unchanged; they became logical garbage, inaccessible through the queue operations. In the linked implementation, `MakeEmpty` must result in an empty queue, but this operation involves more than just setting `front` and `rear` to `NULL`. We must also free the dynamically allocated space in which the queue elements reside, just as we did for the stack items. In fact, the algorithm for destroying the queue is exactly the same as the algorithm for destroying the stack.

As in the case of changing the stack implementation to a linked structure, we change only the declarations and the insides of the queue operations. For a queue-using program, the interfaces to the operations remain the same. Let's look at the declarations first. In our design, we referred to the two queue pointers as `front` and `rear`. These pointers become the data members in our class `QueType`. Each points to a node in the linked queue (or is a `NULL` pointer if the queue is empty). Each queue node has two members, `info` (containing the user's data) and `next` (containing the pointer to the next node or, in the case of the last node, `NULL`). We can implement the FIFO Queue ADT with the following code.

```
// Header file for Queue ADT
class FullQueue
{};

class EmptyQueue
{};
typedef char ItemType
struct NodeType;

class QueType
{
public:
  QueType();
  ~QueType();
  void MakeEmpty();
  void Enqueue(ItemType);
  void Dequeue(ItemType&);
  bool IsEmpty() const;
  bool IsFull() const;
private:
  NodeType* front;
  NodeType* rear;
};

#include <cstddef>                    // For NULL.
#include <new>                        // For bad_alloc.
```

```
struct NodeType
{
  ItemType info;
  NodeType* next;
};

QueType::QueType()          // Class constructor.
// Post:  front and rear are set to NULL.
{
  front = NULL;
  rear = NULL;
}

void QueType::MakeEmpty()
// Post: Queue is empty; all elements have been deallocated.
{
  NodeType* tempPtr;

  while (front != NULL)
  {
    tempPtr = front;
    front = front->next;
    delete tempPtr;
  }
  rear = NULL;
}

// Class destructor.
QueType::~QueType()
{
  MakeEmpty();
}

bool QueType::IsFull() const
// Returns true if there is no room for another NodeType object
//  on the free store and false otherwise.
{
  NodeType* location;
  try
  {
    location = new NodeType;
    delete location;
    return false;
  }
```

```
  catch(std::bad_alloc exception)
  {
    return true;
  }
}

bool QueType::IsEmpty() const
// Returns true if there are no elements on the queue and false otherwise.
{
  return (front == NULL);
}

void QueType::Enqueue(ItemType newItem)
// Adds newItem to the rear of the queue.
// Pre:  Queue has been initialized.
// Post: If (queue is not full), newItem is at the rear of the queue;
//       otherwise, a FullQueue exception is thrown.

{
  if (IsFull())
    throw FullQueue();
  else
  {
    NodeType* newNode;

    newNode = new NodeType;
    newNode->info = newItem;
    newNode->next = NULL;
    if (rear == NULL)
      front = newNode;
    else
      rear->next = newNode;
    rear = newNode;
  }
}

void QueType::Dequeue(ItemType& item)
// Removes front item from the queue and returns it in item.
// Pre:  Queue has been initialized
// Post: If (queue is not empty), the front of the queue has been
//       removed and a copy returned in item;
//       otherwise, an EmptyQueue exception is thrown.
{
  if (IsEmpty())
    throw EmptyQueue();
  else
```

```
  {
    NodeType* tempPtr;

    tempPtr = front;
    item = front->info;
    front = front->next;
    if (front == NULL)
      rear = NULL;
    delete tempPtr;
  }
}
```

A Circular Linked Queue Design

Our `QueType` class contains two pointers, one to each end of the queue. This design is based on the linear structure of the linked queue. Given only a pointer to the front of the queue, we could follow the pointers to reach the rear, but this tactic turns accessing the rear (to `Enqueue` an item) into an $O(N)$ operation. With a pointer to the rear of the queue only, we could not access the front because the pointers go only from front to rear.

If we made the queue *circularly linked*, we could access both ends of the queue from a single pointer. That is, the `next` member of the rear node would point to the front node of the queue (see Figure 5.20). Now `QueType` has only one data member, rather than two. One interesting thing about this queue implementation is that it differs from the logical picture of a queue as a linear structure with two ends. This queue is a circular structure with no ends. What makes it a queue is its support of FIFO access.

To `Enqueue` an element, we access the "rear" node directly through the pointer `rear`. To `Dequeue` an element, we access the "front" node of the queue. We don't have a pointer to this node, but we do have a pointer to the node preceding it—`rear`. The pointer to the "front" node of the queue is in Next(`rear`). An empty queue is represented by `rear = NULL`. Designing and coding the queue operations using a circular linked implementation is left as a programming assignment.

We can test both linked implementations of the Queue ADT by using the same test plan that we wrote for the array-based version.

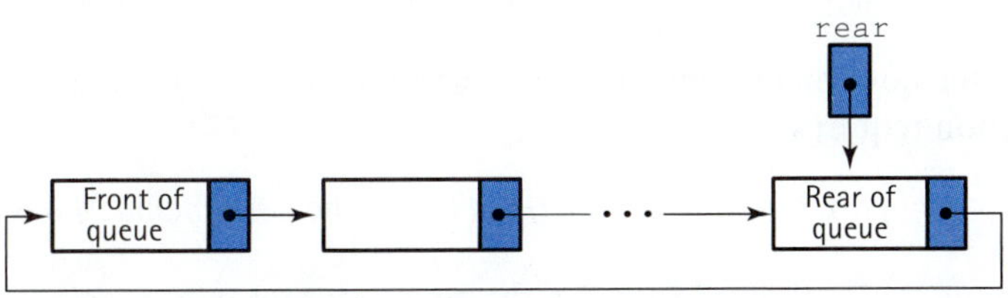

Figure 5.20 *A circular linked queue*

Comparing Queue Implementations

We have now looked at several different implementations of the Queue ADT. How do they compare? As when we compared the stack implementations, we look at two different factors: the amount of memory required to store the structure and the amount of "work" required by the solution, as expressed in Big-O notation. Let's compare the two implementations that we have coded completely: the array-based implementation and the dynamically linked implementation.

An array variable of the maximum queue size takes the same amount of memory, no matter how many array slots are actually used; we need to reserve space for the maximum possible number of elements. The linked implementation using dynamically allocated storage space requires space only for the number of elements actually in the queue at run time. Note, however, that the node elements are larger, because we must store the link (the `next` member) as well as the user's data.

Let's see how these implementations would compare if the queue contains strings (each requiring, say, 80 bytes). If the maximum number of queue elements is 100 strings, `maxQue` must be 101 to account for the reserved space before `front`. On our example system, an array index (type `int`) takes 2 bytes and a pointer takes 4 bytes. The storage requirements of the array-based implementation are

*(80 bytes * 101 array slots) + (2 bytes * 2 indexes) = 8,084 bytes*

no matter how many elements are in the queue at any time. The linked queue implementation requires

80 bytes (the string) + 4 bytes (the "next" pointer) = 84 bytes

per queue node, plus 8 bytes for the two external queue pointers. The storage requirements of these queue implementations are graphed in Figure 5.21a. Note that the linked implementation does not always take less space than the array; when the number of elements in the queue exceeds 96, the linked queue requires more memory, due to the need to store the pointers.

If the queue item type were small, such as a character or an integer, the pointer member could be larger than the user's data member. In this case, the space used by the linked representation exceeds that of the array-based representation much more quickly. Consider a queue that may contain a maximum of 100 integer elements (2 bytes each). The storage requirements for the array-based queue are

*(2 bytes (per element) * 101 array slots) + (2 bytes * 2 indexes) = 206 bytes*

no matter how many elements are in the queue at any time. The linked queue implementation requires

2 bytes (the `info` member) + 4 bytes (the `next` member) = 6 bytes

per queue node, plus 8 bytes for the two external queue pointers. The storage requirements for this queue are graphed in Figure 5.21b. When the number of elements in this

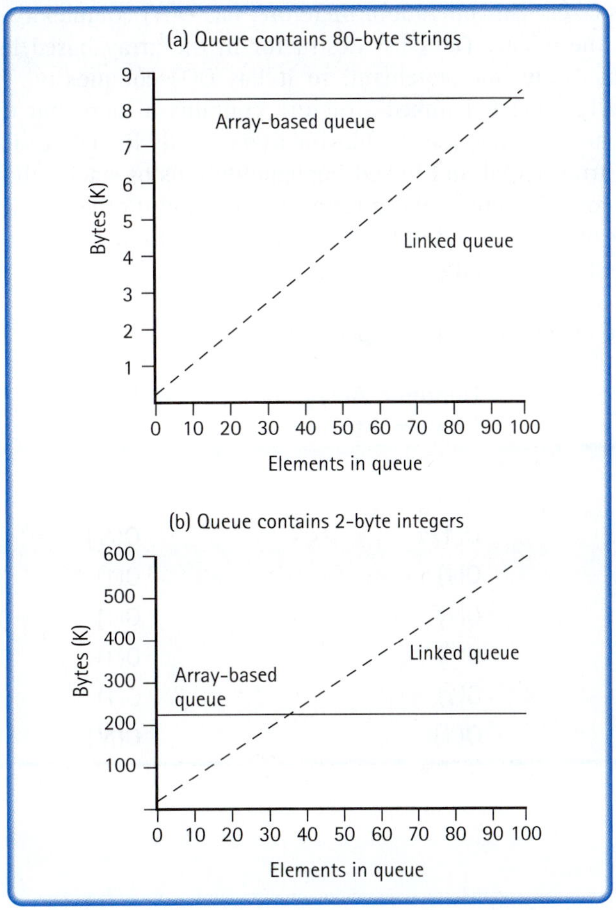

Figure 5.21 *Comparison of storage requirements*

queue exceeds 33, the linked queue requires more memory, due to the need to store pointers that are twice as big as the `ItemType`.

We can also compare the relative "efficiency" of the implementations, in terms of Big-O notation. The class constructors, `IsFull`, and `IsEmpty` operations are clearly O(1); they always take the same amount of work regardless of how many items are on the queue. What about `Enqueue` and `Dequeue`? Does the number of elements in the queue affect the amount of work done by these operations? No, it does not; in both implementations, we can directly access the front and rear of the queue. The amount of work done by these operations is independent of the queue size, so these operations also have O(1) complexity.

Only the `MakeEmpty` operation differs from one implementation to the other. The array-based implementation merely sets the `front` and `rear` indexes, so it is clearly an O(1) operation. The linked implementation must process every node in the queue to free the node space. This operation, therefore, has O(*N*) complexity, where *N* is the number of nodes in the queue. The class destructor in the array-based implementation in dynamic storage has only one statement, so it has O(1) complexity. The class destructor in the dynamically allocated linked structure contains a loop that executes as many times as there are items on the queue. Thus the dynamically linked version has O(*N*) complexity. As with the array-based and linked implementations of stacks, these two queue implementations are roughly equivalent in terms of the amount of work they do, differing only in one of the six operations and in the class destructor. Table 5.2 summarizes the Big-O comparison of the queue operations.

Table 5.2 *Big-O Comparison of Queue Operations*

	Dynamic Array Implementation	Linked Implementation
Class constructor	O(1)	O(1)
`MakeEmpty`	**O(1)**	**O(*N*)**
`IsFull`	O(1)	O(1)
`IsEmpty`	O(1)	O(1)
`Enqueue`	O(1)	O(1)
`Dequeue`	O(1)	O(1)
Destructor	**O(1)**	**O(*N*)**

Case Study

Simulating a Solitaire Game

Problem There is a Solitaire game that you have played for years and never won. Your father assures you that he has won it several times. Is the game winnable or is he teasing you? You decide to simulate the game and see if it is possible to win.

Although this Solitaire is played with a regular Poker or Bridge deck, the rules deal with suits only; the face values (ranks) are ignored. Here are the rules.

1. Take a deck of playing cards and shuffle it.
2. Place four cards, side by side, left to right, face up on the table.
3. If the four cards (or right-most four if there are more than four on the table) are the same suit, remove them to a discard pile. Otherwise, if the first and the fourth (of the right-most cards) are of the same suit, remove the cards between them to a discard pile. Repeat until you cannot move.
4. Take the next card from the shuffled deck and place it face up to the right of the cards already there. Repeat this step if there are fewer than four cards face up.

5. Repeat Steps 3 and 4 until no more cards remain in the deck. You win if all the cards are on the discard pile.

Figure 5.22 walks through the beginning of a typical game to demonstrate how the rules operate. Remember that the game deals with suits only. At least four cards must be face up on the table before the rules can be applied.

Discussion These rules read like those that come with a set of children's toys—only understandable after the toys are put together. Let's try rewriting the rules as an algorithm, but first let's make some general observations about the objects in the simulation. We already have the main objects: a card and a deck to contain them. Here are the other objects mentioned in the rules.

table
discard pile

The table is simply a container that holds the cards where they can be observed. We are always looking at the four most recent cards. "Most recent" cards sounds like a stack might be an appropriate container to represent the table. However, we have to be sure that there are at least four cards face up on the table; that is, in the stack. Our stack ADT doesn't have a length field. We could do what we did with the queue: We could use inheritance to create a counted stack. During the discussion of the stack at the logical level, we said that an alternative approach is to have the `Pop` operation return and remove the top item. Since this application does not look and then remove an item, this alternate approach would be better. We can add a `GetLength` operation. Here is the specification for our new version.

Counted Stack ADT Specification

Structure: Elements are added to and removed from the top of the stack.

Definitions (provided by user):

MAX_ITEMS:	Maximum number of items that might be on the stack.
ItemType:	Data type of the items on the stack.

Operations (provided by the ADT):

MakeEmpty

Function: Sets stack to an empty state.
Preconditions: None
Postcondition: Stack is empty.

Boolean IsEmpty

Function: Determines whether the stack is empty.
Precondition: Stack has been initialized.
Postcondition: Function value = (stack is empty)

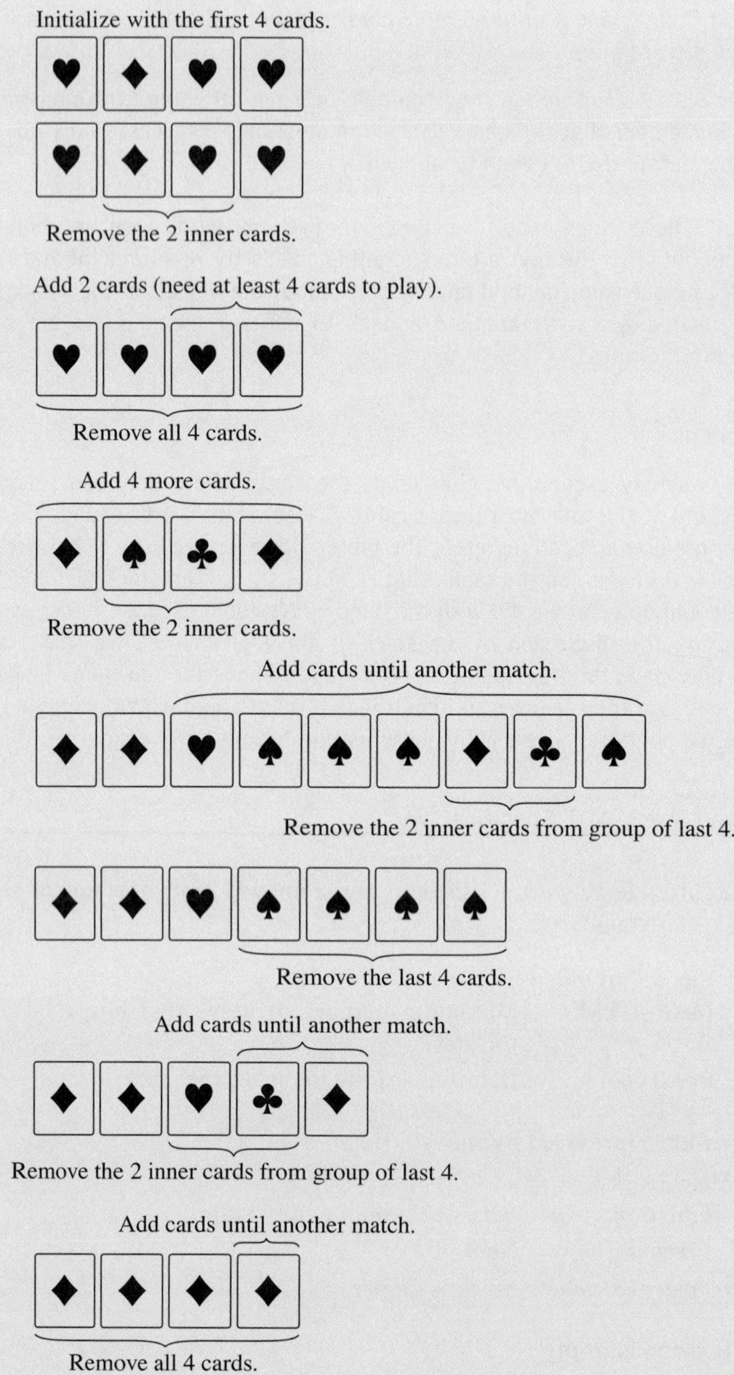

Figure 5.15 *Solitaire Game*

Boolean IsFull

Function:	Determines whether the stack is full.
Precondition:	Stack has been initialized.
Postcondition:	Function value = (stack is full)

Push(ItemType newItem)

Function:	Adds newItem to the top of the stack.
Precondition:	Stack has been initialized.
Postcondition:	If (stack is full) exception FullStack is thrown else newItem is at the top of the stack.

ItemType Pop

Function:	Removes and returns top item from the stack.
Precondition:	Stack has been initialized.
Postconditions:	If (stack is empty) exception EmptyStack is thrown else top element has been removed from stack.

int GetLength

Function:	Returns the number of items on the stack.
Precondition:	Stack has been initialized.
Postcondition:	Stack is unchanged.

What about the discard pile? It is the place where we put the cards in which we are no longer interested. If we win the game, the discard pile will hold all 52 cards in the deck. If we lose the game, there will still be cards on the table. To finish up, the cards remaining on the table get combined with the discard pile to form a new deck. Thus it is convenient to use a deck for the discard pile. Those remaining on the table can be popped and put into the deck. This deck then replaces the original deck.

What will be the input to the simulation? We need to know how many times the game is to be played. We should also have the user input how many times the deck is to be shuffled between games. The output should echo print the input with the number of games won.

Main

```
Prompt for and get number of runs
Prompt for and get number of shuffles
Set won to 0
for RCount going from 1 to number of runs
    for SCount going from 1 to number of shuffles
        deck.Shuffle()
    Play game(deck&, won&)
Print number of games played, number of shuffles, and number won.
```

Now it's time to turn the rules into an algorithm. The shuffling is taken care of in the main simulation. The Play game module takes a deck of cards, plays the game, and increments the number won if appropriate. This module can put the deck back together and return it to the main program to be shuffled again.

PlayGame (Deck& deck, int& won)

```
for counter going from 1 through 52
    Set card to deck.GetNextItem()
    table.Push(card)
    while table.GetLength() >= 4
        Try to remove(table, discardPile)
if table.IsEmpty,
    Increment won
while !table.IsEmpty
    discardPile.PutItem(table.Pop())
Set deck to discardPile
```

Notice that we have put the responsibility of keeping at least four cards on the table into the main loop in *PlayGame*. Once we move two cards to the discard pile, we can apply the *TryToRemove* module again. If we have moved four cards, we do not. Thus, we need a flag within the *TryToRemove* module that is set to `true` if two are removed and `false` if four are removed. If the first and the fourth cards do not match, we must replace them on the stack in the proper order.

TryToRemove(table, discardPile)

```
Set keepTrying to true
Get four
while keepTrying
    if first = fourth
        if first = second = third
            Remove four
            Set keepTrying to false
        else
            Remove two
            if at least two on table
                Set third to first
                Set keepTrying to true
                table.Pop(second)
                table.Pop(first)
            else
                table.Push(first)
                table.Push(fourth)
    else
        Push first, second, third, fourth
```

GetFour(table)

Set fourth to table.Pop()
Set third to table.Pop()
Set second to table.Pop()
Set first to table.Pop()

Before we code *RemoveTwo* and *RemoveFour*, let's reexamine the discard pile. It is a place to put unneeded cards until the end. We put them back with the other cards to reassemble the deck. We really don't need to do that. Our deck is never really empty; we are just looking at the cards one at a time. We can just take that deck and shuffle it again to get a deck with a different order. Thus, *RemoveTwo* and *RemoveFour* aren't needed in our simulation.

We have used a top-down design for the simulation algorithm, using the objects created previously. Which of these modules should be made procedures? All of them, except *GetFour*. As we code our algorithm, we realize that it is very complicated. Maybe not as complicated as toy instructions, but complicated enough for us to realize that testing is going to be difficult.

```
#include <iostream>
#include <time.h>
#include <stdlib.h>
#include "deck.h"
#include "CountedStack.h"
#include <string>
using namespace std;
void PlayGame(Deck& deck, int& won);
void TryToRemove(CountedStack& table);

int main()
{
  // Declarations
  int runs;
  int shuffles;
  int won = 0;
  Deck deck;
  deck.GenerateDeck();
  // Initialize simulation variables
  cout << "Enter number of runs." << endl;
  cin >> runs;
  cout << "Enter number of shuffles between runs." << endl;
  cin >> shuffles;

  // Main simulation module
  for (int count = 1; count <= runs; count++)
```

```
  {
    for (int count = 1; count <= shuffles; count++)
      deck.Shuffle();
    PlayGame(deck, won);
  }

  cout << "Number of games played: " << runs << endl
       << "Number of shuffles: " << shuffles << endl
       << "Number of games won: " << won << endl;
}

// ****************** Helper Functions ********************************

void TryToRemove(CountedStack& table)
// New card has been placed on the table; see if any can be removed.
{
  Card first, second, third, fourth;
  bool keepTrying = true;

  // Get top four
  fourth = table.Pop();
  third = table.Pop();
  second = table.Pop();
  first = table.Pop();

  while (keepTrying)
  {
    if (first.GetSuit() == fourth.GetSuit())  // Are first and fourth the
    {                                         // same?
      if ((first.GetSuit() == second.GetSuit()) &&
          (first.GetSuit() == third.GetSuit()))
         // Top four are the same suit; stop trying
        keepTrying = false;
      else // Only first and fourth are the same
      {
        if (table.GetLength() >= 2)
        {
          // Get a new top four and continue
          third = first;
          second = table.Pop();
          first = table.Pop();
          keepTrying = true;
        }
```

```
        else // Replace first and fourth and stop trying
        {
          keepTrying = false;
          table.Push(first);
          table.Push(fourth);
        }
      }
    }
    else  // No possibility of removing cards; replace four on stack
    {
      table.Push(first);
      table.Push(second);
      table.Push(third);
      table.Push(fourth);
      keepTrying = false;
    }
  }
}

void PlayGame(Deck& deck, int& won)
// Plays the solitaire game, with a new deck of cards
{
  CountedStack table;
  Card card;
  deck.ResetList();
  int limit = deck.GetLength();
  for (int count = 1; count <= limit; count++)
  {
    card = deck.GetNextItem();
    table.Push(card);
    if (table.GetLength() >= 4)
      TryToRemove(table);
  }
  if (table.IsEmpty())
    won++;
}
```

Here is the implementation of `CountedStack`. Since we can "borrow" code from `StackType` no further discussion is necessary.

```
#include "ItemType.h"
//   The user of this file must provide a file "ItemType.h" that defines:
//       ItemType : the class definition of the objects on the stack.
//       MAX_ITEMS: the maximum number of items on the stack.
```

```
class CountedStack
{
public:
  CountedStack();
  // Class constructor.
  bool IsEmpty() const;
  // Function: Determines whether the stack is empty.
  bool IsFull() const;
  // Function: Determines whether the stack is full.
  void Push(ItemType item);
  // Function: Adds newItem to the top of the stack.
  ItemType Pop();
  // Function: Removes and returns a copy of top item on the stack.
  int GetLength();

private:
  int top;
  ItemType  items[MAX_ITEMS];
};

#include "CountedStack.h"

#include <iostream>
CountedStack::CountedStack()
{
  top = -1;
}

bool CountedStack::IsEmpty() const
{
  return (top == -1);
}

bool countedStack::IsFull() const
{
  return (top == MAX_ITEMS - 1);
}

void CountedStack::Push(ItemType newItem)
{
  top++;
  items[top] = newItem;
}
```

```
ItemType CountedStack::Pop()
{
  top--;
  return items[top + 1];
}

int CountedStack::GetLength()
{
  return top + 1;
}
```

Testing We have a clean compile; now it is time to test the program. Fortunately, most of the classes have already been tested: `Card`, `Deck`, and `UnsortedType`. Although `CountedStack` has not been tested, it was taken almost directly from a class that had been thoroughly tested. To exhaustively test the portion of the program that plays the solitaire game, all possible configurations of a deck of 52 cards have to be generated. Although this is theoretically possible, it is impractical. There are 52! (52 factorial) possible arrangements of a deck of cards. This is a *very, very large number*!

Therefore, another method of testing is required. At a minimum, two questions must be considered:

1. Does the program recognize a winning hand?
2. Does the program recognize a losing hand?

To answer these questions, we must examine at least one hand declared to be a winner and several declared to be losers. Since you have never won, this might be difficult. Let's make a compromise. Replace `GenerateDeck` with a procedure that creates a shorter deck that we know should win. For example, a deck of four of the same suit should be a winner. A deck of three of the same suit, two others, and one of the same as the first three should be a winner. Here are two test cases that work, followed by two that do not work.

SPADE, SPADE, SPADE, SPADE
HEART, CLUB, HEART, DIAMOND, HEART, HEART, HEART, HEART
DIAMOND, CLUB, HEART, DIAMOND
SPADE, HEART, CLUB, DIAMOND, HEART

In order for these test cases to remain in this order, we must remember to set the number of shuffles to zero. Here is the output from the four runs.

```
Enter number of runs.
1
Enter number of shuffles between runs.
0
Ace of Spades
Two of Spades
```

```
Three of Spades
Four of Spades

Number of games played: 1
Number of shuffles: 0
Number of games won: 1

Enter number of runs.
1
Enter number of shuffles between runs.
0
Ace of Hearts
Two of Clubs
Three of Hearts
Four of Diamonds
Ace of Hearts
Two of Hearts
Three of Hearts
Four of Hearts

Number of games played: 1
Number of shuffles: 0
Number of games won: 1

Enter number of runs.
1
Enter number of shuffles between runs.
0
Ace of Diamonds
Two of Clubs
Three of Hearts
Four of Diamonds

Number of games played: 1
Number of shuffles: 0
Number of games won: 0

Enter number of runs.
1
Enter number of shuffles between runs.
0
Ace of Spades
Two of Hearts
Three of Clubs
```

```
Four of Diamonds
Ace of Hearts

Number of games played: 1
Number of shuffles: 0
Number of games won: 0
```

Now that we know the program will recognize both losing and winning hands, we run it for various periods of time. Here are the results. It looks like your father was not teasing you after all. It can be won, but it is very difficult to do so.

Number of Games	Number of Shuffles	Games Won
100	7	5
1000	4	0
1000	7	4
10000	7	0
100000	4	798
1000000	3	5390

Summary

We have defined a stack at the logical level as an abstract data type, discussed its use in an application, and presented an implementation encapsulated in a class. Though our logical picture of a stack is a linear collection of data elements with the newest element (the top) at one end and the oldest element at the other end, the physical representation of the stack class does not have to recreate our mental image. The implementation of the stack class must support the last in, first out (LIFO) property; how this property is supported, however, is another matter. For instance, the Push operation could "time stamp" the stack elements and put them into an array in any order. To pop, we would have to search the array, looking for the newest time stamp. This representation is very different from the stack implementation we developed in this chapter, but to the user of the stack class they are functionally equivalent. The implementation is transparent to the program that uses the stack because the stack is encapsulated by the operations in the class that surrounds it.

We also examined the definition and operations of a queue. We discussed some of the design considerations encountered when an array is used to contain the elements of a queue. Though the array itself is a random-access structure, our logical view of the queue as a structure limits us to accessing only the elements in the front and rear positions of the queue stored in the array. We used two pointers, one to the front and one to the rear, for the linked implementation.

There usually is more than one functionally correct design for the same data structure. When multiple correct solutions exist, the requirements and specifications of the problem may determine which solution is the best design.

In the design of data structures and algorithms, you find that there are often trade-offs. A more complex algorithm may result in more efficient execution; a solution that takes longer to execute may save memory space. As always, we must base our design decisions on what we know about the problem's requirements.

Exercises

1. Indicate whether a stack would be a suitable data structure for each of the following applications.
   a. A program to evaluate arithmetic expressions according to the specific order of operators.
   b. A bank simulation of its teller operation to see how waiting times would be affected by adding another teller.
   c. A program to receive data that are to be saved and processed in the reverse order.
   d. An address book to be maintained.
   e. A word processor to have a PF key that causes the preceding command to be redisplayed. Every time the user presses the PF key, the program shows the command that preceded the one currently displayed.
   f. A dictionary of words used by a spelling checker to be built and maintained.
   g. A program to keep track of patients as they check into a medical clinic, assigning patients to doctors on a first come, first served basis.
   h. A data structure used to keep track of the return addresses for nested functions while a program is running.
2. Describe the accessing protocol of a stack at the abstract level.
3. Show what is written by the following segments of code, given that `item1`, `item2`, and `item3` are `int` variables.
   a.
```
StackType<int> stack;
item1 = 1;
item2 = 0;
item3 = 4;
stack.Push(item2);
stack.Push(item1);
stack.Push(item1 + item3);
item2 = stack.Top();
stack.Pop();
stack.Push(item3*item3);
```

```
stack.Push(item2);
stack.Push(3);
item1 = stack.Top();
stack.Pop();
cout  << item1  << endl  << item2  << endl  << item3
      << endl;
while (!stack.IsEmpty())
{
  item1 = stack.Top();
  stack.Pop();
  cout << item1 << endl;
}
```

b.
```
StackType<int> stack;
item1 = 4;
item3 = 0;
item2 = item1 + 1;
stack.Push(item2);
stack.Push(item2 + 1);
stack.Push(item1);
item2 = stack.Top();
stack.Pop();
item1 = item2 + 1;
stack.Push(item1);
stack.Push(item3);
while (!stack.IsEmpty())
{
  item3 = stack.Top();
  cout << item3  << endl;
  stack.Pop();
}
cout << item1 << endl  << item2  << endl  << item3  << endl;
```

Use the following information for Exercises 4–7. The stack is implemented as a class containing an array of items, a data member indicating the index of the last item put on the stack (`top`), and two Boolean data members, `underFlow` and `overFlow`. The stack items are characters and `MAX_ITEM` is 5. In each exercise, show the result of the operation on the stack. Put a *T* or *F* for true or false, respectively, in the Boolean data members.

4. `stack.Push(letter);`

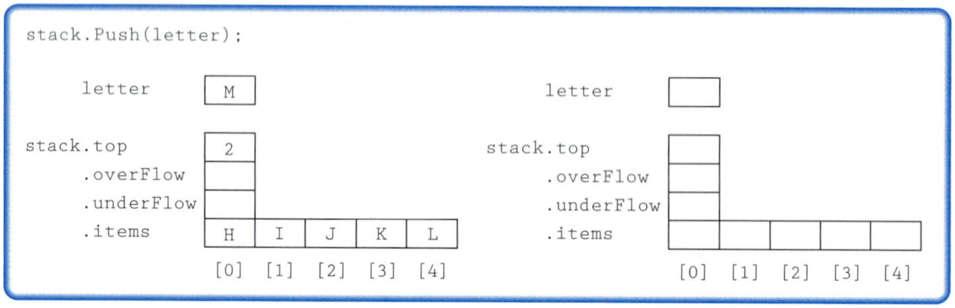

5. `stack.Push(letter);`

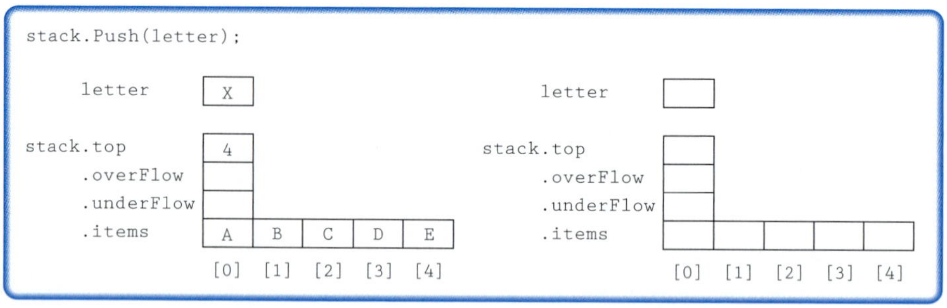

6. `(letter = stack.Top());`
   `stack.Pop();`

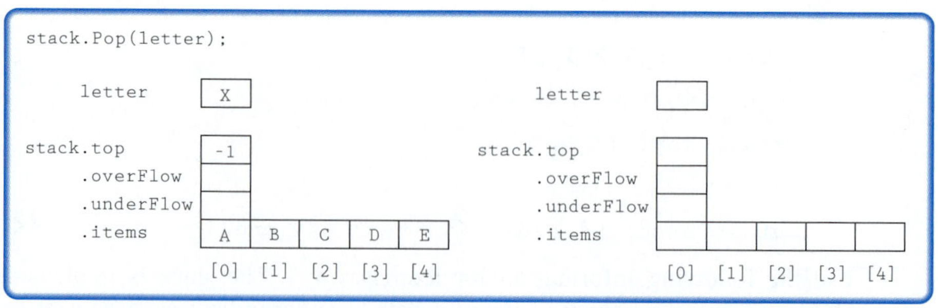

7.
```
(letter = stack.Top());
  stack.Pop();
```

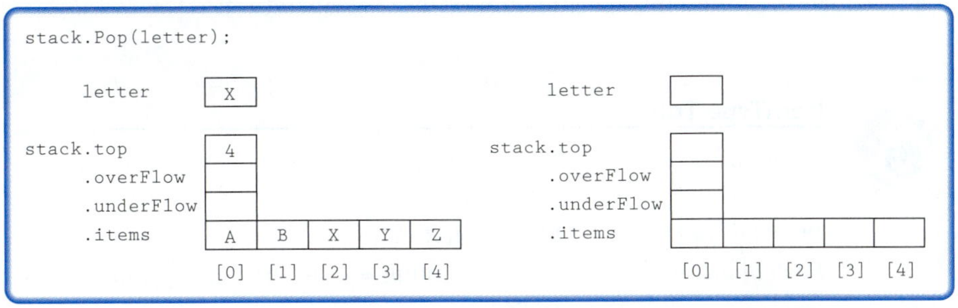

8. Write a segment of code to perform each of the following operations. You may call any of the member functions of `StackType`. The details of the stack type are encapsulated; you may use only the stack operations in the specification to perform the operations. (You may declare additional stack objects.)
   a. Set `secondElement` to the second element in the stack, leaving the stack without its original top two elements.
   b. Set `bottom` equal to the bottom element in the stack, leaving the stack empty.
   c. Set `bottom` equal to the bottom element in the stack, leaving the stack unchanged.
   d. Make a copy of the stack, leaving the stack unchanged.
9. (Multiple choice) The statement

```
stack.items[0] = stack.items[1];
```

   (setting the top element equal to the second element) in a client program of the stack class
   a. would cause a syntax error at compile time.
   b. would cause a run-time error.
   c. would not be considered an error by the computer, but would violate the encapsulation of the stack data type.
   d. would be a perfectly legal and appropriate way to accomplish the intended task.
10. (Multiple choice) The statements

```
stack.Push(item1 + 1);
stack.Pop(item1 + 1);
```

   in the client program
   a. would cause a syntax error at compile time.
   b. would cause a run-time error.

c. would be legal, but would violate the encapsulation of the stack.

d. would be perfectly legal and appropriate.

11. Given the following specification of the `Top` operation:

ItemType Top

Function:	Returns a copy of the last item put onto the stack.
Precondition:	Stack is not empty.
Postconditions:	Function value = copy of item at top of stack.
	Stack is not changed.

Assume `Top` is not a stack operation and `Pop` returns the item removed. Write this function as client code, using operations from the nontemplate version of the `StackType` class. Remember—the client code has no access to the private members of the class.

12. Two stacks of positive integers are needed, one containing elements with values less than or equal to 1,000 and the other containing elements with values larger than 1,000. The total number of elements in the small-value stack and the large-value stack combined are not more than 200 at any time, but we cannot predict how many are in each stack. (All of the elements could be in the small-value stack, they could be evenly divided, both stacks could be empty, and so on.) Can you think of a way to implement both stacks in one array?

    a. Draw a diagram of how the stack might look.

    b. Write the definitions for such a double-stack structure.

    c. Implement the `Push` operation; it should store the new item into the correct stack according to its value (compared to 1,000).

13. A stack of integer elements is implemented as an array. The index of the top element is kept in position 0 in the array, and the stack elements are stored in `stack[1]..stack[stack[0]}`.

    a. How does this implementation fare when assessed against the idea of an array as a homogeneous collection of data elements?

    b. How would this implementation change the stack specifications? How would it change the implementations of the functions?

14. Using one or more stacks, write a code segment to read in a string of characters and determine whether it forms a palindrome. A palindrome is a sequence of characters that reads the same both forward and backward—for example: ABLE WAS I ERE I SAW ELBA.

The character '.' ends the string. Write a message indicating whether the string is a palindrome. You may assume that the data are correct and that the maximum number of characters is 80.

15. Write the body for a function that replaces each copy of an item in a stack with another item. Use the following specification. (This function is in the *client* program.)

ReplaceItem(StackType& stack, ItemType oldItem, ItemType newItem)

Function:	Replaces all occurrences of oldItem with newItem.
Precondition:	stack has been initialized.
Postcondition:	Each occurrence of oldItem in stack has been replaced by newItem.

You may use any of the member functions of the nontemplate version of `StackType`, but you may not assume any knowledge of the stack's implementation.

16. In each plastic container of Pez candy, the colors are stored in random order. Your little brother likes only the yellow ones, so he painstakingly takes out all the candies, one by one, eats the yellow ones, and keeps the others in order, so that he can return them to the container in exactly the same order as before—minus the yellow candies, of course. Write the algorithm to simulate this process. You may use any of the stack operations defined in the Stack ADT, but may not assume any knowledge of the stack's implementation.

17. The specifications for the Stack ADT have been changed. The class representing the stack must now check for overflow and underflow and sets an error flag (a parameter) to true if either occurs.
    a. Rewrite the specifications incorporating this change.
    b. What new data members must you add to the class?
    c. What new member functions must you add to the class?

18. Implement the following specification for a client Boolean function that returns true if two stacks are identical and false otherwise.

Boolean Identical(StackType stack1, StackType stack2)

Function:	Determines if two stacks are identical.
Preconditions:	stack1 and stack2 have been initialized.
Postconditions:	stack1 and stack2 are unchanged. Function value = (stack1 and stack2 are identical)

You may use any of the member functions of `StackType`, but you may not assume any knowledge of the stack's implementation.

The following code segment (used for Exercises 19 and 20) is a count-controlled loop going from 1 through 5. At each iteration, the loop counter is either printed or put on a stack depending on the result of the Boolean function `RanFun()`. (The behavior of `RanFun()` is immaterial.) At the end of the loop, the items on the stack are popped and printed. Because of the logical properties of a stack, this code segment cannot print certain sequences of the values of the loop counter. You are given an output and asked to determine whether the code segment could generate the output.

```
for (count = 1; count <= 5; count++)
  if (RanFun())
     cout << count;
  else
    stack.Push(count);
while (!stack.IsEmpty())
{
    number = stack.Top();
    stack.Pop();
    cout << number;
}
```

19. The following output is possible using a stack: `1 3 5 2 4`
    a. True
    b. False
    c. Not enough information to determine
20. The following output is possible using a stack: `1 3 5 4 2`
    a. True
    b. False
    c. Not enough information to determine
21. Describe the accessing protocol of a queue at the abstract level.
22. Show what is written by the following segments of code, given that `item1`, `item2`, and `item3` are `int` variables.

    a.

```
QueType queue;

item1 = 1;
item2 = 0;
item3 = 4;
queue.Enqueue(item2);
queue.Enqueue(item1);
```

```
queue.Enqueue(item1 + item3);
queue.Dequeue(item2);
queue.Enqueue(item3*item3);
queue.Enqueue(item2);
queue.Enqueue(3);
queue.Dequeue(item1);
cout  << item1  << endl  << item2  << endl  << item3
      << endl;
while (!queue.IsEmpty())
{
  queue.Dequeue(item1);
  cout << item1 << endl;
}
```

b.

```
QueType queue;
item1 = 4;
item3 = 0;
item2 = item1 + 1;
queue.Enqueue(item2);
queue.Enqueue(item2 + 1);
queue.Enqueue(item1);
queue.Dequeue(item2);
item1 = item2 + 1;
queue.Enqueue(item1);
queue.Enqueue(item3);
while (!queue.IsEmpty())
{
  queue.Dequeue(item3);
  cout << item3  << endl;
}
cout << item1 << endl  << item2  << endl  << item3  << endl;
```

23. The specifications for the Queue ADT have been changed. The class representing the queue must now check for overflow and underflow and set an error flag (a parameter) to true if either occurs.
    a. Rewrite the specifications incorporating this change.
    b. What new data members must you add to the class?
    c. What new member functions must you add to the class?

Use the following information for Exercises 24–29. The queue is implemented as a class containing an array of items, a data member indicating the index of the last item put on the queue (`rear`), a data member indicating the index of the location before the first item put on the queue (`front`), and two Boolean data members, `underFlow` and `overFlow`, as discussed in this chapter. The item type is `char` and `maxQue` is 5. For each exercise, show the result of the operation on the queue. Put a *T* or *F* for true or false, respectively, in the Boolean data members.

24. `queue.Enqueue(letter);`

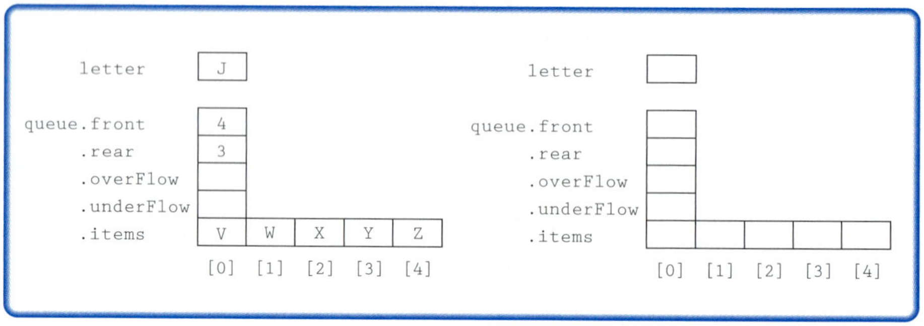

25. `queue.Enqueue(letter);`

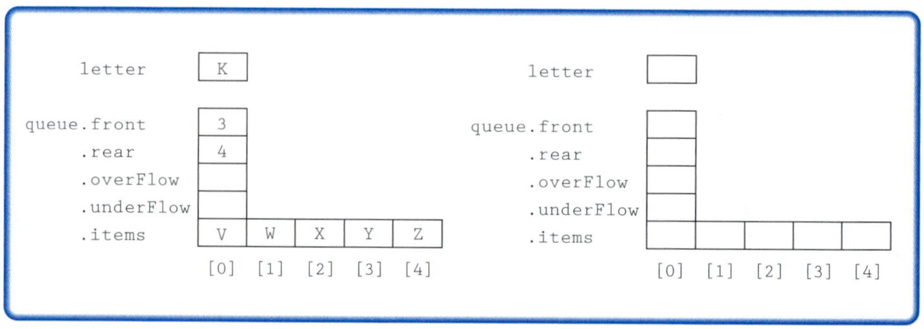

26. `queue.Enqueue(letter);`

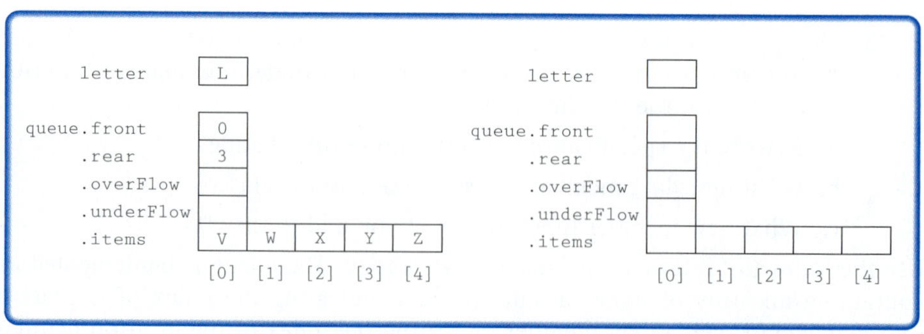

27. `queue.Dequeue(letter);`

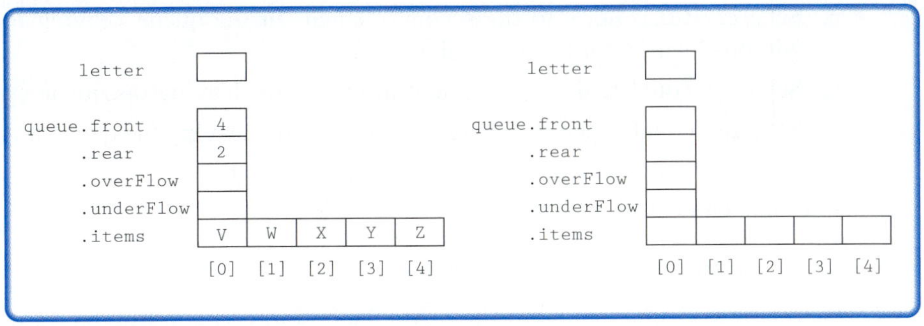

28. `queue.Dequeue(letter);`

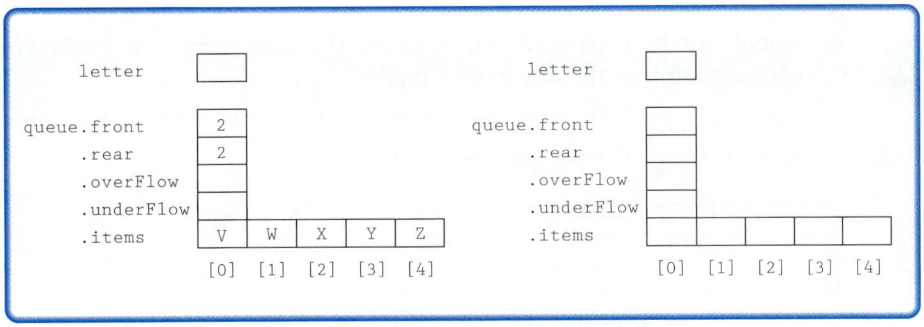

29. `queue.Dequeue(letter);`

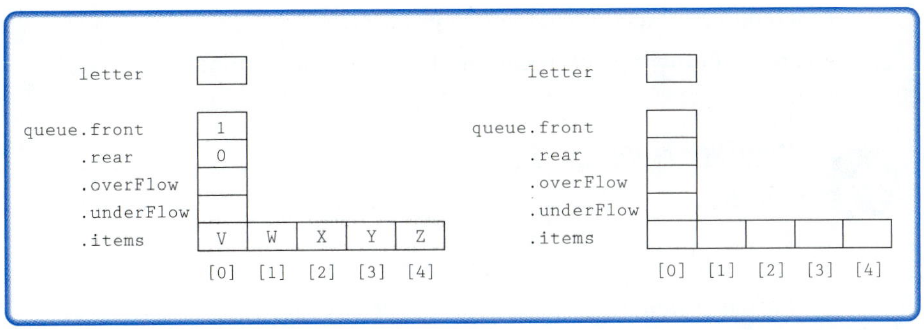

30. Write a segment of code to perform each of the following operations. You may call any of the member functions of `QueType`. The details of the queue are

encapsulated; you may use only the queue operations in the specification to perform the operations. (You may declare additional queue objects.)

a. Set `secondElement` to the second element in the queue, leaving the queue without its original front two elements.
b. Set `last` equal to the rear element in the queue, leaving the queue empty.
c. Set `last` equal to the rear element in the queue, leaving the queue unchanged.
d. Make a copy of the queue, leaving the queue unchanged.

31. (Multiple choice) The statement

```
queue.items[1] = queue.items[2];
```

(setting one element equal to the next element) in a client program of the queue class

a. would cause a syntax error at compile time.
b. would cause a run-time error.
c. would not be considered an error by the computer, but would violate the encapsulation of the queue data type.
d. would be a perfectly legal and appropriate way to accomplish the intended task.

32. (Multiple choice) The statements

```
queue.Enqueue(item1 + 1);
queue.Dequeue(item1 + 1);
```

in the client program

a. would cause a syntax error at compile time.
b. would cause a run-time error.
c. would be legal, but would violate the encapsulation of the queue.
d. would be perfectly legal and appropriate.

33. Given the following specification of a `Front` operation:

ItemType Front

Function:	Returns a copy of the front item on the queue.
Precondition:	Queue is not empty.
Postconditions:	Function value = copy of the front item on the queue. Queue is not changed.

a. Write this function as client code, using operations from the `QueType` class. (Remember—the client code has no access to the private members of the class.)

b. Write this function as a new member function of the `QueType` class.

34. Write the body for a function that replaces each copy of an item in a queue with another item. Use the following specification. (This function is in the client program.)

ReplaceItem(QueType queue, int oldItem, int newItem)

Function:	Replaces all occurrences of oldItem with newItem.
Precondition:	queue has been initialized.
Postcondition:	Each occurrence of oldItem in queue has been replaced by newItem.

You may use any of the member functions of `QueType`, but you may not assume any knowledge of the queue's implementation.

35. Indicate whether each of the following applications would be suitable for a queue.
    a. An ailing company wants to evaluate employee records so as to lay off some workers on the basis of service time (the most recently hired employees are laid off first).
    b. A program is to keep track of patients as they check into a clinic, assigning them to doctors on a first come, first served basis.
    c. A program to solve a maze is to backtrack to an earlier position (the last place where a choice was made) when a dead-end position is reached.
    d. An inventory of parts is to be processed by part number.
    e. An operating system is to process requests for computer resources by allocating the resources in the order in which they are requested.
    f. A grocery chain wants to run a simulation to see how the average customer wait time would be affected by changing the number of checkout lines in its stores.
    g. A dictionary of words used by a spelling checker is to be initialized.
    h. Customers are to take numbers at a bakery and be served in order when their numbers come up.
    i. Gamblers are to take numbers in the lottery and win if their numbers are picked.

36. Implement the following specification for a Boolean function in the client program that returns true if two queues are identical and false otherwise.

Boolean Identical(QueType queue1, QueType queue2)

Function:	Determines if two queues are identical.
Precondition:	queue1 and queue2 have been initialized.
Postconditions:	Queues are unchanged. Function value = (queue1 and queue2 are identical).

You may use any of the member functions of `QueType`, but you may not assume any knowledge of the queue's implementation.

37. Implement the following specification for an integer function in the client program that returns the number of items in a queue. The queue is unchanged.

int GetLength(QueType queue)

Function:	Determines the number of items in the queue.
Precondition:	queue has been initialized.
Postconditions:	queue is unchanged. Function value = number of items in queue.

38. One queue implementation discussed in this chapter dedicated an unused cell before the front of the queue to distinguish between a full queue and an empty queue. Write another queue implementation that keeps track of the length of the queue in a data member `length`.
    a. Write the class definition for this implementation.
    b. Implement the member functions for this implementation. (Which of the member functions have to be changed and which do not?)
    c. Compare this new implementation with the previous one in terms of Big-O notation.
39. Write a queue application that determines if two files are the same.
40. Discuss the difference between the `MakeEmpty` operation in the specification and a class constructor.

The following code segment (used for Exercises 43 and 44) is a count-controlled loop going from 1 through 5. At each iteration, the loop counter is either printed or put on a queue depending on the result of the Boolean function `RanFun()`. (The behavior of `RanFun()` is immaterial.) At the end of the loop, the items on the queue are dequeued and printed. Because of the logical properties of a queue, this code segment cannot print certain sequences of the values of the loop counter. You are given an output and asked to determine whether the code segment could generate the output.

```
for (count = 1; count <= 5; count++)
  if (RanFun())
    cout << count;
  else
    queue.Enqueue(count);
while (!queue.IsEmpty())
{
  queue.Dequeue(number);
  cout << number;
}
```

41. The following output is possible using a queue: `1 2 3 4 5`
    a. True
    b. False
    c. Not enough information to determine
42. The following output is possible using a queue: `1 3 5 4 2`
    a. True
    b. False
    c. Not enough information to determine
43. Change the code for the program `Balanced` on page 284 so that the calls to `Push`, `Pop`, and `Top` are embedded within a *try* clause. The *catch* clause should print an appropriate error message and halt.
44. Define and implement a counted stack, which inherits from `StackType`.
45. Create UML diagrams for the ADTs implemented in this chapter.

chapter 6

Lists Plus

Goals

After studying this chapter, you should be able to

- Use the C++ template mechanism for defining generic data types
- Implement a circular linked list
- Implement a linked list with a header node or a trailer node or both
- Implement a doubly linked list
- Distinguish between shallow copying and deep copying
- Overload C++ operators
- Implement a linked list as an array of records
- Implement dynamic binding with virtual functions

This chapter is a combination of both alternate implementations of lists and new theoretical material accompanied by the C++ implementations of the constructs. The chapter begins by describing the template mechanism in C++ that allows the type of objects on a structure to be defined at run time. Next, three new implementations of lists are discussed: circular linked lists, doubly linked lists, and lists with headers and trailers.

We then introduce the concepts of shallow copying and deep copying, and demonstrate how to force deep copying with the class copy constructor and overloading the assignment operation. Finally, we show how most of the rest of the C++ operators can be overloaded.

Our last linked list implementation uses an array-of-records rather than pointers. This implementation is widely used in operating systems software.

6.1 More about Generics: C++ Templates

In Chapter 3 we defined a generic data type as a type for which the operations are defined but the types of the items being manipulated are not. We have demonstrated how container types can be generic by defining the type of the items to be on the structure in a separate file `ItemType.h` and having the specification files for the containers include that file. This technique works for any language that allows you to include or access other files.

Template A C++ language construct that allows the compiler to generate multiple versions of a class type or a function by allowing parameterized types

However, some languages have special language constructs that allow you to define generic data types. C++ is one of these. The construct is called a *template*. A template allows you to write a description of a class type with "blanks" left in the description to be filled in by the client code. Just as variables are the parameters to functions, types are parameters to templates.

Let's look at how this construct works using the Stack ADT.

```
template<class ItemType>
class StackType
{
public:
  StackType();
  bool IsEmpty() const;
  bool IsFull() const;
  void Push(ItemType item);
  void Pop();
  ItemType Top() const;
private:
  int top;
  ItemType items[MAX_ITEMS];
};
```

This code is known as a *class template*. The definition of `StackType` begins with `template<class ItemType>`, and `ItemType` is called the *formal parameter* to the template. (You could use any identifier for the formal parameter; we use ItemType in this example.) The client program uses code like the following to create several stacks whose components are of different data types:

```
// Client code
StackType<int> myStack;
StackType<float> yourStack;
StackType<char> anotherStack;

myStack.Push(35);
yourStack.Push(584.39);
anotherStack.Push('A');
```

In the definitions of myStack, yourStack, and anotherStack, the data type name enclosed in angle brackets is the *actual parameter* (or *argument*) to the template. At compile time, the compiler generates (*instantiates*) three distinct class types and gives its own internal name to each type. You might imagine that the definitions are transformed internally into something like this:

```
StackType_int myStack;
StackType_flo yourStack;
StackType_char anotherStack;
```

In C++ terminology, the three new class types are called *template classes* (as opposed to the *class template* from which they were created).

When the compiler instantiates a template, it literally substitutes the actual parameter for the formal parameter throughout the class template, just as you would perform a search-and-replace operation in a word processor or text editor. For example, when the compiler encounters StackType<float> in the client code, it generates a new class by substituting float for every occurrence of ItemType in the class template. The result is the same as if we had written the following:

```
class StackType_float
{
  :
  void Push(float item);
  void Pop();
  float Top() const;
private:
  int top;
  float items[MAX_ITEMS];
};
```

A useful perspective on templates is this: An ordinary class definition is a pattern for stamping out individual variables or objects, whereas a class template is a pattern for stamping out individual data types.

There are two things to note about parameters to templates. First, the class template uses the word `class` in its formal parameter list: `template<class ItemType>`. However, the use of `class` is simply required syntax and does not mean that the client's actual parameter must be the name of a class. The actual parameter can consist of the name of any data type, built-in or user-defined. In the client code just shown, we used `int`, `float`, and `char` as actual parameters. Second, observe that when the client passes a parameter to the `StackType` template (as in `StackType<int>`), the parameter is a data type name, not a variable name. This usage seems strange at first, because when we pass parameters to functions, we always pass variable names or expressions, not data type names. Furthermore, note that passing a parameter to a template has an effect at *compile time*, whereas passing a parameter to a function has an effect at *run time*.

Now that we've seen how to write the definition of a class template, how do we handle the definitions of the member functions? We need to write them as *function templates* so that the compiler can associate each one with the proper template class. For example, we code the `Push` function as the following function template:

```
template<class ItemType>
void StackType<ItemType>::Push(ItemType newItem)
{
  if (IsFull())
    throw FullStack();
  top++;
  items[top] = newItem;
}
```

Just as with the class template, we begin the function definition with `template<class ItemType>`. Next, every occurrence of the word `StackType` must have `<ItemType>` appended to it. If the client has declared a type `StackType<float>`, the compiler generates a function definition similar to the following:

```
void StackType<float>::Push(float newItem)
{
  if (IsFull())
    throw FullStack();
  top++;
  items[top] = newItem;
}
```

Finally, when working with templates, we change the ground rules regarding the file(s) into which we put the source code. Previously, we placed the class definition into a header file `StackType.h` and the member function definitions into `StackType.cpp`. As a result, we could compile `StackType.cpp` into object code independently of any client code. This strategy won't work with templates. The compiler cannot instantiate a function template unless it knows the actual parameter to the template, and this actual parameter appears in the client code. Different compilers use different mechanisms to solve this problem. One general solution is to compile the client code and the member functions at the same time. A popular technique is to place *both* the class definition and the member function definitions into the same file: `StackType.h`. Another technique involves giving the *include* directive for the implementation file at the end of the header file. Either way, when the client code specifies `#include "StackType.h"`, the compiler has all the source code–both the member functions and the client code–available to it at once. The following code lists the contents of both the class definition and the function implementations. Pay close attention to the required syntax of the member function definitions.

```
// The class definition for StackType using templates.

class FullStack
// Exception class used by Push when stack is full.
{};

class EmptyStack
// Exception class used by Pop and Top when stack is empty.
{};

#include "MaxItems.h"
// MaxItems.h must be provided by the user of this class.
// This file must contain the definition of MAX_ITEMS,
// the maximum number of items on the stack.

template<class ItemType>
class StackType
{
public:
  StackType();
  bool IsEmpty() const;
  bool IsFull() const;
  void Push(ItemType item);
  void Pop();
  ItemType Top() const;
private:
  int top;
  ItemType items[MAX_ITEMS];
};

// The function definitions for class StackType.
template<class ItemType>
StackType<ItemType>::StackType()
{
  top = -1;
}
```

```
template<class ItemType>
bool StackType<ItemType>::IsEmpty() const
{
  return (top == -1);
}

template<class ItemType>
bool StackType<ItemType>::IsFull() const
{
  return (top == MAX_ITEMS-1);
}

template<class ItemType>
void StackType<ItemType>::Push(ItemType newItem)
{
  if (IsFull())
    throw FullStack();
  top++;
  items[top] = newItem;
}

template<class ItemType>
void StackType<ItemType>::Pop()
{
  if( IsEmpty() )
    throw EmptyStack();
  to--;
}

template<class ItemType>
ItemType StackType<ItemType>::Top()
{
  if (IsEmpty())
    throw EmptyStack();
  return items[top];
}
```

6.2 Circular Linked Lists

The linked list data structures that we implemented in Chapters 3–5 are characterized by a *linear* (line-like) relationship between the elements: Each element (except the first one) has a unique predecessor, and each element (except the last one) has a unique successor. Using linear linked lists does present a problem: Given a pointer to a node anywhere in the list, we can access all the nodes that follow but none of the nodes that precede it. With a singly linked linear list structure (a list whose pointers all point in the same direction), we must always have a pointer to the beginning of the list to be able to access all the nodes in the list.

In addition, the data we want to add to a sorted list may already be in order. Sometimes people manually sort raw data before turning it over to a data entry clerk. Likewise, data produced by other programs are often in some order. Given a Sorted List ADT and sorted input data, we always insert new items at the end of the list. It is ironic that the work done manually to order the data now results in maximum insertion times.

We can, however, change the linear list slightly, making the pointer in the `next` member of the last node point back to the first node instead of containing `NULL` (Figure 6.1). Now our list becomes a circular linked list rather than a linear linked list. We can start at any node in the list and traverse the entire list. If we let our external pointer point to the last item in the list rather than the first, we have direct access to both the first and the last elements in the list (Figure 6.2). `listData->info` references the item in the last node, and `listData->next->info` references the item in the first node. We mentioned this type of list structure in Chapter 5, when we discussed circular linked queues.

Circular linked list A list in which every node has a successor; the "last" element is succeeded by the "first" element

We do not need to change any of the declarations in the class `SortedType` to make the list circular, rather than linear. After all, the members in the nodes are the same; only the value of the `next` member of the last node has changed. How does the circular nature of the list alter the implementations of the list operations? Because an empty circular list has a `NULL` pointer, the `IsEmpty` operation does not change at all. However, using a circular list requires an obvious change in the algorithms that traverse the list. We no longer stop when the traversing pointer becomes `NULL`. Indeed, unless the list is empty, the pointer never becomes `NULL`. Instead, we must look for the external pointer itself as a stop sign. Let's examine these changes in the Sorted List ADT.

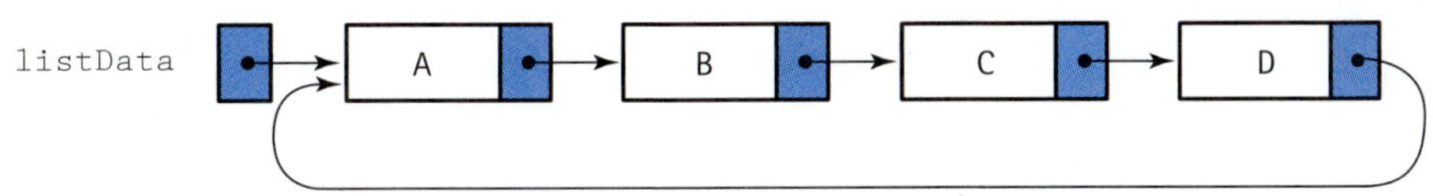

Figure 6.1 *A circular linked list*

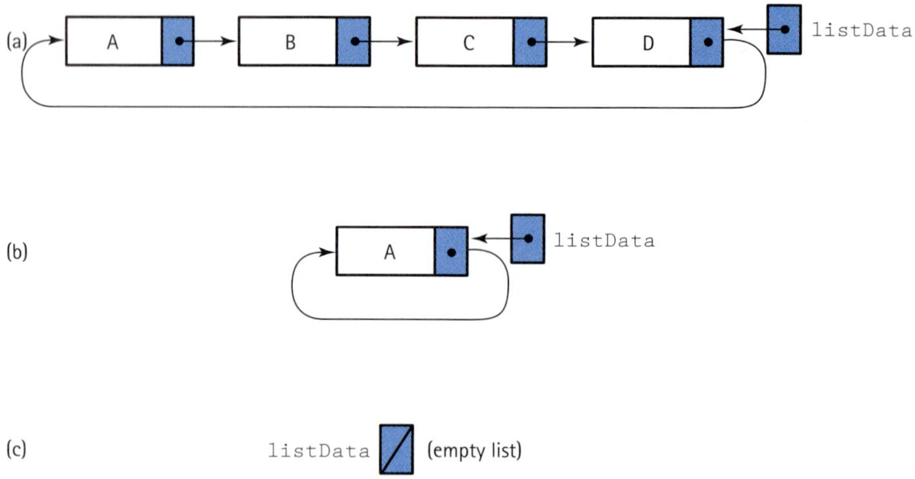

Figure 6.2 *Circular linked lists with the external pointer pointing to the rear element*

Finding a List Item

The `GetItem`, `PutItem`, and `DeleteItem` operations all require a search of the list. Rather than rewriting each of these with minor variations, let's write a general `FindItem` routine that takes `item` as a parameter and returns `location`, `predLoc`, and `found`. `PutItem` and `DeleteItem` need the location of the predecessor node (`predLoc`); `GetItem` can just ignore it.

In the linear list implementation, we searched the list using a pair of pointers, `location` and `predLoc`. (Remember the inchworm?) We modify this approach slightly for the circular list. In the linear list version, we initialized `location` to point to the first node in the list and set `predLoc` to `NULL` (Figure 6.3a). For the circular list search, we initialize `location` to point to the first node and `predLoc` to point to its "predecessor"—the last node in the list (Figure 6.3b).

The search loop executes until (1) a key greater than or equal to the `item`'s key is encountered, or (2) we reach the "end" of the list. In a linear list, the end of the list is detected when `location` equals `NULL`. Because the external pointer to the list points to the last element, we know we have processed all of the items and not found a match when `location` points to the first element again: `location == listData->next`. Because it makes no sense to search an empty list, let's make it a precondition that the list is not empty.

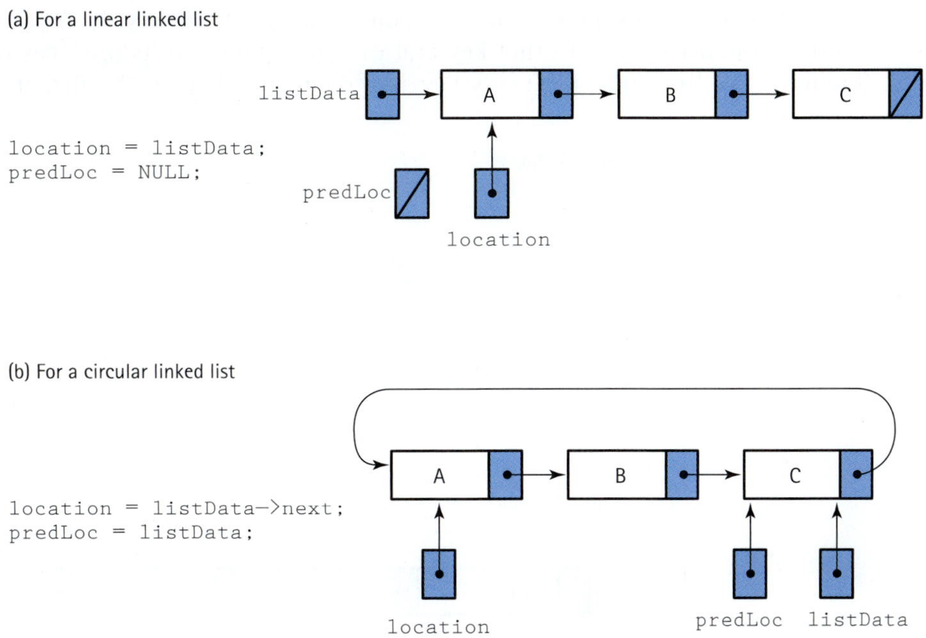

Figure 6.3 *Initializing for `FindItem`*

FindItem

```
Set location to Next(listData)
Set predLoc to listData
Set found to false
Set moreToSearch to true
while moreToSearch AND NOT found DO
    if item.ComparedTo(info(location)) == LESS
        Set moreToSearch to false
    else if item.ComparedTo(info(location)) == EQUAL
        Set found to true
    else
        Set predLoc to location
        Set location to Next(location)
        Set moreToSearch to (location != Next(listData))
```

Following the execution of the loop, if a matching key is found, `location` points to the list node with that key and `predLoc` points to its predecessor in the list (Figure 6.4a). Note that if `item`'s key is the smallest key in the list, then `predLoc`

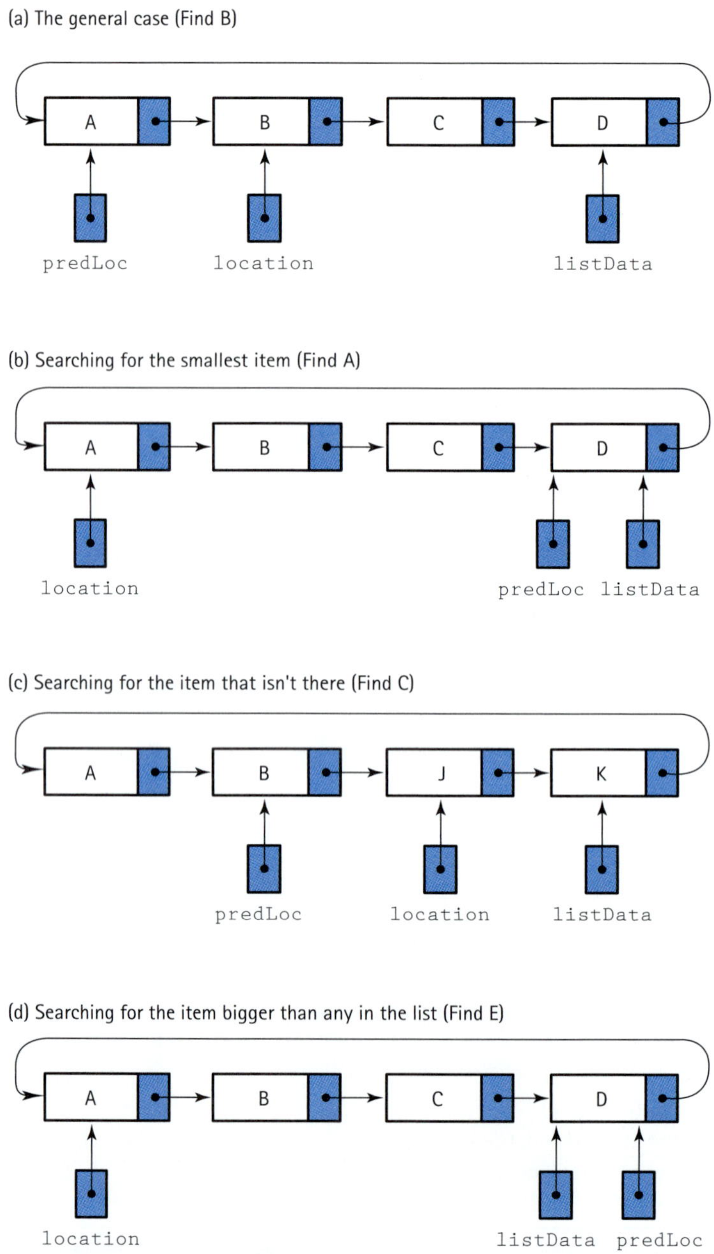

Figure 6.4 *The `FindItem` operation for a circular list*

points to its predecessor—the last node in the circular list (Figure 6.4b). If `item`'s key is not in the list, then `predLoc` points to its logical predecessor in the list and `location` points to its logical successor (Figure 6.4c). Notice that `predLoc` is correct even if `item`'s key is greater than any element in the list (Figure 6.4d). Thus `predLoc` is set correctly for inserting an element whose key is larger than any currently in the list.

The following C++ code implements our `FindItem` algorithm as a *function template*. Notice two things in the function heading. First, `NodeType` was defined in Chapter 5 as a `struct`; here it must be a `struct` template. So each declaration using `NodeType` must include an actual parameter (the name of a data type) in angle brackets. For example, `listData` is declared in the code to be of type `NodeType<ItemType>*` and not simply `NodeType*`. Second, observe the syntax for the declarations of `location` and `predLoc`. You see an asterisk (`*`) and an ampersand (`&`) next to each other. Although this syntax may look strange at first, it is consistent with the usual way we indicate passing-by-reference: Place an `&` after the data type of the parameter. Here we place an `&` after the data type `NodeType<ItemType>*`, which is a pointer to a node.

```
template<class ItemType>
void FindItem(NodeType<ItemType>* listData, ItemType item,
     NodeType<ItemType>*& location, NodeType<ItemType>*& predLoc,
     bool& found)
// Assumption:  ItemType is a type that has a ComparedTo function.
// Pre:  List is not empty.
// Post: If there is an element someItem whose key matches item's
//       key, then found = true; otherwise, found = false.
//       If found, location contains the address of someItem and
//       predLoc contains the address of someItem's predecessor;
//       otherwise, location contains the address of item's logical
//       successor and predLoc contains the address of item's
//       logical predecessor.
{
  bool moreToSearch = true;

  location = listData->next;
  predLoc = listData;
  found = false;
  while (moreToSearch && !found)
  {
    if (item.ComparedTo(location->info) == LESS)
      moreToSearch = false;
    else if (item.ComparedTo(location->info) == EQUAL)
```

```
        found = true;
      else
      {
        predLoc = location;
        location = location->next;
        moreToSearch = (location != listData->next);
      }
    }
}
```

Note that `FindItem` is *not* a member function of the class `SortedType`. It is an auxiliary or "helper" operation, hidden within the implementation, that is used by `SortedType` member functions.

Inserting Items into a Circular List

The algorithm to insert an element into a circular linked list is similar to that for the linear list insertion.

PutItem

Set newNode to address of newly allocated node
Set Info(newNode) to item
Find the place where the new element belongs
Put the new element into the list

The task of allocating space is the same as that carried out for the linear list. We allocate space for the node using the `new` operator and then store `item` into `newNode->info`. The next task is equally simple; we just call `FindItem`:

```
FindItem(listData, item, location, predLoc, found);
```

Of course, we do not find the element because it isn't there; it is the `predLoc` pointer that interests us. The new node is linked into the list immediately after Node(`predLoc`). To put the new element into the list, we store `predLoc->next` into `newNode->next` and `newNode` into `predLoc->next`.

Figure 6.5(a) illustrates the general case. What are the special cases? First, we have the case of inserting the first element into an empty list. In this case, we want to make `listData` point to the new node, and to make the new node point to itself (Figure 6.5b). In the insertion algorithm for the linear linked list, we also had a special case

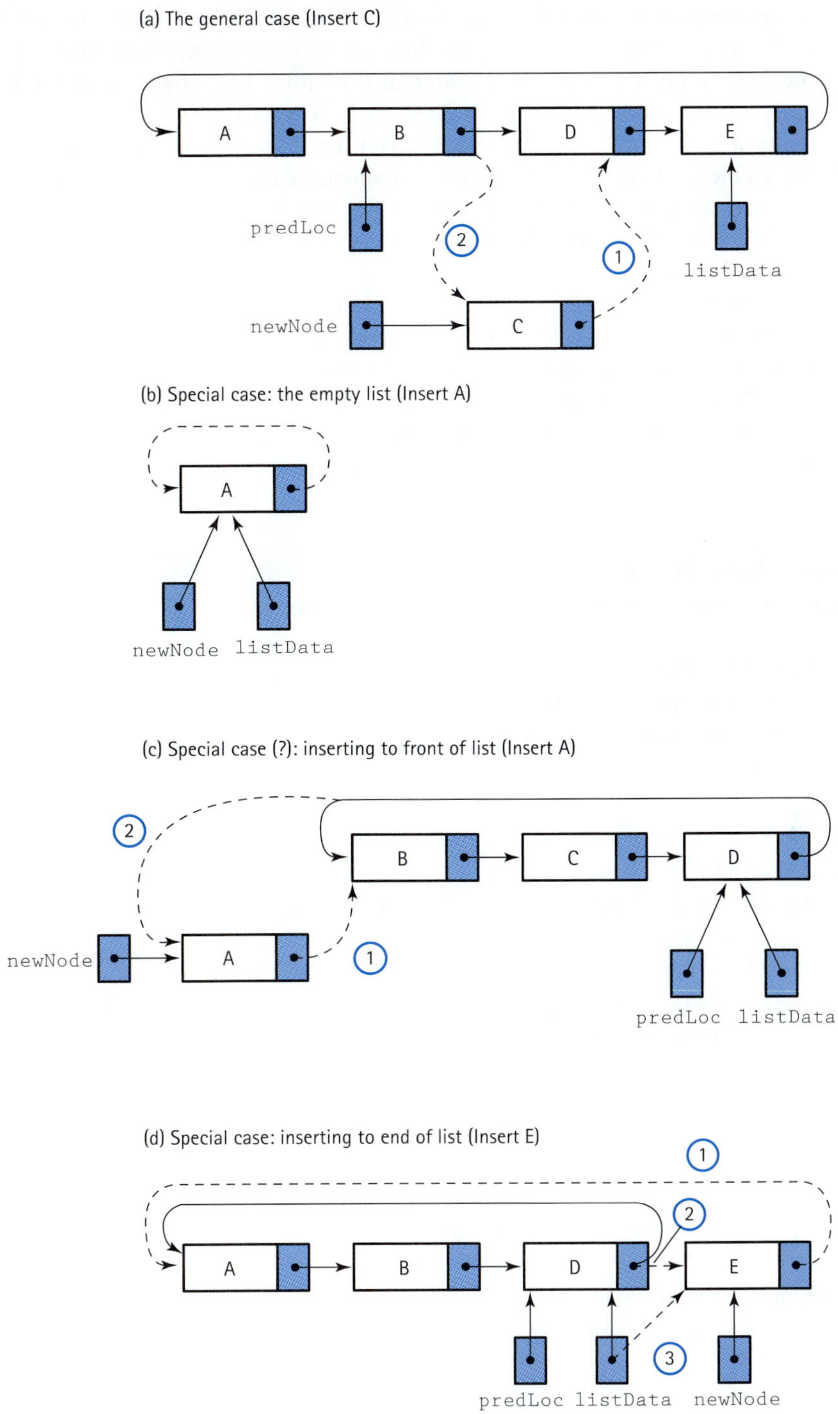

Figure 6.5 *Inserting into a circular linked list*

when the new element key was smaller than any other key in the list. Because the new node became the first node in the list, we had to change the external pointer to point to the new node. The external pointer to a circular list, however, doesn't point to the first node in the list—it points to the last node. Therefore, inserting the smallest list element is not a special case for a circular linked list (Figure 6.5c). However, inserting the largest list element at the end of the list is a special case. In addition to linking the node to its predecessor (previously the last list node) and its successor (the first list node), we must modify the external pointer to point to Node(`newNode`)—the new last node in the circular list (Figure 6.5d).

The statements to link the new node to the end of the list are the same as those for the general case, plus the assignment of the external pointer, `listData`. Rather than checking for this special case before the search, we can treat it together with the general case: Search for the insertion place and link in the new node. Then, if we detect that we have added the new node to the end of the list, we reassign `listData` to point to the new node. To detect this condition, we compare `item` to `listData->info`.

The resulting implementation of `PutItem` is shown here.

```
template<class ItemType>
void SortedType<ItemType>::PutItem(ItemType item)
{
  NodeType<ItemType>* newNode;
  NodeType<ItemType>* predLoc;
  NodeType<ItemType>* location;
  bool found;

  newNode = new NodeType<ItemType>;
  newNode->info = item;
  if ((listData->info.ComparedTo(item)--LESS
  {
    FindItem(listData, item, location, predLoc, found);
    newNode->next = predLoc->next;
    predLoc->next = newNode;

    // If this is last node in list, reassign listData.
    if (listData->info.ComparedTo(item)--LESS
      listData = newNode;
  }
  else          // Inserting into an empty list.
  {
    listData = newNode;
    newNode->next = newNode;
  }
  length++;
}
```

Deleting Items from a Circular List

To delete an element from the circular linked list, we use the same general algorithm we developed for the linear list:

DeleteItem
Find the element in the list
Remove the element from the list
Deallocate the node

For the first task, we use `FindItem`. After the return from `FindItem`, `location` points to the node we wish to delete, and `predLoc` points to its predecessor in the list. To remove Node(`location`) from the list, we simply reset `predLoc->next` to jump over the node we are deleting. That works for the general case, at least (see Figure 6.6a).

What kind of special cases do we have to consider? In the linear list version, we had to check for deleting the first (or first-and-only) element. From our experience with the insertion operation, we might surmise that deleting the smallest element (the first node) of the circular list is *not* a special case; Figure 6.6b shows that guess to be correct. However, deleting the only node in a circular list *is* a special case, as we see in Figure 6.6c. The external pointer to the list must be set to `NULL` to indicate that the list is now empty. We can detect this situation by checking whether `predLoc` equals `location` after the execution of `FindItem`; if so, the node we are deleting is the only one in the list.

We might also guess that deleting the largest list element (the last node) from a circular list is a special case. As Figure 6.6d illustrates, when we delete the last node, we first do the general-case processing to unlink Node(`location`) from the list, then we reset `listData` to point to its predecessor, Node(`predLoc`). We can detect this situation by checking whether `location` equals `listData` after the search.

```
template<class ItemType>
void SortedType<ItemType>::DeleteItem(ItemType item)
{
  NodeType<ItemType>* location;
  NodeType<ItemType>* predLoc;
  bool found;

  FindItem(listData, item, location, predLoc, found);
  if (predLoc == location) // Only node in list?
    listData = NULL;
  else
  {
```

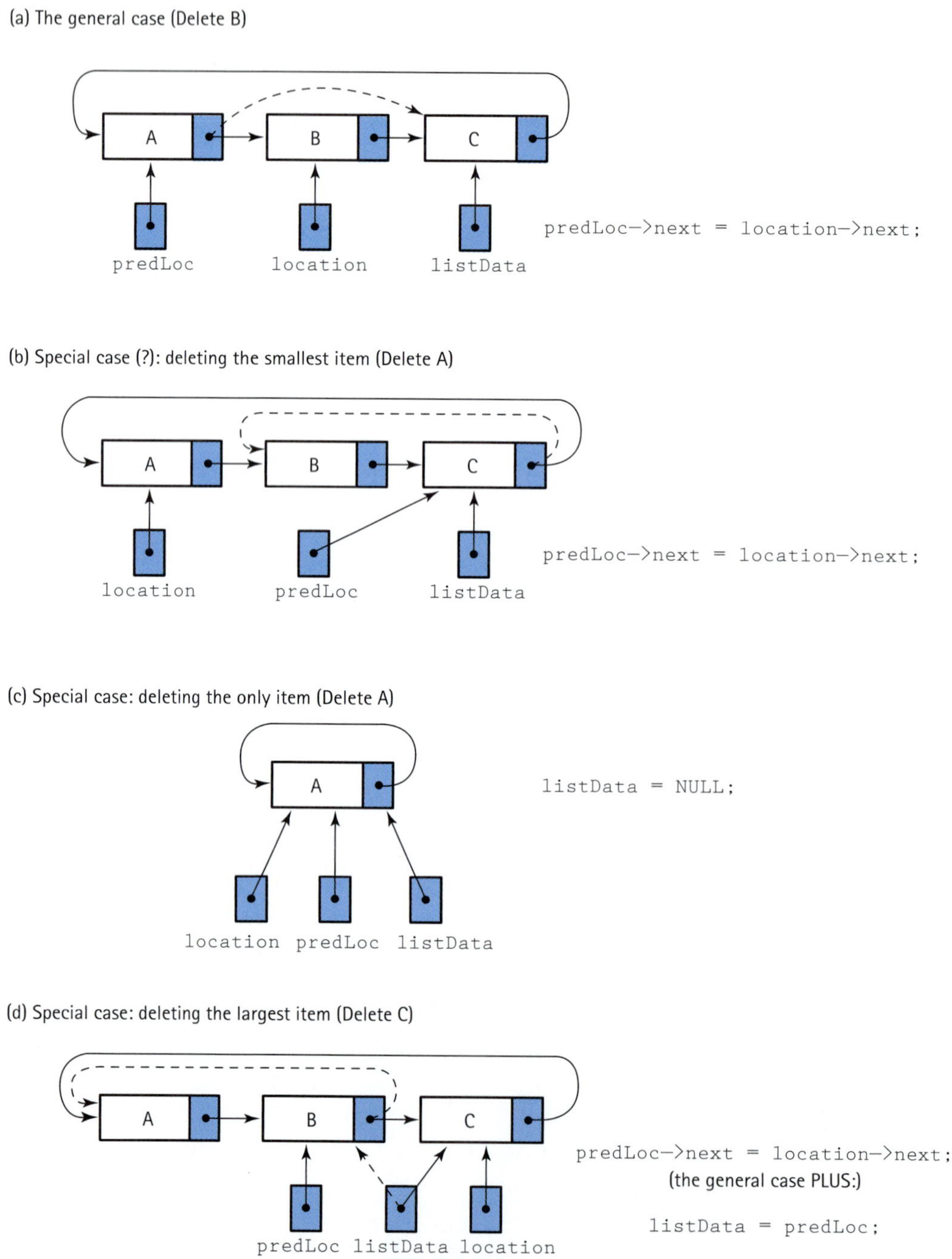

Figure 6.6 *Deleting from a circular linked list*

```
    predLoc->next = location->next;
    if (location == listData)  // Deleting last node in list?
      listData = predLoc;
  }
  delete location;
  length--;
}
```

Having worked through a number of the list operations in detail, we leave the circular implementation of the other Sorted List ADT operations as a programming assignment. None of the operations we have looked at so far has become shorter or much simpler when the implementation changed to a circular list. Why, then, might we want to use a circular, rather than a linear, linked list? Circular lists are useful for applications that require access to both ends of the list. (The circular linked version of the queue in Chapter 5 is a good example of this scenario.)

6.3 Doubly Linked Lists

As noted previously, we can use circular linked lists to reach any node in the list from any starting point. Although this structure offers advantages over a simple linear linked list, it remains too limited for certain types of applications. Suppose we want to delete a particular node in a list, given only a pointer to that node (`location`). This task involves changing the `next` member of the node preceding Node(`location`). As we saw in Chapter 5, however, given only the pointer `location`, we cannot access its predecessor in the list.

Another task that is difficult to perform on a linear linked list is traversing the list in reverse. For instance, suppose we have a list of student records, sorted by grade point average (GPA) from lowest to highest. The dean of students might want a printout of the students' records, sorted from highest to lowest, to use in preparing the Dean's List.

In such a case, where we need to access the node that precedes a given node, a doubly linked list is useful. In a doubly linked list, the nodes are linked in both directions. Each node of a doubly linked list contains three parts:

> **Doubly linked list** A linked list in which each node is linked to both its successor and its predecessor

Info: the data stored in the node
Next: the pointer to the following node
Back: the pointer to the preceding node

Figure 6.7 depicts a linear doubly linked list. Note that the `back` member of the first node, as well as the `next` member of the last node, contains a `NULL`. The following definition might be used to declare the nodes in such a list:

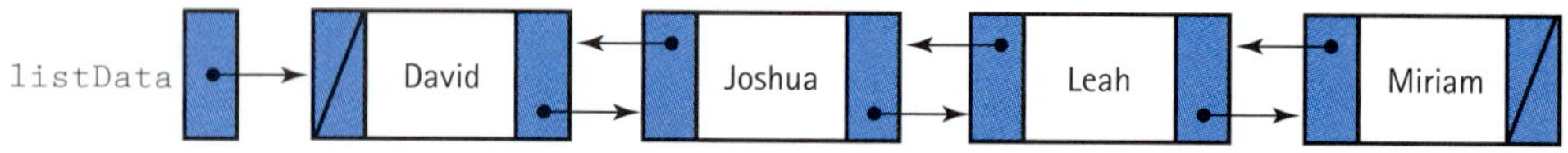

Figure 6.7 *A linear doubly linked list*

```
template<class ItemType>
struct NodeType
{
  ItemType info;
  NodeType<ItemType>* next;
  NodeType<ItemType>* back;
};
```

Using this definition, let's write member functions `PutItem` and `DeleteItem` using the auxiliary function `FindItem`.

Finding an Item in a Doubly Linked List

In the `FindItem` function, we no longer need to use the inchworm search; instead, we can get the predecessor to any node through its `back` member. We change the `FindItem` interface slightly. That is, because we no longer need `predLoc`, we return one pointer, `location`. If `found` is true, `location` points to the node with the same key as `item`; otherwise, `location` points to the node that is the logical successor of `item`. (Recall that `FindItem` is a function template.)

```
template<class ItemType>
void FindItem(NodeType<ItemType>* listData, ItemType item,
     NodeType<ItemType>*& location, bool& found)
// Assumption:  ItemType is a type that has a ComparedTo function.
// Pre:  List is not empty.
// Post: If there is an element someItem whose key matches item's
//       key, then found = true; otherwise, found = false.
//       If found, location contains the address of someItem;
//       otherwise, location contains the address of the logical
//       successor of item.
{
  bool moreToSearch = true;

  location = listData;
  found = false;
  while (moreToSearch && !found)
  {
    if (item.ComparedTo(location->info) == LESS)
```

```
      moreToSearch = false;
    else if (item.ComparedTo(location->info) == EQUAL)
      found = true;
    else
    {
      location = location->next;
      moreToSearch = (location != NULL);
    }
  }
}
```

Operations on a Doubly Linked List

The algorithms for the insertion and deletion operations on a doubly linked list are somewhat more complicated than the corresponding operations on a singly linked list. The reason is clear: There are more pointers to keep track of in a doubly linked list.

As an example, consider the `PutItem` operation. To link the new node, Node(`newNode`), after a given node, Node(`location`), in a singly linked list, we need to change two pointers: `newNode->next` and `location->next` (see Figure 6.8a). The same operation on a doubly linked list requires four pointer changes (see Figure 6.8b).

We allocate space for the new node and call `FindItem` to find the insertion point:

```
FindItem(listData, item, location, found);
```

After the return from `FindItem`, `location` points to the node that should follow the new node. Now we are ready to link Node(`newNode`) into the list. Because of the complexity of the operation, you must be careful about the order in which you change the pointers. For instance, when inserting Node(`newNode`) before Node(`location`), if we change the pointer in `location->back` first, we lose our pointer to Node(`location`)'s predecessor. Figure 6.9 shows the correct order for the pointer changes.

Set Back(newNode) to Back(location)
Set Next(newNode) to location
Set Next(Back(location)) to newNode
Set Back(location) to newNode

We do have to be careful about inserting an item into an empty list, as it is a special case.

One useful feature of a doubly linked list is its elimination of the need for a pointer to a node's predecessor to delete the node. Through the `back` member, we can alter the

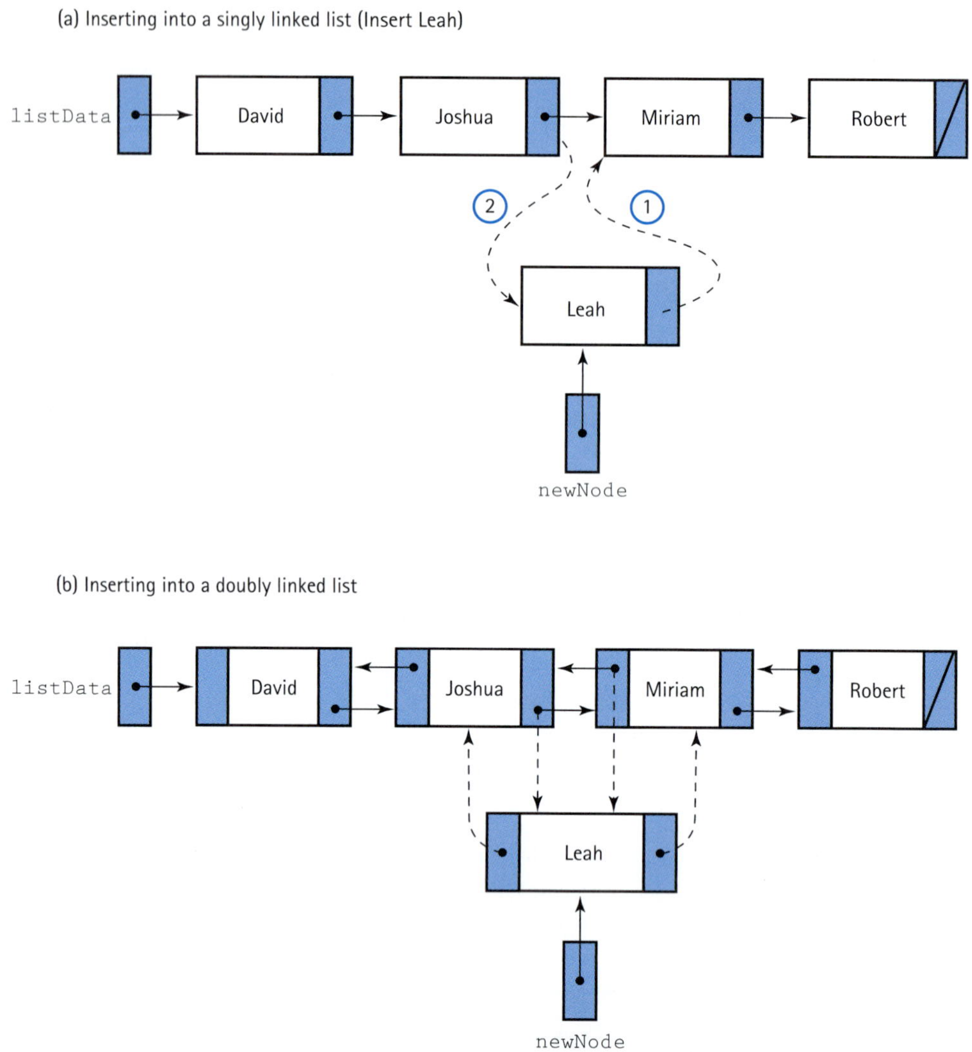

Figure 6.8 *Insertions into singly and doubly linked lists*

`next` member of the preceding node to make it jump over the unwanted node. Then we make the `back` pointer of the succeeding node point to the preceding node.

```
Set Next(Back(location)) to Next(location)
Set Back(Next(location)) to Back(location)
```

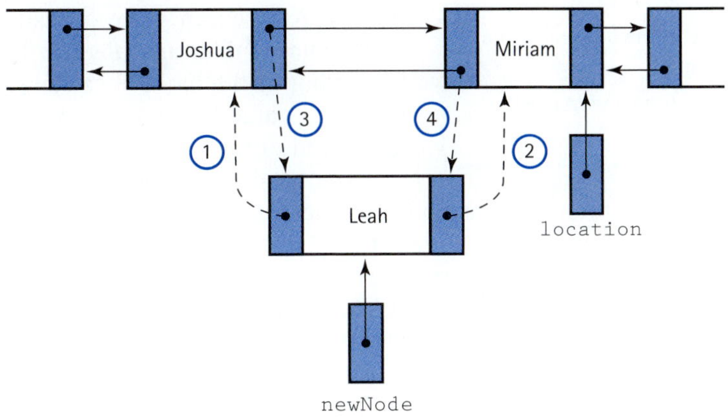

Figure 6.9 *Linking the new node into the list*

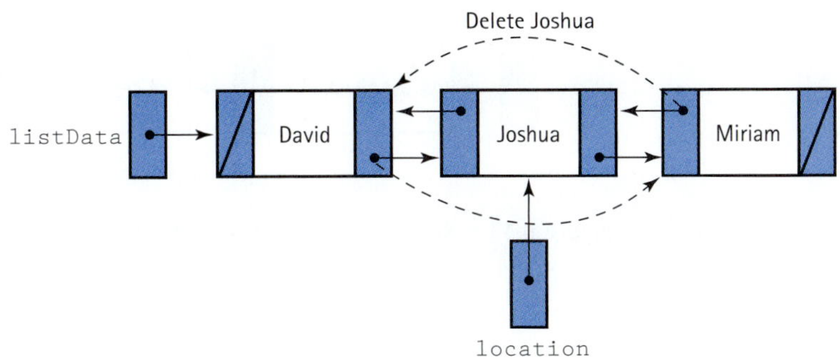

Figure 6.10 *Deleting from a doubly linked list*

We do, however, have to be careful about the end cases. If `location->back` is `NULL`, we are deleting the first node; if `location->next` is `NULL`, we are deleting the last node. If both `location->back` and `location->next` are `NULL`, we are deleting the only node. Figure 6.10 pictures this operation.

We leave the coding of `SortedType` as a programming assignment.

6.4 Linked Lists with Headers and Trailers

In writing the insertion and deletion algorithms for all implementations of linked lists, we see that special cases arise when we are dealing with the first node or the last node. One way to simplify these algorithms is to ensure that we never insert or delete items at the ends of the list.

How can this goal be accomplished? Recall that the elements in a sorted linked list are arranged according to the value in some key—for example, numerically by identification number or alphabetically by name. If we can determine the range of possible values for the key, it is often a simple matter to set up dummy nodes with values outside of

Header node A placeholder node at the beginning of a list; used to simplify list processing

Trailer node A placeholder node at the end of a list; used to simplify list processing

this range. We can place a header node, containing a value smaller than any possible list element key, at the beginning of the list. We can place a trailer node, containing a value larger than any legitimate element key, at the end of the list.

The header and the trailer are regular nodes of the same type as the real data nodes in the list. They have a different purpose, however; instead of storing list data, they act as placeholders.

If a list of students is sorted by last name, for example, we might assume that there are no students named "AAAAAAAAAA" or "ZZZZZZZZZZ." We could therefore initialize our linked list to contain header and trailer nodes with these values as the keys. See Figure 6.11. How can we write a general list algorithm if we must know the minimum and maximum key values? We can use a parameterized class constructor and let the user pass as parameters elements containing the dummy keys. Alternatively, we can just leave the keys undefined and start the search with the second node in the list.

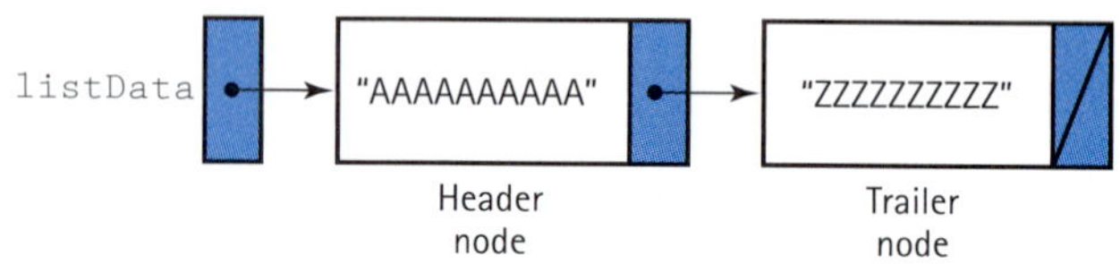

Figure 6.11 *An "empty" list with a header and a trailer*

6.5 Copy Structures

In this section, we reverse the usual order of presentation. We show an example of a problem, and then we give the solution to the general problem. Let's look at an example where a client of the Stack ADT needs a `CopyStack` operation.

CopyStack(StackType oldStack, StackType& copy)

Function:	Makes a copy of a stack.
Precondition:	oldStack has been initialized.
Postconditions:	copy is a duplicate of oldStack.
	oldStack is unchanged.

The client has access to all public member functions of `StackType` but cannot access any of the private data members. To make a copy of a stack, we must take all the items off `oldStack` and store them in a temporary stack. We can then copy the temporary stack back into `copy`.

```
template<class ItemType>
void CopyStack(StackType<ItemType> oldStack,
     StackType<ItemType>& copy)
{
  StackType<ItemType> tempStack;
  ItemType item;

  while (!oldStack.IsEmpty())
  {
    item = oldStack.Top();
    oldStack.Pop();
    tempStack.Push(item);
  }

  // oldStack is now empty; tempStack is the reverse of oldStack.
  while (!tempStack.IsEmpty())
  {
    item = tempStack.Top();
    tempStack.Pop();
    copy.Push(item);
  }
}
```

This situation seems quite straightforward. We realize that `oldStack` is empty because all of the items have been popped, but because `oldStack` is a value parameter, the original stack is not affected. Right? Wrong! If the static, array-based implementation of `StackType` is used, this function works correctly. The array is physically located within a class object. The class object is copied into the value parameter `oldStack`, and the original object is protected from change. But what happens if we use the dynamically linked implementation? The external pointer to the stack is copied into `oldStack` and is not changed, *but the items to which it points change; they are not protected.* See Figure 6.12.

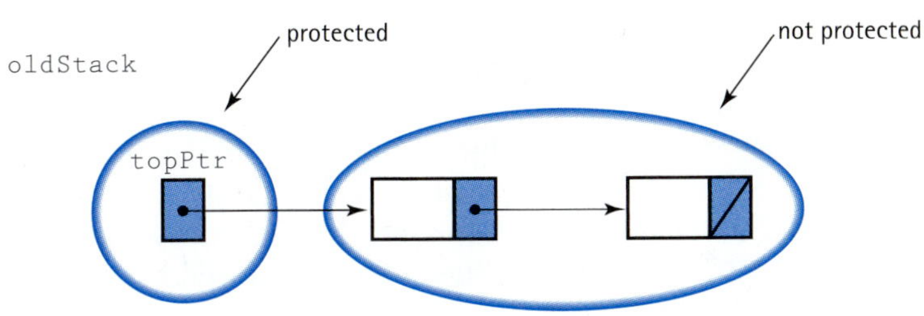

Figure 6.12 *Stack is a value parameter*

Can't we solve this problem by copying `tempStack` back into `oldStack`? Let's consider the code for the `Push` operation and see what happens in the linked implementation. The first item is pushed onto the stack, and its address is stored into the data member `topPtr` of the parameter `oldStack`. As each successive item is placed on the stack, its address is stored into data member `topPtr`. Therefore, the `topPtr` data member of `oldStack` should contain the address of the last item put onto the stack, which is what we want. Because the stack is passed by value, however, only the *copy* of the external pointer to the stack (data member `topPtr` of `oldStack`) is passed to the function; the original pointer does not change. We have recreated the stack, but its external pointer is not transmitted back to the calling code.

Two solutions to this problem are possible: We can make the first parameter a reference parameter and recreate the stack, or we can provide a *copy constructor* as described in the next section.

Shallow Versus Deep Copies

Shallow copy An operation that copies one class object to another without copying any pointed-to data

Deep copy An operation that not only copies one class object to another but also makes copies of any pointed-to data

The problem described in the previous section occurred because when a class object is passed by value, a shallow copy of the parameter is made. With a shallow copy, only the data members in the parameter are copied. In the case of `CopyStack`, only a copy of the external pointer to the stack was passed as the parameter. When pointers are involved, we need a deep copy, one where the data members of the parameter and everything to which the data members point are copied. Figure 6.13 shows the difference.

If the calling code passes an actual parameter `callerStack` to the `CopyStack` function, a shallow copy causes the data member `callerStack.topPtr` to be copied into `oldStack.topPtr`. Both pointers now point to the same linked structure (Figure 6.13a). When the `CopyStack` function removes the items from the stack, it destroys the caller's stack! What we want is a deep copy of the stack so that `CopyStack` works with an identical but *separate* copy of the caller's stack (Figure 6.13b). In this case, the caller's stack remains unchanged by any manipulations within the function.

Class Copy Constructors

C++ uses shallow copying in the following cases: passing parameters by value, initializing a variable in a declaration (`StackType myStack = yourStack;`), returning an object as the value of a function (`return thisStack;`), and implementing the assignment operation (`stack1 = stack2;`). Again, because of the active stance of a class object, C++ supports another special class operation called the copy constructor, which we describe shortly. If present, the copy constructor is used implicitly when a class object is passed by value, when a class object is initialized in a declaration, and when an object is a function return value.

Copy constructor A special member function of a class that is implicitly invoked when passing parameters by value, initializing a variable in a declaration, and returning an object as the value of a function

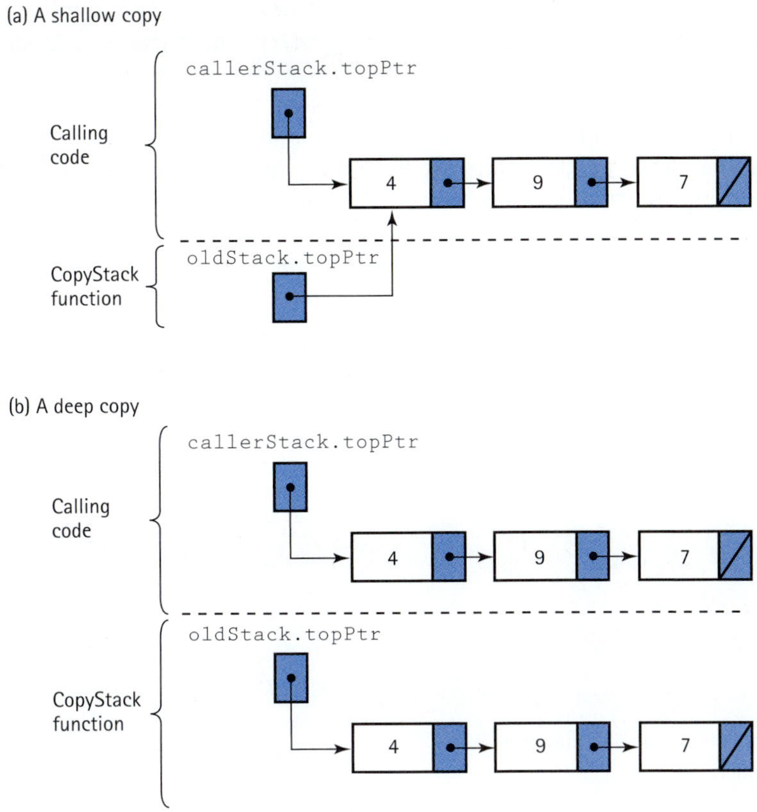

Figure 6.13 *Shallow copy versus deep copy of a stack*

What about the assignment operation? If you want to assign one object to another using a deep copy, you have to (a) write a member function to perform the deep copy and explicitly invoke it rather than use the assignment operator, or (b) overload the assignment operator. We discuss the first alternative in this section and the second alternative in the next section.

The copy constructor has a special syntax. Like the class constructor and destructor, it has no return type, just the class name.

```
template <class ItemType>
class StackType
{
public:
   .
   .
   // Copy constructor.
   StackType(const StackType<ItemType>& anotherStack);
   .
   .
};
```

The pattern that signals a copy constructor is the single reference parameter of the class type. The reserved word `const` protects the parameter from being altered even though it is passed by reference. Because the copy constructor is a class member function, the implementation has direct access to the class data. To copy a linked structure, we must cycle through the structure one node at a time, making a copy of the node's content as we go. Therefore we need two running pointers: one pointing to successive nodes in the structure being copied and one pointing to the last node of the new structure. Remember, in the deep copy of a linked structure, the `info` members are the same but the `next` members are not. In writing the algorithm, we must be sure to take care of the case where the stack being copied is empty.

Copy Constructor

```
if anotherStack.topPtr is NULL
    Set topPtr to NULL
else
    Set topPtr to the address of a newly allocated node
    Set Info(topPtr) to Info(anotherStack.topPtr)
    Set ptr1 to Next(anotherStack.topPtr)

Set ptr2 to topPtr
while ptr1 is not NULL
    Set Next(ptr2) to the address of a newly allocated node
    Set ptr2 to Next(ptr2)
    Set Info(ptr2) to Info(ptr1)
    Set ptr1 to Next(ptr1)
Set Next(ptr2) to NULL
```

Notice that our algorithm avoids using an extra pointer to the new node being inserted by storing its address directly into the structure where the new node will go. `ptr1` points to the node to be copied; `ptr2` points to the last node copied. See Figure 6.14.

```
template <class ItemType>
StackType<ItemType>::StackType(const StackType<ItemType>& anotherStack)
{
  NodeType<ItemType>* ptr1;
  NodeType<ItemType>* ptr2;

  if (anotherStack.topPtr == NULL)
    topPtr = NULL;
  else
  {
```

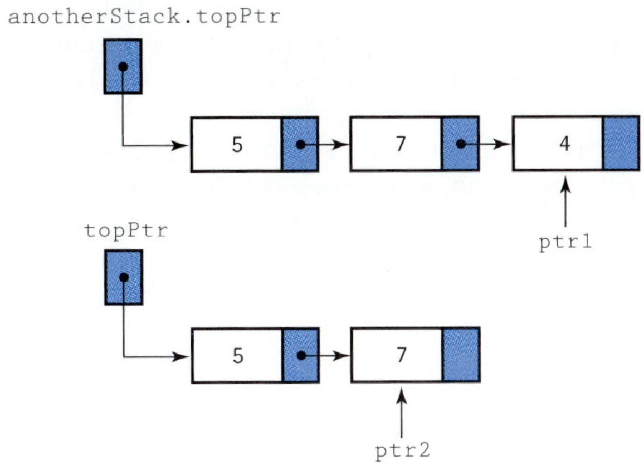

Figure 6.14 *Relative position of pointers at the beginning of each iteration*

```
    topPtr = new NodeType<ItemType>;
    topPtr->info = anotherStack.topPtr->info;
    ptr1 = anotherStack.topPtr->next;
    ptr2 = topPtr;
    while (ptr1 != NULL)
    {
      ptr2->next = new NodeType<ItemType>;
      ptr2 = ptr2->next;
      ptr2->info = ptr1->info;
      ptr1 = ptr1->next;
    }
    ptr2->next = NULL;
  }
}
```

StackType oneStack = anotherStack creates a copy of anotherStack and stores it in oneStack.

Copy Function

We saw how the client program could write a function CopyStack to copy one stack into another, provided a class copy constructor is defined to maintain the integrity of the original stack passed as a value parameter. Alternatively, could we include a member function to copy one stack into another and let the client invoke it explicitly? Sure, but first we must decide whether we are copying self into another object or another object into self. That is, member functions are always applied to an object of the class type. One stack would be the object to which the function is applied, and the other stack would be a parameter of the function. Given the statement

```
myStack.Copy(yourStack);
```

is `myStack` being copied into `yourStack` or the other way around? Of course, we can't answer this question until we see the function declaration. If `yourStack` is being copied into `myStack`, then the code for `Copy` would be nearly identical to the class copy constructor. The difference is that *self* already points to a dynamic structure, and we must deallocate all the nodes of this structure by applying `MakeEmpty` before the copying begins. On the other hand, if `myStack` is being copied into `yourStack`, then we have to rethink the algorithm. We leave this change as an exercise.

There is a third way to implement a copy function. Suppose that we'd like to write a function in which both stacks are parameters to the function.

```
Copy(myStack, yourStack);
```

Compared to dot notation, this syntax is more familiar to (and therefore more comfortable for) some programmers. But we just said that member functions are applied to an object of the class type. How can we do this? C++ provides a syntactic device called a *friend function* that allows this type of construction. A friend function is *not* a member of the class, yet it has permission to access private class members directly. Here is how this friend function would be declared and implemented:

```
template<class ItemType>
class StackType
{
public:
  :
  friend void Copy(StackType<ItemType>, StackType<ItemType>&);
  :
};

template<class ItemType>
void Copy(StackType<ItemType> original, StackType<ItemType>& copy)
{
  if (original.topPtr == NULL)
    copy.topPtr = NULL;
  else
  {
    NodeType<ItemType>* ptr1;
    NodeType<ItemType>* ptr2;

    copy.topPtr = new NodeType<ItemType>;
    copy.topPtr->info = original.topPtr->info;
    ptr1 = original.topPtr->next;
    ptr2 = copy.topPtr;
    while (ptr1 != NULL)
    {

      ptr2->next = new NodeType<ItemType>;
```

```
      ptr2 = ptr2->next;
      ptr2->info = ptr1->info;
      ptr1 = ptr1->next;
    }
    ptr2->next = NULL;
  }
}
```

Notice that we do not preface the name of the function with the class name. `Copy` is a friend function, not a member function. `Copy` does have access to the private data members of its parameters, but access to them must be qualified by the parameter name and a dot. There is no implicit *self* in a friend function. The friend function is declared within a class definition, but it is not a member function of the class.

Overloading Operators

In the last section, we pointed out that the assignment operator (=) normally causes shallow copying. It would be nice if we could write

```
myStack = yourStack;
```

Of course, if the stack is implemented as a dynamic linked structure, this code would result in two pointers pointing to the same stack rather than two distinct stacks. We can solve the problem of shallow copying with the assignment operator by overloading its meaning.

```
template<class ItemType>
class StackType
{
public:
  ⋮
  void operator=(StackType<ItemType>);
  ⋮
};
```

The function definition looks like this:

```
template<class ItemType>
void StackType<ItemType>::operator=
     (StackType<ItemType> anotherStack)
{
  ⋮
}
```

The function body is identical to that of the `Copy` member function that we discussed (but left as an exercise) earlier. Therefore, if we have already written a `Copy` member function, then to overload the assignment operator we make only one small change: Change the function name from `Copy` to `operator=`.

With an `operator=` function provided by the `StackType` class, the client code can use a statement like

```
myStack = yourStack;
```

The compiler implicitly translates this statement into the function call

```
myStack.operator = (yourStack);
```

Thus, the class object to the left of the equals sign in the client code is the object to which the `operator=` function is applied, and the object to the right of the equals sign becomes the parameter to the function.

We can overload the assignment operator for any number of classes. When the compiler sees an assignment operator, it looks at the types of the operands and uses the appropriate code. If the operands are objects of a class that has not overloaded the assignment operator, the default meaning of assignment is used—copying of data members only, yielding a shallow copy.

If we can overload the assignment operator, can we also overload other operators? Yes; all C++ operators may be overloaded except `::`, `.`, `sizeof`, and `?:`. In Chapter 1, we introduced a class `DateType`. Let's expand this class by overloading the relational operators <, >, and ==. We will also update it with a constructor rather than a method `Initialize`. The functions that overload the operators are shaded.

```
class DateType
{
public:
  void  Initialize(int, int, int);
  // Initializes month, day, and year.
  int GetMonth() const;
  // Returns month.
  int GetDay() const;
  // Returns day.
  int GetYear() const;
  // Returns year.
  bool operator<(DateType other) const;
  // Returns true if self comes before other;
  // false otherwise.
  bool operator>(DateType other) const;
  // Returns true if self comes after other;
  // false otherwise.
  bool operator==(DateType other) const;
  // Returns true if self and other are the same;
  // false otherwise.
private:
  int month;
```

```
  int day;
  int year;
};
```

The syntax for overloading a symbol is the word `operator` followed by the symbol to be overloaded. The first operand is the object to which the operator is applied, and the second operand is the parameter. These functions are member functions and are known in C++ as *operator functions*. Here are their implementations.

```
bool DateType::operator<(DateType other) const
{
  if (year < other.year)
    return true;
  else if (year > other.year)
    return false;
  else if (month < other.month)
    return true;
  else if (month > other.month)
    return false;
  else if (day < other.day)
    return true;
  else return false;
}

bool DateType::operator>(DateType other) const
{
  if (year > other.year)
    return true;
  else if (year < other.year)
    return false;
  else if (month > other.month)
    return true;
  else if (month < other.month)
    return false;
  else if (day > other.day)
    return true;
  else return false;
}

bool DateType::operator==(DateType other) const
{
  if (year == other.year
      && month == other.month && day == other.day)
    return true;
  else
    return false;
}
```

If `myBirthday` and `yourBirthday` have been initialized, and the client code includes

```
if (myBirthday < yourBirthday)
```

or

```
if (myBirthday > yourBirthday)
```

or

```
if (myBirthday == yourBirthday)
```

the respective member functions from class `DateType` are invoked.

For our Unsorted ADT, we required `ItemType` to be a class with a member function `ComparedTo`. Now that we know how to overload the relational operators, we could overload "<" and "==" in the `ItemType` class and then rewrite the code for `PutItem`, `GetItem`, and `DeleteItem` using the relational operators. We could, but should we? We cannot use the relational operators as labels on a *switch* statement, so the code would have to be a series of *if-else* clauses. Some programmers find *switch* statements more self-documenting, and others like to use the relational operators. The choice is a matter of personal style.

C++ Further Guidelines for Operator Overloading

1. At least one operand of the overloaded operator must be a class instance.
2. You cannot change the standard order of operator precedence, define new operator symbols, or change the number of operands of an operator.
3. Overloading unary operators: If `data` is of type `SomeClass`, and you want to overload, say, the unary minus operator (-), then `-data` is equivalent to `data.operator-()` if `operator-` is a member function and to `operator-(data)` if `operator-` is a friend function.
4. Overloading binary operators: If `data` is of type `SomeClass` and you want to overload, say, the addition operator (+), then `data + otherData` is equivalent to `data.operator+(otherData)` if `operator+` is a member function and to `operator+(data, otherData)` if `operator+` is a friend function.
5. Overloading the ++ and -- operators requires client code to use the preincrement form: `++someObject` or `--someObject`.
6. Operator functions must be member functions when overloading =, `()`, `[]`, and ->. Other restrictions apply as well. See a C++ reference book before attempting to overload `()`, `[]`, and ->.
7. The stream operators << and >> must be overloaded using a friend function. See a C++ reference book before attempting to overload << and >>.
8. Many meanings for an operator can coexist as long as the compiler can distinguish among the data types of the operands.

One final comment before we leave the problems related to classes in which at least one of the data members is a pointer type: If one of the three–class destructor, copy constructor, or overloaded assignment operator–is necessary, then most likely all three are necessary. This is sometimes called the "Rule of the big 3."

6.6 A Linked List as an Array of Records

We have used both statically allocated arrays and dynamically allocated arrays for our array-based implementations. We have used dynamic memory allocation to obtain the necessary memory for the nodes making up the linked structures developed in this and previous chapters.

The choice between array-based and linked list representations is not the same as the choice between static and dynamic storage allocation. They are separate issues. We typically store arrays in variables that have been declared statically, as illustrated in Figure 6.15a, but an array-based implementation does not necessarily use static storage. The entire array could exist in a dynamically allocated area of memory; that is, we could get space for the whole structure at once using the `new` operator, as illustrated in Figure 6.15b.

(a) A sequential list in static storage

```
struct ListType
{
  int length;
  char info[5];
};
ListType list;
```

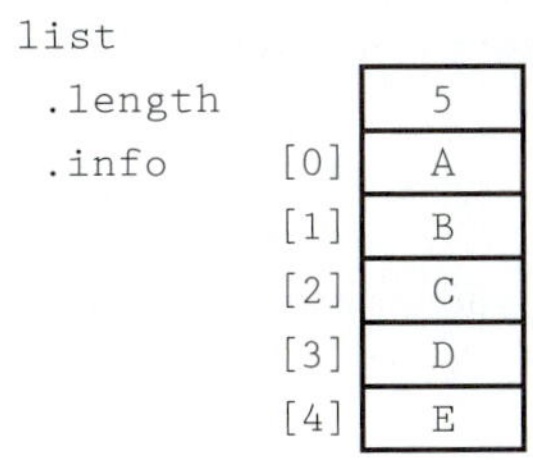

(b) A sequential list in dynamic storage

```
struct ListType
{
  int length;
  char info[5];
};
ListType* list;
list = new ListType;
```

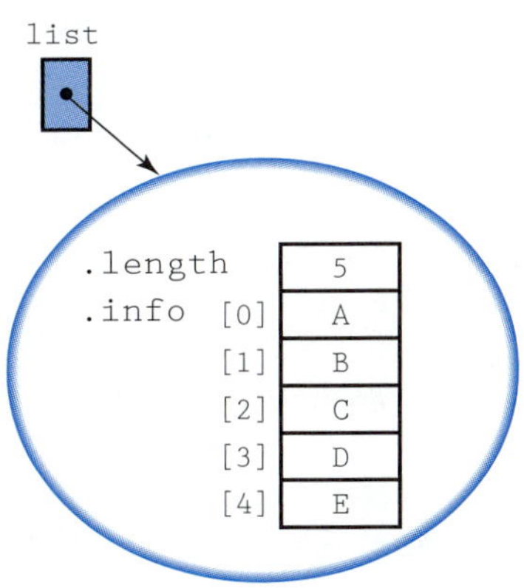

Figure 6.15 *Array-based lists in static and dynamic storage*

We tend to think of linked structures as residing in dynamically allocated storage, as depicted in Figure 6.16b, but this is not a requirement. A linked list could be implemented in an array; the elements might be stored in the array in any order and "linked" by their indexes (see Figure 6.16a). In the following sections, we develop the array-based linked-list implementation.

Why Use an Array?

Dynamic allocation of list nodes offers many advantages, so why would we even discuss using an array-of-records implementation instead? We have noted that dynamic allocation is merely one advantage gained by choosing a linked implementation; another advantage relates to the efficiency of the insertion and deletion algorithms. Most of the algorithms that we have discussed for operations on a linked structure can be used for either an array-based or a dynamic implementation. The main difference involves the requirement that we manage our own free space in an array-based implementation. Managing the free space ourselves gives us greater flexibility.

(a) A linked list in static storage

```
struct NodeType
{
  char info;
  int next;
};
struct ListType
{
  NodeType nodes[5];
  int first;
};
ListType list;
```

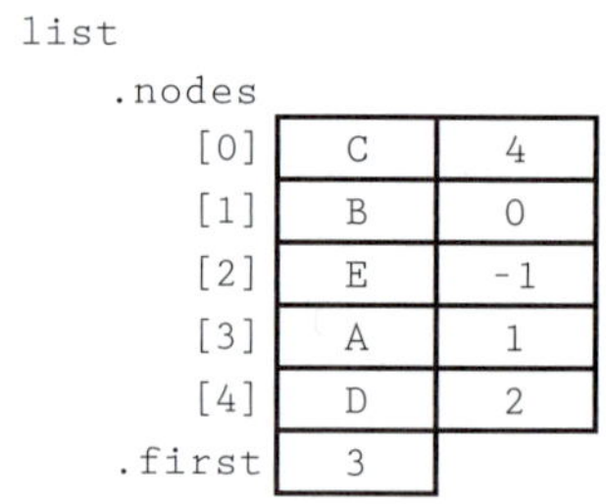

(b) A linked list in dynamic storage

```
struct NodeType
{
  char info;
  NodeType* next;
};

NodeType* list;
list = new NodeType;
```

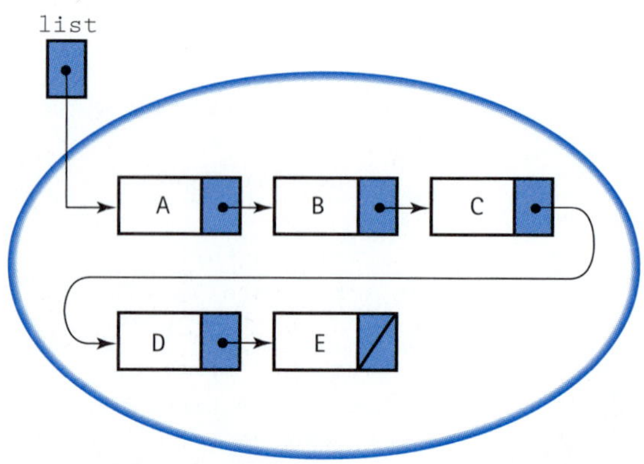

Figure 6.16 *Linked lists in static and dynamic storage*

Another reason to use an array of records is the fact that a number of programming languages do not support dynamic allocation or pointer types. You can still use linked structures when programming in one of these languages, but you would have to represent pointer values as array indexes.

Using pointer variables presents a problem when we need to save the information in a data structure between runs of a program. Suppose we want to write all the nodes in a list to a file and then use this file as input the next time we run the program. If the links are pointer values—containing memory addresses—they are meaningless on the next run of the program because the program may be placed somewhere else in memory the next time. We must save the user data part of each node in the file and then rebuild the linked structure the next time we run the program. An array index, however, remains valid on the next run of the program. We can store the entire array, including the `next` data member (indexes), and then read it back in the next time we run the program.

Most importantly, sometimes dynamic allocation isn't possible or feasible, or dynamic allocation of each node, one at a time, is too costly in terms of time—especially in system software such as operating system code.

How Is an Array Used?

Let's return to our discussion of how we can implement a linked list in an array. As noted earlier, the `next` member of each node tells us the array index of the succeeding node. The beginning of the list is accessed through a "pointer" that contains the array index of the first element in the list. Figure 6.17 shows how a sorted list containing the elements David, Joshua, Leah, Miriam, and Robert might be stored in an array of records called `nodes`. Do you see how the order of the elements in the list is explicitly indicated by the chain of `next` indexes?

What goes in the `next` member of the last list element? Its "null" value must be an invalid address for a real list element. Because the `nodes` array indexes begin at 0, the value -1 is not a valid index into the array; that is, no `nodes[-1]` exists. Therefore -1 makes an ideal value to use as a "null" address. Let's use the constant identifier `NUL` rather than `NULL` to keep the distinction clear. We could use the literal value -1 in our programs,

```
while (location != -1)
```

but it is better programming style to declare a named constant. In fact, we can define `NUL` to be -1.

```
const int NUL = -1;
```

When using an array-of-records implementation to represent a linked list, the programmer must write routines to manage the free space available for new list elements. Where is this free space? Look again at Figure 6.17. All of the array elements that do not contain values in the list constitute free space. Instead of the built-in allocator `new`, which allocates memory dynamically, we must write our own function to allocate nodes from the free space. We call this function `GetNode`.

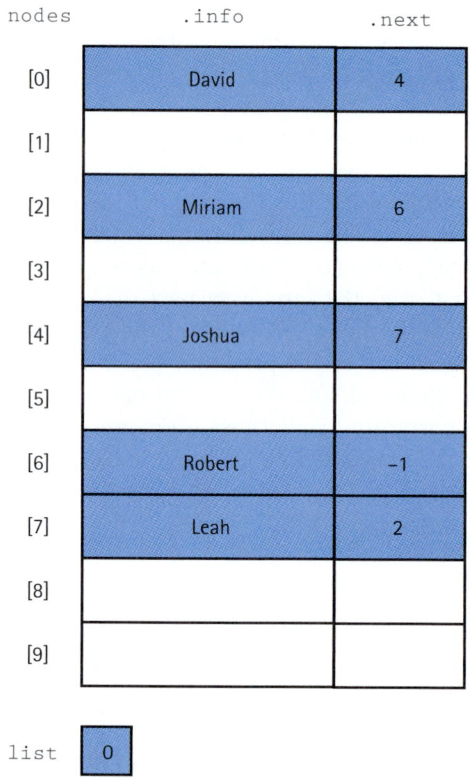

Figure 6.17 *A sorted list stored in an array of records*

When elements are deleted from the list, we need to free the node space. We can't use `delete`, because it only works for dynamically allocated space. We write our own function, `FreeNode`, to return a node to the pool of free space.

This collection of unused array elements can be linked together into a second list, a linked list of free nodes. Figure 6.18 shows the array `nodes` with both the list of values and the list of free space linked through their `next` members. Here `list` is the external pointer to a list that begins at index 0 (containing the value David). Following the links in the `next` member, we see that the list continues with the array slots at index 4 (Joshua), 7 (Leah), 2 (Miriam), and 6 (Robert), in that order. The free list begins at `free`, at index 1. Following the links in the `next` member, we see that the free list also includes the array slots at indexes 5, 3, 8, and 9. Two `NUL` values appear in the `next` column because the `nodes` array contains two linked lists.

Two approaches to using an array-of-records implementation for linked structures are possible. The first is to simulate dynamic memory. One array stores many different linked lists, just as the nodes on the free store can be dynamically allocated for different lists. In this approach, the external pointers to the lists are not part of the storage structure, but the external pointer to the list of free nodes is part of the structure. Figure 6.19 shows an array

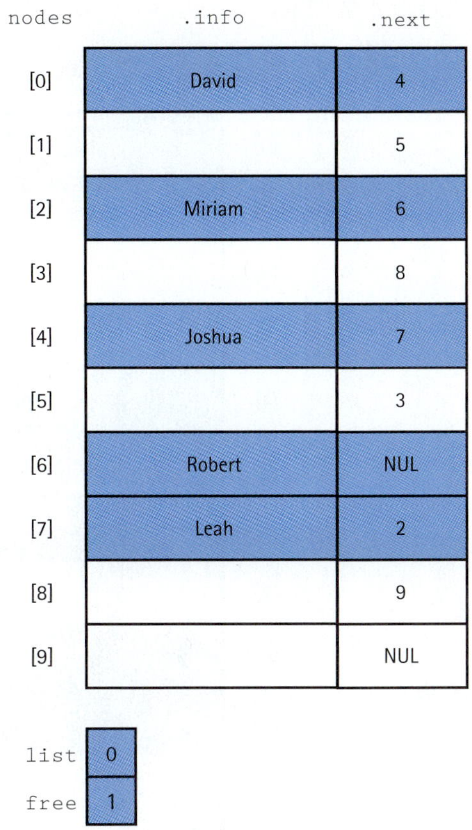

Figure 6.18 *An array with a linked list of values and free space*

that contains two different lists. The list indicated by `list1` contains the values John, Nell, Susan, and Susanne, and the list indicated by `list2` contains the values Mark, Naomi, and Robert. The remaining three array slots in Figure 6.19 are linked together in the free list.

The second approach is to have one array of records for each list. In this approach, the external pointer is part of the storage structure itself (see Figure 6.20). The list constructor takes a parameter that specifies the maximum number of items on the list. This parameter is used to dynamically allocate an array of the appropriate size. Note that the array itself resides in dynamic storage, but the linked structure uses array indexes as "pointers." If the list will be saved between runs of the program, the contents of the array are saved, and the indexes (links) remain valid.

Let's implement this second approach. In implementing our class functions, we need to keep in mind that two distinct processes go on within the array of records: bookkeeping related to the space (such as initializing the array of records, getting a new node, and freeing a node) and the operations on the list that contains the user's data. The bookkeeping operations are transparent to the user. The prototypes of the member functions stay the same, including both a parameterized and a default constructor. The

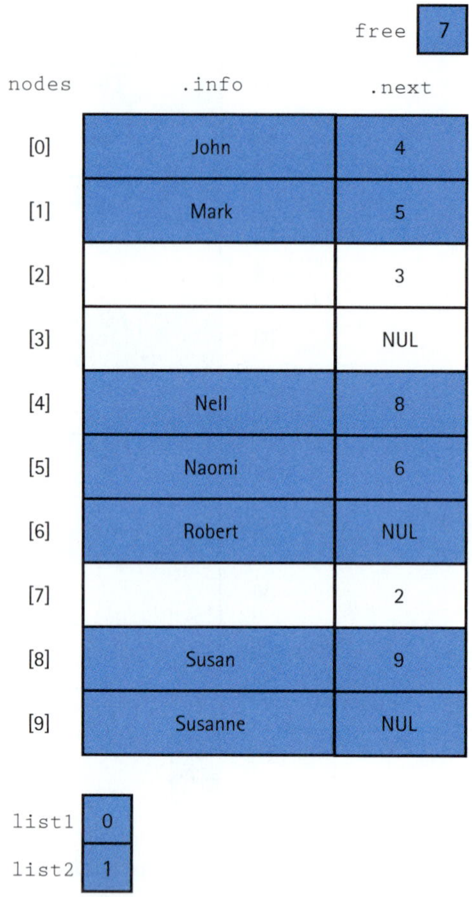

Figure 6.19 *An array with three lists (including the free list)*

private data members, however, change. We need to include the array of records. Let's call this array `nodes` and place it in dynamic storage. `MemoryType`, then, is a struct containing two items: an integer "pointer" to the first free node and a true pointer to the dynamically allocated array of nodes.

To simplify the following discussion and code, we assume that the items on the list are integers rather than using a template class.

```
struct MemoryType;

class ListType
{
public:
  // Member function prototypes go here.
private:
  int listData;
```

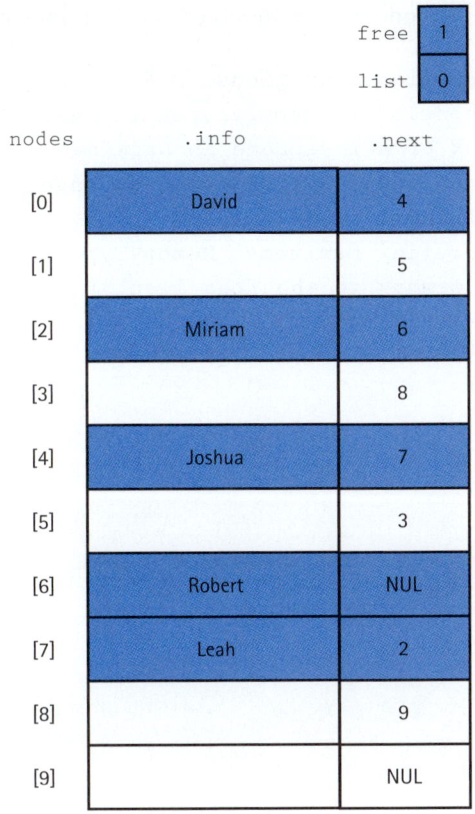

Figure 6.20 *List and linked structure are together*

```
  int currentPos;
  int length;
  int maxItems;
  MemoryType storage;
};
```

The functions that do the bookkeeping are auxiliary ("helper") functions, not class member functions. Member functions are those functions that the user invokes; auxiliary functions are those functions that help to implement the member functions. Let's look first at these bookkeeping functions. The nodes are all free initially, so they must be chained together and the index of the first node stored into `free`. `GetNode` must return the index of the next free node and update `free`. `FreeNode` must take the node index received as a parameter and insert it into the list of free nodes. Because the first item in the list is directly accessible, we have `GetNode` return the first free item and `FreeNode` insert the node being returned at the beginning of the free list. (Yes, we keep the free list as a stack—not because we need the LIFO property but because the code is the simplest for what we need.)

The following code defines `MemoryType` and implements these auxiliary functions:

```
// Prototypes of auxiliary functions.
void GetNode(int& nodeIndex, MemoryType& storage);
// Returns the index of a free node in nodeIndex.
void FreeNode(int nodeIndex, MemoryType& storage);
// Returns nodeIndex to storage.
void InitializeMemory(int maxItems, MemoryType&);
// Initializes all memory to the free list.

// Define end-of-list symbol.
const int NUL = -1;

struct NodeType
{
  int info;
  int next;
};

struct MemoryType
{
  int free;
  NodeType* nodes;
};

void InitializeMemory(int maxItems, MemoryType& storage)
{
  for (int index = 1; index < maxItems; index++)
    storage.nodes[index-1].next = index;
  storage.nodes[maxItems-1] = NUL;
  storage.free = 0;
}

void GetNode(int& nodeIndex, MemoryType& storage)
{
  nodeIndex = storage.free;
  storage.free = storage.nodes[free].next;
}

void FreeNode(int nodeIndex, MemoryType& storage)
{
  storage.nodes[nodeIndex].next = storage.free;
  storage.free = nodeIndex;
}
```

The class constructors for the class `ListType` must allocate the storage for the array of records and call `InitializeMemory`. For the default constructor, we arbitrarily choose an array size of 500.

```
ListType::ListType(int max)
{
  length = 0;
  maxItems = max;
  storage.nodes = new NodeType[max];
  InitializeMemory(maxItems, storage);
  listData = NUL;
}
ListType::ListType()
{
  length = 0;
  maxItems = 500;
  storage.nodes = new NodeType[500];
  InitializeMemory(500, storage);
  listData = NUL;
}

ListType::~ListType()
{
  delete [] storage.nodes;
}
```

Let's look at our design notation, the dynamic pointer-based equivalent, and the array-of-records equivalent. We also need to examine the bookkeeping equivalent of the dynamic pointer-based operations and the array-of-records version. Once we understand all these relationships, coding the member functions of `ListType` is quite straightforward. In fact, it is so straightforward, we leave the code as a programming assignment.

Design Notation/ Algorithm	Dynamic Pointers	Array-of-Records "Pointers"
Node(location)	`*location`	`storage.nodes[location]`
Info(location)	`location->info`	`storage.nodes[location].info`
Next(location)	`location->next`	`storage.nodes[location].next`
Set location to Next(location)	`location = location->next`	`location = storage.nodes[location].next`
Set Info(location) to value	`location->info = value`	`storage.nodes[location].info = value`
Allocate a node	`nodePtr = new NodeType`	`GetNode(nodePtr)`
Deallocate a node	`delete nodePtr`	`FreeNode(nodePtr)`

6.7 Polymorphism with Virtual Functions

In addition to *encapsulation* and *inheritance*, the third capability that must be available in an object-oriented programming language is *polymorphism*. In Chapter 2, we defined polymorphism as the ability to determine which function to apply to a particular object. This determination can be made at compile time (static binding) or at run time (dynamic binding). For a language to be truly object-oriented, it must support both static and dynamic binding; that is, it must support polymorphism. C++ uses *virtual functions* to implement run-time binding.

The basic C++ rule for passing parameters is that the actual parameter and its corresponding formal parameter must be of an identical type. With inheritance, C++ relaxes this rule somewhat. The type of the actual parameter may be an object of a derived class of the formal parameter.* To force the compiler to generate code that guarantees dynamic binding of a member function to a class object, the reserved word `virtual` appears before the function declaration in the declaration of the base class. Virtual functions work in the following way: If a class object is passed *by reference* to some function, and if the body of that function contains a statement

```
formalParameter.MemberFunction(...);
```

then

1. If `MemberFunction` is not a virtual function, the type of the *formal parameter* determines which function to call. (Static binding is used.)
2. If `MemberFunction` is a virtual function, the type of the *actual parameter* determines which function to call. (Dynamic binding is used.)

Let's look at an example. Suppose that `ItemType` is declared as follows:

```
class ItemType
{
public:
  ⋮
  virtual RelationType ComparedTo(ItemType) const;
private:
  char lastName[50];
  ⋮
};
```

*This relaxation allows dynamic binding to occur.

```
RelationType ItemType::ComparedTo(ItemType item) const
{
  int result;

  result = std::strcmp(lastName, item.lastName);
  if (result < 0)
    return LESS;
  else if (result > 0)
    return GREATER;
  else return EQUAL;
}
```

Now let's derive a class `NewItemType` that contains two strings as data members. We want `ComparedTo` to use both of them in the comparison.

```
class NewItemType : public ItemType
{
public:
  :
  RelationType ComparedTo(ItemType) const;
private:
  // In addition to the inherited lastName member
  char firstName[50];
  :
};
RelationType NewItemType::ComparedTo(NewItemType item) const
{
  int result;

  result = std::strcmp(lastName, item.lastName);
  if (result < 0)
    return LESS;
  else if (result > 0)
    return GREATER;
  else
  {
    result = strcmp(firstName, item.firstName);
    if (result < 0)
      return LESS;
    else if (result > 0)
      return GREATER;
    else
      return EQUAL;
  }
}
```

The function `ComparedTo` is marked as virtual in the base class (`ItemType`); according to the C++ language, `ComparedTo` is therefore a virtual function in all derived classes as well. Whenever an object of type `ItemType` or `NewItemType` is passed by reference to a formal parameter of type `ItemType`, the determination of which `ComparedTo` to use within that function is postponed until run time. Let's assume that the client program includes the following function:

```
void PrintResult(ItemType& first, ItemType& second)
{
  using namespace std;
  if (first.ComparedTo(second)==LESS)
    cout << "First comes before second";
  else
    cout << "First does not come before second";
}
```

It then executes the following code:

```
ItemType item1, item2;
NewItemType item3, item4:
  ⋮
PrintResult(item1, item2);
PrintResult(item3, item4);
```

Because `item3` and `item4` are objects of a class derived from `ItemType`, both of the calls to `PrintResult` are valid. `PrintResult` invokes `ComparedTo`. Which one? Is it `ItemType::ComparedTo` or `NewItemType::ComparedTo`? Because `ComparedTo` is a virtual function and the class objects are passed by reference to `PrintResult`, the type of the actual parameter—not the formal parameter—determines which version of `ComparedTo` is called. In the first call to `PrintResult`, `ItemType::ComparedTo` is invoked; in the second call, `NewItemType::ComparedTo` is invoked. This situation is illustrated in the following diagram:

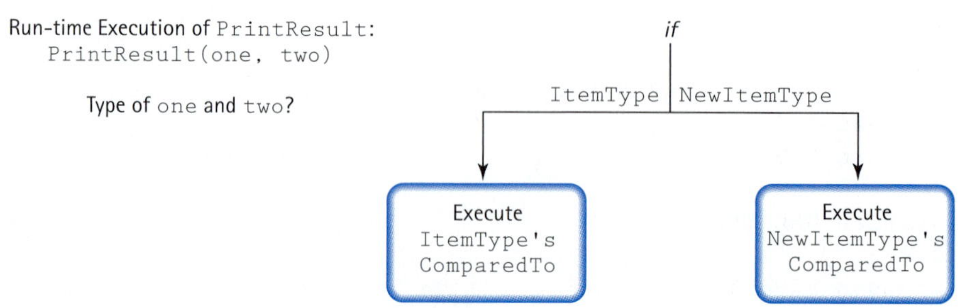

This example demonstrates an important benefit of dynamic binding. The client does not need to have multiple versions of the `PrintResult` function, one for each type of parameter that is passed to it. If new classes are derived from `ItemType` (or even from `NewItemType`), objects of those classes can be passed to `PrintResult` without any modification of `PrintResult`.

If you have a pointer defined as a pointer to a base class and dynamically allocate storage using the base type, the pointer points to a base-class object. If you dynamically allocate storage using the derived type, the pointer points to a derived-class object. Take, for example, the following short program with a base class `One` and a derived class `Two`. Here we allocate an object of (base) class `One` and an object of (derived) class `Two`.

```
#include <iostream>
class One
{
public:
  virtual void Print() const;
};

class Two : public One
{
public:
  void Print() const;
};

void PrintTest(One*);

int main()
{
  using namespace std;
  One* onePtr;
  onePtr = new One;

  cout << "Result of passing an object of class One: ";
  PrintTest(onePtr);

  onePtr = new Two;

  cout << "Result of passing an object of class Two: ";

  PrintTest(onePtr);
  return 0;
}
```

```
void PrintTest(One* ptr)
{
  ptr->Print();
}

void One::Print() const
{
  std::cout  << "Print member function of class One" << endl;
}


void Two::Print() const
{
  std::cout  << "Print member function of class Two " << endl;
}
```

`onePtr` points first to an object of class `One` and then to an object of class `Two`. When the parameter to `PrintTest` points to an object of class `One`, the class `One` member function is applied. When the parameter points to an object of class `Two`, the class `Two` member function is applied. The fact that the type of the run-time object determines which member function is executed is verified by the following output:

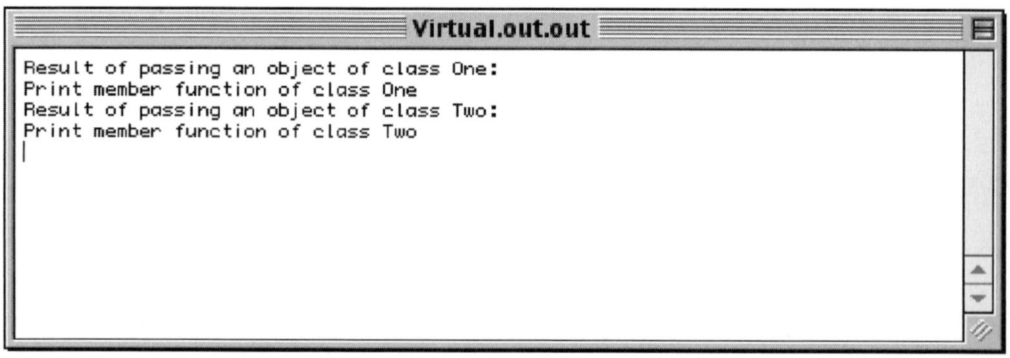

We must issue one word of caution about passing a parameter of a derived type to any function whose formal parameter is of the base type. If you pass the parameter by reference, no problem arises. If you pass the parameter by value, however, only the subobject that is of the base type is actually passed. For example, if the base type has two data members and the derived type has two additional data members, only the two data members of the base type are passed to a function if the formal parameter is of the base type and the actual parameter is of the derived type. This *slicing problem* (any additional data members declared by the derived class are "sliced off") can also occur if we assign an object of the derived type to an object of the base type.

Look back at Figure 5.15, which shows the relationship of objects of `QueType` and `CountedQueType`. If a `CountedQueType` object is passed as a value parameter to a function whose formal parameter is of type `QueType`, only those data members of `Que-`

`Type` are copied; `length`, a member of `CountedQueType`, is not. Although this slicing does not present a problem in this case, be aware of this situation when designing your hierarchy of classes.

6.8 A Specialized List ADT

We have defined Unsorted and Sorted List ADTs and given several implementations of each. Our lists can be used for many applications. However, some applications always need special-purpose lists. Perhaps they require specific list operations that are not defined by our List ADTs, or perhaps the specific qualities of our lists (unique elements) do not mesh well with the requirements of the application. In such cases, we may be able to extend one of our list classes to create a new list that meets the needs of the application. Alternatively, we might create a new list class customized for the application in question.

In the Case Study later in this chapter, we need lists with a unique set of properties and operations. The lists must hold elements of the type `int`; duplicate elements are allowed. The lists need not support IsFull, GetItem, or DeleteItem. In fact, the only list operations that we have been using that this new list construct requires are the GetLength operation and the iterator operations. For the Case Study, we will need to process elements from left to right and from right to left, so we need to support two iterators. In addition, we plan to insert items at the front and at the back of our lists. The reasons for these requirements are made clear in the Case Study; for now, we just accept the requirements as stated and consider how to implement the new list.

Let's summarize these specifications in a CRC card.

Class Name: SpecializedList	Superclass:	Subclasses:
Responsibilities	**Collaborations**	
MakeEmpty		
GetLength( ) returns int		
Reset for forward traversal		
GetNextItem( ) returns int		
Reset for backward traversal		
GetPriorItem( ) returns int		
Put at the front of the list		
Put at the rear of the list		
. . .		

Given this unique set of requirements, we decide to start from scratch for our new List ADT. Of course, we can reuse our knowledge of lists and perhaps even reuse (cut and paste) some of the code from the previous list implementations. Because the new list construct creates a specialized list for a specific application, we call the list class `SpecializedList`. To satisfy the requirement that we be able to iterate through the list in both directions, instead of our standard "current position" property, lists of the class `SpecializedList` have both a "current forward position" and a "current backward position" and provide iterator operations for traversing the list in either direction. Note that this statement does not mean that an iteration can change directions—rather, two separate iterations can be going on at the same time, one forward and one backward.

One advantage of a doubly linked structure is that it supports the ability to traverse a structure in both directions. When a structure is linked in only one direction, it is not simple to traverse it in the other direction. Because a doubly linked list is linked in both directions, traversing the list forward or backward is equally easy. On the other hand, a circular structure with the external pointer pointing to the last item in the structure gives direct access to both the front element and the last element. A doubly linked circular structure would be ideal (see Figure 6.21).

```
struct NodeType;

class SpecializedList
{
public:
  SpecializedList();                        // Class constructor.
  ~SpecializedList();                       // Class destructor.
  SpecializedList(const SpecializedList& someList);
  // Copy constructor.

  void ResetForward();
  // Initializes current position for an iteration
  //  through the list from first item to last item.

  void GetNextItem(int& item, bool& finished);
  // Gets the next item in the structure.
  //  finished is true if all items have been accessed.
```

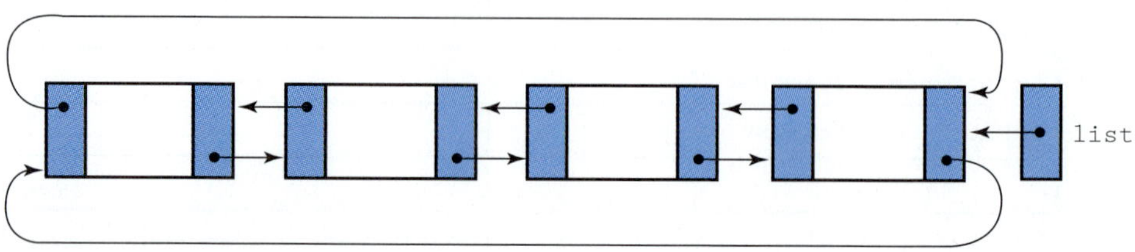

Figure 6.21 *A circular doubly linked list*

```
  // GetNextItem and GetPriorItem are independent; a forward
  //  iteration and a backward iteration may be in progress
  //  at the same time.

  void ResetBackward();
  // Initializes current position for an iteration
  //  through the list from last item to first item.

  void GetPriorItem(int& item, bool& finished);
  // Gets the previous item in the structure.
  //  finished is true if all items have been accessed.

  void PutFront(int item);
  // Inserts item as the first item in the structure.

  void PutEnd(int item);
  // Inserts item as the last item in the structure.

  int GetLength();
  // Returns the number of items in the structure.
private:
  NodeType* list;
  NodeType* currentNextPos;
  NodeType* currentBackPos;
  int length;
};
:
struct NodeType
{
  NodeType* next;
  NodeType* back;
  int info;
};
```

The constructor must set the list pointer to NULL and the length to 0.

```
SpecializedList::SpecializedList()
{
  length = 0;
  list = NULL;
}
```

Although we provide a length operation, we give the user another way of determining when the last item has been accessed. GetNextItem and GetPriorItem both have two parameters, a returned item and a Boolean flag. This flag is set to `true` when the last item has been returned. `ResetForward` sets `currentNextPos` to `NULL`, and `GetNextItem` returns the next item in the structure, setting `finished` to `true` when `currentNextPos` equals `list`. `ResetBackward` sets `currentBackPos` to `NULL`, and `GetPriorItem` returns the previous item in the structure, setting `finished` to `true` when `currentBackPos` equals `list->next`.

```
void SpecializedList::ResetForward()
// Post: currentNextPos has been initialized for a forward
//       traversal.
{
  currentNextPos = NULL;
}


void SpecializedList::GetNextItem(int& item,
     bool& finished)
// Pre:  ResetForward has been called before the first call to
//       this function.
// Post: item is a copy of the next item in the list.
//       finished is true if item is the last item in the list and
//       false otherwise.
{
  if (currentNextPos == NULL)
    currentNextPos = list->next;
  else
    currentNextPos = currentNextPos->next;
  item = currentNextPos->info;
  finished = (currentNextPos == list);
}


void SpecializedList::ResetBackward()
// Post: currentBackPos has been initialized for a backward
//       traversal.
{
  currentBackPos = NULL;
}


void SpecializedList::GetPriorItem(int& item,
     bool& finished)
// Post: item is a copy of the previous item in the list.
//       finished is true if item is the first item in the list;
//       false otherwise.
{
  if (currentBackPos == NULL)
```

```
      currentBackPos = list;
    else
      currentBackPos = currentBackPos->back;
    item = currentBackPos->info;
    finished = (currentBackPos == list->next);
}
int SpecializedList::GetLength()
{ return length; }
```

`PutFront` inserts the new item as the first item in the list (see Figure 6.22a). `PutEnd` inserts the new item as the last item in the list (see Figure 6.22b). The results look quite different in the diagram, but a careful examination reveals that they are identical *except for the external pointer* `list`. Inserting an item at the beginning does not change `list`; inserting one at the end does. We can use the same insertion routine for both, but have `PutEnd` move `list`.

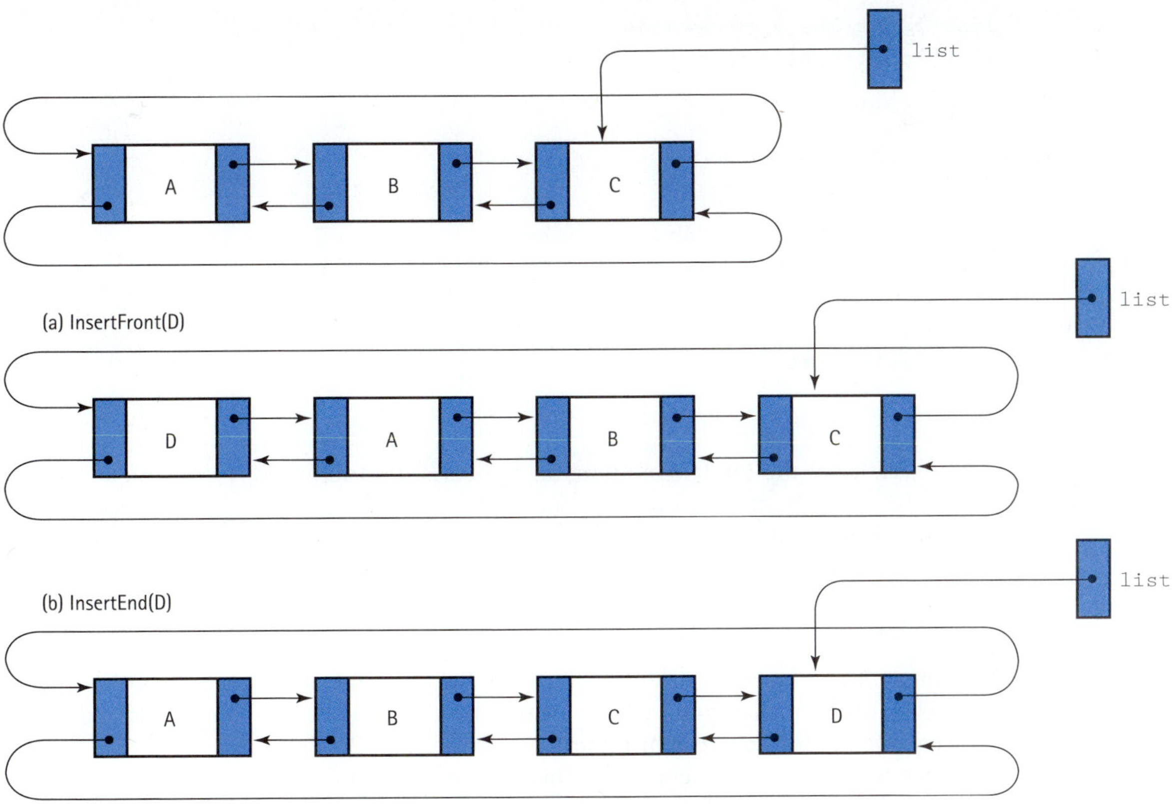

Figure 6.22 *Putting at the front and at the rear*

```
void SpecializedList::PutFront(int item)
// Post: item has been inserted at the front of the list.
{
  NodeType* newNode;

  newNode = new NodeType;
  newNode->info = item;
  if (list == NULL)
  { // list is empty.
    newNode->back = newNode;
    newNode->next = newNode;
    list = newNode;
  }
  else
  {
    newNode->back = list;
    newNode->next = list->next;
    list->next->back = newNode;
    list->next = newNode;
  }
  length++;
}

void SpecializedList::PutEnd(int item)
// Post: item has been inserted at the end of the list.
{
  PutFront(item);
  list = list->next;
}
```

We leave the implementations of the class destructor, copy constructor, and overloaded assignment operator plus functions `LengthIs` and `MakeEmpty` as a programming assignment.

Test Plan

Items must be inserted at both ends of the list, and traversals must go both forward and backward. Note that some of the operations have not been implemented. For example, we can't test the constructor by printing the length. But how *can* we test it? Well, if the other operations work correctly, then the constructor can be assumed to be correct. Rather than testing all the front insertions and then all the end insertions, let's change the pattern somewhat and mix them up.

Operation to Be Tested and Description of Action	Input Values	Expected Output
`PutFront` Insert five items	1, 2, 3, 4, 5	
`PutEnd` Insert two items	0, –1	
`PutFront` Insert one item	6	
`PutEnd` Insert one item	–2	
`ResetForward`		
`GetNextItem` Call nine times, print each time		6, 5, 4, 3, 2, 1, 0, –1, –2
`ResetBackward`		
`GetPriorItem` Call nine times, print each time		–2, –1, 0, 1, 2, 3, 4, 5, 6

We should also test each time `GetNextItem` and `GetPriorItem` are called to see whether we have reached the end of the traversal. On the Web, the file `SpecialDr.cpp` is the driver for this class, `Special1.in` is the input file representing this test plan, and `Special1.out` is the output. The file `SpecializedList.h` contains the code from this chapter.

Case Study

Implementing a Large Integer ADT

The range of integer values that can be supported varies from one computer to another. In most C++ environments, file `<climits>` shows you the limits. For example, `long` integers range from -2,147,483,648 to +2,147,483,647 on many machines. However long they may be on a particular machine, some user is bound to want to represent integers with even larger values. Let's design and implement a class `LargeInt` that allows the user to manipulate integers where the number of digits is limited only by the size of the free store.

Because we are providing an alternative implementation for a mathematical object, an integer number, most of the operations are already specified: addition, subtraction, multiplication, division, assignment, and the relational operators. For this Case Study, we limit our attention to addition, subtraction, equality, and less than. Enhancing this ADT with the other operations is left as a programming assignment.

In addition to the standard mathematical operations, we need an operation that constructs a number one digit at a time. This operation cannot be a parameterized constructor because the integer parameter might be too large to represent in the machine—after all, that is the idea of this ADT. Instead, we need a special member function that can be called within a loop that inserts the digits one at a time. We also need an operation that writes the integer to a file, one digit at a time, from most significant digit to least significant digit.

Before we can begin to look at the algorithms for these operations, we need to decide on our representation. Earlier we were designing the class `SpecializedList` for use in this Case Study, so you know that we will use a circular, doubly linked list. Why doubly linked? Because we need to access the digits from most significant to least significant to write them to a file, and we need to access the digits from least significant to most significant to manipulate them arithmetically. Why circular? Because we need to insert digits from most significant to least significant when constructing an object, and we need to insert digits from least significant to most significant when constructing an object that is the result of an arithmetic operation.

Figure 6.23 shows several examples of numbers in a singly linked list and an addition. Figure 6.23a and 6.23c show one digit per node; Figure 6.23b shows several digits per node. We develop the algorithms for a single digit per node. You are asked in the exercises to explore the necessary changes to include more than one digit in each node.

Here is the first approximation of the class `LargeInt`:

```
#include "SpecializedList.h"
#include <fstream>
class LargeInt
```

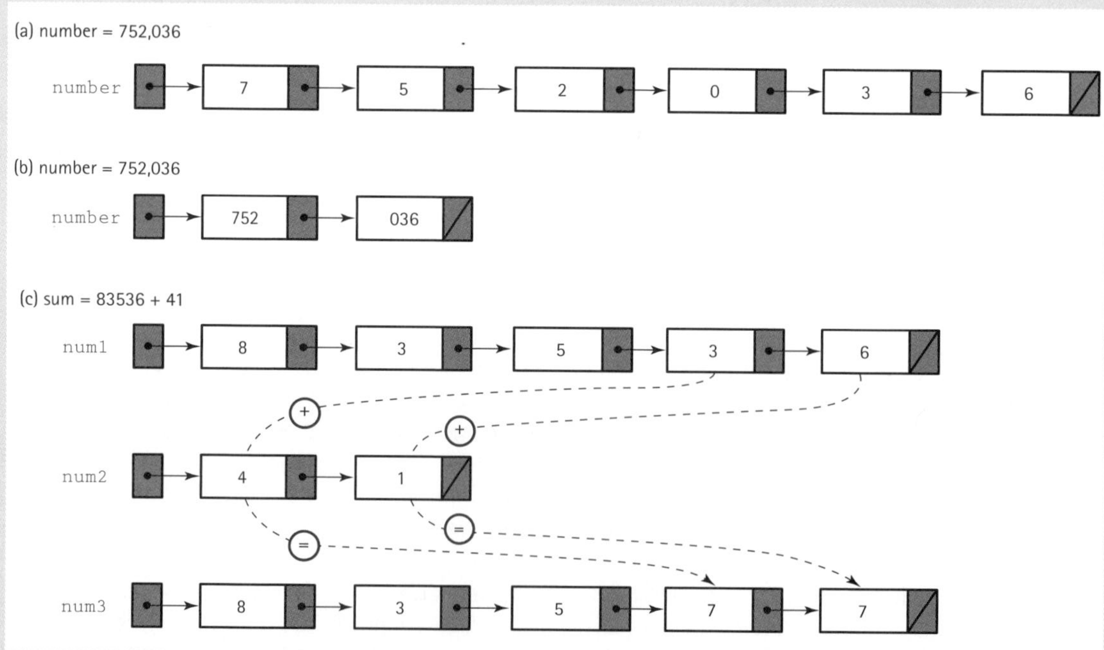

Figure 6.23 *Representing large integers with linked lists*

```
{
public:
  LargeInt();
  ~LargeInt();
  LargeInt(const LargeInt&);
  bool operator<(LargeInt second);
  bool operator==(LargeInt second);
  LargeInt operator+(LargeInt second);
  LargeInt operator-(LargeInt second);
  void InsertDigit(int);
  void Write(std::ofstream&);
private:
  SpecializedList number;
};
```

Earlier we said that classes in a program typically exhibit one of the following relationships: They are independent of each other, they are related by composition, or they are related by inheritance. The classes `LargeInt` and `SpecializedList` are related by composition. As you see in the private part of the class definition, a `LargeInt` object is composed of (or contains) a `SpecializedList` object. Just as inheritance expresses an *is a* relationship (a `CountedQueType` object is a `QueType` object [and more]), composition expresses a *has a* relationship (a `LargeInt` object *has a* `SpecializedList` object inside it).

Addition and Subtraction Let's look at addition of positive integers first, and then look at the role of the sign. We begin by adding the two least significant digits (the units position). Next, we add the digits in the tens position (if present) plus the carry from the sum of the least significant digits (if any). This process continues until one of three things happens: (1) the first operand runs out of digits; (2) the second operand runs out of digits; or (3) both run out of digits simultaneously. Rather than try to determine which operand is self at this stage, let's summarize these observations in an algorithm with three parameters of type `SpecializedList`: `first`, `second`, and `result` where `result = first + second`.

Add(first, second, result)

```
Set carry to 0
Set finished1 to false
Set finished2 to false

first.ResetBackward()
second.ResetBackward()
while (!finished1 AND !finished2)
    first.GetPriorItem(digit1, finished1)
    second.GetPriorItem(digit2, finished2)
    Set temp to digit1 + digit2 + carry
```

```
    Set carry to temp / 10
    result.InsertFront(temp % 10)
Finish up digits in first, adding carries as necessary
Finish up digits in second, adding carries as necessary
if (carry != 0)
    result.InsertFront(carry)
```

Apply the algorithm to the following examples.

```
322    388    399     999     3     1     988    0
 44    108      1      11    44    99     100    0
---    ---    ---    ----    --   ---    ----    -
366    496    400    1010    47   100    1088    0
```

Now let's examine subtraction in the simplest case: Both integers are positive and the smaller one (`second`) is subtracted from the larger one (`first`). Again, we begin with the digits in the units position. Let's call the digit in `first` `digit1` and the digit in `second` `digit2`. If `digit2` is less than `digit1`, we subtract and insert the resulting digit at the front of the result. If `digit2` is greater than `digit1`, we borrow 10 and subtract. Then we access the digits in the tens position. If we have borrowed, we subtract 1 from the new `digit1` and proceed as before. Because we have limited our problem to the case where `first` is larger than `second`, they either run out of digits together or `first` still contains digits when `second` has been processed. Note also that this constraint guarantees that borrowing does not extend beyond the most significant digit of `first`.

Sub(first, second, result)

```
Set borrow to false
Set finished1 to false
Set finished2 to false

first.ResetBackward()
second.ResetBackward()
while (!finished1 AND ! finished2)
    first.GetPriorItem(digit1, finished1)
    if (borrow)
        if (digit1 != 0)
            Set digit1 to digit1 - 1
            Set borrow to false
        else
            Set digit1 to 9
            Set borrow to true
  second.GetPriorItem(digit2, finished2)
```

```
    if (digit2 <= digit1)
        result.PutFront(digit1 - digit2)
    else
        Set borrow to true
        result.PutFront(digit1 + 10 - digit2)
while (!finished1)
    first.GetPriorItem(digit1, finished1)
    if (borrow)
        if (digit1 != 0)
            Set digit1 to digit1 - 1
            Set borrow to false
        else
            Set digit1 to 9;
            Set borrow to true
    result.PutFront(digit1)
```

By now you are wondering about the usefulness of a subtraction algorithm that is so restricted. With these restricted subtraction and addition algorithms, we can implement addition and subtraction with all combinations of signs. Here are the rules.

Addition Rules

1. If both operands are positive, use the addition algorithm.
2. If one operand is negative and one operand is positive, subtract the smaller absolute value from the larger absolute value and give the result the sign of the larger absolute value.
3. If both operands are negative, use the addition algorithm and give the result a minus sign.

Subtraction Rules

Remember how subtraction seemed more difficult than addition when you were first learning arithmetic? Not anymore. We need to use only one subtraction rule: "Change the sign of the subtrahend and add." We do have to be careful about how we change the sign because we do not want to actually change the sign of the argument passed to subtract, as that would produce an unwanted side effect. Therefore, we create a new `LargeInt` object, make it a copy of the second parameter, invert its sign, and then add.

These rules indicate that the signs should be manipulated separately from the actual addition or subtraction. Therefore, we must add a `sign` data member to our `LargeInt` class. How shall we represent the sign? Let's define an enumeration type `SignType` having two constants (`MINUS` and `PLUS`) and adopt the convention that zero has the sign `PLUS`. Let's encode our simplified addition and subtraction algorithms into the auxiliary functions `Add` and `Sub`, which take three arguments each of type `SpecializedList`. The code for each overloaded arithmetic symbol applies the rules for its operation and calls either `Add` or `Sub`. `Sub` should not be called, however, if the two operands are the same, as the result would be zero. Here are the algorithms for `operator+` and `operator-`.

operator+(LargeInt second)

```
// self is first operand
if sign = second.sign
   Add(number, second.number, result.number)
   Set result.sign to sign
else
   if |self| < |second|
      Sub(second.number, number, result.number)
      Set result.sign to second.sign
   else if |second| < |self|
      Sub(number, second.number, result.number)
      Set result.sign to sign
return result
```

operator–(LargeInt second)

```
Set copy to a copy of second
Set copy.sign to !second.sign
Add(number, copy.number, result.number)
return result
```

Relational Operators When comparing strings, we compare the characters in each character position, one at a time, from left to right. The first characters that do not match determine which string comes first. When comparing numbers, we simply compare the numbers digit by digit if they have the same sign and are the same length (have the same number of digits). Here are the rules:

1. A negative number is less than a positive number.
2. If the signs are positive and one number has more digits than the other, then the number with fewer digits is the smaller value.
3. If the signs are both negative and one number has more digits than the other, then the number with more digits is the smaller value.
4. If the signs are the same and the number of digits is the same, compare the digits from left to right. The first unequal pair determines the result.

Look at the following examples carefully and convince yourself that all the cases for "less than" are represented.

True	False
`-1 < 1`	`1 < -1`
`5 < 10`	`10 < 5`
`-10 < -5`	`-5 < -10`
`54 < 55`	`55 < 54`
`-55 < -54`	`-54 < -55`
	`-55 < -55`
	`55 < 55`

Let's summarize these observations for the "less than" operation. Because we have only one digit per node, the class `SpecializedList`'s `GetLength` function gives us the number of digits in the number. It is a member function, so the first operand is self and the second operand is `second`.

operator<(second)

```
if (sign is MINUS AND second.sign is PLUS)
    return true
else if (sign is PLUS AND second.sign is MINUS)
    return false
else if (sign is PLUS AND number.GetLength() < second.number.GetLength())
    return true
else if (sign is PLUS AND number.GetLength() > second.number.GetLength())
    return false
else if (sign is MINUS AND number.GetLength() > second.number.GetLength())
    return true
else if (sign is MINUS AND number.GetLength() < second.number.GetLength())
    return false
else    // Must compare digit by digit
    Set relation to CompareDigits(number, second.number)
    if (sign is PLUS AND relation is LESS)
        return true
    else if (sign is PLUS AND relation is GREATER)
        return false
    else if (sign is MINUS AND relation is GREATER)
        return true
    else return false
```

This algorithm calls the function `GetLength` of class `SpecializedList` eight times. We should make the number of digits be a data member of the class `LargeInt` and avoid these function calls. Thus each operation that defines a new large integer must call `GetLength` once and store this value in the `LargeInt` object. Let's call the new data member `numDigits`. We now need to specify an operation that compares the digits in two equal-length lists and returns `LESS`, `GREATER`, or `EQUAL` depending on the relationship of its two arguments. We pass the list of digits only, so this function compares the absolute values of its two arguments.

RelationType CompareDigits(operand1, operand2)

```
operand1.ResetForward()
operand2.ResetForward()
Set same to true
Set finished to false
while !finished
    operand1.GetNextItem(digit1, finished)
    operand2.GetNextItem(digit2, finished)
    if (digit1 < digit2)
        return LESS
    else if (digit1 > digit2)
        return GREATER
return EQUAL
```

The algorithm for `operator==` is very similar. If the signs are not the same, it returns `false`. If the signs are the same, it calls `CompareDigits`.

operator==(second)

```
if (sign is MINUS AND second.sign is PLUS) OR
    (sign is PLUS AND second.sign is MINUS)
    return false
else
    return (CompareDigits(number, second.number) == EQUAL)
```

Other Operations We have now examined all of the algorithms for the linked long integer representation except for `Write` and `InsertDigit` and the class constructors and destructor. Before we look at which implicit operations we need, we should examine the relationship between the classes `LargeInt` and `SpecializedList`. The only data member in `LargeInt` that contains dynamic pointers is `number`, which is of type `SpecializedList`. Because `SpecializedList` has a destructor, we do not need one for `LargeInt`. For the same reason, we do not need a class copy constructor. We can delete these constructors from our preliminary class definition, but we should retain the default class constructor to set the object to 0. Figure 6.24 shows our final objects and their interactions.

The following code shows the revised class definition, the complete addition operation, and the "less than" operator. We have implemented the changes that were made in the algorithm discussions. We leave the completion of the other operations as a programming assignment.

```
#include "SpecializedList.h" // Gain access to SpecializedList
#include <fstream>
enum SignType {PLUS, MINUS};
```

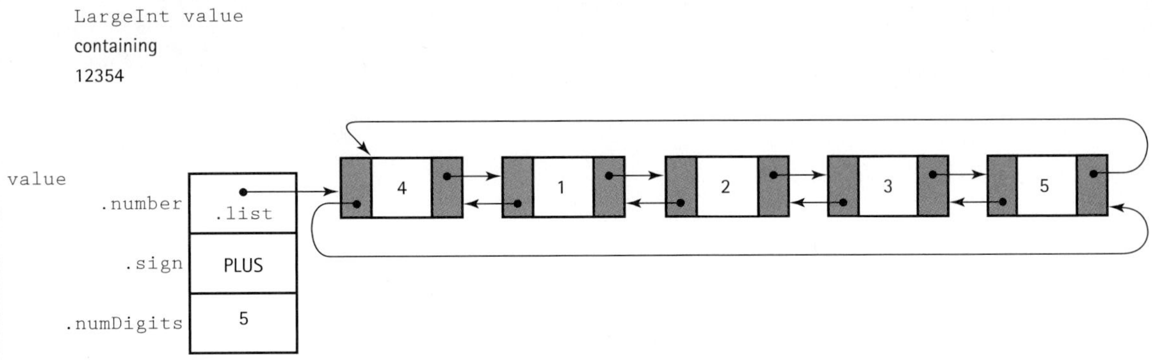

Explicit member functions applicable to `value`:
`operator<`
`operator==`
`operator+`
`operator-`
`InsertDigit`
`Write`

Explicit member functions applicable to `number`:
`ResetForward`
`GetNextItem`
`ResetBackward`
`GetPriorItem`
`PutFront`
`PutEnd`
`GetLength`

Figure 6.24 *An instance of class* `LargeInt`

```
class LargeInt
{
public:
  LargeInt();
  bool operator<(LargeInt second);
  bool operator==(LargeInt second);
  LargeInt operator+(LargeInt second);
  LargeInt operator-(LargeInt second);
  void InsertDigit(int);
  void Write(std::ofstream&);
private:
  SpecializedList number;
  SignType sign;
  int numDigits;
};

void Add(SpecializedList first, SpecializedList second,
     SpecializedList& result)
// Post:  result = first + second.
{
```

```
  int carry = 0;
  bool finished1 = false;
  bool finished2 = false;
  int temp;
  int digit1;
  int digit2;

  first.ResetBackward();
  second.ResetBackward();

  while ( !finished1 && !finished2)
  {
    first.GetPriorItem(digit1, finished1);
    second.GetPriorItem(digit2, finished2);
    temp = digit1 + digit2 + carry;
    carry = temp / 10;
    result.PutFront(temp % 10);
  }
  while ( !finished1)
  {// Adds remaining digits (if any) in first to the sum.
    first.GetPriorItem(digit1, finished1);
    temp = digit1 + carry;
    carry = temp / 10;
    result.PutFront(temp % 10);
  }
  while ( !finished2)
  {// Adds remaining digits (if any) in second to the sum.
    second.GetPriorItem(digit2, finished2);
    temp = digit2 + carry;
    carry = temp / 10;
    result.PutFront(temp % 10);
  }
  if (carry != 0)          // Adds in carry (if any).
    result.PutFront(carry);
}

LargeInt LargeInt::operator+(LargeInt second)
// self is first operand.
{
  SignType selfSign;
  SignType secondSign;
  LargeInt result;
```

```
  if (sign == second.sign)
  {
    Add(number, second.number, result.number);
    result.sign = sign;
  }
  else
  {
    selfSign = sign;
    secondSign = second.sign;
    sign = PLUS;
    second.sign = PLUS;
    if (*this < second)
    {
      Sub(second.number, number, result.number);
      result.sign = secondSign;
    }
    else if (second < *this)
    {
      Sub(number, second.number, result.number);
      result.sign = selfSign;
    }
    sign = selfSign;
  }
  result.numDigits = result.number.GetLength();
  return result;
}

enum RelationType  {LESS, GREATER, EQUAL};
RelationType CompareDigits(SpecializedList first,
     SpecializedList second);

bool LargeInt::operator<(LargeInt second)
{
  RelationType relation;

  if (sign == MINUS && second.sign == PLUS)
    return true;
  else if (sign == PLUS && second.sign == MINUS)
    return false;
  else if (sign == PLUS && numDigits < second.numDigits)
```

```
    return true;
  else if (sign == PLUS && numDigits > second.numDigits)
    return false;
  else if (sign == MINUS && numDigits > second.numDigits)
    return true;
  else if (sign == MINUS && numDigits < second.numDigits)
    return false;
  else // Must compare digit by digit.
  {
    relation = CompareDigits(number, second.number);
    if (sign == PLUS && relation == LESS)
      return true;
    else if (sign == PLUS && relation == GREATER)
      return false;
    else if (sign == MINUS && relation == GREATER)
      return true;
    else return false;
  }
}

RelationType CompareDigits(SpecializedList first,
     SpecializedList second)
{
  bool same = true;
  bool finished = false;
  int digit1;
  int digit2;

  first.ResetForward();
  second.ResetForward();
  while ( !finished)
  {
    first.GetNextItem(digit1, finished);
    second.GetNextItem(digit2, finished);
    if (digit1 < digit2)
      return LESS;
    if (digit1 > digit2)
      return GREATER;
  }
  return EQUAL;
}
```

Explicit Reference to Self

The object to which a member function is applied can reference its data members directly. On some occasions, an object needs to refer to itself as a whole, not just to its data members. An example occurs in the code for overloading the plus operator. Within this function, we have to determine whether self is less than the other operand. Here is that segment of the algorithm:

```
if |self |< |second|
    Sub(second.number, number, result.number)
    Set result.sign to second.sign
```

We need to apply the relational operator "less than" to two `LargeInt` objects from within a member function. How do we reference self? C++ has a hidden pointer called `this`. When a class member function is invoked, `this` points to the object to which the function is applied. The `this` pointer is available for use by the programmer. The algorithm segment shown here can be implemented by substituting `*this` for self.

```
secondSign = second.sign;
sign = PLUS;
second.sign = PLUS;
if (*this < second)
{
  Sub(second.number, number, result.number);
  result.sign = secondSign;
}
```

Look at the layers of abstraction represented in this Case Study. The application programmer uses the class `LargeInt` to define and manipulate very large integers in an application program. The `LargeInt` programmer uses `SpecializedList` to define and manipulate large integers represented as a linked list of digits. The `SpecializedList` programmer creates a utility that inserts items of type `int` into a circular, doubly linked list and traverses the list in either direction.

Test Plan Each `LargeInt` operation must be unit tested. The complexity of the code for each operation is evident in the number of *if* statements found in the algorithms. The more complex the code, the more test cases are necessary to test it. A white-box testing strategy would require going through the code of each operation and identifying data to test at least all branches. A black-box testing strategy would involve choosing data that test the various possible inputs. It would require varying combinations of signs and relative relationships between operands. In the case of "less than," addition, and subtraction, the examples used in the discussion would serve as test data for those operations. Other end cases should be included as well, such as cases where one or both of the operands are zero.

Of course, this discussion presupposes that `SpecializedList` has been thoroughly tested!

Summary

This chapter is a collection of theoretical material and implementation techniques. Rather than requiring the user to provide a file containing information about the items on the structure, C++ provides a way to provide this information when a structure is declared in a program. Templates are a C++ construct that allow the client to specify the type of the items to be on the structure in angle brackets beside the type name in the declaration statement.

The idea of linking the elements in a list has been extended to include lists with header and trailer nodes, circular lists, and doubly linked lists. The idea of linking the elements is a possibility to consider in the design of many types of data structures.

A shallow copy is a copy where items are copied but not the items to which they might point. A deep copy is a copy where items and the items to which they may point are copied. C++ provides a construct called a copy constructor, which can be used to force a deep copy. The relational operators can be overloaded, so that values of different types can be compared using the standard symbols. The assignment operator can also be overloaded.

In addition to using dynamically allocated nodes to implement a linked structure, we looked at a technique for implementing linked structures in an array of records. In this technique the links are not pointers into the free store but indexes into the array of records. This type of linking is used extensively in systems software.

Polymorphism is revisited in this chapter with an example of how to use the C++ virtual function construct to implement dynamic binding. We also examined the concept of deep versus shallow copying and assignment operator overloading.

The Case Study at the end of the chapter designed a Large Integer ADT. The number of digits is bounded only by the size of memory. Several relational and arithmetic operators were overloaded to work with objects of this type.

Exercises

1. Dummy nodes are used to simplify list processing by eliminating some "special case."
   a. What special case is eliminated by a header node in a linear linked list?
   b. What special case is eliminated by a trailer node in a linear linked list?
   c. Would dummy nodes be useful in implementing a linked stack? That is, would their use eliminate a special case?
   d. Would dummy nodes be useful in implementing a linked queue with a pointer to both head and rear elements?
   e. Would dummy nodes be useful in implementing a circular linked queue?
2. Implement the class constructor, destructor, and copy constructor for the circular linked list class.

3. If you were going to implement the FIFO Queue ADT as a circular linked list, with the external pointer accessing the "rear" node of the queue, which member functions would you need to change?
4. Write a member function `PrintReverse` that prints the elements on a list in reverse order. For instance, for the list `X Y Z`, `list.PrintReverse()` would output `Z Y X`. The list is implemented as a circular list with `listData` pointing to the first element in the list. You may assume that the list is not empty.
5. Can you derive a type `DLList` from the class `SpecializedList` that has a member function `PutItem` that inserts the item into its proper place in the list? If so, derive the class and implement the function. If not, explain why not.
6. If you were to rewrite the implementation of the Sorted List ADT using a doubly linked list, would you have to change the class definition? If so, how?
7. Outline the changes to the member functions that would be necessary to implement the Sorted List ADT as a doubly linked list.
8. Write a member function `Copy` of the Stack ADT, assuming that the stack named in the parameter list is copied into self.
9. Write a member function `Copy` of the Stack ADT, assuming that self is copied into the stack named in the parameter list.
10. Using the circular doubly linked list shown here, give the expression corresponding to each of the following descriptions.

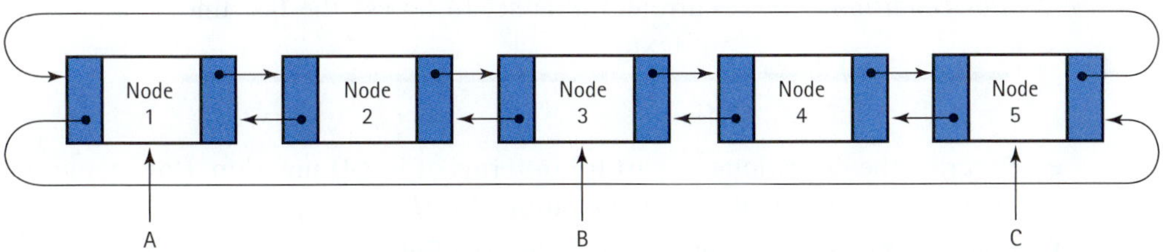

(For example, the expression for the `info` member of Node 1, referenced from pointer A, would be `A->info`.)

a. The `info` member of Node 1, referenced from pointer C
b. The `info` member of Node 2, referenced from pointer B
c. The `next` member of Node 2, referenced from pointer A
d. The `next` member of Node 4, referenced from pointer C
e. Node 1, referenced from pointer B
f. The `back` member of Node 4, referenced from pointer C
g. The `back` member of Node 1, referenced from pointer A

11. The text edited by a line editor is represented by a doubly linked list of nodes, each of which contains an 80-column line of text (type `LineType`). There is one external pointer (type `LineType*`) to this list, which points to the "current" line in the text being edited. The list has a header node, which contains the string "`- - - Top of File - - -`" and a trailer node, which contains the string "`- - - Bottom of File - - -`".

    a. Draw a sketch of this data structure.
    b. Write the type declarations to support this data structure.
    c. Write the class constructor, which sets up the header and trailer nodes.
    d. Code the following operations:

GoToTop(LineType* linePtr)

Function:	Goes to top of the list.
Postcondition:	currentLine is set to access the first line of text.

GoToBottom(LineType* linePtr)

Function:	Goes to bottom of the list.
Postcondition:	currentLine is set to access the last line of text.

    e. Describe the operations in part (d) in terms of Big-O notation. How could you change the list to make these operations O(1)?
    f. Code the `InsertLine` operation, using the following specification:

InsertLine(LinePtrType linePtr, LineType newLine)

Function:	Inserts newLine at the current line.
Postconditions:	newLine has been inserted after current-Line. currentLine points to newLine

    g. What other member functions should be included?

12. Of the three variations of linked lists (circular, with header and trailer nodes, and doubly linked), which would be most appropriate for each of the following applications?

    a. You want to search a list for a key and return the keys of the two elements that come before it and the keys of the two elements that come after it.

    b. A text file contains integer elements, one per line, *sorted* from smallest to largest. You must read the values from the file and create a sorted linked list containing the values.

    c. A list is short and frequently becomes empty. You want a list that is optimal for inserting an element into the empty list and deleting the last element from the list.

13. What is the Big-O measure for initializing the free list in the array-based linked implementation? For the functions `GetNode` and `FreeNode`?

14. Use the linked lists contained in the array pictured in Figure 6.19 to answer the following questions:

    a. What elements are in the list pointed to by `list1`?

    b. What elements are in the list pointed to by `list2`?

    c. What array positions (indexes) are part of the free space list?

    d. What would the array look like after the deletion of Nell from the first list?

    e. What would the array look like after the insertion of Anne into the second list? Assume that before the insertion the array is as pictured in Figure 6.19.

15. An array of records (nodes) is used to contain a doubly linked list, with the `next` and `back` members indicating the indexes of the linked nodes in each direction.

    a. Show how the array would look after it was initialized to an empty state, with all the nodes linked into the free-space list. (The free-space nodes have to be linked in only one direction.)

free

list

nodes

	.info	.next	.back
[0]			
[1]			
[2]			
[3]			
[4]			
[5]			
[6]			
[7]			
[8]			
[9]			

b. Draw a box-and-arrow picture of a doubly linked list into which the following numbers are inserted into their proper places: 17, 4, 25.

c. Fill in the contents of the array on the next page after the following numbers are inserted into their proper places in the doubly linked list: 17, 4, 25.

free	
list	

nodes

	.info	.next	.back
[0]			
[1]			
[2]			
[3]			
[4]			
[5]			
[6]			
[7]			
[8]			
[9]			

d. Show how the array in part (c) would look after 17 is deleted.

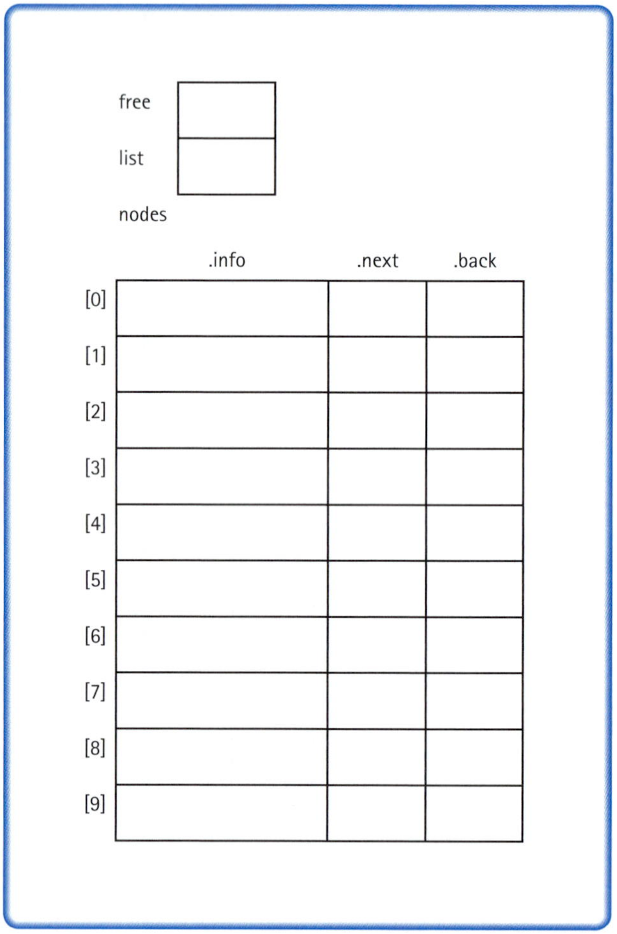

16. Discuss the changes that would be necessary if more than one digit is stored per node in the `LargeInt` class.
17. Distinguish between static and dynamic binding of functions.
18. Rewrite `SortedType` (array-based) using templates.
19. Rewrite `SortedType` (linked) using templates.
20. Rewrite `StackType` (linked) using templates.
21. Rewrite `QueType` (linked) using templates.
22. Replace function `ComparedTo` in an array-based `UnsortedList` by assuming that member functions of class `ItemType` overload the relational operators.
23. Create the UML diagrams for class `LargeInt`.
24. True or False? A double linked list has two pointers in each node.

25. True or False? A header node is a placeholder node at the beginning of a list, used to simplify list processing.
26. True or False? A trailer node is not syntactically different from the other nodes in the list.
27. True or False? A trailer node is not logically different from the other nodes in the list.
28. True or False? A trailer node is a placeholder node at the end of a list, used to simplify list processing.
29. True or False? A programmer, using inheritance to specialize a class X, needs access to the source code for X's implementation.
30. True or False? In C++, a derived class's constructor is executed after its base class constructor is executed.
31. True or False? For a C++ derived class to override an inherited member function, the base class is required to declare the function to be virtual.

chapter 7

Programming with Recursion

Goals

After studying this chapter, you should be able to

- Discuss recursion as another form of repetition
- Do the following tasks, given a recursive routine:
  - Determine whether the routine halts
  - Determine the base case(s)
  - Determine the general case(s)
  - Determine what the routine does
  - Determine whether the routine is correct and, if it is not, correct it
- Do the following tasks, given a simple recursive problem:
  - Determine the base case(s)
  - Determine the general case(s)
  - Design and code the solution as a recursive void or value-returning function
- Verify a recursive routine, according to the Three-Question Method
- Decide whether a recursive solution is appropriate for a problem
- Compare and contrast dynamic storage allocation and static storage allocation in relation to using recursion
- Explain how recursion works internally by showing the contents of the run-time stack
- Replace a recursive solution with iteration and/or the use of a stack
- Explain why recursion may or may not be a good choice to implement the solution of a problem

This chapter introduces the topic of recursion—a unique problem-solving approach supported by many computer languages (C++ included). With recursion, you solve a problem by repeatedly breaking it into smaller versions of the same problem, until you reduce the subproblems to a trivial size that can be easily solved. You then repeatedly combine your solutions to the subproblems until you arrive at a solution to the original problem.

Although recursion may at first appear unwieldy and awkward, when applied properly it represents an extremely powerful and useful problem-solving tool.

7.1 What Is Recursion?

You may have seen a set of gaily painted Russian dolls that fit inside one another. Inside the larger doll is a smaller doll, inside of which is an even smaller doll, inside of which is yet a smaller doll, and so on. A recursive definition is like such a set of Russian dolls. It reproduces itself in the form of smaller and smaller versions of itself until a version is reached that can no longer be subdivided—that is, until the smallest doll is reached. The recursive algorithm is implemented by using a function that makes recursive calls to itself, which is analogous to taking the dolls apart one by one. The solution often depends on passing back larger and larger subsolutions from the recursive calls, which is analogous to putting the dolls back together again.

Recursive call A function call in which the function being called is the same as the one making the call

In C++, any function can invoke another function. A function can even invoke itself! When a function invokes itself, it makes a *recursive call*. The word *recursive* means "having the characteristic of coming up again, or repeating." In this case, a function invocation is repeated by the function itself. This type of recursion is sometimes called direct recursion, because the function directly calls itself. All of the examples in this chapter involve direct recursion. Indirect recursion occurs when function A calls function B, and function B calls function A; the chain of function calls could be even longer, but if it eventually leads back to function A, then it involves indirect recursion.

Direct recursion When a function directly calls itself

Indirect recursion When a chain of two or more function calls returns to the function that originated the chain

Recursion is a powerful programming technique, but you must be careful when using it. Recursive solutions can be less efficient than iterative solutions to the same problem. In fact, some of the examples used in this chapter are better suited to iterative methods. Nevertheless, many problems lend themselves to simple, elegant, recursive solutions and are exceedingly cumbersome to solve iteratively. Some programming languages, such as early versions of FORTRAN, BASIC, and COBOL, do not allow recursion. Other languages are especially oriented to recursive approaches–LISP, for example. C++ lets us make a choice; we can implement both iterative and recursive algorithms in C++.

7.2 The Classic Example of Recursion

Mathematicians often define concepts in terms of the process used to generate them. For instance, $n!$ (read "n factorial") is used to calculate the number of permutations of n elements. One mathematical description of $n!$ is

$$n! = \begin{cases} 1, & \text{if } n = 0 \\ n * (n-1) * (n-2) * \cdots * 1, & \text{if } n > 0 \end{cases}$$

Consider the case of 4!. Because $n > 0$, we use the second part of the definition:

$$4! = 4 * 3 * 2 * 1 = 24$$

This description of $n!$ provides a different definition for each value of n, as the three dots stand in for the intermediate factors. That is, the definition of 2! is 2 * 1, the definition of 3! is 3 * 2 * 1, and so forth.

We can also express $n!$ with a single definition for any nonnegative value of n:

$$n! = \begin{cases} 1, & \text{if } n = 0 \\ n * (n-1)! & \text{if } n > 0 \end{cases}$$

This definition is a recursive definition, because we express the factorial function in terms of itself.

> **Recursive definition** A definition in which something is defined in terms of a smaller version of itself

Let's consider the recursive calculation of 4! intuitively. Because 4 is not equal to 0, we use the second half of the definition:

$$4! = 4 * (4 - 1)! = 4 * 3!$$

Of course, we can't do the multiplication yet, because we don't know the value of 3!. So we call up our good friend Sue Ann, who has a Ph.D. in math, to find the value of 3!.

Sue Ann has the same formula we have for calculating the factorial function, so she knows that

$$3! = 3 * (3 - 1)! = 3 * 2!$$

She doesn't know the value of 2!, however, so she puts us on hold and calls up her friend Max, who has an M.S. in math.

Max has the same formula Sue Ann has, so he quickly calculates that

$$2! = 2 * (2 - 1)! = 2 * 1!$$

But Max can't complete the multiplication because he doesn't know the value of 1! He puts Sue Ann on hold and calls up his mother, who has a B.A. in math education.

Max's mother has the same formula Max has, so she quickly figures out that

$$1! = 1 * (1 - 1)! = 1 * 0!$$

Of course, she can't perform the multiplication, because she doesn't have the value of 0!. So Mom puts Max on hold and calls up her colleague Bernie, who has a B.A. in English literature.

Bernie doesn't need to know any math to figure out that 0! = 1 because he can read that information in the first clause of the formula ($n! = 1$, if $n = 0$). He reports the answer immediately to Max's mother. She can now complete her calculations:

$$1! = 1 * 0! = 1 * 1 = 1$$

She reports back to Max, who now performs the multiplication in his formula and learns that

$$2! = 2 * 1! = 2 * 1 = 2$$

He reports back to Sue Ann, who can now finish her calculation:

$$3! = 3 * 2! = 3 * 2 = 6$$

Sue Ann calls you with this exciting bit of information. You can now complete your calculation:

$$4! = 4 * 3! = 4 * 6 = 24$$

> **Base case** The case for which the solution can be stated nonrecursively
>
> **General (recursive) case** The case for which the solution is expressed in terms of a smaller version of itself
>
> **Recursive algorithm** A solution that is expressed in terms of (1) smaller instances of itself and (2) a base case

Notice when the recursive calls stop—when we reach a case for which we know the answer without resorting to a recursive definition. In this example, Bernie knew that 0! = 1 directly from the definition without having to resort to recursion. The case (or cases) for which an answer is explicitly known is called the base case. The case for which the solution is expressed in terms of a smaller version of itself is called the recursive or general case. A recursive algorithm expresses the solution in terms of a call to itself—that is, a recursive call. A recursive algorithm must terminate; that is, it must have a base case.

7.3 Programming Recursively

Of course, the use of recursion is not limited to mathematicians with telephones. Computer languages such as C++ that support recursion give the programmer a powerful tool for solving certain kinds of problems by reducing the complexity or hiding the details of the problem.

In this chapter, we consider recursive solutions to several simple problems. In our initial discussion, you may wonder why a recursive solution would ever be preferred to an iterative, or nonrecursive, one because the iterative solution may seem simpler and more efficient. Don't worry. As you will see later, in some situations the use of recursion produces a much simpler—and more elegant—program.

Coding the Factorial Function

As noted earlier, a recursive function is one that calls itself. In the previous section, Sue Ann, Max, Max's mom, and Bernie all had the same formula for solving the factorial function. When we construct a recursive C++ function `Factorial` for solving $n!$, we know where we can get the value of $(n - 1)!$ that we need in the formula. We already have a function for doing this calculation: `Factorial`. Of course, the actual parameter (`number - 1`) in the recursive call is different than the parameter in the original call (`number`). (The recursive call is the one within the function.) As we see, this difference is an important and necessary consideration.

```
int Factorial(int number)
// Pre:  number is nonnegative.
// Post: Function value = factorial of number.
{
  if (number == 0)                          // Line 1
    return 1;                               // Line 2
  else
    return number * Factorial(number-1);    // Line 3
}
```

Notice the use of `Factorial` in line 3. `Factorial` involves a recursive call to the function, with the parameter `number - 1`.

Let's walk through the calculation of 4! using the function `Factorial`. The original value of `number` is 4. Table 7.1 shows the steps in the calculation.

For purposes of comparison, let's look at the recursive and iterative solutions to this problem side by side:

```
int Factorial(int number)
{
  if (number == 0)
    return 1;
  else
    return number *
      Factorial(number - 1);
}
```

```
int Factorial(int number)
{
  int fact = 1;

  for (int count = 2;
    count <= number; count++)
    fact = fact * count;
  return fact;
}
```

Table 7.1 *Walk-through of Factorial(4)*

Recursive Call	Line	Action
	1	4 is not 0, so skip to *else* clause.
	3	return `number * Factorial(4 2 1)`
		First recursive call returns us to the beginning of the function with `number` = 3.
1	1	3 is not 0, so skip to *else* clause.
	3	return `number * Factorial(3 – 1)`
		Second recursive call returns us to the beginning of the function with `number` = 2.
2	1	2 is not 0, so skip to *else* clause.
	3	return `number * Factorial(2 – 1)`
		Third recursive call returns us to the beginning of the function with `number` = 1.
3	1	1 is not 0, so skip to *else* clause.
	3	return `number * Factorial(1 – 1)`
		Fourth recursive call returns us to the beginning of the function with `number` = 0.
4	1	0 is 0, so go to line 2.
	2	return 1
3	3	1 replaces call to `Factorial`; `number` is 1.
		return 1
2	3	1 replaces call to `Factorial`; `number` is 2.
		return 2
1	3	2 replaces call to `Factorial`; `number` is 3.
		return 6
	3	6 replaces call to `Factorial`; `number` is 4.
		return 24

These two versions of `Factorial` illustrate some of the differences between recursive and iterative functions. First, an iterative algorithm uses a *looping construct* such as the *for* loop (or *while* or *do . . . while* loop) to control the execution. In contrast, the recursive solution uses a *branching structure* (*if* or *switch* statement). The iterative version needs a couple of local variables, whereas the recursive version uses the parameters of the function to provide all its information. Sometimes, as we will see later, the recursive solution needs more parameters than the equivalent iterative one. Data values used in the iterative solution are usually initialized inside the routine, above the loop. Similar data values used in a recursive solution are typically initialized by the choice of parameter values in the initial call to the routine.

Let's summarize the vocabulary of recursive solutions. A *recursive definition* is a definition in which something is defined in terms of smaller versions of itself. The definition of the factorial function certainly fits this description. A *recursive call* is a call made to the function from within the function itself. Line 3 in the function `Factorial` is an example of a recursive call.

In a recursive algorithm there is always at least one case for which the answer is known; the solution is not stated in terms of smaller versions of itself. In the case of the factorial, the answer is known if the number is 0. The case for which the answer is known is called the *base case*. The case that is stated recursively is the *general* or *recursive case.*

7.4 Verifying Recursive Functions

The kind of walk-through we did in the previous section, to check the validity of a recursive function, is time-consuming, tedious, and often confusing. Furthermore, simulating the execution of `Factorial(4)` tells us that the function works when `number` = 4, but it doesn't tell us whether the function is valid for *all* nonnegative values of `number`. It would be useful to have a technique that would help us determine inductively whether a recursive algorithm works.

The Three-Question Method

We use the Three-Question Method to verify recursive functions. To confirm that a recursive solution works, you must be able to answer yes to all three of the following questions:

1. *The Base-Case Question:* Is there a nonrecursive way out of the function, and does the routine work correctly for this base case?
2. *The Smaller-Caller Question:* Does each recursive call to the function involve a smaller case of the original problem, leading inescapably to the base case?
3. *The General-Case Question:* Assuming that the recursive call(s) works correctly, does the entire function work correctly?

Let's apply these three questions to the function `Factorial`. (We use the mathematical N here rather than the variable `number`.)

1. *The Base-Case Question:* The base case occurs when $N = 0$. `Factorial` is then assigned the value of 1, which is the correct value of 0!, and no further (recursive) calls to `Factorial` are made. The answer is yes.
2. *The Smaller-Caller Question:* To answer this question, we must look at the parameters passed in the recursive call. In the function `Factorial`, the recursive call passes $N - 1$. Each subsequent recursive call sends a decremented value of the parameter, until the value sent is finally 0. At this point, as we verified with the base-case question, we have reached the smallest case, and no further recursive calls are made. The answer is yes.

3. *The General-Case Question:* In the case of a function like `Factorial`, we need to verify that the formula we are using actually results in the correct solution. Assuming that the recursive call `Factorial(N - 1)` gives us the correct value of $(n - 1)!$, the `return` statement computes $N * (N - 1)!$. This is the definition of a factorial, so we know that the function works for all positive integers. In answering the first question, we have already ascertained that the function works for $N = 0$. (The function is defined only for nonnegative integers.) Thus the answer is yes.

Those of you who are familiar with *inductive proofs* should recognize what we have done. Having made the assumption that the function works for some base case $(n - 1)$, we can now show that applying the function to the next value, $(n - 1) + 1$, or n, results in the correct formula for calculating $n!$.

7.5 Writing Recursive Functions

The questions used for verifying recursive functions can also serve as a guide for *writing* recursive functions. You can use the following approach to write any recursive routine:

1. Get an exact definition of the problem to be solved. (This, of course, is the first step in solving any programming problem.)
2. Determine the *size* of the problem to be solved on this call to the function. On the initial call to the function, the size of the whole problem is expressed in the value(s) of the parameter(s).
3. Identify and solve the *base case(s)* in which the problem can be expressed nonrecursively. This ensures a yes answer to the base-case question.
4. Identify and solve the *general case(s)* correctly in terms of a smaller case of the same problem—a recursive call. This ensures yes answers to the smaller-caller and general-case questions.

In the case of `Factorial`, the definition of the problem is summarized in the definition of the factorial function. The size of the problem is the number of values to be multiplied: N. The base case occurs when $N = 0$, in which case we take the nonrecursive path. Finally, the general case occurs when $N > 0$, resulting in a recursive call to `Factorial` for a smaller case: `Factorial(N - 1)`.

Writing a Boolean Function

Let's apply this approach to writing a Boolean function, `ValueInList`, that searches for a value in a list of integers and returns true or false to indicate whether the value is found. The list is declared as follows and is passed as a parameter to `ValueInList`:

```
struct ListType
{
  int length;
```

```
  int info[MAX_ITEMS];
};
ListType list;
```

The recursive solution to this problem is as follows:

Return (value is in the first position?) OR (value is in the rest of the list?)

We can answer the first question just by comparing the value to `list.info[0]`. But how do we know whether the value is in the rest of the list? If only we had a function that would search the rest of the list. *But we do have one!* The function `ValueInList` searches for a value in a list. We simply need to start searching at the first position, instead of the zeroth position (a smaller case). To do so, we need to pass the search-starting place to `ValueInList` as a parameter. We know that the end of the list is at position `list.length - 1`, so we can stop searching if the value isn't there. Thus we use the following function specification:

bool ValueInList (list, value, startIndex)

Function:	Searches list for value between positions startIndex and list.length - 1.
Precondition:	list.info[startIndex]..list.info[list.length - 1] contain values to be searched.
Postcondition:	Function value = (value exists in list.info[startIndex]..list.info[list.length - 1]).

To search the whole list, we would invoke the function with the statement

```
if (ValueInList(list, value, 0))
```

The general case of this algorithm is the part that searches the rest of the list. This case involves a recursive call to `ValueInList`, specifying a smaller part of the array to be searched:

```
return ValueInList(list, value, startIndex + 1)
```

By using the expression `startIndex + 1` as the parameter, we have effectively diminished the size of the problem to be solved by the recursive call. That is, searching the list from `startIndex + 1` to `list.length - 1` is a smaller task than searching from `startIndex` to `list.length - 1`. Figure 7.1 shows the function `ValueInList` frozen in midexecution.

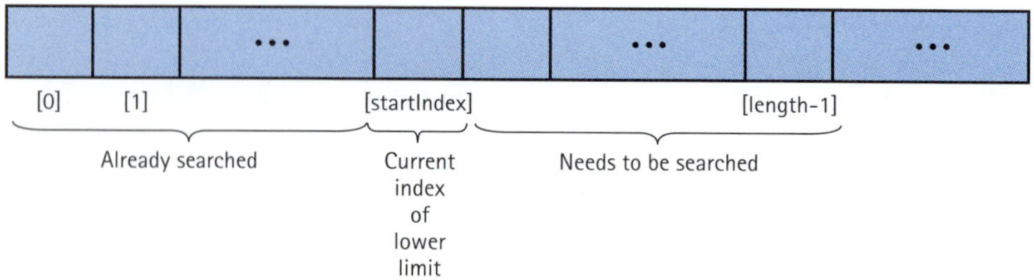

Figure 7.1 *Function* `ValueInList` *in midexecution*

Finally, we need to know when to stop searching. This problem involves two base cases: (1) the value is found (return true), and (2) we reach the end of the list without finding the value (return false). In either case, we can stop making recursive calls to `ValueInList`.

Let's summarize what we have discussed and then write the function `ValueInList`.

Function ValueInList

Definition:	Search list for value. Return true if value is found and return false otherwise.
Size:	The number of slots to search in list.info[startIndex]..list.info[list.length - 1].
Base Cases:	(1) If list.info[startIndex] equals value, return true. (2) If startIndex equals list.length - 1 and list.info[list.length - 1] does not equal value, return false.
General Case:	Search the rest of the list for value. This is a recursive invocation of ValueInList with the parameter startIndex + 1 (smaller caller).

The code for function `ValueInList` follows:

```
bool ValueInList(ListType list, int value, int startIndex)
{
  if (list.info[startIndex] == value)
    return true;                                // Base case 1
  else if (startIndex == list.length-1)
    return false;                               // Base case 2
  else return ValueInList(list, value, startIndex+1);
}
```

The parameter `startIndex` acts as an index through the array; it is initialized in the original invocation of `ValueInList` and incremented on each recursive call. The equivalent iterative solution would use a local counter, initialized inside the function above the loop and incremented inside the loop.

Let's use the Three-Question Method to verify this function.

1. *The Base-Case Question:* One base case occurs when this call finds the value and the function is exited without any further calls to itself. A second base case occurs when we reach the end of the list without the value being found and the function is exited without any further recursive calls. The answer is yes.
2. *The Smaller-Caller Question:* The recursive call in the general case increments the value of `startIndex`, making the part of the list left to be searched smaller. The answer is yes.
3. *The General-Case Question:* Let's assume that the recursive call in the general case correctly tells us whether the value is found in the second through last elements in the list. Then Base Case 1 gives us the correct answer (true) if the value is found in the first element in the list, and Base Case 2 gives us the correct answer (false) if the value is not in the first element and the first element is the *only* element in the list. The only other possible case is that the value exists somewhere in the rest of the list. Assuming that the general case works correctly, the entire function works, so the answer to this question is also yes.

7.6 Using Recursion to Simplify Solutions

So far, we have looked at examples that could just as easily (or more easily) have been written as iterative routines. At the end of the chapter, we talk more about choosing between iterative and recursive solutions. For many problems, though, using recursion simplifies the solution.

The first problem we consider is a function, `Combinations`, that tells us how many combinations of a certain size can be made out of a total group of elements. For instance, if we have 20 different books to pass out to 4 students, we can easily see that—to be equitable—we should give each student 5 books. But how many combinations of 5 books can be made out of a group of 20 books?

A mathematical formula can be used for solving this problem. Given that *C* is the total number of combinations, *group* is the total size of the group from which to pick, *members* is the size of each subgroup, and *group* >= *members*,

$$C(group,\ members) = \begin{cases} group, & \text{if } members = 1 \\ 1, & \text{if } members = group \\ C(group-1,\ members-1) + C(group-1,\ members), & \text{if } group > members > 1 \end{cases}$$

Because this definition of *C* is recursive, it is easy to see how a recursive function could be used to solve the problem.

Let's summarize our problem.

Function Combinations

Definition:	Calculates how many combinations of members size can be made from the total group size.
Size:	Sizes of group, members.
Base Case:	(1) If members = 1, return group.
	(2) If members = group, return 1.
General Case:	If group > members > 1, return Combinations(group − 1, members - 1) + Combinations(group − 1, members)

The resulting recursive function, `Combinations`, is listed here.

```
int Combinations(int group, int members)
// Pre:  group and members are positive.
// Post: Function value = number of combinations of members size
//       that can be constructed from the total group size.
{
  if (members == 1)
    return group;              // Base case 1
  else if (members == group)
    return 1;                  // Base case 2
  else
    return (Combinations(group-1, members-1) +
            Combinations(group-1, members));
}
```

Figure 7.2 shows the processing of this function to calculate the number of combinations of 3 elements that can be made from a set of 4.

Returning to our original problem, we can now find out how many combinations of 5 books can be made from the original set of 20 books with the statement

```
std::cout  << "Number of combinations = "  << Combinations(20, 5)
           << std::endl;
```

Writing a recursive solution to a problem that is characterized by a recursive definition, like `Combinations` or `Factorial`, is fairly straightforward.

7.7 Recursive Linked List Processing

Let's look next at a different kind of problem—a function that prints out the elements in a dynamically allocated linked list. The list has been implemented using the following declarations. For this example, `ListType` is a class rather than a class template. `NodeType` is a struct rather than a struct template, and the `info` member of type `NodeType` is of type `int`.

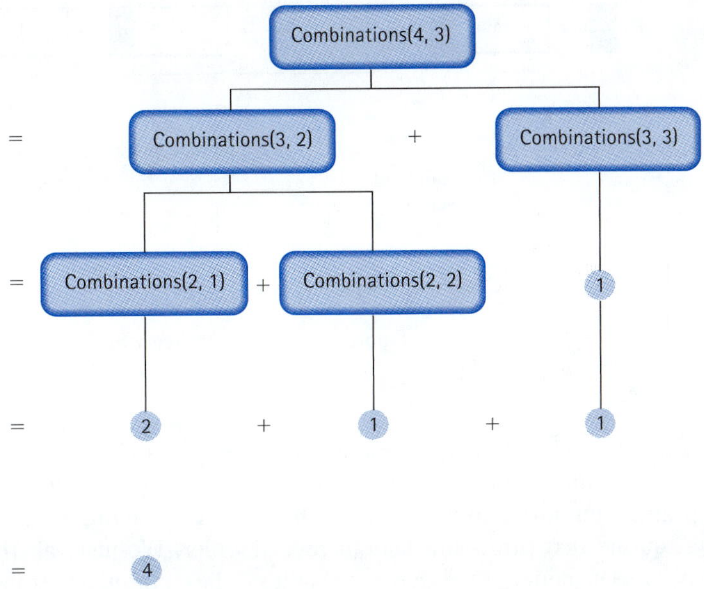

Figure 7.2 *Calculating* `Combinations(4,3)`

```
struct NodeType;
class ListType
{
public:
  // Prototypes of member functions
private:
  NodeType* listData;
};
```

By now you are probably protesting that this task is so simple to accomplish iteratively (`while (ptr != NULL)`) that it does not make any sense to write it recursively. So let's make the task more fun: Print out the elements in the list in *reverse order*. This problem is much more easily and "elegantly" solved recursively.

What is the task to be performed? The algorithm follows and is illustrated in Figure 7.3.

RevPrint

Print out the second through last elements in the list in reverse order
Print the first element in the list

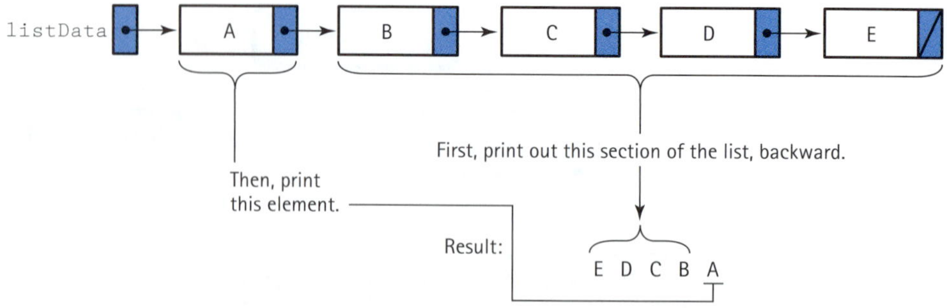

Figure 7.3 *Recursive RevPrint*

The second part of the task is simple. If `listPtr` points to the first node in the list, we can print out its contents with the statement `cout << listPtr->info`. The first part of the task—printing out all the other nodes in the list in reverse order—is also simple, because we have a routine that prints out lists in reverse order: We just call the function `RevPrint` recursively. Of course, we have to adjust the parameter somewhat, to `RevPrint (listPtr->next)`. This call says "Print, in reverse order, the linked list pointed to by `listPtr->next`." This task, in turn, is accomplished recursively in two steps:

```
RevPrint the rest of the list (third through last elements)
Then print the second element in the list.
```

Of course, the first part of this task is accomplished recursively. Where does it all end? We need a base case. We can stop calling `RevPrint` when we have completed its smallest case: `RevPrint`-ing a list of one element. Then the value of `listPtr->next` is `NULL`, and we can stop making recursive calls. Let's summarize the problem.

Function RevPrint

Definition:	Print out the list in reverse order.
Size:	Number of elements in the list pointed to by listPtr.
Base Case:	If the list is empty, do nothing.
General Case:	RevPrint the list pointed to by listPtr->next, then print listPtr->info.

The other recursive routines that we have written have been value-returning functions. `RevPrint`, however, is a void function. Each function call simply performs an action (printing the contents of a list node) without returning a value to the calling code.

```
void RevPrint(NodeType* listPtr)
{
  if (listPtr != NULL)
  {
    RevPrint(listPtr->next);
    std::cout  << listPtr->info  << std::endl;
  }
}
```

Given our `ListType` class, can we make `RevPrint` become a public member function of the class? The answer is no, and here is the reason: To print the entire linked list, the client's initial call to `RevPrint` must pass as a parameter the pointer to the first node in the list. In the `ListType` class, this pointer (`listPtr`) is a *private* member of the class, so the following client code is not permitted:

```
list.RevPrint(list.listData);      // Not allowed; listData is private
```

Therefore, we must treat `RevPrint` as an auxiliary, nonmember function and define a member function, say, `PrintReversed`, that calls `RevPrint`:

```
void PrintReversed();          // Prototype in ListType class declaration
   .
   .
   .
void ListType::PrintReversed()
{
  RevPrint(listData);
}
```

Given this design, the client can print the entire list with the following function call:

```
list.PrintReversed();
```

Let's verify `RevPrint` using the Three-Question Method.

1. *The Base-Case Question:* The base case is implied. When `listPtr` is equal to `NULL`, we return to the statement following the last recursive call to `RevPrint`, and no further recursive calls are made. The answer is yes.
2. *The Smaller-Caller Question:* The recursive call passes the list pointed to by `listPtr->next`, which is one node smaller than the list pointed to by `listPtr`. The answer is yes.

3. *The General-Case Question:* We assume that `RevPrint (listPtr->next)` correctly prints out the rest of the list in reverse order; this call, followed by the statement printing the value of the first element, gives us the whole list, printed in reverse order. The answer is yes.

How would you change the function `RevPrint` (in addition to changing its name) to make it print out the list in forward rather than reverse order? We leave this modification as an exercise.

7.8 A Recursive Version of Binary Search

In the chapter on sorted lists (Chapter 4), we developed a binary search algorithm for the member function `RetrieveItem` in our Sorted List ADT. Let's review the algorithm:

```
BinarySearch
Set first to 0
Set last to length − 1
Set found to false
Set moreToSearch to (first <= last)
while moreToSearch AND NOT found
    Set midPoint to (first + last) / 2
    switch (item.ComparedTo(info[midPoint]))
        case LESS    : Set last to midPoint - 1
                       Set moreToSearch to (first <= last)
        case GREATER : Set first to midPoint + 1
                       Set moreToSearch to (first <= last)
        case EQUAL   : Set found to true
```

Although the function that we wrote in Chapter 4 was iterative, this really is a *recursive algorithm.* The solution is expressed in smaller versions of the original problem: If the answer isn't found in the middle position, perform `BinarySearch` (a recursive call) to search the appropriate half of the list (a smaller problem). Let's summarize the problem in terms of a Boolean function that simply returns true or false to indicate whether the desired item is found. We assume that it is not a public member function of the class `ListType` but rather an auxiliary function of the class that takes the array `info` as a parameter.

bool BinarySearch

Definition:	Searches the list to see if item is present.
Size:	The number of elements in list.info[fromLocation]..list.info[toLocation].
Base Cases:	(1) If fromLocation > toLocation, return false. (2) If item.ComparedTo(list.info[midPoint]) = EQUAL, return true.
General Case:	If item.ComparedTo(list.info[midPoint]) = LESS, BinarySearch the first half of the list. If item.ComparedTo(list.info[midPoint]) = GREATER, BinarySearch the second half of the list.

The recursive version of the function follows. Because each branch of the *switch* statement includes only one statement, we use the relational operators. Notice that we had to make `fromLocation` and `toLocation` become parameters to the function rather than local index variables. An initial call to the function would be of the form `BinarySearch(info, item, 0, length - 1)`.

```
template<class ItemType>
bool BinarySearch(ItemType info[], ItemType item,
                  int fromLocation, int toLocation)
{
  if (fromLocation > toLocation)          // Base case 1
    return false;
  else
  {
    int midPoint;
    midPoint = (fromLocation + toLocation) / 2;
    if (item < info[midPoint])
      return
        BinarySearch(info, item, fromLocation, midPoint - 1);
    else if (item == info[midPoint])
      return true;
    else                                  // Base case 2
      return
        BinarySearch(info, item, midPoint + 1, toLocation);
  }
}
```

7.9 Recursive Versions of `PutItem` and `DeleteItem`

Function `PutItem`

Inserting an item into a linked implementation of a sorted list requires two pointers: one pointing to the node being examined and one pointing to the node behind it. We need this trailing pointer because by the time we discover where to insert a node, we are beyond the node that needs to be changed. The recursive version is actually simpler because we let the recursive process take care of the trailing pointer. We develop the algorithm here; in the next section, we demonstrate why it works.

Let's begin by looking at an example where the item type is `int`.

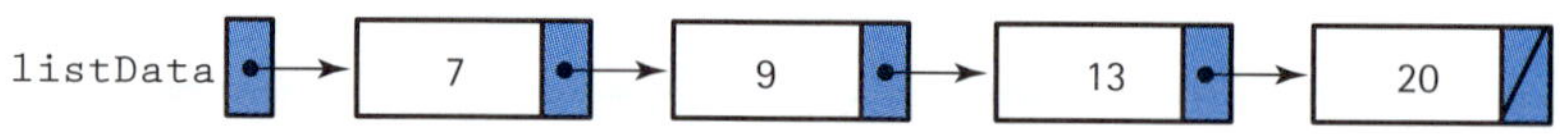

If we insert 11, we begin by comparing 11 to the value in the first node of the list, 7. Eleven is greater than 7, so we look for the insertion point in the list pointed to by the `next` member of the first node. This new list is one node shorter than the original list. We compare 11 to the value in the first node in this list, 9. Eleven is greater than 9, so we look for the insertion point in the list pointed to by the `next` member of the first node. This new list is one node shorter than the current list. We compare 11 with the value in the first node of this new list, 13. Eleven is less than 13, so we have found the insertion point. We insert a new node with 11 as the value of the first node in the list we are examining.

What if the value we are inserting is greater than the value in the last node of the list? In this case, the list is empty and we insert the value into the empty list. `Insert` is not a member function of `ListType`; it is an auxiliary function called by `PutItem` with the pointer to the list as a parameter. We make it a template function.

Function Insert

Definition:	Insert item into a sorted list.
Size:	The number of items in the list.
Base Cases:	(1) If the list is empty, insert item into the empty list.
	(2) If item < listPtr->info, insert item as the first node.
General Case:	Insert(listPtr->next, item).

The function is coded on the next page. Note that the pointer to the list is a reference parameter; that is, the function receives the actual address of the pointer to the current node, not just a copy of the pointer. We show why this must be true in the next sections.

```
template<class ItemType>
void Insert(NodeType<ItemType>*& listPtr, ItemType item)
{
  if (listPtr == NULL || item < listPtr->info)
  {
    // Save current pointer.
    NodeType<ItemType>* tempPtr = listPtr;
    // Get a new node.
    listPtr = new NodeType<ItemType>;
    listPtr->info = item;
    listPtr->next = tempPtr;
  }
  else Insert(listPtr->next, item);
}
```

Function `DeleteItem`

The `Delete` function is a mirror image of the `Insert` function. In the iterative version, we find the node to delete only after we have gone past the node containing a pointer to it. We solved that problem in the recursive `Insert` by passing the address of the pointer to the list. Does the same approach work for the deletion operation? Let's delete 13 from the same list.

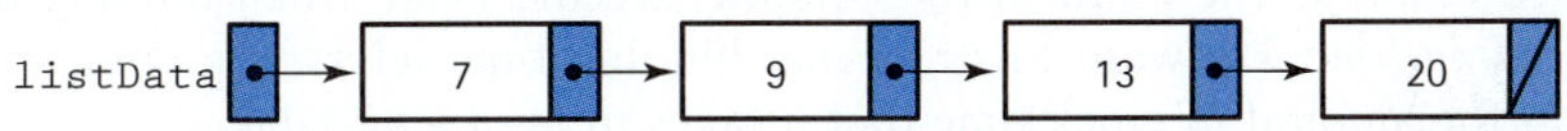

The precondition to the operation is that the item is in the list, so we compare 13 with the value in the first node in the list, 7. They are not equal, so we look for 13 in the list pointed to by the `next` member of the first node in the list. We compare 13 with 9; they are not equal, so we look for 13 in the list pointed to by the `next` member of the first node. We compare 13 with the value in the first node in the list, and they are equal. We save the pointer to the node containing 13 (to deallocate the node later) and set the pointer to the list equal to the `next` member of the first node.

Function Delete

Definition:	Deletes item from list.
Size:	The number of items in the list.
Base Case:	If item = (listPtr->info), delete node pointed to by listPtr.
General Case:	Delete(listPtr->next, item).

Once again, the function must receive the address in the structure where the pointer to the current node is stored.

```
template<class ItemType>
void Delete(NodeType<ItemType>*& listPtr, ItemType item)
{
  if (item == listPtr->info)
  {
    NodeType<ItemType>* tempPtr = listPtr;
    listPtr = listPtr->next;
    delete tempPtr;
  }
  else
    Delete(listPtr->next, item)
}
```

7.10 How Recursion Works

To understand how recursion works and why some programming languages allow it but others do not, we have to take a detour and look at how languages associate places in memory with variable names. The association of a memory address with a variable name is called *binding*. The point in the compile/execute cycle when binding occurs is called the *binding time*. We want to stress that binding time refers to a point of time in a process, not the amount of clock time that it takes to bind a variable.

Static storage allocation associates variable names with memory locations at compile time; dynamic storage allocation associates variable names with memory locations at execution time. As we look at how static and dynamic storage allocation work, consider the following question: *When are the parameters of a function bound to a particular address in memory?* The answer to this question tells us something about whether a language can support recursion.

Static Storage Allocation

As a program is translated, the compiler creates a *symbol table*. When a variable is declared, it is entered into the symbol table, and a memory location—an address—is assigned to it. As an example, let's see how the compiler would translate the following C++ global declarations:

```
int girlCount, boyCount, totalKids;
```

To simplify this discussion, we assume that integers take only one memory location. This statement causes three entries to be made in the symbol table. (The addresses used are arbitrary.)

Symbol	*Address*
`girlCount`	0000
`boyCount`	0001
`totalKids`	0002

That is, *at compile time*,

> `girlCount` is *bound* to address 0000.
> `boyCount` is *bound* to address 0001.
> `totalKids` is *bound* to address 0002.

Whenever a variable is used later in the program, the compiler searches the symbol table for its actual address and substitutes that address for the variable name. After all, meaningful variable names are intended for the convenience of the human reader; addresses, however, are meaningful to computers. For example, the assignment statement

```
totalKids = girlCount + boyCount;
```

is translated into machine instructions that execute the following actions:

- Get the contents of address 0000.
- Add it to the contents of address 0001.
- Put the result into address 0002.

The object code itself is then stored in a different part of memory. Suppose that the translated instructions begin at address 1000. At the beginning of execution, control is transferred to address 1000. The instruction stored there is executed, then the instruction in address 1001 is executed, and so on.

Where are the parameters of functions stored? With static storage allocation, the formal parameters of a function are assumed to reside in a particular place; for instance, the compiler might set aside space for the parameter values immediately preceding the code for each function. Consider a function with two `int` parameters, `girlCount` and `boyCount`, as well as a local variable, `totalKids`. Let's assume that the function's code begins at an address called `CountKids`. The compiler leaves room for the two formal parameters and the local variable at addresses `CountKids - 1`, `CountKids - 2`, and `CountKids - 3`, respectively. Given the function definition

```
void CountKids(int girlCount, int boyCount)
{
  int totalKids;
  .
  .
}
```

the statement

```
totalKids = girlCount + boyCount;
```

in the body of the function would generate the following actions:

- Get the contents of address `CountKids - 1`.
- Add it to the contents of address `CountKids - 2`.
- Store the result in address `CountKids - 3`.

Figure 7.4 shows how a program with three functions might be arranged in memory.

This discussion has been simplified somewhat, because the compiler actually sets aside space not only for the parameters and local variables, but also for the return address (the location in the calling code of the next instruction to process, following the completion of the function) and the computer's current register values. It has, however, drawn attention to the main point: The function's formal parameters and local variables are bound to actual addresses in memory at compile time.

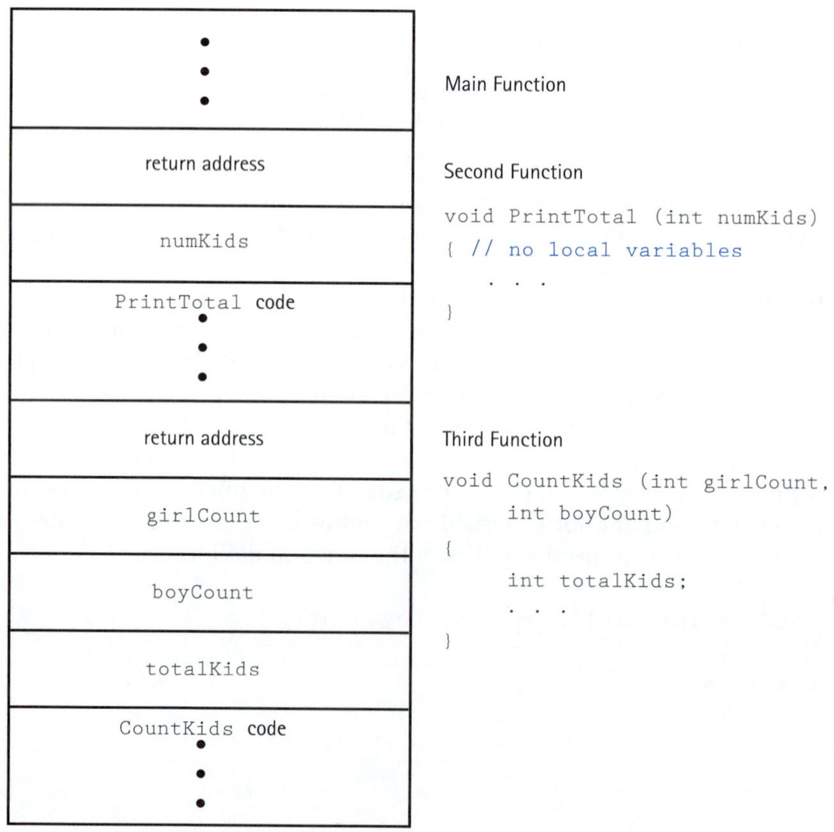

Figure 7.4 *Static allocation of space for a program with three functions*

We can compare the static allocation scheme to one way of allocating seats in an auditorium where a lecture will be held. A finite number of invitations are issued for the event, and the exact number of chairs needed are set up before the lecture. Each invited guest has a reserved seat. If anyone brings friends, however, there is nowhere for the invited friends to sit.

What is the implication of binding variable names to memory locations before the program executes? Each parameter and local variable has only a single location assigned to it at compile time. (They are like invited guests with reserved seats.) If each call to a function is an independent event, then no problem arises. But in the case of recursion, each recursive call depends on the state of the values in the previous call. Where is the storage for the multiple versions of the parameters and local variables generated by recursive calls? Because the intermediate values of the parameters and local variables must be retained, the recursive call cannot store its arguments (actual parameters) in the fixed number of locations that were set up at compile time. The values from the previous recursive call would be overwritten and lost. Thus a language that uses only static storage allocation *cannot* support recursion.

Dynamic Storage Allocation

The situation we have described is also analogous to a class of students that must share one copy of a workbook. Joe writes his exercise answers in the space provided in the workbook, then Mary erases his answers, and writes hers in the same space. This process continues until each student in the class writes his or her answers into the workbook, obliterating all the answers that came before. Obviously, this situation is not practical. What is needed is for each student to read from the single copy of the workbook, then to write his or her answers on a separate piece of paper. In computer terms, each invocation of a function needs its own work space. Dynamic storage allocation provides this solution.

With dynamic storage allocation, variable names are not bound to actual addresses in memory until *run time*. The compiler references variables not by their actual addresses, but by relative addresses. Of particular interest to us, the compiler references the parameters and local variables of a function relative to some address known at run time, not relative to the location of the function's code.

Let's look at a simplified version of how this situation might work in C++. (The actual implementation depends on the particular machine and compiler.) When a function is invoked, it needs space to keep its formal parameters, its local variables, and the return address (the address in the calling code to which the computer returns when the function completes its execution). Just like the students sharing one copy of a workbook, each invocation of a function needs its own work space. This work space is called an activation record or stack frame. A simplified version of an activation record for function `Factorial` might have the following "declarations":

> **Activation record (stack frame)** A record used at run time to store information about a function call, including the parameters, local variables, register values, and return address

```
struct ActivationRecordType
{
  AddressType returnAddr;      // Return address
  int result;                  // Returned value
  int number;                  // Formal parameter
  .
  .
  .
};
```

Each call to a function, including recursive calls, generates a new activation record. Within the function, references to the parameters and local variables use the values in the activation record. When the function ends, the activation record is released. How does this happen? Your source code doesn't need to allocate and free activation records; instead, the compiler adds a "prologue" to the beginning of each function and an "epilogue" to the end of each function. Table 7.2 compares the source code for `Factorial`

Table 7.2 *Run-time Version of* `Factorial` *(Simplified)*

What Your Source Code Says	What the Run-time System Does
`int Factorial(int number)`	`// Function prologue`
`{`	`actRec = new ActivationRecordType;`
	`actRec->returnAddr = retAddr;`
	`actRec->number = number;`
	`// actRec->result is undefined`
`  if (number == 0)`	`if (actRec->number == 0)`
`    return 1;`	`  actRec->result = 1;`
`  else`	`else`
`    return number *`	`  actRec->result =`
`     Factorial(number - 1);`	`    actRec->number *`
`}`	`    Factorial(actRec->number-1);`
	`// Function epilogue`
	`returnValue = actRec->result;`
	`retAddr = actRec->returnAddr;`
	`delete actRec;`
	`Jump (goto) retAddr`

with a simplified version of the "code" executed at run time. (Of course, the code executed at run time is object code, but we are listing the source code "equivalent" so that it makes sense to the reader.)

What happens to the activation record of one function when a second function is invoked? Consider a program whose `main` function calls `Proc1`, which then calls `Proc2`. When the program begins executing, it generates the "main" activation record. (The `main` function's activation record persists for the entire execution of the program.) At the first function call, an activation record is generated for `Proc1`:[1]

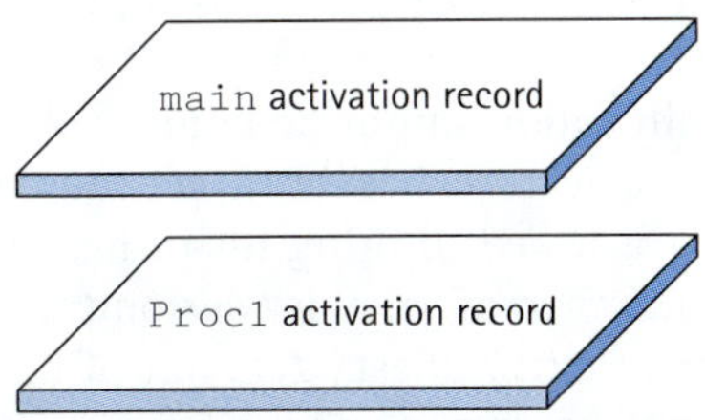

When `Proc2` is called from within `Proc1`, its activation record is generated. Because `Proc1` has not finished executing, its activation record still exists; just like the mathematicians with telephones, one waits "on hold" until the next call is finished:

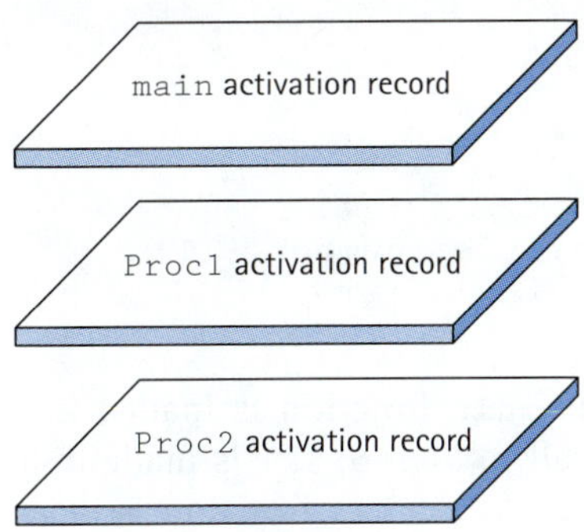

When `Proc2` finishes executing, its activation record is released. But which of the other two activation records becomes the active one—`Proc1`'s or `main`'s? `Proc1`'s activation record should now be active, of course. The order of activation follows the last in, first out

[1]The drawings in this chapter that represent the run-time stack have the top of the stack at the bottom of the picture, because we generally think of memory as being allocated in increasing address order.

Run-time stack A data structure that keeps track of activation records during the execution of a program

rule. We know of a structure that supports LIFO access—the stack—so it should come as no surprise that the structure that keeps track of the activation records at run time is called the run-time stack.

When a function is invoked, its activation record is pushed onto the run-time stack. Each nested level of function calls adds another activation record to the stack. As each function completes its execution, its activation record is popped from the stack. Recursive function calls, like calls to any other functions, generate a new activation record. The level of recursive calls in a program determines how many activation records for this function are pushed onto the run-time stack at any one time.

Using dynamic allocation might be compared to another way of allocating seats in an auditorium where a lecture has been scheduled. A finite number of invitations is issued, but each guest is asked to bring his or her own chair. In addition, each guest can invite an unlimited number of friends, as long as they all bring their own chairs. Of course, if the number of extra guests gets out of hand, the space in the auditorium runs out, and there may not be enough room for any more friends or chairs. Similarly, the level of recursion in a program must eventually be limited by the amount of memory available in the run-time stack.

Let's walk through the function `Factorial` again, to see how its execution affects the run-time stack. Here is the function:

```
int Factorial(int number)
{
  if (number == 0)
    return 1;
  else
    return number * Factorial(number - 1);
}
```

Suppose that the `main` function is loaded in memory beginning at location 5000, and that the initial call to `Factorial` is made in a statement at memory location 5200. Suppose also that the `Factorial` function is loaded in memory at location 1000, with the recursive call made in the statement at location 1010. Figure 7.5 shows a simplified version of how this example program is loaded in memory. (The location numbers have been picked arbitrarily, so that we have actual numbers to show in the return address field of the activation record.)

When `Factorial` is called the first time from the statement in the `main` function at address 5200,

```
answer = Factorial(4);
```

an activation record is pushed onto the run-time stack to hold three pieces of data: the return address (5200), the formal parameter `number` (4), and the value returned from the function (`result`), which has not yet been evaluated. Rather than showing our activa-

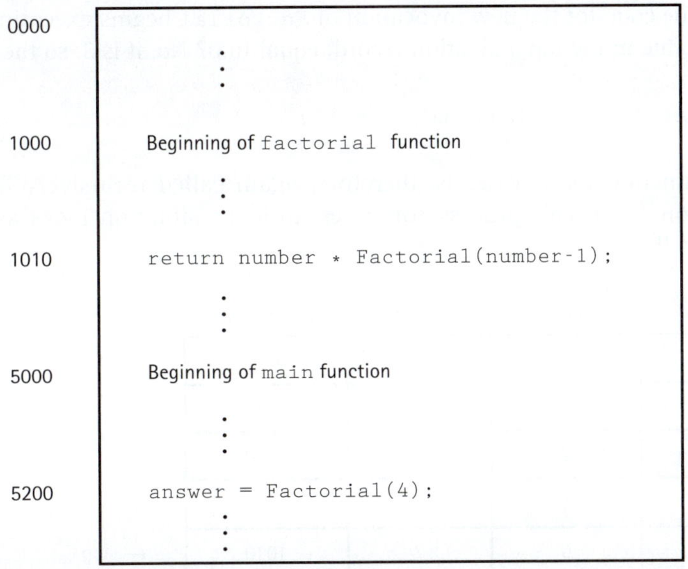

Figure 7.5 *The sample program loaded in memory*

tion records as pictures, let's show them as a table. Each new activation record constitutes a new row of the table. The activation record in the last row of the table is now on the top of the run-time stack. We have added a column on the left that identifies which call it is.

Call	*number*	*result*	*returnAddr*	
1	4	?	5200	← top

The code is now executed. Is `number` (the `number` value in the top activation record) equal to 0? No, it is 4, so the `else` branch is taken:

```
return number * Factorial(number - 1);
```

This time the function `Factorial` is called from a different place—recursively from within the function, from the statement at location 1010. After the value of `Factorial(number - 1)` is calculated, we want to return to this location to multiply the result times `number`. A new activation record is pushed onto the run-time stack:

Call	*number*	*result*	*returnAddr*	
1	4	?	5200	
2	3	?	1010	← top

The code for the new invocation of `Factorial` begins executing. Is `number` (the `number` value in the top activation record) equal to 0? No, it is 3, so the `else` branch is taken:

```
return number * Factorial(number - 1);
```

The function `Factorial` is, therefore, again called recursively from the instruction at location 1010. This process continues until the situation looks as shown here with the fifth call.

Call	*number*	*result*	*returnAddr*	
1	4	?	5200	
2	3	?	1010	
3	2	?	1010	
4	1	?	1010	
5	0	?	1010	← top

As the fifth call is executed, we again ask the question: Is `number` (the `number` value in the top activation record) equal to 0? *Yes*. This time we perform the *then* clause, storing the value 1 into `result` (the instance of `result` in the top activation record, that is). The fifth invocation of the function has executed to completion, and the function returns the value of `result` in the top activation record. The run-time stack is popped to release the top activation record, leaving the activation record of the fourth call to `Factorial` at the top of the run-time stack. We don't restart the fourth function call from the beginning, however. As with any function call, we return to the place where the function was called—namely, the return address (location 1010) stored in the activation record.

Next, the returned value (1) is multiplied by the value of `number` in the top activation record (1) and the result (1) is stored into `result` (the instance of `result` in the top activation record, that is). Now the fourth invocation of the function is complete, and the function returns the value of `result` in the top activation record. Again, the run-time stack is popped to release the top activation record, leaving the activation record of the third call to `Factorial` at the top of the run-time stack.

Call	*number*	*result*	*returnAddr*	
1	4	?	5200	
2	3	?	1010	
3	2	2	1010	← top

We return to the place where we made the recursive call to `Factorial`.

This process continues until we reach the first call:

Call	*number*	*result*	*returnAddr*	
1	4	?	5200	← top

At this point, 6 has just been returned as the value of `Factorial(number - 1)`. This value is multiplied by the value of `number` in the top activation record (that is, 4) and the result, 24, is stored into the `result` field of the top activation record. This assignment completes the execution of the initial call to the function `Factorial`. The value of `result` in the top activation record (24) is returned to the place of the original call (address 5200), and the activation record is popped. This action leaves the main activation record at the top of the run-time stack. The final value of `result` is stored into the variable `answer`, and the statement following the original call is executed.

The number of recursive calls constitutes the *depth* of the recursion. Notice the relationship between the complexity of the iterative version in terms of Big-O notation and the depth of recursion for the factorial: Both are based on the parameter `number`. Is it a coincidence that the depth of recursion is the same as the complexity of the iterative version? No. Recursion represents another way of doing repetition, so you would expect that the depth of recursion would be approximately the same as the number of iterations for the iterative version of the same problem. In addition, both are based on the size of the problem.

7.11 Tracing the Execution of Recursive Function `Insert`

Earlier we wrote a recursive `Insert` function that inserts a new node into a dynamically allocated linked list. To follow the execution of `Insert`, let's put addresses on the nodes in the list. In the following diagram, the number above a node is the base address of the node. The number beneath the `next` member is the address of the `next` data member only. The external pointer to the list is stored in location 010.

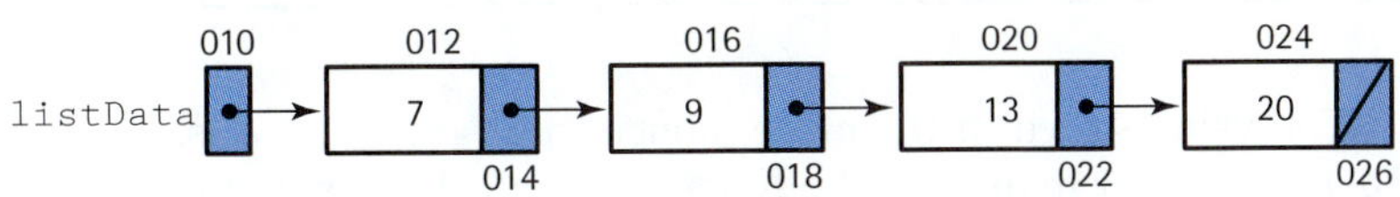

Here is the function template we will trace:

```
template<class ItemType>
void Insert(NodeType<ItemType>*& listPtr, ItemType item)
{
  if (listPtr == NULL || item < listPtr->info)
```

```
    {
      // Save current pointer.
      NodeType<ItemType>* tempPtr = listPtr;
      // Get new node.
      listPtr = new NodeType<ItemType>;
      listPtr->info = item;
      listPtr->next = tempPtr;
    }
    else Insert(listPtr->next, item);
}
```

Our trace must keep track of `listPtr`, `item`, and the return address. The local variable `tempPtr` also has a place in the activation record. Rather than give a specific return address, however, we use the convention that R0 is the return address from the nonrecursive call and R1 is the return address from the recursive call. We trace `Insert(listData, item)`, where `item` is 11. Recall that the formal parameter `listPtr` is passed by reference and `item` is passed by value. Here is what the activation record looks like after the nonrecursive call:

Call	*listPtr*	*item*	*tempPtr*	*returnAddr*	
1	010	11	?	R0	← top

As the code begins its execution, the value stored in the place named in `listPtr` (location 010) is examined (because `listPtr` is a reference parameter). This value is not NULL, so `item` is compared with the `info` data member of the node pointed to by location 010. Eleven is greater than 7, so the function is called again recursively.

Call	*listPtr*	*item*	*tempPtr*	*returnAddr*	
1	010	11	?	R0	
2	014	11	?	R1	← top

The value stored in the place named in `listPtr` (that is, location 014) is not NULL and 11 is greater than 9, so the function is called again recursively.

Call	*listPtr*	*item*	*tempPtr*	*returnAddr*	
1	010	11	?	R0	
2	014	11	?	R1	
3	018	11	?	R1	← top

The value stored in the place named in `listPtr` is not `NULL` but 11 is less than 13, so the *then* clause is executed and the following steps are performed. The value in the place named in `listPtr` is copied into `tempPtr`. The `new` operator is executed and the address of a node of type `NodeType` is stored into the place named in `listPtr`. The stack now looks as follows assuming that the address of the new node is 028:

Call	*listPtr*	*item*	*tempPtr*	*returnAddr*	
1	010	11	?	R0	
2	014	11	?	R1	
3	018	11	020	R1	← top

`listPtr` has not changed! Didn't we just store the address 028 there? No, we stored 028 into the place *named* in `listPtr`: in location 018, the `next` member of the previous node. Our list now looks like this:

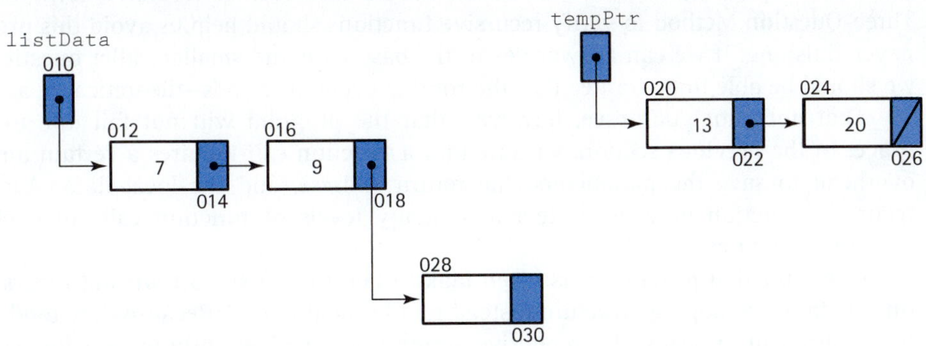

The next two statements store `item` into `listPtr->info` and `tempPtr` into `listPtr->next`, completing the insertion.

Let's see what the activation records would look like at this point if we had passed `listPtr` as a value parameter:

Call	*listPtr*	*item*	*tempPtr*	*returnAddr*	
1	012	11	?	R0	
2	016	11	?	R1	
3	028	11	020	R1	← top

When the `new` operator is executed, the address of a node of type `NodeType` is stored into `listPtr`—not the place *named* in `listPtr`. Therefore 028 is stored into the activation record member `listPtr`, not in the `next` data member of the preceding node as is the case when `listPtr` is a reference parameter. The `next` data member of the new node is set properly, but the pointer to the new node is stored in the activation record that is removed when the function exits. Thus the rest of the list is lost. In fact, if you use this incorrect version to build the list, the list is empty. (Can you explain why?)

Our recursive `Insert` function works properly because the first parameter is the *address* in memory of either the external pointer to the list or the `next` data member of a node in the list.

7.12 Debugging Recursive Routines

Because of their nested calls to themselves, recursive routines can prove confusing to debug. The most serious problem relates to the possibility that the routine recurses forever. A typical symptom of this problem is an error message noting that the system has run out of space in the run-time stack, due to the level of recursive calls. Using the Three-Question Method to verify recursive functions should help us avoid this problem of never finishing. If we can answer yes to the base-case and smaller-caller questions, then we should be able to guarantee that the routine eventually ends—theoretically, at least.

That does not guarantee, however, that the program will not fail due to lack of space. In the previous section, we saw that a function call requires a certain amount of overhead to save the parameters, the return address, and the local data. A call to a recursive function may generate many, many levels of function calls to itself—more than the system can handle.

One error that programmers often make when they first start writing recursive routines is to use a looping structure instead of a branching one. Because they tend to think of the problem in terms of a repetitive action, they inadvertently use a *while* statement rather than an *if* statement. The main body of the recursive routine should always break down into base and recursive cases. Hence, we use a branching statement, not a looping statement. It's a good idea to double-check your recursive functions to make sure that you used an *if* or *switch* statement to achieve a branching effect.

Recursive routines are good places to put debug output statements during testing. Print out the parameters and local variables, if any, at the beginning and end of the function. Be sure to print out the values of the parameters on the recursive call(s) to verify that each call attempts to solve a problem smaller than the previous one.

7.13 Removing Recursion

In cases where a recursive solution is not desired, either because the language doesn't support recursion or because the recursive solution is deemed too costly in terms of space or time, you can implement a recursive algorithm as a nonrecursive function. Two general techniques are often substituted for recursion: iteration and stacking.

Iteration

When the recursive call is the last action executed in a recursive function, an interesting situation occurs. The recursive call causes an activation record to be put on the run-time stack to hold the function's parameters and local variables. When this recursive call finishes executing, the run-time stack is popped and the previous values of the variables are restored. But because the recursive call is the last statement in the function, the function terminates without using these values. Thus the pushing and popping of activation records is a superfluous activity. All we really need to do is to change the "smaller-caller" variable(s) on the recursive call's parameter list and then "jump" back to the beginning of the function. In other words, we really need a *loop*.

For instance, as explained later in this chapter, the function `ValueInList` is a poor use of recursion. It is a simple matter to remove the recursion from this function. The last statement executed in the general case is the recursive call to itself, so let's replace this recursion with a loop.

The recursive solution has two base cases: (1) we find the value and (2) we reach the end of the list without finding the value. The base cases solve the problem without further executions of the function. In the iterative solution, the base cases become the terminating conditions of the loop:

```
while (!found && moreToSearch)
```

When the terminating conditions are met, the problem is solved without further executions of the loop body.

In the general case of the recursive solution, `ValueInList` is called to search the remaining, unsearched part of the list. Each recursive execution of the function processes a smaller version of the problem. The smaller-caller question is answered affirmatively because `startIndex` is incremented, shrinking the unsearched part of the list on each recursive call. Similarly, in an iterative solution, each subsequent execution of the loop body processes a smaller version of the problem. The unsearched part of the list shrinks with each execution of the loop body because `startIndex` is incremented.

```
if value = list.info[startIndex]
    Set found to true
else
    Increment startIndex
```

Here is the iterative version of the function:

```
bool ValueInList(ListType list, int value, int startIndex)
{
  bool found = false;

  while (!found && startIndex < list.length)
    if (value == list.info[startIndex])
      found = true;
    else startIndex++;
  return found;
}
```

Tail recursion The case in which a function contains only a single recursive invocation and it is the last statement to be executed in the function

Cases where the recursive call is the last statement executed are called tail recursion. Note that the recursive call is not necessarily the last statement in the function. For instance, the recursive call in the following version of `ValueInList` is still tail recursion, even though it is *not* the last statement in the function:

```
bool ValueInList(ListType list, int value, int startIndex)
{
  if (list.info[startIndex] == value)
    return true;
  else if (startIndex != list.length-1)
    return ValueInList(list, value, startIndex+1);
  else return false;
}
```

The recursive call is the last statement *executed* in the general case—thus it involves tail recursion. To remove recursion from the solution, tail recursion is usually replaced by iteration. In fact, many compilers catch tail recursion and automatically replace it with iteration.

Stacking

When the recursive call is *not* the last action executed in a recursive function, we cannot simply substitute a loop for the recursion. For instance, in the function `RevPrint` we make the recursive call and then print the value in the current node. In such a case, we must replace the stacking performed by the *system* with stacking performed by the *programmer.*

How would we write `RevPrint` nonrecursively? As we traverse the list, we must keep track of the pointer to each node, until we reach the end of the list (when our traversing pointer equals `NULL`). We then print the `info` data member of the last node. Next, we back up and print again, back up and print again, and so on, until we have printed the first list element.

We already know of a data structure in which we can store pointers and retrieve them in reverse order: the stack. The general task for `RevPrint` is as follows:

RevPrint (iterative)

Create an empty stack of pointers.
Set ptr to point to first node in list
while the list is not empty
    Push ptr onto the stack
    Advance ptr
while the stack is not empty
    Pop the stack to get ptr (to previous node)
    Print Info(ptr)

A nonrecursive `RevPrint` function may be coded as shown here. Note that we now make `RevPrint` be a member function of the class `ListType` instead of a helper function. Because `RevPrint` no longer has a parameter, we don't have to deal with the problem of having the client pass the (inaccessible) pointer to the beginning of the linked list.

```
#include "StackType.h"
void ListType::RevPrint()
{
  StackType<NodeType*> stack;
  NodeType* listPtr;

  listPtr = listData;

  while (listPtr != NULL)  // Put pointers onto the stack.
  {
    stack.Push(listPtr);
    listPtr = listPtr->next;
  }
  // Retrieve pointers in reverse order and print elements.
  while (!stack.IsEmpty())
  {
    listPtr = stack.Top();
    stack.Pop();
    std::cout << listPtr->info;
  }
}
```

Notice that the nonrecursive version of `RevPrint` is quite a bit longer than its recursive counterpart, especially if we add in the code for the stack routines `Push`, `Pop`, `Top`, and `IsEmpty`. This verbosity reflects our need to stack and unstack the pointers explicitly. In the recursive version, we just called `RevPrint` recursively, and let the run-time stack keep track of the pointers.

7.14 Deciding Whether to Use a Recursive Solution

You must consider several factors in deciding whether to use a recursive solution to a problem. The main issues are the clarity and the efficiency of the solution. Let's focus on efficiency first.

In general, a recursive solution is more costly in terms of both computer time and space. (This is not an absolute decree; it really depends on the computer and the compiler.) A recursive solution usually requires more "overhead" because of the nested recursive function calls, in terms of both time (the function prologues and epilogues must be run for each recursive call) and space (an activation record must be created). A call to a recursive routine may hide many layers of internal recursive calls. For instance, the call to an iterative solution to `Factorial` involves a single function invocation, causing one activation record to be put on the run-time stack. Invoking the recursive version of `Factorial`, however, requires $N + 1$ function calls and $N + 1$ activation records to be pushed onto the run-time stack, where N represents the formal parameter `number`. That is, the depth of recursion is $O(N)$. For some problems, the system may not have enough space in the run-time stack to run a recursive solution.

As an extreme example, consider the original version of the recursive function `ValueInList`. Every time it is invoked, it saves copies of the parameters, including the entire list that is passed as a value parameter. As we search farther and farther in the list, nesting more and more levels of recursive calls, the amount of memory needed for the run-time stack becomes considerable. If the list contains 100 elements and the item we are seeking is not in the list, we end up saving 100 copies of the 100-element list. Eventually we use up so much memory that we may run out of space altogether! This case is an extreme example of one of the "overhead" problems associated with recursive calls. In this particular instance, we might make the list be a reference parameter (something generally not done in value-returning functions) so that every invocation of `ValueInList` would not generate new copies of the array-based list. (The address of the one and only copy of `list` would be passed instead.) Even so, the level of recursion is $O(N)$ and the iterative solution is about the same length and just as clear. Thus `ValueInList` is a poor use of recursion.

Another potential problem is the possibility that a particular recursive solution might be *inherently* inefficient. Such inefficiency is not a reflection of how we choose to implement the algorithm; rather, it is an indictment of the algorithm itself. For instance, look back at the function `Combinations`, which we discussed earlier in this chapter. The example of this function illustrated in Figure 7.2, `Combinations(4,3)`

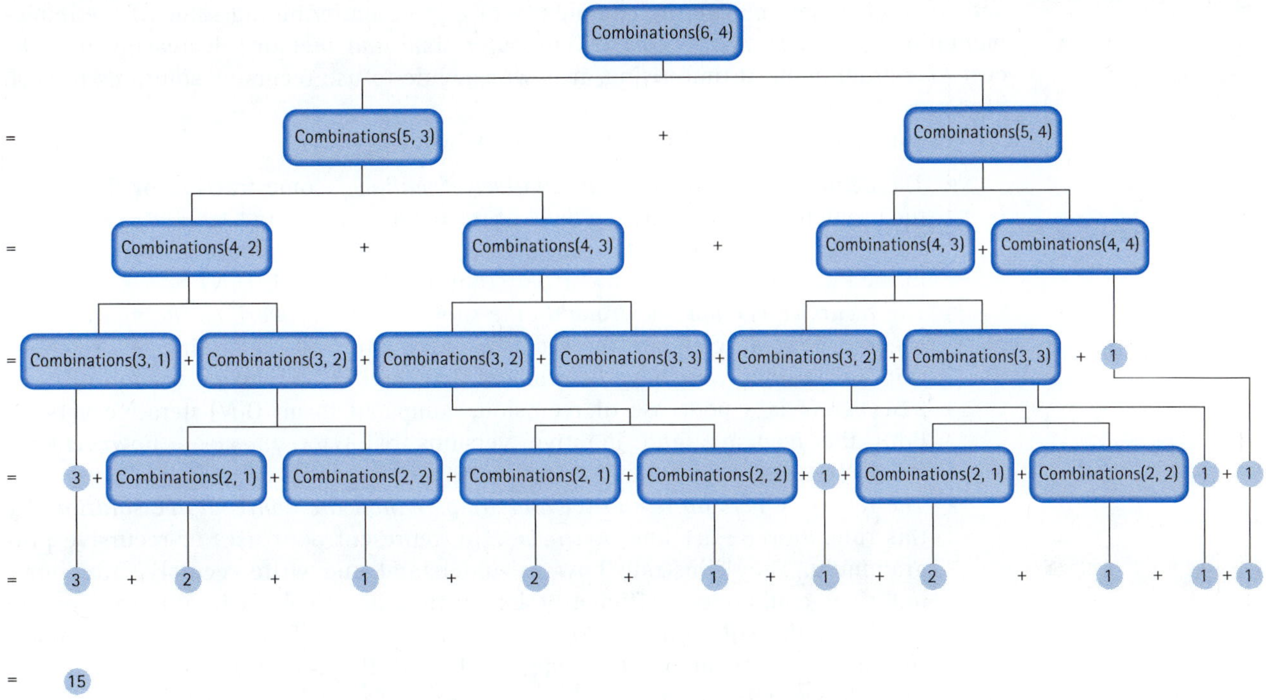

Figure 7.6 *Calculating* `Combinations(6,4)`

seems straightforward enough. But consider the execution of `Combinations(6,4)`, as illustrated in Figure 7.6. The inherent problem with this function is that it calculates the same values over and over. `Combinations(4,3)` is calculated in two different places, and `Combinations(3,2)` is calculated in three places, as are `Combinations(2,1)` and `Combinations(2,2)`. It is unlikely that we could solve a combinatorial problem of any large size using this function. The problem is that the program runs "forever"—or until it exhausts the capacity of the computer; it is an exponential-time, $O(2^N)$ solution to a linear time, $O(N)$, problem. Although our recursive function is very easy to understand, it was not a practical solution. In such cases, you should seek an iterative solution.

The issue of the clarity of the solution remains an important factor, however. For many problems, a recursive solution is simpler and more natural for the programmer to write. The total amount of work required to solve a problem can be envisioned as an iceberg. By using recursive programming, the applications programmer may limit his or her view to the tip of the iceberg. The system takes care of the great bulk of the work below the surface. Compare, for example, the recursive and nonrecursive versions of the function `RevPrint`. In the recursive version, the system takes care of the stacking that we had to do explicitly in the nonrecursive function. Thus recursion can act as a tool to help reduce the complexity of a program by hiding some of the implementation details. With the cost of computer time and memory decreasing and the cost of a programmer's time rising, it is worthwhile to use recursive solutions to such problems.

To summarize, it is good to use recursion when:

- *The depth of recursive calls is relatively "shallow,"* some fraction of the size of the problem. For instance, the level of recursive calls in the `BinarySearch` function is $O(\log_2 N)$; it is a good candidate for recursion. The depth of recursive calls in the `Factorial` and `ValueInList` routines, however, is $O(N)$.
- *The recursive version does roughly the same amount of work as the nonrecursive version.* You can compare the Big-O approximations to determine this relationship. For instance, we have determined that the $O(2^N)$ recursive version of `Combinations` is a poor use of recursion, compared to an $O(N)$ iterative version. Both the recursive and iterative versions of `BinarySearch`, however, are $O(\log_2 N)$. `BinarySearch` is a good example of a recursive function.
- *The recursive version is shorter and simpler than the nonrecursive solution.* By this rule, `Factorial` and `ValueInList` represent poor uses of recursive programming. They illustrate how to understand and write recursive functions, but they could more efficiently be written iteratively—without any loss of clarity in the solution. `RevPrint` is a better use of recursion. Its recursive solution is very simple to understand, and the nonrecursive equivalent is much less elegant.

Case Study

Escaping from a Maze

Problem: As a child, did you ever dream of playing in a maze? How fun and scary it would have been to get lost and then, just at sundown, to find your way out. If you had thought about it, you might have come up with the idea of marking your path as you went along. If you were trapped, you could then go back to the last crossing and take another path.

This technique of going back to the last decision point and trying another way is called *backtracking.* We illustrate this very useful problem-solving technique in the context of trying to get out of a maze.

Given a maze and a starting point within it, you are to determine whether there is a way out. There is only one exit from the maze. You may move horizontally or vertically (but not diagonally) in any direction in which there is an open path, but you may not move in a direction that is blocked. If you move into a position where you are blocked on three sides, you must go back the way you came (backtrack) and try another path.

Brainstorming: This is a different kind of problem because the situation doesn't represent something in real life with which many of us are familiar. Clearly, the central object is a maze that has one exit. Positions can be blocked, which implies that positions can be open or free. Let's examine what such a structure might look like, using a 'O' to represent an Open position, a '+' to represent a blocked position, and an 'E' to represent the exit. The directions say to find a way out from a starting point, so let's mark the starting point with an 'S'.

O	O	+	E	O
O	+	S	O	+
O	O	O	O	+
+	+	O	+	+

From the starting point, we can go to the right or down but not to the left or up because both of these positions are blocked. So let's try going down. Ok; we are now—where? We need a way of determining where we are. Let's assume that the maze is on a grid, where the row and column numbers begin at one. We can specify a position by its row and column number. So we are now at position [3,3], shaded here.

O	O	+	E	O
O	+	S	O	+
O	O	O	O	+
+	+	O	+	+

We are not at the exit, so we face the same decision as before—where to go next. We can go left, right, and down. What about up? Well, that's the starting position and we don't want to go there again. Let's go down.

O	O	+	E	O
O	+	S	O	+
O	O	O	O	+
+	+	O	+	+

We can't go right or left and we can't go down or we would fall out of the problem. Note: We must look at this problem later. (How do we get the program to recognize the edge of the maze?) We could go up, but we've been there before. In fact, this is the same situation we faced before, when we decided not to go back into the starting position. This time it is just another open position. How do we know not to go back?

If you were hiking in an uncharted area, you might mark your trail by breaking twigs or leaving stones in the path you had traveled. We can use the same idea here. We mark the trail of positions that we've already tried by replacing the Open symbol with a special symbol for Tried. We use a little stone ('*') for this symbol.

O	O	+	E	O
O	+	*	O	+
O	O	*	O	+
+	+	O	+	+

Our rules are slightly modified: We can go in any direction that is not blocked or *already tried.* We are trapped.

We don't know for sure that there is no way to get out of the maze. We only know that the path we tried doesn't get us there. We passed a couple of Open positions [3,2] and [3,4] as we were going along the path that led us to the dead end. We could go back to one of them and try another path from there. Let's go back to [3,4].

O	O	+	E	O
O	+	*	O	+
O	O	*	O	+
+	+	*	+	+

Now, we have only one choice: We go up.

O	O	+	E	O
O	+	*	O	+
O	O	*	*	+
+	+	*	+	+

Again, we have only one choice: Up.

O	O	+	E	O
O	+	*	*	+
O	O	*	*	+
+	+	*	+	+

We have escaped!

In our simulation of trying to escape from a maze, we didn't come up with any new objects, so we can skip the filtering phase and look at the responsibilities of the maze. It must create itself and determine if we can reach the exit given a starting position. Notice that the maze is changed as we try to escape from it. Because we might want to try to escape from different positions within the maze, we should allow the maze to copy itself.

Class Name: Maze	Superclass:	Subclasses:

Responsibilities	Collaborations
Create maze(file)	ifstream
Try to escape (starting position) returns boolean	
Print	
Copy returns a copy	

Data Structure: There are many problems for which the choice of data structure can be postponed until after the responsibility algorithms are written. In this case, however, the structure and the processing are so intertwined we need to choose our data structure first. We drew our picture using rows and columns so we could talk about the different places, so a two-dimensional array seems a natural choice to represent the maze. We can set the array up to a maximum size (say 10 x 10) and let the actual size be read in as the first values on the file containing the maze.

We might as well use the same symbols that we used in the discussion. Do we need any other data fields? Yes, we need to know the actual size of the maze stored in the array in order to process it. Here are our class data fields.

```
private:
  char maze[10][10];
  int maxRows;          // Maximum number of rows
  int maxCols;          // Maximum number of columns
```

Constructor(ifstream inFile)

Because the format of the maze input was not given as part of the problem, we can determine how the file should look. For ease of processing, the data should be one row of the maze per line with no embedded blanks. We can read the line using the >> operator and then loop through the string using `[]` to move each character into the array.

In our hand simulation we recognized the border of the maze. How do we simulate that? We can put a border of Blocked symbols around the maze array. An alternative is to check for the end of a row or column during the processing. Either is fine, but bordering the maze makes the code a little easier. Let's look at what a bordered array would look like if maxRow is 4 and maxCol is 5.

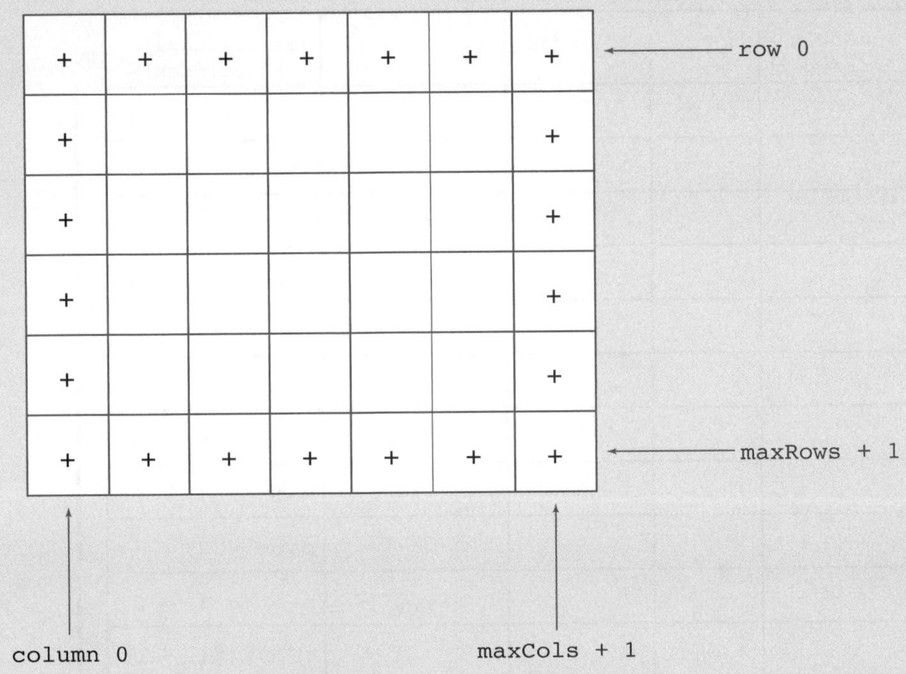

Because of the border, the first row read goes into the second row of the array, the second row read goes into the third row of the array, and so on; beginning at the second column.

```
inFile >> maxRows >> maxCols
for rowIndex going from 1 through maxRows
        inFile >> row
        for colIndex going from 1 through maxCols
                Set maze[rowIndex][colIndex] to row[colIndex-1]
        // Set the side borders
        Set maze[rowIndex][0] to '+';
        Set maze[rowIndex][maxCols + 1] to '+'
// Set the top and bottom borders
for colIndex going 0 through maxCols + 1
        Set maze[0][colIndex ] to '+'
        Set maze[maxRows+1][colIndex ] to '+'
```

This algorithm is quite complex. Let's hand-simulate it to be sure it does what we think it does. We can use the same maze we used for our brainstorming, but put an O where the starting position was. `maxRows` is 4 and `maxCols` is 5.

```
OO+EO
O+OO+
OOOO+
++O++
```

rowIndex [colIndex]	row	colIndex	row	max[rowIndex] [colIndex]
1	OO+EO	1	0	maze[1][1] = O
		2	0	maze[1][2] = O
		3	+	maze[1][3] = +
		4	E	maze[1][4] = E
		5	0	maze[1][5] = O
				maze[1][0] = +
				maze[1][6] = +
2	O+OO+	1	0	maze[2][1] = O
		2	+	maze[2][2] = +
		3	0	maze[2][3] = O
		4	0	maze[2][4] = O
		5	+	maze[2][5] = +
				maze[2][0] = +
				maze[2][6] = +
...				
4	++O++	5	+	maze[4][5] = +
				maze[4][0] = +
				maze[4][6] = +
		0		maze[0][0] = +
				maze[5][0] = +
		1		maze[0][1] = +
				maze[5][1] = +
...				
		6		maze[0][6] = +
				maze[5][6] = +

first loop (rows 1 through maze[4][6])

second loop (maze[0][0] through maze[5][6])

Yes, this algorithm runthrough seems fine.

Print

We do not need to print the border, only the actual maze.

```
for rowIndex going 1 through maxRows
        for colIndex going 1 through maxCols
                cout << " " << maze[rowIndex][colIndex]
        cout << endl
```

boolean TryToEscape(startRow, startCol)

Let's summarize what we learned in our brainstorming session, using variable `free` to record the outcome.

If the contents of the current position contains E, set `free` to true.

If the contents of the current position contains "*", we "retreat".

If the contents of the current position is '+', we "retreat".

If the contents of the current position is 'O', we "process".

The first case is clear: We have escaped and we return `free` as true. The second and third cases cause us to retreat or backtrack. This clearly sounds like a recursive situation. To retreat would be to exit that call. "Process" is the general case: Mark the space with a '*' and try the cells around it.

TryToEscape is a non-recursive function that takes the starting row and column as parameters. Its chore is to call a recursive helper function to search for the way out. This helper function needs the maze (the structure to be searched), the starting position, and `free`, a Boolean field in which to return the result. The Boolean data field is initialized to false before the first recursive call. Within the recursion (if this variable is true), we just return.

```
Set free to false
Try(maze, row, col, free)
return free
```

Try(maze, row, col, free)

We just return when the maze position contains '*' or '+' or free is true.

```
if not free AND maze[row,col] <> '*' AND maze[row][col] <> '+'
        if maze[row,col] is 'E'
                Set free to true
        else
                Set maze[row][col] to '*'
                try(maze, row+1, col, free)
                try(maze, row-1, col, free)
                try(maze, row, col+1, free)
                try(maze, row, col-1, free)
```

Can you see a way to cut down the run time? This algorithm works, but can you see a way to make it more efficient? There are four recursive calls made, one after the other, even if "free" has been set to true in the first, second, or third call. If we guard the last three recursive calls with an *if* statement, we can avoid unnecessary recursive calls. We code it that way.

Before we code this algorithm though, we verify the design with our three questions.

1. *The Base-Case Question:* The base cases occur when the current position is not an Open path, in which case we should stop searching this path (i.e., do nothing). When free is already true on entrance to the function, we already know the answer to the problem and can quit.
2. *The Smaller-Caller Question:* We need to show here that the portion of the maze left to be searched is smaller on each recursive call. As we process each Open position, we set the value of this position to the Tried symbol. As Open positions are found, therefore, the size of the maze that is left to process (represented by Open symbols) becomes smaller. We usually look at the parameters of the recursive call to see how the size of the problem is changing. In this case we can see that the row and column parameters are adjusted to guide the search for the exit into new paths adjacent to the current position. Because the maze is bordered by Blocked positions, we are guaranteed that we do not go off the edge.
3. *The General-Case Question:* Let's assume that a call to Try correctly tells us whether an escape can be made from a given position. If we can escape from some known position in the maze, then we can also escape from an Open position adjacent to that position. So if we check all the positions adjacent to the starting point (the four calls to Try) and find that any of them leads to an escape, then we know that we can escape from the starting point. The converse is also true. If none of the adjacent positions leads to the exit, then the starting point cannot lead to an exit. So the general case should solve the problem, assuming that the recursive calls do what they are supposed to do.

We can now code our algorithm, confident that it is correct. The specification and implementation files are shown here.

```
// Specification file for class Maze
// This class determines if there is a
// way out of the maze.
#include <fstream>
class Maze
{
public:
  Maze(std::ifstream& inFile);
  void Print();
  bool TryToEscape(int startRow, int startCol);
  Maze(const Maze& anotherMaze);

private:
  char maze[10][10];
  int maxRows;                // Maximum number of rows
  int maxCols;                // Maximum number of columns
};
```

```
// Implementation file for class Maze.
#include "Maze.h"

#include <iostream>
#include <fstream>
#include <string>

Maze::Maze(std::ifstream& inFile)
{
  using namespace std;
  int rowIndex, colIndex;
  inFile >> maxRows >> maxCols;
  string row;
  for (rowIndex = 1; rowIndex <= maxRows; rowIndex++)
  {
    inFile >> row;
    for (colIndex = 1; colIndex <= maxCols; colIndex++)
      maze[rowIndex][colIndex] = row[colIndex-1];
    maze[rowIndex][0] = '+';
    maze[rowIndex][maxCols+1] = '+';
  }
  for (colIndex = 0; colIndex <= maxCols+1; colIndex++)
  {
    maze[0][colIndex] = '+';
    maze[maxRows+1][colIndex] = '+';
  }
}

Maze::Maze (const Maze& anotherMaze)
{
  maxRows = anotherMaze.maxRows;
  maxCols = anotherMaze.maxCols;
  for (int rowIndex = 0; rowIndex <= maxRows+1; rowIndex++)
    for (int colIndex = 0; colIndex <= maxCols+1; colIndex++)
      maze[rowIndex][colIndex] = anotherMaze.maze[rowIndex][colIndex];
}

void Maze::Print()
{
  using namespace std;
  int rowIndex, colIndex;

  cout << "Maze" << endl;
  for (rowIndex = 1; rowIndex <= maxRows; rowIndex++)
  {
    for (colIndex = 1; colIndex <= maxCols; colIndex++)
      cout << " " << maze[rowIndex][colIndex];
    cout << endl;
  }
}
```

```
void Try(char[][10], int row, int col, bool& free);

bool Maze::TryToEscape(int startRow, int startCol)
{
  bool free = false;
  Try(maze, startRow, startCol, free);
  return free;
}

void Try(char maze[][10] , int row, int col, bool& free)
{
  if (!free && (maze[row][col]) != '*' && (maze[row][col]) != '+')
    if (maze[row][col] == 'E')
      free = true;
    else
    {
      maze[row][col] = '*';
      Try(maze, row+1, col, free);
      if (!free)
        Try(maze, row-1, col, free);
      if (!free)
        Try(maze, row, col+1, free);
      if (!free)
        Try(maze, row,col-1, free);
    }
}
```

Testing: We need to build a test driver for class `Maze`. Because this class does not represent an ADT used as a structure in other problems, our driver will be different. We need to create the maze and try different starting positions to see if the function `TryToEscape` gives the correct answer. Let's prompt for the row outside the loop, and use a negative row as a flag to stop the processing.

```
Open data file
Create the maze
Prompt for starting positions
Read row
While row > 0
        Read col
        Set anotherMaze to copy of maze
        if (anotherMaze.TryToEscape(row,col)
                Print "Free"
        else
                Print "Trapped"
        Prompt for starting position
        Read row
```

Here is the code for the driver followed by the run log from a variety of starting positions. The maze is the one that we used during our brainstorming phase.

```
#include <fstream>
#include <iostream>
#include <string>
#include "Maze.h"
int main()
{
  using namespace std;
  ifstream inFile;
  string fileName;
  int row, col;
  cout << "Enter file name" << endl;
  cin >> fileName;
  inFile.open(fileName.c_str());
  Maze maze(inFile);
  maze.Print();
  cout << "Enter row and col of starting position: "
       << endl<< "negative row stops the processing." << endl;
  cin >> row;
  while (row > 0)
  {
    Maze anotherMaze = maze;
    cin >> col;
    if (anotherMaze.TryToEscape(row, col))
      cout << "Free" << endl;
    else
      cout << "Trapped" << endl;
      cout << "Enter row and col of starting position: "
        << endl<< "negative row stops the processing."
        << endl;
    cin >> row;
  }
  return 0;
}
```

```
Enter file name
maze1
Maze
 O O + E O
 O + O O +
 O O O O +
 + + O + +
Enter row and col of starting position;
negative row stops the processing.
1 1
```

```
Free
Enter row and col of starting position;
negative row stops the processing.
1 5
Free
Enter row and col of starting position;
negative row stops the processing.
4 1
Trapped
Enter row and col of starting position;
negative row stops the processing.
1 5
Free
Enter row and col of starting position;
negative row stops the processing.
1 4
Free
Enter row and col of starting position;
negative row stops the processing.
2 2
Trapped
Enter row and col of starting position;
negative row stops the processing.
3 3
Free
Enter row and col of starting position;
negative row stops the processing.
-1

Process has exited with status 0.
```

If you look at the maze used as an example, you can tell that all Open cells lead to the exit; only starting positions that contain a hedge return "Trapped." You are asked in the exercises to design a maze that contains a starting point that is Open and returns "Trapped."

Summary

Recursion is a very powerful computing tool. Used appropriately, it can simplify the solution of a problem, often resulting in shorter, more easily understood source code. As usual in computing, tradeoffs are necessary: Recursive functions are often less efficient, in terms of both time and space, due to the overhead associated with many levels of function calls. How expensive this cost is depends on the computer system and the compiler.

A recursive solution to a problem must have at least one base case—that is, a case where the solution is derived nonrecursively. Without a base case, the function will recurse forever (or at least until the computer runs out of memory). The recursive solution also has one or more general cases that include recursive calls to the function. The recursive calls must involve a "smaller caller." One (or more) of the actual parameter values must change in each recursive call to redefine the problem to be smaller than it was on the previous call. Thus each recursive call leads the solution of the problem toward the base case(s).

A typical implementation of recursion involves the use of a stack. Each call to a function generates an activation record to contain its return address, parameters, and local variables. The activation records are accessed in a last in, first out manner. Thus a stack is the choice of data structure.

Recursion can be supported by systems and languages that use dynamic storage allocation. The function parameters and local variables are not bound to addresses until an activation record is created at run time. Thus multiple copies of the intermediate values of recursive calls to the function can be supported, as new activation records are created for them.

With static storage allocation, in contrast, a single location is reserved at compile time for each parameter and local variable of a function. No place is provided to store any intermediate values calculated by repeated nested calls to the same function. Therefore, systems and languages with only static storage allocation cannot support recursion.

When recursion is not possible or appropriate, a recursive algorithm can be implemented nonrecursively by using a looping structure and, in some cases, by pushing and popping relevant values onto a stack. This programmer-controlled stack explicitly replaces the system's run-time stack. While such nonrecursive solutions are often more efficient in terms of time and space, they usually involve a tradeoff in terms of the elegance of the solution.

Exercises

1. Explain what is meant by the following:
   a. base case
   b. general (or recursive) case
   c. run-time stack
   d. binding time
   e. tail recursion
2. True or false? If false, correct the statement. *Recursive functions:*
   a. often have fewer local variables than the equivalent nonrecursive routines.
   b. generally use *while* or *for* statements as their main control structure.
   c. are possible only in languages with static storage allocation.
   d. should be used whenever execution speed is critical.
   e. are always shorter and clearer than the equivalent nonrecursive routines.
   f. must always contain a path that does not contain a recursive call.
   g. are always less "efficient," in terms of Big-O complexity.

3. Use the Three-Question Method to verify the `ValueInList` function described in this chapter.
4. Describe the Three-Question Method of verifying recursive routines in relation to an inductive proof.
5. Which data structure would you most likely see in a nonrecursive implementation of a recursive algorithm?
6. Using the recursive function `RevPrint` as a model, write the recursive function `PrintList`, which traverses the elements in the list in forward order. Does one of these routines constitute a better use of recursion? If so, which one?

Use the following function in answering Exercises 7 and 8:

```
int Puzzle(int base, int limit)
{
  if (base > limit)
    return -1;
  else
    if (base == limit)
      return 1;
    else
      return base*Puzzle(base+1, limit);
}
```

7. Identify the following:
   a. the base case(s) of the function `Puzzle`
   b. the general case(s) of the function `Puzzle`
8. Show what would be written by the following calls to the recursive function `Puzzle`:
   a. `cout << Puzzle(14, 10);`
   b. `cout << Puzzle(4, 7);`
   c. `cout << Puzzle(0, 0);`
9. Given the following function:

```
int Func(int num)
{
  if (num == 0)
    return 0;
  else
    return num + Fun(num + 1);
}
```

a. Is there a constraint on the values that can be passed as a parameter for this function to pass the smaller-caller test?
b. Is `Func(7)` a good call? If so, what is returned from the function?
c. Is `Func(0)` a good call? If so, what is returned from the function?
d. Is `Func(-5)` a good call? If so, what is returned from the function?

10. Put comments on the following routines to identify the base and general cases and explain what each routine does.

a.
```
int Power(int base, int exponent)
{
  if (exponent == 0)
    return 1;
  else
    return base * Power(base, exponent-1);
}
```

b.
```
int Factorial(int number)
{
  if (num > 0)
    return num * Factorial(num - 1);
  else
    if (num == 0)
      return 1;
}
```

c.
```
void Sort(int values[], int fromIndex, int toIndex)
{
  int maxIndex;

  if (fromIndex != toIndex)
  {
    maxIndex =  MaxPosition(values, fromIndex, toIndex);
    Swap(values[maxIndex], values[toIndex]);
    Sort(values, fromIndex, toIndex - 1);
  }
}
```

11. a. Fill in the blanks to complete the following recursive function:

```
int Sum(int info[], int fromIndex, int toIndex)
// Computes the sum of the items between fromIndex and toIndex.
{
  if (fromIndex __________ toIndex)
    return ________________________;
  else
    return ________________________;
}
```

b. Which is the base case and which is the general case?

c. Show how you would call this function to sum all the elements in an array called `numbers`, which contains elements indexed from 0 to `MAX_ITEMS - 1`.

d. What run-time problem might you experience with this function as it is now coded?

12. You must assign the grades for a programming class. The class is studying recursion, and students have been given this simple assignment: Write a recursive function `SumSquares` that takes a pointer to a linked list of integer elements and returns the sum of the squares of the elements.

Example:

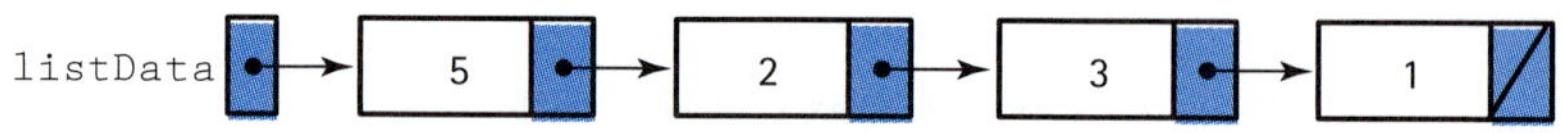

`SumSquares(listPtr)` yields (5 * 5) + (2 * 2) + (3 * 3) + (1 * 1) = 39

Assume that the list is not empty.

You have received quite a variety of solutions. Grade the functions that follow, marking errors where you see them.

a.
```
int SumSquares(NodeType* list)
{
  return 0;
  if (list != NULL)
    return (list->info*list->info) + SumSquares(list->next));
}
```

b.
```
int SumSquares(NodeType* list)
{
  int sum = 0;
  while (list != NULL)
  {
    sum = list->info + sum;
    list = list->next;
  }
  return sum;
}
```

c.
```
int SumSquares(NodeType* list)
{
  if (list == NULL)
    return 0;
  else
    return list->info*list->info + SumSquares(list->next);
}
```

d.
```
int SumSquares(NodeType* list)
{
  if (list->next == NULL)
    return list->info*list->info;
  else
    return list->info*list->info + SumSquares(list->next);
}
```

e.
```
int SumSquares(NodeType* list)
{
  if (list == NULL)
    return 0;
  else
    return (SumSquares(list->next) * SumSquares(list->next));
}
```

13. The Fibonacci sequence is the series of integers

`0, 1, 1, 2, 3, 5, 8, 21, 34, 55, 89 ...`

See the pattern? Each element in the series is the sum of the preceding two items. There is a recursive formula for calculating the *n*th number of the sequence (the 0th number if Fib(0) = 0):

$$\text{Fib}(N) = \begin{cases} N, & \text{if } N = 0 \text{ or } 1 \\ \text{Fib}(N-2) + \text{Fib}(N-1), & \text{if } N > 1 \end{cases}$$

a. Write a recursive version of the function `Fibonacci`.

b. Write a nonrecursive version of the function `Fibonacci`.

c. Write a driver to test the recursive and iterative versions of the function `Fibonacci`.

d. Compare the recursive and iterative versions for efficiency. (Use words, not Big-O notation.)

e. Can you think of a way to make the recursive version more efficient?

14. The following defines a function that calculates an approximation of the square root of a number, starting with an approximate answer (`approx`), within the specified tolerance (`tol`).

$$\text{SqrRoot(number, approx, tol)} = \begin{cases} \text{approx}, & \text{if } |\text{approx}^2 - \text{number}| <= \text{tol} \\ \text{SqrRoot(number, (approx}^2 + \text{number})/(2*\text{approx}), \text{tol}), & \text{if } |\text{approx}^2 - \text{number}| > \text{tol} \end{cases}$$

a. What limitations must be made on the values of the parameters if this method is to work correctly?

b. Write a recursive version of the function `SqrRoot`.

c. Write a nonrecursive version of the function `SqrRoot`.

d. Write a driver to test the recursive and iterative versions of the function `SqrRoot`.

15. A sequential search member function of `SortedType` has the following prototype:

```
void SortedType::Search(int value, bool& found);
```

a. Write the function definition as a recursive search, assuming a linked list implementation.

b. Write the function definition as a recursive search, assuming an array-based implementation.

16. We want to count the number of possible paths to move from row 1, column 1 to row *N*, column *N* in a two-dimensional grid. Steps are restricted to going up or to the right, but not diagonally. The illustration that follows shows three of many paths, if $N = 10$:

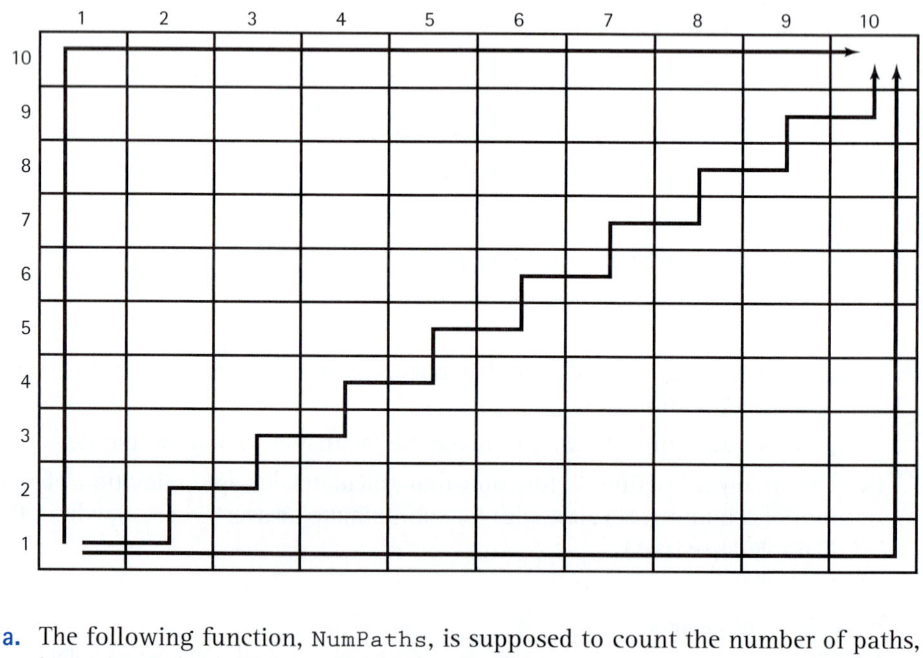

a. The following function, `NumPaths`, is supposed to count the number of paths, but it has some problems. Debug the function.

```
int NumPaths(int row, int col, int n)
{
  if (row == n)
```

```
        return 1;
      else
        if (col == n)
          return NumPaths + 1;
        else
          return NumPaths(row + 1, col) * NumPaths(row, col + 1);
    }
```

b. After you have corrected the function, trace the execution of `NumPaths` with `n = 4` by hand. Why is this algorithm inefficient?

c. You can improve the efficiency of this operation by keeping intermediate values of `NumPaths` in a two-dimensional array of integer values. This approach keeps the function from having to recalculate values that it has already figured out. Design and code a version of `NumPaths` that uses this approach.

d. Show an invocation of the version of `NumPaths` you developed in part (c), including any array initialization necessary.

e. How do the two versions of `NumPaths` compare in terms of time efficiency? Space efficiency?

17. Given the following function:[2]

```
int Ulam(int num)
{
  if (num < 2)
    return 1;
  else
    if (num % 2 == 0)
      return Ulam(num / 2);
    else
      return Ulam (3 * num + 1);
}
```

a. What problems come up in verifying this function?

b. How many recursive calls are made by the following initial calls:

```
cout   << Ulam(7)   << endl;
cout   << Ulam(8)   << endl;
cout   << Ulam(15)  << endl;
```

18. Explain the relationship between dynamic storage allocation and recursion.

---

[2]One of our reviewers pointed out that the proof of termination of this algorithm is a celebrated open question in mathematics. See *Programming Pearls* by Jon Bentley for a discussion and further references.

19. What do we mean by binding time, and what does it have to do with recursion?

20. Given the following values in `list`:

`list`

`.length` 10

	[0]	[1]	[2]	[3]	[4]	[5]	[6]	[7]	[8]	[9]
`.info`	2	6	9	14	23	65	92	96	99	100

Show the contents of the run-time stack during the execution of this call to `BinarySearch`:

```
BinarySearch(info, 99, 0, 9);
```

21. The parameter to the following two recursive routines is a pointer to a singly linked list of numbers, whose elements are unique (no duplicates) and unsorted. Each node in the list contains two members, `info` (a number) and `next` (a pointer to the next node).

    a. Write a recursive value-returning function, `MinLoc`, that receives a pointer to a list of unsorted numbers and returns a pointer to the node that contains the minimum value in the list.

    b. Write a recursive void function, `Sort`, that receives a pointer to an unsorted list of numbers and reorders the values in the list from smallest to largest. This function may call the recursive `MinLoc` function that you wrote in part (a). (*Hint:* It is easier to swap the values in the `info` part of the nodes than to reorder the nodes in the list.)

22. True or false? If false, correct the statement. *A recursive solution should be used when:*

    a. computing time is critical.

    b. the nonrecursive solution would be longer and more difficult to write.

    c. computing space is critical.

    d. your instructor says to use recursion.

23. Design a maze in which there are starting positions that return "Trapped" when the starting position is Open.

24. True or False? All recursive algorithms need a base case even if it is "do nothing."

25. True or False? The general case is what allows recursion to terminate.

26. True or False? The base case is what allows recursion to terminate.

27. A recursive function must always contain both a base case and a general case although the base case may be empty.

28. Both void and value-returning functions can be recursive.

29. The body of a recursive function can include many calls to itself.
30. If a program halts and an error message similar to "RUN-TIME STACK OVERFLOW" appears, the cause may be infinite recursion.
31. In general, a nonrecursive solution to a problem is more memory efficient than a recursive solution.
32. Tail recursion often indicates that the problem could be solved more efficiently using iteration.
33. There usually are more local variables in a recursive routine than in the equivalent iterative routine.

chapter 8

Binary Search Trees

Goals

After studying this chapter, you should be able to

- Define and use the following terminology:
  - Binary tree
  - Binary search tree
  - Ancestor
  - Root
  - Parent
  - Child
  - Descendant
  - Level
  - Height
  - Subtree
- Define a binary search tree at the logical level
- Show what a binary search tree would look like after a series of insertions and deletions
- Implement the following binary search tree algorithms in C++:
  - Putting an element into the tree
  - Deleting an element from the tree
  - Getting an element from the tree
  - Modifying an element in the tree
  - Copying a tree
  - Traversing a tree in preorder, inorder, and postorder
- Discuss the Big-O efficiency of a given binary search tree operation
- Describe an algorithm for balancing a binary search tree
- Show how a binary tree can be represented in an array, with implicit positional links between the elements
- Define the terms *full binary tree* and *complete binary tree*

So far, we have discussed some of the advantages of using a linear linked list to store sorted information. One drawback of using a linear linked list, however, is the time it takes to search a long list. A sequential or linear search of (possibly) all the nodes in the entire list is an O(*N*) operation. In Chapter 3, we saw how a binary search could find an element in a sorted list stored sequentially in an array; this kind of search is an $O(\log_2 N)$ operation. It would be nice if we could binary search a linked list, but no practical way exists to find the midpoint of a linked list of nodes. We can, however, reorganize the list's elements into a linked structure that is just perfect for binary searching: the *binary search tree*. The binary search tree provides us with a structure that retains the flexibility of a linked list but allows for quicker $O(\log_2 N)$ access to any node in the list.

This chapter introduces some basic tree vocabulary and then develops the algorithms and implementations of the operations needed to use a binary search tree.

8.1 Trees

A binary search tree is a structure with two properties: a shape property and a property that relates the keys of the elements in the structure. We look first at the shape property.

Each node in a singly linked list may point to one other node: the one that follows it. Thus a singly linked list is a *linear* structure; each node in the list (except the last) has a unique successor. In contrast, a binary tree is a structure in which each node is capable of having two successor nodes, called *children*. Each of the children, being nodes in the binary tree, can also have two child nodes, and these children can also have two children, and so on, giving the tree its branching structure. The "beginning" of the tree is a unique starting node called the root.

Binary tree A structure with a unique starting node (the root), in which each node is capable of having two child nodes, and in which a unique path exists from the root to every other node

Root The top node of a tree structure; a node with no parent

Leaf node A tree node that has no children

Figure 8.1 depicts a binary tree. The root node of this binary tree contains the value A. Each node in the tree may have 0, 1, or 2 children. The node to the left of a node, if it exists, is called its *left child*. For instance, the left child of the root node contains the value B. The node to the right of a node, if it exists, is its *right child*. The right child of the root node contains the value C. The root node is the parent of the nodes containing B and C. (Earlier textbooks used the terms *left son, right son,* and *father* to describe these relationships.) If a node in the tree has no children, it is called a leaf. For instance, the nodes containing G, H, E, I, and J are leaf nodes.

In addition to specifying that a node may have as many as two children, the definition of a binary tree states that a unique path exists from the root to every other node. Thus every node (except the root) has a unique parent. In the structure pictured at the top of the next page, the nodes have the correct number of children, but the unique path rule is violated: Two paths from the root to the node containing D exist. Therefore this structure is not a tree at all, let alone a binary tree.

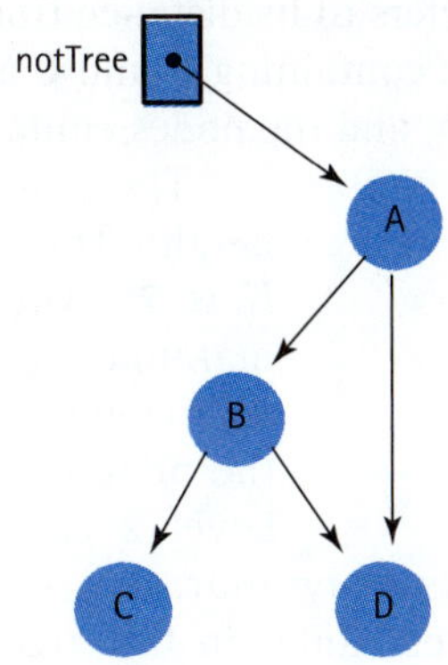

In Figure 8.1, each of the root node's children is itself the root of a smaller binary tree, or subtree. The root node's left child, containing B, is the root of its *left subtree*, and the right child, containing C, is the root of its *right subtree*. In fact, any node in the tree can be considered the root node of a subtree. The subtree whose root node has the value B also includes the nodes with values D, G, H, and E. These nodes are the *descendants* of the node containing B. The descendants of the node containing C are the nodes with the values F, I, and J. A node is the *ancestor* of another node if it is the parent of the node, or the parent of some other ancestor of that node. (Yes, this is a recursive definition.) In Figure 8.1, the ancestors of the node with the value G are the nodes containing D, B, and A. Obviously, the root of the tree is the ancestor of every other node in the tree.

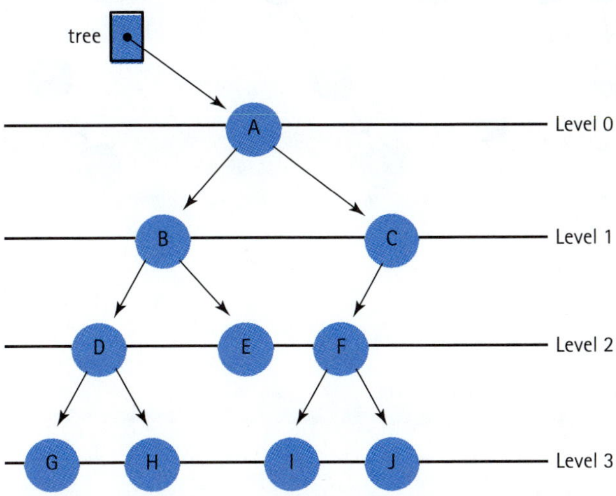

Figure 8.1 *A binary tree*

The level of a node refers to its distance from the root. If we designate the level of the root as 0 (zero), the nodes containing B and C are Level 1 nodes; the nodes containing D, E, and F are Level 2 nodes; and the nodes containing G, H, I, and J are Level 3 nodes.

Level The distance of a node from the root; the root is level 0

Height The maximum level

The maximum level in a tree determines its height. The maximum number of nodes at any level N is 2^N. Often, however, levels do not contain the maximum number of nodes. For instance, in Figure 8.1, Level 2 could contain four nodes, but because the node containing C in Level 1 has only one child, Level 2 contains three nodes. Level 3, which could contain eight nodes, has only four. We could construct many differently shaped binary trees out of the ten nodes in this tree. Figure 8.2 illustrates a few variations. You can readily see that the maximum number of levels in a binary tree with N nodes is N. What is the minimum number of levels? If we fill the tree by giving every node in each level two children until we run out of nodes, the tree has $\log_2 N + 1$ lev-

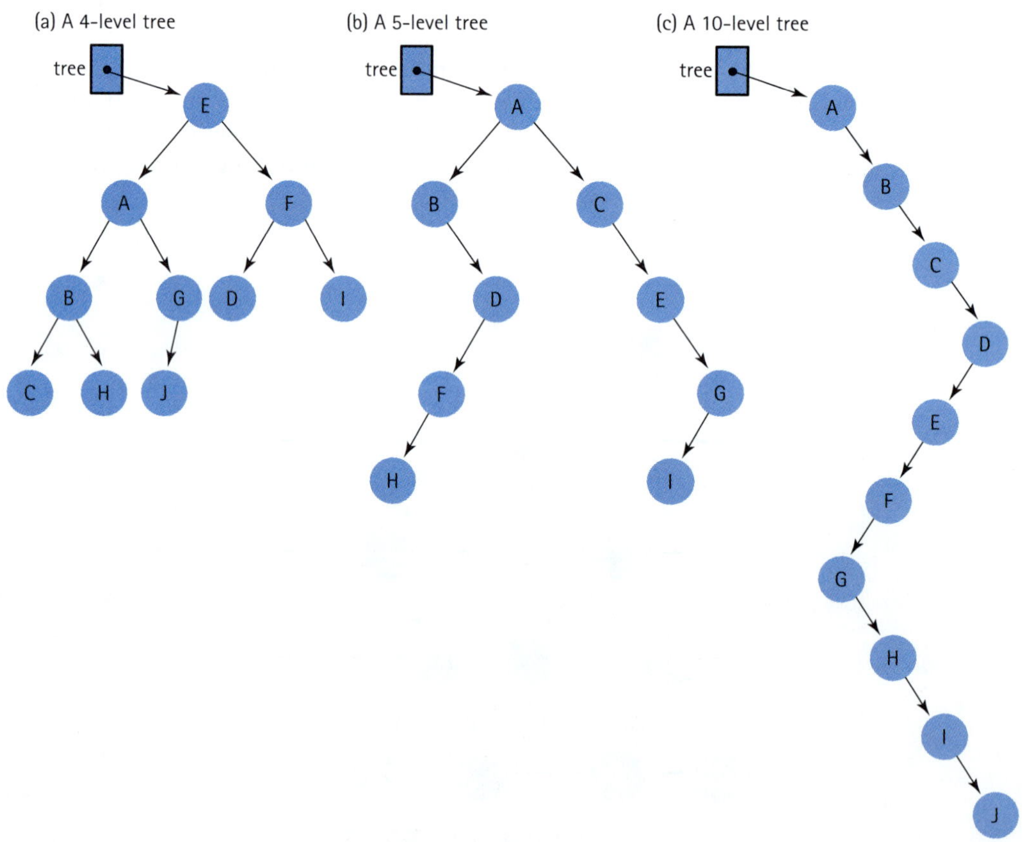

Figure 8.2 *Binary trees with ten nodes*

els (Figure 8.2a). Demonstrate this fact to yourself by drawing "full" trees with 8 [$\log_2(8) = 3$] and 16 [$\log_2(16) = 4$] nodes. What if there are 7, 12, or 18 nodes?

The height of a tree is the critical factor in determining how efficiently we can search for elements. Consider the maximum-height tree in Figure 8.2c. If we begin searching at the root node and follow the pointers from one node to the next, accessing the node with the value J (the farthest from the root) is an $O(N)$ operation—no better than searching a linear list! On the other hand, given the minimum-height tree depicted in Figure 8.2a, to access the node containing J, we have to look at only three other nodes—the ones containing E, A, and G—before we find J. Thus, if the tree is of minimum height, its structure supports $O(\log_2 N)$ access to any element.

The arrangement of the values in the tree pictured in Figure 8.2a does not actually lend itself to quick searching. Suppose we want to find the value G. We begin searching at the root of the tree. This node contains E, not G, so we need to keep searching. But which of its children should we examine next, the right or the left? The nodes are not organized in any special order, so we have to check both subtrees. We could search the tree, level by level, until we come across the desired value. That is an $O(N)$ search operation, which is no better than searching a linked list!

To support $O(\log_2 N)$ searching, we add a special property based on the relationship among the keys of the items in the tree. We put all the nodes with values smaller than the value in the root into its left subtree, and all the nodes with values larger than the value in the root into its right subtree. Figure 8.3 shows the nodes from Figure 8.2a

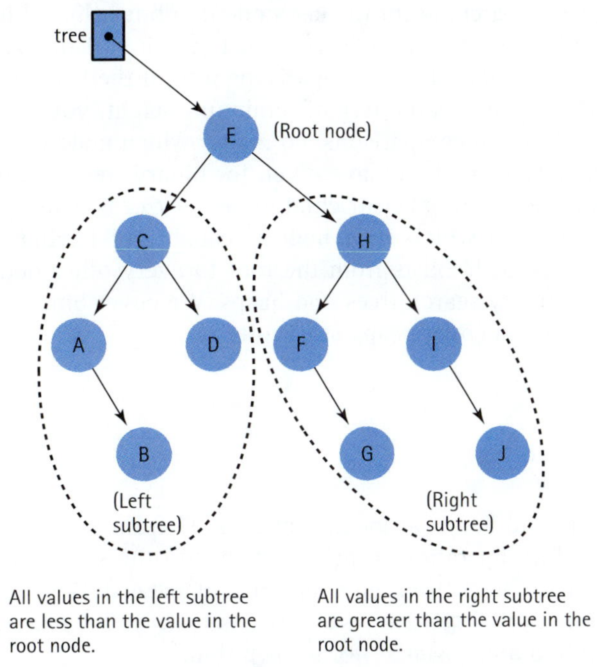

Figure 8.3 *A binary search tree*

rearranged to satisfy this property. The root node, which contains E, accesses two subtrees. The left subtree contains all values smaller than E and the right subtree contains all values larger than E.

To search for the value G, we look first in the root node. G is larger than E, so we know that G must be in the root node's right subtree. The right child of the root node contains H. Now what? Do we go to the right or to the left? This subtree is also arranged according to the binary search property: The nodes with smaller values are found to the left and the nodes with larger values are found to the right. The value of this node, H, is greater than G, so we search to its left. The left child of this node contains the value F, which is smaller than G, so we reapply the rule and move to the right. The node to the right contains G; we have found the node we were seeking.

> **Binary search tree** A binary tree in which the key value in any node is greater than the key value in its left child and any of its children (the nodes in the left subtree) and less than the key value in its right child and any of its children (the nodes in the right subtree)

A binary tree with this special property is called a binary search tree. Like any binary tree, it achieves its branching structure by allowing each node to have a maximum of two child nodes. It achieves its easy-to-search structure by maintaining the binary search property: The left child of any node (if one exists) is the root of the subtree that contains only values smaller than the node. The right child of any node (if one exists) is the root of the subtree that contains only values that are larger than the node.

Four comparisons instead of ten doesn't sound like such a big deal, but as the number of elements in the structure increases, the difference becomes more impressive. In the worst case—searching for the last node in a linear linked list—you must look at every node in the list; on the average, you must search half the list. If the list contains 1,000 nodes, you must make 1,000 comparisons to find the last node! If the 1,000 nodes were arranged in a binary search tree of minimum height, you would never make more than 10 ($\log_2(1{,}000) < 10$) comparisons, no matter which node you were seeking!

The definitions that we have given for binary trees can be extended to trees whose nodes can have any number of child nodes. A *tree* is a structure with a unique starting node (the root), in which each node is capable of having many child nodes, and in which a unique path exists from the root to every other node. In this book we restrict ourselves to binary search trees and heaps. We cover binary search trees in great depth in this chapter and cover heaps in Chapter 9.

8.2 Logical Level

We should be old hands at looking at an ADT from the logical level by now. We know that we need an operation to put an item into the structure (`PutItem`). We need to be able to delete an item from the structure (`DeleteItem`). We need the usual complement of observer functions (`GetItem`, `IsEmpty`, `IsFull`, and `GetLength`). Let's also include a `Print` operation and a `MakeEmpty` operation.

Traversals are more complicated in a binary search tree. In the List ADTs we have examined so far, we have traversed the structure in only two ways: from front to back or from back to front. In all but the `SpecializedList` class, we have started at the beginning of the list and continued until we accessed all the items. In fact, there are many ways to traverse the items in a tree. We let the client determine which way to traverse the tree by passing a traversal name as a parameter to the ResetTree and GetNextItem operations. We discuss traversals in much more detail later in the chapter.

Binary Search Tree Specification

Structure: The placement of each element in the binary tree must satisfy the binary search property: The value of the key of an element is greater than the value of the key of any element in its left subtree, and less than the value of the key of any element in its right subtree.

Operations (provided by TreeADT):

Assumption: Before any call is made to a tree operation, the tree has been declared and a constructor has been applied.

MakeEmpty

Function: Initializes tree to empty state.

Postcondition: Tree exists and is empty.

Boolean IsEmpty

Function: Determines whether tree is empty.

Postcondition: Function value = (tree is empty).

Boolean IsFull

Function: Determines whether tree is full.

Postcondition: Function value = (tree is full).

int GetLength

Function: Determines the number of elements in tree.

Postcondition: Function value = number of elements in tree.

int GetLength(ItemType item, Boolean& found)

Function: Retrieves item whose key matches item's key (if present).

Precondition: Key member of item is initialized.

Postconditions: If there is an element someItem whose key matches item's key, then found = true and a copy of someItem is returned; otherwise, found = false and item is returned. Tree is unchanged.

PutItem(ItemType item)

Function: Adds item to tree.

Preconditions: Tree is not full.
item is not in tree.

Postconditions: item is in tree.
Binary search property is maintained.

DeleteItem(ItemType item)

Function: Deletes the element whose key matches item's key.

Preconditions: Key member of item is initialized.
One and only one element in tree has a key matching item's key.

Postcondition: No element in tree has a key matching item's key.

Print(ofstream& outFile)

Function: Prints the values in the tree in ascending key order on outFile.

Precondition: outFile has been opened for writing.

Postconditions: Items in the tree have been printed in ascending key order.
outFile is still open.

ResetTree(OrderType order)

Function: Initializes current position for an iteration through the tree in OrderType order.

Postcondition: Current position is prior to root of tree.

ItemType GetNextItem(OrderType order, Boolean& finished)

Function: Gets the next element in tree.

Preconditions: Current position is defined.
Element at current position is not last in tree.

Postconditions: Current position is one position beyond current position at entry to GetNextItem.
finished = (current position is last in tree).
A copy of element at current position is returned.

8.3 Application Level

Although our implementation structure is quite different from any we have used before, we have changed the name of only one list operation: ResetTree has replaced ResetList. Of course, the algorithms we develop to implement the operations differ from those used for the list operations.

Replace the list operations with the corresponding tree operations in any of the applications that we have written for the other List ADTs and you have an application of the Binary Search Tree ADT. Although binary search trees are interesting mathematical objects, they are used mainly in computing as implementation structures for lists.

8.4 Implementation Level

We develop the algorithms for the operations specified for the Binary Search Tree ADT and represent the tree as a linked structure whose nodes are allocated dynamically. Because the binary search tree is inherently a recursive structure, we first implement the algorithms using recursive solutions. We then take the `PutItem` and `DeleteItem` functions and show how they can be implemented iteratively. Here is the first approximation for the class `TreeType`. If we need more data members, we can add them at a later time.

As with our first brush with linked lists, we choose not to make the class generic. Let's make this implementation be a tree of `char` values. You are asked to convert the class into a template class in the exercises.

```
#include <iostream>

struct TreeNode;

typedef char ItemType;
// Assumption:  ItemType is a type for which the operators "<"
//  and "==" are defined--either an appropriate built-in type or
//  a class that overloads these operators.

enum OrderType {PRE_ORDER, IN_ORDER, POST_ORDER};

class TreeType
{
public:
  TreeType();                        // Constructor.
  ~TreeType();                       // Destructor.
  TreeType(const TreeType& originalTree);  // Copy constructor.
  void operator=(TreeType& originalTree);
  void MakeEmpty();
  bool IsEmpty() const;
```

```
  bool IsFull() const;
  int GetLength() const;
  ItemType GetItem(ItemType item, bool& found);
  void PutItem(ItemType item);
  void DeleteItem(ItemType item);
  void ResetTree(OrderType order);
  ItemType GetNextItem (OrderType order,
       bool& finished);
  void Print(std::ofstream& outFile) const;
private:
  TreeNode* root;
};
```

Before we go on, we need to decide just what a node in the tree will look like. In our discussion of trees, we talked about right and left children. These structural pointers hold the tree together. We also need a place to store the user's data in the node, which we'll continue to call `info`. Figure 8.4 shows a picture of a node.

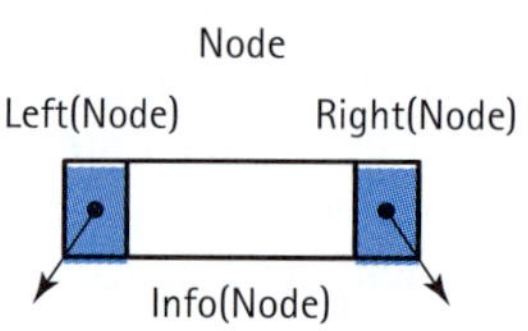

Figure 8.4 *Node terminology for a tree node*

Here is the definition of `TreeNode` that corresponds with the picture in Figure 8.4:

```
struct TreeNode
{
  ItemType info;
  TreeNode* left;
  TreeNode* right;
};
```

8.5 Recursive Binary Search Tree Operations

The `TreeType` class contains the external pointer to the list of nodes as a data member (`root`). The recursive implementations of the tree operations should recurse on nodes. Therefore each member function calls a secondary recursive function that takes `root` as a parameter. The names of the secondary functions make it clear which operations they help to implement. Because we must declare a function before we can use it, we must list each recursive function before the class function or we must list its prototype. Because it is easy to forget to place them in what seems like reverse order, it is a good idea to list the prototypes at the beginning of the implementation. We now develop these recursive functions.

Functions `IsFull` and `IsEmpty`

The observer functions are identical to those used in a linear linked implementation. We can just borrow the code, using the appropriate variable names.

```
bool TreeType::IsFull() const
// Returns true if the free store has no room for another node
//  and false otherwise.
{
  TreeNode* location;
  try
  {
    location = new TreeNode;
    delete location;
    return false;
  }
  catch(std::bad_alloc exception)
  {
    return true;
  }
}

bool TreeType::IsEmpty() const
// Returns true if the tree is empty and false otherwise.
{
  return root == NULL;
}
```

Function `GetLength`

In the function `Factorial`, we could determine the factorial of N if we knew the factorial of $N - 1$. The analogous statement here is that we can determine the number of nodes in the tree if we know the number of nodes in the left subtree and the number of nodes in the right subtree. That is, the number of nodes in a tree is

Number of nodes in left subtree + number of nodes in right subtree + 1

This is easy. Given a function `CountNodes` and a pointer to a tree node, we know how to calculate the number of nodes in a subtree; we call `CountNodes` recursively with the pointer to the subtree as the argument! Thus we know how to write the general case. What about the base case? A leaf node has no subtrees, so the number of nodes is 1. How do we determine that a node has no subtrees? The pointers to its children are

NULL. Let's try summarizing these observations into an algorithm, where `tree` is a pointer to a node.

```
CountNodes Version 1
if (Left(tree) is NULL) AND (Right(tree) is NULL)
    return 1
else
    return CountNodes(Left(tree)) + CountNodes(Right(tree)) + 1
```

Let's try this algorithm on a couple of examples to be sure that it works (see Figure 8.5).

We call `CountNodes` with the tree in Figure 8.5a. The left and right children of the root node (M) are not `NULL`, so we call `CountNodes` with the node containing A as the root. Because both the left and right children are `NULL` on this call, we send back the answer 1. Now we call `CountNodes` with the tree containing Q as the root. Both of its children are `NULL`, so we send back the answer 1. Now we can calculate the number of nodes in the tree with M in the root:

$$1 + 1 + 1 = 3$$

This seems to work correctly.

The tree in Figure 8.5b is not balanced; let's see if this condition poses a problem. It is not true that both children of the root (L) are `NULL`, so `CountNodes` is called with the left child as the argument. Oops—we do have a problem. The first statement checks

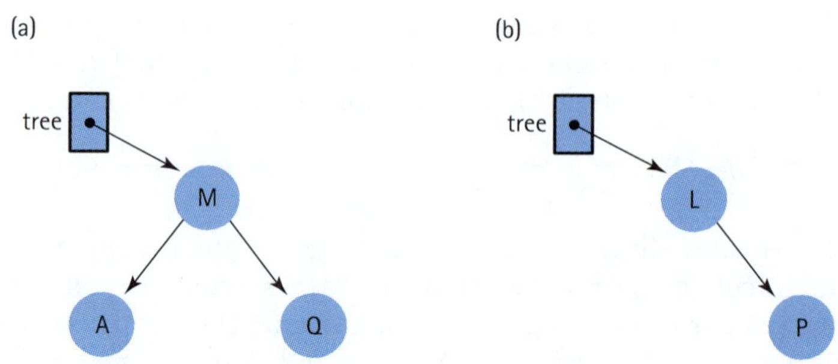

Figure 8.5 *Two binary search trees*

whether the children of the root are `NULL`, but the root itself is `NULL`. The function crashes when we try to access `tree->left` when `tree` is `NULL`. Well, we can check whether the left or right child is `NULL`, and not call `CountNodes` if it is.

CountNodes Version 2

```
if (Left(tree) is NULL) AND (Right(tree) is NULL)
    return 1
else if Left(tree) is NULL
    return CountNodes(Right(tree)) + 1
else if Right(tree) is NULL
    return CountNodes(Left(tree)) + 1
else return CountNodes(Left(tree)) + CountNodes(Right(tree)) + 1
```

Version 2 works correctly if the function `CountNodes` has a precondition that the tree is not empty. However, an initially empty tree causes a crash. We must check whether the tree is empty as the first statement in the algorithm and, if it is, return zero.

CountNodes Version 3

```
if tree is NULL
    return 0
else if (Left(tree) is NULL) AND (Right(tree) is NULL)
    return 1
else if Left(tree) is NULL
    return CountNodes(Right(tree)) + 1
else if Right(tree) is NULL
    return CountNodes(Left(tree)) + 1
else return CountNodes(Left(tree)) + CountNodes(Right(tree)) + 1
```

This algorithm certainly looks complicated. There must be a simpler solution—and there is. We can collapse the two base cases into one. There is no need to turn the leaf node into a special case. We can simply have one base case: An empty tree returns zero.

CountNodes Version 4

```
if tree is NULL
    return 0
else
    return CountNodes(Left(tree)) + CountNodes(Right(tree)) + 1
```

We have taken the time to work through the versions containing errors because they illustrate two important points about recursion with trees: (1) always check for the empty tree first, and (2) leaf nodes do not need to be treated as separate cases. Table 8.1 reviews the design notation and the corresponding C++ code.

Table 8.1 *Comparing Node Design Notation to C++ Code*

Design Notation	C++ Code
Node(location)	*location
Info(location)	location->info
Right(location)	location->right
Left(location)	location->left
Set Info(location) to value	location->info = value

Here is the function specification:

Function CountNodes

Definition:	Counts the number of nodes in tree.
Size:	Number of nodes in tree.
Base Case:	If tree is NULL, return 0.
General Case:	Return CountNodes(Left(tree)) + CountNodes(Right(tree)) + 1.

```
int CountNodes(TreeNode* tree);

int TreeType::GetLength() const
// Calls the recursive function CountNodes to count the
//  nodes in the tree.
{
```

```
  return CountNodes(root);
}

int CountNodes(TreeNode* tree)
// Post: Returns the number of nodes in the tree.
{
  if (tree == NULL)
    return 0;
  else
    return CountNodes(tree->left) + CountNodes(tree->right) + 1;
}
```

Function `GetItem`

At the beginning of this chapter, we demonstrated how to search for an element in a binary search tree. That is, we first check whether the item is in the root. If it is not, we compare the element with the root and look in either the left or the right subtree. This statement looks recursive. Let's apply the general guidelines for determining recursive solutions.

We have two choices for the size of the problem: the number of nodes in the tree or the number of nodes in the path from the root to the node for which we are searching (or until we reach an empty tree). Either is acceptable. The first is easier to say; the second is more precise. One base case arises when we find the element with the same key; another occurs when we determine that an element with the same key is not in the tree. The general case is either to retrieve the element from the left subtree or to retrieve it from the right subtree. Because the left or right subtree is at least one node smaller than the original tree and one level deeper, the size decreases with each call.

Only one question remains: How do we know there is no item with the same key in the tree? If the tree is empty, then it cannot contain an item with the same key as `item`'s key. Let's summarize these observations. We define a recursive routine `Retrieve`, which is invoked by the `GetItem` member function.

Function Retrieve

Definition:	Searches for an element with the same key as item's key. If it is found, store it into item.
Size:	Number of nodes in tree (or number of nodes in the path).
Base Cases:	(1) If item's key matches key in Info(tree), item is set to Info(tree) and found is true. (2) If tree = NULL, found is false.
General Case:	If item's key is less than key in Info(tree), Retrieve(Left(tree), item, found); else Retrieve(Right(tree), item, found).

```
void Retrieve(TreeNode* tree,
     ItemType& item, bool& found);

ItemType TreeType::GetItem(ItemType item, bool& found) const
// Calls recursive function Retrieve to search the tree for item.
{
  Retrieve(root, item, found);
  return item;
}

void Retrieve(TreeNode* tree,
     ItemType& item, bool& found)
// Recursively searches tree for item.
// Post: If there is an element someItem whose key matches item's,
//       found is true and item is set to a copy of someItem;
//       otherwise, found is false and item is unchanged.
{
  if (tree == NULL)
    found = false;                     // item is not found.
  else if (item < tree->info)
    Retrieve(tree->left, item, found); // Search left subtree.
  else if (item > tree->info)
    Retrieve(tree->right, item, found);// Search right subtree.
  else
  {
    item = tree->info;                 // item is found.
    found = true;
  }
}
```

Let's trace this operation, using the tree in Figure 8.6. We want to find the element with the key 18, so the nonrecursive call is

```
Retrieve(root, 18, found)
```

`root` is not `NULL`, and `18 > tree->info`, so we issue the first recursive call:

```
Retrieve(tree->right, 18, found)
```

`tree` now points to the node whose key is 20 so `18 < tree->info`. The next recursive call is

```
Retrieve(tree->left, 18, found)
```

Now `tree` points to the node with the key 18 so `18 = tree->info`. We set `found` and `item`, and the recursion halts.

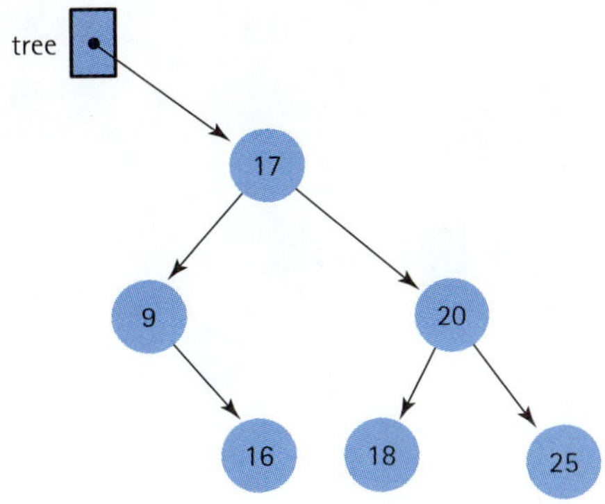

Figure 8.6 *Tracing the Retrieve operation*

Next, let's look at an example where the key is not found in the tree. We want to find the element with the key 7. The nonrecursive call is

```
Retrieve(root, 7, found)
```

`tree` is not `NULL` and `7 < tree->info`, so the first recursive call is

```
Retrieve(tree->left, 7, found)
```

`tree` points to the node that contains 9. `tree` is not `NULL`, and we issue the second recursive call:

```
Retrieve(tree->left, 7, found)
```

Now `tree` is `NULL`; we set `found` to `false`, and `item` is unchanged.

Function `PutItem`

To create and maintain the information stored in a binary search tree, we need an operation that inserts new nodes into the tree. We use the following insertion approach. A new node is always inserted into its appropriate position in the tree *as a leaf.* Figure 8.7 shows a series of insertions into a binary tree.

We want to write a function `Insert` that inserts an item into the tree, given a pointer to the root of the whole tree:

```
Insert(tree, item);
```

Before developing the algorithm, we want to reiterate that every node in a binary search tree is the root node of a binary search tree. In Figure 8.8a, we want to insert a node with the key value 13 into the tree whose root is the node containing 7. Because

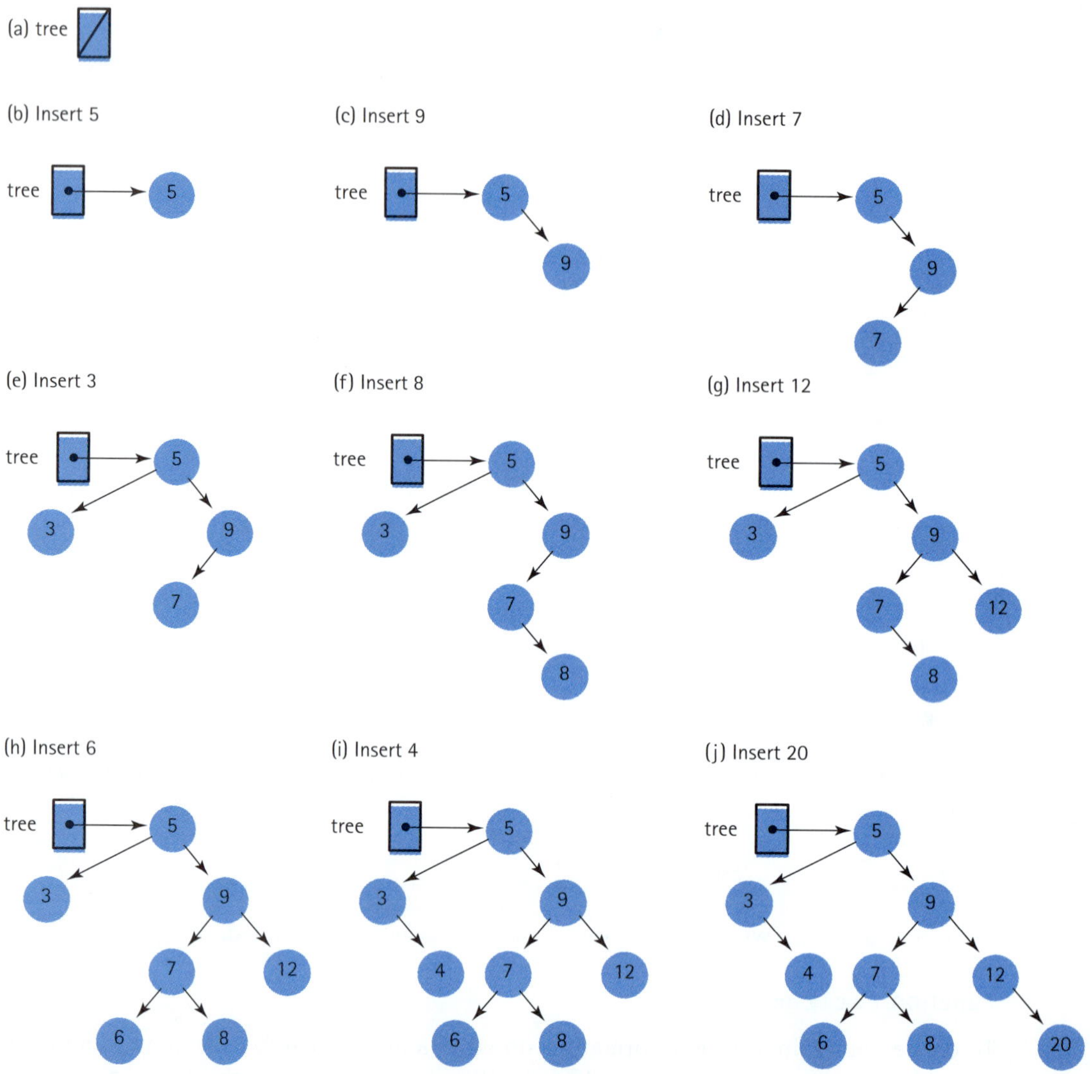

Figure 8.7 *Insertions into a binary search tree*

13 is greater than 7, we know that the new node belongs in the root node's right subtree. We have now redefined a smaller version of our original problem: We want to insert a node with the key value 13 into the tree *whose root is* `tree->right` (Figure 8.8b). Of course, we already have a function to insert elements into a binary search tree: `Insert`. `Insert` is called recursively:

```
Insert(tree->right, item);
```

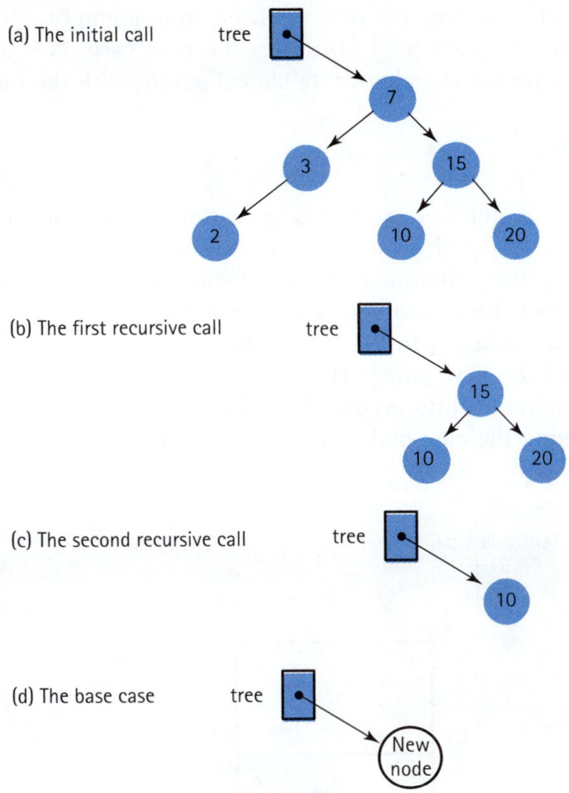

Figure 8.8 *The recursive Insert operation*

`Insert` begins its execution, looking for the place to insert `item` in the tree whose root is the node with the key value 15. We compare the key of `item` (13) to the key of the root node; 13 is less than 15, so we know that the new `item` belongs in the tree's left subtree. Again, we have redefined a smaller version of the problem: We want to insert a node with the key value 13 into the tree *whose root is tree->left* (Figure 8.8c). We call `Insert` recursively to perform this task. Remember that in this (recursive) execution of `Insert`, `tree` points to the node whose key is 15, not the original `tree` root:

```
Insert(tree->left, item);
```

Again, we recursively execute `Insert`. We compare the key of `item` to the key of the (current) root node and then call `Insert` to insert `item` into the correct subtree—the left subtree if `item`'s key is less than the key of the root node, and the right subtree if `item`'s key is greater than the key of the root node.

Where does it all end? There must be a base case, in which space for the new element is allocated and the value of `item` is copied into it. This case occurs when `tree` is

`NULL`, when the subtree we wish to insert into is empty. (Remember—we will add `item` as a leaf node.) Figure 8.8d illustrates the base case. We can create the new node and link it to the correct member of its logical parent with the following statement:

```
tree = new TreeNode;
```

Wait a minute! How does this execution of `new` link the new node to the existing tree? To understand this point, we must consider the meaning of `tree` in a recursive execution of the function. The last recursive call (Figure 8.9a) is `Insert(tree->right, item)`. Because `tree` is a reference parameter, in the final recursive execution of `Insert`, `tree` refers to the `right` data member of the node containing 10 (the logical parent of the new node). The statement executing `new` gets the address of the new node and stores it into `tree`, the `right` data member of the node containing 10, thereby linking the new node into the tree structure (Figure 8.9b). It is critical that `tree`

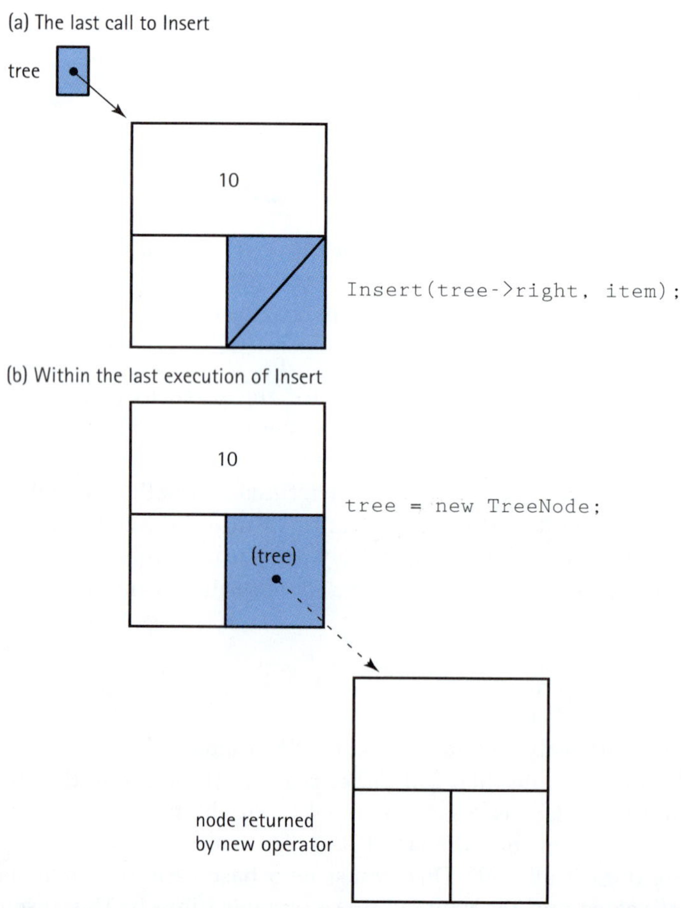

Figure 8.9 *The tree parameter is a pointer within the tree*

be a reference parameter. If it is not, the pointer passed to `Insert` will be a copy of the root of the subtree and not the location of the root itself.

This technique should sound familiar. We used it in Chapter 7 when we inserted an element into a linked implementation of a sorted list recursively. The important point to remember is that passing a pointer by *value* allows the function to change what the caller's pointer points to; passing a pointer by *reference* allows the function to change the caller's pointer as well as to change what the pointer points to. The recursive function is summarized as follows:

Function Insert

Definition:	Inserts item into binary search tree.
Size:	The number of elements in path from root to insertion place.
Base Case:	If tree is NULL, then allocate a new leaf to contain item.
General Cases:	(1) If item < Info(tree), then Insert(Left(tree), item). (2) If item > Info(tree), then Insert(Right(tree), item).

Here is the code that implements this recursive algorithm:

```
void Insert(TreeNode*& tree, ItemType item);

void TreeType::PutItem(ItemType item)
// Calls the recursive function Insert to insert item into tree.
{
  Insert(root, item);
}

void Insert(TreeNode*& tree, ItemType item)
// Inserts item into tree.
// Post:  item is in tree; search property is maintained.
{
  if (tree == NULL)
  {// Insertion place found.
    tree = new TreeNode;
    tree->right = NULL;
    tree->left = NULL;
    tree->info = item;
  }
  else if (item < tree->info)
```

```
    Insert(tree->left, item);      // Insert in left subtree.
  else
    Insert(tree->right, item);     // Insert in right subtree.
}
```

Insertion Order and Tree Shape Because we always add nodes as leaves, the order in which we insert nodes determines the shape of the tree. Figure 8.10 illustrates

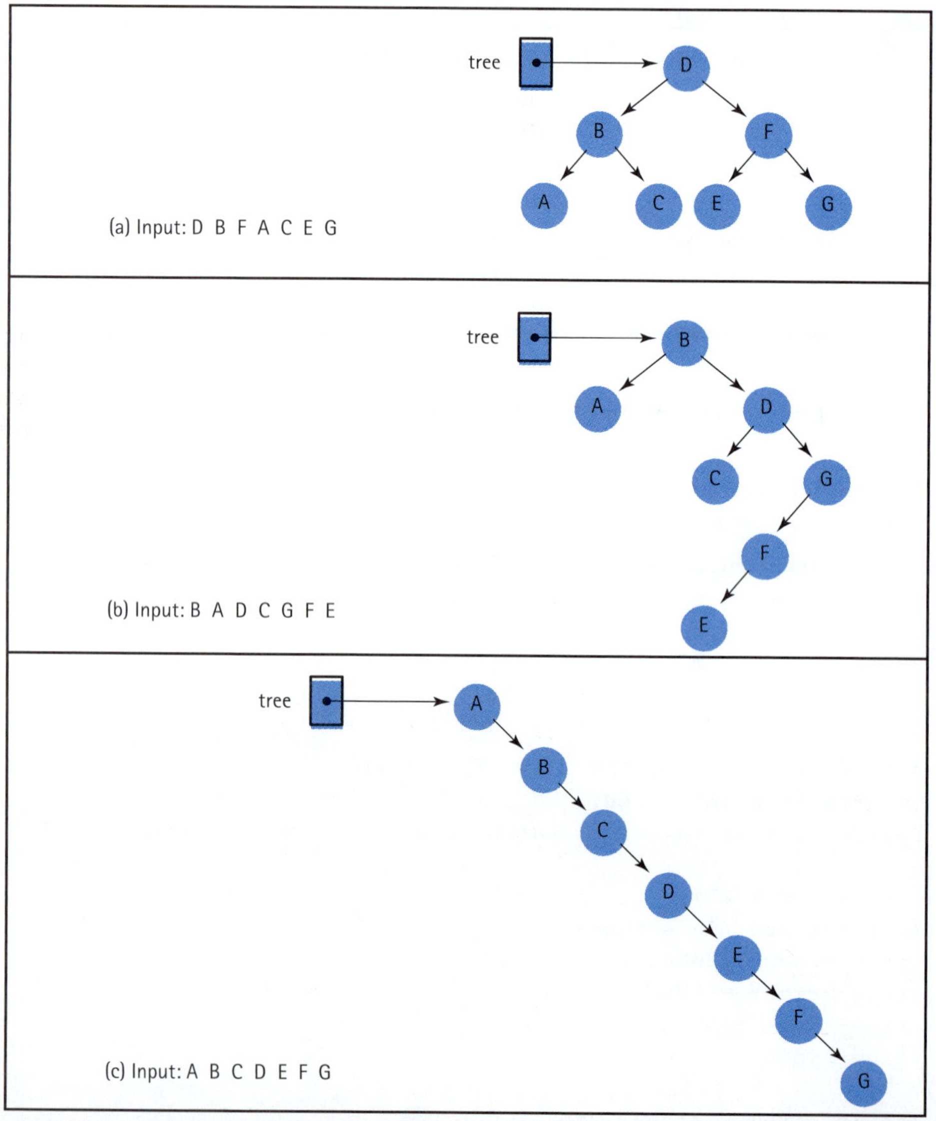

Figure 8.10 *The input order determines the shape of the tree*

how the same data, inserted in different orders, produce very differently shaped trees. If the values are inserted in order (or in reverse order), the tree will be very skewed. A random mix of the elements produces a shorter, "bushy" tree. Because the height of the tree determines the maximum number of comparisons in a search, the tree's shape has very important implications. Obviously, minimizing the height of the tree maximizes the efficiency of the search. Some algorithms adjust a tree to make its shape more desirable; these schemes are subjects for more advanced courses.

Function `DeleteItem`

`Delete` (the recursive helper function for `DeleteItem`) receives the external pointer to a binary search tree and an item, and then finds and deletes the node matching the item's key from the tree. According to the specifications of the operation, an item with the same key exists in the tree. These specifications suggest a two-part operation:

Delete
Find the node in the tree
Delete the node from the tree

We know how to find the node; we did it in `Retrieve`. The second part of the operation—deleting this node from the tree—is more complicated. This task varies according to the position of the node in the tree. Obviously, it is simpler to delete a leaf node than to delete the root of the tree. In fact, we can break down the deletion algorithm into three cases, depending on the number of children linked to the node we want to delete:

1. *Deleting a leaf (no children):* As shown in Figure 8.11, deleting a leaf is simply a matter of setting the appropriate link of its parent to `NULL` and then disposing of the unnecessary node.
2. *Deleting a node with only one child:* The simple solution for deleting a leaf does not suffice for deleting a node with a child, because we don't want to lose all of its descendants from the tree. Instead, we want the pointer from the parent to skip over the deleted node and point to the child of the node we intend to delete. We then dispose of the unwanted node (see Figure 8.12).
3. *Deleting a node with two children:* This case is the most complicated because we cannot make the parent of the deleted node point to *both* of the deleted node's children. The tree must remain a binary tree, and the search property must remain intact. We have several ways to accomplish this deletion. The method we use does

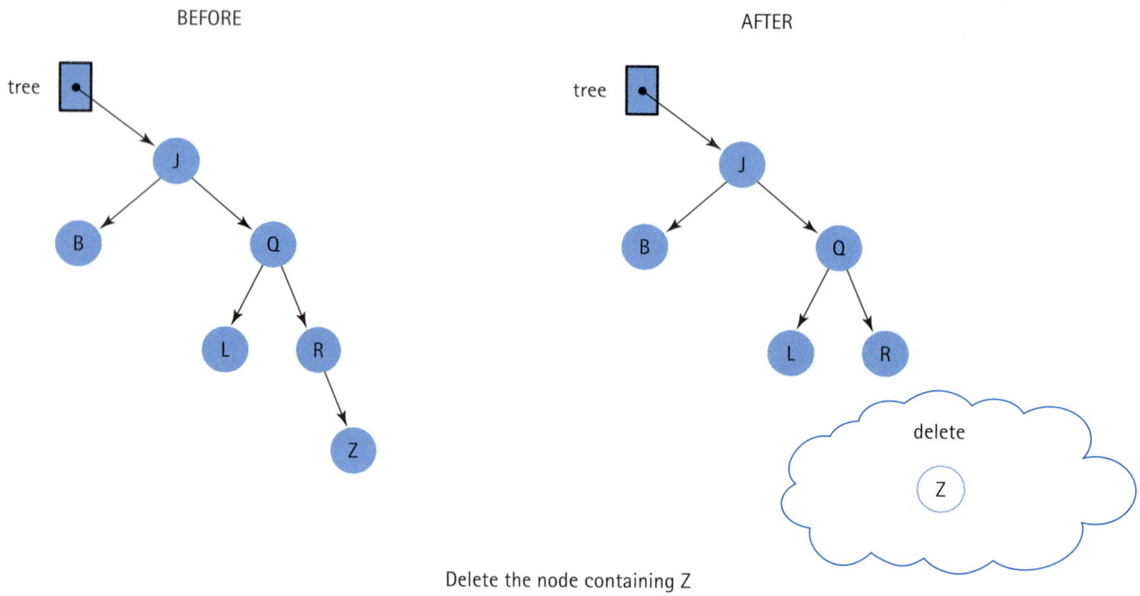

Delete the node containing Z

Figure 8.11 *Deleting a leaf node*

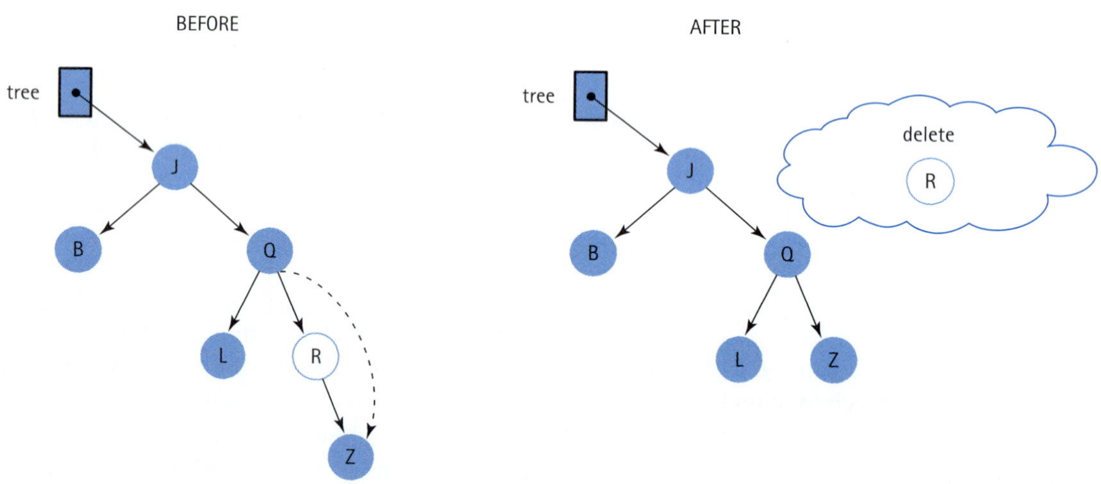

Delete the node containing R

Figure 8.12 *Deleting a node with one child*

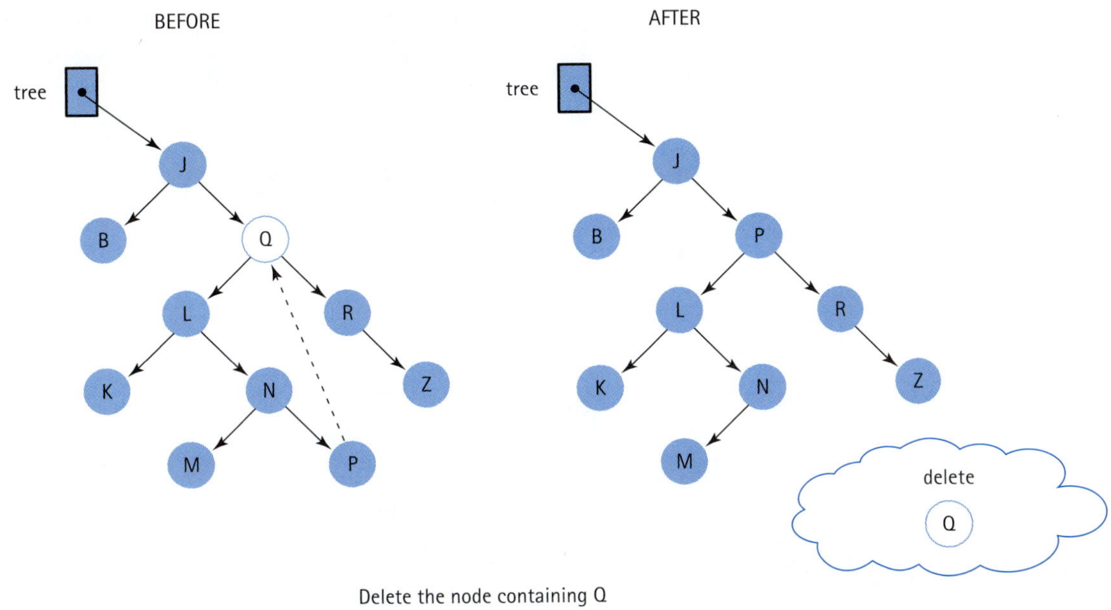

Figure 8.13 *Deleting a node with two children*

not delete the *node* but rather replaces its `info` data member with the `info` data member from another node in the tree that maintains the search property. We then delete this other node.

Which element could we use to replace the deleted `item` that would maintain the search property? The elements whose keys immediately precede or follow `item`'s—that is, `item`'s logical predecessor or successor. We replace the `info` data member of the node we wish to delete with the `info` data member of its logical predecessor—the node whose key is closest in value to, but less than, the key of the node to be deleted. Look at Figure 8.7j and locate the logical predecessor of nodes 5, 9, and 7. Do you see the pattern? The logical predecessor of 5 is the largest value in 5's left subtree. The logical predecessor of 9 is the largest value in 9's left subtree. The logical predecessor of 7 is 6, the largest value in 7's left subtree. This replacement value is found in a node with either zero or one child. We then delete the node originally containing the replacement value by changing one of its parent's pointers (see Figure 8.13). Figure 8.14 shows examples of all of these types of deletions.

Clearly, the delete task involves changing pointers of the *parent* of the node to be deleted. If our recursive algorithm passes `tree` as a reference parameter, then `tree` itself is the parent that we must change. Let's look at the three cases in terms of our implementation.

If both child pointers are `NULL`, the node is a leaf, so we just set `tree` to `NULL`. If one child pointer is `NULL`, we set `tree` to the other child pointer. If neither child pointer is `NULL`, we replace the `info` data member of `tree` with the `info` data member of the

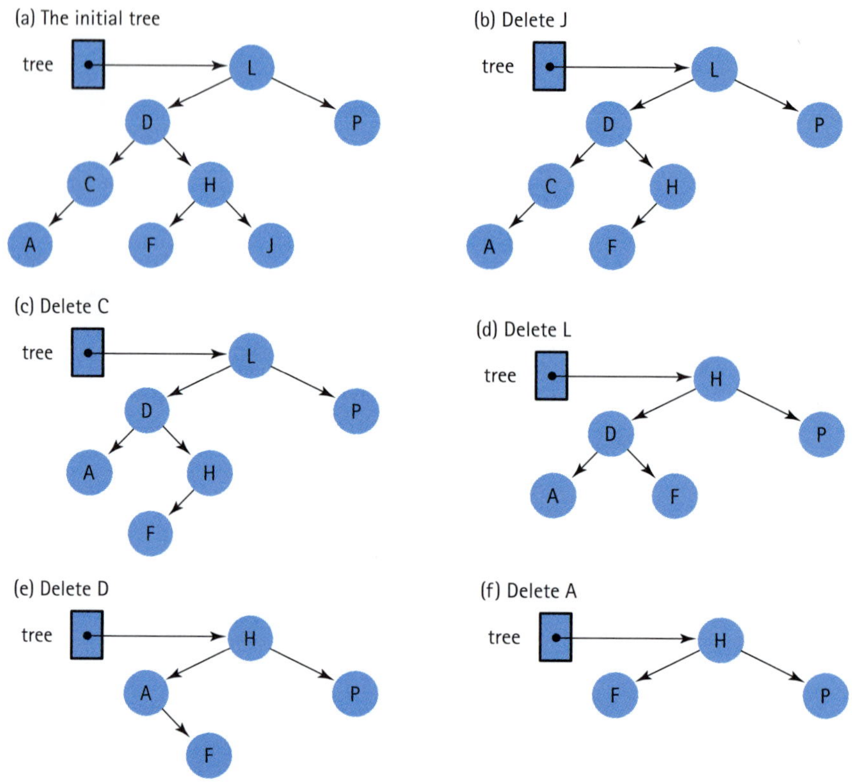

Figure 8.14 *Deletions from a binary search tree*

node's logical predecessor and delete the node containing the predecessor. Let's summarize this algorithm as `DeleteNode`.

DeleteNode

```
if (Left(tree) is NULL) AND (Right(tree) is NULL)
    Set tree to NULL
else if Left(tree) is NULL
    Set tree to Right(tree)
else if Right(tree) is NULL
    Set tree to Left(tree)
else
    Find predecessor
    Set Info(tree) to Info(predecessor)
    Delete predecessor
```

Now we can write the recursive definition and code for `Delete`.

Function Delete

Definition:	Removes someItem from tree where item equals someItem.
Size:	The number of nodes in the path from the root to the node to be deleted.
Base Case:	If item's key matches key in Info(tree), delete node pointed to by tree.
General Case:	If item < Info(tree), Delete(Left(tree), item); else Delete(Right(tree), item).

```
void DeleteNode(TreeNode*& tree);

void Delete(TreeNode*& tree, ItemType item);

void TreeType::DeleteItem(ItemType item)
// Calls the recursive function Delete to delete item from tree.
{
  Delete(root, item);
}

void Delete(TreeNode*& tree, ItemType item)
// Deletes item from tree.
// Post:  item is not in tree.
{
  if (item < tree->info)
    Delete(tree->left, item);     // Look in left subtree.
  else if (item > tree->info)
    Delete(tree->right, item);    // Look in right subtree.
  else
    DeleteNode(tree);             // Node found; call DeleteNode.
}
```

Before we code `DeleteNode`, let's look at it again. We can remove one of the tests if we notice that the action taken when the left child pointer is `NULL` also takes care of the case in which both child pointers are `NULL`. When the left child pointer is `NULL`, the right child pointer is stored into `tree`. If the right child pointer is also `NULL`, then `NULL` is stored into `tree`, which is what we want if both are `NULL`.

In good top-down fashion, let's now write the code for `DeleteNode` using `GetPredecessor` as the name of an operation that returns a copy of the `info` data member of the predecessor of the node with two children.

```
void GetPredecessor(TreeNode* tree, ItemType& data);

void DeleteNode(TreeNode*& tree)
// Deletes the node pointed to by tree.
// Post: The user's data in the node pointed to by tree is no
//       longer in the tree.  If tree is a leaf node or has only one
//       non-NULL child pointer, the node pointed to by tree is
//       deleted; otherwise, the user's data is replaced by its
//       logical predecessor and the predecessor's node is deleted.
{
  ItemType data;
  TreeNode* tempPtr;

  tempPtr = tree;
  if (tree->left == NULL)
  {
    tree = tree->right;
    delete tempPtr;
  }
  else if (tree->right == NULL)
  {
    tree = tree->left;
    delete tempPtr;
  }
  else
  {
    GetPredecessor(tree->left, data);
    tree->info = data;
    Delete(tree->left, data);  // Delete predecessor node.
  }
}
```

Next, we look at the operation for finding the logical predecessor. We know that the logical predecessor is the maximum value in `tree`'s left subtree. Where is this node found? The maximum value in a binary search tree is located in its *rightmost node*. Therefore, given `tree`'s left subtree, we just keep moving right until the right child is `NULL`. When this event occurs, we set `data` to the `info` member of the node. We have no reason to look for the predecessor recursively in this case. A simple iteration until `tree->right` is `NULL` suffices.

```
void GetPredecessor(TreeNode* tree, ItemType& data)
// Sets data to the info member of the rightmost node in tree.
{
  while (tree->right != NULL)
    tree = tree->right;
```

```
  data = tree->info;
}
```

Function `Print`

To traverse a linear linked list, we set a temporary pointer equal to the start of the list and then follow the links from one node to the other until we reach a node whose pointer value is `NULL`. Similarly, to traverse a binary tree, we initialize our pointer to the root of the tree. But where do we go from there—to the left or to the right? Do we access the root or the leaves first? The answer is “all of these.” There are only two ways to traverse a list: forward and backward. In contrast, there are many ways to traverse a tree.

An *inorder traversal* accesses the nodes in such a way that the values in the nodes are accessed in order from the smallest to the largest. This technique is the one we want for `Print`.

First, we print the root’s left subtree—that is, all values in the tree that are smaller than the value in the root node. Next, we print the value in the root node. Finally, we print the values in the root’s right subtree—that is, all the values that are larger than the value in the root node (see Figure 8.15).

Let’s describe this problem again, thinking recursively (and writing a recursive helper function named `Print`). We want to print the elements in the binary search tree rooted at `tree` in order; that is, first we print the left subtree in order, then we print the root, and finally we print the right subtree in order. Of course, `tree->left` points to the root of the left subtree. Because the left subtree is also a binary search tree, we can call the function `Print` to print it, using `tree->left` as the root parameter. When `Print` finishes printing the left subtree, we print the value in the root node. Then we call `Print` to print the right subtree with `tree->right` as the root parameter.

Both calls to the function `Print` use the same approach to print the subtree: Print the left subtree with a call to `Print`, print the root, and then print the right subtree with another call to `Print`. What happens if the incoming parameter is `NULL` on one of the recursive calls? This event signals that the parameter is the root of an empty tree. In this case, we just want to exit the function—clearly, there’s no point to printing an empty subtree.

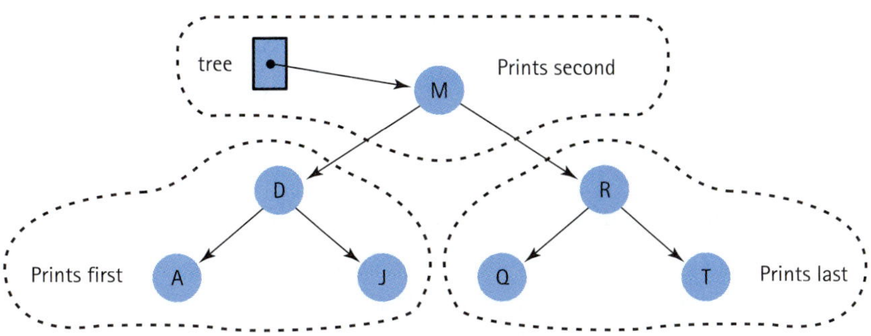

Figure 8.15 *Printing all the nodes in order*

Function Print

Definition:	Prints the items in the binary search tree in order from smallest to largest.
Size:	The number of nodes in the tree whose root is tree.
Base Case:	If tree = NULL, do nothing.
General Case:	Traverse the left subtree in order. Then print Info(tree). Then traverse the right subtree in order.

This description can be coded into the following recursive function. For simplicity, we assume that `tree->info` can be output directly using the stream insertion operator. Here is the helper function that does the printing.

```
void PrintTree(TreeNode* tree, std::ofstream& outFile)
// Prints info member of items in tree in sorted order on outFile.
{
  if (tree != NULL)
  {
    PrintTree(tree->left, outFile);    // Print left subtree.
    outFile << tree->info;
    PrintTree(tree->right, outFile);   // Print right subtree.
  }
}
```

This traversal is called an *inorder traversal* because it accesses each node's left subtree before it processes (prints) the information in the node itself, and then accesses the node's right subtree.

Finally, the `Print` member function of the `TreeType` class invokes `PrintTree` as follows:

```
void TreeType::Print(std::ofstream& outFile) const
// Calls recursive function Print to print items in the tree.
{
  PrintTree(root, outFile);
}
```

The Class Constructor and Destructor

The default class constructor simply creates an empty tree by setting `root` to `NULL`. As there is no other logical way of constructing an empty tree, we do not provide a parameterized constructor.

```
TreeType::TreeType()
{
  root = NULL;
}
```

In the same way that the class constructor takes care of each class object's initialization, the class destructor takes care of deallocating dynamic nodes when a class object goes out of scope. The operation invokes a recursive routine with the pointer to a binary search tree as a parameter and destroys all the nodes, leaving the tree empty. To delete the elements, we have to traverse the tree. Instead of printing each element, as we did in the previous section, we remove the node from the tree. We said that there is more than one way to traverse a binary tree. Is there a preferred way to destroy the tree?

While any of the traversals would result in the function working correctly, one traversal order is more efficient than the others. Knowing that the `DeleteNode` operation does less work to delete a leaf node than a node with children, we want to delete leaves first. The traversal that allows us to access leaf nodes first is called a *postorder traversal*: We access each node's left subtree and its right subtree before we process the node itself. If you delete the nodes in postorder, each node is a leaf by the time it is its turn to be deleted. The code for the destructor follows:

```
void Destroy(TreeNode*& tree);

TreeType::~TreeType()
// Calls recursive function Destroy to destroy the tree.
{
  Destroy(root);
}

void Destroy(TreeNode*& tree)
// Post: tree is empty; nodes have been deallocated.
{
  if (tree != NULL)
  {
    Destroy(tree->left);
    Destroy(tree->right);
    delete tree;
  }
}
```

The body of the `MakeEmpty` member function is identical to that of the class destructor, with one exception: After the call to `Destroy`, it must set `root` to `NULL`.

Copying a Tree

Both the copy constructor and the overloading of the assignment operator involve making a copy of a tree. Copying a tree may be the most interesting—and complex—

algorithm associated with trees. Clearly, it entails a recursive algorithm. We must do what we did with all the other member functions: Call an auxiliary recursive function with `root` as a parameter. Both the copy constructor and the assignment operator must call this function.

```
void CopyTree(TreeNode*& copy,
     const TreeNode* originalTree);

TreeType::TreeType(const TreeType& originalTree)
// Calls the recursive function CopyTree to copy originalTree
//  into root.
{
  CopyTree(root, originalTree.root);
}

void TreeType::operator=
     (const TreeType& originalTree)
// Calls the recursive function CopyTree to copy originalTree
//  into root.
{
  {
    if (&originalTree == this)
      return;                // Ignore assigning self to self.
    Destroy(root);           // Deallocate existing tree nodes.
    CopyTree(root, originalTree.root);
  }
}
```

The recursive function `CopyTree` has two parameters, both pointers to tree nodes. Let's call them `copy` and `otherTree`. What is the base case? If `otherTree` is `NULL`, then `copy` is `NULL`. What is `copy` if `otherTree` is not `NULL`? We get a node for `copy` to point to and put `otherTree->info` into it. We then store a copy of `otherTree`'s left subtree into `copy`'s left child and store a copy of `otherTree`'s right subtree into `copy`'s right child. Where do we get a copy of the subtrees? We use `CopyTree` recursively, of course.

```
void CopyTree(TreeNode*& copy,
     const TreeNode* originalTree)
// Post: copy is the root of a tree that is a duplicate
//       of originalTree.
{
  if (originalTree == NULL)
    copy = NULL;
```

```
    else
    {
      copy = new TreeNode;
      copy->info = originalTree->info;
      CopyTree(copy->left, originalTree->left);
      CopyTree(copy->right, originalTree->right);
    }
}
```

Be sure you understand how this code works before going on to the next section. Like many recursive algorithms, this short function is elegant but not obvious. In fact, let's trace `CopyTree` on the following tree:

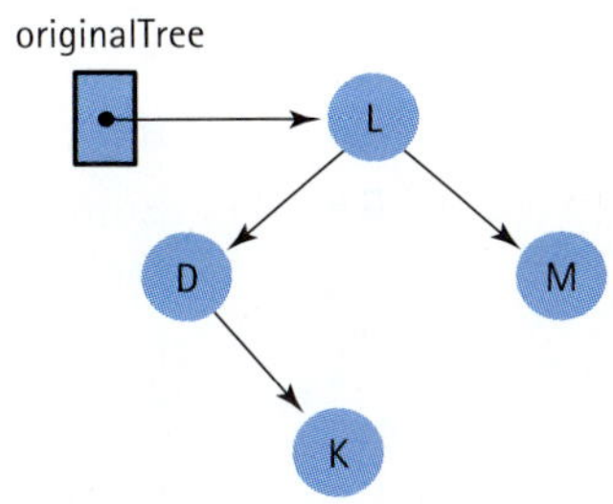

As in Chapter 7, R0 stands for the nonrecursive call, R1 stands for the first recursive call (`copy->left`), and R2 stands for the second recursive call (`copy->right`). In the trace, an arrow pointing to the contents of a node stands for the pointer to that node. A Comments column in the table shows the trace.

Call	copy	originalTree	Return	Comment
1	external pointer to new tree	→L	R0	`copy` is given a node to point to; L is copied into the `info` member; R1 is executed
2	left of node allocated in call 1	→D	R1	`copy` is given a node to point to; D is copied into the `info` member; R1 is executed
3	left of node allocated in call 2	NULL	R1	`NULL` is copied into `copy` (i.e., left of node allocated in call 2) and call 3 is completed

At this point the third call is finished, and `copy` looks like this:

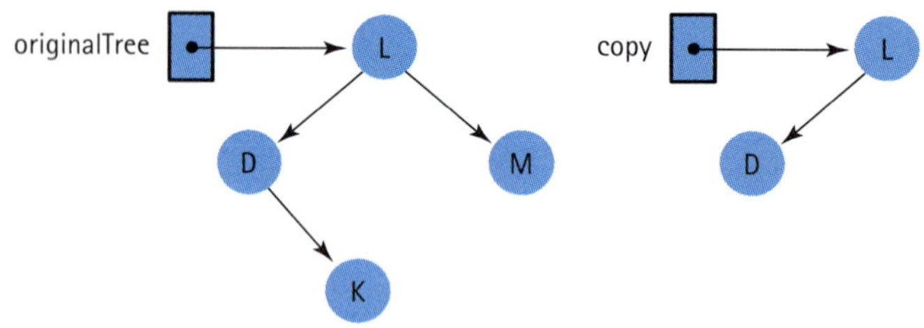

We return to finish the second call. We shade the completed calls to show that the execution of that call has finished and that activation record is no longer on the stack.

Call	copy	originalTree	Return	Comment
1	external pointer to new tree	→L	R0	copy is given a node to point to; L is copied into the info member; R1 is executed
2	left of node allocated in call 1	→D	R1	copy is given a node to point to; D is copied into the info member; R1 is executed
3	left of node allocated in call 2	NULL	R1	NULL is copied into copy (i.e., left of node allocated in call 2) and call 3 is completed
4	right of node allocated in call 2	→K	R2	copy is given a node to point to; K is copied into the info member; R1 is executed
5	left of node allocated in call 4	NULL	R1	NULL is copied into copy (i.e., left of node in call 4) and call 5 is completed

After the completion of the fifth call, control returns to the fourth call. Because the fifth call came from R1, R2 must be executed.

Call	copy	originalTree	Return	Comment
1	external pointer to new tree	→L	R0	copy is given a node to point to; L is copied into the info member; R1 is executed
2	left of node allocated in call 1	→D	R1	copy is given a node to point to; D is copied into the info member; R1 is executed
3	left of node allocated in call 2	NULL	R1	NULL is copied into copy (i.e., left of node allocated in call 2) and call 3 is completed
4	right of node allocated in call 2	→K	R2	copy is given a node to point to; K is copied into the info member; R1 is executed
5	left of node allocated in call 4	NULL	R1	NULL is copied into copy (i.e., left of node allocated in call 4) and call 5 is completed
6	right of node allocated in call 4	NULL	R2	NULL is copied into copy (i.e., right of node allocated in call 4) and call 6 is completed

Because the sixth call came from R2, the fourth call is now finished, and `copy` looks like this:

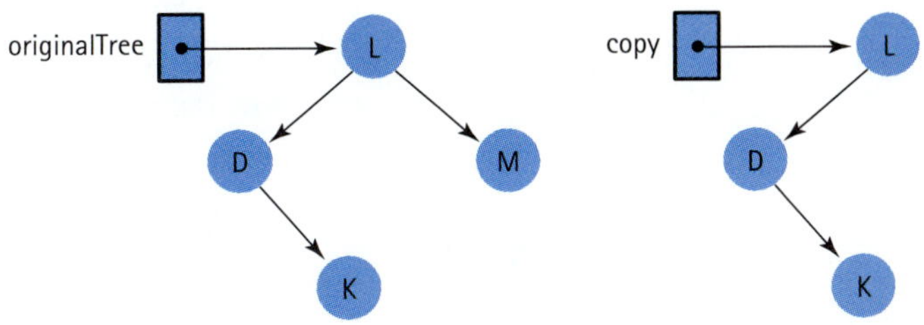

But as the fourth call came from R2, call 4 is also finished, leaving only the activation record from the original call on the stack. Execution continues with the second recursive call from call 1.

Call	copy	originalTree	Return	Comment
1	external pointer to new tree	→L	R0	`copy` is given a node to point to; L is copied into the `info` member; R1 is executed
2	left of node allocated in call 1	→D	R1	`copy` is given a node to point to; D is copied into the `info` member; R1 is executed
3	left of node allocated in call 2	NULL	R1	`NULL` is copied into `copy` (i.e., left of node allocated in call 2) and call 3 is completed
4	right of node allocated in call 2	→K	R2	`copy` is given a node to point to; K is copied into the `info` member; R1 is executed
5	left of node allocated in call 4	NULL	R1	`NULL` is copied into `copy` (i.e., left of node allocated in call 4) and call 5 is completed
6	right of node allocated in call 4	NULL	R2	`NULL` is copied into `copy` (i.e., right of node allocated in call 4) and call 6 is completed
7	right of node allocated in call 1	→M	R2	`copy` is given a node to point to; M is copied into the `info` member; R1 is executed
8	left of node allocated in call 7	NULL	R1	`NULL` is copied into `copy` (i.e., left of node allocated in call 7) and call 8 is completed

All we have left to do is the second recursive call from call 7.

Call	copy	originalTree	Return	Comment
1	external pointer to new tree	→L	R0	`copy` is given a node to point to; L is copied into the `info` member; R1 is executed
2	left of node allocated in call 1	→D	R1	`copy` is given a node to point to; D is copied into the `info` member; R1 is executed
3	left of node allocated in call 2	NULL	R1	`NULL` is copied into `copy` (i.e., left of node allocated in call 2) and call 3 is completed
4	right of node allocated in call 2	→K	R2	`copy` is given a node to point to; K is copied into the `info` member; R1 is executed
5	left of node allocated in call 4	NULL	R1	`NULL` is copied into `copy` (i.e., left of node allocated in call 4) and call 5 is completed
6	right of node allocated in call 4	NULL	R2	`NULL` is copied into `copy` (i.e., right of node allocated in call 4) and call 6 is completed
7	right of node allocated in call 1	→M	R2	`copy` is given a node to point to; M is copied into the `info` member; R1 is executed
8	left of node allocated in call 7	NULL	R1	`NULL` is copied into `copy` (i.e., left of node allocated in call 7) and call 8 is completed
9	right of node allocated in call 7	NULL	R2	`NULL` is copied into `copy` (i.e., right of node allocated in call 7) and call 9 is completed

Call 9's completion finishes up call 7, which then finishes up call 1. Because call 1 is the nonrecursive call, the process is finished. At last, `copy` is a duplicate of `originalTree`.

More about Traversals

Inorder traversal A systematic way of visiting all nodes in a binary tree that visits the nodes in the left subtree of a node, then visits the node, and then visits the nodes in the right subtree of the node

Postorder traversal A systematic way of visiting all nodes in a binary tree that visits the nodes in the left subtree of a node, then visits the nodes in the right subtree of the node, and then visits the node

Preorder traversal A systematic way of visiting all nodes in a binary tree that visits a node, then visits the nodes in the left subtree of the node, and then visits the nodes in the right subtree of the node

In the `Print` function, we conducted an inorder traversal of a binary search tree: The value in a node was printed *in between* the printing of the values in its left subtree and the values in its right subtree. An inorder traversal prints the values in a binary search tree in ascending key order. When implementing the destructor for the binary search tree, we introduced a postorder traversal: A node was deleted *after* destroying its left subtree and its right subtree. One more important traversal exists: the preorder traversal. In a preorder traversal, the values in a node are visited *before* the values in its left subtree and the values in its right subtree.

Compare the algorithms for these three traversals to be sure you understand the difference among them.

```
Inorder(tree)
if tree is not NULL
    Inorder(Left(tree))
    Visit Info(tree)
    Inorder(Right(tree))
```

```
Postorder(tree)
if tree is not NULL
    Postorder(Left(tree))
    Postorder(Right(tree))
    Visit Info(tree)
```

```
Preorder(tree)
if tree is not NULL
    Visit Info(tree)
    Preorder(Left(tree))
    Preorder(Right(tree))
```

When we say "visit," we mean that the algorithm does whatever it needs to do with the values in the node–print them, sum certain data members, or delete them, for example. Notice that the name given to each traversal specifies where the node itself is processed in relation to its subtrees.

If you are having trouble visualizing these traversals, try the following exercise. Visualize each traversal order by drawing a "loop" around a binary tree as in Figure 8.16. Before drawing the loop, extend the nodes of the tree that have fewer than two

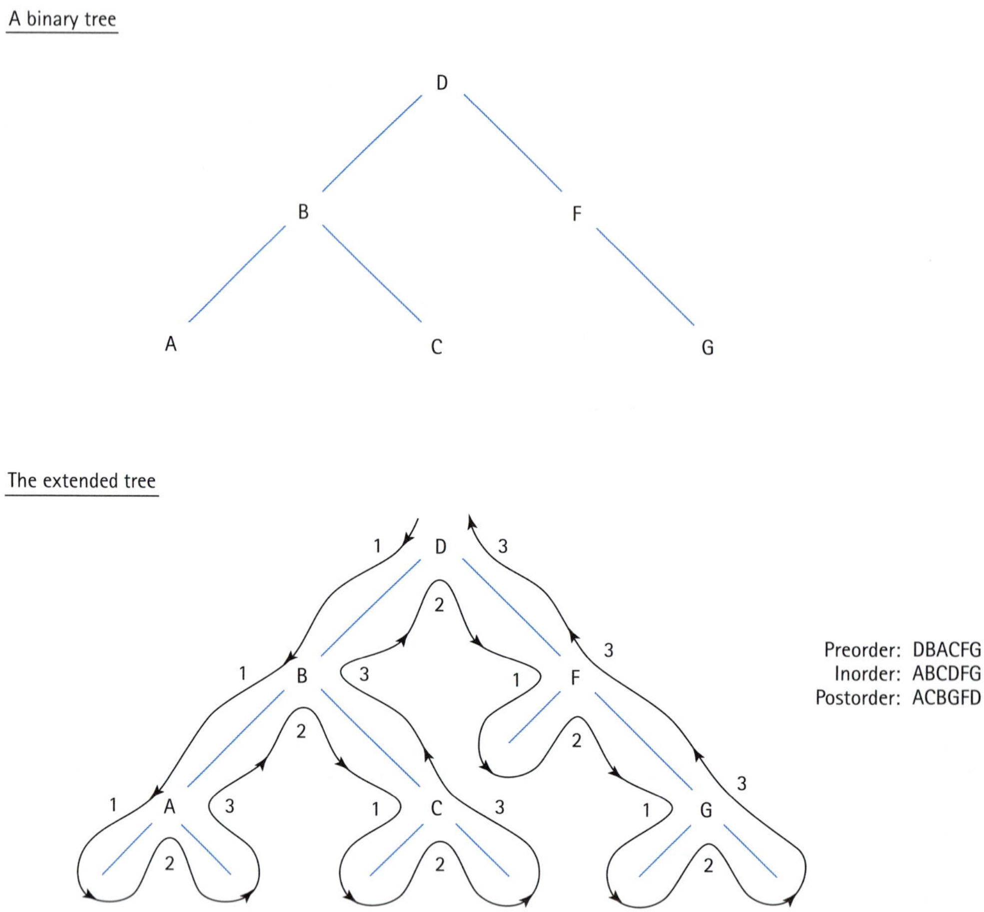

Figure 8.16 *Visualizing binary tree traversals*

children with short lines so that every node has two "edges." Then draw the loop from the root of the tree, down the left subtree, and back up again, hugging the shape of the tree as you go. Each node of the tree is "touched" three times by the loop (the touches are numbered in the figure): once on the way down before the left subtree is reached, once after finishing the left subtree but before starting the right subtree, and once on the way up, after finishing the right subtree.

To generate a preorder traversal, follow the loop and visit each node the first time it is touched (before visiting the left subtree). To generate an inorder traversal, follow the loop and visit each node the second time it is touched (in between visiting the two subtrees). To generate a postorder traversal, follow the loop and visit each node the third time it is touched (after visiting the right subtree). Use this method on the tree in Figure 8.17 and see if you agree with the listed traversal orders.

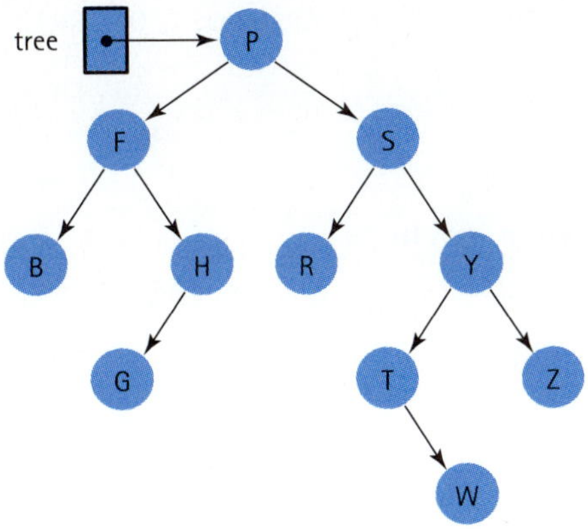

Inorder: B F G H P R S T W Y Z
Preorder: P F B H G S R Y T W Z
Postorder: B G H F R W T Z Y S P

Figure 8.17 *Three tree traversals*

An inorder traversal allows us to print the values in ascending order; a postorder traversal allows us to destroy a tree more efficiently. Where is a preorder traversal useful? This traversal is not particularly useful when dealing with binary search trees; however, in other applications of binary trees it is very useful.

Functions `ResetTree` and `GetNextItem`

`ResetTree` gets the "current position" ready for a traversal; `GetNextItem` moves the current position to the next node and returns the value stored there. We have looked at three kinds of traversals, so what does "next node" mean here? Both `ResetTree` and `GetNextItem` have a parameter of type `OrderType` that allows the user to specify which traversal to use.

When traversing a linear structure, moving from one item to the next one is specified explicitly. Our tree traversals are recursive, so the location of the next item is a function of the current item and the run-time stack. We could use an auxiliary stack to implement the traversal, thereby saving the history that we need to find the next item. However, an even simpler way exists: We let `ResetTree` generate a queue of node contents in the proper order and let `GetNextItem` process the node contents from the queue. Recall that `OrderType` is specified as follows:

```
enum OrderType {PRE_ORDER, IN_ORDER, POST_ORDER};
```

We let `ResetTree` call one of three recursive functions depending on the value of the parameter `order`. Each function implements a recursive traversal storing the node contents onto a queue. Thus we must have three queues declared in the private section of `TreeType`.

```
enum OrderType {PRE_ORDER, IN_ORDER, POST_ORDER};

class TreeType
{
public:
  // Function prototypes go here.
private:
  TreeNode* root;
  QueType preQue;
  QueType inQue;
  QueType postQue;
}
// Function prototypes for auxiliary functions.

void PreOrder(TreeNode*, QueType&);
// Enqueues tree items in preorder.

void InOrder(TreeNode*, QueType&);
// Enqueues tree items in inorder.

void PostOrder(TreeNode*, QueType&);
// Enqueues tree items in postorder.

void TreeType::ResetTree(OrderType order)
// Calls a function to create a queue of the tree elements in
// the desired order.
{
  switch (order)
  {
    case PRE_ORDER : PreOrder(root, preQue);
                     break;
    case IN_ORDER  : InOrder(root, inQue);
                     break;
    case POST_ORDER: PostOrder(root, postQue);
                     break;
  }
}

void PreOrder(TreeNode* tree,
     QueType& preQue)
// Post: preQue contains the tree items in preorder.
{
  if (tree != NULL)
  {
    preQue.Enqueue(tree->info);
```

```
    PreOrder(tree->left, preQue);
    PreOrder(tree->right, preQue);
  }
}

void InOrder(TreeNode* tree,
     QueType& inQue)
// Post: inQue contains the tree items in inorder.
{
  if (tree != NULL)
  {
    InOrder(tree->left, inQue);
    inQue.Enqueue(tree->info);
    InOrder(tree->right, inQue);
  }
}

void PostOrder(TreeNode* tree,
     QueType& postQue)
// Post: postQue contains the tree items in postorder.
{
  if (tree != NULL)
  {
    PostOrder(tree->left, postQue);
    PostOrder(tree->right, postQue);
    postQue.Enqueue(tree->info);
  }
}

ItemType TreeType::GetNextItem(OrderType order, bool& finished)
// Returns the next item in the desired order.
// Post: For the desired order, item is the next item in the queue.
//       If item is the last one in the queue, finished is true;
//       otherwise, finished is false.
{
  ItemType item;
  finished = false;
  switch (order)
  {
    case PRE_ORDER   : preQue.Dequeue(item);
                       if (preQue.IsEmpty())
                         finished = true;
                       break;
    case IN_ORDER    : inQue.Dequeue(item);
                       if (inQue.IsEmpty())
                         finished = true;
```

```
                         break;
    case   POST_ORDER:   postQue.Dequeue(item);
                         if (postQue.IsEmpty())
                           finished = true;
                         break;
  }
  return item;
}
```

8.6 Iterative Insertion and Deletion

Searching a Binary Search Tree

In the recursive versions of the tree operations, we embedded the search task within the function that needed it. The other alternative is to have a general search function; let's take that approach here. The function `FindNode` receives a pointer to a binary search tree and an item with the key initialized. It sends back a pointer to the desired node (`nodePtr`) and a pointer to the node's parent (`parentPtr`) if an item with a matching key is found.

What do we do if no item has a key that matches `item`'s, as is the case when we are inserting a new element? We set `nodePtr` to `NULL`. In this case, `parentPtr` points to the node into which the new element must be inserted as a right or left child. One other case arises: What if we find a matching key in the root node? Because no parent node exists, we set `parentPtr` to `NULL`.

Here is the specification for the *internal* tree function, `FindNode`:

FindNode(TreeNode* tree, ItemType item, TreeNode*& nodePtr, TreeNode*& parentPtr)

Function:	Searches for a node whose key matches item's key.
Precondition:	tree points to the root of a binary search tree.
Postconditions:	If a node is found with the same key as item's, then nodePtr points to that node and parentPtr points to its parent node. If the root node has the same key as item's, parentPtr is NULL. If no node has the same key, then nodePtr is NULL and parentPtr points to the node in the tree that is the logical parent of item.

Let's look at the search algorithm in detail. We use `nodePtr` and `parentPtr` (the outgoing parameters) to search the tree. Because we access the tree through its root, we initialize `nodePtr` to the external pointer, `tree`. We initialize `parentPtr` to `NULL`. We compare `item` and `nodePtr->info`. If the keys are equal, we have found the desired node. If `item`'s key is less, we look in the left subtree; if `item`'s key is greater, we look in the right subtree. This operation is exactly like a recursive search except that we change pointer values to move left and right rather than making recursive calls.

```
FindNode
Set nodePtr to tree
Set parentPtr to NULL
Set found to false

while more elements to search AND NOT found
    if item < Info(nodePtr)
        Set parentPtr to nodePtr
        Set nodePtr to Left(nodePtr)
    else if item > Info(nodePtr)
        Set parentPtr to nodePtr
        Set nodePtr to Right(nodePtr)
    else
        Set found to true
```

When does the loop terminate? Two terminating conditions are possible. First, we stop searching if we find the correct node. In this case, `nodePtr` points to the node containing the same key as `item`'s, and `parentPtr` points to this node's parent. Second, if no element in the tree has the same key as `item`'s, we search until we fall out of the tree. At this point, `nodePtr = NULL`, and `parentPtr` points to the node that would be the `item`'s parent—if it existed in the tree. (We use this value of `parentPtr` when we insert an item into a tree.) The resulting loop condition is

```
while (nodePtr != NULL && !found)
```

The algorithm illustrates that the maximum number of comparisons in a binary search tree equals the height of the tree. As discussed earlier, this number may range from $\log_2 N$ to N (where N is the number of tree elements), depending on the shape of the tree.

The complete function follows.

```
void FindNode(TreeNode* tree, ItemType item,
     TreeNode*& nodePtr, TreeNode*& parentPtr)
```

```
// Post: If a node is found with the same key as item's, then
//       nodePtr points to that node and parentPtr points to its
//       parent node. If the root node has the same key as item's,
//       parentPtr is NULL. If no node has the same key, then
//       nodePtr is NULL and parentPtr points to the node in the
//       tree that is the logical parent of item.

{
  nodePtr = tree;
  parentPtr = NULL;
  bool found = false;
  while (nodePtr != NULL && !found)
  {
    if (item < nodePtr->info)
    {
      parentPtr = nodePtr;
      nodePtr = nodePtr->left;
    }
    else if (item > nodePtr->info)
    {
      parentPtr = nodePtr;
      nodePtr = nodePtr->right;
    }
    else
      found = true;
  }
}
```

Let's trace this function, using the tree in Figure 8.6 on page 509. We want to find the element with the key 18. `nodePtr` is initially set to `tree`, the external pointer. Because `item`'s key (18) is greater than `nodePtr->info` (17), we advance the pointers. Now `parentPtr` points to the root node and we move `nodePtr` to the right; it then points to the node with the key 20. Because `item`'s key (18) is less than this key (20), we advance the pointers. Now `parentPtr` points to the node with the key 20, and we move `nodePtr` to the left; `nodePtr` then points to the node with the key 18. Now 18 is equal to `nodePtr->info` and `found` is true, so we stop looping. We exit the function with `nodePtr` pointing to the node with the desired key and `parentPtr` pointing to this node's parent.

Next, let's look at an example where the key is not found in the tree. We want to find the element with the key 7. `nodePtr` is initially set to `tree`. Because `item`'s key (7) is less than `nodePtr->info` (17), we move to the left. Now `nodePtr` points to the node containing 9 and `parentPtr` points to the root node. Because `item`'s key is less than `nodePtr->info`, we move again to the left. Now `nodePtr = NULL`; it has fallen out of the tree. Because no more is left to search in this subtree, we stop looping. We exit the function with `nodePtr` equal to `NULL` and `parentPtr` pointing to the node with the key 9. If we were calling `FindNode` with the intention of subsequently inserting a node with the key 7, we would now know two things:

1. Because `nodePtr` = `NULL`, the tree does not include a node with the key 7.
2. Because `parentPtr` points to the last node visited before we fell out of the tree, the new node, with a key value of 7, must be attached to the node at `parentPtr`. This information will prove very helpful when we develop the iterative `PutItem` operation.

Function `PutItem`

The algorithm for the iterative `PutItem` operation must carry out the same three tasks that any insert operation performs:

PutItem

Create a node to contain the new item.
Find the insertion place.
Attach the new node.

Creating a node works in the same way as in the recursive version. Finding the insertion point and inserting the node are different, however. Let's see how the function `FindNode` can perform the search for us. We call `FindNode`, asking it to find the node with the same key as `item`'s:

```
FindNode(tree, item, nodePtr, parentPtr);
```

Suppose we want to insert an element with the key value 13 into the binary search tree pictured in Figure 8.18. In the function `FindNode`, `nodePtr` is initialized to point to the root of the tree, and `parentPtr` is initialized to `NULL` (Figure 8.18a). Because `item`'s key (13) is larger than the key of the root node (7), we move `nodePtr` to the right, dragging `parentPtr` along behind it (Figure 8.18b). Now `item`'s key is less than `nodePtr->info`, so we move `nodePtr` to the left, with `parentPtr` following (Figure 8.18c). Because `item`'s key is greater than `nodePtr->info`, `parentPtr` catches up and `nodePtr` moves to the right (Figure 8.18d). At this point, `nodePtr` is `NULL`, so we exit `FindNode` with the pointers positioned as shown in Figure 8.18d.

Of course, a node with `item`'s key is not supposed to be found, for we are just now inserting its node. The good news is that `nodePtr` has fallen out of the tree just at the spot where the new node should be inserted. Because `parentPtr` trails immediately behind `nodePtr`, we can simply attach the new node to the node pointed to by `parentPtr` (Figure 8.18e).

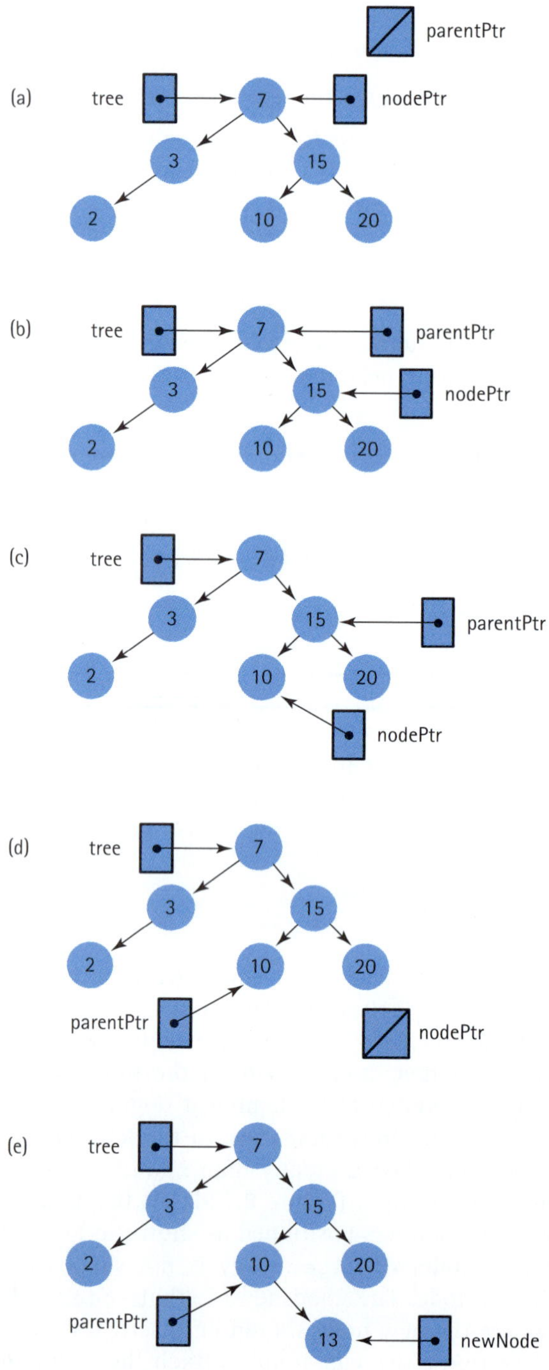

Figure 8.18 *Using the function `FindNode` to find the insertion point*

Now we're ready for the third task: to fix the pointers in the node pointed to by `parentPtr` so as to attach the new node. In the general case, we compare the key of the new element to the key of `parentPtr->info`. Either `parentPtr->left` or `parentPtr->right` must be set to point to the new node:

AttachNewNode
if item < Info(parentPtr)
    Set Left(parentPtr) to newNode
else
    Set Right(parentPtr) to newNode

When we are inserting the first node into an empty tree, however, `parentPtr` still equals `NULL` and dereferencing `parentPtr` is illegal. We need to make inserting the first node into the tree become a special case. We can test for `parentPtr = NULL` to determine whether the tree is empty; if so, we change `tree` to point to the new node.

AttachNewNode(revised)
if parentPtr equals NULL
    Set tree to newNode
else if item < Info(parentPtr)
    Set Left(parentPtr) to newNode
else
    Set Right(parentPtr) to newNode

Taken together, the pieces of the insertion operation design can be coded as the function `PutItem`, with the interface described in the Binary Search Tree ADT specification.

```
void TreeType::PutItem(ItemType item)
// Post: item is in tree.
{
  TreeNode* newNode;
  TreeNode* nodePtr;
  TreeNode* parentPtr;
```

```
  newNode = new TreeNode;
  newNode->info = item;
  newNode->left = NULL;
  newNode->right = NULL;

  FindNode(root, item, nodePtr, parentPtr);

  if (parentPtr == NULL)          // Insert as root.
    root = newNode;
  else if (item < parentPtr->info)
    parentPtr->left = newNode;
  else parentPtr->right = newNode;
}
```

Function DeleteItem

The same three cases exist for the iterative DeleteItem operation that existed for the recursive Delete: deleting a node with no children, one child, or two children. We can use FindNode to locate the node (pointed to by nodePtr) to delete and its parent node (pointed to by parentPtr).

The actual deletion in the recursive version occurs in DeleteNode. Can we use it to delete the node pointed to by nodePtr? DeleteNode takes only one parameter, the place in the tree where the pointer to the node to be deleted resides. We can use the DeleteNode function developed for the recursive version if we can determine the *place in the structure* to pass to DeleteNode. That is, given nodePtr and parentPtr, we must determine whether the node pointed to by nodePtr is the right or left child of the node pointed to by parentPtr. If the value of nodePtr is the same as the value of parentPtr->left, then we pass parentPtr->left to DeleteNode; otherwise, we pass parentPtr->right.

```
void TreeType::DeleteItem(ItemType item)
// Post: There is no node in the tree whose info member
//       matches item.
{
  TreeNode* nodePtr;
  TreeNode* parentPtr;

  FindNode(root, item, nodePtr, parentPtr);

  if (nodePtr == root)
    DeleteNode(root);
  else
    if (parentPtr->left == nodePtr)
      DeleteNode(parentPtr->left);
    else DeleteNode(parentPtr->right);
}
```

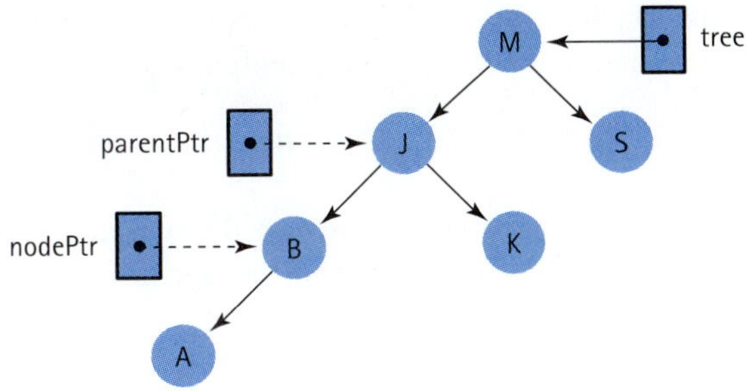

Figure 8.19 *Pointers `nodePtr` and `parentPtr` are external to the tree*

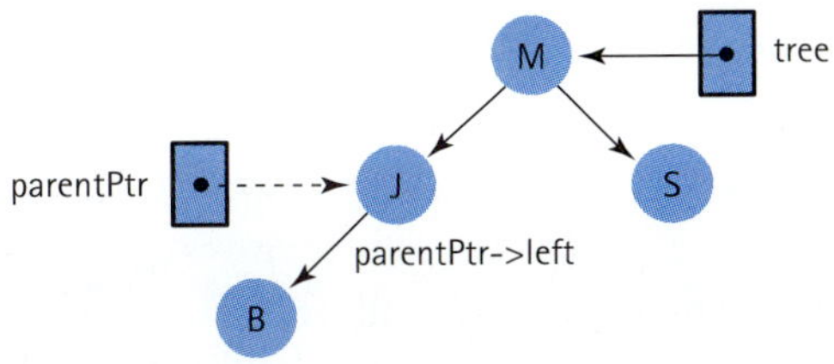

Figure 8.20 *Pointer `parentPtr` is external to the tree, but `parentPtr->left` is an actual pointer in the tree*

It is very important to recognize the difference between passing `nodePtr` to `DeleteNode` and passing either `parentPtr->right` or `parentPtr->left`. See Figures 8.19 and 8.20.

Test Plan

Because we use the Binary Search Tree ADT to represent items in a list, we can employ the same strategy that we have used to test the other list ADTs for it. However, testing the traversals is much more difficult than testing a simple linear traversal. The tree in Figure 8.17 is a good tree to use as a test because we already have the answers. We need to insert the items, retrieve items found and not found in the tree, print the tree, reset the tree for each traversal, use `GetNextItem` to get each of the items in each traversal, delete all the items, and call each of the other functions where appropriate.

On the Web, the program `TreeDr.cpp` contains the driver for the test. The recursive version of `TreeType` is located in file `TreeType.cpp`; the iterative version is found in file `ITreeType.cpp`. The input file is `TreeType.in` and the output files are `TreeType.out` and `TreeType.screen` for the recursive version and `ITreeType.out` and `ITreeType.screen` for the iterative version.

Recursion or Iteration?

Now that we have looked at both the recursive and the iterative versions of inserting and deleting nodes, can we determine which approach is better? In Chapter 7, we gave some guidelines for determining when recursion is appropriate. Let's apply these guidelines to the use of recursion with binary search trees.

Is the depth of recursion relatively shallow?

Yes. The depth of recursion depends on the height of the tree. If the tree is well balanced (relatively short and bushy, not tall and stringy), the depth of recursion is closer to $O(\log_2 N)$ than to $O(N)$.

Is the recursive solution shorter or clearer than the nonrecursive version?

Yes. The recursive solutions are certainly shorter than the combination of the nonrecursive functions plus the supporting function `FindNode`. Is it clearer? Once you accept that in every recursive execution, the parameter `tree` is actually a pointer member within a node of the tree, the recursive version becomes intuitively obvious.

Is the recursive version much less efficient than the nonrecursive version?

No. Both the recursive and the nonrecursive versions of inserting and deleting are $O(\log_2 N)$ operations, assuming a well-balanced tree. The only efficiency issue of concern relates to space. `item` is a value parameter; our functions pass a copy of it on each recursive call. If `item` is a large struct or class object, these copies may cause an overflow of the run-time stack. (It would be better to make `item` be a `const` reference parameter if `ItemType` is large and the tree has great height.)

We give the recursive versions of the functions an "A"; they represent a good use of recursion.

8.7 Comparing Binary Search Trees and Linear Lists

A binary search tree is an appropriate structure for many of the same applications discussed previously in conjunction with other sorted list structures. The special advantage of using a binary search tree is that it facilitates searching, while conferring the benefits of linking the elements. It provides the best features of both the sorted array-based list and the linked list. Like a sorted array-based list, it can be searched quickly, using a binary search. Like a linked list, it allows insertions and deletions without having to move data. Thus this structure is particularly suitable for applications in which search time must be minimized or in which the nodes are not necessarily processed in sequential order.

As usual, a tradeoff exists. The binary search tree, with its extra pointer in each node, takes up more memory space than a singly linked list does. In addition, the algorithms for manipulating the tree are somewhat more complicated. If all of the list's uses involve sequential rather than random processing of the elements, the tree may not be as good a choice as a linked list.

Suppose we have 100,000 customer records in a list. If our main activity is to send out updated monthly statements to the customers and if the order in which the statements are printed matches the order in which the records appear on the list, a linked list would be suitable. But suppose we decide to keep a terminal available to give out account information to the customers whenever they ask. If the data are kept in a linked list, the first customer on the list can be given information almost instantly, but the last customer has to wait while the application examines the other 99,999 records. When direct access to the records is a requirement, a binary search tree represents a more appropriate structure.

Big-O Comparisons

Finding the node to process (`FindNode`), as we would expect in a structure dedicated to searching, is the most interesting operation to analyze. In the best case—if the order in which the elements were inserted results in a short, bushy tree—we can find any node in the tree with at most $\log_2 N + 1$ comparisons. We would expect to locate a random element in such a tree much faster than we could find such an element in a sorted linked list. In the worst case—if the elements were inserted in order from smallest to largest, or vice versa—the tree won't really be a tree at all; it is a linear list, linked through either the `left` or `right` data members. *This structure is called a "degenerate" tree.* In this case, the tree operations should perform much the same as the operations on a linked list. Therefore, in a *worst-case* analysis, the complexity of the tree operations is identical to the comparable linked-list operations. In the following analysis, however, we assume that the items are inserted into the tree in random order to produce a balanced tree.

The `PutItem`, `DeleteItem`, and `GetItem` operations basically involve finding the node [$O(\log_2 N)$] plus tasks that are O(1)—for instance, creating a node, resetting pointers, or copying data. These operations are all described as $O(\log_2 N)$. The `DeleteItem` operation consists of finding the node plus `DeleteNode`. In the worst case (deleting a node with two children), `DeleteNode` must find the replacement value, an $O(\log_2 N)$ operation. (Actually, the two tasks add up to $\log_2 N$ comparisons, because if the delete node is higher in the tree, fewer comparisons are needed to find it, and more comparisons may be needed to find its replacement node.) Otherwise, if the deleted node has zero or one child, `DeleteNode` is an O(1) operation. Thus `DeleteItem` may also be described as $O(\log_2 N)$.

The observer operations `IsFull` and `IsEmpty` have O(1) complexity because the number of items in the structure does not affect these operations. `GetLength`, however, is different. As we said in Chapter 5, the `length` data member *must* be present in array-based implementations, but is a design choice in linked implementations. In the implementations in Chapter 5, we chose to keep a `length` field rather than counting the number of items when the `GetLength` member function is called. In our tree implementation, we have the same choice; we chose to count the number of items on the list when `GetLength` is called. Therefore, the order of the tree implementation is $O(N)$.

The `MakeEmpty`, `Print`, and destructor operations require the tree to be traversed, processing each element once. Thus they have $O(N)$ complexity. Table 8.2 compares the

Table 8.2 *Big-O Comparison of List Operations*

	Binary Search Tree	Array-Based Linear List	Linked List
Class constructor	O(1)	O(1)	O(1)
Destructor	O(N)	O(1)*	O(N)
`MakeEmpty`	O(N)	O(1)*	O(N)
`GetLength`	O(N)	O(1)	O(1)
`IsFull`	O(1)	O(1)	O(1)
`IsEmpty`	O(1)	O(1)	O(1)
`GetItem`			
Find	O($\log_2 N$)	O($\log_2 N$)	O(N)
Process	O(1)	O(1)	O(1)
Total	O($\log_2 N$)	O($\log_2 N$)	O(N)
`PutItem`			
Find	O($\log_2 N$)	O($\log_2 N$)	O(N)
Process	O(1)	O(N)	O(1)
Total	O($\log_2 N$)	O(N)	O(N)
`DeleteItem`			
Find	O($\log_2 N$)	O($\log_2 N$)	O(N)
Process	O(1)	O(N)	O(1)
Total	O($\log_2 N$)	O(N)	O(N)

*If the items in the array-based list could possibly contain pointers, the items must be deallocated, making this an O(N) operation.

orders of magnitude for the tree and list operations as we have coded them. The binary search tree operations are based on a random insertion order of the items; the find operation in the array-based implementation is based on a binary search.

8.8 A Nonlinked Representation of Binary Trees

Our discussion of the implementation of binary trees has so far remained limited to a scheme in which the pointers from parent to children are *explicit* in the data structure. That is, a member was declared in each node for the pointer to the left child and the pointer to the right child.

A binary tree can be stored in an array in such a way that the relationships in the tree are not physically represented by link members, but rather are *implicit* in the algorithms that manipulate the tree stored in the array. The code is, of course, much less self-documenting, but we might save memory space because we have no pointers.

Let's take a binary tree and store it in an array in such a way that we do not lose the parent–child relationships. We store the tree elements in the array, level by level, left to right. If the number of nodes in the tree is `numElements`, we can package the array and `numElements` into a struct as illustrated in Figure 8.21. The tree elements are stored with the root in `tree.nodes[0]` and the last node in `tree.nodes[numElements - 1]`.

To implement the algorithms that manipulate the tree, we must be able to find the left and right child of a node in the tree. Comparing the tree and the array in Figure 8.21, we see that

- `tree.nodes[0]`'s children are in `tree.nodes[1]` and `tree.nodes[2]`.
- `tree.nodes[1]`'s children are in `tree.nodes[3]` and `tree.nodes[4]`.
- `tree.nodes[2]`'s children are in `tree.nodes[5]` and `tree.nodes[6]`.

Do you see the pattern? For any node `tree.nodes[index]`, its left child is in `tree.nodes[index * 2 + 1]` and its right child is in `tree.nodes[index * 2 + 2]` (provided that these child nodes exist). Notice that the nodes in the array from `tree.nodes[tree.numElements/2]` to `tree.nodes[tree.numElements - 1]` are leaf nodes.

Not only can we easily calculate the location of a node's children, but we can also determine the location of its *parent* node. This task is not an easy one in a binary tree linked together with pointers from parent to child nodes, but it is very simple in our

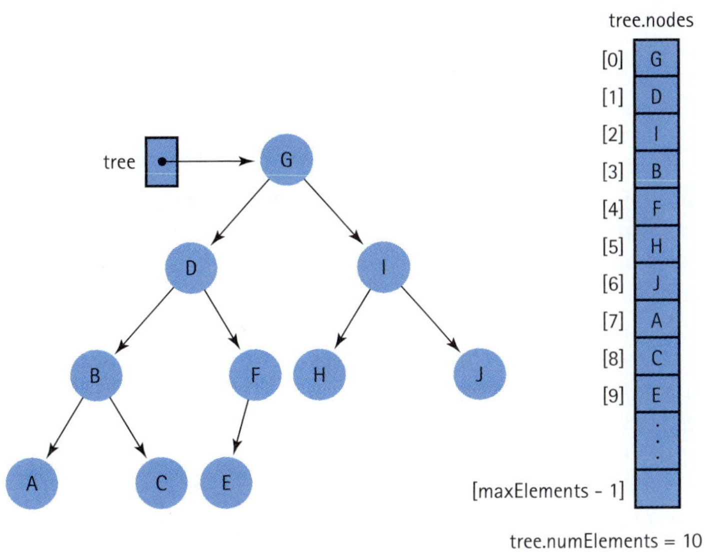

Figure 8.21 *A binary tree and its array representation*

implicit link implementation: `tree.nodes[index]`'s parent is in `tree.nodes[(index - 1)/2]`.

Because integer division truncates any remainder, `(index - 1)/2` is the correct parent index for either a left or a right child. Thus this implementation of a binary tree is linked in both directions—from parent to child and from child to parent. We take advantage of this fact later in the next chapter.

Full binary tree A binary tree in which all of the leaves are located on the same level and every nonleaf node has two children

This tree representation works well for any binary tree that is full or complete. A full binary tree is a binary tree in which all of the leaves are located on the same level and every nonleaf node has two children. The basic shape of a full binary tree is triangular:

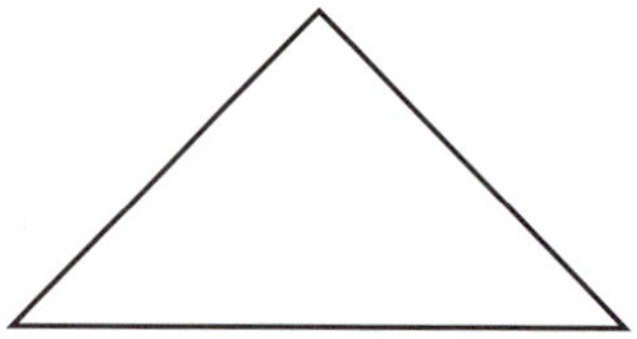

Complete binary tree A binary tree that is either full or full through the next-to-last level, with the leaves on the last level located as far to the left as possible

A complete binary tree is a binary tree that is either full or full through the next-to-last level, with the leaves on the last level located as far to the left as possible. The shape of a complete binary tree is either triangular (if the tree is full) or something like the following:

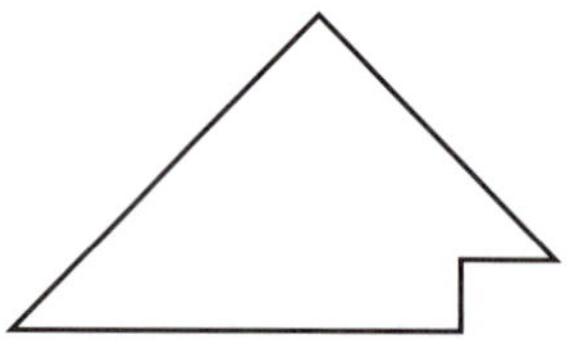

Figure 8.22 shows some examples of binary trees.

The array-based representation is simple to implement for trees that are full or complete, because the elements occupy contiguous array slots. If a tree is not full or complete, however, we must account for the gaps created by missing nodes. To use the array representation, we must store a dummy value in those positions in the array so as to maintain the proper parent–child relationship. The choice of a dummy value depends on what information is stored in the tree. For instance, if the elements in the tree are nonnegative integers, we can store a negative value in the dummy nodes.

Figure 8.23 illustrates a tree that is not complete as well as its corresponding array. Some of the array slots do not contain actual tree elements, but rather hold dummy values. The algorithms to manipulate the tree must reflect this situation. For example, to determine whether the node in `tree.nodes[index]` has a left child, you must check whether `index * 2 + 1 < tree.numElements`, and then check whether the value in `tree.nodes[index * 2 + 1]` is the dummy value.

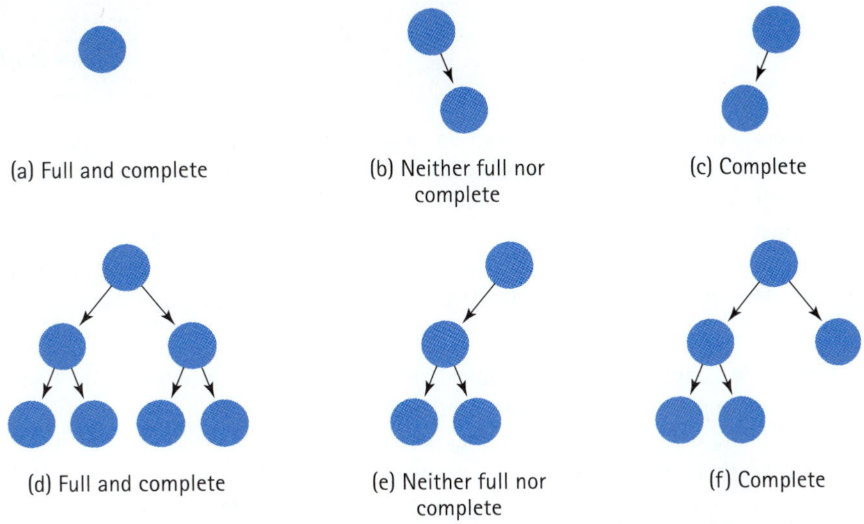

Figure 8.22 *Examples of binary trees*

We have seen how we can use an array to represent a binary tree. We can also reverse this process, creating a binary tree from the elements in an array. In fact, we can regard *any* one-dimensional array as representing the nodes in a tree, although the data values that happen to be stored in it may not match this structure in a meaningful way. In Chapter 9, we use this binary tree representation to implement a *heap*, a new ADT.

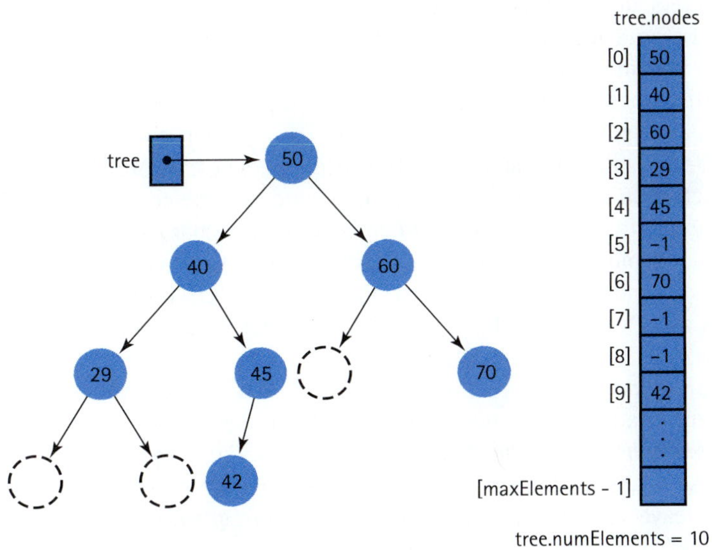

Figure 8.23 *A binary search tree stored in an array with dummy values*

Case Study

Building an Index

Problem Our publisher has asked us to produce an index for this book. The first step in this process is to decide which words should go into the index; the second step is to produce a list of the pages where each word occurs.

Instead of trying to choose words out of our heads (thin air), we decided to let the computer produce a list of all unique words used in the manuscript and their frequency of occurrence. We could then review the list and choose which words to include in the index.

Discussion Clearly, the main object in this problem is a word with associated frequency. Therefore, the first thing we must do is define a "word."

Looking back over the preceding paragraphs, what is a tentative definition of word in this context? How about "something between two blanks"? Or better yet, a "character string between two blanks"? That definition works for most of the words. However, all words before '.' and ',' would have the '.' and ',' attached. Also, words surrounded by quotes would cause a problem.

Does the following definition take care of the problem?

A word is a string of alphanumeric characters between markers where markers are whitespace and all punctuation marks.

Yes, it is a good working definition of the kind of word that would be a candidate for an index term. We can use function `isalnum`, available in `<cctype>`, to determine if a character is an alphanumeric character. We can skip leading non-numeric characters and store and read characters until we encounter a non-alphanumeric character (`isalnum` returns false) or `inFile` goes into the fail state. If we do not encounter any alphanumeric characters, we return the empty string.

This process ignores quotation marks, but leaves contractions as a problem. Let's examine a few and see if we can find a solution. The common contractions "let's," "couldn't," "can't," and "that's" all have only one letter after the single quote. The algorithm would return the characters up to the single quote as one word and the character following the single quote as one word. What we really want to do is ignore the characters after the single quote. By saying that words must be at least three characters long to be considered for the index, we solve this problem. Ignoring words of fewer than three letters also removes from consideration such words as "a," "is," "to," "do," and "by" that do not belong in an index.

Brainstorming As usual, our first step is to list objects that might be useful in solving the problem. Scanning the problem statement, we identify the following nouns: *publisher, index, text, word, list, pages, heads, computer, manuscript, frequency,* and *occurrence.* Clearly, some of these nouns set the stage for the problem and are not part of the solution. Removing those nouns leave us with *manuscript, word, list,* and *frequency.*

Scenarios There is really only one scenario for this problem: Read a file (the manuscript), break it into words, process the words, and output the results. To process each word, we check its length. If it is three characters or longer, we check whether it is a word that we have processed before. If it is, we increment its frequency; if not, we add it to the list of words with a frequency of 1. The limit of three characters is rather arbitrary, however. Let's let the user enter the minimum number of characters.

Although *frequency* is a noun, it is a property of a word in this case. Let's combine *word* and *frequency* into a WordType object. We need a container object (list) in which to store the items of WordType. We can use any of the list ADTs we have written. To have the output file list the words in alphabetic order, we should use the Sorted List ADT. Here, then, are the CRC cards for WordType and ListType:

Class Name: WordType	Superclass:	Subclasses:

Responsibilities	Collaborations
Initialize (word1)	
Increment frequency	
GetWord	
GetFrequency	

Class Name: ListType	Superclass:	Subclasses:

Responsibilities	Collaborations
Initialize	
Put Item (item)	WordType
Get Item (item)	WordType
Tell a word to increment its frequency	WordType
Print its contents in alphabetical order	WordType

We are now ready to summarize our discussion in the main driver function.

Driver (Main)

```
Open input file
Open output file
Get file label
Print file label on output file
Get minimum word length
Set letters to GetString(input file)
while more data
    if letters.GetLength() >= minimum word length
        Initialize WordType object with letters
        list.GetItem(wordObject, found)
        if found
            Increment count of wordObject
        else
            list.PutItem(wordObject)
    Set letters to GetString (input file)
list.Print(output file)
```

Oops! Our design has a major flaw. Regardless of which list ADT we use, `GetItem` returns a *copy* of the item in the list. Incrementing the returned item simply increments a copy of the item in the list. Therefore, all the frequencies would end up being 1. In fact, this problem really doesn't lend itself to using one of our list ADTs. The processing would be much more efficient if we write a single function that searches the list for a string and increments the count if it finds it and inserts a node with the string if it doesn't. When the search finds that the string is not there, it is already at the point where the node belongs.

This discussion brings up a very important point: Sometimes it is not appropriate to use an off-the-shelf container class. Using library classes—whether one provided by C++ or your own user-defined class—allows you to write more reliable software in a shorter amount of time. These classes are already tested and debugged. If they fit the needs of your problem, use them. If they do not, then write a special-purpose function to do the job. In this case, we need to write our own. The revised CRC card for the container object follows.

Class Name: ListType	Superclass:	Subclasses:

Responsibilities	Collaborations
Initialize	
PutOrIncrement	WordType
Print its contents in alphabetical order	String
. . .	

Here is a revised main function:

```
Open input file
Open output file
Get file label
Print file label on output file
Get minimum word length
Set letters to GetString (input file)
while more data
    if letters.GetLength() >= minimum word length
        list.InsertOrIncrement(tree, letters)
    Set letters to GetString (input file)
list.Print(output file)
```

GetString(inFile) returns string

```
Set letters to empty string
Get a letter
while (NOT isalnum(letter)  AND inFile)
        Get a letter
if (NOT inFile)
        return letters
else
    do
        Set letter to tolower(letter);
        Set letters to letters + letter;
        Get a letter
    while (isalnum(letter) AND inFile);
```

Before going any further, we must decide on an implementation structure for `ListType`. No limit has been placed on the number of items in the list, so a linked implementation is appropriate. For each word, the list must be searched, either to insert a new word or to increment an already identified word's frequency. A tree-based list would be the most efficient because its search has O(log2*N*) complexity.

In our original design, we made WordType a class with member functions to initialize itself, compare itself, and increment its frequency. Because the container class is being designed especially for this problem, let's make `WordType` a struct rather than a class and let the list be responsible for the processing.

PutOrIncrement

```
if tree is NULL
    Get a new node for tree to point to
    Set word member of Info(tree) to letters
    Set count member of Info(tree) to 1
    Set Left(tree) to NULL
    Set Right(tree) to NULL
else if word member of Info(tree) is equal to letters
    Increment count member of Info(tree)
else if letters is less than the word member of Info(tree)
    PutOrIncrement(Left(tree), letters)
else
    PutOrIncrement(Right(tree), letters)
```

Print

```
if tree is not NULL
    Print(tree, outFile)
    word member of Info(tree).PrintToFile(TRUE, outFile)
    outFile << word
    Print(tree, outFile)
```

We are now ready to code our algorithms.

```
#include <fstream>
#include <cstddef>
#include <iostream>
#include <string>

using namespace std;
struct WordType
{
```

```
public:
  string word;
  int count;
};

struct TreeNode
{
  WordType info;
  TreeNode* left;
  TreeNode* right;
};

class ListType
{
public:
  ListType();
  void PutOrIncrement(string letters);
  void PrintList(ofstream&);
private:
  TreeNode* root;
};

string GetString(ifstream&);
const int MAX_LETTERS = 20;
int main()
{
  ListType list;
  string inFileName;
  string outFileName;
  string outputLabel;
  ifstream inFile;
  ofstream outFile;
  string letters;
  int minimumLength;

  // Prompt for file names, read file names, and prepare files
  cout << "Enter name of input command file; press return." << endl;
  cin  >> inFileName;
  inFile.open(inFileName.c_str());
  if (!inFile)
    cout << "file not found";

  cout << "Enter name of output file; press return." << endl;
  cin  >> outFileName;
  outFile.open(outFileName.c_str());
```

```
  cout << "Enter name of test run; press return." << endl;
  cin  >> outputLabel;
  outFile << outputLabel << endl;

  cout << "Enter the minimum size word to be considered." << endl;
  cin >> minimumLength;

  // Read the text stripping of words and inserting them into
  // list.  If a word is already there, its count is incremented.
  letters = GetString(inFile);
  while (inFile)
  {
    if (letters.length() >= minimumLength)
      list.PutOrIncrement(letters);
    letters = GetString(inFile);
  }

  list.PrintList(outFile);
  outFile.close();
  inFile.close();
  return 0;
}

string GetString(ifstream& inFile)
// Post: Non-alphanumeric characters are skipped. Alphanumeric characters are
//       read and concatenated on a string until a non-alphanumeric character
//       is read or end of file is reached. Letters are all converted to
//       lowercase.
{
  char letter;
  string letters = "";

  inFile.get(letter);
  while (inFile && !isalnum(letter))
    inFile.get(letter);

  if (!inFile)
    // No legal character found; empty string returned.
     return letters;
  else
  {// Read and collect characters.
    do
    {
       letter = tolower(letter);
```

```
      letters = letters + letter;
      inFile.get(letter);
    } while (isalnum(letter) && inFile);

  }
  return letters;
}

ListType::ListType()
{
  root = NULL;
}

void Process(TreeNode*& tree, std::string letters)
{
  if (tree == NULL)
  {
    tree = new TreeNode;
    tree->info.word = letters;
    tree->info.count = 1;
    tree->left = NULL;
    tree->right = NULL;
  }
  else if (tree->info.word == letters)
    tree->info.count++;
  else if (tree->info.word > letters)
    Process(tree->left, letters);
  else
    Process(tree->right, letters);
}

void ListType::PutOrIncrement(string letters)
{
  Process(root, letters);
}

void Print(TreeNode*& tree, ofstream& outFile)
{
  if (tree != NULL)
  {
    Print(tree->left, outFile);
    outFile << tree->info.word;
```

```
    outFile  << "  " << tree->info.count;
    outFile << endl;
    Print(tree->right, outFile);
  }
}

void ListType::PrintList(ofstream& outFile)
{
  Print(root, outFile);
}
```

We leave the rest of the problem of creating the index as a programming assignment.

Testing As a test plan for this program, we can take a text file, manually calculate the words and frequencies, and run the program to check the answers. On the Web, the file `Frequency.out` contains the result of running the program on the file `Words.cpp`, using the file `History.in` as input data.

Summary

In this chapter, we saw how we can use a binary tree to structure sorted information so as to reduce the search time for any particular element. For applications requiring direct access to the elements in a sorted structure, the binary search tree is a very useful data type. If the tree is balanced, we can access any node in the tree with an $O(\log_2 N)$ operation. The binary search tree combines the advantages of quick random access (like a binary search on a linear list) with the flexibility of a linked structure.

We also saw that we can implement the tree operations very elegantly and concisely using recursion. This result makes sense, because a binary tree is itself a "recursive" structure: Any node in the tree is the root of another binary tree. Each time we move down a level in the tree, taking either the right or the left path from a node, we cut the size of the (current) tree in half, a clear case of the smaller-caller. We also saw cases of iteration that replaced recursion (`PutItem` and `DeleteItem`).

Exercises

1. a. What does the level of a binary search tree mean in relation to its searching efficiency?
   b. What is the maximum number of levels that a binary search tree with 100 nodes can have?
   c. What is the minimum number of levels that a binary search tree with 100 nodes can have?
2. Which of these formulas gives the maximum total number of nodes in a tree that has N levels? (Remember that the root is Level 0.)
   a. $N^2 - 1$ b. 2^N c. $2^N - 1$ d. 2^{N+1}

3. Which of these formulas gives the maximum number of nodes in the *N*th level of a binary tree?

   a. N^2 b. 2^N c. 2^{N+1} d. $2^N - 1$

4. How many ancestors does a node in the *N*th level of a binary search tree have?

5. a. How many different *binary trees* can be made from three nodes that contain the key values 1, 2, and 3?

   b. How many different *binary search trees* can be made from three nodes that contain the key values 1, 2, and 3?

6. Draw all possible binary trees that have four leaves where all nonleaf nodes have two children.

7. The `TreeType` class used a queue as an auxiliary storage structure for iterating through the elements in the tree. Discuss the relative merits of using a dynamically allocated array-based queue versus a dynamically allocated linked queue.

Answer the questions in Exercises 8–10 independently, using the following tree.

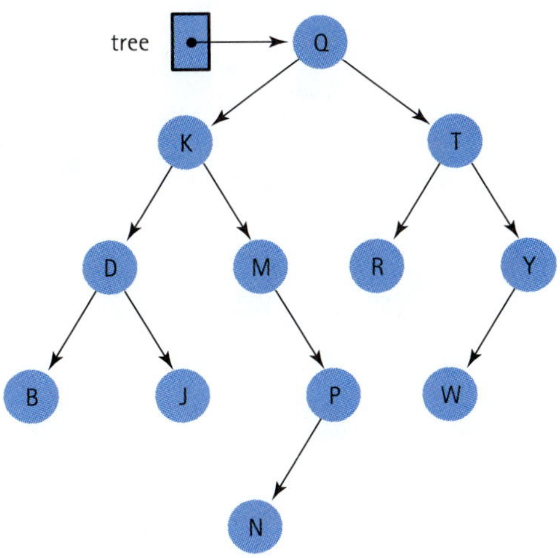

8. a. What are the ancestors of node P?

   b. What are the descendants of node K?

   c. What is the maximum possible number of nodes in the tree at the level of node W?

   d. What is the maximum possible number of nodes in the tree at the level of node N?

   e. Insert node O. How many nodes would be in the tree if it were completely full down to and including the level of node O?

9. Show what the tree would look like after each of the following changes. (Use the original tree to answer each part.)
   a. Add node C.
   b. Add node Z.
   c. Add node X.
   d. Delete node M.
   e. Delete node Q.
   f. Delete node R.
10. Show the order in which the nodes in the tree are processed by
   a. an inorder traversal of the tree.
   b. a postorder traversal of the tree.
   c. a preorder traversal of the tree.
11. Draw the binary search tree whose elements are inserted in the following order:

    50 72 96 94 107 26 12 11 9 2 10 25 51 16 17 95

Exercises 12–16 use the following tree.

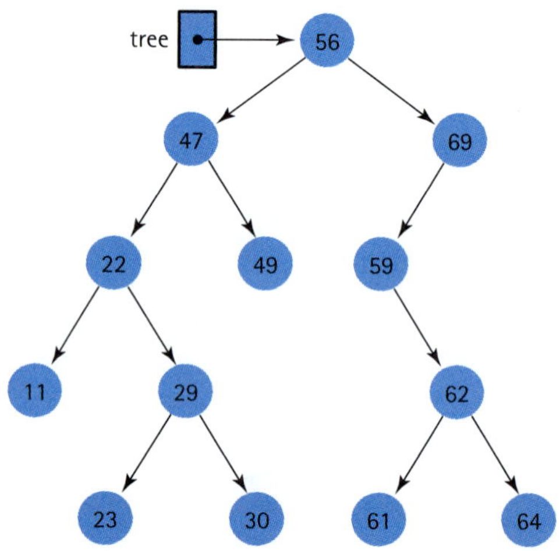

12. a. What is the height of the tree?
   b. What nodes are on Level 3?
   c. Which levels have the maximum number of nodes that they could contain?
   d. What is the maximum height of a binary search tree containing these nodes? Draw such a tree.
   e. What is the minimum height of a binary search tree containing these nodes? Draw such a tree.
13. a. Trace the path that would be followed in searching for a node containing 61.

b. Trace the path that would be followed in searching for a node containing 28.

14. Show the order in which the nodes in the tree are processed by
    a. an inorder traversal of the tree.
    b. a postorder traversal of the tree.
    c. a preorder traversal of the tree.
15. Show how the tree would look after the deletion of 29, 59, and 47.
16. Show how the (original) tree would look after the insertion of nodes containing 63, 77, 76, 48, 9, and 10 (in that order).
17. True or false?
    a. Invoking the delete function in this chapter might create a tree with more levels than the original tree had.
    b. A preorder traversal processes the nodes in a tree in the exact reverse order that a postorder traversal processes them.
    c. An inorder traversal always processes the elements of a tree in the same order, regardless of the order in which the elements were inserted.
    d. A preorder traversal always processes the elements of a tree in the same order, regardless of the order in which the elements were inserted.
18. If you wanted to traverse a tree, writing all the elements to a file, and later (the next time you ran the program) rebuild the tree by reading and inserting, would an inorder traversal be appropriate? Why or why not?
19. a. One hundred integer elements are chosen at random and inserted into a sorted linked list and a binary search tree. Describe the efficiency of searching for an element in each structure, in terms of Big-O notation.
    b. One hundred integer elements are inserted in order, from smallest to largest, into a sorted linked list and a binary search tree. Describe the efficiency of searching for an element in each structure, in terms of Big-O notation.
20. The key of each node in a binary search tree is a short character string.
    a. Show how such a tree would look after the following words were inserted (in the order indicated):

       monkey canary donkey deer zebra yak walrus vulture penguin quail

    b. Show how the tree would look if the same words were inserted in this order:

       quail walrus donkey deer monkey vulture yak penguin zebra canary

    c. Show how the tree would look if the same words were inserted in this order:

       zebra yak walrus vulture quail penguin monkey donkey deer canary

21. Write a function called `PtrToSuccessor` that finds a node with the smallest key value in a tree, unlinks it from the tree, and returns a pointer to the unlinked node.

22. Modify the `DeleteNode` function so that it uses the immediate successor (rather than the predecessor) of the value to be deleted in the case of deleting a node with two children. You should call the function `PtrToSuccessor` that you wrote in Exercise 21.
23. Use the Three-Question Method to verify the recursive function `Insert`.
24. Use the Three-Question Method to verify the recursive function `Delete`.
25. Write `IsFull` and `IsEmpty` for the iterative version of class `TreeType`.
26. Add a `TreeType` member function `Ancestors` that prints the ancestors of a given node whose `info` member contains `value`. Do not print `value`.
    a. Write the declaration.
    b. Write the iterative implementation.
27. Write a recursive version of the function `Ancestors` described in Exercise 26.
28. Write a recursive version of `Ancestors` (see Exercise 27) that prints out the ancestors in reverse order (first the parent, then the grandparent, and so on).
29. Add a Boolean member function `IsBST` to the class `TreeType` that determines whether a binary tree is a binary search tree.
    a. Write the declaration of the function `IsBST`. Include adequate comments.
    b. Write a recursive implementation of this function.
30. Extend the Binary Search Tree ADT to include the member function `LeafCount` that returns the number of leaf nodes in the tree.
31. Extend the Binary Search Tree ADT to include the member function `SingleParentCount` that returns the number of nodes in the tree that have only one child.
32. Write a client function that returns a count of the nodes that contain a value less than the parameter `value`.
33. Extend the Binary Search Tree ADT to include a Boolean function `SimilarTrees` that receives pointers to two binary trees and determines whether the shapes of the trees are the same. (The nodes do not have to contain the same values, but each node must have the same number of children.)
    a. Write the declaration of the function `SimilarTrees` as a `TreeType` member function. Include adequate comments.
    b. Write the body of the function `SimilarTrees`.
34. The `TreeType` member function `MirrorImage` creates and returns a mirror image of the tree.
    a. Write the declaration of the function `MirrorImage`. Include adequate comments.
    b. Write the body of the function `MirrorImage`.
    c. Can the binary tree returned from this function be used for binary searching? If so, how?

35. Write a client function `MakeTree` that creates a binary search tree from the elements in a sorted list of integers. You cannot traverse the list inserting the elements in order, as that would produce a tree that has *N* levels. You must create a tree with at most $\log_2 N + 1$ levels.

36. Write a client Boolean function `MatchingItems` that determines whether a binary search tree and a sequential list contain the same values.

Examine the following binary search tree and answer the questions in Exercises 37–40. The numbers on the nodes are *labels* so that we can talk about the nodes; they are not key values within the nodes.

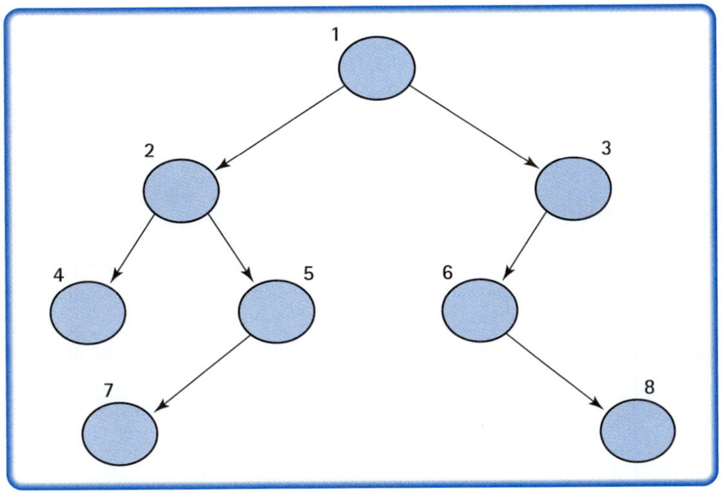

37. If an item is to be inserted whose key value is less than the key value in node 1 but greater than the key value in node 5, where would it be inserted?

38. If node 1 is to be deleted, the value in which node could be used to replace it?

39. 4 2 7 5 1 6 8 3 is a traversal of the tree in which order?

40. 1 2 4 5 7 3 6 8 is a traversal of the tree in which order?

41. In Chapter 6, we discussed how to store a linked list in an array of nodes using index values as "pointers" and managing our list of free nodes. We can use these same techniques to store the nodes of a binary search tree in an array, rather than using dynamic storage allocation. Free space is linked through the `left` member.

a. Show how the array would look after these elements had been inserted in this order:

Q L W F M R N S

Be sure to fill in all the spaces. If you do not know the contents of a space, use "?".

free	
root	

	.info	.left	.right
nodes [0]			
[1]			
[2]			
[3]			
[4]			
[5]			
[6]			
[7]			
[8]			
[9]			

b. Show the contents of the array after "B" has been inserted and "R" has been deleted.

`free`	
`root`	

	`.info`	`.left`	`.right`
`nodes` [0]			
[1]			
[2]			
[3]			
[4]			
[5]			
[6]			
[7]			
[8]			
[9]			

42. a. Which of the following trees are complete?
    b. Which of the following trees are full?

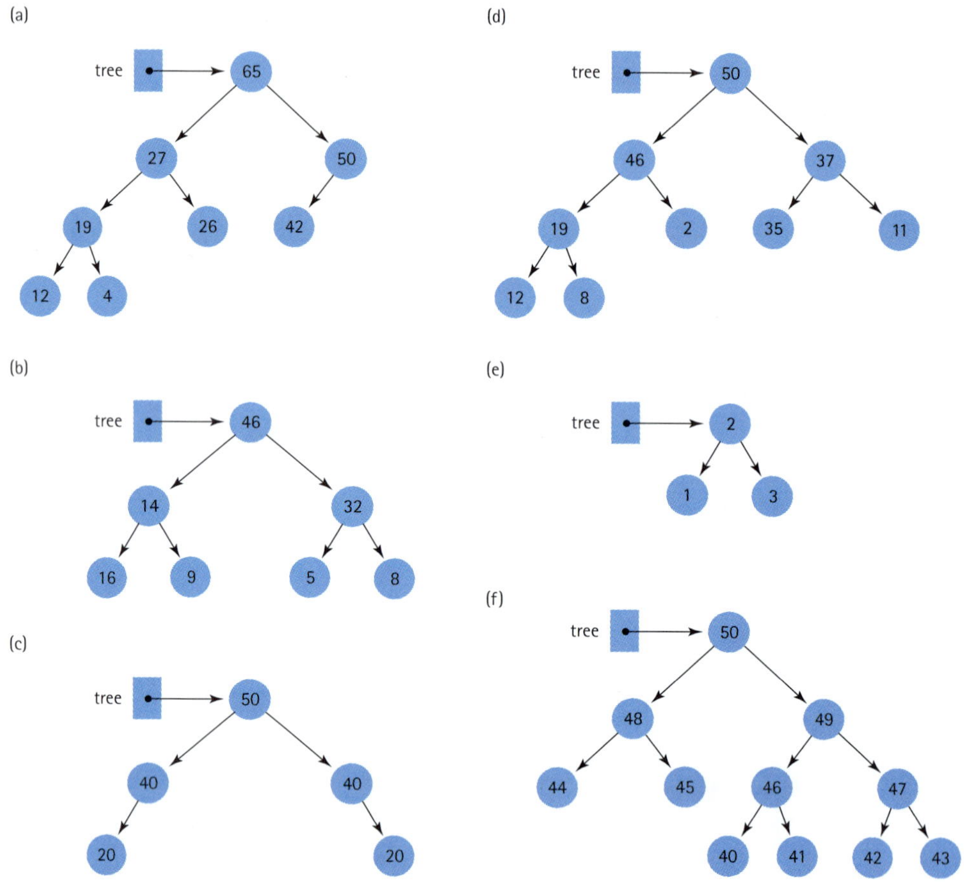

43. The elements in a binary tree are to be stored in an array, as described in the chapter. Each element is a nonnegative `int` value.

    a. What value can you use as the dummy value, if the binary tree is not complete?

    b. Show the contents of the array, given the following tree.

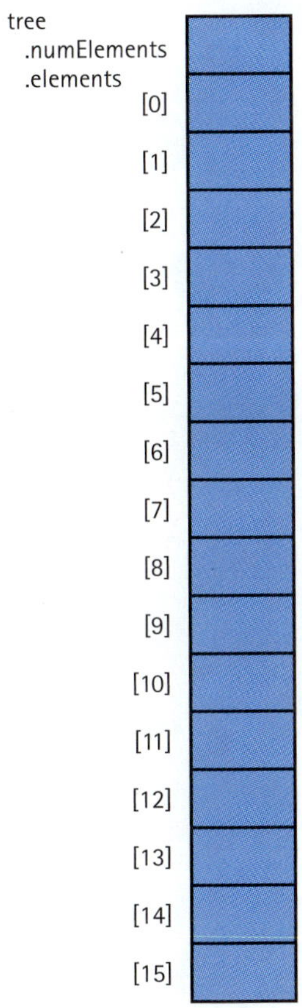

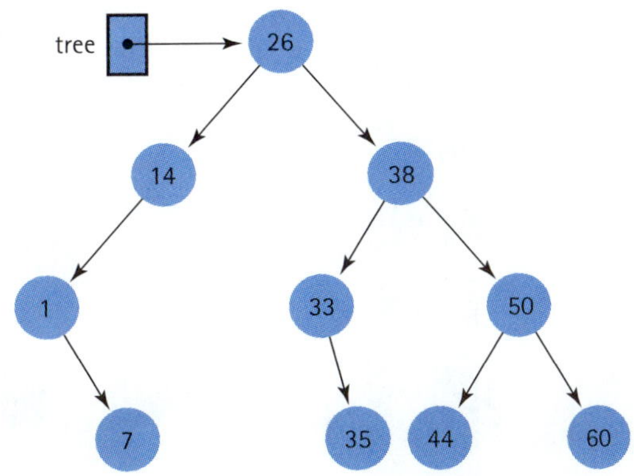

44. The elements in a complete binary tree are to be stored in an array, as described in the chapter. Each element is a nonnegative `int` value. Show the contents of the array, given the following tree.

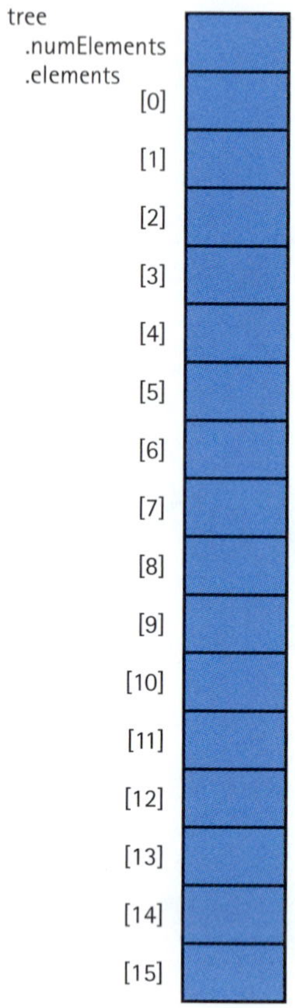

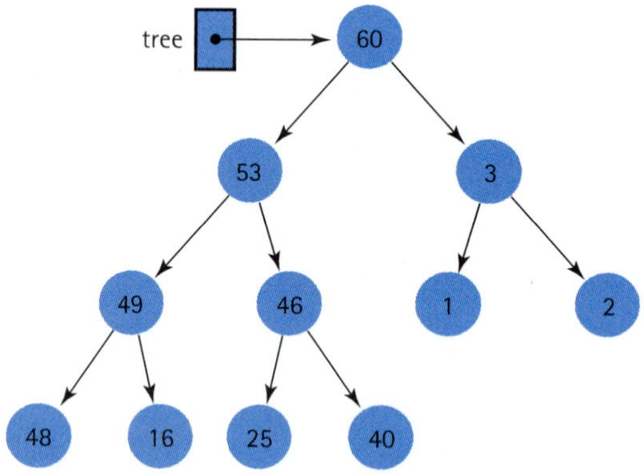

45. Given the following array, draw the binary tree that can be created from its elements. The elements are arranged in the array as discussed in the chapter.

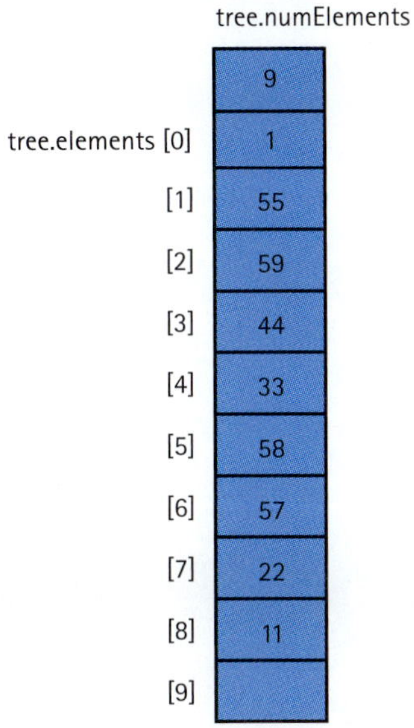

46. A binary tree is stored in an array called `treeNodes`, which is indexed from 0 to 99, as described in the chapter. The tree contains 85 elements. Mark each of the following statements as True or False, and correct any false statements.

   a. `treeNodes[42]` is a leaf node.
   b. `treeNodes[41]` has only one child.
   c. The right child of `treeNodes[12]` is `treeNodes[25]`.
   d. The subtree rooted at `treeNodes[7]` is a full binary tree with four levels.
   e. The tree has seven levels that are full, and one additional level that contains some elements.

47. Implement the Binary Search Tree ADT as a template class.

chapter 9

Priority Queues, Heaps, Graphs, and Sets

Goals

After studying this chapter, you should be able to

- Describe a priority queue at the logical level and implement a priority queue as a list
- Describe the shape and order properties of a heap, and implement a heap in a nonlinked tree representation in an array
- Implement a priority queue as a heap
- Compare the implementations of a priority queue using a heap, a linked list, and a binary search tree
- Define the following terms related to graphs:
  - Directed graph
  - Undirected graph
  - Vertex
  - Edge
  - Path
  - Complete graph
  - Weighted graph
  - Adjacency matrix
  - Adjacency list
- Implement a graph using an adjacency matrix to represent the edges
- Explain the difference between a depth-first and a breadth-first search, and implement these searching strategies using stacks and queues for auxiliary storage
- Implement a shortest-path operation, using a priority queue to access the edge with the minimum weight
- Describe a set at the logical level and implement a set both explicitly and implicitly

We have examined several basic data types in depth, discussing their uses and operations, and investigating one or more implementations of each. As we have constructed these programmer-defined data structures out of the built-in types provided by our high-level language, we have noted variations that adapt them to the needs of different applications. In Chapter 8, we saw how a tree structure, the binary search tree, facilitates searching data stored in a linked structure. In this chapter, we consider how other branching structures are used to model a variety of applications.

We end the chapter by looking at the Set ADT, an abstract data type that models the mathematical entity called a *set*.

9.1 ADT Priority Queue

A priority queue is an abstract data type with an interesting accessing protocol: Only the *highest-priority* element can be accessed. "Highest priority" can mean different things, depending on the application. Consider, for example, a small company with one secretary. When the other employees leave work on the secretary's desk, which jobs are done first? The jobs are processed in order of the employee's importance in the company; the secretary completes the president's work before starting the vice-president's job, and does the marketing director's work before staff programmers' tasks. The *priority* of each job relates to the level of the employee who initiated it.

In a telephone answering system, calls are answered in the order in which they are received; that is, the highest-priority call is the one that has been waiting the longest. Thus a FIFO queue can be considered a priority queue whose highest-priority element is the one that has been queued the longest time.

Logical Level

As you would expect, the Priority Queue ADT has exactly the same operations as a FIFO queue. The only difference relates to the postcondition of the `Dequeue` operation. Thus, we do not need to use a CRC card and can go directly to the specification.

Priority Queue ADT Specification

Structure: The priority queue is arranged to support access to the highest-priority item.

Operations:

Assumption: Before any call is made to a priority queue operation, the queue has been declared and a constructor has been applied.

MakeEmpty

Function:	Initializes the queue to an empty state.
Postcondition:	Queue is empty.

Boolean IsEmpty

Function:	Tests whether the queue is empty.
Postcondition:	Function value = (queue is empty).

Boolean IsFull

Function:	Tests whether the queue is full.
Postcondition:	Function value = (queue is full).

Enqueue(ItemType newItem)

Function:	Adds newItem to the queue.
Postconditions:	If (the priority queue is full), exception FullPQ is thrown; else newItem is in the queue.

Dequeue(ItemType& item)

Function:	Removes element with highest priority and returns it in item.
Postconditions:	If (the priority queue is empty), exception EmptyPQ is thrown; else highest priority element has been removed from queue. item is a copy of removed element.

Application Level

In discussing FIFO queue applications in Chapter 5, we said that the operating system of a multiuser computer system may use job queues to save user requests in the order in which they are made. Such requests might also be handled according to the importance of the job request. That is, the head of the company might get higher priority than the junior programmer. An interactive program might get higher priority than a job to print out a report that isn't needed until the next day. To handle these requests efficiently, the operating system may use a priority queue.

Hospital emergency rooms see patients in priority queue order; the patient with the most severe injuries sees the doctor first. Graduating seniors go to the head of the waiting list (priority queue) when trying to register for classes that are full. See Figure 9.1.

Priority queues are also useful in sorting. Given a set of elements to sort, we can enqueue the elements into a priority queue, and then dequeue them in sorted order (from largest to smallest). We look more closely at how priority queues can be used in sorting in Chapter 10.

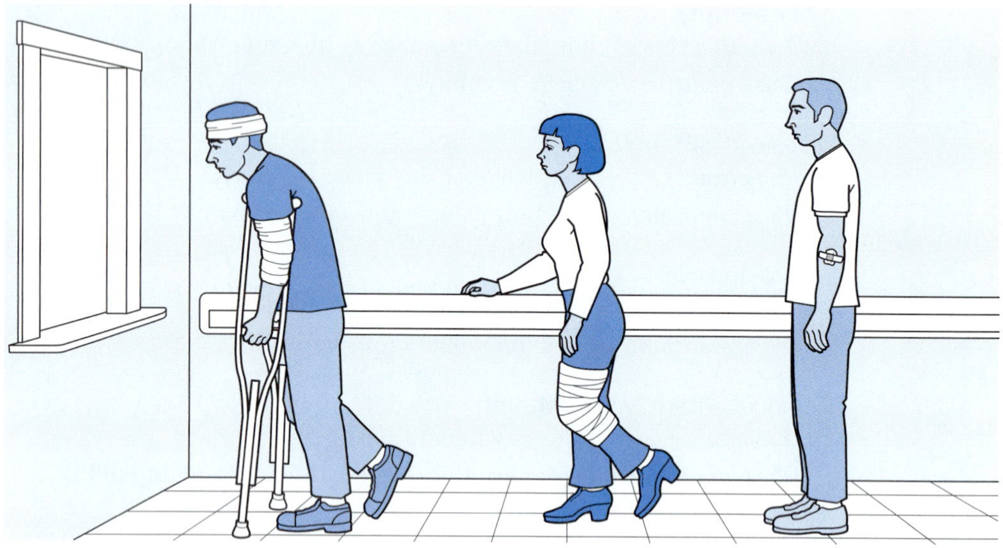

Figure 9.1 *Real-life priority queue*

Implementation Level

There are many ways to implement a priority queue. In any implementation, we want to access the element with the highest priority quickly and easily. Let's briefly consider some possible approaches:

Unsorted List Enqueuing an item would be very easy—simply insert it at the end of the list. Dequeuing would require searching through the entire list to find the item with the highest priority.

Array-Based Sorted List Dequeuing is very easy with this approach—simply return the item with the highest priority, which would be in the `length - 1` position (provided the array is kept in increasing order of priority). Thus, dequeuing is an O(1) operation. Enqueuing, however, would be more expensive. We have to find the place to enqueue the item—$O(\log_2 N)$ if we use a binary search—and rearrange the elements of the list after inserting the new item—$O(N)$.

Linked Sorted List Assume that the linked list is kept sorted from largest to smallest. Dequeuing simply requires removing and returning the first list element, an operation that requires only a few steps. But enqueuing again is $O(N)$ because we must search the list one element at a time to find the insertion location.

Binary Search Tree For this approach, the `Enqueue` operation would be implemented as a standard binary search tree `Insert` operation. We know that it requires $O(\log_2 N)$

steps on average. Assuming we have access to the underlying data structure of the tree, we can implement the `Dequeue` operation by returning the rightmost tree element. We follow the right subtree down, maintaining a trailing pointer as we go, until we reach a node with an empty right subtree. The trailing reference allows us to "unlink" the node from the tree. We then return the node. This is also an $O(\log_2 N)$ operation on average.

9.2 Heaps

Logical Level

Like a binary search tree, a heap is a binary tree that satisfies two properties, one concerning its shape and the other concerning the order of its elements. The *shape property* is simple: A heap must be a complete binary tree. The *order property* says that, for every node in the heap, the value stored in that node is greater than or equal to the value in each of its children. (The heap as a data structure is not to be confused with an unrelated concept of the same name. *Heap* is also a synonym for the free store—the area of memory available for dynamically allocated data.)

> **Heap** A complete binary tree, each of whose elements contains a value that is greater than or equal to the value of each of its children

Figure 9.2 shows two heaps that contain the letters "A" through "J." Notice that the placement of the values differs in the two trees, but the shape remains the same: a complete binary tree of ten elements. Note also that both heaps have the same root node. A group of values can be stored in a binary tree in many ways and still satisfy the order property of heaps. Because of the shape property, we know that the shape of all heaps with a given number of elements is the same. Because of the order property, we know that the root node always contains the largest value in the heap. This fact gives us a hint as to how we might use this data structure. The special feature of heaps is that we always know the location of the maximum value: It is in the root node.

When we refer to a "heap" in this section, we mean the structure defined above. It might also be called a "maximum heap," because the root node contains the maximum value in the structure. We can also create a "minimum heap," each of whose elements contains a value that is *less* than or equal to the value of each of its children.

Suppose we want to remove the element with the largest value from a heap. The largest element resides in the root node, so we can easily remove it, as illustrated in Figure 9.3a on page 575. Of course, its removal leaves a hole at the root position. Because the heap's tree must be complete, we decide to fill the hole with the bottom rightmost element from the heap; now the structure satisfies the shape property (Figure 9.3b). However, the replacement value came from the bottom of the tree, where the smaller values are located; the tree no longer satisfies the order property of heaps.

This situation suggests one of the basic heap operations: Given a complete binary tree whose elements satisfy the heap order property *except in the root position*, repair

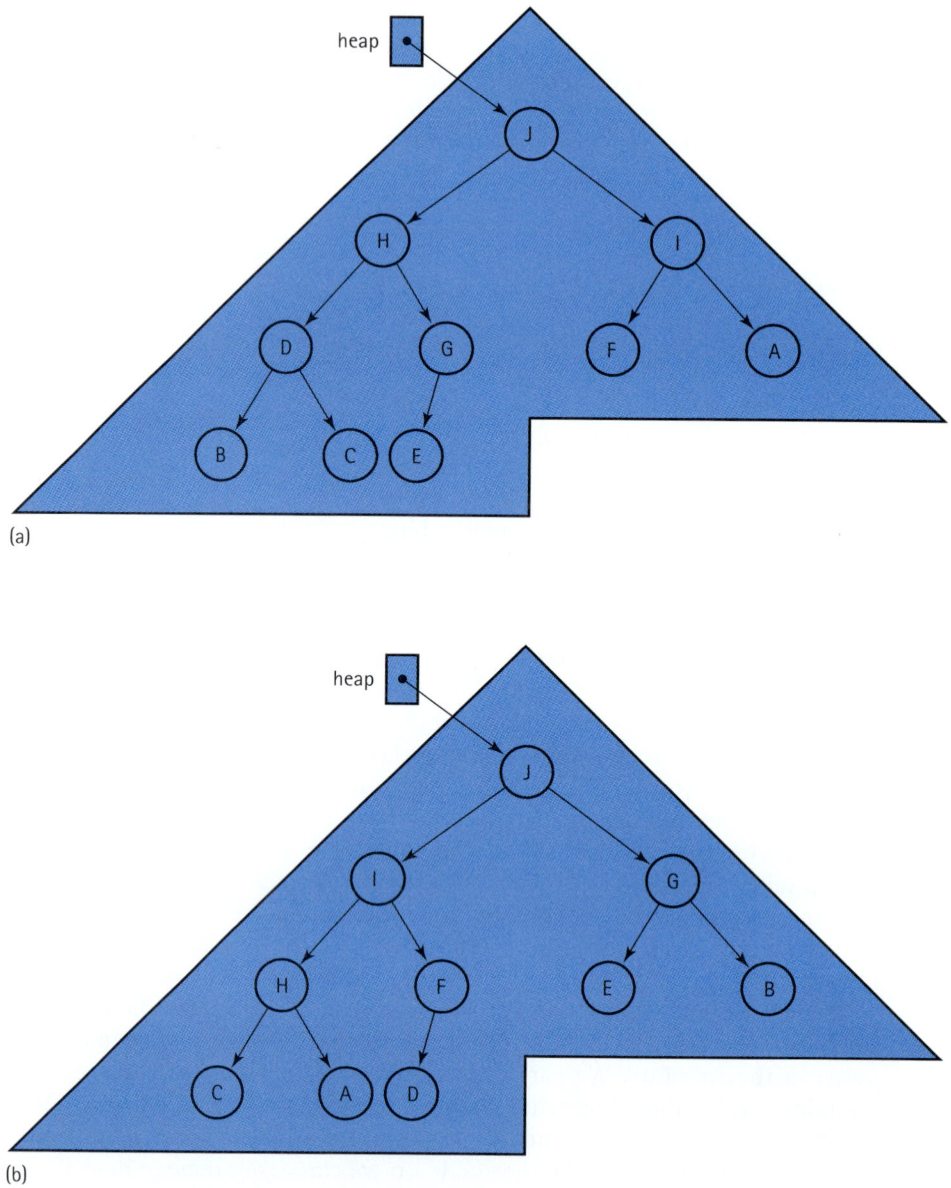

Figure 9.2 *Two heaps containing the letters "A" through "J"*

the structure so that it again becomes a heap. This operation, called `ReheapDown`, involves moving the element down from the root position until it ends up in a position where the order property is satisfied (see Figure 9.3c). `ReheapDown` has the following specification.

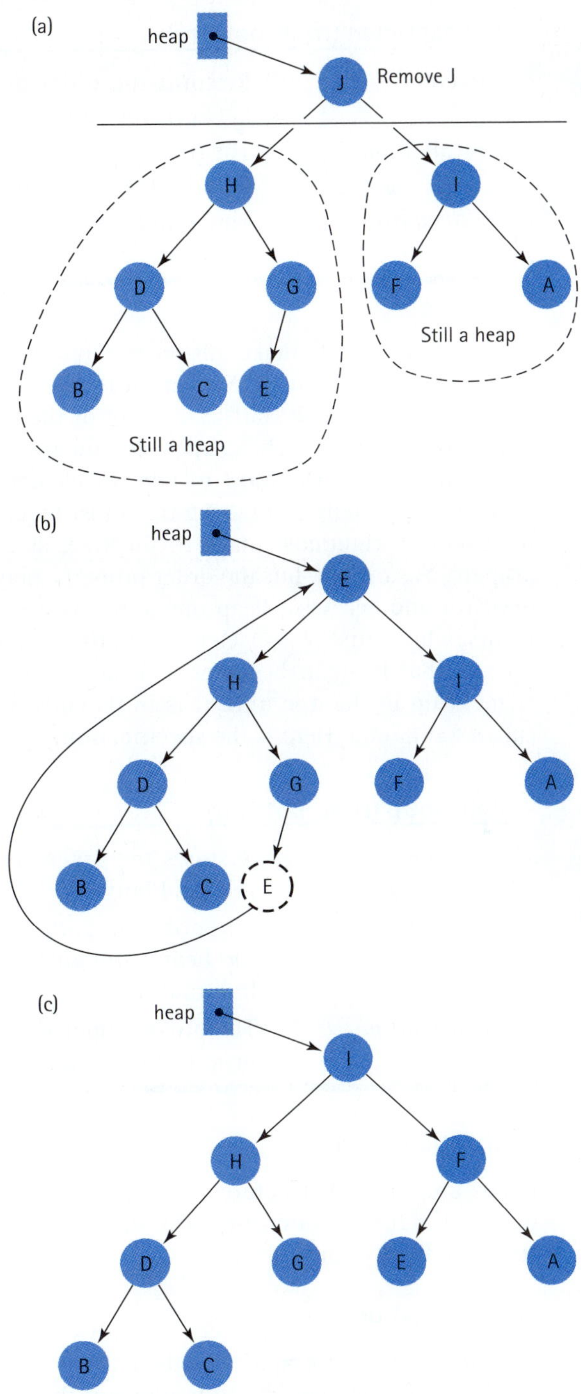

Figure 9.3 *The* `ReheapDown` *operation*

ReheapDown (root, bottom)

Function:	Restores the order property of heaps to the tree between root and bottom.
Precondition:	The order property of heaps may be violated only by the root node of the tree.
Postcondition:	The order property applies to all elements of the heap.

We have tried to make this operation fairly general, by telling it where to find the root and the bottom rightmost element of the heap. Letting the root be a parameter, instead of just assuming that we start at the root of the whole heap, generalizes this routine, allowing us to perform the reheap operation on any subtree as well as on the original heap.

Now suppose we want to add an element to the heap. Where do we put it? The shape property tells us that the tree must be complete, so we put the new element in the next bottom rightmost place in the tree, as illustrated in Figure 9.4a. Now the shape property is satisfied, but the order property may be violated. This situation illustrates the need for another basic heap operation: Given a complete binary tree containing N elements, whose first $N - 1$ elements satisfy the order property of heaps, repair the structure so that it again becomes a heap. To fix this structure, we need to float the Nth element up in the tree until it is in its correct place (see Figure 9.4b). This operation is called `ReheapUp`. Here is the specification:

ReheapUp (root, bottom)

Function:	Restores the order property to the heap between root and bottom.
Precondition:	The order property is satisfied from the root of the heap through the next-to-last node; the last (bottom) node may violate the order property.
Postcondition:	The order property applies to all elements of the heap from root through bottom.

Application Level

Heaps are unusual structures. Like arrays, they are used only as implementation structures for higher-level classes. The main application for a heap is as an implementation structure for a priority queue.

Implementation Level

Although we have graphically depicted heaps as binary trees with nodes and links, it would be very impractical to implement the heap operations using the usual linked-tree

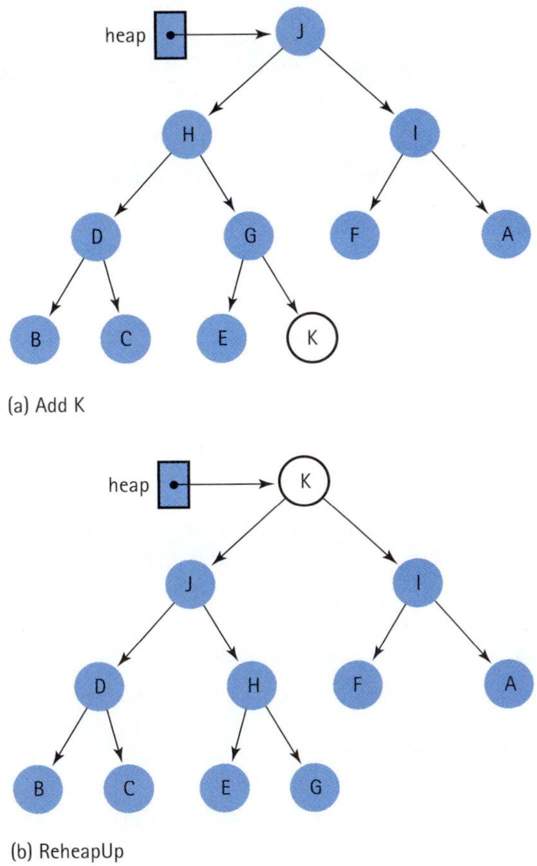

Figure 9.4 *The* `ReheapUp` *operation*

representation. The shape property of heaps tells us that the binary tree is complete, so we know that it never has any holes in it. Thus we can easily store the tree in an array with implicit links, as discussed in Chapter 8. Figure 9.5 shows how the values in a heap would be stored in such a representation. If a heap with `numElements` elements is implemented this way, the shape property says that the heap elements are stored in `numElements` consecutive slots in the array, with the root element placed in the first slot (index 0) and the last leaf node placed in the slot with index `numElements - 1`. The order property says that, for every nonleaf node `heap.elements[index]`,

```
heap.elements[index] >= heap.elements[index * 2 + 1]
```

and, if there is a right child,

```
heap.elements[index] >= heap.elements[index * 2 + 2]
```

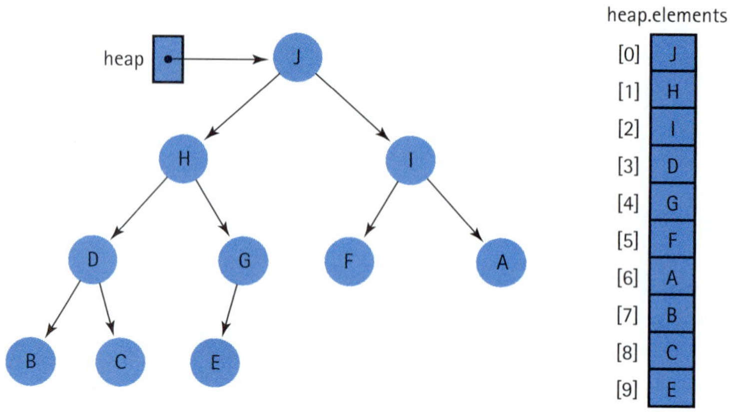

Figure 9.5 *Heap values in an array representation*

We use the following declarations to support this heap implementation:

```
template<class ItemType>
// Assumes ItemType is either a built-in simple type or a class
// with overloaded relational operators.
struct HeapType
{
  void ReheapDown(int root, int bottom);
  void ReheapUp(int root, int bottom);
  ItemType* elements;   // Array to be allocated dynamically
  int numElements;
};
```

This declaration is somewhat different from anything we have used so far. We are making `HeapType` be a struct with member functions. Why not make it into a class? Because heaps are seldom used alone. They are acted upon by other structures rather than being active. We define the functions that restore the heap property as part of the struct, but we also allow access to the data members. Our algorithms are very general, with the positions of both the root and the bottom elements passed as parameters. Additionally, we have chosen to include the data member `numElements` to record the number of elements on the heap, although our example algorithms do not use it.

We've specified the utility operations `ReheapDown` and `ReheapUp` to fix heaps that are "broken" at one end or the other. Now let's look at these operations in more detail.

When `ReheapDown` is first called, two possibilities arise. If the value in the root node (`heap.elements[0]`) is greater than or equal to the values in its children, the order property remains intact and we don't have to do anything. Otherwise, we know that the maximum value of the tree is in either the root node's left child (`heap.elements[1]`) or the right child (`heap.elements[2]`). We must swap one of these values with the smaller value in the root. Now the subtree rooted at the node that is swapped is a heap—except (possibly) for *its* root node. We apply the same process again, asking whether the value in this node is greater than or equal to the values in its children. We continue to test smaller and smaller subtrees of the original heap, moving our original root node down, until (1) the root of the current subtree is a leaf node or (2) the value in the root of the current subtree is greater than or equal to the values in both its children.

The algorithm for this function is given here and illustrated with an example in Figure 9.6. At the start, `root` is the index of the node that (possibly) violates the heap order property.

ReheapDown(heap, root, bottom)

```
if heap.elements[root] is not a leaf
    Set maxChild to index of child with larger value
    if heap.elements[root] < heap.elements[maxChild]
        Swap(heap.elements[root], heap.elements[maxChild])
        ReheapDown(heap, maxChild, bottom)
```

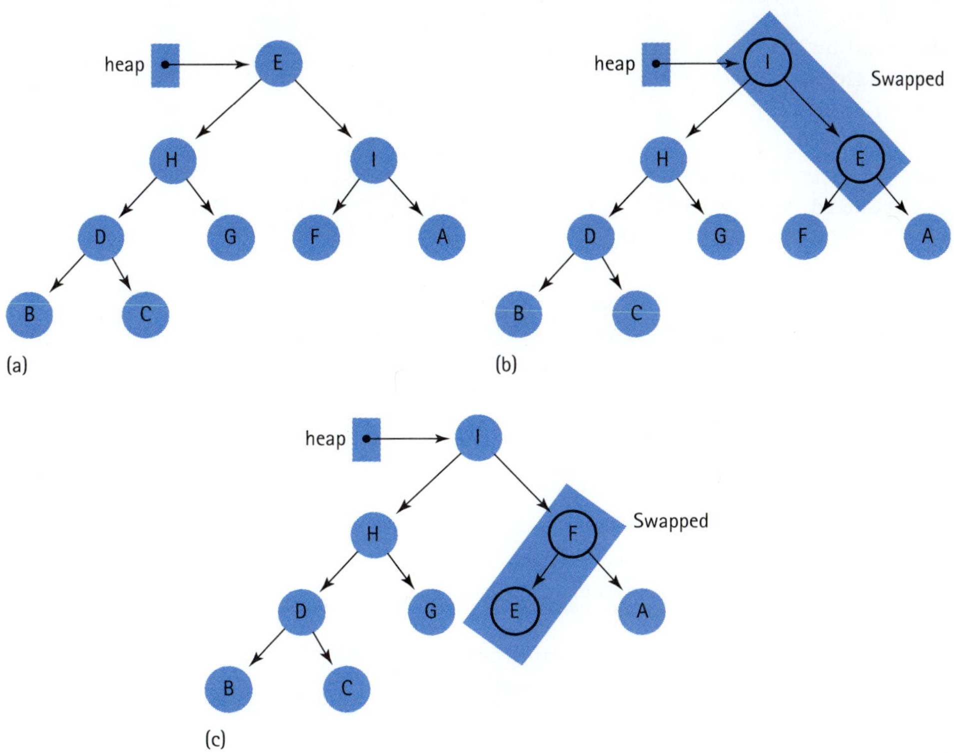

Figure 9.6 *The `ReheapDown` operation*

This algorithm is recursive. In the general case, we swap the value in the root node with its larger child, and then repeat the process. On the recursive call, we specify `maxChild` as the root of the heap; this shrinks the size of the tree still to be processed, satisfying the smaller-caller question. Two base cases exist: (1) if `heap.elements[root]` is a leaf, and (2) if the heap order property is already intact. In either of these cases, we do nothing. How can we tell if `heap.elements[root]` is a leaf? If the calculated position of the left child is greater than `bottom`, then it is a leaf node. Look back at Figure 9.5. The node with F is the first leaf node. The index of the node with F is 5, so its left child would be in index position 11 if it exists. Because 11 is greater than 9 (`bottom`), F's left child is not in the heap, so F is a leaf node.

To determine `maxChild`, we first check whether the current root node has only a single child. If so, it is a left child (because the tree is complete), and we set `maxChild` to its index. Otherwise, we compare the values in the two child nodes and set `maxChild` to the index of the node that has the larger value.

The following code gives the whole function. It uses a utility function, `Swap`, that swaps the values of its two parameters. (Because this function is trivial, we do not show its implementation here.)

```
template<class ItemType>
void HeapType<ItemType>::ReheapDown(int root, int bottom)
// Post: Heap property is restored.
{
  int maxChild;
  int rightChild;
  int leftChild;

  leftChild = root*2+1;
  rightChild = root*2+2;
  if (leftChild <= bottom)
  {
    if (leftChild == bottom)
      maxChild = leftChild;
    else
    {
      if (elements[leftChild] <= elements[rightChild])
        maxChild = rightChild;
      else
        maxChild = leftChild;
    }
    if (elements[root] < elements[maxChild])
    {
      Swap(elements[root], elements[maxChild]);
      ReheapDown(maxChild, bottom);
    }
  }
}
```

The complementary operation, ReheapUp, takes a leaf node that violates the order property of heaps and moves it up until its correct position is found. We compare the value in the bottom node with the value in its parent node. If the parent's value is smaller, the order property is violated, so we swap the two nodes. Then we examine the parent, repeating the process until (1) the current node is the root of the heap or (2) the value in the current node is less than or equal to the value in its parent node. The algorithm for this function is given here and illustrated in Figure 9.7.

```
ReheapUp(heap, root, bottom)
if bottom > root
    Set parent to index of parent of bottom node
    if heap.elements[parent] < heap.elements[bottom]
        Swap(heap.elements[parent], heap.elements[bottom])
        ReheapUp(heap, root, parent)
```

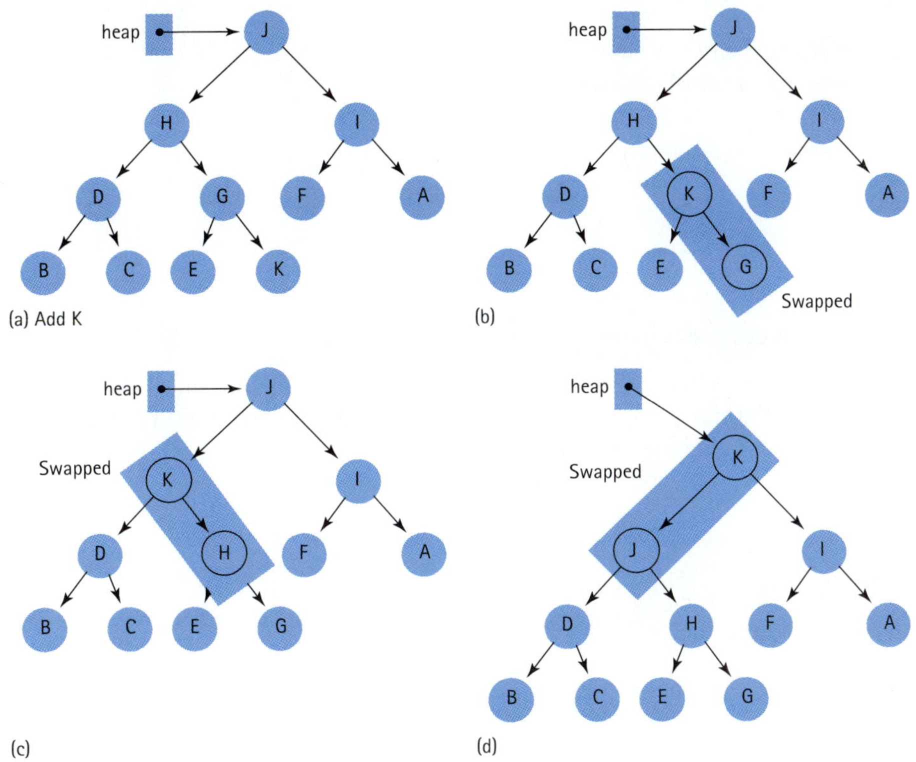

Figure 9.7 *The* ReheapUp *operation*

This algorithm is also recursive. In the general case, we swap the (current) "bottom" node with its parent and reinvoke the function. On the recursive call, we specify `parent` as the bottom node; this shrinks the size of the tree still to be processed, so the smaller-caller question can be answered affirmatively. Two base cases exist: (1) if we have reached the root node or (2) if the heap order property is satisfied. In either case, we exit the function without doing anything.

How do we find the parent node? This task is not an easy one in a binary tree linked together with pointers from parent to child nodes. As we saw earlier, however, it is very simple in our implicit link implementation:

```
parent = (index - 1) / 2;
```

We can now code the whole function:

```
template<class ItemType>
void HeapType<ItemType>::ReheapUp(int root, int bottom)
// Post: Heap property is restored.
{
  int parent;

  if (bottom > root)
  {
    parent = (bottom-1) / 2;
    if (elements[parent] < elements[bottom])
    {
      Swap(elements[parent], elements[bottom]);
      ReheapUp(root, parent);
    }
  }
}
```

Application Level Revisited

A heap is an excellent way to implement a priority queue. The following code shows how we declare our `PQType` class. For brevity, we omit the copy constructor and leave its coding as an exercise.

```
class FullPQ()
{};
class EmptyPQ()
{};
template<class ItemType>
class PQType
{
public:
  PQType(int);
```

```
  ~PQType();
  void MakeEmpty();
  bool IsEmpty() const;
  bool IsFull() const;
  void Enqueue(ItemType newItem);
  void Dequeue(ItemType& item);
private:
  int length;
  HeapType<ItemType> items;
  int maxItems;
};

template<class ItemType>
PQType<ItemType>::PQType(int max)
{
  maxItems = max;
  items.elements = new ItemType[max];
  length = 0;
}

template<class ItemType>
void PQType<ItemType>::MakeEmpty()
{
  length = 0;
}

template<class ItemType>
PQType<ItemType>::~PQType()
{
  delete [] items.elements;
}
```

We keep the number of elements in a priority queue in the data member `length`. Using the heap implementation described earlier, the elements are stored in the first `length` slots of the array `items.elements`. Because of the order property, we know that the largest element is in the root—that is, in the first array slot (index 0).

Let's look first at the `Dequeue` operation. The root element is returned to the caller. After we remove the root, we are left with two subtrees, each of which satisfies the heap property. Of course, we cannot leave a hole in the root position, as that would violate the shape property. Because we have removed an element, `length - 1` elements are now left in the priority queue, stored in array slots 1 through `length - 1`. If we fill the hole in the root position with the bottom element, array slots 0 through `length - 2` contain the heap elements. The heap shape property is now intact, but the order property may be violated. The resulting structure is not a heap, but it is *almost* a heap—all of the nodes *except the root node* satisfy the order property. This problem is an easy one to correct, as we already have a heap operation to perform exactly this task: `ReheapDown`. Here is our algorithm for `Dequeue`:

Dequeue

Set item to root element from queue
Move last leaf element into root position
Decrement length
items.ReheapDown(0, length - 1)

The `Enqueue` operation involves adding an element in its "appropriate" place in the heap. Where is this place? If the new element's priority is larger than the current root element's priority, we know that the new element belongs in the root. But that's not the typical case; we want a more general solution. To start, we can put the new element at the bottom of the heap, in the next available leaf position (review Figure 9.4). Now the array contains elements in the first `length + 1` slots, preserving the heap shape property. The resulting structure is probably not a heap, but it's *almost* a heap—the order property is violated in the last leaf position. This problem is easy to solve using the `ReheapUp` operation. Here is our algorithm for `Enqueue`:

Enqueue

Increment length
Put newItem in next available position
items.ReheapUp(0, length - 1)

```
template<class ItemType>
void PQType<ItemType>::Dequeue(ItemType& item)
// Post: element with highest priority has been removed
//       from the queue; a copy is returned in item.
{
  if (length == 0)
    throw EmptyPQ();
  else
  {
```

```
    item = items.elements[0];
    items.elements[0] = items.elements[length-1];
    length--;
    items.ReheapDown(0, length-1);
  }
}

template<class ItemType>
void PQType<ItemType>::Enqueue(ItemType newItem)
// Post: newItem is in the queue.
{
  if (length == maxItems)
    throw FullPQ();
  else
  {
    length++;
    items.elements[length-1] = newItem;
    items.ReheapUp(0, length-1);
  }
}
template<class ItemType>
bool PQType<ItemType>::IsFull() const
// Post: Returns true if the queue is full and false otherwise.
{
  return length == maxItems;
}

template<class ItemType>
bool PQType<ItemType>::IsEmpty() const
// Post: Returns true if the queue is empty and false otherwise.
{
  return length == 0;
}
```

Heaps Versus Other Priority Queue Representations

How efficient is the heap implementation of a priority queue? The `MakeEmpty`, `IsEmpty`, and `IsFull` operations are trivial, so we examine only the operations to add and remove elements.

`Enqueue` puts the new element into the next free leaf node in the heap. This array position can be accessed directly, so this part of the operation has O(1) complexity. Next, we invoke `ReheapUp` to correct the order. This operation moves the new element up the tree, level by level; because a complete tree is of minimum height, at most $\log_2 N$ levels exist above the new element (N = `length`). Thus `Enqueue` is an $O(\log_2 N)$ operation.

Table 9.1 *Comparison of Priority Queue Implementations*

	`Enqueue`	`Dequeue`
Heap	$O(\log_2 N)$	$O(\log_2 N)$
Linked list	$O(N)$	$O(1)$
Binary search tree		
Balanced	$O(\log_2 N)$	$O(\log_2 N)$
Skewed	$O(N)$	$O(N)$

`Dequeue` removes the element in the root node and replaces it with the bottom rightmost leaf node. Both of these elements in the array can be accessed directly, so this part of the operation has O(1) complexity. Next, we invoke `ReheapDown` to correct the order. This operation moves the root element down in the tree, level by level. At most $\log_2 N$ levels exist below the root, so `Dequeue` is also an $O(\log_2 N)$ operation.

How does this implementation compare to the others mentioned earlier in this section? If we implement the priority queue with a linked list, sorted from largest to smallest priority, `Dequeue` merely removes the first node from the list—an O(1) operation. `Enqueue`, however, may have to search all the elements in the list to find the appropriate insertion place; it is an $O(N)$ operation.

If we implement the priority queue using a binary search tree, the efficiency of the operations depends on the shape of the tree. When the tree is bushy, both `Dequeue` and `Enqueue` are $O(\log_2 N)$ operations. In the worst case, if the tree degenerates to a linked list sorted from smallest to largest priority, both `Dequeue` and `Enqueue` have $O(N)$ complexity. Table 9.1 summarizes the efficiency of the various implementations.

Overall, the binary search tree looks good, if it is balanced. It can, however, become skewed, which reduces the efficiency of the operations. The heap, on the other hand, is always a tree of minimum height. It is not a good structure for accessing a randomly selected element, but that is not one of the operations defined for priority queues. The accessing protocol of a priority queue specifies that only the largest (or highest-priority) element can be accessed. The linked list is a good choice for this operation (assuming the list is sorted from largest to smallest), but we may have to search the entire list to find the place to add a new element. For the operations specified for priority queues, therefore, the heap represents an excellent choice.

9.3 Graphs

Logical Level

Binary trees provide a very useful way of representing relationships in which a hierarchy exists. That is, a node is pointed to by at most one other node (its parent), and each node points to at most two other nodes (its children). If we remove the restriction that each node can have at most two children, we have a general tree, as pictured here:

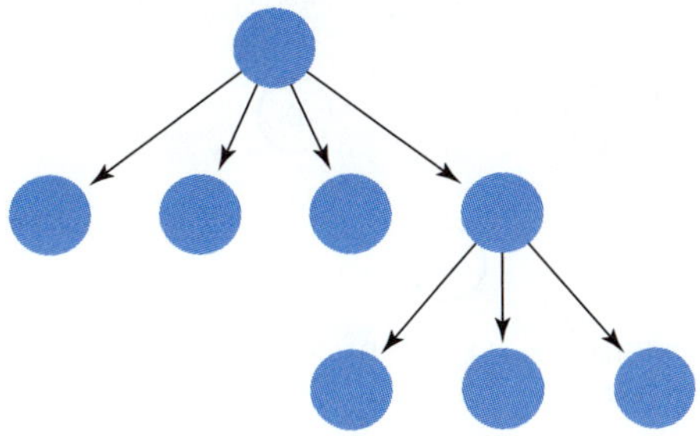

If we also remove the restriction that each node may have only one parent node, we have a data structure called a graph. A graph is made up of a set of nodes called vertices and a set of lines called edges (or arcs) that connect the nodes.

Graph A data structure that consists of a set of nodes and a set of edges that relate the nodes to one another

Vertex A node in a graph

Edge (arc) A pair of vertices representing a connection between two nodes in a graph

Undirected graph A graph in which the edges have no direction

Directed graph (digraph) A graph in which each edge is directed from one vertex to another (or the same) vertex

The set of edges describes relationships among the vertices. For instance, if the vertices are the names of cities, the edges that link the vertices could represent roads between pairs of cities. Because the road that runs between Houston and Austin also runs between Austin and Houston, the edges in this graph have no direction. This structure is called an undirected graph. However, if the edges that link the vertices represent flights from one city to another, the direction of each edge *is* important. The existence of a flight (edge) from Houston to Austin does not assure the existence of a flight from Austin to Houston. A graph whose edges are directed from one vertex to another is called a directed graph, or digraph.

From a programmer's perspective, vertices represent whatever is the subject of our study: people, houses, cities, courses, and so on. Mathematically, vertices are the undefined concept upon which graph theory rests. In fact, a great deal of formal mathematics is associated with graphs. In other computing courses, you will probably analyze graphs and prove theorems about them. This textbook introduces the graph as an abstract data type, explains some basic terminology, discusses how you might implement a graph, and describes how algorithms that manipulate graphs make use of stacks, queues, and priority queues.

Formally, a graph G is defined as follows:

$$G = (V, E)$$

where

V(G) is a finite, nonempty set of vertices

E(G) is a set of edges (written as pairs of vertices)

To specify the set of vertices, list them in set notation, within { } braces. The following set defines the four vertices of the graph pictured in Figure 9.8a:

$$V(Graph1) = \{A, B, C, D\}$$

(a) Graph1 is an undirected graph.

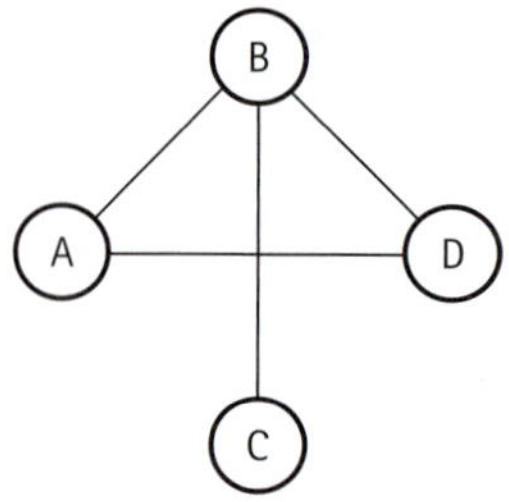

V(Graph1) = {A, B, C, D}
E(Graph1) = {(A, B), (A, D), (B, C), (B, D)}

(b) Graph2 is a directed graph.

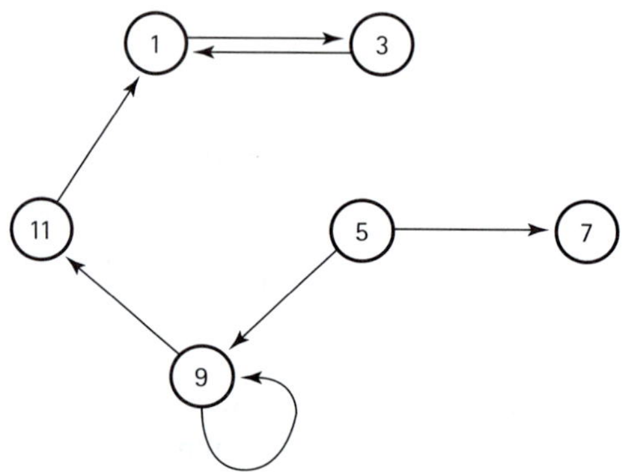

V(Graph2) = {1, 3, 5, 7, 9, 11}
E(Graph2) = {(1, 3), (3, 1), (5, 7), (5, 9), (9, 11), (9, 9), (11, 1)}

(c) Graph3 is a directed graph.

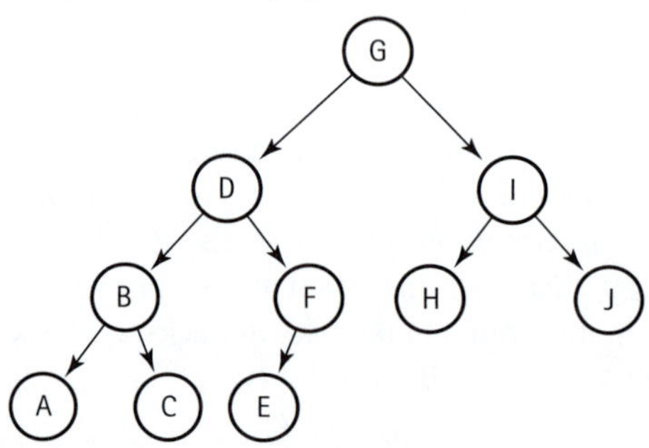

V(Graph3) = {A, B, C, D, E, F, G, H, I, J}
E(Graph3) = {(G, D), (G, I), (D, B), (D, F), (I, H), (I, J), (B, A), (B, C), (F, E)}

Figure 9.8 *Some examples of graphs*

The set of edges is specified by listing a sequence of edges. To denote each edge, write the names of the two vertices it connects in parentheses, with a comma between them. For instance, the vertices in Graph1 in Figure 9.8a are connected by the four edges described here:

$$E(Graph1) = \{(A, B), (A, D), (B, C), (B, D)\}$$

Because Graph1 is an undirected graph, the order of the vertices in each edge is unimportant. The set of edges in Graph1 can also be described as follows:

$$E(Graph1) = \{(B, A), (D, A), (C, B), (D, B)\}$$

If the graph is a digraph, the direction of the edge is indicated by which vertex is listed first. For instance, in Figure 9.8b, the edge (5, 7) represents a link from vertex 5 to vertex 7. However, Graph2 does not contain corresponding edge (7, 5). Note that in pictures of digraphs, the arrows indicate the direction of the relationship.

If two vertices in a graph are connected by an edge, they are said to be adjacent. In Graph1 (Figure 9.8a), vertices A and B are adjacent, but vertices A and C are not. If the vertices are connected by a directed edge, then the first vertex is said to be *adjacent to* the second, and the second vertex is said to be *adjacent from* the first. For example, in Graph2 (in Figure 9.8b), vertex 5 is *adjacent to* vertices 7 and 9, while vertex 1 is *adjacent from* vertices 3 and 11.

Adjacent vertices Two vertices in a graph that are connected by an edge

Path A sequence of vertices that connects two nodes in a graph

Complete graph A graph in which every vertex is directly connected to every other vertex

Weighted graph A graph in which each edge carries a value

Graph3 in Figure 9.8c may look familiar; it is the tree we examined earlier in connection with the nonlinked representation of a binary tree. A tree is a special case of a directed graph, in which each vertex may be adjacent from only one other vertex (its parent node) and one vertex (the root) is not adjacent from any other vertex.

A path from one vertex to another consists of a sequence of vertices that connect them. For a path to exist, an uninterrupted sequence of edges must go from the first vertex, through any number of vertices, to the second vertex. For example, in Graph2, a path goes from vertex 5 to vertex 3, but not from vertex 3 to vertex 5. Note that in a tree, such as Graph3 (Figure 9.8c), a unique path exists from the root to every other node in the tree.

In a complete graph, every vertex is adjacent to every other vertex. Figure 9.9 shows two complete graphs. If there are N vertices, there will be $N * (N - 1)$ edges in a complete directed graph and $N * (N - 1) / 2$ edges in a complete undirected graph.

In a weighted graph, each edge carries a value. Weighted graphs can be used to represent applications in which the *value* of the connection between the vertices is important, not just the *existence* of a connection. For instance, in the weighted graph pictured in Figure 9.10, the vertices represent cities and the edges indicate the Air

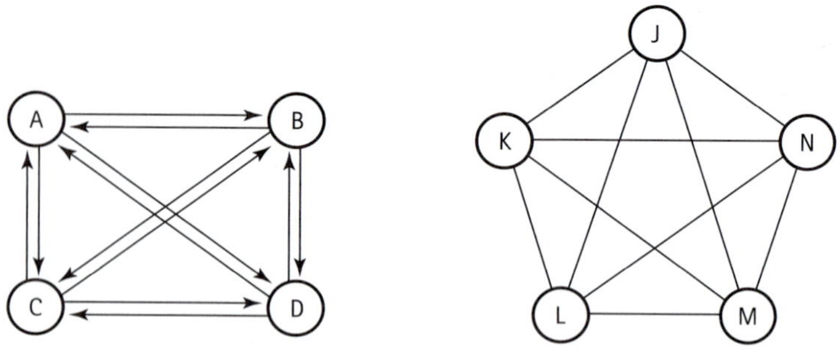

(a) Complete directed graph. (b) Complete undirected graph.

Figure 9.9 *Two complete graphs*

Busters Airlines flights that connect the cities. The weights attached to the edges represent the air distances between pairs of cities.

To see whether we can get from Denver to Washington, we look for a path between the two cities. If the total travel distance is determined by the sum of the distances between each pair of cities along the way, we can calculate the travel distance by adding the weights attached to the edges that constitute the path between them. Note that multiple paths may connect two vertices. Later in this chapter, we discuss a way to find the shortest path between two vertices.

We have described a graph at the abstract level as a set of vertices and a set of edges that connect some or all of the vertices to one another. What kind of operations are defined on a graph? In this chapter, we specify and implement a small set of useful graph operations. Many other operations on graphs can be defined; we have chosen operations that are useful in the graph applications described later in the chapter. First, however, we must define the operations necessary to build and process the graph.

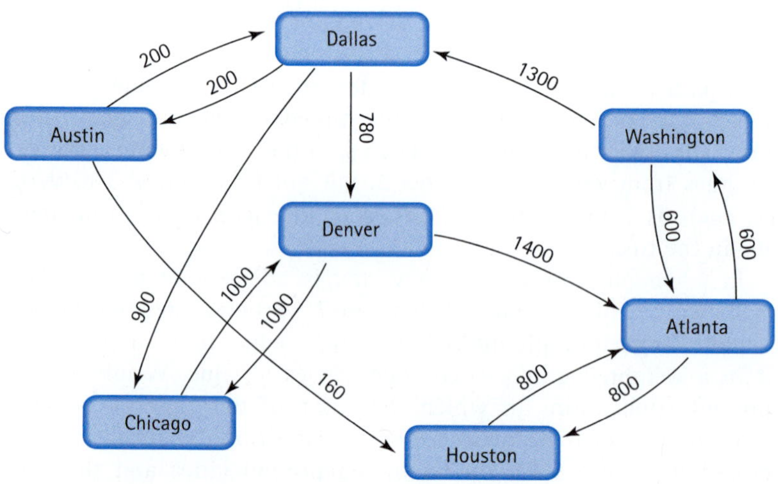

Figure 9.10 *A weighted graph*

We need to add vertices and edges, determine the weight on an edge, and get access to vertices that are adjacent from a vertex. Let's collect our observations about creating a graph into a CRC card:

Class Name: GraphType	Superclass:	Subclasses:

Responsibilities	Collaborations
Initialize	
IsFull returns Boolean	
IsEmpty returns Boolean	
Add vertex to graph (vertex)	VertexType
Add edge to graph (vertex, vertex, weight)	VertexType
Return value weight (vertex, vertex)	VertexType, QueType
Get a queue of to vertices (vertex, queue)	

Here is the specification for the Graph ADT:

Graph ADT Specification

Structure:

The graph consists of a set of vertices and a set of weighted edges that connect some or all of the vertices to one another.

Operations:

Assumption: Before any call is made to a graph operation, the graph has been declared and a constructor has been applied.

MakeEmpty

Function: Initializes the graph to an empty state.

Postcondition: Graph is empty.

Boolean IsEmpty

Function: Tests whether the graph is empty.

Postcondition: Function value = (graph is empty).

Boolean IsFull

Function:	Tests whether the graph is full.
Postcondition:	Function value = (graph is full).

AddVertex(VertexType vertex)

Function:	Adds vertex to the graph.
Precondition:	Graph is not full.
Postcondition:	vertex is in V(graph).

AddEdge(VertexType fromVertex, VertexType toVertex, EdgeValueType weight)

Function:	Adds an edge with the specified weight from fromVertex to toVertex.
Precondition:	fromVertex and toVertex are in V(graph).
Postcondition:	(fromVertex, toVertex) is in E(graph) with the specified weight.

EdgeValueType GetWeight(VertexType fromVertex, VertexType toVertex)

Function:	Determines the weight of the edge from fromVertex to toVertex.
Precondition:	fromVertex and toVertex are in V(graph).
Postconditions:	Function value = weight of edge from fromVertex to toVertex, if edge exists. If edge does not exist, function value = special "null-edge" value.

GetToVertices(VertexType vertex, QueType& vertexQ)

Function:	Returns a queue of the vertices that are adjacent from vertex.
Precondition:	vertex is in V(graph).
Postcondition:	vertexQ contains the names of all vertices that are adjacent from vertex.

Application Level

Our Graph ADT specification includes only the most basic operations. It provides no traversal operations. As you might imagine, we can traverse a graph in many different orders. As a result, we consider traversal to be a graph application rather than an innate operation. The basic operations given in our specification allow us to implement different traversals *independently* of how the graph itself is implemented.

In Chapter 8, we discussed the postorder tree traversal, which goes to the deepest level of the tree and works up. This strategy of going down a branch to its deepest point and moving up is called a *depth-first* strategy. Another systematic way to visit each vertex in a tree is to visit each vertex on Level 0 (the root), then each vertex on Level 1, then each vertex on Level 2, and so on. Visiting each vertex by level in this way is called a *breadth-first* strategy. With graphs, both depth-first and breadth-first strategies are useful. We outline both algorithms within the context of the airline example.

Depth-First Searching One question we can answer with the graph in Figure 9.10 is, "Can I get from city X to city Y on my favorite airline?" This is equivalent to asking, "Does a path exist in the graph from vertex X to vertex Y?" Using a depth-first strategy, let's develop an algorithm that finds a path from `startVertex` to `endVertex`.

We need a systematic way to keep track of the cities as we investigate them. With a depth-first search, we examine the first vertex that is adjacent from `startVertex`; if it is `endVertex`, the search ends. Otherwise, we examine all vertices that can be reached in one step (are adjacent from) this vertex. Meanwhile, we need to store the other vertices that are adjacent from `startVertex`. If a path does not exist from the first vertex, we come back and try the second vertex, third vertex, and so on. Because we want to travel as far as we can down one path, backtracking if we do not find the `endVertex`, a stack is a good structure for storing the vertices.

Here is the algorithm we use:

DepthFirstSearch

```
Set found to false
stack.Push(startVertex)
do
    stack.Pop(vertex)
    if vertex = endVertex
        Write final vertex
        Set found to true
    else
        Write this vertex
        Push all adjacent vertices onto stack
while !stack.IsEmpty() AND !found
if (!found)
    Write "Path does not exist"
```

Let's apply this algorithm to the airline-route graph depicted in Figure 9.10. We want to fly from Austin to Washington. We initialize our search by pushing our starting

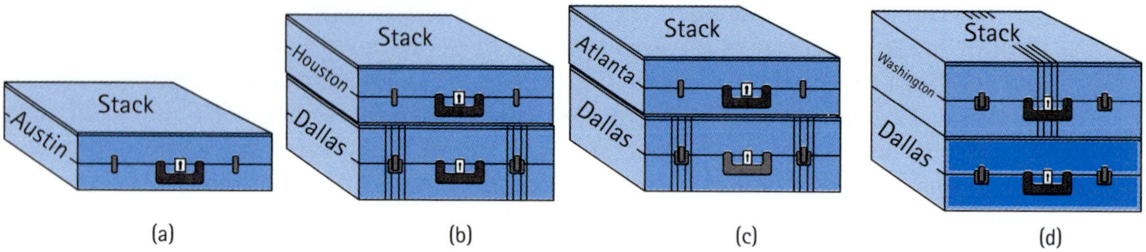

Figure 9.11 *Using a stack to store the routes*

city onto the stack (Figure 9.11a). At the beginning of the loop, we pop the current city, Austin, from the stack. The places we can reach directly from Austin are Dallas and Houston; we push both these vertices onto the stack (Figure 9.11b). At the beginning of the second iteration, we pop the top vertex from the stack—Houston. Houston is not our destination, so we resume our search from there. There is only one flight out of Houston, to Atlanta; we push Atlanta onto the stack (Figure 9.11c). Again we pop the top vertex from the stack. Atlanta is not our destination, so we continue searching from there. Atlanta has flights to two cities: Houston and Washington.

But we just came from Houston! We don't want to fly back to cities that we have already visited; this could cause an infinite loop. Our algorithm must take care of cycling. That is, we must mark a city as having been visited so that it is not investigated a second time. Let's assume that we have marked the cities that have already been tried, and continue our example. Houston has already been visited, so we ignore it. The second adjacent vertex, Washington, has not been visited so we push it onto the stack (Figure 9.11d). Again we pop the top vertex from the stack. Washington is our destination, so the search is complete. The path from Austin to Washington, using a depth-first search, is illustrated in Figure 9.12.

This search is called a depth-first search because we go to the deepest branch, examining all paths beginning at Houston before we come back to search from Dallas. When

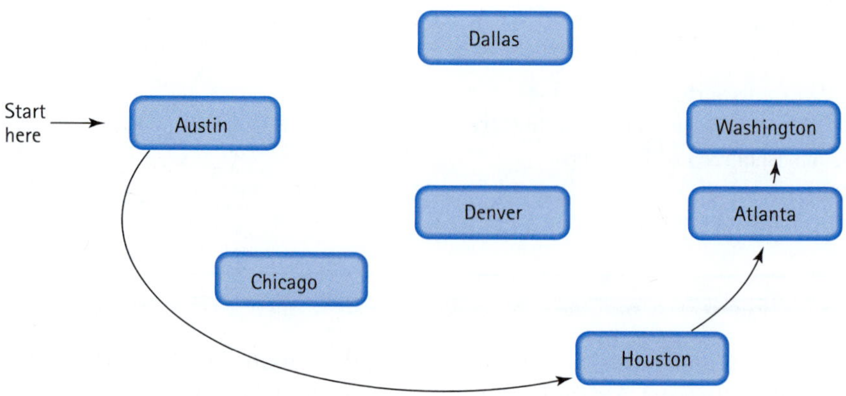

Figure 9.12 *The depth-first search*

you have to backtrack, you take the branch closest to where you dead-ended. That is, you go as far as you can down one path before you take alternative choices at earlier branches.

Before we look at the source code of the depth-first search algorithm, let's talk a little more about "marking" vertices on the graph. Before we begin the search, we must clear any marks in the vertices to indicate they are not yet visited. Let's call this function `ClearMarks`. As we visit each vertex during the search, we mark it. Let's call this function `MarkVertex`. Before we process each vertex, we can ask, "Have we visited this vertex before?" The answer to this question is returned by the function `IsMarked`. If we have already visited this vertex, we ignore it and go on. We must add these three functions to the specifications of the Graph ADT.

Additions to Graph ADT

ClearMarks

Function: Sets marks for all vertices to false.

Postcondition: All marks have been set to false.

MarkVertex(VertexType vertex)

Function: Sets mark for vertex to true.

Precondition: vertex is in V(graph).

Postcondition: IsMarked(vertex) is true.

Boolean IsMarked(VertexType vertex)

Function: Determines if vertex has been marked.

Precondition: vertex is in V(graph).

Postcondition: Function value = (vertex is marked true).

The function `DepthFirstSearch` receives a graph object, a starting vertex, and a target vertex. It uses the depth-first strategy to determine whether a path connects the starting city to the ending city, displaying the names of all cities visited in the search. Note that nothing in the function depends on the implementation of the graph. The function is implemented as a graph application; it uses the Graph ADT operations (including the mark operations) without knowing how the graph is represented.

In the following function, we assume that the header files for `StackType` and `QueType` have been included. We also assume that `VertexType` is a type for which the "==" and the "<<" operators are defined.

```
template<class VertexType>
void DepthFirstSearch(GraphType<VertexType> graph,
     VertexType startVertex, VertexType endVertex)
// Assumes VertexType is a type for which the "==" and "<<"
```

```
// operators are defined.
{
  using namespace std;
  StackType<VertexType> stack;
  QueType<VertexType> vertexQ;

  bool found = false;
  VertexType vertex;
  VertexType item;

  graph.ClearMarks();
  stack.Push(startVertex);
  do
  {
    stack.Pop(vertex);
    if (vertex == endVertex)
    {
      cout << vertex;
      found = true;
    }
    else
    {
      if (!graph.IsMarked(vertex))
      {
        graph.MarkVertex(vertex);
        cout << vertex;
        graph.GetToVertices(vertex, vertexQ);

        while (!vertexQ.IsEmpty())
        {
          vertexQ.Dequeue(item);
          if (!graph.IsMarked(item))
            stack.Push(item);
        }
      }
    }
  } while (!stack.IsEmpty() && !found);
  if (!found)
    cout << "Path not found." << endl;
}
```

Breadth-First Searching A breadth-first search looks at all possible paths at the same depth before it goes to a deeper level. In our flight example, a breadth-first search checks all possible one-stop connections before checking any two-stop connections. For most travelers, this is the preferred approach for booking flights.

When we come to a dead end in a depth-first search, we back up as *little* as possible. We try another route from a recent vertex—the route on top of our stack. In a breadth-first search, we want to back up as *far* as possible to find a route originating from the earliest vertices. The stack is not an appropriate structure for finding an early route because it keeps track of things in the order opposite of their occurrence—the latest route is on top. To keep track of things in the order in which they happened, we use a FIFO queue. The route at the front of the queue is a route from an earlier vertex; the route at the back of the queue is from a later vertex.

To modify the search to use a breadth-first strategy, we change all calls to stack operations to the analogous FIFO queue operations. Searching for a path from Austin to Washington, we first enqueue all cities that can be reached directly from Austin: Dallas and Houston (Figure 9.13a). Then we dequeue the front queue element. Dallas is not the destination we seek, so we enqueue all adjacent cities that have not yet been visited: Chicago and Denver (Figure 9.13b). (Austin has been visited already, so it is not enqueued.) Again we dequeue the front element from the queue. This element is the other "one-stop" city, Houston. Houston is not the desired destination, so we continue the search. Only one flight goes out of Houston, to Atlanta. Because we haven't visited Atlanta before, it is enqueued (Figure 9.13c).

Figure 9.13 *Using a queue to store the routes*

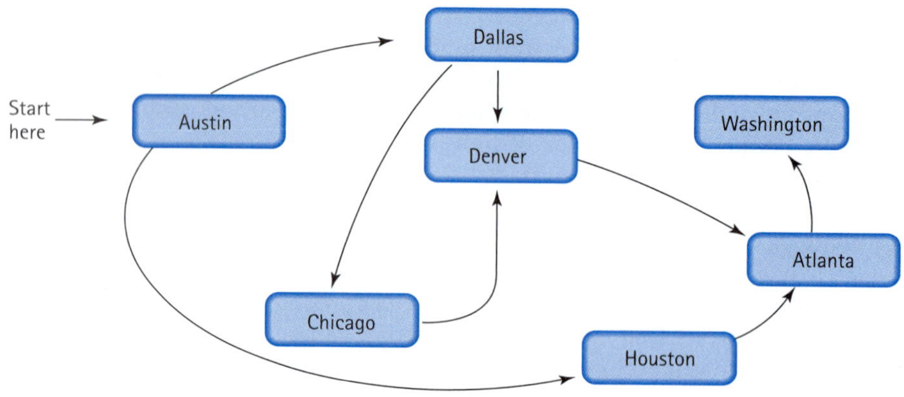

Figure 9.14 *The breadth-first search*

Now we know that we cannot reach Washington with one stop, so we start examining the two-stop connections. We dequeue Chicago; this is not our destination, so we put its adjacent city, Denver, into the queue (Figure 9.13d). Now an interesting situation arises: Denver is in the queue twice. Should we mark a city as having been visited when we put it in the queue or after it has been dequeued, when we are examining its outgoing flights? If we mark it only after it is dequeued, the queue may include multiple copies of the same vertex (so we need to check whether a city is marked *after* it is dequeued).

An alternative approach is to mark the city as having been visited before it is put into the queue. Which technique is better? It depends on the processing. You may want to know whether alternative routes exist, in which case you would want to put a city into the queue more than once.

Back to our example. We have put Denver into the queue in one step and removed its previous entry at the next step. Denver is not our destination, so we put its adjacent cities that we haven't already marked (only Atlanta) into the queue (Figure 9.13e). This processing continues until Washington is put into the queue (from Atlanta) and finally dequeued. We have found the desired city, and the search is complete. This search is illustrated in Figure 9.14.

The source code for the `BreadthFirstSearch` function is identical to that for the depth-first search, except for the replacement of the stack with a FIFO queue.

```
template<class VertexType>
void BreadthFirstSearch(GraphType<VertexType> graph,
     VertexType startVertex, VertexType endVertex)
// Assumption: VertexType is a type for which the "==" and
//             "<<" operators are defined.
{
  using namespace std;
  QueType<VertexType> queue;
  QueType<VertexType> vertexQ;
```

```
  bool found = false;
  VertexType vertex;
  VertexType item;

  graph.ClearMarks();
  queue.Enqueue(startVertex);

  do
  {
    queue.Dequeue(vertex);

    if (vertex == endVertex)
    {
      cout  << vertex;
      found = true;
    }
    else
    {
      if (!graph.IsMarked(vertex))
      {
        graph.MarkVertex(vertex);
        cout  << vertex;
        graph.GetToVertices(vertex, vertexQ);

        while (!vertexQ.IsEmpty())
        {
          vertexQ.Dequeue(item);
          if (!graph.IsMarked(item))
            queue.Enqueue(item);
        }
      }
    }
  } while (!queue.IsEmpty() && !found);
  if (!found)
    cout << "Path not found." << endl;
}
```

The Single-Source Shortest-Path Problem We know from the two search operations just discussed that multiple paths may connect one vertex to another. Suppose that we want to find the *shortest path* from Austin to each of the other cities that Air Busters serves. By "shortest path," we mean the path whose edge values (weights), when added together, have the smallest sum. Consider the following two paths from Austin to Washington:

Austin	
Houston	160 miles
Atlanta	800 miles
Washington	600 miles
Total miles	1560 miles

Austin	
Dallas	200 miles
Denver	780 miles
Atlanta	1400 miles
Washington	600 miles
Total Miles	2980 miles

Clearly, the first path is preferable, unless you want to collect frequent-flyer miles.

Let's develop an algorithm that displays the shortest path from a designated starting city to *every other city* in the graph—this time we will not search for a path between a starting city and an ending city. As in the two graph searches described earlier, we need an auxiliary structure for storing cities that we process later. By retrieving the city that was most recently put into the structure, the depth-first search tries to keep going "forward." It tries a one-flight solution, then a two-flight solution, then a three-flight solution, and so on. It backtracks to a fewer-flight solution only when it reaches a dead end. In contrast, by retrieving the city that has been in the structure for the longest time, the breadth-first search tries all one-flight solutions, then all two-flight solutions, and so on. The breadth-first search finds a path with a minimum number of flights.

But the minimum *number* of flights does not necessarily mean the minimum total distance. Unlike the depth-first and breadth-first searches, the shortest-path traversal must use the number of miles (edge weights) between cities. We want to retrieve the vertex that is *closest* to the current vertex—that is, the vertex connected with the minimum edge weight. If we consider minimum distance to be the highest priority, then we know of a perfect structure—the priority queue. Our algorithm can use a priority queue whose elements are flights (edges) with the distance from the starting city as the priority. That is, the items on the priority queue are struct variables with three data members: `fromVertex`, `toVertex`, and `distance`.

ShortestPath

```
graph.ClearMarks()
Set item.fromVertex to startVertex
Set item.toVertex to startVertex
Set item.distance to 0
pq.Enqueue(item)
```

(continued)

```
do
    pq.Dequeue(item)
    if item.toVertex is not marked
        Mark item.toVertex
        Write item.fromVertex, item.toVertex, item.distance
        Set item.fromVertex to item.toVertex
        Set minDistance to item.distance
        Get queue vertexQ of vertices adjacent from item.fromVertex
        while more vertices in vertexQ
            Get next vertex from vertexQ
            if vertex not marked
                Set item.toVertex to vertex
                Set item.distance to minDistance + graph.GetWeight(fromVertex, vertex)
                pq.Enqueue(item)
while !pq.IsEmpty()
```

The algorithm for the shortest-path traversal is similar to those we used for the depth-first and breadth-first searches, albeit with two major differences:

1. We use a priority queue rather than a FIFO queue or a stack.
2. We stop only when there are no more cities to process; we have no destination.

Here is the source code for the shortest-path algorithm. This code assumes that the header files for `QueType` and `PQType` have been included. Notice that `ItemType` (the type of the items to be placed into the priority queue) must overload the relational operators such that a smaller distance indicates a *higher* priority. As a result, the priority queue is implemented with a *minimum heap*. That is, for every item in the heap, `item.distance` is less than or equal to the `distance` member of each of its children.

```
template<class VertexType>
struct ItemType
{
  bool operator<(ItemType otherItem);
  // "<" means shorter distance.
  bool operator==(ItemType otherItem);
  bool operator<=(ItemType otherItem);
  VertexType fromVertex;
  VertexType toVertex;
  int distance;
};
```

```
template<class VertexType>
void ShortestPath(GraphType<VertexType> graph,
     VertexType startVertex)
{
  using namespace std;
  ItemType item;
  int minDistance;
  PQType<VertexType> pq(10);      // Assume at most 10 vertices.
  QueType<VertexType> vertexQ;
  VertexType vertex;

  graph.ClearMarks();
  item.fromVertex = startVertex;
  item.toVertex = startVertex;
  item.distance = 0;
  pq.Enqueue(item);
  cout  << "Last Vertex  Destination   Distance" << endl;
  cout  << "------------------------------------" << endl;

  do
  {
    pq.Dequeue(item);
    if (!graph.IsMarked(item.toVertex))
    {
      graph.MarkVertex(item.toVertex);
      cout << item.fromVertex;
      cout << "  ";
      cout << item.toVertex;
      cout << "  " << item.distance << endl;
      item.fromVertex = item.toVertex;
      minDistance = item.distance;
      graph.GetToVertices(item.fromVertex, vertexQ);

      while (!vertexQ.IsEmpty())
      {
        vertexQ.Dequeue(vertex);
        if (!graph.IsMarked(vertex))
        {
          item.toVertex = vertex;
          item.distance = minDistance +
              graph.GetWeight(item.fromVertex, vertex);
          pq.Enqueue(item);
        }
      }
    }
  } while (!pq.IsEmpty());
}
```

The output from this function is a table of city pairs (edges), showing the total distance from `startVertex` to each of the other vertices in the graph, as well as the last vertex visited before the destination. If `graph` contains the information shown in Figure 9.10, the function call

```
ShortestPath(graph, startVertex);
```

where `startVertex` corresponds to Washington, would print a table like this:

Last Vertex	Destination	Distance
Washington	Washington	0
Washington	Atlanta	600
Washington	Dallas	1300
Atlanta	Houston	1400
Dallas	Austin	1500
Dallas	Denver	2080
Dallas	Chicago	2200

The shortest-path distance from Washington to each destination appears in the second and third columns. For example, our flights from Washington to Chicago total 2,200 miles. The first column shows which city immediately preceded the destination in the traversal.

Let's figure out the shortest path from Washington to Chicago. We see from the first column that the next-to-last vertex in the path is Dallas. Now we look up Dallas in the Destination (second) column: The vertex before Dallas is Washington. The whole path is Washington–Dallas–Chicago. (We might want to consider another airline for a more direct route!)

Implementation Level

Array-Based Implementation A simple way to represent V(graph), the vertices in the graph, is with an array where the elements are of the type of the vertices (`VertexType`). For example, if the vertices represent cities, `VertexType` would be some representation of strings. A simple way to represent E(graph), the edges in a graph, is with an adjacency matrix, a two-dimensional array of edge values (weights). Thus a graph consists of a data member `numVertices`, a one-dimensional array `vertices`, and a two-dimensional array `edges`. Figure 9.15 depicts the implementation of the graph of Air Busters flights between seven cities. For simplicity, we omit

Adjacency matrix For a graph with N nodes, an N by N table that shows the existence (and weights) of all edges in the graph

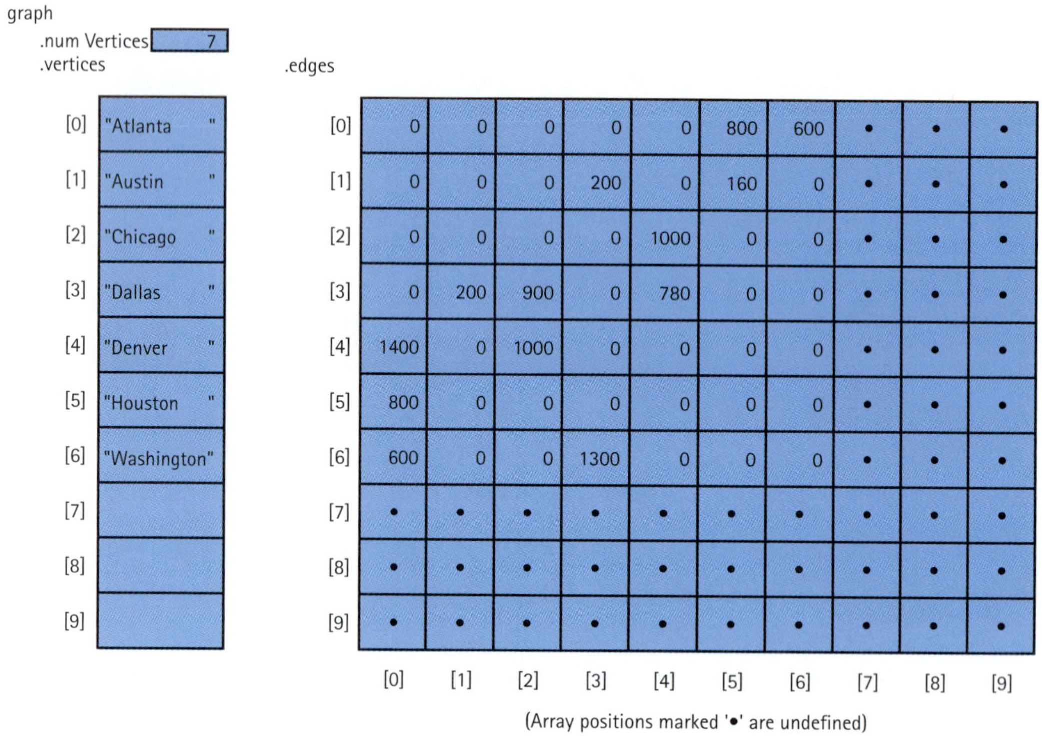

Figure 9.15 *Graph of flight connections between cities*

additional Boolean data needed to mark vertices as "visited" during a traversal. While the city names in Figure 9.15 are in alphabetical order, there is no requirement that the elements in this array be sorted.

At any time, within this representation of a graph,

- `numVertices` is the number of vertices in the graph.
- V(graph) is contained in `vertices[0]..vertices[numVertices - 1]`.
- E(graph) is contained in the square array `edges[0][0]..edges[numVertices - 1][numVertices - 1]`.

The names of the cities are contained in `graph.vertices`. The weight of each edge in `graph.edges` represents the air distance between two cities that are connected by a flight. For example, the value in `graph.edges[1][3]` tells us that a direct flight goes between Austin and Dallas, and that the air distance is 200 miles. A `NULL_EDGE` value (0) in `graph.edges[1][6]` tells us that the airline has no direct flights between Austin and Washington. Because this is a weighted graph with the weights consisting of air distances, we use the `int` type for `EdgeValueType`. If this were not a weighted graph, `EdgeValueType` would be `bool`, and each position in the adjacency matrix would be true if an edge exists between the pair of vertices and false if no edge exists.

Here is the definition of the class `GraphType`. For simplicity, we assume that `EdgeValueType` is `int`.

```
template<class VertexType>
// Assumption: VertexType is a type for which the "=",
// "==", and "<<" operators are defined.
class GraphType
{
public:
  GraphType();                  // Default is 50 vertices
  GraphType(int maxV);          // maxV <= 50
  ~GraphType();
  void MakeEmpty();
  bool IsEmpty() const;
  bool IsFull() const;
  void AddVertex(VertexType);
  void AddEdge(VertexType, VertexType, int);
  int GetWeight(VertexType, VertexType);
  void GetToVertices(VertexType, QueType<VertexType>&);
  void ClearMarks();
  void MarkVertex(VertexType);
  bool IsMarked(VertexType);
private:
  int numVertices;
  int maxVertices;
  VertexType* vertices;
  int edges[50][50];
  bool* marks;       // marks[i] is the mark for vertices[i].
};
```

The class constructors are usually the easiest operations to write, but not for `GraphType`. We have to allocate the space for `vertices` and `marks` (the Boolean array indicating whether a vertex has been marked). The default constructor sets up space for 50 `vertices` and `marks`. The parameterized constructor lets the user specify the maximum number of vertices. Why don't we put `edges` in dynamic storage? We could, but allocating storage for a two-dimensional array is rather complex, and we do not wish to divert our attention from the main issue: the Graph ADT.

```
template<class VertexType>
GraphType<VertexType>::GraphType()
// Post: Arrays of size 50 are dynamically allocated for
//       marks and vertices. numVertices is set to 0;
//       maxVertices is set to 50.
{
  numVertices = 0;
  maxVertices = 50;
  vertices = new VertexType[50];
  marks = new bool[50];
}
```

```
template<class VertexType>
GraphType<VertexType>::GraphType(int maxV)
// Post: Arrays of size maxV are dynamically allocated for
//       marks and vertices.
//       numVertices is set to 0; maxVertices is set to maxV.
{
  numVertices = 0;
  maxVertices = maxV;
  vertices = new VertexType[maxV];
  marks = new bool[maxV];
}

template<class VertexType>
GraphType<VertexType>::~GraphType()
// Post: Arrays for vertices and marks have been deallocated.
{
  delete [] vertices;
  delete [] marks;
}
```

The `AddVertex` operation puts `vertex` into the next free space in the array of vertices. Because the new vertex has no edges defined yet, we also initialize the appropriate row and column of `edges` to contain `NULL_EDGE` (0 in this case).

```
const int NULL_EDGE = 0;

template<class VertexType>
void GraphType<VertexType>::AddVertex(VertexType vertex)
// Post: vertex has been stored in vertices.
//       Corresponding row and column of edges have been set
//       to NULL_EDGE.
//       numVertices has been incremented.
{
  vertices[numVertices] = vertex;

  for (int index = 0; index < numVertices; index++)
  {
    edges[numVertices][index] = NULL_EDGE;
    edges[index][numVertices] = NULL_EDGE;
  }
  numVertices++;
}
```

To add an edge to the graph, we must first locate the `fromVertex` and `toVertex` that define the edge we want to add. These parameters to `AddEdge` are of type `VertexType`. To index the correct matrix slot, we need the *index* in the `vertices` array that corresponds to each vertex. Once we know the indexes, it is a simple matter to set the weight of the edge in the matrix. Here is the algorithm:

AddEdge

Set fromIndex to index of fromVertex in V(graph)
Set toIndex to index of toVertex in V(graph)
Set edges[fromIndex][toIndex] to weight

To find the index of each vertex, let's write a search function that receives the name of a vertex and returns its location (index) in `vertices`. Because the precondition of `AddEdge` states that `fromVertex` and `toVertex` are in V(graph), the search function is very simple. We code it as the helper function `IndexIs`:

```
template<class VertexType>
int IndexIs(VertexType* vertices, VertexType vertex)
// Post: Returns the index of vertex in vertices.
{
  int index = 0;

  while (!(vertex == vertices[index]))
    index++;
  return index;
}

template<class VertexType>
void GraphType<VertexType>::AddEdge(VertexType fromVertex,
     VertexType toVertex, int weight)
// Post: Edge (fromVertex, toVertex) is stored in edges.
{
  int row;
  int col;

  row = IndexIs(vertices, fromVertex);
  col = IndexIs(vertices, toVertex);
  edges[row][col] = weight;
}
```

The `GetWeight` operation is the mirror image of `AddEdge`:

```
template<class VertexType>
int GraphType<VertexType>::GetWeight
     (VertexType fromVertex, VertexType toVertex)
// Post: Returns the weight associated with the edge
```

```
//         (fromVertex, toVertex).
{
  int row;
  int col;

  row = IndexIs(vertices, fromVertex);
  col = IndexIs(vertices, toVertex);
  return edges[row][col];
}
```

The last graph operation that we specified is `GetToVertices`. This function takes a vertex as a parameter, and returns a queue of vertices that are adjacent from the designated vertex. That is, it returns a queue of all vertices that you can reach from this vertex in one step. Using an adjacency matrix to represent the edges, it is a simple matter to determine the nodes to which the `vertex` is adjacent. We merely loop through the appropriate row in `edges`; whenever a value is found that is not `NULL_EDGE`, we add another vertex to the queue.

```
template<class VertexType>
void GraphType<VertexType>::GetToVertices(VertexType vertex,
     QueType<VertexType>& adjVertices)
// Post: Returns a queue of vertices adjacent from vertex.
{
  int fromIndex;
  int toIndex;

  fromIndex = IndexIs(vertices, vertex);
  for (toIndex = 0; toIndex < numVertices; toIndex++)
    if (edges[fromIndex][toIndex] != NULL_EDGE)
      adjVertices.Enqueue(vertices[toIndex]);
}
```

We leave the completion and testing of this implementation as a programming assignment.

Linked Implementation The advantages to representing the edges in a graph with an adjacency matrix relate to its speed and simplicity. Given the indexes of two vertices, determining the existence (or the weight) of an edge between them is an O(1) operation. The problem with adjacency matrices is that their use of *space* is $O(N^2)$, where N is the *maximum* number of vertices in the graph. If the maximum number of vertices is large, adjacency matrices may waste a lot of space.

In the past, we have tried to save space by allocating memory as we need it at run time, using linked structures. We can use a similar approach when implementing graphs. Adjacency lists are linked lists, one list per vertex, that identify the vertices to which each vertex is connected. You can implement adjacency lists in several ways. Figure 9.16 shows two adjacency list representations of the graph in Figure 9.10.

Adjacency list A linked list that identifies all vertices to which a particular vertex is connected; each vertex has its own adjacency list

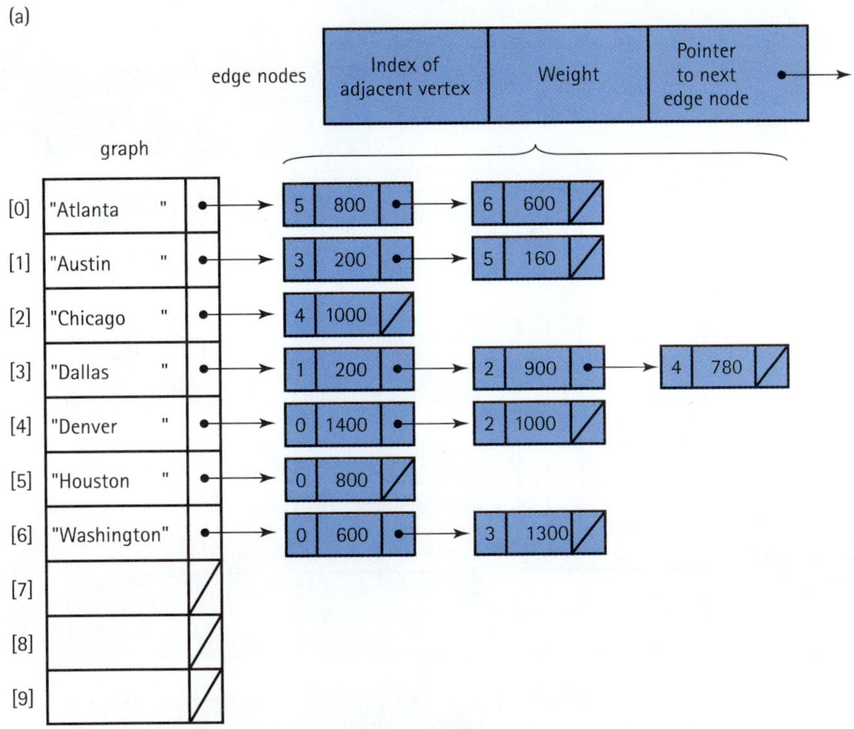

Figure 9.16 *Adjacency list representation of graphs*

In Figure 9.16a, the vertices are stored in an array. Each component of this array contains a pointer to a linked list of edge nodes. Each node in these linked lists contains an index number, a weight, and a pointer to the next node in the adjacency list. Let's look at the adjacency list for Denver. The first node in the list indicates that a 1,400-mile flight goes from Denver to Atlanta (the vertex whose index is 0) and a 1,000-mile flight goes from Denver to Chicago (the vertex whose index is 2).

The implementation illustrated in Figure 9.16b does not use any arrays. Instead, the list of vertices is implemented as a linked list. Now each node in the adjacency lists contains a pointer to the vertex information rather than the index of the vertex. Because so many of these pointers appear in Figure 9.16b, we have used text to describe the vertex that each pointer designates rather than draw them as arrows.

We leave the implementation of the `GraphType` member functions using these implementations as Programming Assignments 3 and 4 in Chapter 9 of the Instructor's Guide.

9.4 Sets

Graphs and sets differ from the other ADTs that we have studied in that they are modeled on mathematical objects. The operations that are defined on them come from mathematics. In fact, we use the concept of a *set* to define a graph: A graph is a set of nodes

(b)

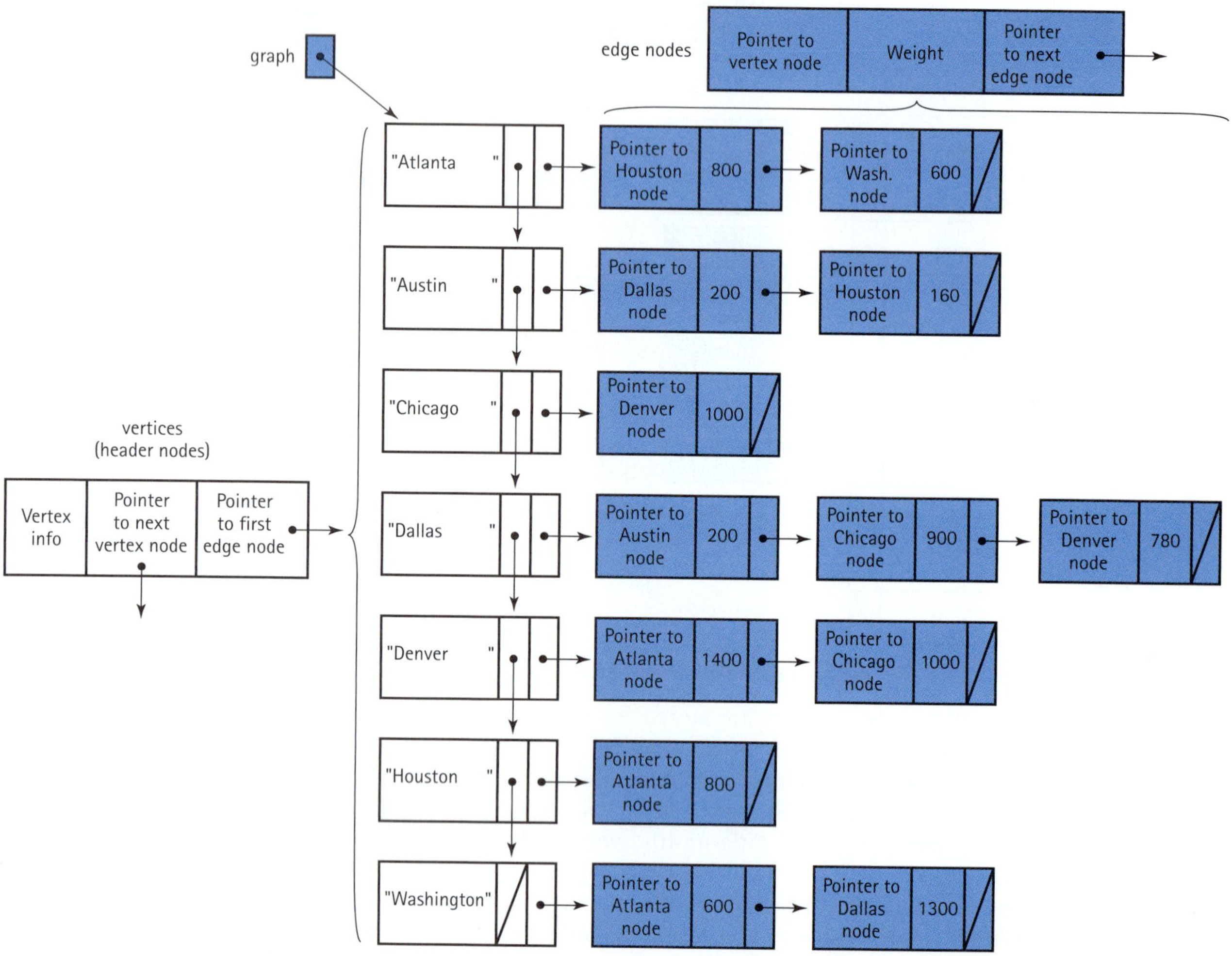

Figure 9.16 *(continued)*

and a set of edges that relate nodes to one another. In this definition, we rely on our intuitive definition of a set as a collection. In this section, however, we will view a set as an abstract data type.

Set An unordered collection of distinct values (items or components), chosen from the possible values of a single data type, called the component (base) type

Logical Level

In mathematics, a set is a collection or group of items, each of which can itself be a set or an item. For our ADT, we define a set as an unordered collection of distinct values, chosen from the possible values of an atomic data type or a composite data type called the component or base type. All of the items in the set are of the same data type.

Three special types of sets are important:

- The subset, a set contained within another set
- The universal set, a set that contains all the values of the base type
- The empty set, which contains no values

We define two transformers for the Set ADT: `Store`, which puts an item into a set, and `Delete`, which removes an item from the set. Three mathematical operations are defined on sets: union, intersection, and difference. Union takes two sets and creates a third set that contains all the elements in either of the input sets. Intersection takes two sets and creates a third set that contains only the elements in both sets. Difference takes two sets and creates a third set that contains all the items in the first set that are not in the second set. In set terminology, the number of items in the set is called the set's cardinality.

Component (base) type The data type of the components or items in a set

Subset A set X is a subset of set Y if each item of X is an element of Y; if at least one element of Y is not in X, then X is a *proper* subset of Y

Universal set The set containing all the values of the component type

Empty set A set with no members

Union A binary set operation that returns a set made up of all the items that are in either of the input sets

Intersection A binary set operation that returns a set made up of all the items that are in both of the input sets

Difference A binary set operation that returns a set made up of all the items that are in the first set but not the second set

Cardinality The number of items in a set

Let's review these set operations with concrete examples. SetA and SetB are as follows:

SetA = {A, B, D, Q, G, S}
SetB = {A, D, S, P, Z}

SetA ∪ SetB (union) returns a set with the items (letters in this case) that are in either SetA or SetB. If a letter is in both, only one is in the resulting set.

ResultSet = {A, B, D, Q, G, S, P, Z}

SetA ∩ SetB (intersection) returns a set with the letters that are in both sets.

ResultSet = {A, D, S}

SetA – SetB (difference) returns a set that contains the letters in SetA that are not in SetB.

ResultSet = {B, Q, G}

Note that set union and set intersection are commutative, but set difference is not. That is, SetA ∪ SetB is the same as SetB ∪ SetA and SetA ∩ SetB is the same as SetB ∩ SetA, but SetA – SetB is not the same as SetB – SetA.

We need observer operations to test whether the set is empty or full, to return the cardinality, and to make the set empty. Here is the CRC card summarizing our operations that mirror the mathematical definitions:

Class Name: SetType	Superclass:	Subclasses:

Responsibilities	Collaborations
MakeEmpty	
IsFull returns Boolean	
CardinalityIs returns integer	
IsEmpty returns Boolean	ItemType
Store (item)	ItemType
Delete (item)	ItemType
Intersection (A, B) returns SetType	ItemType
Union (A, B) returns SetType	ItemType
Difference (A, B) returns SetType	ItemType
Print set members on outFile	

Here is the specification for these responsibilities:

Set ADT Specification

Structure: Items are inserted and deleted; there is no inherent order in the items.

Operations:

Assumptions: Before any call is made to a set operation, the set has been declared and a constructor has been applied. The "==" and "<<" operators apply to values of ItemType.

MakeEmpty

Function: Initializes the set to an empty state.

Postcondition: Set is empty.

Boolean IsEmpty

Function: Tests whether the set is empty.

Postcondition: Function value = (set is empty).

Boolean IsFull

Function: Tests whether the set is full.

Postcondition: Function value = (set is full).

int CardinalityIs

Function: Returns the number of items in the set.

Postcondition: Function value = number of items in the set.

Store(ItemType newItem)

Function: Adds newItem to the set.

Postconditions: If (the set is full and newItem is not there), exception FullSet is thrown; else newItem is in the set only once.

Delete(ItemType item)

Function: Removes an item from the set if it is there.

Postcondition: The item is not in the set.

SetType Union(SetType A, SetType B)

Function: Takes the union of A and B.

Postcondition: Returns the union of set A and set B.

SetType Intersection(SetType A, SetType B)

Function: Takes the intersection of A and B.

Postcondition: Returns the intersection of set A and set B.

SetType Difference(SetType A, SetType B)

Function: Takes the difference of A and B.

Postcondition: Returns the difference of set A and set B.

Print(ofstream& outFile)

Function: Prints the items in a set.

Postcondition: The items in the set are printed on outFile.

Notice that the definitions for the mathematical set say nothing about the set being full. However, to implement the Set ADT, we must consider that possibility. `Store` and `Delete` are actually not necessary. We could create an empty set and a set with one item and perform a union of the two to implement `Store`. We could create a set containing the item to be deleted and perform a difference of the set and the set with the one item to implement `Delete`. However, having `Store` and `Delete` makes processing easier.

Application Level

A set could be the implementation structure for the vertices and/or edges in a graph. One property of a set is that putting an item, which is already there, into the set does not change the set. (Did you realize that is what the specification said?) Also, deleting an item that is not there does not change the set. These properties can prove useful in determining whether items occur in a passage of text, for example. All the characters in the text could be put into a set. When the process is finished, the set contains exactly one copy of every item that appeared in the text.

Implementation Level

There are two basic ways to implement sets. The first explicitly records the presence or absence of each item in the base type (`ItemType`) in the representation of the set variable. The second records only those items that are in a set variable at a particular time. If an item is not listed as being in the set, it is not in the set. That is, the presence of each item in the set is explicitly recorded; the absence of an item is implicit.

Explicit Representation The explicit representation of each item in the base type in each set variable is called a bit vector representation. A one-to-one mapping matches each item in the base type (`ItemType`) with a Boolean flag. If the item is in a set variable, the flag is true; if the item is not in the set variable, the flag is false. Languages that have a built-in set data type use this technique where the Boolean flag is represented by a bit—hence the name "bit vector."

Bit vector A representation that maps each item in the component type to a Boolean flag

We can use an array-based implementation for the bit vector because the cardinality of the base type gives us the size of the array. Of course, this technique does not work for infinite base types or even fairly large base types. However, it would work very well for a limited base type. For example, if we want to implement a set type, with a base type of the uppercase letters, we could represent each set instance with a Boolean array indexed from 0 through 25. The flag in position 0 represents the presence or absence of the letter "A," the flag in position 1 represents the presence or absence of the letter "B," and so on. The empty set would be an array of all `false` values; the universal set would be an array of all `true` values. The constructor would create an array and set each position to `false`. All of the binary operations could be accomplished using Boolean operators.

Here is the class definition for the explicit implementation. Because the base type can be anything, we need a function to map the item into an index within the array size. We leave this mapping function to the user of the set.

```
#include "map.h"
// File map.h must include a definition of ItemType and a function named
//  "map" that maps an item of ItemType into an index between 0 and max - 1
//  if the parameterized constructor is used and between 0 and 399 if
//  the default constructor is used.
class SetType
{
```

```
public:
  SetType();          // Default constructor: Array size is 400.
  SetType(int max); // Parameterized constructor
  ~SetType();         // Destructor
  SetType(const SetType anotherSet);  // Copy constructor
  void MakeEmpty();
  void Store(ItemType item);
  void Delete(ItemType item);
  bool IsEmpty();
  bool IsFull();
  int CardinalityIs();
  SetType Union(SetType setB);
  SetType Intersection(SetType setB);
  SetType Difference(SetType setB);
  void Print(std::ofstream& outFile);
private:
  int maxItems;
  ItemType* items;
};
```

Store(ItemType item)

```
Set items[map(item)] to true
```

Delete(ItemType item)

```
Set items[map(item)] to false
```

int Cardinality()

```
Set count to 0
for counter going from 0 to maxItems - 1
    if (items[counter])
        count++
return count
```

In the following algorithms, `setA` is self.

```
SetType Union(SetType setB)
Set result.maxItems to maxItems
for counter going from 0 to maxItems - 1
    Set result.items[counter] to items[counter] OR setB.items[counter]
return result
```

```
SetType Intersection(SetType setB)
Set result.maxItems to maxItems
for counter going from 0 to maxItems - 1
    Set result.items[counter] to items[counter] AND setB.items[counter]
return result
```

```
SetType Difference(SetType setB)
Set result.maxItems to maxItems
for counter going from 0 to maxItems - 1
    Set result.items[counter] to items[counter] AND NOT setB.items[counter]
return result
```

`IsFull` has no meaning in this implementation, but `IsEmpty` and `MakeEmpty` do. We leave the rest of the algorithms as exercises.

Implicit Representation Set variables implemented as bit vectors (explicit set representation) use the same amount of space regardless of how many items are in the set. The space is proportional to the cardinality of the universal set. (Actually, the space equals the size of the universal set.) This fact can limit the base type to comparatively small finite sets.

A second approach to implementing sets involves keeping a list of the items in the set. The empty set is an empty list. If an item is stored in a set, we store the item in the list. Implicit set representation requires only space that is proportional to the number of items in a set at any one time. The limit in this case is the cardinality of the individual sets rather than the cardinality of the universal set.

With implicit set representation, we implement the set algorithms as list algorithms. We use `ListType` in the following definition, because we do not at the moment know which implementation we should use.

```
class SetType           // Set ItemType using a typedef statement.
{
public:
  SetType();            // Default constructor: Array size is 400.
  SetType(int max);     // Parameterized constructor.
  ~SetType();           // Destructor.
  void MakeEmpty();
  void Store(ItemType item);
  void Delete(ItemType item);
  bool IsEmpty();
  bool IsFull();
  int CardinalityIs();
  SetType Union(SetType setB);
  SetType Intersection(SetType setB);
  SetType Difference(SetType setB);
private:
  ListType items;
};
```

The `SetType` constructor calls the `ListType` constructor. `MakeEmpty`, `IsEmpty`, `IsFull`, and `CardinalityIs` just call the corresponding list operations. The constraint on the `Store` operation says that only one copy exists. Thus the `RetrieveItem` list operation must be called before `Store`. If the item is in the set, the function returns without doing anything. If the item is not in the set, `InsertItem` is called. The constraint on `Delete` says to delete the item if it is in the set. Again `RetrieveItem` is called. If the item is in the set, it is deleted; if it is not there, the function returns without doing anything further.

Let's consider how to implement `Intersection`, one of the binary operations using `ListType`. So far, we have not decided which of the lists we should use. In our algorithm, we say `setA`, but we are referring to the `items` member of `setA`, which is a list.

Recall that the intersection of two sets consists of the set made up of those items that are found in both of the other sets. If we were doing this operation by hand, one algorithm might be to take an item from the first set and scan the second set to see if it is there. If it is, the item goes into the result. We repeat this algorithm for every item in the first set. That's easy to express using our list operations.

```
SetType Intersection(SetType setB)
Reset self
for counter going from 1 to length
    GetNextItem(item) from self
    setB.RetrieveItem(item, found)
    if found
        result.Store(item)
return result
```

The Big-O complexity of this algorithm is $O(N * N)$ or $O(N\log N)$, depending on how `RetrieveItem` is implemented. A little thought produces an algorithm that has $O(N)$ complexity. Assume that the lists are sorted. Rather than looking at one item from the first list (set) and checking whether it is in the second list, let's look at the first item from each list. Three situations can occur:

- The item from setA comes before the item from setB.
- The item from setB comes before the item from setA.
- The items are equal.

If the items are equal, the item from one of the sets goes into the result, and we get a new item from both setA and setB. If the item from setA comes before the item from setB, we know that the item from setA cannot be in the result, so we get another item from setA. If the item from setB comes before the item from setA, we know that the item from setB cannot be in the result, so we get another item from setB.

Here is the revised algorithm based on the assumption that the items are sorted within the container:

```
SetType Intersection(SetType setB)
Reset self
Reset setB
while NOT (self is empty OR setB.IsEmpty)
    GetNextItem(itemA) from self
    setB.GetNextItem(itemB)
```

(continued)

```
    if (itemA < itemB)
        GetNextlem(itemA) from self
    else if itemB < itemA
        setB.GetNextItem(itemB)
    else
        result.Store(itemA)
        GetNextItem(itemA) from self
        setB.GetNextItem(itemB)
return result
```

Be very careful: Sets are *unordered* collections, but the implementation structure that contains the sets can be ordered—and we can take advantage of that ordering to produce an O(*N*) algorithm for the intersection operation. This process of moving down two ordered lists in parallel is called a *merge*. This very useful algorithm can be used to implement the other binary operations in O(*N*) time. We leave the design of these algorithms as exercises.

Both implementations are left as programming assignments.

Summary

In this chapter, we discussed several branching structures: trees, heaps, and graphs. Branching structures are very versatile and offer a good way to model many real-world objects and situations. Because these data structures are appropriate for many different types of applications, all kinds of variations and generalizations of trees and graphs exist. These topics are introduced here to highlight the wide variety of applications for which programmers must select and create appropriate data structures. They are generally covered in detail in more advanced computer science courses.

We also developed the Set ADT. Two types of implementation structures are possible for this ADT: explicit, in which each item of the base type is associated with a Boolean flag, and implicit, in which the items in the set are kept in a list.

Exercises

1. A priority queue containing characters is implemented as a heap stored in an array. The precondition states that this priority queue cannot contain duplicate elements. Currently, the priority queue holds 10 elements, as shown on the next page. What values might be stored in array positions 7–9 so that the properties of a heap are satisfied?

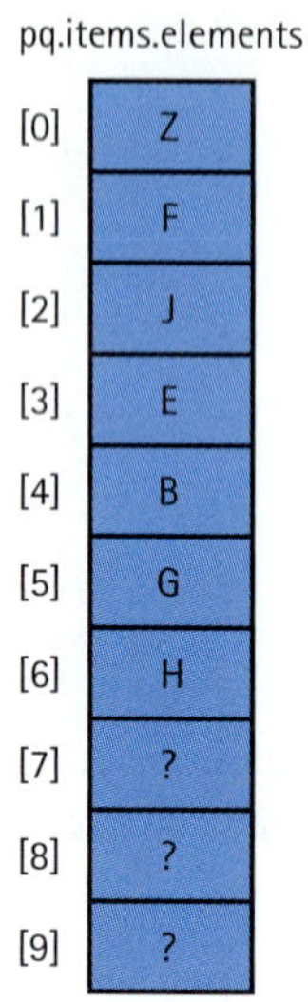

2. A *minimum heap* has the following order property: The value of each element is less than or equal to the value of each of its children. What changes must be made in the heap operations given in this chapter?
3. a. Write a nonrecursive version of `ReheapDown`.
   b. Write a nonrecursive version of `ReheapUp`.
   c. Describe the nonrecursive versions of these operations in terms of Big-O notation.
4. A priority queue is implemented as a heap:

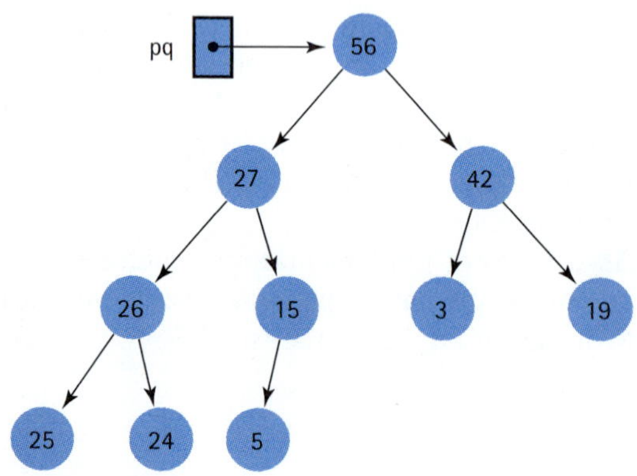

   a. Show how the heap would look after this series of operations:

```
pq.Enqueue(28);
pq.Enqueue(2);
```

```
pq.Enqueue(40);
pq.Dequeue(x);
pq.Dequeue(y);
pq.Dequeue(z);
```

b. What would the values of `x`, `y`, and `z` be after the series of operations in part (a)?

5. A priority queue is implemented as a linked list, sorted from largest to smallest element.
   a. How would the definition of `PQType` change?
   b. Write the `Enqueue` operation, using this implementation.
   c. Write the `Dequeue` operation, using this implementation.
   d. Compare the `Enqueue` and `Dequeue` operations to those for the heap implementation, in terms of Big-O notation.
6. A priority queue is implemented as a binary search tree.
   a. How would the definition of `PQType` change?
   b. Write the `Enqueue` operation, using this implementation.
   c. Write the `Dequeue` operation, using this implementation.
   d. Compare the `Enqueue` and `Dequeue` operations to those for the heap implementation, in terms of Big-O notation. Under what conditions would this implementation be better or worse than the heap implementation?
7. A priority queue is implemented as a sequential array-based list. The highest-priority item is in the first array position, the second-highest priority item is in the second array position, and so on.
   a. Write the declarations in the private part of the priority queue class definition needed for this implementation.
   b. Write the `Enqueue` operation, using this implementation.
   c. Write the `Dequeue` operation, using this implementation.
   d. Compare the `Enqueue` and `Dequeue` operations to those for the heap implementation, in terms of Big-O notation. Under what conditions would this implementation be better or worse than the heap implementation?
8. A stack is implemented using a priority queue. Each element is time-stamped as it is put into the stack. (The time stamp is a number between 0 and `INT_MAX`. Each time an element is pushed onto the stack, it is assigned the next larger number.)
   a. What is the highest-priority element?
   b. Write the `Push` and `Pop` algorithms, using the specifications in Chapter 4.
   c. Compare these `Push` and `Pop` operations to the ones implemented in Chapter 4, in terms of Big-O notation.
9. A FIFO queue is implemented using a priority queue. Each element is time-stamped as it is put into the queue. (The time stamp is a number between 0 and

`INT_MAX`. Each time an element is enqueued, it is assigned the next larger number.)

a. What is the highest-priority element?

b. Write the `Enqueue` and `Dequeue` operations, using the specifications in Chapter 4.

c. Compare these `Enqueue` and `Dequeue` operations to the ones implemented in Chapter 4, in terms of Big-O notation.

10. A priority queue of strings is implemented using a heap. The heap contains the following elements:

.numElements 10
.elements

[0]	"introspective"
[1]	"intelligent"
[2]	"intellectual"
[3]	"intimate"
[4]	"intensive"
[5]	"interesting"
[6]	"internal"
[7]	"into"
[8]	"in"
[9]	"intro"

a. What feature of these strings is used to determine their priority in the priority queue?

b. Show how this priority queue is affected by adding the string "interviewing."

Use the following description of an *undirected graph* for Exercises 11–14.

EmployeeGraph = (V, E)

V(EmployeeGraph) = {Susan, Darlene, Mike, Fred, John, Sander, Lance, Jean, Brent, Fran}

E(EmployeeGraph) = {(Susan, Darlene), (Fred, Brent), (Sander, Susan), (Lance, Fran), (Sander, Fran), (Fran, John), (Lance, Jean), (Jean, Susan), (Mike, Darlene), (Brent, Lance), (Susan, John)}

11. Draw a picture of `EmployeeGraph`.

12. Draw `EmployeeGraph`, implemented as an adjacency matrix. Store the vertex values in alphabetical order.
13. Using the adjacency matrix for `EmployeeGraph` from Exercise 12, describe the path from Susan to Lance
    a. using a breadth-first strategy.
    b. using a depth-first strategy.
14. Which one of the following phrases best describes the relationship represented by the edges between the vertices in `EmployeeGraph`?
    a. "works for"
    b. "is the supervisor of"
    c. "is senior to"
    d. "works with"

Use the following specification of a *directed graph* for Exercises 15–18.

ZooGraph = (V, E)

V(ZooGraph) = {dog, cat, animal, vertebrate, oyster, shellfish, invertebrate, crab, poodle, monkey, banana, dalmatian, dachshund}

E(ZooGraph) = {(vertebrate, animal), (invertebrate, animal), (dog, vertebrate), (cat, vertebrate), (monkey, vertebrate), (shellfish, invertebrate), (crab, shellfish), (oyster, shellfish), (poodle, dog), (dalmatian, dog), (dachshund, dog)}

15. Draw a picture of `ZooGraph`.
16. Draw the adjacency matrix for `ZooGraph`. Store the vertices in alphabetical order.
17. To tell if one element in `ZooGraph` has relation X to another element, you look for a path between them. Show whether the following statements are true, using the picture or adjacency matrix.
    a. dalmatian X dog
    b. dalmatian X vertebrate
    c. dalmatian X poodle
    d. banana X invertebrate
    e. oyster X invertebrate
    f. monkey X invertebrate
18. Which of the following phrases best describes relation X in Exercise 17?
    a. "has a"
    b. "is an example of"
    c. "is a generalization of"
    d. "eats"

Use the following graph for Exercises 19–21.

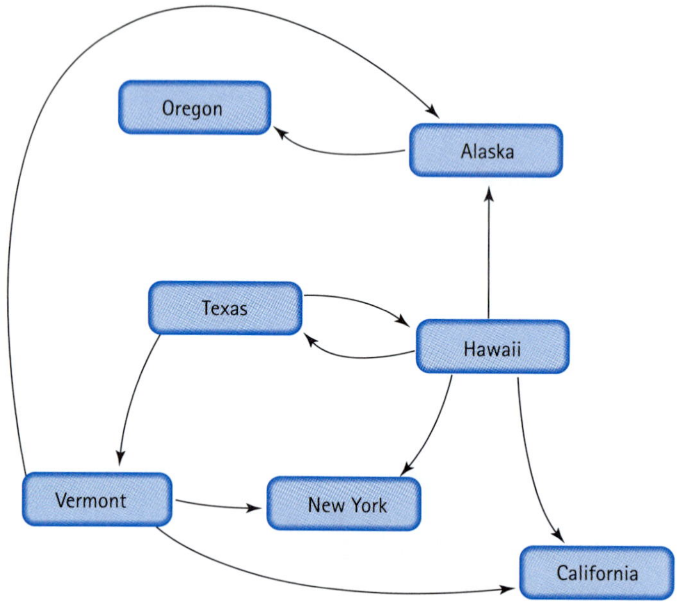

19. Describe the graph pictured above, using the formal graph notation.

    V(StateGraph) =

    E(StateGraph) =

20. a. Is there a path from Oregon to any other state in the graph?
    b. Is there a path from Hawaii to every other state in the graph?
    c. From which state(s) in the graph is there a path to Hawaii?
21. a. Show the adjacency matrix that would describe the edges in the graph. Store the vertices in alphabetical order.
    b. Show the array-of-pointers adjacency lists that would describe the edges in the graph.
22. Extend the class `GraphType` in this chapter to include a Boolean `EdgeExists` operation, which determines whether two vertices are connected by an edge.
    a. Write the declaration of this function. Include adequate comments.
    b. Using the adjacency matrix implementation developed in the chapter and the declaration from part (a), implement the body of the function.
23. Extend the class `GraphType` in this chapter to include a `DeleteEdge` operation, which deletes a given edge.
    a. Write the declaration of this function. Include adequate comments.

b. Using the adjacency matrix implementation developed in the chapter and the declaration from part (a), implement the body of the function.

24. Extend the class `GraphType` in this chapter to include a `DeleteVertex` operation, which deletes a vertex from the graph. Deleting a vertex is more complicated than deleting an edge from the graph. Discuss why.

25. The `DepthFirstSearch` operation can be implemented without a stack by using recursion.

    a. Name the base case(s). Name the general case(s).

    b. Write the algorithm for a recursive depth-first search.

26. Distinguish between set representations that are implicit and those that are explicit.

27. Finish designing the algorithms for the explicit set representation.

28. Finish designing the algorithms for the implicit set representation.

29. Implement the copy constructor for PQType.

30. Did you notice that we did not include a copy constructor from `GraphType`? Discuss the issues involved in implementing this copy constructor.

31. True or False? A full binary tree has all the leaf nodes on the same level, and every nonleaf node has one or two children.

32. True or False? A heap is built using pointer variables.

33. True or False? A heap must be a complete binary tree.

34. True or False? There are only two general ways of representing a graph: adjacency matrix and adjacency lists.

35. True or False? The explicit representation of a set uses a bit vector.

36. True or False? The implicit representation of a set uses the list ADT.

37. True or False? Set operations using the explicit representation use Boolean operations.

38. True or False? The explicit representation of a set uses the list ADT.

39. True or False? The Big-O complexity of implicitly represented binary set operations is the same for `SortedList` and `UnsortedList`.

chapter 10

Sorting and Searching Algorithms

Goals

After studying this chapter, you should be able to

- Design and implement the following sorting algorithms:
  - Straight selection sort
  - Bubble sort (two versions)
  - Insertion sort
  - Merge sort
  - Quick sort
  - Heap sort
  - Radix sort
- Compare the efficiency of the sorting algorithms, in terms of Big-O complexity and space requirements
- Discuss other efficiency considerations: sorting small numbers of elements, programmer time, and sorting arrays of large data elements
- Sort on several keys
- Discuss the performances of the following search algorithms:
  - Sequential search of an unsorted list
  - Sequential search of a sorted list
  - Binary search
  - Searching a high-probability sorted list
- Define the following terms:
  - Hashing
  - Rehashing
  - Collisions
  - Linear probing
  - Clustering
- Design and implement an appropriate hashing function for an application
- Design and implement a collision-resolution algorithm for a hash table
- Discuss the efficiency considerations for the searching and hashing algorithms, in terms of Big-O notation

At many points in this book, we have gone to great trouble to keep lists of elements in sorted order: student records sorted by ID number, integers sorted from smallest to largest, words sorted alphabetically. The goal of keeping sorted lists, of course, is to facilitate searching. Given an appropriate data structure, a particular list element can be found more quickly if the list is sorted.

In this chapter, we examine strategies for sorting and searching, two tasks that are fundamental to a variety of computing problems. In fact, we challenge you to look back at the programs you have written so far. Are there any that do *not* include a sort or a search?

10.1 Sorting

Putting an unsorted list of data elements into order—*sorting*—is a very common and useful operation. Entire books have been written about various sorting algorithms and algorithms for searching a sorted list to find a particular element. The goal is to come up with better, more efficient sorts. Because sorting a large number of elements can be extremely time-consuming, a good sorting algorithm is very desirable. This is one area in which programmers are sometimes encouraged to sacrifice clarity in favor of speed of execution.

How do we describe efficiency? We pick an operation central to most sorting algorithms: the operation that compares two values to see which is smaller. In our study of sorting algorithms, we relate the number of comparisons to the number of elements in the list (N) as a rough measure of the efficiency of each algorithm. The number of swaps made is another measure of sorting efficiency. In the exercises, we ask you to analyze the sorting algorithms developed in this chapter in terms of data movements.

Another efficiency consideration is the amount of memory space required. In general, memory space is not a very important factor in choosing a sorting algorithm. We look at only one sort in which space would be a serious consideration. The usual time versus space tradeoff applies to sorts—more space often means less time, and vice versa.

Because processing time is the factor that applies most often to sorting algorithms, we consider it in detail here. Of course, as in any application, the programmer must determine goals and requirements before selecting an algorithm and starting to write code.

We review the straight selection sort and the bubble sort, two simple sorts that students often write in their first programming course. Then we review a more complex sorting algorithm that we examined in Chapter 7 (the quick sort algorithm) and introduce two additional complex sorts: merge sort and heap sort. We assume that the actual data type that replaces the template parameter `ItemType` in the rest of the chapter is either a simple built-in type or a class that overloads the relational operators. For simplicity, we assume that the keys are unique.

As we pointed out in Chapter 7, at the logical level, sorting algorithms take an unsorted list object and convert it into a sorted list object. At the implementation level, sorting algorithms take an array and reorganize the values in the array so that they are in order by key. The number of values to be sorted and the array in which they are stored are parameters to our sorting algorithms. Note that we are not sorting an object of type `UnsortedType` but rather the values stored in an array. We call the array `values`, and its elements are of type `ItemType`.

Straight Selection Sort

If you were handed a list of names and asked to put them in alphabetical order, you might use this general approach:

1. Find the name that comes first in the alphabet, and write it on a second sheet of paper.
2. Cross the name out on the original list.
3. Continue this cycle until all names on the original list have been crossed out and written onto the second list, at which point the second list is sorted.

This algorithm is simple to translate into a computer program, but it has one drawback: It requires space in memory to store two complete lists. Although we have not talked a great deal about memory space considerations, this duplication is clearly wasteful. A slight adjustment to this manual approach does away with the need to duplicate space, however. As you cross a name off the original list, a free space opens up. Instead of writing the minimum value on a second list, you can exchange it with the value currently in the position where the crossed-off item should go. Our "by-hand list" is represented in an array.

Let's look at an example—sorting the five-element array shown in Figure 10.1a. Because of this algorithm's simplicity, it is usually the first sorting method that students learn. Therefore, we go straight to the algorithm:

SelectionSort

```
Set current to the index of first item in the array
while more items in unsorted part of array
    Find the index of the smallest unsorted item
    Swap the current item with the smallest unsorted one
    Shrink the unsorted part of the array by incrementing current
```

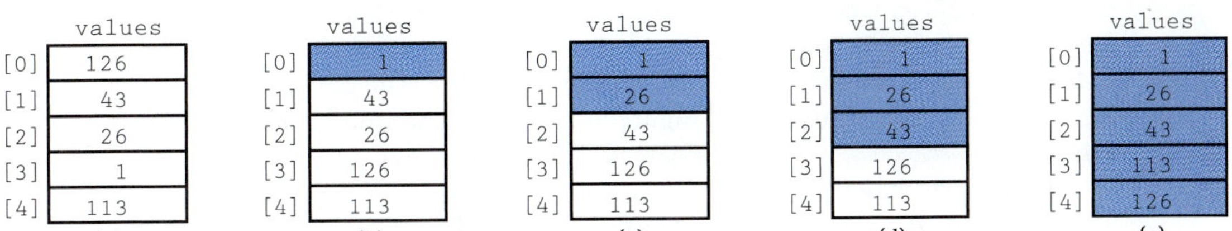

Figure 10.1 *Example of straight selection sort (sorted elements are shaded)*

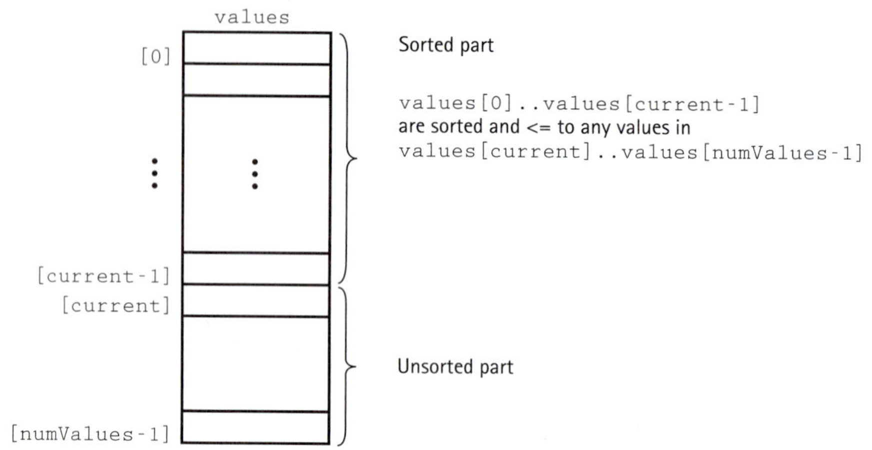

Figure 10.2 *A snapshot of the selection sort algorithm*

Although you could immediately begin writing the code, we will use this algorithm to practice designing correct loops.

We use a variable, `current`, to mark the beginning of the unsorted part of the array. We start out by setting `current` to the index of the first position (index 0). The unsorted part of the array then goes from the index `current` to `numValues - 1`.

The main sort processing occurs in a loop. In each iteration of the loop body, the smallest value in the unsorted part of the array is swapped with the value in the `current` location. After the swap, `current` is in the sorted part of the array, so we shrink the size of the unsorted part by incrementing `current`. The loop body is now complete.

At the top of the loop body, the unsorted part of the array goes from the (now incremented) `current` index to `numValues - 1`. We know that every value in the unsorted part is greater than (or equal to, if duplicates are permitted) any value in the sorted part of the array.

How do we know when "there are more elements in the unsorted part"? As long as `current <= numValues - 1`, the unsorted part of the array (`values[current] .. values[numValues - 1]`) contains values. In each iteration of the loop body, `current` is incremented, shrinking the unsorted part of the array. When `current` = `numValues - 1`, the "unsorted" part contains only one element, and we know that this value must be greater than (or equal to) any value in the sorted part. Thus the value in `values[numValues - 1]` is in its correct place, and we are done. The condition for the *while* loop is `current < numValues - 1`. Figure 10.2 gives a snapshot of the selection sort algorithm.

Now all we have to do is to locate the smallest value in the unsorted part of the array. Let's write a function to perform this task. The function `MinIndex` receives the array elements and the first and last indexes of the unsorted part, and returns the index of the smallest value in this part of the array.

int MinIndex(values, startIndex, endIndex)
Set indexOfMin to startIndex
for index going from startIndex + 1 to endIndex
    if values[index] < values[indexOfMin]
        Set indexOfMin to index
return indexOfMin

Now that we know where the smallest unsorted element is located, we swap it with the element at index `current`. Because swapping data values between two array locations is common in many sorting algorithms, let's write a little function, `Swap`, to accomplish this task.

```
template<class ItemType>
inline void Swap(ItemType& item1, ItemType& item2)
// Post: Contents of item1 and item2 have been swapped.
{
  ItemType tempItem;

  tempItem = item1;
  item1 = item2;
  item2 = tempItem;
}
```

The word `inline` before the function heading is called a *specifier*. `inline` suggests that the compiler insert the code for the function body every time a call is issued rather than actually making a function call. We "suggest" rather than "tell," because compilers are not obliged to implement the `inline` specifier.

Here are the rest of the function templates for this sorting algorithm:

```
template<class ItemType>
int MinIndex(ItemType values[], int startIndex, int endIndex)
// Post: Returns the index of the smallest value in
//       values[startIndex]..values[endIndex].
{
  int indexOfMin = startIndex;
  for (int index = startIndex + 1; index <= endIndex; index++)
    if (values[index] < values[indexOfMin])
      indexOfMin = index;
  return indexOfMin;
}
```

```
template<class ItemType>
void SelectionSort(ItemType values[], int numValues)
// Post: The elements in the array values are sorted by key.
{
  int endIndex = numValues-1;
  for (int current = 0; current < endIndex; current++)
    Swap(values[current],
         values[MinIndex(values, current, endIndex)]);
}
```

Analyzing the Selection Sort Now let's try measuring the amount of "work" required by this algorithm. We describe the number of comparisons as a function of the number of items in the array. To be concise, in this discussion we refer to `numValues` as N.

The comparison operation occurs in the function `MinIndex`. We know from the loop condition in the `SelectionSort` function that `MinIndex` is called $N - 1$ times. Within `MinIndex`, the number of comparisons varies, depending on the values of `startIndex` and `endIndex`:

```
for (int index = startIndex + 1; index <= endIndex; index++)
  if (values[index] < values[indexOfMin])
    indexOfMin = index;
```

In the first call to `MinIndex`, `startIndex` is 0 and `endIndex` is `numValues - 1`, so $N - 1$ comparisons occur; in the next call, $N - 2$ comparisons occur; and so on. In the last call, only one comparison takes place. The total number of comparisons is

$$(N - 1) + (N - 2) + (N - 3) + \cdots + 1 = N(N - 1)/2$$

To accomplish our goal of sorting an array of N elements, the straight selection sort requires $N(N - 1)/2$ comparisons. Note that the particular arrangement of values in the array does not affect the amount of work done. Even if the array is in sorted order *before* the call to `SelectionSort`, the function still makes $N(N - 1)/2$ comparisons.

Table 10.1 shows the number of comparisons required for arrays of various sizes. Note that doubling the array size roughly quadruples the number of comparisons.

How do we describe this algorithm in terms of Big-O notation? If we express $N(N - 1)/2$ as $\frac{1}{2}^2 - \frac{1}{2}$, it is easy to see. In Big-O notation, we consider only the term $\frac{1}{2}^2$, because it increases fastest relative to N. (Remember the elephants and goldfish?) Further, we ignore the constant, $\frac{1}{2}$, making this algorithm become $O(N^2)$. Thus, for large values of N, the computation time is *approximately proportional* to N^2. Looking again at Table 10.1, we see that multiplying the number of elements by 10 increases the number of comparisons by a factor of more than 100; that is, the number of comparisons is multiplied by approximately the square of the increase in the number of elements. Looking at this table makes us appreciate why sorting algorithms are the subject of so much

Table 10.1 *Number of Comparisons Required to Sort Arrays of Different Sizes Using the Selection Sort*

Number of Items	Number of Comparisons
10	45
20	190
100	4,950
1,000	499,500
10,000	49,995,000

attention: Using `SelectionSort` to sort an array of 1,000 elements requires almost one-half million comparisons!

The identifying feature of a selection sort is that, on each pass through the loop, one element is put into its proper place. In the straight selection sort, each iteration finds the smallest unsorted element and puts it into its correct place. If we had made the function find the largest value, instead of the smallest, the algorithm would have sorted in descending order. We could also have made the loop go down from `numValues - 1` to `1`, putting the elements into the bottom of the array first. All these algorithms are variations on the straight selection sort. The variations do not change the basic way that the minimum (or maximum) element is found.

Bubble Sort

The bubble sort is a selection sort that uses a different scheme for finding the minimum (or maximum) value. Each iteration puts the smallest unsorted element into its correct place, but it also changes the locations of the other elements in the array. The first iteration puts the smallest element in the array into the first array position. Starting with the last array element we compare successive pairs of elements, swapping them whenever the bottom element of the pair is smaller than the one above it. In this way, the smallest element "bubbles up" to the top of the array. The next iteration puts the smallest element in the unsorted part of the array into the second array position, using the same technique. As you look at the example in Figure 10.3, note that in addition to putting

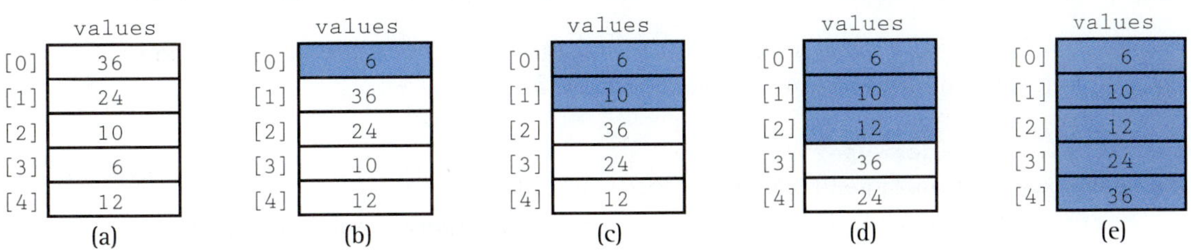

Figure 10.3 *Example of bubble sort (sorted elements are shaded)*

one element into its proper place, each iteration produces some intermediate changes in the array.

The basic algorithm for the bubble sort follows:

BubbleSort
Set current to the index of first item in the array
while more items in unsorted part of array
    "Bubble up" the smallest item in the unsorted part,
        causing intermediate swaps as needed
    Shrink the unsorted part of the array by incrementing current

The structure of the loop is much like that in the `SelectionSort` function. The unsorted part of the array is the area from `values[current]` to `values[numValues - 1]`. The value of `current` begins at 0, and we loop until `current` reaches `numValues - 1`, with `current` incremented in each iteration. On entrance to each iteration of the loop body, the first `current` values are already sorted, and all elements in the unsorted part of the array are greater than or equal to the sorted elements.

The inside of the loop body is different, however. Each iteration of the loop "bubbles up" the smallest value in the unsorted part of the array to the `current` position. The algorithm for the bubbling task follows:

BubbleUp(values, startIndex, endIndex)
for index going from endIndex DOWNTO startIndex + 1
    if values[index] < values[index - 1]
        Swap(values[index], values[index - 1])

Figure 10.4 gives a snapshot of this algorithm. Using the `Swap` function coded earlier, the code for the function `BubbleSort` follows.

```
template<class ItemType>
void BubbleUp(ItemType values[], int startIndex, int endIndex)
// Post: Adjacent pairs that are out of order have been switched
//       between values[startIndex]..values[endIndex] beginning at
//       values[endIndex].
{
```

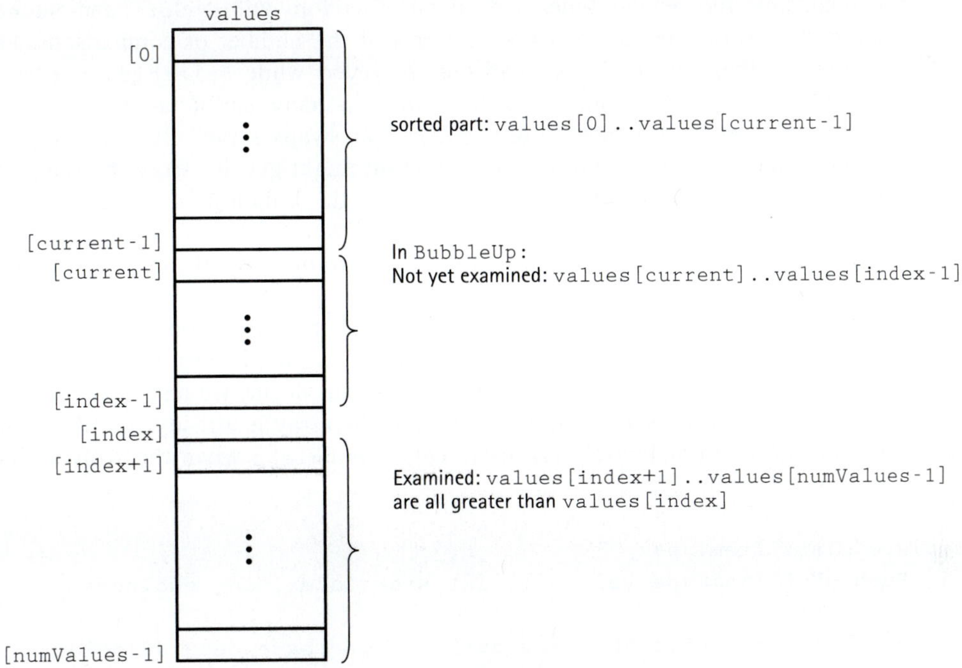

Figure 10.4 *Snapshot of bubble sort*

```
  for (int index = endIndex; index > startIndex; index--)
    if (values[index] < values[index-1])
      Swap(values[index], values[index-1]);
}

template<class ItemType>
void BubbleSort(ItemType values[], int numValues)
// Post: The elements in the array values are sorted by key.
{
  int current = 0;

  while (current < numValues - 1)
  {
    BubbleUp(values, current, numValues-1);
    current++;
  }
}
```

Analyzing the Bubble Sort It is easy to analyze the work required by `BubbleSort`—it is the same as that for the straight selection sort algorithm. The comparisons occur in `BubbleUp`, which is called $N - 1$ times. There are $N - 1$ comparisons the first time, $N - 2$

comparisons the second time, and so on. Therefore `BubbleSort` and `SelectionSort` require the same amount of work, in terms of the number of comparisons. `BubbleSort` does more than just make comparisons, however: while `SelectionSort` performs only one data swap per iteration, `BubbleSort` may do many additional data swaps.

What purpose do these intermediate data swaps serve? By reversing out-of-order pairs of data as they are noticed, the function might get the array in order before $N - 1$ calls to `BubbleUp`. However, this version of the bubble sort makes no provision for stopping when the array is completely sorted. Even if the array is already in sorted order when `BubbleSort` is called, this function continues to call `BubbleUp` (which changes nothing) $N - 1$ times.

We could quit before the maximum number of iterations if `BubbleUp` returns a Boolean flag, `sorted`, to tell us when the array is sorted. Within `BubbleUp`, we initially set `sorted` to true; then in the loop, if any swaps occur, we reset `sorted` to false. If no elements have been swapped, we know that the array is already in order. Now the bubble sort needs to make only *one* extra call to `BubbleUp` when the array is in order. This version of the bubble sort follows:

```
template<class ItemType>
void BubbleUp2(ItemType values[], int startIndex, int endIndex,
     bool& sorted)
// Post: Adjacent pairs that are out of order have been switched
//       between values[startIndex]..values[endIndex] beginning at
//       values[endIndex].
//       sorted is false if a swap was made and true otherwise.
{
  sorted = true;
  for (int index = endIndex; index > startIndex; index--)
    if (values[index] < values[index-1])
    {
      Swap(values[index], values[index-1]);
      sorted = false;
    }
}

template<class ItemType>
void ShortBubble(ItemType values[], int numValues)
// Post: The elements in the array values are sorted by key.
//       The process stops as soon as values is sorted.
{
  int current = 0;
  bool sorted = false;
  while (current < numValues - 1 && !sorted)
  {
    BubbleUp2(values, current, numValues-1, sorted);
```

```
        current++;
    }
}
```

The analysis of ShortBubble is more difficult. Clearly, if the array is initially sorted in order, one call to BubbleUp2 tells us so. In this best-case scenario, ShortBubble is $O(N)$; only $N - 1$ comparisons are required for the sort. What if the original array was actually sorted in *descending* order before the call to ShortBubble? This is the worst possible case: ShortBubble requires as many comparisons as BubbleSort and SelectionSort, not to mention the "overhead" consisting of the many extra swaps and setting and resetting of the sorted flag. Can we calculate an average case? In the first call to BubbleUp2, when current is 0, numValues - 1 comparisons occur; on the second call, when current is 1, numValues - 2 comparisons occur. The number of comparisons in any call to BubbleUp2 is numValues - current - 1. If we let N indicate numValues and K indicate the number of calls to BubbleUp2 executed before ShortBubble finishes its work, the total number of comparisons required is

$$\underbrace{(N-1)}_{\text{1st call}} + \underbrace{(N-2)}_{\text{2nd call}} + \underbrace{(N-3)}_{\text{3rd call}} + \cdots + \underbrace{(N-K)}_{K\text{th call}}$$

A little algebra[1] changes this to

$$(2KN - K^2 - K)/2$$

In Big-O notation, the term that is increasing the fastest relative to N is $2KN$. We know that K is between 1 and $N - 1$. On average, over all possible input orders, K is proportional to N. Therefore, $2KN$ is proportional to N^2; that is, the ShortBubble algorithm is also $O(N^2)$.

Why do we even bother to mention the bubble sort algorithm if it is $O(N^2)$ and requires extra data movements? Because ShortBubble is the only sorting algorithm that recognizes when the array is already sorted and stops. If the original array is already sorted when the program calls ShortBubble, only one pass is made through the array. If you plan to sort a file that you know is almost in order, ShortBubble is a good choice.

---

[1]For those of you who want to see the algebra:

$$\begin{aligned} & (N-1) + (N-2) + \cdots + (N-K) \\ = \; & KN - (\text{sum of 1 through } K) \\ = \; & KN - [K(K+1)] \\ = \; & KN - (K^2 + K) \\ = \; & (2KN - K^2 - K)\,/\,2 \end{aligned}$$

Insertion Sort

In Chapter 3, we created a sorted list by inserting each new element into its appropriate place in an array. We can use a similar approach for sorting an array. The principle of the insertion sort is quite simple: Each successive element in the array to be sorted is inserted into its proper place with respect to the other, already-sorted elements. As with the previous sorts, we divide our array into a sorted part and an unsorted part. Initially, the sorted portion contains only one element: the first element in the array. Now we take the second element in the array and put it into its correct place in the sorted part; that is, `values[0]` and `values[1]` are in order with respect to each other. Now the value in `values[2]` is put into its proper place, so `values[0] . . values[2]` are in order with respect to each other. This process continues until all the elements have been sorted. Figure 10.5 illustrates this process, which we describe in the following algorithm, and Figure 10.6 shows a snapshot of the algorithm.

In Chapter 3, our strategy was to search for the insertion point from the beginning of the array and shift the elements from the insertion point down one slot to make room for the new element. We can combine the searching and shifting by beginning at the *end* of the sorted part of the array. We compare the item at `values[current]` to the one before it. If it is less, we swap the two items. We then compare the item at

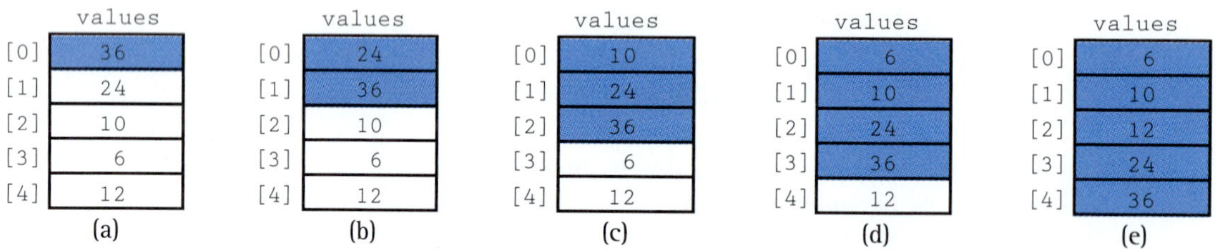

Figure 10.5 *Example of the insertion sort algorithm*

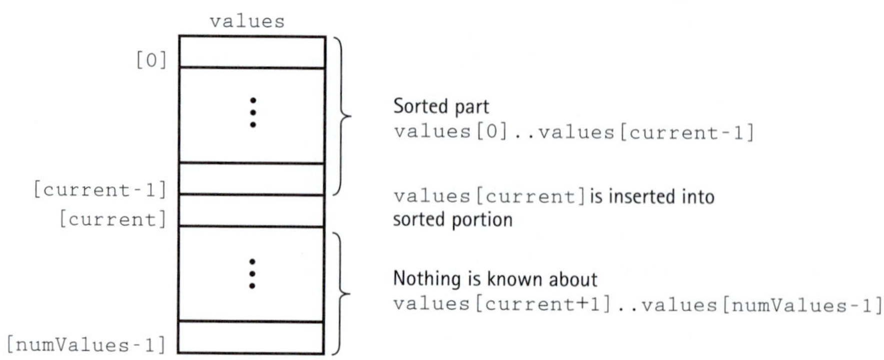

Figure 10.6 *A snapshot of the insertion sort algorithm*

values[current - 1] to the one before it, and swap them if necessary. The process stops when the comparison shows that the values are in order or we have swapped into the first place in the array.

```
InsertionSort
for count going from 0 through numValues - 1
    InsertItem(values, 0, count)
```

```
InsertItem(values, startIndex, endIndex)
Set finished to false
Set current to endIndex
Set moreToSearch to (current does not equal startIndex)
while moreToSearch AND NOT finished
    if values[current] < values[current - 1]
        Swap(values[current], values[current - 1])
        Decrement current
        Set moreToSearch to (current does not equal startIndex)
    else
        Set finished to true
```

Here are the coded versions of InsertItem and InsertionSort:

```
template<class ItemType>
void InsertItem(ItemType values[], int startIndex, int endIndex)
// Post: values[0]..values[endIndex] are now sorted.
{
  bool finished = false;
  int current = endIndex;
  bool moreToSearch = (current != startIndex);

  while (moreToSearch && !finished)
  {
```

```
      if (values[current] < values[current-1])
      {
        Swap(values[current], values[current-1]);
        current--;
        moreToSearch = (current != startIndex);
      }
      else
        finished = true;
    }
}

template<class ItemType>
void InsertionSort(ItemType values[], int numValues)
// Post: The elements in the array values are sorted by key.
{
  for (int count = 0; count < numValues; count++)
    InsertItem(values, 0, count);
}
```

Analyzing the Insertion Sort The general case for this algorithm mirrors that for the `SelectionSort` and the `BubbleSort`, so the general case is $O(N^2)$. Like `ShortBubble`, `InsertionSort` also has a best case: the data are already sorted in ascending order. When the data are in ascending order, `InsertItem` is called N times, but only one comparison is made each time and no swaps occur. The maximum number of comparisons is made only when the elements in the array are in reverse order.

If we know nothing about the original order in the data to be sorted, `SelectionSort`, `ShortBubble`, and `InsertionSort` are all $O(N^2)$ sorts and are too time-consuming for sorting large arrays. Thus we need sorting methods that work better when N is large.

$O(N \log_2 N)$ Sorts

Considering how rapidly N^2 grows as the size of the array increases, can't we do better? We note that N^2 is a lot larger than $(\frac{1}{2})^2 + (\frac{1}{2})^2$. If we could cut the array into two pieces, sort each segment, and then merge the two pieces again, we should end up sorting the entire array with a lot less work. Figure 10.7 shows an example of this approach.

The idea of "divide and conquer" has been applied to the sorting problem in different ways, resulting in a number of algorithms that can do the job much more efficiently than $O(N^2)$. In fact, an entire category of sorting algorithms are $O(N\log_2 N)$. We looked at one of these in Chapter 7: `QuickSort`. Here we examine two other sorting algorithms: `MergeSort` and `HeapSort`. As you might guess, the efficiency of these algorithms is

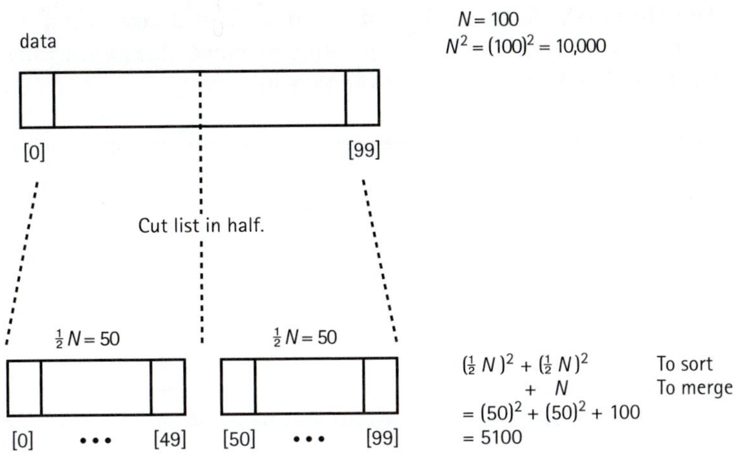

Figure 10.7 *Rationale for divide-and-conquer sorts*

achieved at the expense of the simplicity seen in the straight selection, bubble, and insertion sorts.

Merge Sort

The merge sort algorithm is taken directly from the idea in the previous section:

MergeSort
Cut the array in half
Sort the left half
Sort the right half
Merge the two sorted halves into one sorted array

Merging the two halves together is an $O(N)$ task: We merely go through the sorted halves, comparing successive pairs of values (one in each half) and putting the smaller value into the next slot in the final solution. Even if the sorting algorithm used for each half is $O(N^2)$, we should see some improvement over sorting the whole array at once.

Actually, because `MergeSort` is itself a sorting algorithm, we might as well use it to sort the two halves. That's right—we can make `MergeSort` be a recursive function and let it call itself to sort each of the two subarrays:

MergeSort—Recursive

Cut the array in half
MergeSort the left half
MergeSort the right half
Merge the two sorted halves into one sorted array

This is the general case, of course. What is the base case, which does not involve any recursive calls to `MergeSort`? If the "half" to be sorted doesn't have more than one element, we can consider it already sorted and just return.

Let's summarize `MergeSort` in the format we used for other recursive algorithms. The initial function call would be `MergeSort(values, 0, numValues - 1)`.

Function MergeSort(values, first, last)

Definition:	Sorts the array items in ascending order.
Size:	values[first]..values[last].
Base Case:	If fewer than two items in values[first]..values[last], do nothing.
General Case:	Cut the array in half. MergeSort the left half. MergeSort the right half. Merge the two sorted halves into one sorted array.

Cutting the array in half is simply a matter of finding the midpoint between the first and last indexes:

```
middle = (first + last) / 2;
```

Then, in the smaller-caller tradition, we can make the recursive calls to `MergeSort`:

```
MergeSort(values, first, middle);
MergeSort(values, middle+1, last);
```

So far this is simple enough. Now we merely have to merge the two halves and we're done.

Merging the Sorted Halves Obviously, the serious work occurs in the merge step. Let's look first at the general algorithm for merging two sorted arrays, and then at the specific problem of our subarrays.

To merge two sorted arrays, we compare successive pairs of elements, one from each array, moving the smaller of each pair to the "final" array. We can stop when the shorter array runs out of elements, and then move all remaining elements (if any) from the other array to the final array. Figure 10.8 illustrates the general algorithm. We use a similar approach in our specific problem, in which the two "arrays" to be merged are actually subarrays of the original array (Figure 10.9). Just as in Figure 10.8, where we merged array1 and array2 into a third array, we need to merge our two subarrays into some auxiliary data structure. We need this data structure, another array, only temporarily. After the merge step, we can copy the now-sorted elements back into the original array. Figure 10.10 shows the entire process.

Let's specify a function, `Merge`, to perform this task:

Merge(ItemType values[ ], int leftFirst, int leftLast, int rightFirst, int rightLast)

Function:	Merges two sorted subarrays into a single sorted piece of the array.
Preconditions:	values[leftFirst]..values[leftLast] are sorted; values[rightFirst]..values[rightLast] are sorted.
Postcondition:	values[leftFirst]..values[rightLast] are sorted.

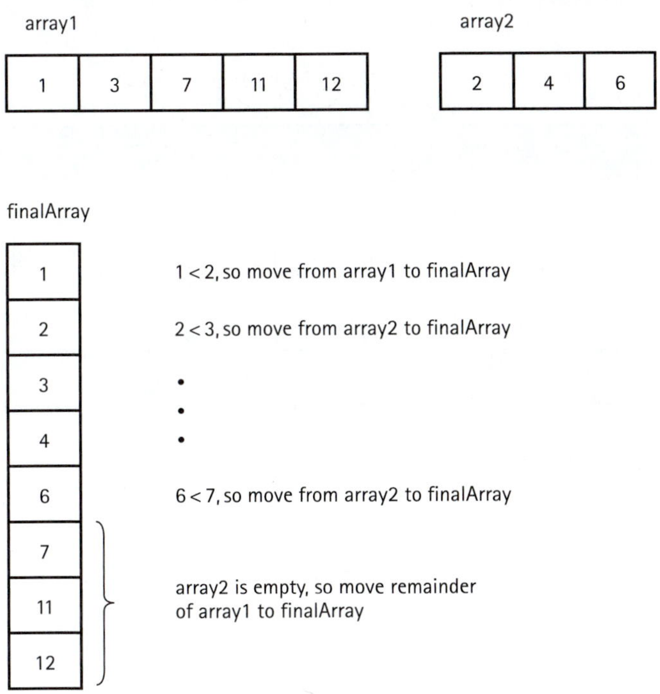

Figure 10.8 *Strategy for merging two sorted arrays*

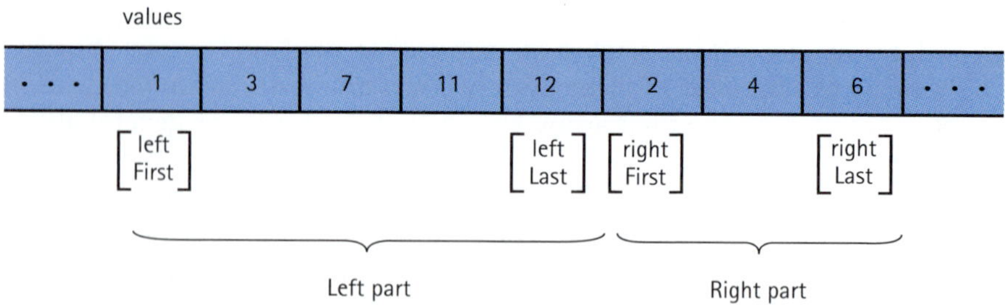

Figure 10.9 *Two subarrays*

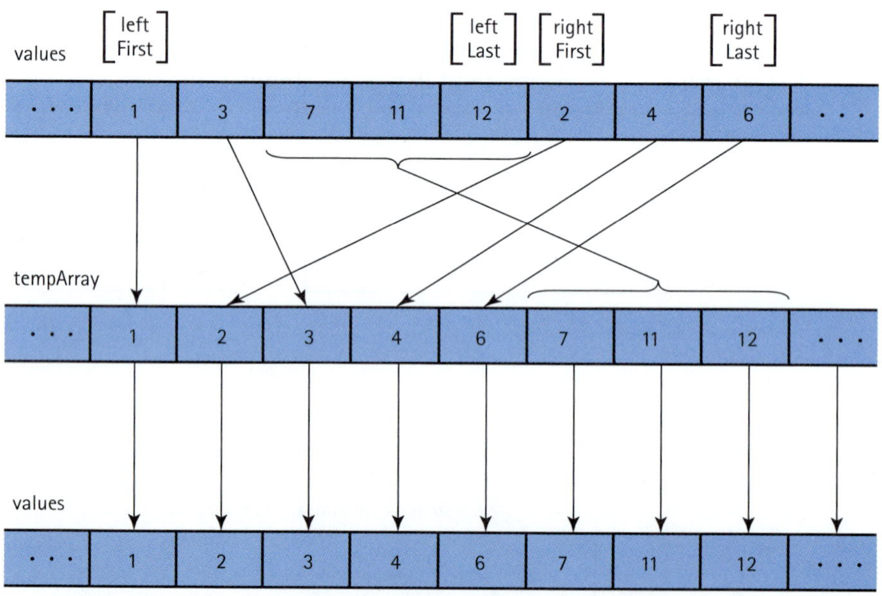

Figure 10.10 *Merging sorted halves*

Here is the algorithm for `Merge`:

```
Merge (uses a local array, tempArray)
Set saveFirst to leftFirst        // To know where to copy back
Set index to leftFirst
while more items in left half AND more items in right half
    if values[leftFirst] < values[rightFirst]
        Set tempArray[index] to values[leftFirst]
        Increment leftFirst
    else
        Set tempArray[index] to values[rightFirst]
        Increment rightFirst
    Increment index
Copy any remaining items from left half to tempArray
Copy any remaining items from right half to tempArray
Copy the sorted elements from tempArray back into values
```

In the coding of the function `Merge`, we use `leftFirst` and `rightFirst` to indicate the "current" position in the left and right halves, respectively. Because they are not reference parameters, copies of these parameters are passed to `Merge`. The copies are changed in the function, but the changed values are not passed out of `Merge`. Note that both of the "copy any remaining items . . ." loops are included. During the execution of this function, one of these loops never executes. Can you explain why?

```
template<class ItemType>
void Merge(ItemType values[], int leftFirst, int leftLast,
     int rightFirst, int rightLast)
// Post: values[leftFirst]..values[leftLast] and
//       values[rightFirst]..values[rightLast] have been merged.
//       values[leftFirst]..values[rightLast] are now sorted.
{
  ItemType tempArray[MAX_ITEMS];
  int index = leftFirst;
  int saveFirst = leftFirst;

  while ((leftFirst <= leftLast) && (rightFirst <= rightLast))
  {
    if (values[leftFirst] < values[rightFirst])
    {
```

```
      tempArray[index] = values[leftFirst];
      leftFirst++;
    }
    else
    {
      tempArray[index] = values[rightFirst];
      rightFirst++;
    }
    index++;
  }

  while (leftFirst <= leftLast)
  // Copy remaining items from left half.
  {
    tempArray[index] = values[leftFirst];
    leftFirst++;
    index++;
  }

  while (rightFirst <= rightLast)
  // Copy remaining items from right half.
  {
    tempArray[index] = values[rightFirst];
    rightFirst++;
    index++;
  }

  for (index = saveFirst; index <= rightLast; index++)
    values[index] = tempArray[index];
}
```

The `MergeSort` *Function* As we said, most of the work takes place in the merge task. The actual `MergeSort` function is short and simple:

```
template<class ItemType>
void MergeSort(ItemType values[], int first, int last)
// Post: The elements in values are sorted by key.
{
  if (first < last)
  {
    int middle = (first + last) / 2;
    MergeSort(values, first, middle);
    MergeSort(values, middle + 1, last);
    Merge(values, first, middle, middle + 1, last);
  }
}
```

Analyzing the Merge Sort The `MergeSort` function splits the original array into two halves. First it sorts the first half of the array, using the divide-and-conquer approach; then it sorts the second half of the array using the same approach; finally it merges the two halves. To sort the first half of the array it follows the same approach, splitting and merging. During the sorting process, the splitting and merging operations are intermingled. To simplify the analysis, however, we imagine that all of the splitting occurs first. We can view the process in this way without affecting the correctness of the algorithm.

We view the `MergeSort` algorithm as continually dividing the original array (of size N) in two, until it has created N one-element subarrays. Figure 10.11 shows this point of view for an array with an original size of 16. The total work needed to divide the array in half, over and over again until we reach subarrays of size 1, is $O(N)$. After all, we end up with N subarrays of size 1.

Each subarray of size 1 is obviously a sorted subarray. The real work of the algorithm comes in merging the smaller sorted subarrays back into the larger sorted subarrays. To merge two sorted subarrays of size X and size Y into a single sorted subarray using the `Merge` operation requires $O(X + Y)$ steps. We can see this fact because each time through the *while* loops of the `Merge` function we advance either the `leftFirst` index or the `rightFirst` index by 1. Because we stop processing when these indexes become greater than their "last" counterparts, we know that we take a total of `(leftLast - leftFirst + 1) + (rightLast - rightFirst + 1)` steps. This expression represents the sum of the lengths of the two subarrays being processed.

How many times is the `Merge` function called? And what are the sizes of the subarrays involved? Let's work from the bottom up. The original array of size N is eventually

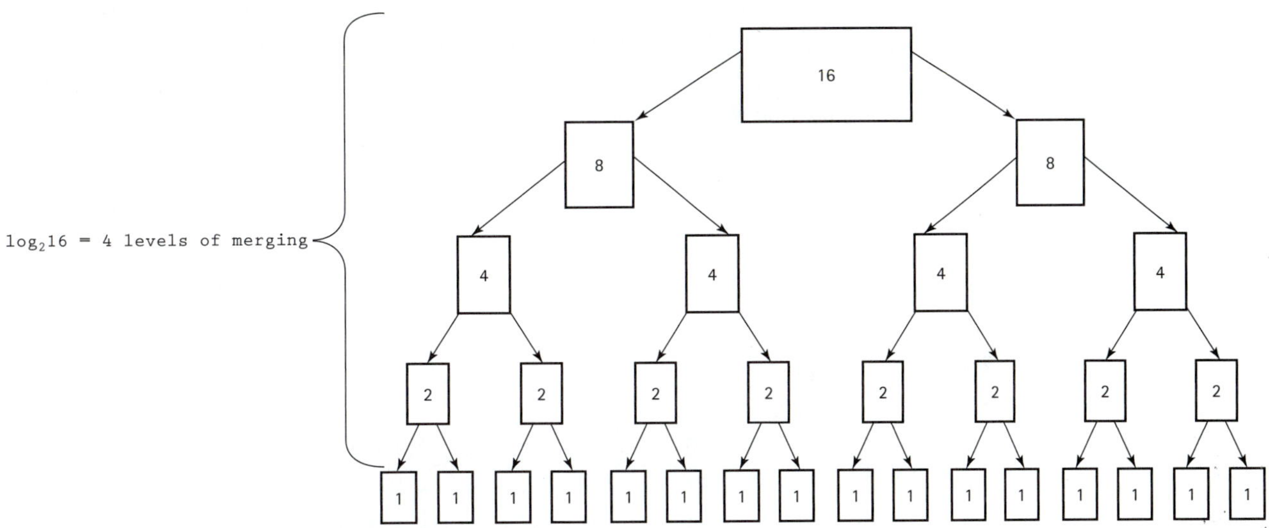

Figure 10.11 *Analysis of the function `MergeSort` with N = 16*

split into N subarrays of size 1. Merging two of those subarrays into a subarray of size 2 requires $O(1 + 1) = O(2)$ steps based on the analysis given in the preceding paragraph. That is, we must perform this merge operation a total of $\frac{1}{2}$ times (we have N one-element subarrays and we are merging them two at a time). Thus the total number of steps to create all of the sorted two-element subarrays is $O(N)$.

We repeat this process to create four-element subarrays. It takes four steps to merge two two-element subarrays. We must perform this merge operation a total of $\frac{1}{4}$ times (we have $\frac{1}{2}$ two-element subarrays and we are merging them two at a time). The total number of steps to create all of the sorted four-element subarrays is $O(N)$ $(4 * \frac{1}{4} = N)$.

The same reasoning leads us to conclude that each of the other levels of merging also requires $O(N)$ steps. At each level, the sizes of the subarrays double, but the number of subarrays is cut in half, balancing out.

We now know that it takes a total of $O(N)$ steps to perform merging at each "level" of merging. How many levels are there? The number of levels of merging is equal to the number of times we can split the original array in half. If the original array is size N, we have $\log_2 N$ levels (this is just like the analysis of the binary search algorithm). For example, in Figure 10.11 the size of the original array is 16 and the number of levels of merging is 4. Because we have $\log_2 N$ levels, and we require N steps at each level, the total cost of the merge operation is $O(N\log_2 N)$. Because the splitting phase was only $O(N)$, we conclude that `MergeSort` has $O(N\log_2 N)$ complexity. Table 10.2 illustrates that, for large values of N, $O(N\log_2 N)$ represents a big improvement over $O(N^2)$.

The disadvantage of `MergeSort` derives from the fact that it requires an auxiliary array that is as large as the original array to be sorted. If the array is large and space is a critical factor, this sort may not be an appropriate choice. Next, we discuss two sorts that move elements within the original array and do not need an auxiliary array.

Quick Sort

The quick sort algorithm is based on the idea that it is faster and easier to sort two small lists than one larger one. The name comes from the fact that, in general, quick sort can

Table 10.2 *Comparing N^2 and $N\log_2 N$*

N	$\log_2 N$	N^2	$N\log_2 N$
32	5	1,024	160
64	6	4,096	384
128	7	16,384	896
256	8	65,536	2,048
512	9	262,144	4,608
1024	10	1,048,576	10,240
2048	11	4,194,304	22,528
4096	12	16,777,216	49,152

sort a list of data elements quite rapidly. The basic strategy of this sorting algorithm is to divide and conquer.

If you were given a large stack of final exams to sort by name, you might use the following approach: pick a splitting value, say L, and divide the stack of tests into two piles, A-L and M-Z. (Note that the two piles do not necessarily contain the same number of tests.) Then take the first pile and subdivide it into two piles, A-F and G-L. The A-F pile can be further broken down into A-C and D-F. This division process goes on until the piles are small enough to be easily sorted. The same process is applied to the M-Z pile.

Eventually, all the small sorted piles can be stacked one on top of the other to produce a sorted set of tests. (See Figure 10.12.)

This strategy is based on recursion—on each attempt to sort the stack of tests, the stack is divided and then the same approach is used to sort each of the smaller stacks (a smaller case). This process continues until the small stacks do not need to be further divided (the base case). The parameter list of the `QuickSort` function reflects the part of the list that is currently being processed: We pass the array and the first and last indexes that define the part of the array to be processed on this call. The initial call to `QuickSort` is

```
QuickSort(values, 0, numberOfValues-1);
```

Function QuickSort

Definition:	Sorts the items in array values.
Size:	values[first]..values[last].
Base Case:	If less than 2 items in values[first]..values[last], do nothing.
General Case:	Split the array according to splitting value. QuickSort the elements <= splitting value. QuickSort the elements > splitting value.

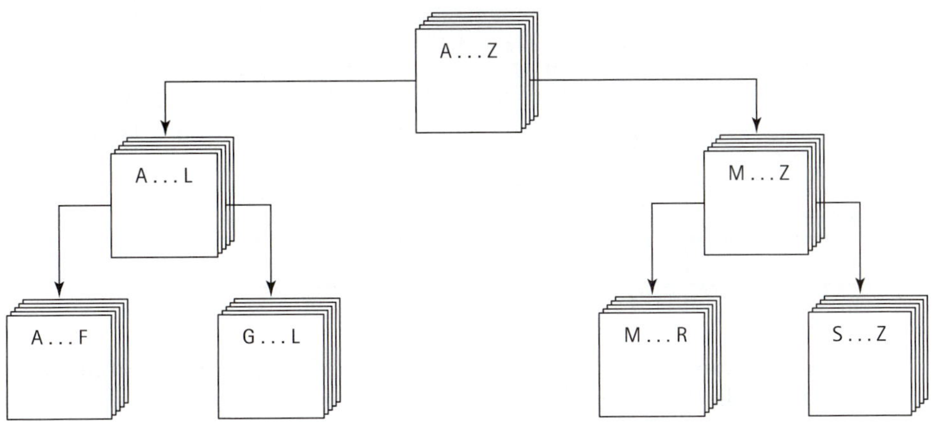

Figure 10.12 *Ordering a list using the quick sort algorithm*

QuickSort

```
if there is more than one item in values[first]..values[last]
    Select splitVal
    Split the array so that
        values[first]..values[splitPoint-1] <= splitVal
        values[splitPoint] = splitVal
        values[splitPoint+1]..values[last] > splitVal
    QuickSort the left half
    QuickSort the right half
```

How do we select `splitVal`? One simple solution is to use the value in `values[first]` as the splitting value. (We show a better value later.)

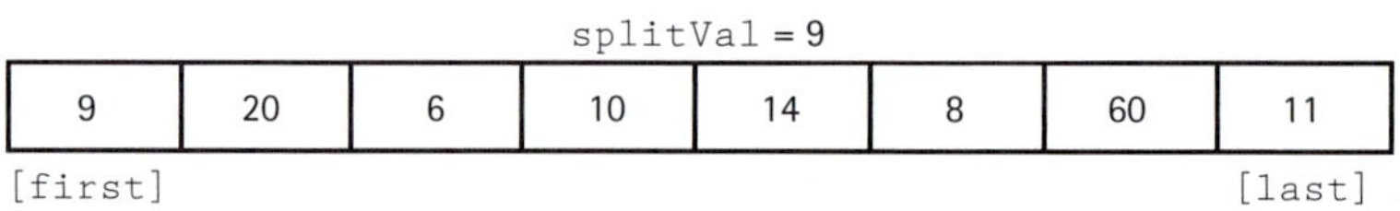

After the call to `Split`, all items less than or equal to `splitVal` are on the left side of the array and all items greater than `splitVal` are on the right side of the array.

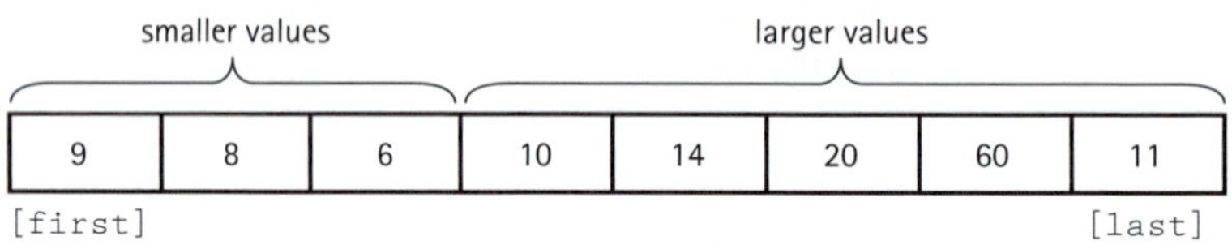

The two "halves" meet at `splitPoint`, the index of the last item that is less than or equal to `splitVal`. Note that we don't know the value of `splitPoint` until the splitting process is complete. We can then swap `splitVal` with the value at `splitPoint`.

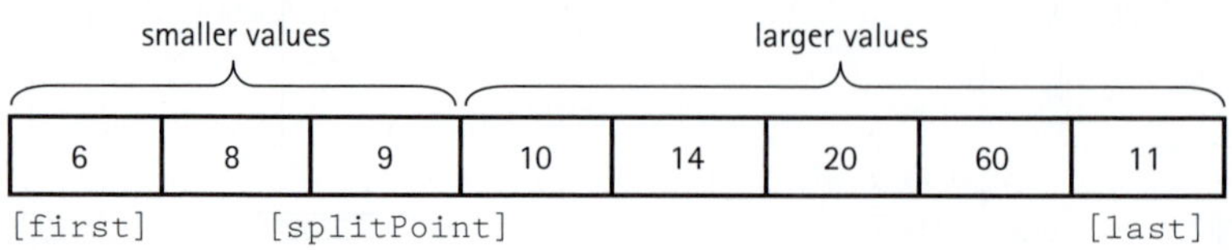

Our recursive calls to `QuickSort` use this index (`splitPoint`) to reduce the size of the problem in the general case.

`QuickSort(values, first, splitPoint - 1)` sorts the left "half" of the array. `QuickSort(values, splitPoint + 1, last)` sorts the right "half" of the array. (The “halves” are not necessarily the same size.) `splitVal` is already in its correct position in `values[splitPoint]`.

What is the base case? When the segment being examined has less than two items, we do not need to continue. So “there is more than one item in `values[first]..values[last]`” can be translated into “`if (first < last)`”. We can now code the function `QuickSort`.

```
template<class ItemType>
void QuickSort(ItemType values[], int first, int last)
{
  if (first < last)
  {
    int splitPoint;

    Split(values, first, last, splitPoint);
    // values[first]..values[splitPoint-1] <= splitVal
    // values[splitPoint] = splitVal
    // values[splitPoint+1]..values[last] > splitVal

    QuickSort(values, first, splitPoint-1);
    QuickSort(values, splitPoint+1, last);
  }
}
```

Let’s verify `QuickSort` using the Three-Question Method.

1. *Is there a nonrecursive base case?* Yes. When `first >= last` (the segment contains at most one element), `QuickSort` does nothing.
2. *Does each recursive call involve a smaller case of the problem?* Yes. `Split` divides the segment into two not necessarily equal pieces, and each of these smaller pieces is then quick sorted. Note that even if `splitVal` is the largest or smallest value in the segment, the two pieces are still smaller than the original one. If `splitVal` is smaller than all other values in the segment, then `QuickSort (values, first, splitPoint - 1)` terminates immediately, because `first > splitPoint - 1`. `QuickSort (values, splitPoint + 1, last)` quick sorts a segment one element smaller than the original.
3. *Assuming that the recursive calls succeed, does the entire function work?* Yes. We assume that `QuickSort (values, first, splitPoint - 1)` actually sorts the first `splitPoint - 1` elements, whose values are less than or equal to `splitVal`. `values[splitPoint]`, which contains `splitVal`, is in its correct place. We also assume that `QuickSort (values, splitPoint + 1, last)` has correctly sorted the rest of the list, whose values are all greater than `splitVal`. In this way, we determine that the whole list is sorted.

In good top-down fashion, we have shown that our algorithm works *if the function `Split` works*. Now we must develop our splitting algorithm. We must find a way to get all elements equal to or less than `splitVal` on one side of `splitVal` and all elements greater than `splitVal` on the other side.

We achieve this goal by moving the indexes, `first` and `last`, toward the middle of the array, looking for items that are on the wrong side of the split point (Figure 10.13). We make `first` and `last` be value parameters, so we can change their values without affecting the calling function. We save the original value of `first` in a local variable, `saveFirst`. (See Figure 10.13a.)[2]

We start by moving `first` to the right, toward the middle, comparing `values[first]` to `splitVal`. If `values[first]` is less than or equal to `splitVal`, we keep incrementing `first`; otherwise, we leave `first` where it is and begin moving `last` toward the middle. (See Figure 10.13b.)

Now we compare `values[last]` to `splitVal`. If it is greater, we continue decrementing `last`; otherwise, we leave `last` in place. (See Figure 10.13c.) At this point, it is clear that `values[last]` and `values[first]` are each on the wrong side of the array. Note that the elements to the left of `values[first]` and to the right of `values[last]` are not necessarily sorted; they are just on the correct side *with respect to* `splitVal`. To put `values[first]` and `values[last]` into their correct sides, we merely swap them, then increment `first` and decrement `last`. (See Figure 10.13d.)

Now we repeat the whole cycle, incrementing `first` until we encounter a value that is greater than `splitVal`, then decrementing `last` until we encounter a value that is less than or equal to `splitVal`. (See Figure 10.13e.)

When does the process stop? When `first` and `last` meet each other, no further swaps are necessary. They meet at `splitPoint`, the location where `splitVal` belongs. We swap `values[saveFirst]`, which contains `splitVal`, with the element at `values[splitPoint]`. (See Figure 10.13f.) The index `splitPoint` is returned from the function, to be used by `QuickSort` to set up the next recursive call.

```
void Split(ItemType values[], int first, int last, int& splitPoint)
{
  ItemType splitVal = values[first];
  int saveFirst = first;
  bool onCorrectSide;

  first++;
  do
  {
    onCorrectSide = true;
    while (onCorrectSide)              // Move first toward last.
      if (values[first] > splitVal)
        onCorrectSide = false;
      else
      {
        first++;
        onCorrectSide = (first <= last);
      }
```

[2]We assume that the relational operators are defined on values of `ItemType`.

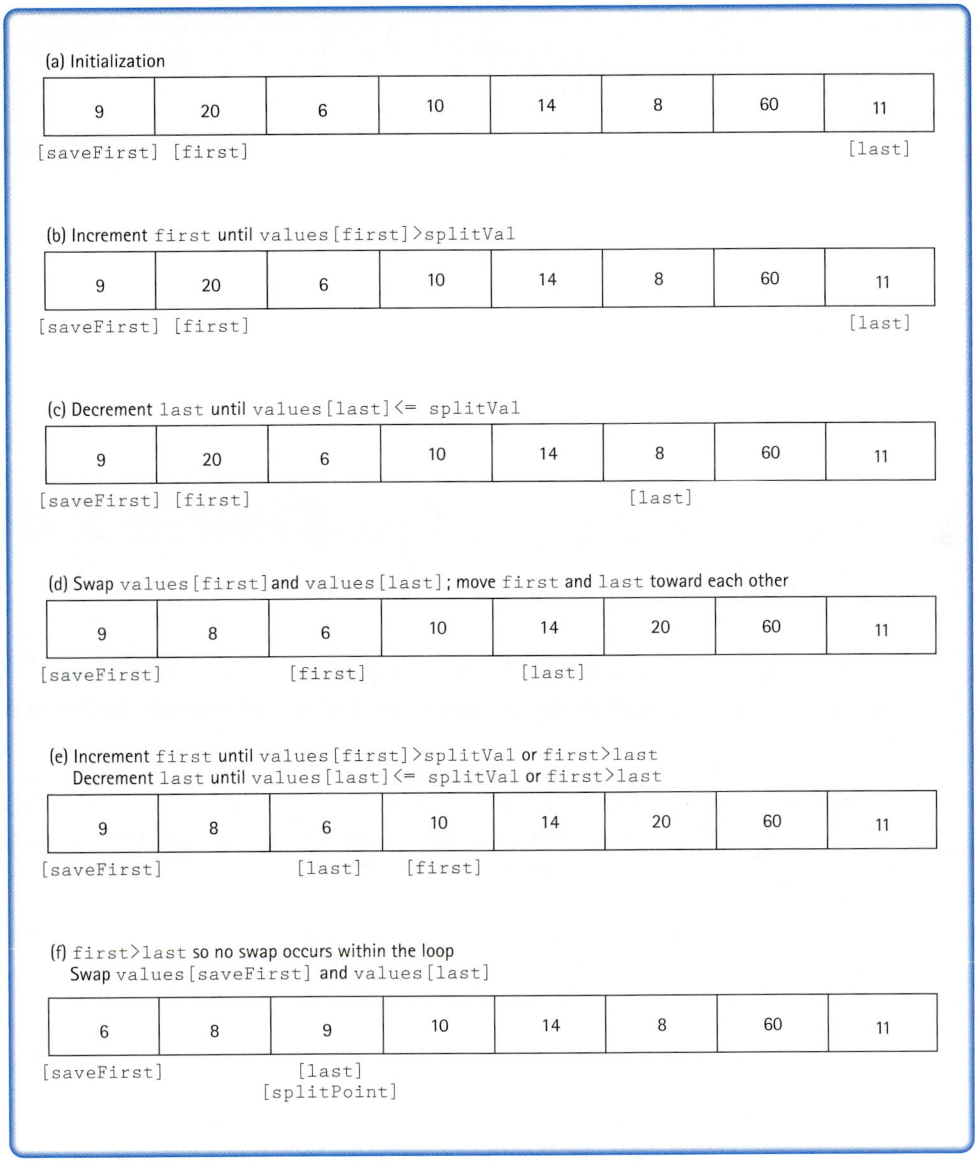

Figure 10.13 *Function split*

```
    onCorrectSide = (first <= last);
    while (onCorrectSide)              // Move last toward first.
      if (values[last] <= splitVal)
        onCorrectSide = false;
      else
      {
        last--;
        onCorrectSide = (first <= last);
      }

    if (first < last)
    {
      Swap(values[first], values[last]);
      first++;
      last--;
    }
  } while (first <= last);

  splitPoint = last;
  Swap(values[saveFirst], values[splitPoint]);
}
```

What happens if our splitting value is the largest or the smallest value in the segment? The algorithm still works correctly, but because of the lopsided splits it is not so quick.

Is this situation likely to occur? That depends on our choice of a splitting value and on the original order of the data in the array. If we use `values[first]` as the splitting value and the array is already sorted, then *every* split is lopsided. One side contains one element, while the other side contains all except one of the elements. Thus our `QuickSort` is not a quick sort. Such a splitting algorithm favors an array in random order.

It is not unusual, however, to want to sort an array that is already in nearly sorted order. In such a case, a better splitting value would be the middle value,

```
values[(first + last) / 2]
```

This value could be swapped with `values[first]` at the beginning of the function.

Many possible splitting algorithms exist. One that represents a slight variation of the one we have just developed follows. It uses the value in the middle of the array as the splitting value without moving it to the first slot. As a result, the value in `values[splitPoint]` may or may not be in its permanent place.

```
void Split2(ItemType values[], int first, int last,
            int& splitPt1, int& splitPt2)
{
  ItemType splitVal = values[(first+last)/2];
  bool onCorrectSide;
```

```
  do
  {
    onCorrectSide = true;
    while (onCorrectSide)      // Move first toward last.
      if (values[first] >= splitVal)
        onCorrectSide = false;
      else
        first++;

    onCorrectSide = true;
    while (onCorrectSide)           // Move last toward first.
      if (values[last] <= splitVal)
        onCorrectSide = false;
      else
        last--;
    if (first <= last)
    {
      Swap(values[first], values[last]);
      first++;
      last--;
    }
  } while (first <= last);

  splitPt1 = first;
  splitPt2 = last;
}
```

If we use this algorithm, `QuickSort` must be adjusted slightly.

```
void QuickSort2(ItemType values[], int first, int last)
{
  if (first < last)
  {
    int splitPt1;
    int splitPt2;

    Split2(values, first, last, splitPt1, splitPt2);
    // values[first]..values[splitPt2] <= splitVal
    // values[splitPt1+1]..values[last] > splitVal

    if (splitPt1 < last)
      QuickSort2(values, splitPt1, last);
    if (first < splitPt2)
      QuickSort2(values, first, splitPt2);
  }
}
```

The analysis of `QuickSort` is very similar to that of `MergeSort`. On the first call, every element in the array is compared to the dividing value (the "split value"), so the work done is $O(N)$. The array is divided into two parts (not necessarily halves), which are then examined.

Each of these pieces is then divided in two, and so on. If each piece is split approximately in half, $O(\log_2 N)$ splits occur. At each split, we make $O(N)$ comparisons. Thus `QuickSort` is also an $O(N\log_2 N)$ algorithm, which is quicker than the $O(N^2)$ sorts we discussed earlier in this chapter.

But `QuickSort` isn't *always* quicker. Note that $\log_2 N$ splits take place *if* each split divides the segment of the array approximately in half. As we've seen, `QuickSort` is sensitive to the order of the data.

What happens if the array is already sorted when we call our first version of `QuickSort`? The splits are very lopsided, and the subsequent recursive calls to `QuickSort` break into a segment of one element and a segment containing all the rest of the array. This situation produces a sort that is not at all quick. In fact, $N - 1$ splits occur; in this case, `QuickSort` has $O(N^2)$ complexity.

Such a situation is very unlikely to arise by chance. By way of analogy, consider the odds of shuffling a deck of cards and coming up with a sorted deck. On the other hand, in some applications you may know that the original array is likely to be sorted or nearly sorted. In such cases, you would want to use either a different splitting algorithm or a different sort—maybe even `ShortBubble`!

What about space requirements? `QuickSort` does not require an extra array, as `MergeSort` does. Does it have any extra space requirements, besides the few local variables? Yes—remember that `QuickSort` uses a recursive approach. Many levels of recursion can be "saved" on the system stack at any time. On average, the algorithm requires $O(\log_2 N)$ extra space to hold this information and in the worst case requires $O(N)$ extra space, the same as `MergeSort`.

Heap Sort

In each iteration of the selection sort, we searched the array for the next-smallest element and put it into its correct place in the array. Another way to write a selection sort is to find the maximum value in the array and swap it with the last array element, then find the next-to-largest element and put it into its place, and so on. Most of the work in this sorting algorithm comes from searching the remaining part of the array in each iteration, looking for the maximum value.

In Chapter 9, we discussed the *heap*, a data structure with a very special feature: We always know where to find its greatest element. Because of the order property of heaps, the maximum value of a heap is located in the root node. We can take advantage of this situation by using a heap to help us sort. The general approach of the heap sort is as follows:

1. Take the root (maximum) element off the heap, and put it into its place.
2. Reheap the remaining elements. (This action puts the next-largest element into the root position.)
3. Repeat until no more elements are left.

The first part of this algorithm sounds a lot like the straight selection sort. What makes the heap sort fast is the second step: finding the next-largest element. Because the shape property of heaps guarantees a binary tree of minimum height, we make only $O(\log_2 N)$ comparisons in each iteration, as compared with $O(N)$ comparisons in each iteration of the selection sort.

Building a Heap By now you are probably protesting that we are dealing with an unsorted array of elements, not a heap. Where does the original heap come from? Before we go on, we must convert the unsorted array, `values`, into a heap.

Let's look at how the heap relates to our array of unsorted elements. In Chapter 9, we saw how heaps can be represented in an array with implicit links. Because of the shape property, we know that the heap elements take up consecutive positions in the array. In fact, the unsorted array of data elements already satisfies the shape property of heaps. Figure 10.14 shows an unsorted array and its equivalent tree.

We also need to make the unsorted array elements satisfy the order property of heaps. First, let's see whether any part of the tree already satisfies the order property. All of the leaf nodes (subtrees with only a single node) are heaps. In Figure 10.15a, the subtrees whose roots contain the values 19, 7, 3, 100, and 1 are heaps because they are root nodes.

Next, let's look at the first *nonleaf* node, the one containing the value 2 (Figure 10.15b). The subtree rooted at this node is not a heap, but it is *almost* a heap—all of the nodes *except the root node* of this subtree satisfy the order property. We know how to fix this problem. In Chapter 9, we developed a heap utility function, `ReheapDown`, that we can use to correct this exact situation. Given a tree whose elements satisfy the order property of heaps except (perhaps) at the root node, `ReheapDown` rearranges the nodes, leaving the (sub)tree as a heap.

We apply this function to all subtrees on this level, then move up a level in the tree and continue reheaping until we reach the root node. After `ReheapDown` has been called for the root node, the entire tree should satisfy the order property of heaps. Figure 10.15 illustrates this heap-building process; Figure 10.16 shows the changing contents of the array.

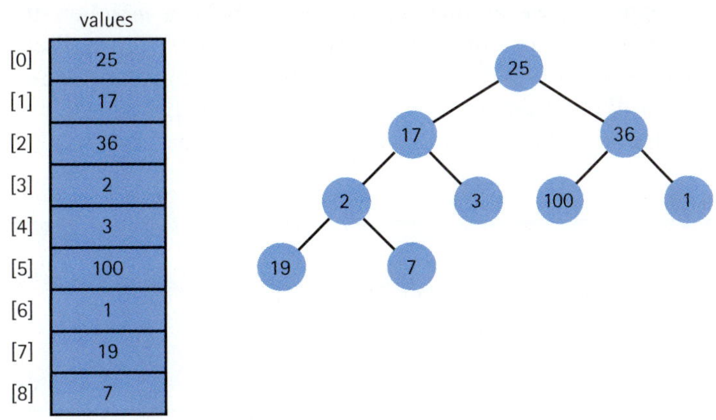

Figure 10.14 *An unsorted array and its tree*

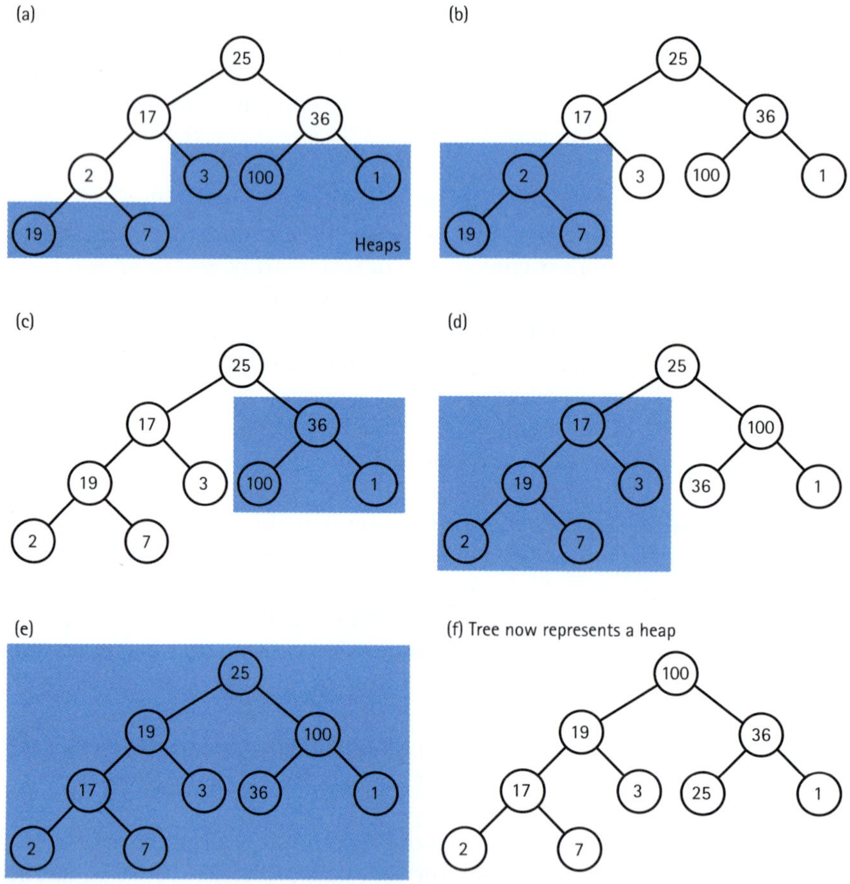

Figure 10.15 *The heap-building process*

(In Chapter 9, we defined `ReheapDown` to be a member function of `HeapType`, a struct type. There, the function had two parameters: the indexes of the root node and the bottom node. Here, we assume a slight variation: `ReheapDown` is a global function that takes a third parameter—an array that is treated as a heap.)

The algorithm for building a heap is summarized here:

BuildHeap

```
for index going from first nonleaf node up to the root node
    ReheapDown(values, index, numValues - 1)
```

	[0]	[1]	[2]	[3]	[4]	[5]	[6]	[7]	[8]
Original values	25	17	36	2	3	100	1	19	7
After ReheapDown index = 3	25	17	36	19	3	100	1	2	7
After index = 2	25	17	100	19	3	36	1	2	7
After index = 1	25	19	100	17	3	36	1	2	7
After index = 0	100	19	36	17	3	25	1	2	7
Tree is a heap.									

Figure 10.16 *Changing contents of the array*

We know where the root node is stored in our array representation of heaps—in `values[0]`. Where is the first nonleaf node? Because half the nodes of a complete binary tree are leaves (prove this yourself), the first nonleaf node may be found at position `numValues/2 - 1`.

Sorting Using the Heap Now that we are satisfied that we can turn the unsorted array of elements into a heap, let's take another look at the sorting algorithm.

We can easily access the largest element from the original heap—it's in the root node. In our array representation of heaps, that location is `values[0]`. This value belongs in the last-used array position `values[numValues - 1]`, so we can just swap the values in these two positions. Because `values[numValues - 1]` contains the largest value in the array (its correct sorted value), we want to leave this position alone. Now we are dealing with a set of elements, from `values[0]` through `values[numValues - 2]`, that is almost a heap. We know that all of these elements satisfy the order property of heaps, except (perhaps) the root node. To correct this condition, we call our heap utility, `ReheapDown`.

At this point we know that the next-largest element in the array is located in the root node of the heap. To put this element in its correct position, we swap it with the element in `values[numValues - 2]`. Now the two largest elements are in their final correct positions, and the elements in `values[0]` through `values[numValues - 3]` are almost a heap. We call `ReheapDown` again, and now the third-largest element is placed in the root of the heap.

We repeat this process until all of the elements are in their correct positions—that is, until the heap contains only a single element, which must be the smallest item in the array, `values[0]`. This location is its correct position, so the array is now completely sorted from the smallest to the largest element. Notice that at each iteration the size of the unsorted portion (represented as a heap) becomes smaller and the size of the sorted portion becomes larger. At the end of the algorithm, the size of the sorted portion matches the size of the original array.

The heap sort algorithm, as we have described it, sounds like a recursive process. Each time through, we swap and reheap a smaller portion of the total array. Because it uses tail recursion, we can code the repetition just as clearly using a simple *for* loop. The node-sorting algorithm follows:

Sort Nodes

```
for index going from last node up to next-to-root node
    Swap data in root node with values[index]
    ReheapDown(values, 0, index - 1)
```

The function `HeapSort` first builds the heap and then sorts the nodes, using the algorithms just discussed. Notice that `HeapSort` does not actually use the struct `HeapType`. Rather, it uses the `ReheapDown` function with the array of values passed as a parameter.

```
template<class ItemType>
void HeapSort(ItemType values[], int numValues)
// Assumption: Function ReheapDown is available.
// Post: The elements in the array values are sorted by key.
{
  int index;

  // Convert the array of values into a heap.
  for (index = numValues/2 - 1; index >= 0; index--)
    ReheapDown(values, index, numValues-1);

  // Sort the array.
  for (index = numValues-1; index >=1; index--)
  {
    Swap(values[0], values[index]);
    ReheapDown(values, 0, index-1);
  }
}
```

Figure 10.17 shows how each iteration of the sorting loop (the second *for* loop) would change the heap created in Figure 10.16. Each line represents the array after one operation. The sorted elements are shaded.

We entered the `HeapSort` routine with a simple array of unsorted values and returned to the caller with an array of the same values sorted in ascending order. Where did the heap go? The heap in `HeapSort` is just a temporary structure, internal to the sorting algorithm. It is created at the beginning of the function, to aid in the sorting process, and then is methodically diminished element by element as the sorted part of the array grows. At the end of the function, the sorted part fills the array and the heap has completely disappeared. When we used heaps to implement priority queues in

	[0]	[1]	[2]	[3]	[4]	[5]	[6]	[7]	[8]
values	100	19	36	17	3	25	1	2	7
Swap	7	19	36	17	3	25	1	2	100
ReheapDown	36	19	25	17	3	7	1	2	100
Swap	2	19	25	17	3	7	1	36	100
ReheapDown	25	19	7	17	3	2	1	36	100
Swap	1	19	7	17	3	2	25	36	100
ReheapDown	19	17	7	1	3	2	25	36	100
Swap	2	17	7	1	3	19	25	36	100
ReheapDown	17	3	7	1	2	19	25	36	100
Swap	2	3	7	1	17	19	25	36	100
ReheapDown	7	3	2	1	17	19	25	36	100
Swap	1	3	2	7	17	19	25	36	100
ReheapDown	3	1	2	7	17	19	25	36	100
Swap	2	1	3	7	17	19	25	36	100
ReheapDown	2	1	3	7	17	19	25	36	100
Swap	1	2	3	7	17	19	25	36	100
ReheapDown	1	2	3	7	17	19	25	36	100
Exit from sorting loop	1	2	3	7	17	19	25	36	100

Figure 10.17 *Effect of* `HeapSort` *on the array*

Chapter 9, the heap structure stayed around for the duration of the use of the queue. The heap in `HeapSort`, in contrast, is not a retained data structure. It exists only for a while inside the `HeapSort` function.

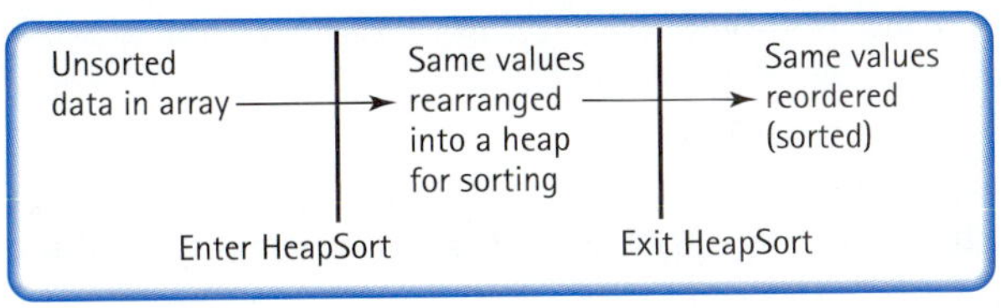

Analyzing the Heap Sort The code for `HeapSort` is very short—only a few lines of new code plus the utility function `ReheapDown`, which we developed in Chapter 9. These few lines of code, however, do quite a bit. All of the elements in the original array are rearranged to satisfy the order property of heaps, moving the largest element up to the top of the array, only to put it immediately into its place at the bottom. It's difficult to believe from a small example such as the one in Figure 10.17 that `HeapSort` is really very efficient.

In fact, for small arrays, `HeapSort` is not very efficient because of its "overhead." For large arrays, however, `HeapSort` is very efficient. Consider the sorting loop. We loop through $N - 1$ times, swapping elements and reheaping. The comparisons occur in `ReheapDown`. A complete binary tree with N nodes has $O(\log_2(N + 1))$ levels. In the worst case, then, if the root element has to be bumped down to a leaf position, the `ReheapDown` function would make $O(\log_2 N)$ comparisons; the function `ReheapDown` is $O(\log_2 N)$. Multiplying this activity by the $N - 1$ iterations, $O(N)$, shows that the sorting loop is $O(N\log_2 N)$.

Combining the original heap build operation, which is $O(N)$, and the sorting loop, we can see that `HeapSort` requires $O(N\log_2 N)$ comparisons. Note that, unlike `QuickSort`, `HeapSort`'s efficiency is *not* affected by the initial order of the elements. `HeapSort` is just as efficient in terms of space; it uses only one array to store the data.

Testing

We have examined several sorting algorithms: selection sort, two versions of bubble sort, insertion sort, merge sort, two versions of quick sort, and heap sort. Before we examine other issues involved in sorting, we need to verify that our algorithms are correct. We can use the same pattern that we have used for earlier ADTs. We can take as input the name of a sorting algorithm, apply that algorithm to an array of values, and print the results. We need to initialize an array with random numbers, refresh the array after it has been sorted, and generate an array of new values.

On the Web, the file `SortDr.cpp` contains the test driver. The file `Sorts.in` contains a test plan that generates an array, applies each of the algorithms to it, generates a second array, and applies one of the algorithms. `Sorts.out` holds the output from the driver, and `Sorts.screen` holds what was written on the screen. Examine these files carefully. Be sure you understand them. You are asked to design a more involved test plan in the exercises.

Other Efficiency Considerations

When N Is Small Throughout this chapter, we have based our analysis of efficiency on the number of comparisons made by a sorting algorithm. This number gives us a rough estimate of the computation time involved. The other activities that accompany the comparison (swapping, keeping track of Boolean flags, and so forth) contribute to the "constant of proportionality" of the algorithm.

In comparing Big-O evaluations, we ignored constants and smaller-order terms, because we wanted to know how the algorithm would perform for large values of N. In general, an $O(N^2)$ sort requires few extra activities in addition to the comparisons, so its constant of proportionality is fairly small. On the other hand, an $O(N\log_2 N)$ sort may be more complex, with more overhead and thus a larger constant of proportionality. This situation may cause anomalies in the relative performances of the algorithms when the value of N is small. In such a case, N^2 is not much greater than $N\log_2 N$, and the constants may dominate instead, causing an $O(N^2)$ sort to run faster than an $O(N\log_2 N)$ sort.

We have discussed sorting algorithms that have a complexity of either $O(N^2)$ or $O(N\log_2 N)$. The obvious question is: Are some algorithms better than $O(N\log_2 N)$? No, it has been proven theoretically that we cannot do better than $O(N\log_2 N)$ for sorting algorithms that are based on comparing keys.

Eliminating Calls to Functions At the beginning of this chapter, we mentioned that it may be desirable, for efficiency reasons, to streamline the code as much as possible, even at the expense of readability. For instance, we have consistently written

```
Swap(item1, item2)
```

instead of the corresponding inline expansion:

```
tempItem = item1;
item1 = item2;
item2 = temp;
```

Similarly, in `SelectionSort`, we coded the operation to find the minimum element as a function, `MinIndex`; in `BubbleSort`, we coded a function `BubbleUp`. Coding such operations as functions made the code simpler to write and to understand, avoiding a more complicated nested loop structure.

Although the function calls are clearer, in the actual coding it may be better to use the inline expansion. Function calls require extra overhead that you may prefer to avoid in a sort, where these routines are called within a loop.

The recursive sorting functions, `MergeSort` and `QuickSort`, lead to a similar situation: They require the extra overhead involved in executing recursive calls. You may want to avoid this overhead by writing nonrecursive versions of these functions.

Programmer Time If the recursive calls are less efficient, why would anyone ever decide to use a recursive version of a sort? The decision involves a choice between types of efficiency. Until now, we have been concerned only with minimizing computer time. While computers are becoming faster and cheaper, however, it is not clear that computer *programmer*s are following that trend. In some situations, programmer time may be an important consideration in choosing a sort algorithm and its implementation. In this respect, the recursive version of `QuickSort` is more desirable than its nonrecursive counterpart, which requires the programmer to simulate the recursion explicitly.

Space Considerations Another efficiency consideration relates to the amount of memory space required. In general, memory space is not a very important factor in choosing a sorting algorithm. We looked at only one sort, `MergeSort`, in which space would be a major factor. The usual time versus space tradeoff applies to sorts—more space often means less time, and vice versa.

Because processing time is the factor that applies most often to sorting algorithms, we have considered it in detail here. Of course, as in any application, the programmer must determine his or her goals and requirements before selecting an algorithm and starting to code.

More about Sorting in General

Keys In our descriptions of the various sorts, we showed examples of sorting arrays using unique keys. A record may also contain secondary keys, which may or may not be unique. For instance, a student record may contain the following data members:

`studentNumber`	*Primary unique key*

`name`
`address`
`major`
	Secondary keys

If the data elements are only single integers, it doesn't matter whether you maintain the original order of duplicate values. However, preserving the original order of records with identical key values may be desirable. If a sort preserves this order, it is said to be stable.

Stable sort A sorting algorithm that preserves the order of duplicates

Suppose the items on our array are student records with the following declarations:

```
struct AddressType
{
  .
  .
  .
  StrType city;
  long zip;
};

struct NameType
{
  StrType firstName;
  StrType lastName;
};

struct PersonType
{
  long studentNumber;
  NameType name;
  AddressType address;
};
```

The list may normally be sorted by the unique key `studentNumber`. For some purposes, we might want to see a listing in order by name. In this case, the sort key would consist of the `name` data member. To sort by ZIP code, we would sort on the `address.zip` data member.

If the sort is stable, we can get a listing by ZIP code, with the names in alphabetical order within each ZIP code, by sorting twice: the first time by name and the second time by ZIP code. A stable sort preserves the order of the records when a match on the key is found. The second sort, by ZIP code, produces many such matches, but preserves the alphabetical order imposed by the first sort.

To get a listing by city, with the ZIP codes in order within each city and the names alphabetically sorted within each ZIP code, we would sort three times, on the following keys:

```
name
address.zip
address.city
```

The file would first be put into alphabetical order by name. The output from the first sort would serve as input to a sort on ZIP code. The output from this sort would serve as input to a sort on city name. If the sorting algorithms used were stable, the final sort would give us the desired result.

Of the sorts that we have discussed in this book, only `HeapSort` is inherently unstable. The stability of the other sorts depends on how the code manages duplicate values. In the exercises you are asked to examine the code for the other sorts as we have coded them and determine whether they are stable.

Sorting with Pointers Sorting large records using some kind of sort that swaps the contents of two places may require a lot of computer time just to move sections of memory from one place to another every time we make a swap. We can reduce this move time by setting up an array of *pointers* to the records and then rearranging the pointers instead of the actual records. Figure 10.18 illustrates this scheme. After the sort, the records are still in the same physical arrangement, but they may be accessed in order through the rearranged array of pointers.

We may extend this scheme to keep a large array of data sorted on more than one key. The data can be physically stored according to the primary key, and auxiliary arrays can contain pointers to the same data but be sorted on secondary keys.

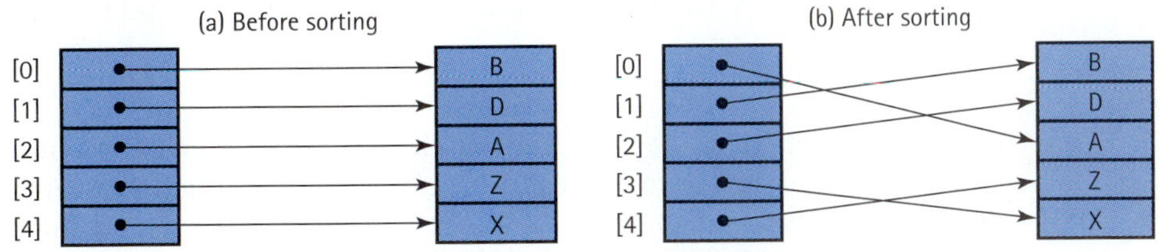

Figure 10.18 *Sorting arrays with pointers*

10.2 Searching

As discussed in Chapter 2, for each particular structure used to hold data, the functions that allow access to elements in the structure must be defined. In some cases, access is limited to the elements in specific positions in the structure, such as the top element in a stack or the front element in a queue. Often, when data are stored in a list or a table, we want to be able to access any element in the structure.

Sometimes the retrieval of a specified element can be performed directly. For instance, the fifth element of the list stored *sequentially* in an array-based list called `list` is found in `list.info[4]`. Often, however, you want to access an element according to some key value. For instance, if a list contains student records, you may want to find the record of the student named Suzy Brown or the record of the student whose ID number is 203557. In cases such as these, you need some kind of *searching technique* to retrieve the desired record.

For each of the techniques we review or introduce, our algorithm must meet the following specifications. Note that we are talking about techniques within the class, not client code.

FindItem(item, location)

Function:	Determines whether an item in the list has a key that matches item's.
Preconditions:	List has been initialized. item's key has been initialized.
Postconditions:	location = position of element whose key matches item's key, if it exists; otherwise, location = NULL.

This specification applies to both array-based and linked lists, where `location` would be either an index in an array-based list or a pointer in a linked list, and `NULL` would be either −1 in an array-based list or the null pointer in a linked list.

Linear Searching

We cannot discuss efficient ways to find an element in a list without considering how the elements were inserted into the list. Therefore, our discussion of search algorithms must deal with the issue of the list's `InsertItem` operation. Suppose that we want to insert elements as quickly as possible, and we are not equally concerned with how long it takes to find them. We would put the element into the last slot in an array-based list and the first slot in a linked list. These are O(1) insertion algorithms. The resulting list is sorted according to the time of insertion, not according to key value.

To search this list for the element with a given key, we must use a simple *linear* (or *sequential*) *search*. Beginning with the first element in the list, we search for the desired element by examining each subsequent item's key until either the search is successful or the list is exhausted.

```
LinearSearch (unsorted data)
Initialize location to position of first item
Set found to false
Set moreToSearch to (have not examined Info(last))
while moreToSearch AND NOT found
    if item equals Info(location)
        Set found to true
    else
        Set location to Next(location)
        Set moreToSearch to (have not examined Info(last))
if NOT found
    Set location to NULL
```

Based on the number of comparisons, it should be obvious that this search is $O(N)$, where N represents the number of elements. In the worst case, in which we are looking for the last element in the list or for a nonexistent element, we make N key comparisons. On the average, assuming that there is an equal probability of searching for any item in the list, we make $N/2$ comparisons for a successful search; that is, we search half of the list.

High-Probability Ordering

The assumption of equal probability for every element in the list is not always valid. Sometimes certain list elements are in much greater demand than others. This observation suggests a way to improve the search: Put the most-often-desired elements at the beginning of the list. Using this scheme, you are more likely to have a hit in the first few tries, and rarely do you have to search the whole list.

If the elements in the list are not static or if you cannot predict their relative demand, you need some scheme to keep the most frequently used elements at the front of the list. One way to accomplish this goal is to move each element accessed to the front of the list. Of course, this scheme offers no guarantee that this element is later frequently used. If the element is not retrieved again, however, it drifts toward the end of the list as other elements move to the front. This scheme is easy to implement for linked lists, requiring only a couple of pointer changes, but it is less desirable for lists kept sequentially in arrays, because of the need to move all the other elements down to make room at the front.

A second approach, which causes elements to move toward the front of the list gradually, is appropriate for either linked or sequential list representations. As an element is found, it is swapped with the element that precedes it. Over many list retrievals, the most frequently desired elements tend to be grouped at the front of the list. To implement this approach, we need to modify only the end of the algorithm to exchange the found element with the one before it in the list (unless it is the first element). If the search operation was implemented as a `const` function and we made this modification, we would have to remove the `const` declaration, as the search operation actually changes the list. This modification should be documented; it is an unexpected side effect of searching the list.

Keeping the most active elements at the front of the list does not affect the worst case; if the search value is the last element or is not in the list, the search still takes N comparisons. It is still an $O(N)$ search. The *average* performance on successful searches should improve, however. Both of these algorithms depend on the assumption that some elements in the list are used much more often than others. If this assumption does not hold true, a different ordering strategy is needed to improve the efficiency of the search technique.

Lists in which the relative positions of the elements are changed in an attempt to improve search efficiency are called *self-organizing* or *self-adjusting* lists.

Key Ordering

If a list is sorted according to the key value, we can write more efficient search routines. To support a sorted list, we must either insert the elements in order or sort the list before searching it. (Inserting the elements in order is an $O(N^2)$ process, as each insertion is $O(N)$. If we insert each element into the next free slot and then sort the list with a "good" sort, the process has $O(N\log_2 N)$ complexity.)

If the list is sorted, a sequential search no longer needs to search the whole list to discover that an element does *not* exist. Rather, it needs to search only until it has passed the element's logical place in the list—that is, until it encounters an element with a larger key value. Versions of the Sorted List ADT in Chapters 3 and 5 implement this search technique.

The advantage of linear searching of a sorted list is the ability to stop searching before the list is exhausted if the element does not exist. Again, the search is $O(N)$—the worst case, searching for the largest element, still requires N comparisons. The average number of comparisons for an unsuccessful search is now $N/2$, however, instead of a guaranteed N.

The advantage of linear searching lies in its simplicity. The disadvantage relates to its performance: In the worst case, you make N comparisons. If the list is sorted and stored in an array, however, you can improve the search time to a worst case of $O(\log_2 N)$ with a binary search. In this instance, efficiency is improved at the expense of simplicity.

Binary Searching

We have seen a way to improve searching efficiency from $O(N)$ to $O(\log_2 N)$. If the data elements are sorted and stored sequentially in an array, we can use a *binary* search. The binary search algorithm improves the search efficiency by limiting the search to the area where the element might be. It takes a divide-and-conquer approach, continually paring down the area to be searched until either the element is found or the search area is gone (the element is not in the list). We developed the `BinarySearch` function in Chapter 3 and converted it to a recursive function in Chapter 7.

The binary search is not guaranteed to be faster for searching very small lists. Even though the binary search generally requires fewer comparisons, each comparison involves more computation. When N is very small, this extra work (the constants and smaller terms that we ignore in determining the Big-O approximation) may dominate. Although the algorithm requires fewer comparisons, each involves more processing. For instance, in one assembly-language program, the linear search required 5 time units per comparison, whereas the binary search took 35. For a list containing 16 elements, therefore, the worst-case linear search would require 5 * 16 = 80 time units. The worst-case binary search requires only 4 comparisons, but at 35 time units each, the comparisons take 140 time units. In cases where the list contains a small number of elements, a linear search is certainly adequate and sometimes faster than a binary search.

As the number of elements increases, however, the disparity between the linear search and the binary search grows very quickly. Look back at Table 3.1 to compare the rates of growth for the two algorithms.

The binary search discussed here is appropriate only for list elements stored in a sequential array-based representation. After all, how can you efficiently find the midpoint of a linked list? However, you already know of a structure that allows you to perform a binary search on a linked data representation, the binary search tree. The operations used to search a binary tree are discussed in Chapter 8.

10.3 Hashing

So far, we have succeeded in paring down our $O(N)$ search to $O(\log_2 N)$ complexity by keeping the list sorted sequentially with respect to the key value. That is, the key in the first element is less than (or equal to) the key in the second element, which is less than the key in the third element, and so on. Can we do even better? Is it possible to design a search of $O(1)$—that is, one that has a constant search time, no matter where the element is located in the list?

In theory, that goal is not an impossible dream. Let's look at an example, a list of employees of a fairly small company. Each of the 100 employees has an ID number in the range 0 to 99, and we want to access the employee records using the key `idNum`. If we store the elements in an array that is indexed from 0 to 99, we can directly access any employee's record through the array index. There is a one-to-one correspondence between the element keys and the array index; in effect, the array index functions as the key of each element.

In practice, however, this perfect relationship between the key value and the location of an element is not easy to establish or maintain. Consider a similar small company that uses its employees' five-digit ID number as the primary key. Now the range of key values goes from 00000 to 99999. Obviously, it is impractical to set up an array of 100,000 elements, of which only 100 are needed, just to make sure that each employee's element is in a perfectly unique and predictable location.

What if we keep the array size down to the size that we actually need (an array of 100 elements) and use just the last two digits of the key to identify each employee? For instance, the element of employee 53374 is in `employeeList.info[74]`, and the element of employee 81235 is in `employeeList.info[35]`. Note that the elements are not sorted according to the *value* of the key as they were in our earlier discussion; the position of employee 81235's record precedes that of employee 53374 in the array, even though the value of its key is larger. Instead, the elements are sorted with respect to some *function* of the key value.

This function is called a hash function, and the search technique we are using is called hashing. In the case of the employee list, the hash function is (Key % 100). The key (`idNum`) is divided by 100, and the remainder is used as an index into the array of employee elements, as illustrated in Figure 10.19. This function assumes that the array is indexed from 0 to 99 (`MAX_ITEMS` = 100). The function to perform the conversion of key values to indexes is very simple:

Hash function A function used to manipulate the key of an element in a list to identify its location in the list

Hashing The technique used for ordering and accessing elements in a list in a relatively constant amount of time by manipulating the key to identify its location in the list

```
int ItemType::Hash() const
// Post: Returns an integer between 0 and MAX_ITEMS - 1.
{
  return (idNum % MAX_ITEMS);
}
```

Here we assume that `Hash` is a member function of `ItemType`, the type of the items in the list, and that `idNum` is a data member of `ItemType`.

This hash function has two uses. First, it is used as a method of accessing the list element. The result of the hash function tells us where to *look* for a particular element—information we need to retrieve, modify, or delete the element. Here, for example, is a

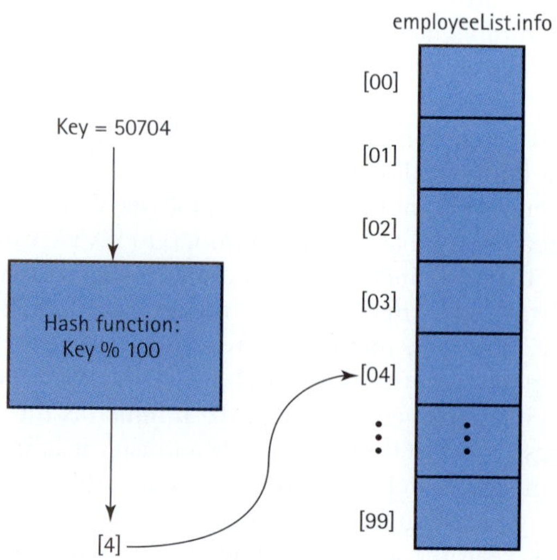

Figure 10.19 *Using a hash function to determine the location of the element in an array*

simple version of the function `RetrieveItem`, which assumes that the element is present in the list:

```
template<class ItemType>
void ListType<ItemType>::RetrieveItem(ItemType& item)
// Post: Returns the element in the array at position
//       item.Hash().
{
  int location;

  location = item.Hash();
  item = info[location];
}
```

Second, the hash function determines where in the array to *store* the element. If the employee list elements were inserted into the list using an insert operation from Chapter 3—into sequential array slots or into slots with their relative order determined by the key value—we could not use the hash function to retrieve them. We have to create a version of an insert operation that puts each new element into the correct slot *according to the hash function.* Here is a simple version of `InsertItem`, which assumes that the array slot at the index returned from the hash function is not in use:

```
template<class ItemType>
void ListType<ItemType>::InsertItem(ItemType item)
// Post: item is stored in the array at position item.Hash().
{
  int location;

  location = item.Hash();
  info[location] = item;
  length++;
}
```

Figure 10.20a shows an array whose elements—records for the employees with the key values (unique ID numbers) 12704, 31300, 49001, 52202, and 65606—were added using `InsertItem`. Note that this function does not fill the array positions sequentially. Because we have not yet inserted any elements whose keys produce the hash values 3 and 5, the array slots [3] and [5] are logically "empty." This technique differs from the approach we used in Chapter 3 to create a sorted list. In Figure 10.20b, the same employee records have been inserted into a sorted list using the `InsertItem` operation from Chapter 3. Note that, unless the hash function was used to determine where to insert an element, the hash function is *useless* for finding the element.

	(a) Hashed		(b) Linear
[00]	31300	[00]	12704
[01]	49001	[01]	31300
[02]	52202	[02]	49001
[03]	Empty	[03]	52202
[04]	12704	[04]	65606
[05]	Empty	[05]	Empty
[06]	65606	[06]	Empty
[07]	Empty	[07]	Empty
⋮	⋮	⋮	⋮

Figure 10.20 *Comparing hashed and sequential lists of identical elements*

Collisions

By now you are probably objecting to this scheme on the grounds that it does not guarantee unique hash locations. For example, ID number 01234 and ID number 91234 both "hash" to the same location: `list.info[34]`. The problem of avoiding these collisions represents the biggest challenge in designing a good hash function. A good hash function *minimizes collisions* by spreading the elements uniformly throughout the array. We say "minimizes collisions," because it is extremely difficult to avoid them completely.

Collision The condition resulting when two or more keys produce the same hash location

Assuming that some collisions will occur, where do you store the elements that cause them? We briefly describe several popular collision-handling algorithms in the next sections. Note that the scheme used to find the place to store an element determines the method subsequently used to retrieve it.

Linear Probing A simple approach to resolving collisions is to store the colliding element in the next available space. This technique is known as linear probing. In the situation depicted in Figure 10.21, we want to add the employee element with the key ID number 77003. The hash function returns 3. But there is already an element stored in this array slot, the record for Employee 50003. We increment `location` to 4 and examine the next array slot. The `list.info[4]` entry is also in use, so we increment `location` again. This time we find an empty slot, so we store the new element into `list.info[5]`.

Linear probing Resolving a hash collision by sequentially searching a hash table beginning at the location returned by the hash function

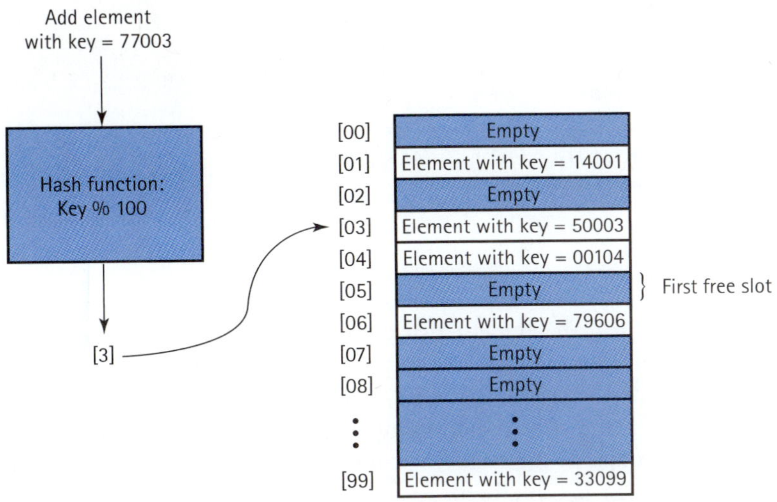

Figure 10.21 *Handling collisions with linear probing*

What happens if the key hashes to the last index in the array and that space is in use? We can consider the array to be a circular structure and continue looking for an empty slot at the beginning of the array. This situation is similar to the circular array-based queue we developed in Chapter 4. There we used the `%` operator when we incremented our index. We can use similar logic here.

How do we know whether an array slot is "empty"? We can initialize the array slot to contain a special `emptyItem` value. This value (a parameter to the class constructor) must be syntactically legal, but semantically illegal. For instance, if all employees have nonnegative integer `idNum` keys, we can use –1 as the key value for an "empty" slot. Now it is easy to tell whether the slot is free: We just compare the value in the position to `emptyItem`.

The following version of `InsertItem` uses linear probing to find a place to store a new element. It assumes that the array has room for another element; that is, the client checks for `IsFull` before calling the function. (We have retained the `length` member of `ListType`. Even though it no longer tells us where to find the end of the list, it is still useful in determining whether the list is full.)

```
template<class ItemType>
void ListType<ItemType>::InsertItem(ItemType item)
// Post: item is stored in the array at position item.Hash()
//       or the next free spot.
{
```

```
  int location;

  location = item.Hash();
  while (info[location] != emptyItem)
    location = (location + 1) % MAX_ITEMS;
  info[location] = item;
  length++;
}
```

To search for an element using this collision-handling technique, we perform the hash function on the key, then compare the desired key to the actual key in the element at the designated location. If the keys do not match, we use linear probing, beginning at the next slot in the array. Following is a version of the function `RetrieveItem` that uses this approach. If the element is not found in the list, the outgoing parameter `found` is false, and `item` is undefined.

```
template<class ItemType>
void ListType<ItemType>::RetrieveItem(ItemType& item, bool& found)
{
  int location;
  int startLoc;
  bool moreToSearch = true;

  startLoc = item.Hash();
  location = startLoc;
  do
  {
    if (info[location] == item || info[location] == emptyItem)
      moreToSearch = false;
    else
      location = (location + 1) % MAX_ITEMS;
  } while (location != startLoc && moreToSearch);
  found = (info[location] == item);
  if (found)
    item = info[location];
}
```

We have discussed the insertion and retrieval of elements in a hash table, but we have not yet mentioned how to delete an element from the table. If we did not need to concern ourselves with collisions, the deletion algorithm would be simple:

Delete

Set location to item.Hash()
Set info[location] to emptyItem

Collisions, however, complicate matters. We can find the element using the same search approach as we used for `RetrieveItem`. But when we locate the element in the hash table, we cannot merely replace the item with `emptyItem`. A review of `RetrieveItem` shows the problem. In the loop, the detection of an empty slot ends the search. If `DeleteItem` "empties" the slot occupied by a deleted element, we may terminate a subsequent search prematurely.

Let's look at an example. In Figure 10.22, suppose we delete the element with the key 77003 by setting the array slot [5] to `emptyItem`. A subsequent search for the element with the key 42504 would begin at the hash location [4]. The record in this slot is not the one we are looking for, so we increment the hash location to [5]. This slot, which was formerly occupied by the record that we deleted, is now empty (contains `emptyItem`), so we terminate the search. We haven't really finished searching, however—the record that we want is found in the next slot.

One solution to this problem is to create a third constant value, `deletedItem`, to use in slots that were occupied by deleted records. If a slot contains `deletedItem`, it means that this slot is currently free but was previously occupied.

With this change, we must modify both the insertion and the retrieval operations to process slots correctly. The insertion algorithm treats a slot with `deletedItem` and `emptyItem` in the same way; the search for an available slot for the new element ends. `emptyItem` halts the search in the function `RetrieveItem`, but `deletedItem` does not.

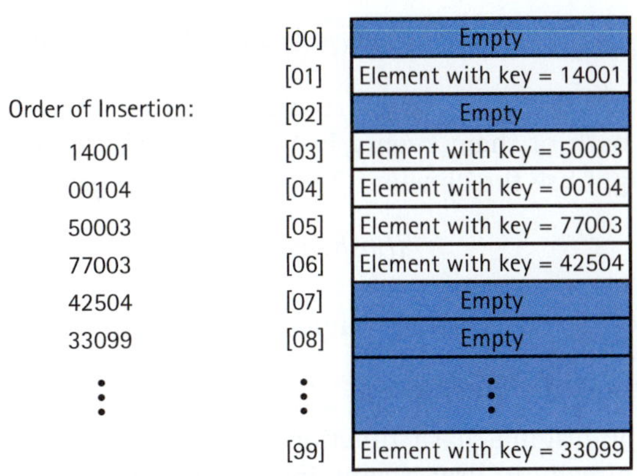

Figure 10.22 *A hash program with linear probing*

This solution corrects the search problem, but produces another dilemma: After many deletions, the search "path" to a record may travel through many array slots with `deletedItem`. This "wandering" may cause the efficiency of retrieving an element to deteriorate. These problems illustrate that a hash table, in the forms that we have studied thus far, is not the most effective data structure for implementing lists whose elements may be deleted.

Clustering One problem with linear probing is that it results in a situation called clustering. A good hash function produces a uniform distribution of indexes throughout the array's index range. Initially, therefore, records are inserted throughout the array, with each slot being equally likely to be filled. Over time, after a number of collisions have been resolved, the distribution of records in the array becomes less and less uniform. The records tend to cluster together, as multiple keys begin to compete for a single hash location.

Clustering The tendency of elements to become unevenly distributed in the hash table, with many elements clustering around a single hash location

Consider the hash table in Figure 10.22. Only a record whose key produces the hash value 8 would be inserted into array slot [8]. However, any records with keys that produce the hash values 3, 4, 5, 6, or 7 would be inserted into array slot [7]. That is, array slot [7] is five times as likely as array slot [8] to be filled. Clustering results in inconsistent efficiency of insertion and retrieval operations.

Rehashing The technique of linear probing discussed here is an example of collision resolution by rehashing. If the hash function produces a collision, the hash value serves as the input to a *rehash function* to compute a new hash value. In the previous section, we added 1 to the hash value to create a new hash value; that is, we used the rehash function:

Rehashing Resolving a collision by computing a new hash location from a hash function that manipulates the original location rather than the element's key

(HashValue + 1) % 100

For rehashing with linear probing, you can use any function

(HashValue + constant) % array-size

as long as *constant* and *array-size* are relatively prime—that is, if the largest number that divides both of them evenly is 1. For instance, given the 100-slot array in Figure 10.21, we might use the constant 3 in the rehash function:

(HashValue + 3) % 100

(Although 100 is not a prime number, 3 and 100 are relatively prime; they have no common factor larger than 1.)

Suppose that we want to add a record with the key 14001 to the hash table in Figure 10.21. The original hash function (`Key % 100`) returns the hash value 1, but this array slot is already in use; it contains the record with the key 44001. To determine the

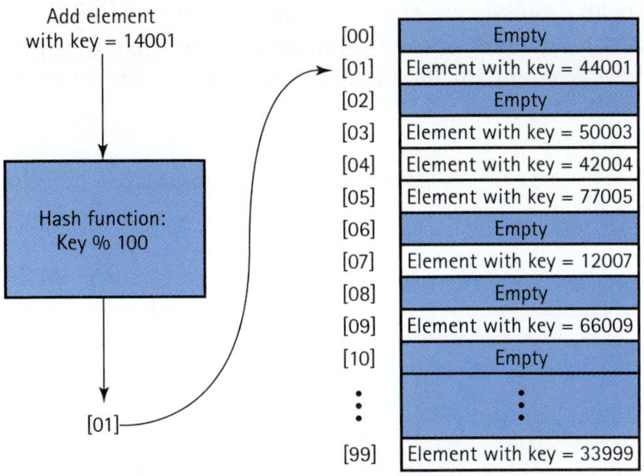

Figure 10.23 *Handling collisions with rehashing*

next array slot to try, we apply the rehash function using the results of the first hash function as input: `(1 + 3) % 100 = 4`. The array slot at index [4] is also in use, so we reapply the rehash function until we find an available slot. Each time, we use the value computed from the previous rehash as input to the rehash function. The second rehash gives us `(4 + 3) % 100 = 7`; this slot is in use, too. The third rehash gives us `(7 + 3) % 100 = 10`; the array slot at index [10] is empty, so the new element is inserted there.

To understand why the constant and the number of array slots must be relatively prime, consider the rehash function

(HashValue + 2) % 100

We want to add the record with the key 14001 to the hash table pictured in Figure 10.23. The original hash function, `Key % 100`, returns the hash value 1. This array slot is already occupied. We resolve the collision by applying the rehash function above, examining successive odd-numbered indexes until a free slot is found. What happens if *all* of the slots with odd-numbered indexes are already in use? The search would fail—even though the hash table includes free slots with even-numbered indexes. This rehash function does not cover the full index range of the array. However, if the constant and the number of array slots are relatively prime (like 3 and 100), the function produces successive rehashes that eventually cover *every* index in the array.

Rehash functions that use linear probing do not eliminate clustering (although the clusters are not always visually apparent in a figure). For example, in Figure 10.23, any record with a key that produces the hash value 1, 4, 7, or 10 would be inserted into the slot at index [10].

In linear probing, we add a constant (usually 1) in each successive application of the rehash function. A second approach, called quadratic probing, makes the result of rehashing dependent on how many times the rehash function has been applied. In the *I*th rehash, the function is

$$(HashValue \pm I^2)\ \%\ array\text{-}size$$

Quadratic probing Resolving a hash collision by using the rehashing formula (`HashValue` ± I^2) % `array-size`, where I is the number of times that the rehash function has been applied

Random probing Resolving a hash collision by generating pseudorandom hash values in successive applications of the rehash function

The first rehash adds 1 to `HashValue`, the second rehash subtracts 1 from `HashValue`, the third rehash adds 4, the fourth subtracts 4, and so on. Quadratic probing reduces clustering, but it does not necessarily examine every slot in the array. For example, if array-size is a power of 2 (512 or 1,024, for example), relatively few array slots are examined. If array-size is a prime number of the form (4 * some-integer + 3), however, quadratic probing does examine every slot in the array.

A third approach uses a pseudorandom number generator to determine the increment to `HashValue` in each application of the rehash function. Random probing is an excellent technique for eliminating clustering, but it tends to be slower than the other techniques we have discussed.

Buckets and Chaining Another alternative for handling collisions is to *allow* multiple element keys to hash to the same location. One solution is to let each computed hash location contain slots for multiple elements, rather than just a single element. Each of these multi-element locations is called a bucket. Figure 10.24 shows a hash table with buckets that can hold three elements each. Using this approach, we can allow collisions to produce duplicate entries at the same hash location, up to a point. When the bucket becomes full, we must again deal with the problem of handling collisions.

Bucket A collection of elements associated with a particular hash location

Chain A linked list of elements that share the same hash location

Another solution, which avoids this problem, is to use the hash value not as the actual location of the element, but rather as the index into an array of pointers. Each pointer accesses a chain of elements that share the same hash location. Figure 10.25 illustrates this solution to the problem of collisions. Rather than rehashing, we simply allow both elements to share hash location [3]. The entry in the array at this location contains a pointer to a linked list that includes both elements.

To search for a given element, you first apply the hash function to the key and then search the chain for the element. Searching is not eliminated, but it is limited to elements that actually share a hash location. In contrast, with linear probing you may have to search through many additional elements if the slots following the hash location are filled with elements from collisions on other hash locations.

Figure 10.26 compares the chaining and hash-and-search schemes. The elements were added in the order shown on the next page.

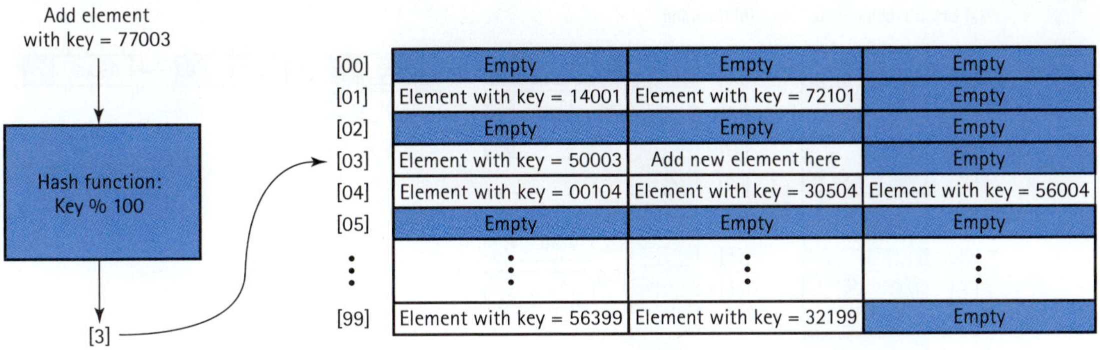

Figure 10.24 *Handling collisions by hashing with buckets*

45300
20006
50002
40000
25001
13000
65905
30001
95000

Figure 10.26a depicts the linear probing approach to collision handling; Figure 10.26b shows the result of chaining the colliding elements. Let's search for the element with the key 30001.

Using linear probing, we apply the hash function to get the index [1]. Because `list.info[1]` does not contain the element with the key 30001, we search sequentially until we find the element in `list.info[7]`.

Using the chaining approach, we apply the hash function to get the index [1]. `list.info[1]` directs us to a chain of elements whose keys hash to 1. We search this linked list until we find the element with the desired key.

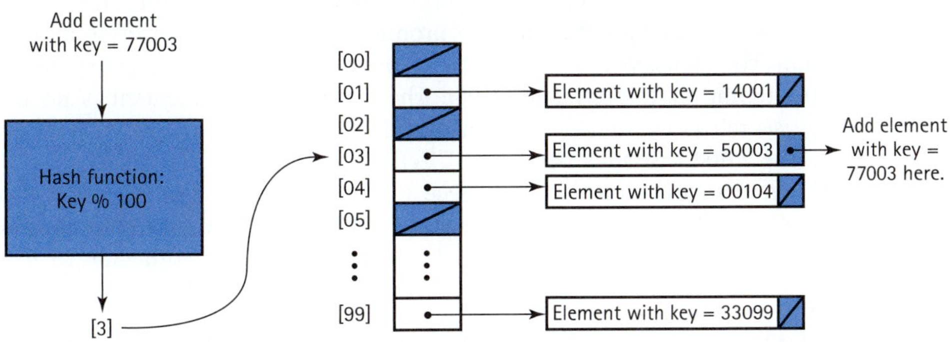

Figure 10.25 *Handling collisions by hashing with chaining*

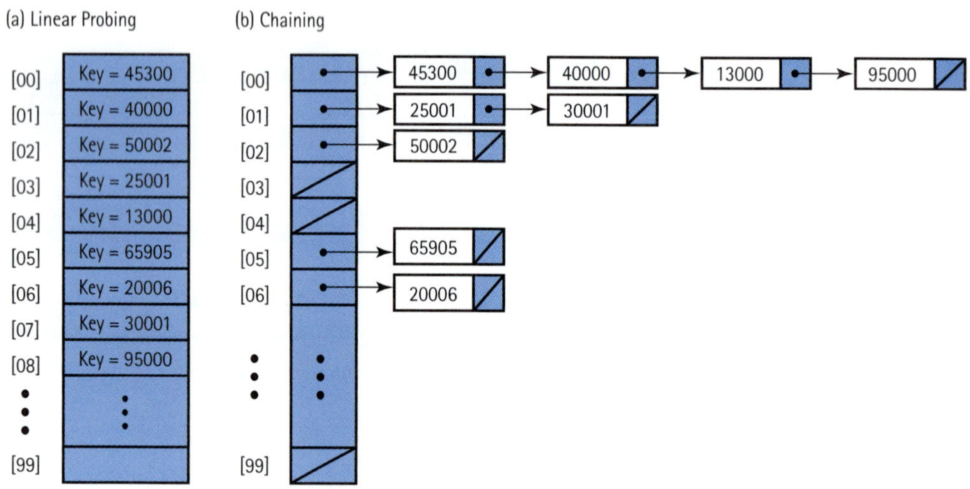

Figure 10.26 *Comparison of linear probing and chaining schemes*

Another advantage of chaining is that it simplifies the deletion of records from the hash table. We apply the hash function to obtain the index of the array slot that contains the pointer to the appropriate chain. The node can then be deleted from this chain using the linked-list algorithm from Chapter 5.

Choosing a Good Hash Function

One way to minimize collisions is to use a data structure that has more space than is actually needed for the number of elements, so as to increase the range of the hash function. In practice it is desirable to have the array size somewhat larger than the number of elements required, thereby reducing the number of collisions.

Selecting the table size involves a space versus time tradeoff. The larger the range of hash locations, the less likely that two keys will hash to the same location. However, allocating an array that contains a large number of empty slots wastes space.

More importantly, you can design your hash function to minimize collisions. The goal is to distribute the elements as uniformly as possible throughout the array. Therefore you want your hash function to produce unique values as often as possible. Once you admit collisions, you must introduce some sort of searching, either through array or chain searching or through rehashing. The access to each element is no longer direct, and the search is no longer O(1). In fact, if the collisions cause very disproportionate chains, the worst case may be almost O(N)![3]

To avoid such a situation, you need to know something about the statistical distribution of keys. Imagine a company whose employee records are sorted based on a six-digit company ID. The company has 500 employees, and we decide to use a chained

---

[3]This is O(N) "exclamation point," not O(N) factorial, as one long-ago student complained when he got the answer wrong on a quiz.

approach to handle collisions. We set up 100 chains (expecting an average of five elements per chain) and use the hash function

idNum % 100

That is, we use the last two digits of the six-digit ID number as our index. The planned hash scheme is shown in Figure 10.27a. Figure 10.27b shows what happened when we implemented the hash scheme. How could the distribution of the elements have

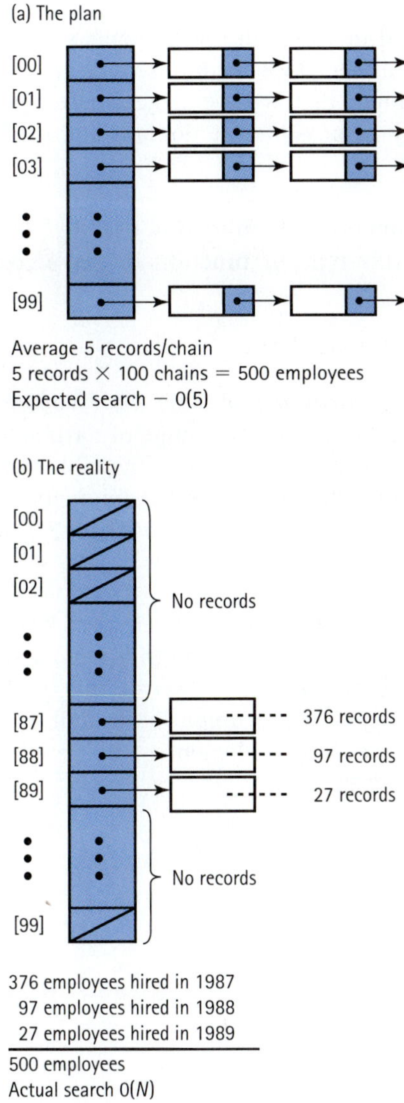

Figure 10.27 *Hash scheme to handle employee records*

come out so skewed? It turns out that the company's ID number is a concatenation of three fields:

XXX	X	XX
3 digits, unique number (000–999)	1 digit, dept. number (0–9)	2 digits, year hired (e.g., 89)

The hash scheme depended solely on the year hired to produce hash values. Because the company was founded in 1987, all the elements were crowded very disproportionately into a small subset of the hash locations. A search for an employee element, in this case, is O(N). Although this is an exaggerated example, it illustrates the need to understand as completely as possible the domain and predicted values of keys in a hash scheme.

Division Method The most common hash functions use the division method (%) to compute hash values. We used this type of function in the preceding examples. The general function is

Key % TableSize

We have already mentioned the idea of making the table somewhat larger than the number of elements required, so as to increase the range of hash values. In addition, better results are produced with the division method when the table size is a prime number.

The advantage of the division hash function is its simplicity. Sometimes, however, it is necessary to use a more complicated (or even exotic) hash function to get a good distribution of hash values.

Other Hash Methods How can we use hashing if the element key is a string instead of an integer? One approach is to use the internal representations of the string's characters to create a number that can serve as an index. (Recall that each ASCII character is represented in memory as an integer in the range 0 through 127.) For instance, the following simple hash function takes a five-element `char` array and produces a hash value in the range 0 through `MAX_ITEMS - 1`:

```
int Hash(char letters[])
Post: Returns an integer between 0 and MAX_ITEMS - 1.
{
  int sum = 0;

  for (int index = 0; index < 5; index++)
    sum = sum + int(letters[index]);
  return sum % MAX_ITEMS;
}
```

A hash method called folding involves breaking the key into several pieces and concatenating or exclusive-OR'ing some of the pieces to form the hash value. Another method is to square the key and then use some of the digits (or bits) of the key as a hash value. A number of other techniques exist, all of which are intended to make the hash location as unique and random (within the allowed range) as possible.

> **Folding** A hash method that breaks the key into several pieces and concatenates or exclusive-ORs some of the pieces to form the hash value

Let's look at an example of folding. Suppose we want to devise a hash function that results in an index between 0 and 255, and the internal representation of the `int` key is a bit string of 32 bits. We know that it takes 8 bits to represent the 256 index values ($2^8 = 256$). A folding algorithm to create a hash function might

1. Break the key into four bit strings of 8 bits each,
2. Exclusive-OR the first and last bit strings,
3. Exclusive-OR the two middle bit strings, and
4. Exclusive-OR the results of Steps 2 and 3 to produce the 8-bit index into the array.

We illustrate this scheme using the key 618403. The binary representation of this key is

```
00000000000010010110111110100011
```

We break this bit string into four 8-bit strings:

```
00000000  (leftmost 8 bits)
00001001  (next 8 bits)
01101111  (next 8 bits)
10100011  (rightmost 8 bits)
```

The next step is to exclusive-OR the first and last bit strings. The exclusive OR of two bits is 0 if the two bits are the same, and 1 if they are different. To exclusive-OR (denoted as XOR) bit strings, we apply this rule to successive pairs of bits.

```
      00000000
(XOR) 10100011
--------------
      10100011
```

Next, we exclusive-OR the middle two bit strings:

```
      00001001
(XOR) 01101111
--------------
      01100110
```

Finally, we exclusive-OR the results of the preceding two steps:

```
       10100011
(XOR)  01100110
---------------
       11000101
```

This binary number is equivalent to the decimal number 197, so the key 618403 hashes into the index 197. We leave the implementation of this hash function as an exercise.

The relationship between the key and the index is not intuitively obvious, but the indexes produced are likely to be uniformly distributed through the range of possible values.

When using an exotic hash function, you should keep two considerations in mind. First, you should consider the efficiency of calculating the function. Even if a hash function always produces unique values, it is not a good hash function if it takes longer to calculate the hash value than to search half the list. Second, you should consider programmer time. An extremely exotic function that somehow produces unique hash values for all of the known key values may fail if the domain of possible key values changes in a later modification. The programmer who has to modify the program may then waste a lot of time trying to find another hash function that is equally clever.

Of course, if you know all of the possible keys ahead of time, it is possible to determine a *perfect* hash function. For example, if you needed a list of elements whose keys were the reserved words in a computer language, you could find a hash function that hashes each word to a unique location. In general, it takes a great deal of work to discover a perfect hash function. And usually, we find that its computational complexity is very high, perhaps comparable to the effort required to execute a binary search.

Complexity

We began the discussion of hashing by trying to find a list implementation where the insertion and deletion had O(1) complexity. If our hash function never produces duplicates or if the array size is very large compared to the expected number of items in the list, then we have reached our goal. In general, this will not be the case. Clearly, as the number of elements approaches the array size, the efficiency of the algorithms deteriorates. A precise analysis of the complexity of hashing is beyond the scope of this book. Informally we can say that the larger the array relative to the expected number of elements, the more efficient the algorithms.

10.4 Radix Sort

We have placed the radix sort in a section by itself after sorting, searching, and hashing for two reasons.

First, the radix sort is not a *comparison* sort; that is, the algorithm does not compare two items in a list. Therefore, we cannot analyze the amount of work done in terms of comparisons. In fact, the only thing that the radix sort has in common with the other sorts is that it takes an unsorted list as input and returns a sorted list as output.

Second, the radix sort is to sorting as hashing is to searching. That is, it makes use of the *values* in the individual keys to order the items just as hashing makes use of the values in the individual keys to determine where to place items. As in the other sorting algorithms, the number of values to be sorted and the array in which they are stored serve as parameters.

Radix The number of possibilities for each position; the digits in a number system

The idea behind the radix sort is to divide the values to be sorted into as many subgroups as there are possible alternatives for each position in the key. For example, if the key is an integer number, each position is a digit and has ten possibilities: 0 . . 9. If the key is a string of letters and case is not important, then each position has 26 possibilities: "a" . . "z". The number of possibilities is called the radix. After subdividing the values into radix subgroups, we combine them again into one array and repeat the process. If we begin with the *least-significant* position in the key, regroup the values in order, and repeat the process as many times as there are positions in the key, moving one position to the left each time, the array will be sorted when we finish.

Let's illustrate this algorithm by sorting three-digit positive integers. Within a three-digit number, let's refer to the ones, tens, and hundreds positions as positions 1, 2, and 3, respectively. We divide the values into ten subgroups based on the digit in the ones position (position 1). Let's create an array of queues, `queues[0]..queues[9]`, to hold the groups. All items with 0 in the ones position are enqueued into `queues[0]`; all items with a 1 in the ones position are enqueued into `queues[1]`; and so on. After the first pass through the array, we collect the subgroups (queues) with the `queues[0]` subgroup on top and the `queues[9]` subgroup on the bottom. We repeat the process using the tens position and the hundreds position. When we collect the queues the last time, the values in the array are in order. This algorithm is illustrated in Figures 10.28 and 10.29.

Original array	*Array after 1st pass*	*Array after 2nd pass*	*Array after 3rd pass*
762	800	800	001
124	100	100	100
432	761	001	124
761	001	402	402
800	762	124	432
402	432	432	761
976	402	761	762
100	124	762	800
001	976	976	976
999	999	999	999

Figure 10.28 *Array after each pass*

[0]	[1]	[2]	[3]	[4]	[5]	[6]	[7]	[8]	[9]
800	761	762		124		976			999
100	001	432							
		402							

(a) Queues after 1st pass

[0]	[1]	[2]	[3]	[4]	[5]	[6]	[7]	[8]	[9]
800		124	432			761	976		999
100						762			
001									
402									

(b) Queues after 2nd pass

[0]	[1]	[2]	[3]	[4]	[5]	[6]	[7]	[8]	[9]
001	100			402			761	800	976
	124			432			762		999

(c) Queues after 3rd pass

Figure 10.29 *Queues after each pass*

Look at the array after each pass; the digits in the position that corresponds to the pass number are sorted (Figure 10.28). Likewise, the digits in the pass-number position are the same as the index of the queue that it is in (Figure 10.29).

Let's first write the algorithm for the radix sort that matches our example and then examine ways to make it more general.

RadixSort(values, numValues)

```
for position going from 1 to 3
    for counter going from 0 to numValues - 1
        Set whichQueue to digit at position "position" of values[counter]
        queues[whichQueue].Enqueue(values[counter])
    Collect queues
```

In this algorithm, each iteration of the outer loop corresponds to one pass in Figures 10.28 and 10.29. In the first pass, we use the ones digit of an integer item to determine the appropriate queue for the item. In the second pass, we use the tens digit. In the third pass, we use the hundreds digit. Next, we need to write the Collect Queues step of the algorithm. Here we collect the items from all of the queues and put them back into the `values` array.

```
Collect Queues
Set index to 0
for counter going from 0 to 9
    while !queues[counter].IsEmpty()
        queues[counter].Dequeue(item)
        Set values[index] to item
        Increment index
```

Now that we understand the algorithm for three-digit integer keys, let's look at how we can make it more general before we code it. When we examined the insertion of an item into a sorted list in Chapter 3, we required the comparison of two items to be a member function of `ItemType`. The corresponding idea here is to make accessing the correct position in the key become a function. For example, with an integer key, we must extract the digits using / and `%`. If the key is a string, then we need access into an array of characters. The point is that *only the user knows*, so the user should provide a member function for `ItemType` to access successive positions in the key. This function (`SubKey`) takes the position number as a parameter.

The radix sort function itself, however, must know the number of positions in the key (`numPositions`) and the number of possible values for each position in the key (`radix`). We make `numPositions` and `radix` be parameters to the function.

```
template<class ItemType>
void RadixSort(ItemType values[], int numValues,
     int numPositions, int radix)
// Post: Elements in values are in order by key.
{
  QueType<ItemType> queues[radix];
  // With default constructor, each queue size is 500.
  int whichQueue;

  for (int position = 1; position <= numPositions; position++)
  {
    for (int counter = 0; counter < length; counter++)
    {
      whichQueue = values[counter].SubKey(position);
```

```
        queues[whichQueue].Enqueue(values[counter]);
      }
      CollectQueues(values, queues, radix);
    }
}

template<class ItemType>
void CollectQueues(ItemType values[], QueType<ItemType> queues[],
     int radix)
// Post: queues are concatenated with queue[0]'s on top and
//       queue[9]'s on the bottom and copied into values.
{
  int index = 0;
  ItemType item;

  for (int counter = 0; counter < radix; counter++)
  {
    while (!queues[counter].IsEmpty())
    {
      queues[counter].Dequeue(item);
      values[index] = item;
      index++;
    }
  }
}
```

If the keys are integer values, then the function `SubKey` must take the position number and extract the digit in that position. Let's calculate a few positions and look for a pattern. Assume `itemKey` is the four-digit integer 8749.

Position is 1: `itemKey % 10` = 9
Position is 2: `(itemKey / 10) % 10` = 4
Position is 3: `(itemKey / 100) % 10` = 7
Position is 4: `(itemKey / 1000) % 10` = 8

Notice that as the position number gets larger, the second operand of the / operation increases. If we rewrite the first calculation as

Position is 1: `(itemKey / 1) % 10`

the pattern becomes even clearer:

$$Result = (itemKey / 10^{position - 1}) \% 10$$

If the key is alphabetic, then `SubKey` must take each character and convert it to a number between 0 and 25 (if case does not count) or between 0 and 51 (if case does matter). The algorithm that you use depends on the character set of the machine you are using.

Analyzing the Radix Sort

The amount of work done by the radix sort is more complicated than any scenario we have examined so far. Each item in the array is processed `numPositions` times, making the Big-O analysis a function of two variables: N (the number of items to be sorted) and P (the number of positions in the key). The processing includes extracting a value from the key, inserting the item into a queue, dequeueing each item, and copying each item back into the array. We know that each operation is O(1). So an approximation is $O(N * P)$. However, when N is large, it dominates P. (N is the elephant and P is the goldfish, to use our familiar analogy.)

In each iteration of the radix sort, the queues are collected, meaning that each item to be sorted is processed twice on each iteration: once to put it into a queue and once when the queues are collected. We could streamline the processing in the radix sort somewhat by using the linked queue implementation and accessing the queues directly to re-create the intermediate list in linked form. However, this approach would require copying the final linked version back into the array-based form.

What about space requirements? Our `RadixSort` function requires space for at least two copies of each element: one place in the array and one place in the queue. If the queues are array-based, the amount of space is prohibitive because each queue must have room for every element. If the queues are linked, additional space for N pointers is required. We can cut the space requirements if we realize that this algorithm works just as well if the values to be sorted are in linked form. Nodes can be removed from the linked structure and moved to the appropriate queue; then the linked structure can be re-created by concatenating the queues. In this way, only one copy of an item (plus a pointer) exists: either in the linked structure or in a subgroup (queue).

Hence, both time and space requirements can be improved in the radix sort, if we use the linked versions of the queue and list.

Summary

We have not attempted in this chapter to describe every known sorting algorithm. Instead, we have presented a few of the most popular sorts, of which many variations exist. It should be clear from this discussion that no single sort works best for all applications. The simpler, generally $O(N^2)$ sorts work as well, and sometimes better, for fairly small values of N. Because they are simple, they require relatively little programmer time to write and maintain. As you add features to improve sorts, you also add to the complexity of the algorithms, increasing both the work required by the routines and the programmer time needed to maintain them.

Another consideration in choosing a sort algorithm is the order of the original data. If the data are already sorted (or almost sorted), `ShortBubble` is $O(N)$, whereas some versions of a `QuickSort` are $O(N^2)$.

As always, the first step in choosing an algorithm is to determine the goals of the particular application. This step usually narrows down the options considerably. After that, knowledge of the strong and weak points of the various algorithms assists you in making a choice.

Table 10.3 compares the sorts discussed in this chapter, in terms of Big-O.

Table 10.3 *Comparison of Sorting Algorithms*

	Order of Magnitude		
Sort	Best Case	Average Case	Worst Case
`SelectionSort`	$O(N^2)$	$O(N^2)$	$O(N^2)$
`BubbleSort`	$O(N^2)$	$O(N^2)$	$O(N^2)$
`ShortBubble`	$O(N)$ (*)	$O(N^2)$	$O(N^2)$
`InsertionSort`	$O(N)$ (*)	$O(N^2)$	$O(N^2)$
`MergeSort`	$O(N\log_2 N)$	$O(N\log_2 N)$	$O(N\log_2 N)$
`QuickSort`	$O(N\log_2 N)$	$O(N\log_2 N)$	$O(N^2)$ (depends on split)
`HeapSort`	$O(N\log_2 N)$	$O(N\log_2 N)$	$O(N\log_2 N)$

*Data almost sorted.

The radix sort is not shown in Table 10.3 because it is not based on key comparisons. This sort algorithm uses the values in different key positions to successively divide the list into sublists, then collects the sublists back together. After this process is repeated as many times as there are positions in the key, the list is sorted.

Searching, like sorting, is a topic that is closely tied to the goal of efficiency. We speak of a sequential search as an $O(N)$ search, because it may require as many as N comparisons to locate an element. (N refers to the number of elements in the list.) Binary searches are considered to be $O(\log_2 N)$ and are appropriate for arrays only if they are sorted. A binary search tree may be used to allow binary searches on a linked structure. The goal of hashing is to produce a search that approaches $O(1)$. Because of collisions involving hash locations, some searching or rehashing is usually necessary. A good hash function minimizes collisions and distributes the elements randomly throughout the table.

To solve a problem, most programmers would rather create a new algorithm than review someone else's solution. Why, then, have we devoted an entire chapter to a discussion of well-known sorting and searching algorithms? First, it is important to be familiar with the basic sorting and searching techniques. You will use these tools over and over again in a programming environment, and you need to know which ones are appropriate solutions to different problems. Second, a review of sorting and searching techniques gives us another opportunity to examine a measuring tool—the Big-O approximation—that helps us determine how much work is required by a particular algorithm. Both building and measuring tools are needed to construct sound program solutions.

Exercises

1. Show the contents of the array

43	7	10	23	18	4	19	5	66	14
[0]	[1]	[2]	[3]	[4]	[5]	[6]	[7]	[8]	[9]

after the fourth iteration of

a. `BubbleSort`

b. `SelectionSort`

c. `InsertionSort`

2. a. Show how the values in the array in Exercise 1 would have to be rearranged to satisfy the heap property.

b. Show how the array would look with four values in the sorted portion after reheaping.

3. a. Show how the values in the array in Exercise 1 would be arranged immediately before the execution of the function `Merge` in the original (nonrecursive) call to `MergeSort`.

b. Show how the values in the array in Exercise 1 would be arranged immediately before the first recursive call to `QuickSort`.

4. Given the array

26	24	3	17	25	24	13	60	47	1
[0]	[1]	[2]	[3]	[4]	[5]	[6]	[7]	[8]	[9]

tell which sorting algorithm would produce the following results after four iterations:

a.

[0]	[1]	[2]	[3]	[4]	[5]	[6]	[7]	[8]	[9]
1	3	13	17	26	24	24	25	47	60

b.

[0]	[1]	[2]	[3]	[4]	[5]	[6]	[7]	[8]	[9]
1	3	13	17	25	24	24	60	47	26

c.

[0]	[1]	[2]	[3]	[4]	[5]	[6]	[7]	[8]	[9]
3	17	24	26	25	24	13	60	47	1

5. How many comparisons would be needed to sort an array containing 100 elements using `ShortBubble`
   a. in the worst case?
   b. in the best case?
6. A sorting function is called to sort a list of 100 integers that have been read from a file. If all 100 values are zero, what would the execution requirements (in terms of Big-O notation) be if the sort used was
   a. `QuickSort`, with the first element used as the split value?
   b. `ShortBubble`?
   c. `SelectionSort`?
   d. `HeapSort`?
   e. `InsertionSort`?
   f. `MergeSort`?
7. How many comparisons would be needed to sort an array containing 100 elements using `SelectionSort` if the original array values were already sorted?
   a. 10,000
   b. 9,900
   c. 4,950
   d. 99
   e. None of the above
8. A merge sort is used to sort an array of 1,000 test scores in descending order. Which of the following statements is true?
   a. The sort is fastest if the original test scores are sorted from smallest to largest.
   b. The sort is fastest if the original test scores are in completely random order.
   c. The sort is fastest if the original test scores are sorted from largest to smallest.
   d. The sort is the same, no matter what the order of the original elements.

9. A list is sorted from smallest to largest when a sort algorithm is called. Which of the following sorts would take the longest time to execute, and which would take the shortest time?
   a. `QuickSort`, with the first element used as the split value
   b. `ShortBubble`
   c. `SelectionSort`
   d. `HeapSort`
   e. `InsertionSort`
   f. `MergeSort`
10. a. In what case(s), if any, is the bubble sort $O(N)$?
    b. In what case(s), if any, is the selection sort $O(\log_2 N)$?
    c. In what case(s), if any, is quick sort $O(N^2)$?
11. A very large array of elements is to be sorted. The program will be run on a personal computer with limited memory. Which sort would be a better choice: a heap sort or a merge sort? Why?
12. Use the Three-Question Method to verify `MergeSort`.
13. True or false? Correct the false statements.
    a. `MergeSort` requires more space to execute than `HeapSort`.
    b. `QuickSort` (using the first element as the split value) is better for nearly sorted data than `HeapSort`.
    c. The efficiency of `HeapSort` is not affected by the order of the elements on entrance to the function.
14. Which of the following is true about `QuickSort`?
    a. A recursive version executes faster than a nonrecursive version.
    b. A recursive version has fewer lines of code than a nonrecursive version.
    c. A nonrecursive version takes more space on the run-time stack than a recursive version.
    d. It can be programmed only as a recursive function.
15. What is meant by the statement that "programmer time is an efficiency consideration"? Give an example of a situation in which programmer time is used to justify the choice of an algorithm, possibly at the expense of other efficiency considerations.
16. Identify one or more correct answers: Reordering an array of pointers to list elements, rather than sorting the elements themselves, is a good idea when
    a. the number of elements is very large.
    b. the individual elements are large in size.
    c. the sort is recursive.
    d. there are multiple keys on which to sort the elements.

17. Go through the sorting algorithms coded in this chapter and determine which ones are stable as coded. If there are unstable algorithms (other than `HeapSort`), make them stable.

18. Give arguments for and against using functions (such as `Swap`) to encapsulate frequently used code in a sorting routine.

19. Write a version of the bubble sort algorithm that sorts a list of integers in descending order.

20. We said that `HeapSort` is inherently unstable. Explain why.

21. Sooey County is about to have its annual Big Pig Contest. Because the sheriff's son, Wilbur, is majoring in computer science, the county hires him to computerize the Big Pig judging. Each pig's name (string) and weight (integer) are to be read in from the keyboard. The county expects 500 entries this year.

    The output needed is a listing of the ten heaviest pigs, sorted from biggest to smallest. Because Wilbur has just learned some sorting methods in school, he feels up to the task of writing this "pork-gram." He writes a program to read in all the entries into an array of records, then uses a selection sort to put the entire array in order based on the `pigWeight` member. He then prints the ten largest values from the array.

    Can you think of a more efficient way to write this program? If so, write the algorithm.

22. State University needs a listing of the overall SAT percentiles of the 14,226 students it has accepted in the past year. The data are in a text file, with one line per student. That line contains the student's ID number, SAT overall percentile, math score, English score, and high school grade point average. (At least one blank separates each two fields.) The output needed is a listing of all the percentile scores, one per line, sorted from highest to lowest. Duplicates should be printed. Outline an $O(N)$ algorithm to produce the listing.

23. Which sorting algorithm would you *not* use under the following conditions?
    a. The sort must be stable.
    b. Data are in descending order by key.
    c. Data are in ascending order by key.
    d. Space is very limited.

24. Determine the Big-O measure for `SelectionSort` based on the number of elements moved rather than the number of comparisons,
    a. for the best case.
    b. for the worst case.

25. Determine the Big-O measure for `BubbleSort` based on the number of elements moved rather than the number of comparisons,
    a. for the best case.
    b. for the worst case.

26. Determine the Big-O measure for `QuickSort` based on the number of elements moved rather than the number of comparisons,
    a. for the best case.
    b. for the worst case.
27. Determine the Big-O measure for `MergeSort` based on the number of elements moved rather than the number of comparisons,
    a. for the best case.
    b. for the worst case.
28. Fill in the following table, showing the number of comparisons needed either to find the value or to determine that the value is not in the array, given the following array of values.

`dataValues`

14	27	95	12	26	5	33	15	9	99
[0]	[1]	[2]	[3]	[4]	[5]	[6]	[7]	[8]	[9]

Values	Search dataValues Sequentially	Search sortedValues Sequentially	Binary Search sortedValues	Search Tree
15				
17				
14				
5				
99				
100				
0				

For Exercises 29–32, use the following values:

66 47 87 90 126 140 145 153 177 285 393 395 467 566 620 735

29. Store the values into a hash table with 20 positions, using the division method of hashing and the linear probing method of resolving collisions.

30. Store the values into a hash table with 20 positions, using rehashing as the method of collision resolution. Use `key % tableSize` as the hash function, and `(key + 3) % tableSize` as the rehash function.

31. Store the values into a hash table with ten buckets, each containing three slots. If a bucket is full, use the next (sequential) bucket that contains a free slot.

32. Store the values into a hash table that uses the hash function `key % 10` to determine into which of ten chains to put the value.

33. Fill in the following table, showing the number of comparisons needed to find each value using the hashing representations given in Exercises 29–32.

Number of Comparisons

Value	Exercise 29	Exercise 30	Exercise 31	Exercise 32
66				
467				
566				
735				
285				
87				

34. If you know the index of an element stored in an array of N unsorted elements, which of the following best describes the order of the algorithm to retrieve the element?

    a. $O(1)$

    b. $O(N)$

    c. $O(\log_2 N)$

    d. $O(N^2)$

    e. $O(0.5N)$

35. The element being searched for is *not* in an array of 100 elements. What is the *average* number of comparisons needed in a sequential search to determine that the element is not present

    a. if the elements are completely unsorted?

    b. if the elements are sorted from smallest to largest?

    c. if the elements are sorted from largest to smallest?

36. The element being searched for is *not* in an array of 100 elements. What is the *maximum* number of comparisons needed in a sequential search to determine that the element is not present

    a. if the elements are completely unsorted?

    b. if the elements are sorted from smallest to largest?

    c. if the elements are sorted from largest to smallest?

37. The element being searched for *is* in an array of 100 elements. What is the *average* number of comparisons needed in a sequential search to determine the position of the element

    a. if the elements are completely unsorted?

    b. if the elements are sorted from smallest to largest?

    c. if the elements are sorted from largest to smallest?

38. Choose the answer that correctly completes the following sentence: The elements in an array may be sorted by highest probability of being requested so as to reduce

    a. the average number of comparisons needed to find an element in the list.

    b. the maximum number of comparisons needed to detect that an element is not in the list.

    c. the average number of comparisons needed to detect that an element is not in the list.

    d. the maximum number of comparisons needed to find an element that is in the list.

39. True or false? Correct any false statements.

    a. A binary search of a sorted set of elements in an array is always faster than a sequential search of the elements.

    b. A binary search is an $O(N\log_2 N)$ algorithm.

    c. A binary search of elements in an array requires that the elements be sorted from smallest to largest.

    d. A high-probability ordering scheme would be a poor choice for arranging an array of elements that are equally likely to be requested.

    e. When a hash function is used to determine the placement of elements in an array, the order in which the elements are added does not affect the resulting array.

    f. When hashing is used, increasing the size of the array always reduces the number of collisions.

    g. If we use buckets in a hashing scheme, we do not have to worry about collision resolution.

    h. If we use chaining in a hashing scheme, we do not have to worry about collision resolution.

i. The functions in this chapter are used only for external searching (i.e., not for disk searching).

j. The goal of a successful hashing scheme is an O(1) search.

40. Choose the answer that correctly completes the following sentence: The number of comparisons required to find an element in a hash table with *N* buckets, of which *M* are full,

a. is always 1.

b. is usually only slightly less than *N*.

c. may be large if *M* is only slightly less than *N*.

d. is approximately $\log_2 M$.

e. is approximately $\log_2 N$.

41. How might you order the elements in a list of C++'s reserved words to use the idea of high-probability ordering?

42. How would you modify the radix sort algorithm to sort the list in descending order?

43. The radix sort algorithm uses an array of queues. Would an array of stacks work just as well?

44. On the Web, the file `Sorts.in` contains a minimal test plan for the sorting algorithms we have studied. Design a more comprehensive test plan and apply it using `SortDr.cpp`.

appendices

Appendix A Reserved Words

The following identifiers are *reserved words*—identifiers with predefined meanings in the C++ language. The programmer cannot declare them for other uses (for example, variable names) in a C++ program.

`and`	`double`	`not`	`this`
`and_eq`	`dynamic_cast`	`not_eq`	`throw`
`asm`	`else`	`operator`	`true`
`auto`	`enum`	`or`	`try`
`bitand`	`explicit`	`or_eq`	`typedef`
`bitor`	`export`	`private`	`typeid`
`bool`	`extern`	`protected`	`typename`
`break`	`false`	`public`	`union`
`case`	`float`	`register`	`unsigned`
`catch`	`for`	`reinterpret_cast`	`using`
`char`	`friend`	`return`	`virtual`
`class`	`goto`	`short`	`void`
`compl`	`if`	`signed`	`volatile`
`const`	`inline`	`sizeof`	`wchar_t`
`const_cast`	`int`	`static`	`while`
`continue`	`long`	`static_cast`	`xor`
`default`	`mutable`	`struct`	`xor_eq`
`delete`	`namespace`	`switch`	
`do`	`new`	`template`	

Appendix B Operator Precedence

The following table summarizes C++ operator precedence. In the table, the operators are grouped by precedence level (highest to lowest), and a horizontal line separates each precedence level from the next-lower level. In general, the binary operators group from left to right; the unary operators, from right to left; and the `?:` operator, from right to left. Exception: The assignment operators group from right to left.

Precedence (highest to lowest)

Operator	*Associativity*	*Remarks*
`::`	Left to right	Scope resolution (binary)
`::`	Right to left	Global access (unary)
`()`	Left to right	Function call and function-style cast
`[] -> .`	Left to right	
`++ --`	Right to left	++ and -- as postfix operators
`typeid dynamic_cast`	Right to left	
`static_cast const_cast`	Right to left	
`reinterpret_cast`	Right to left	
++ -- ! Unary + Unary -	Right to left	++ and -- as prefix operators
~ Unary * Unary &	Right to left	
(cast) `sizeof new delete`	Right to left	
`->* .*`	Left to right	
`* / %`	Left to right	
`+ -`	Left to right	
`<< >>`	Left to right	
`< <= > >=`	Left to right	
`== !=`	Left to right	
`&`	Left to right	
`^`	Left to right	
`|`	Left to right	
`&&`	Left to right	
`||`	Left to right	
`?:`	Right to left	
`= += -= *= /= %=`	Right to left	
`<<= >>= &= |= ^=`	Right to left	
`throw`	Right to left	
`,`	Left to right	The sequencing operator, not the separator

Appendix C A Selection of Standard Library Routines

The C++ standard library provides a wealth of data types, functions, and named constants. This appendix details only some of the more widely used library facilities. It is a good idea to consult the manual for your particular system to see what other types, functions, and constants the standard library provides.

This appendix is organized alphabetically according to the header file your program must `#include` before accessing the listed items. For example, to use a mathematics routine such as `sqrt`, you would `#include` the header file `cmath` as follows:

```
#include <cmath>
using namespace std;
 ⋮
y = sqrt(x);
```

Note that every identifier in the standard library is defined to be in the namespace `std`. Without the `using` directive above, you would write

```
y = std::sqrt(x);
```

C.1 The Header File `cassert`

`assert(booleanExpr)`

Argument: A logical (Boolean) expression

Effect: If the value of `booleanExpr` is `true`, execution of the program simply continues. If the value of `booleanExpr` is `false`, execution terminates immediately with a message stating the Boolean expression, the name of the file containing the source code, and the line number in the source code.

Function return value: None (a void function)

Note: If the preprocessor directive `#define NDEBUG` is placed before the directive `#include <cassert>`, all `assert` statements are ignored.

C.2 The Header File `cctype`

`isalnum(ch)`

Argument: A `char` value `ch`

Function return value: An `int` value that is

- nonzero (`true`), if `ch` is a letter or a digit character ('A'–'Z', 'a'–'z', '0'–'9')
- 0 (`false`), otherwise

`isalpha(ch)`

Argument: A `char` value `ch`

Function return value: An `int` value that is
- nonzero (`true`), if `ch` is a letter ('A'–'Z', 'a'–'z')
- 0 (`false`), otherwise

`iscntrl(ch)`

Argument: A `char` value `ch`

Function return value: An `int` value that is
- nonzero (`true`), if `ch` is a control character (in ASCII, a character with the value 0–31 or 127)
- 0 (`false`), otherwise

`isdigit(ch)`

Argument: A `char` value `ch`

Function return value: An `int` value that is
- nonzero (`true`), if `ch` is a digit character ('0'–'9')
- 0 (`false`), otherwise

`isgraph(ch)`

Argument: A `char` value `ch`

Function return value: An `int` value that is
- nonzero (`true`), if `ch` is a nonblank printable character (in ASCII, '!' through '~')
- 0 (`false`), otherwise

`islower(ch)`

Argument: A `char` value `ch`

Function return value: An `int` value that is
- nonzero (`true`), if `ch` is a lowercase letter ('a'–'z')
- 0 (`false`), otherwise

`isprint(ch)`

Argument: A `char` value `ch`

Function return value: An `int` value that is
- nonzero (`true`), if `ch` is a printable character, including the blank (in ASCII, ' ' through '~')
- 0 (`false`), otherwise

`ispunct(ch)`

Argument: A `char` value `ch`

Function return value: An `int` value that is
- nonzero (`true`), if `ch` is a punctuation character (equivalent to `isgraph(ch) && !isalnum(ch)`)
- 0 (`false`), otherwise

`isspace(ch)`

Argument: A `char` value `ch`

Function return value: An `int` value that is

- nonzero (`true`), if `ch` is a whitespace character (blank, newline, tab, carriage return, form feed)
- 0 (`false`), otherwise

`isupper(ch)`

Argument: A `char` value `ch`

Function return value: An `int` value that is

- nonzero (`true`), if `ch` is an uppercase letter ('A'–'Z')
- 0 (`false`), otherwise

`isxdigit(ch)`

Argument: A `char` value `ch`

Function return value: An `int` value that is

- nonzero (`true`), if `ch` is a hexadecimal digit ('0'–'9', 'A'–'F', 'a'–'f')
- 0 (`false`), otherwise

`tolower(ch)`

Argument: A `char` value `ch`

Function return value: A character that is

- the lowercase equivalent of `ch`, if `ch` is an uppercase letter
- `ch`, otherwise

`toupper(ch)`

Argument: A `char` value `ch`

Function return value: A character that is

- the uppercase equivalent of `ch`, if `ch` is a lowercase letter
- `ch`, otherwise

C.3 The Header File `cfloat`

This header file supplies named constants that define the characteristics of floating-point numbers on your particular machine. Among these constants are the following:

`FLT_DIG`	Approximate number of significant digits in a `float` value on your machine
`FLT_MAX`	Maximum positive `float` value on your machine
`FLT_MIN`	Minimum positive `float` value on your machine
`DBL_DIG`	Approximate number of significant digits in a `double` value on your machine
`DBL_MAX`	Maximum positive `double` value on your machine
`DBL_MIN`	Minimum positive `double` value on your machine
`LDBL_DIG`	Approximate number of significant digits in a `long double` value on your machine
`LDBL_MAX`	Maximum positive `long double` value on your machine
`LDBL_MIN`	Minimum positive `long double` value on your machine

C.4 The Header File `climits`

This header file supplies named constants that define the limits of integer values on your particular machine. Among these constants are the following:

`CHAR_BITS`	Number of bits in a byte on your machine (8, for example)
`CHAR_MAX`	Maximum `char` value on your machine
`CHAR_MIN`	Minimum `char` value on your machine
`SHRT_MAX`	Maximum `short` value on your machine
`SHRT_MIN`	Minimum `short` value on your machine
`INT_MAX`	Maximum `int` value on your machine
`INT_MIN`	Minimum `int` value on your machine
`LONG_MAX`	Maximum `long` value on your machine
`LONG_MIN`	Minimum `long` value on your machine
`UCHAR_MAX`	Maximum `unsigned char` value on your machine
`USHRT_MAX`	Maximum `unsigned short` value on your machine
`UINT_MAX`	Maximum `unsigned int` value on your machine
`ULONG_MAX`	Maximum `unsigned long` value on your machine

C.5 The Header File `cmath`

In the `math` routines listed below, the following notes apply.

1. Error handling for incalculable or out-of-range results is system dependent.
2. All arguments and function return values are technically of type `double` (double-precision floating-point). However, single-precision (`float`) values may be passed to the functions.

`acos(x)`

Argument:	A floating-point expression `x`, where $-1.0 \le x \le 1.0$
Function return value:	Arc cosine of `x`, in the range 0.0 through π

`asin(x)`

Argument:	A floating-point expression `x`, where $-1.0 \le x \le 1.0$
Function return value:	Arc sine of `x`, in the range $-\pi/2$ through $\pi/2$

`atan(x)`

Argument:	A floating-point expression `x`
Function return value:	Arc tangent of `x`, in the range $-\pi/2$ through $\pi/2$

`ceil(x)`

Argument:	A floating-point expression `x`
Function return value:	"Ceiling" of `x` (the smallest whole number $\ge$ x)

`cos(angle)`
Argument: A floating-point expression `angle`, measured in radians
Function return value: Trigonometric cosine of `angle`

`cosh(x)`
Argument: A floating-point expression `x`
Function return value: Hyperbolic cosine of `x`

`exp(x)`
Argument: A floating-point expression `x`
Function return value: The value *e*(2.718...) raised to the power `x`

`fabs(x)`
Argument: A floating-point expression `x`
Function return value: Absolute value of `x`

`floor(x)`
Argument: A floating-point expression `x`
Function return value: "Floor" of `x` (the largest whole number ≤ `x`)

`log(x)`
Argument: A floating-point expression `x`, where `x` > 0.0
Function return value: Natural logarithm (base *e*) of `x`

`log10(x)`
Argument: A floating-point expression `x`, where `x` > 0.0
Function return value: Common logarithm (base 10) of `x`

`pow(x, y)`
Arguments: Floating-point expressions `x` and `y`. If `x` = 0.0, `y` must be positive; if `x` ≤ 0.0, `y` must be a whole number
Function return value: `x` raised to the power `y`

`sin(angle)`
Argument: A floating-point expression `angle`, measured in radians
Function return value: Trigonometric sine of `angle`

`sinh(x)`
Argument: A floating-point expression `x`
Function return value: Hyperbolic sine of `x`

`sqrt(x)`
Argument: A floating-point expression `x`, where `x` ≥ 0.0
Function return value: Square root of `x`

`tan(angle)`

Argument: A floating-point expression `angle`, measured in radians

Function return value: Trigonometric tangent of `angle`

`tanh(x)`

Argument: A floating-point expression `x`

Function return value: Hyperbolic tangent of `x`

C.6 The Header File `cstddef`

This header file defines a few system-dependent constants and data types. From this header file, the only item we use in this book is the following symbolic constant:

`NULL` The null pointer constant `0`

C.7 The Header File `cstdlib`

`abs(i)`

Argument: An `int` expression `i`

Function return value: An `int` value that is the absolute value of `i`

`atof(str)`

Argument: A C string (null-terminated `char` array) `str` representing a floating point number, possibly preceded by whitespace characters and a '+' or '–'

Function return value: A `double` value that is the floating-point equivalent of the characters in `str`

Note: Conversion stops at the first character in `str` that is inappropriate for a floating-point number. If no appropriate characters were found, the return value is system dependent.

`atoi(str)`

Argument: A C string (null-terminated `char` array) `str` representing an integer number, possibly preceded by whitespace characters and a '+' or '–'

Function return value: An `int` value that is the integer equivalent of the characters in `str`

Note: Conversion stops at the first character in `str` that is inappropriate for an integer number. If no appropriate characters were found, the return value is system dependent.

`atol(str)`

Argument: A C string (null-terminated `char` array) `str` representing a long integer, possibly preceded by whitespace characters and a '+' or '–'

Function return value: A `long` value that is the long integer equivalent of the characters in `str`

Note: Conversion stops at the first character in `str` that is inappropriate for a `long` integer number. If no appropriate characters were found, the return value is system dependent.

`exit(exitStatus)`

Argument: An `int` expression `exitStatus`

Effect: Program execution terminates immediately with all files properly closed

Function return value: None (a void function)

Note: By convention, `exitStatus` is 0 to indicate normal program completion and is nonzero to indicate an abnormal termination.

`labs(i)`

Argument: A `long` expression `i`

Function return value: A `long` value that is the absolute value of `i`

`rand()`

Argument: None

Function return value: A random `int` value in the range 0 through `RAND_MAX`, a constant defined in `cstdlib` (`RAND_MAX` is usually the same as `INT_MAX`)

Note: See `srand` below.

`srand(seed)`

Argument: An `int` expression `seed`, where `seed` ≥ 0

Effect: Using `seed`, the random number generator is initialized in preparation for subsequent calls to the `rand` function.

Function return value: None (a void function)

Note: If `srand` is not called before the first call to `rand`, a `seed` value of 1 is assumed.

`system(str)`

Argument: A C string (null-terminated `char` array) `str` representing an operating system command, exactly as it would be typed by a user on the operating system command line

Effect: The operating system command represented by `str` is executed.

Function return value: An `int` value that is system dependent

Note: Programmers often ignore the function return value, using the syntax of a void function call rather than a value-returning function call.

C.8 The Header File `cstring`

The header file `cstring` (not to be confused with the header file named `string`) supports manipulation of C strings (null-terminated `char` arrays).

`strcat(toStr, fromStr)`

Arguments:	C strings (null-terminated `char` arrays) `toStr` and `fromStr`, where `toStr` must be large enough to hold the result
Effect:	`fromStr`, including the null character '\0', is concatenated (joined) to the end of `toStr`.
Function return value:	The base address of `toStr`
Note:	Programmers usually ignore the function return value, using the syntax of a void function call rather than a value-returning function call.

`strcmp(str1, str2)`

Arguments:	C strings (null-terminated `char` arrays) `str1` and `str2`
Function return value:	An `int` value < 0, if `str1` < `str2` lexicographically The `int` value 0, if `str1` = `str2` lexicographically An `int` value > 0, if `str1` > `str2` lexicographically

`strcpy(toStr, fromStr)`

Arguments:	`toStr` is a `char` array and `fromStr` is a C string (null-terminated `char` array), and `toStr` must be large enough to hold the result
Effect:	`fromStr`, including the null character '\0', is copied to `toStr`, overwriting what was there.
Function return value:	The base address of `toStr`
Note:	Programmers usually ignore the function return value, using the syntax of a void function call rather than a value-returning function call.

`strlen(str)`

Argument:	A C string (null-terminated `char` array) `str`
Function return value:	An `int` value ≥ 0 that is the length of `str` (excluding the '\0')

C.9 The Header File `string`

This header file supplies a programmer-defined data type (specifically, a *class*) named `string`. Associated with the `string` type are a data type, `string::size_type`, and a named constant, `string::npos`, defined as follows:

`string::size_type`	An unsigned integer type related to the number of characters in a string
`string::npos`	The maximum value of type `string::size_type`

There are dozens of functions associated with the `string` type. Below are several of the most important ones. In the descriptions, `s` is assumed to be a variable (an *object*) of type `string`.

`s.c_str()`

Arguments:	None
Function return value:	The base address of a C string (null-terminated `char` array) corresponding to the characters stored in `s`

`s.find(arg)`

Argument:	An expression of type `string` or `char`, or a C string (such as a literal string)
Function return value:	A value of type `string::size_type` that gives the starting position in `s` where `arg` was found. If `arg` was not found, the return value is `string::npos`.
Note:	Positions of characters within a string are numbered starting at 0.

`getline(inStream, s)`

Arguments:	An input stream `inStream` (of type `istream` or `ifstream`) and a `string` object `s`
Effect:	Characters are input from `inStream` and stored into `s` until the newline character is encountered. (The newline character is consumed but not stored into `s`.)
Function return value:	Although the function technically returns a value (which we do not discuss here), programmers usually invoke the function as though it were a void function.

`s.length()`

Arguments:	None
Function return value:	A value of type `string::size_type` that gives the number of characters in the string

`s.size()`

Arguments:	None
Function return value:	The same as `s.length()`

`s.substr(pos, len)`

Arguments:	Two unsigned integers, `pos` and `len`, representing a position and a length. The value of `pos` must be less than `s.length()`.
Function return value:	A temporary `string` object that holds a substring of at most `len` characters, starting at position `pos` of `s`. If `len` is too large, it means "to the end" of the string in `s`.
Note:	Positions of characters within a string are numbered starting at 0.

Appendix D Character Sets

The following charts show the ordering of characters in two widely used character sets: ASCII (American Standard Code for Information Interchange) and EBCDIC (Extended Binary Coded Decimal Interchange Code). The internal representation for each character is shown in decimal. For example, the letter *A* is represented internally as the integer 65 in ASCII and as 193 in EBCDIC. The space (blank) character is denoted by a "□".

Left Digit(s) / *Right Digit*	*ASCII*									
	0	*1*	*2*	*3*	*4*	*5*	*6*	*7*	*8*	*9*
0	NUL	SOH	STX	ETX	EOT	ENQ	ACK	BEL	BS	HT
1	LF	VT	FF	CR	SO	SI	DLE	DC1	DC2	DC3
2	DC4	NAK	SYN	ETB	CAN	EM	SUB	ESC	FS	GS
3	RS	US	□	!	"	#	$	%	&	'
4	(	)	*	+	,	−	.	/	0	1
5	2	3	4	5	6	7	8	9	:	;
6	<	=	>	?	@	A	B	C	D	E
7	F	G	H	I	J	K	L	M	N	O
8	P	Q	R	S	T	U	V	W	X	Y
9	Z	[	\	]	^	_	`	a	b	c
10	d	e	f	g	h	i	j	k	l	m
11	n	o	p	q	r	s	t	u	v	w
12	x	y	z	{	|	}	~	DEL		

Codes 00–31 and 127 are the following nonprintable control characters:

NUL	Null character	VT	Vertical tab	SYN	Synchronous idle
SOH	Start of header	FF	Form feed	ETB	End of transmitted block
STX	Start of text	CR	Carriage return	CAN	Cancel
ETX	End of text	SO	Shift out	EM	End of medium
EOT	End of transmission	SI	Shift in	SUB	Substitute
ENQ	Enquiry	DLE	Data link escape	ESC	Escape
ACK	Acknowledge	DC1	Device control one	FS	File separator
BEL	Bell character (beep)	DC2	Device control two	GS	Group separator
BS	Back space	DC3	Device control three	RS	Record separator
HT	Horizontal tab	DC4	Device control four	US	Unit separator
LF	Line feed	NAK	Negative acknowledge	DEL	Delete

Left Digit(s) \ *Right Digit*	*EBCDIC* 0	1	2	3	4	5	6	7	8	9
6					□					
7					¢	.	<	(	+	|
8	&									
9	!	$	*	)	;	¬	–	/		
10							^	,	%	_
11	>	?								
12		`	:	#	@	'	=	"		a
13	b	c	d	e	f	g	h	i		
14						j	k	l	m	n
15	o	p	q	r						
16		~	s	t	u	v	w	x	y	z
17								\	{	}
18	[	]								
19				A	B	C	D	E	F	G
20	H	I								J
21	K	L	M	N	O	P	Q	R		
22							S	T	U	V
23	W	X	Y	Z						
24	0	1	2	3	4	5	6	7	8	9

In the EBCDIC table, nonprintable control characters—codes 00–63, 250–255, and those for which empty spaces appear in the chart—are not shown.

Appendix E The Standard Template Library

Overview

The Standard Template Library (STL) is a subset of the ISO/ANSI C++ standard library. The STL provides three kinds of facilities for C++ programmers to use: *containers*, *iterators*, and *generic algorithms*.

An **STL container** holds other objects, much like the containers you have studied in this text: lists, stacks, queues, and so on. Specifically, the STL supplies many useful container classes, some of which are the following:

`list`	A sequential-access list that can be traversed both forward and backward.
`vector`	An abstraction of a one-dimensional array providing, as expected, random access to the array elements.
`stack`	A stack, with the usual LIFO access.
`queue`	A queue, with the usual FIFO access.
`deque`	A double-ended queue (insertions and deletions can occur at both ends) with the uncommon additional property of random access.
`set`	An abstraction of a mathematical set.

The container classes are template classes so that, for example, we declare objects of type `list<int>`, `stack<float>`, and so forth.

To introduce the concepts of *STL iterator* and *STL algorithm*, we begin with the following code segment, which inputs several integer values and outputs them in reverse order. The lines of code are numbered so that we can refer to them in the discussion that follows the code segment.

```
1  #include <iostream>
2  #include <list>          // For list<T> class
3  #include <algorithm>     // For reverse() function
     ⋮
4  using namespace std;

5  list<int> nums;
6  list<int>::iterator iter;
7  int number;

8  cin >> number;
9  while (number != -9999)
10 {
11   nums.push_back(number);
12   cin >> number;
13 }
14 for (iter = nums.begin(); iter != nums.end(); iter++)
15   cout << *iter << endl;
```

```
16 reverse(nums.begin(), nums.end());

17 for (iter = nums.begin(); iter != nums.end(); iter++)
18   cout << *iter << endl;
```

In this code, lines 2 and 3 cause insertion of the header files `list` and `algorithm`, allowing us to use the template class `list` and the function named `reverse`. Line 5 creates a list named `nums` whose components are of type `int`. The list is initially empty. Line 6 declares `iter` to be of type `list<int>::iterator`, a data type defined inside the `list<int>` class. We discuss its usage in a moment.

Lines 8 through 13 read integer values from the standard input device and insert them into the list. The `push_back` function, a member of the `list` class, takes the value in its argument list and appends it to the back (rear) of the list. (Note that the verb *push*, traditionally used only for insertion into a stack, is used throughout the STL container classes to mean *insert*.) The loop continues until the sentinel (trailer) value –9999 is read, after which the `nums` list contains the input values in the order in which they were read.

Next, the loop in lines 14 and 15 traverses the `nums` list from front to back, printing each list item in turn. The variable `iter`, which was declared in line 6, is an **STL iterator.** In one sense, an STL iterator is similar to the iterator concept you have studied in this text (a class member function named something like `GetNext`). Both STL iterators and `GetNext` operations enable cycling through a container, one item at a time. On the other hand, an STL iterator is a lower-level concept than a `GetNext` operation: It simply represents the *location* of an item within a container. Thus, an STL iterator is a generalization of the notion of a pointer. Iterators allow C++ programs to access a container's stored items without having to know the internal structure of the container. The syntax for manipulating an iterator is very nearly the same as for a pointer. To access an item referred to by an iterator `iter`, one writes `*iter`. To step the iterator forward to refer to the next item in the container, one writes `iter++`. The inner workings of the iterator, such as the detail of advancing the position in the container, are hidden from the user and are specific to the container being used. Each STL container class defines one or more iterator types, such as `list<int>::iterator`. An iterator may be implemented as an ordinary pointer or a class object, depending on the particular container.

Now, back to lines 14 and 15. In line 14, the variable `iter` is initialized to the value returned by the function call `nums.begin()`. The function named `begin`, a member of the `list` class, returns the location of the first item in the list. (In the C++ literature—and even in places within this appendix—the phrase "returns an iterator to the first item" is used. What is really meant is "returns the location of." You can even say "returns a pointer to" or "returns the address of," although there is no guarantee that a particular iterator is implemented as a C++ pointer variable.) In the heading of the `for` statement of line 14, the loop condition is `iter != nums.end()`. The function named `end`, a member of the `list` class, returns the location of an imaginary list item that is just beyond the last actual list item. (This position is often called the *past-the-end* position.) The third piece of the `for` statement heading, which is `iter++`, says to advance the iterator to point to the next list item. Therefore, each time through the loop, we obtain the location of the next list item, and we keep looping until we've gone past the end of the list. In each loop iteration, we perform the loop body seen in line 15: We output the value referred to (or "pointed to") by the iterator `iter`. Note that the output statement uses the expression `*iter`, not `iter`. That is, we want to print the list item, not its location.

Next, look at line 16 of the program. The `reverse` function, available through the header file `algorithm`, takes as arguments two iterators—a beginning and an ending position in a container—and puts into reverse order all the items from the beginning position up to, but not including, the ending position. So in line 16, *all* of the items in the `nums` list are processed because the second argument, `nums.end()`, specifies the past-the-end position. Finally, lines 17 and 18 traverse the `nums` list, printing out the new contents of the list.

The `reverse` function is an example of an **STL algorithm**. In computer science terminology, an algorithm is an abstract procedural concept, a recipe for solving a problem. An algorithm implemented in a programming language is a program. Every program implements one or more algorithms. In contrast, the STL defines the term *algorithm* in a much narrower sense. An STL algorithm (or simply an *algorithm*) is a template function that has iterators for its parameter types. The description of each algorithm specifies the kinds of iterators it requires as its parameters. Later in the appendix, we describe a variety of algorithms supplied by the STL.

Let's look at another example of an STL container class: `vector`. A `vector` object is an abstraction of a one-dimensional array and can be used in the same manner as a built-in array:

```
#include <vector>            // For vector<T> class
  :
vector<float> arr(100);      // A 100-element array
  :
arr[24] = 9.86;              // Random access is allowed through
arr[i+j] = arr[k];           // a subscript (index) expression
```

However, the `vector` class is far more versatile than a built-in array. A major limitation of built-in arrays is that the array size is fixed at compile time and cannot grow or shrink while the program is running. In contrast, the size of a vector can vary at run time. Suppose we want to input an unknown number of integer values at run time and store them into an array. With a built-in array, we have to estimate its size in advance, and our estimate may be too large (a waste of memory) or too small (our program is in trouble). With a vector, we don't need to specify its size and can let it grow as needed:

```
vector<int> vec;                          // Initial size is 0
int inputVal;

cin >> inputVal;
while (cin)                               // Assume 50 numbers are
{                                         // input before EOF occurs
  vec.push_back(inputVal);
  cin >> inputVal;
}
cout << vec.size() << endl;               // Outputs 50

for (int i = 0; i < vec.size(); i++)  // We can still use
  cout << vec[i] << endl;                 // indexing
```

In the preceding code, the size of the vec object keeps increasing as needed, with memory implicitly being allocated dynamically. Notice also in the code that push_back is a member of the vector<int> class as well as the list<int> class. In fact, many of the STL container classes have member functions with the same name (for example, push_back) and the same semantics. Because of this uniformity, it is incredibly easy to reuse code from one context in another context. For example, how might we input several integer values into a vector and then output them in reverse order? The answer: Go back to our first code example with lines numbered 1 through 18 and change only lines 2, 5, and 6:

```
2  #include <vector>          // For vector<T> class
5  vector<int> nums;
6  vector<int>::iterator iter;
```

All of the other lines in the program remain absolutely identical because

- both list and vector have member functions push_back, begin, and end with identical semantics.
- the reverse algorithm doesn't care what kind of container it's processing, as long as it receives a beginning position in the container and a past-the-end position.

The first time you study the STL in depth, it will likely be hard to know where to start. In the STL, containers form the heart of the library, but it is difficult to understand containers without some knowledge of the STL algorithms and the iterator requirements, and vice versa. In the STL, algorithms extend the functionality of the containers, and the iterators enable containers and algorithms to work together. In fact, if the user wishes to build his or her own container with iterators or create algorithms that meet the STL requirements, these structures will interact correctly with the STL components.

A problem some have when first learning the STL is that some of the terminology used there (such as *iterator* and *algorithm*) is different from common usage in computer science. As in every new subject in computer science, the new vocabulary must be learned. The STL is well worth learning, for it is a fast, flexible, and useful library.

The ISO/ANSI C++ Standard requires that the full Standard Template Library be provided by every compliant compiler. The STL components are nicely designed to work together well. They are as fast as anything a journeyman programmer can create in the time it takes to learn to use the library.

We should point out that in the design of the STL, the Standards committee made a deliberate decision to provide speed rather than safety, so most STL components do not throw exceptions. Most STL member functions either succeed or do nothing. We do not provide further discussion of exceptions in the STL containers and algorithms except for the at() member function supported by the random access containers. We refer you to the 1998 ISO/ANSI C++ Standard 14882 and to Josuttis's *The C++ Standard Library* for further discussion of this topic. (See the references at the end of this appendix.)

We now examine in more detail the STL components in the following order: iterators, containers, and algorithms.

Iterators

In many data structures and containers, we need some idea of the position or location of an item in the structure. In C, and in C++ before the STL, the pointer met this need. Pointers have the advantage of speed but require great care to avoid pitfalls. The STL provides the iterator as a replacement for pointers that is as efficient as pointers but is much safer. Each STL container provides one or more iterator types appropriate to the internal structure of the container.

We have seen that iterators are objects that specify position in STL containers and allow STL algorithms to cycle through the items in a container. This is done through a common interface through which an iterator is manipulated. Specifically, every iterator type must support at least the following operations:

Prefix *	Dereference (access the item currently pointed to)
++	Increment (point to the next item)

Additional operations are required for different categories of iterators.

An essential point is that behavior defines iterators. Anything that *acts* like an iterator *is* an iterator. It turns out that a variable of type int* (pointer to int) can serve as an iterator for a built-in int array. This fact enables many of the generic STL algorithms to be used directly with built-in arrays. In contrast, a pointer cannot serve as an iterator into a list container. If the list object happens to be implemented with a linked list of dynamically allocated nodes, the pointer operation p++ almost certainly doesn't point to the next node in the linked list (because list nodes are not likely to reside in consecutive memory locations). Therefore, a class like list<int> supplies a data type list<int>::iterator, which overloads the ++ operator in its own way to advance the iterator to the next item in the list.

In summary, an iterator can be either an ordinary pointer (if the container is a built-in array) or an object of a class that defines pointer-like operations that meet the STL requirements.

Iterator Categories

Different STL containers have different properties, so iterators for the various containers also have different properties. Similarly, different STL algorithms require different properties of the iterators they use. For example, sorting a container requires random access; otherwise, performance suffers. Consequently, iterators are classified in increasing "strength" of properties into *input iterators, output iterators, forward iterators, bidirectional iterators*, and *random access iterators*. Figure A.1 displays the relationships among the iterator categories. As we'll see later, if an

Below, the arrow means "is stronger than"

Random access → Bidirectional → Forward → Input
Output

Figure A.1 *Relationships among iterator categories*

STL algorithm requires an iterator of a particular category, then the programmer can use an iterator of that category or of any stronger category, but not of a weaker category.

Some additional types of iterators are *reverse iterators*, *stream iterators*, *insertion iterators*, and *raw storage iterators*. Reverse iterators allow iteration through containers from the back to the front. Stream iterators allow you to read and write files from STL algorithms. Insertion iterators allow adding new items to the container rather than overwriting the position referred to by the iterator. We are able to discuss only the first of these in the space of this appendix. However, the references at the end of the appendix allow you to explore the others and more.

Input Iterators

Input iterators can only be stepped forward by one item per step. Furthermore, they may be dereferenced only to fetch (but not store into) an item from a collection. Table A.1 displays the allowable operations on an input iterator.

An example of an input iterator is a stream iterator that treats the keyboard input stream as a "container" and iterates through the stream, fetching one input character after the next. (The `iostream` header file provides such iterators.) We do not explore input stream iterators in this appendix.

Output Iterators

As with input iterators, output iterators can only be stepped forward by one item per step. However, output iterators may be dereferenced only to store a value at (but not fetch a value from) the specified location. Table A.2 shows the allowable operations on an output iterator.

At first, it might seem strange that we can modify something but not fetch it, but it begins to make more sense if you consider that output iterators are often used for sending data to an output stream such as `cout`. (The `iostream` header file provides output stream iterators.) The idea is to treat an output stream as a "container" of characters and, using an output iterator, write each new character to the stream, one by one. We do not discuss stream iterators further in this appendix.

Table A.1 *Operations on Input Iterators*

Below, `r` and `r2` are input iterators.	
`*r`	Provides read access to the item at the position denoted by `r`
`r++`	Steps `r` forward one position in the container; returns the old position
`++r`	Steps `r` forward one position in the container; returns the new position
`r == r2`	Returns `true` if `r` and `r2` denote the same position, else returns `false`
`r != r2`	Returns `true` if `r` and `r2` denote different positions, else returns `false`

Table A.2 *Operations on Output Iterators*

Below, r is an output iterator.

`*r = value`	Stores `value` at the position denoted by `r`
`r++`	Steps `r` forward one position in the container; returns the old position
`++r`	Steps `r` forward one position in the container; returns the new position

Forward Iterators

We have looked at two categories of iterators that step forward through a container, one permitting only fetching, the other permitting only storing. Often we would like to both fetch and store a value at a particular position as we step through a container. Forward iterators allow us to do so. Specifically, the valid operations on a forward iterator are the same as those of an input iterator plus the ability to store into the referenced item (see Table A.3).

The following is a generic algorithm that illustrates the use of forward iterators.

```
// In any container that supports forward iterators,
// replace every occurrence of an x value by a y value.

template <class ForwardIterator, class T>
void replace( ForwardIterator first, ForwardIterator pastLast,
              const T& x, const T& y)
{
  while (first != pastLast)
  {
    if (*first == x)
      *first = y;
    ++first;
  }
}
```

Table A.3 *Operations on Forward Iterators*

Below, r and r2 are forward iterators.

`*r`	Provides read access to the item at the position denoted by `r`
`*r = value`	Stores `value` at the position denoted by `r`
`r++`	Steps `r` forward one position in the container; returns the old position
`++r`	Steps `r` forward one position in the container; returns the new position
`r == r2`	Returns `true` if `r` and `r2` denote the same position, else returns `false`
`r != r2`	Returns `true` if `r` and `r2` denote different positions, else returns `false`

Notice that the second parameter, `pastLast`, must denote a position that is one past that of the last item to be considered. In other words, the `replace` function replaces items in the container beginning at the position denoted by `first` and continuing up to *but not including* the position denoted by `pastLast`. Alternatively, we can say it this way: The algorithm processes items in the range [`first`, `pastLast`), a mathematical notation meaning an interval that is closed on the left (it includes the left endpoint) but open on the right (it does not include the right endpoint).

A call to the `replace` function might look like this:

```
list<int> lst;
  ⋮
replace(lst.begin(), lst.end(), 25, 125);
```

Recall from earlier in this appendix that `lst.begin()` returns the location of the first list item and `lst.end()` returns the past-the-end location.

The STL implements algorithms such as `replace` with the weakest iterator that is capable of carrying out the task at hand. In `replace`, the forward iterator is sufficient. Any stronger iterator may be used where a forward iterator is specified.

Bidirectional Iterators

Bidirectional iterators have all the properties of forward iterators but allow backward as well as forward movement through a container (see Table A.4).

Adding the decrement operator makes some algorithms easier to implement. We will see that all the STL containers support either bidirectional iterators or random access iterators. The `list` container provides bidirectional iterators. (Hence, some people like to think of `list` as an abstraction of a doubly-linked list because it allows efficient traversal in either direction.)

Random Access Iterators

Random access iterators have all the properties of bidirectional iterators but support additional operations to allow random (direct) access to any item in a container (see Table A.5).

The `vector` container provides random access iterators, which makes sense because `vector` is an abstraction of a one-dimensional array.

Table A.4 *Operations on Bidirectional Iterators*

To the operations on forward iterators, add the following operations.	
`r--`	Steps `r` backward one position in the container; returns the old position
`--r`	Steps `r` backward one position in the container; returns the new position

Table A.5 *Operations on Random Access Iterators*

To the operations on bidirectional iterators, add the following operations.	
`r[i]`	Provides indexed read or store access to the item at the position denoted by `r`
`r += i`	Steps `r` forward by `i` positions in the container
`r -= i`	Steps `r` backward by `i` positions in the container
`r + i`	Returns an iterator value that is `i` positions beyond `r` in the container
`r - i`	Returns an iterator value that is `i` positions prior to `r` in the container
`r - r2`	Returns the number of items that exist between the positions denoted by `r` and `r2`
`r < r2`	Returns `true` if and only if the position denoted by `r` is before the position denoted by `r2`
`r > r2`	Returns `true` if and only if the position denoted by `r` is after the position denoted by `r2`
`r <= r2`	Returns `true` if and only if the position denoted by `r` is not after the position denoted by `r2`
`r >= r2`	Returns `true` if and only if the position denoted by `r` is not before the position denoted by `r2`

We have not yet mentioned reverse iterators, which are of considerable importance. We delay introducing these iterators until we discuss `vector` containers, because `vector` supports reverse iterators as well as random access iterators.

Containers

The STL provides three kinds of containers: *sequence containers*, *container adapters*, and *associative containers.*

In a sequence container, every item in the container has a position, which depends on the time and place of insertion but *not on the item's value*. The sequence containers are `vector`, `list`, and `deque`. These containers are sometimes referred to as "first class containers." Each STL container provides a different set of operations that have different tradeoffs in terms of time and space complexity. Selection of a container should be made accordingly. The `vector` provides random access to its elements, and insertions and deletions at the back (but not in the middle) are very efficient. The C++ Standard suggests that `vector` is the sequence type that should be used by default. If your program requires frequent insertions and deletions in the middle of a sequence, the `list` should be used. The `deque` should be used if frequent insertions and deletions are needed at the beginning and the end of the sequence.

The associative containers are `map`, `multimap`, `set`, and `multiset`. These containers are based on the concept of an *associative array*, a data structure that holds pairs of values: a key and a value associated with that key. We discuss associative containers later but do not explore them in detail in this appendix.

The container adapters are `queue`, `stack`, and `priority_queue`. These are called adapters because they use one of the three sequence containers (`vector`, `list`, or `deque`) to actually hold the items and simply present a different interface (stack, queue, or priority queue) to the programmer.

We begin by looking at the sequence containers `vector`, `list`, and `deque`, along with another class provided by the standard library: `string`.

The `vector<T>` Class

The `vector` container provides fast random access into sequences of varying length, as well as fast insertion and deletion at the end of the vector. `vector<T>` is a template class implemented with a dynamically allocated array that may be used with any type `T` that is assignable and copyable. This means that if `T` is a class or struct type, both `operator=` and a copy constructor must be defined for `T`.

A `vector`'s behavior is similar to the C++ array, the main difference being that a built-in array is of fixed size that must be known at compile time, whereas the `vector` automatically expands to accommodate new entries. As with the List ADT from Chapter 3, a `vector` divides its storage into an initial segment that contains the inserted items and a final segment of unused items called the *reserve*. Unlike the List ADT, when the reserve is exhausted, the `vector` allocates new memory space twice of that currently allocated, copies the data to the new memory, then deallocates the old memory space. This operation is called a **resize.** There is a member function that is available to carry out this operation, but most often it occurs implicitly. This process of allocating more memory is sometimes referred to as **reallocation**, especially when done implicitly.

We speak of the first position in the `vector` as the **front** and the last used position as the **back**. The `vector` container supports insertion and deletion at the back of the container in amortized time of O(1). The term **amortized time** to do a task is a weighted average of two things: the time to do just the primary task (which usually takes a short time and occurs frequently) and the additional time to carry out another associated task (which usually takes considerably longer but occurs infrequently). For the `vector`, the insertion operation takes a very short time but has high probability. The additional task is to reallocate memory and copy data *when the reserve is exhausted*, which takes a fairly long time but has a very low probability.

The following are some properties of `vector` containers:

- `vectors` provide random access, either through an unchecked index (`[]`) or through a range-checked `at()` member function.
- `vector` iterators are random access iterators. Therefore, the behavior is essentially that of C++ pointers. The iterators may be indexed, and pointer arithmetic may be applied. An iterator is of a type defined within class `vector<T>` and may be declared by writing

```
vector<T>::iterator vIter;
```

- Insertion and deletion can be done in O(1) time at the back of a `vector` and O(N) time elsewhere.
- Insertion and deletion invalidate any iterators referring to items beyond the deletion position.

There are two sizes associated with a `vector v`. One, the value returned by `v.size()`, is the number of items that have been inserted into the `vector`. The other, the value returned from `v.capacity()`, is the number of items inserted plus the number of places in the reserve. In Figure A.2, the capacity is 9, and the size is 4.

	Inserted items				Reserve				
Iterator position	`begin()`				`end()`				
Conceptual position	Front			Back					
Index	0	1	2	3	4	5	6	7	8
Value	8	2	34	2					

Figure A.2 `vector` *memory allocation*

The function call `v.front()` returns the first item in the `vector`, and `v.back()` returns the last item. The values stored in the reserve section are inaccessible. The position referred to by `v.begin()` is the position of index 0, which is also from where the `v.front()` function fetches. The position referred to by `v.end()` is the one-past-the-end position. It is one beyond the position from where the `v.back()` function fetches.

To describe the member functions of the `vector<T>` class, we now present a series of tables along with examples. Please note that we include only a representative sample of the available

Table A.6 `vector` *Constructors and Destructor*

`vector<T> v;`	Default constructor. Creates an empty `vector` object, `v`
`vector<T> vNew(vOld);`	Copy constructor. Creates a vector, `vNew`, as a copy of another vector, `vOld`, of the same type. All members are copied
`vector<T> v(n);`	Creates a vector of size `n`, with each element constructed by the default constructor for type `T`
`vector<T> v(n, value);`	Creates a vector of size `n`, with each element initialized to `value`, which is of type `T`
`vector<T> v(first, pastLast);`	Creates a vector whose elements are copies of a subrange of another container of any type having the same base type `T`. The subrange is [`first`, `pastLast`)—that is, from the position denoted by the iterator `first` up to *but not including* the position denoted by the iterator `pastLast`
`v.~vector<T>()`	Destructor. Deallocates storage for `v` and invokes destructors (if any) for its elements of type `T`. Not usually called explicitly; the destructor is called automatically when `v` goes out of scope

member functions. For a comprehensive list, you should consult one of the references at the end of the appendix.

Here is a short program illustrating the uses of several of the constructors.

```
// Code to illustrate vector constructors using primitive types and a
// user-defined type as base types.

#include <vector>     // For vector<T> class
#include <cassert>    // For assert() function

struct node
{
  node()
  {
    iValue = 0;
    dValue = 0.0;
  }

  int iValue;
  double dValue;
};

int main()
{
  using namespace std;

  vector<double> doubleVec;       // Empty vector of doubles
  vector<int> intVec(5, 999);     // Vector of 5 int values, each
                                  // initialized to 999
  vector<node> nodeVec(100);      // Vector of 100 nodes, each
                                  // initialized with default
                                  // constructor node()
  assert(doubleVec.size() == 0);
  assert(intVec.size() == 5);
  assert(intVec[0] == 999);
  assert(nodeVec.size() == 100);
  assert(nodeVec[9].iValue == 0);
  assert(nodeVec[9].dValue == 0.0);
    ⋮
}
```

Table A.7 *`vector` Element Access*

`v[index]`	Indexed access with no range checking. Index range is 0 through `v.size()` – 1. The expression `v[index]` may return a value or have a value assigned to it
`v.at(index)`	Indexed access with range checking. Index range is 0 through `v.size()` – 1. Throws an `out_of_range` exception if `index` ≥ `v.size()`. The expression `v.at(index)` may return a value or have a value assigned to it
`v.front()`	Returns the first item in the vector. Same as `v[0]` or `v.at(0)`
`v.back()`	Returns the last item in the vector. Same as `v[v.size() - 1]`

```
// Illustrates use of vector element access

#include <vector>      // For vector<T> class
#include <iostream>

int main ()
{
  using namespace std;

  const int SIZE = 12;
  int array[SIZE] = {1, 2, 3, 5, 8, 13, 21, 25, 16, 9, 4, 1};
  vector<int> v(12);

  for (int i = 0; i < SIZE; i++)
    v[i] = array[i];

  cout << v.at(SIZE);  // Would generate an exception

  for (int i = 0; i < SIZE; i++)  // Or use i <= v.size()
    cout << v.at(i) << endl;

  // Illustrates use of front and back member functions
  cout << v.front() << " same as " << v[0] << endl;
  cout << v.back () << " same as " << v[SIZE - 1] << endl;
}
```

Table A.8 *`vector` Member Functions for Insertion*

`v.push_back(item);`	Inserts `item` onto the back of the vector. (If needed, resize. Store into first reserve location, and adjust internal pointers)
`v.insert(iter, item);`	Inserts `item` into the vector before the position denoted by iterator `iter`. (Copy last item into reserve, resizing if needed. Successively copy items until position denoted by `iter` is reached. Copy `item` into position denoted by `iter`)
`v.insert(iter, n, item);`	Inserts `n` copies of `item`, starting at the position denoted by `iter`
`v.swap(vOther);`	Swaps the contents of vectors `v` and `vOther`. The vectors must be of the same type. This operation is fast, as only internal pointers are changed

```
// Illustrates use of vector member functions for insertion

#include <vector>      // For vector<T> class
#include <iostream>

int main ()
{
  using namespace std;

  const int SIZE = 12;
  int array[SIZE] = {1, 2, 3, 5, 8, 13, 21, 25, 16, 9, 4, 1};
  vector<int> v(12);
  vector<int> w(12);

  // Give v the items from array using the push_back member
  for (int i = 0; i < SIZE; i++)
    v.push_back(array[i]);

  // Give w the values 0 through SIZE - 1
  for (int i = 0; i < SIZE; i++)
    w.push_back(i);

  // Display v
  for (int i = 0; i < SIZE; i++)
    cout << v[i] << endl;

  // Exchange the identities of v and w
  v.swap(w);
```

```
    //  and display v, then w
    for (int i = 0; i < SIZE; i++)
      cout << v[i] << endl;

    for (int i = 0; i < SIZE; i++)
      cout << v[i] << endl;
}
```

Table A.9 *`vector` Member Functions for Item Removal*

`v.pop_back();`	Removes the last item from `v`. (This only changes internal pointers)
`v.erase(iter);`	Removes the item at the position denoted by `iter`. (Copies data from the position following the one denoted by `iter` to the position denoted by `iter`, then copies successively until the last item is copied. Internal pointers are adjusted)
`v.erase(first, pastLast);`	Removes all items in the range [`first`, `pastLast`]

Table A.10 *`vector` Member Functions Related to Size*

`v.empty()`	Returns `true` if `v` contains no items, else returns `false`
`v.size()`	Returns the number of items currently in `v`
`v.capacity()`	Returns number of items in container + number of available positions in reserve memory
`v.reserve(n);`	Increases container capacity to `n`

`v.resize(n, value);`	`if (n > v.size())`
	`  v.insert(v.end(), n - v.size(), value);`
	`else if (n < v.size())`
	`  v.erase(v.begin() + n, v.end());`

Reallocation invalidates all references, pointers, and iterators into a vector that were set prior to reallocation, because those iterator values all point into the old (previously allocated) memory. It is guaranteed that no reallocation takes place for insertions that take place after a call to `reserve()`until the vector reaches a size specified in the call to `reserve()`.

Table A.11 *`vector` Member Functions Related to Iterators*

`vector<T>::iterator itr;`	Creates a random access iterator for a `vector<T>`
`vector<T>::reverse_iterator itr;`	Creates a (random access) reverse iterator for a `vector<T>`
`v.begin()`	Returns a random access iterator value denoting the position of the first item
`v.end()`	Returns a random access iterator value denoting the position of the imaginary past-the-end item
`v.rbegin()`	Returns a reverse iterator value denoting the position of the first item of a reverse iteration (i.e., the last item in the container)
`v.rend()`	Returns a reverse iterator value denoting the position of the imaginary past-the-end item of a reverse iteration (i.e., the imaginary before-the-first item in the container)

Before we look at the next sequence container, `list`, we examine the `string` class, which is somewhat similar to `vector<char>` but has member functions and optimizations more appropriate to character strings.

The `string` Class

This section presents the `string` class from the C++ standard library. Although `string` is not part of the STL, it is an integral part of the standard library. A knowledge of the `string` class is essential in a programmer's toolbox.

The standard library defines a class `char_traits` that defines properties of ordinary characters (type `char`) and wide characters (type `wchar_t`, which is the wide [16-bit] character type in which the Unicode character set is encoded). Although the C++ Standard deals with character traits, we do not in this appendix. We deal only with the simpler situation in which the character type is `char`.

The word *string* can be a source of confusion in Standard C++. By *string*, do we mean the strings that are inherited from the C language—namely, null-terminated `char` arrays? Or do we mean Standard C++ `string` class objects? To help remove some of this ambiguity, we will consistently use *string* to refer only to the class `string`. In contrast, we use the term **cstring** to refer to the kind of strings that C++ inherits from C (null-terminated `char` arrays). We do so partly because the header file that provides functions that manipulate C-style strings is the file `<cstring>`, and partly because cstrings are inherited from the C language.

Standard C++ provides two string types, `string` and `wstring`. The names are created by two `typedef` statements that specialize the template class `basic_string`:

```
typedef basic_string<char> string;      // Usual string using ASCII
                                        // characters
typedef basic_string<wchar_t> wstring;  // Wide character string
```

We mention this fact so that you might better understand compiler error messages that mention `basic_string`. Also, you may need to deal with wide character strings (type `wstring`) at some time in the future. We do not discuss `wstring` any further in this appendix.

We begin our discussion of the `string` class by presenting a program that uses both `vector` and `string`. The program reads a line from standard input, splits the line into words, and then outputs the words in reverse order from which they appeared in the input. First we present the program, and then we explain the details.

```
#include <iostream>
#include <string>      // For string class
#include <vector>      // For vector<T> class

using std::string;
using std::vector;

void parse(string& line, string& delimiters, vector<string>& strVec)
// Action: Splits line into words using delimiters,
//         returns words in strVec
// Pre:  line and delimiters have been initialized,
//         and strVec is empty
// Post: strVec contains the words
{
  using namespace std;
  int lineLength = line.length();
  int wordPastEnd;
  int wordStart = line.find_first_not_of(delimiters, 0);

  while ( wordStart >= 0 && wordStart < lineLength )
  {
    wordPastEnd = line.find_first_of(delimiters, wordStart);

    if (wordPastEnd < 0 || wordPastEnd > lineLength)
      wordPastEnd = lineLength;

    strVec.push_back(line.substr(wordStart, wordPastEnd - wordStart));

    // Find first character not in the delimiter list after the 2nd arg
    wordStart = line.find_first_not_of(delimiters, wordPastEnd + 1);
  }
}


int main()
{
  using namespace std;
```

```
    string line;
    string delimiters(" ,.?!:;");
    vector<string> wordVec;

    getline(cin, line, '\n');
    parse(line, delimiters, wordVec);

    vector<string>::iterator itr;

    // Output words in the order that the words appear in wordVec
    for (itr = wordVec.begin(); itr < wordVec.end(); itr++)
      cout << *itr << endl;

    // Output words in the reverse order that they appear in wordVec
    vector<string>::reverse_iterator revItr;
    for (revItr = wordVec.rbegin(); revItr < wordVec.rend(); revItr++)
      cout << *revItr << endl;
}
```

Given the input

```
Now is the time for
```

the program produces this output:

```
Now
is
the
time
for
for
time
the
is
Now
```

The `main` function declares the `string` object `line` to hold the input from the keyboard, and the `string` object `delimiters` holds the separator characters space, comma, period, question mark, exclamation mark, colon, and semicolon. The `getline` stand-alone function, available through the header file `<string>`, has prototype

```
ostream& getline( istream& is, string str, char delim);
```

The effect of getline is to extract characters from the input stream is until one of the following occurs: the end of file on the stream is encountered, the delimiter character is extracted from the input stream, or str.max_size() characters have been extracted. The value str.max_size() is the size of the largest possible string container. The value is implementation dependent but is about 4 x 10^9 for a typical 32-bit C++ implementation.

The function with signature

```
void parse(string& line, string& delimiters,
           vector<string>& strVec);
```

is called to split line into words separated by characters from the string delimiters. The parse function uses the string member function find_first_of, which returns an int value that is the index of the first character in line that matches any character of the delimiter string. Similarly, find_first_not_of returns the int value that is the index of the first character in line that is *not* in the delimiter string. These two numbers are used to locate the start and past-the-end indexes of successive words. Successive substrings are extracted from line using the substr member function and are inserted at the end of strVec using the push_back member function of vector.

Back in the main function, when control returns from the parse function, the argument wordVec contains the successive substrings of line. The successive strings are extracted first to last by use of a vector<string> iterator. A vector iterator is declared, then initialized in a for statement to the location of the front item in wordVec that is returned by the begin() member function. The iterator's referent is output, and the iterator is stepped forward with the ++ operator and compared to the past-the-end value obtained from the end() member function. The result is to display the substrings from line in front to back order.

Next, the strings in strVec are output last to first. An iterator of type vector<string>::reverse_iterator is declared and then initialized in a second for statement to a reverse iterator value that refers to the last item in wordVec by means of the rbegin() member function. The iterator's referent is output. Then the iterator is stepped forward with the ++ operator. (The operator ++ is overloaded to move the iterator's position toward the *front* of the list.) Then the iterator is compared to an iterator value obtained from the rend() member function. This value behaves as if it were a "before-the-first" position, enabling the iteration from back to front to terminate. The result is that the substrings from line are displayed in reverse order.

In this example, we have used the following features of string and vector:

- The use of vector with string as a base type
- The getline function for strings
- The string member functions find_first_of, find_first_not_of, length, and substr
- The use of the type vector<T>::iterator
- The use of the type vector<T>::reverse_iterator

Now let's look in more detail at the string class. Figure A.3 depicts a string that contains the characters in "Bill" and has a size of 4 and a capacity of 9. The string class has members begin() and end() that return iterator values denoting the front and past-the-end positions of the string. A

	Inserted items				Reserve				
Iterator position	`begin()`				`end()`				
Index	0	1	2	3	4	5	6	7	8
Value	'B'	'i'	'l'	'l'					

Figure A.3 `string` *memory allocation*

difference between `vector` and `string` is that the `vector` members `front()` and `back()` are missing from `string`. On the other hand, `string` has several useful search members that, if needed in a `vector`, must be imitated by generic "find" and "conditional find" STL algorithms.

As we did with the `vector<T>` class, we now present a series of tables describing many (but not all) of the available `string` member functions, interspersed with remarks.

Table A.12 `string` *Constructors and Destructor*

`string s;`	Default constructor. Creates an empty string
`string s(str);`	Copy constructor. Creates a new string `s` as a copy of another string, `str`
`string s(str, indx);`	Creates a new string `s` from characters starting at index `indx` of `str`
`string s(str, indx, count);`	Creates a new string `s` initialized by at most `count` characters from `str`, starting at index `indx` in `str`
`string s(cstr);`	Creates a new string `s` initialized with characters from the cstring `cstr`
`string s(charArray, count);`	Creates a new string `s` initialized with at most `count` characters from `char` array `charArray`
`string s(count, ch);`	Creates a new string `s` initialized with `count` instances of character `ch`
`string s(first, pastLast);`	Creates a new string `s` initialized with characters in the iterator range [`first`, `pastLast`) of any `char` container
`s.~string();`	Destructor. Frees the memory allocated to string `s`

Here is a short code segment demonstrating some of the `string` constructors.

```
std::string s0("string"); // Create string s0 containing
                          // 's' 't' 'r' 'i' 'n' 'g'
std::string s1;           // Create empty string s1
std::string s2(s0);       // Create string s2 with characters from s0
```

```
std::string s3(s0, 3);     // Create string s3 with the characters
                           // starting at index 3 from s0: characters
                           // 'i' 'n' 'g'
char x[] = "string";       // Create a cstring
std::string s4(x, x+3);    // Create s4 as a string with 's' 't' 'r'
    // x and x + 3 are pointers into cstring x. Pointers behave as
    // random access iterators.
```

Table A.13 *`string` Element Access*

`s[i]`	Indexed access with no range checking. Character at index `i` may be fetched or stored
`s.at(i)`	Indexed access with range checking. Character at index `i` may be fetched or stored. Throws an `out_of_range` exception if `i` ≥ `s.size()`
`s.c_str()`	Returns a pointer (type `const char *`) to a cstring representing the data in string `s`. The cstring is terminated by a null character (`'\0'`)
`s.data()`	Returns a pointer (type `const char *`) to `s[0]`. *Warning:* The pointed-to sequence should not be treated as a cstring because it is not guaranteed to be terminated by a null character (`'\0'`)

Table A.14 *`string` Member Functions Related to Size*

`s.length()`	Returns the number of characters currently in `s`
`s.size()`	Same as `s.length()`
`s.resize(newSize, padChar);`	Changes the size of `s` to `newSize`, filling with repetitions of the character `padChar` if necessary
`s.empty()`	Returns `true` if `s` is empty, else returns `false`
`s.capacity()`	Returns the number of characters that `s` can contain without having to reallocate (i.e., number of characters in reserve + size of `s`)

Table A.15 *string Member Functions for Searching and Substrings*

`s.find(str)`	Returns the integer index of the first position of the first occurrence of string `str` in `s`
`s.find(str, pos)`	Returns the integer index of the first position of the first occurrence of string `str` in `s`, with the search starting at position `pos` of `s`
`s.find_first_of(delim, pos)`	Returns the integer index of the first position of the first occurrence of any character from the string `delim`, with the search starting at position `pos` of `s`
`s.find_first_not_of(delim, pos)`	Returns the integer index of the first position of the first occurrence of any character *not* in the string `delim`, with the search starting at position `pos` of `s`
`s.substr(pos, len)`	Returns a `string` object that represents a substring of `s` of at most `len` characters, starting at position `pos` of `s`. If `len` is too large, it means "to the end" of string `s`. If `pos` is too large, an `out_of_range` exception is thrown

Note: If any version of `find` fails to find the search value, the function's return value is the constant `string::npos`, which is the largest possible value of type `string::size_type`, an unsigned integer type defined by the `string` class.

Table A.16 *string Comparisons*

`s1 == s2`	Returns `true` if all characters of `s1` and `s2` are pairwise equal, else returns `false`
`s1 != s2`	Returns `true` if not all characters of `s1` and `s2` are pairwise equal, else returns `false`
`s1 < s2`	Returns `true` if `s1` comes before `s2` lexicographically, else returns `false`
`s1 > s2`	Returns `true` if `s1` comes after `s2` lexicographically, else returns `false`
`s1 <= s2`	Same as `!(s1 > s2)`
`s1 >= s2`	Same as `!(s1 < s2)`

Lexicographic ordering compares characters at corresponding positions sequentially until a position `i` is found where `s1[i]` ≠ `s2[i]`. Then the expression `s1 < s2` has the same Boolean value as `s1[i] < s2[i]`.

Table A.17 *`string` I/O Operations*

This table assumes the following declarations:

```
ostream os;
istream is;
```

`os << str`	Places characters from string `str` onto stream `os`
`is >> str`	Extracts characters from stream `is` into string `str`. Leading whitespace characters are skipped, and input stops at the first trailing whitespace character
`getline(is, str, delimiter)`	Reads characters from stream `is` into string `str` up to end-of-file or until the character `delimiter` is extracted. The delimiter is removed from `is` and discarded. *Note:* `getline` is not a member function of the `string` class. It is a stand-alone, global function

The `list<T>` Class

The `list` is the second of the three STL sequence containers. A `list` is a sequential access container that is optimized for insertions and deletions anywhere in the list. Although the C++ Standard does not require any particular implementation, the requirements of fast insertion and deletion and support for bidirectional iterators, together with the lack of a requirement of random access, suggest that the implementation be a doubly linked list.

To create an object of type `list<T>`, the data type `T` must be assignable and copyable. That is, if `T` is a class or struct type, both `operator=` and a copy constructor must be defined for `T`.

The following are some properties of `list` containers:

- `lists` provide sequential access, so there is no indexed access and no `at()` member
- Iterators are bidirectional
- Insertion and deletion can be done in O(1) time at any location in the list.
- Insertion and deletion do not invalidate iterators referring to items not involved in the deletion.
- There are many member functions that do the same task that external STL algorithms do, but they are faster for `lists`, because internal pointers are changed instead of data being moved.
- The `list` provides the best exception safety in that more of its operations either succeed or have no effect than in other containers

As we have done with `vector` and `string`, we now present a series of tables detailing many (but not all) of the `list` member functions.

Reminder: The iterator range [`first`, `pastLast`) refers to the container position denoted by `first` up to but not including the position denoted by `pastLast`.

Table A.18 *`list` Constructors and Destructor*

`list<T> lst;`	Default constructor. Creates `lst` as an empty list
`list<T> lst(oldList);`	Copy constructor. Creates `lst` as a copy of `oldList`
`list<T> lst(count);`	Creates a list of `count` items, each constructed by the default constructor for type `T`
`list<T> lst(count, typeTobj);`	Creates a list of `count` items, each one a copy of `typeTobj`, an object of type `T`
`list<T> lst(first, pastLast);`	Creates a list initialized with type `T` objects from the range [`first`, `pastLast`) in another container
`lst.~list<T>();`	Destructor. Frees the memory allocated to `lst`

A `list` does not provide random access. In addition to dereferencing iterators, list elements are accessed through the member functions `front()` and `back()`.

Table A.19 *`list` Element Access*

`lst.front()`	Returns the first item in the list
`lst.back()`	Returns the last item in the list

Table A.20 describes `list` insertion and deletion operations. Note that class `list<T>` provides member functions for deletion, but there is also a generic STL algorithm for this purpose. However, a member function is preferred to the algorithm because it changes internal pointers instead of moving data, so it is likely to be faster.

Table A.20 *list Member Functions for Insertion and Removal*

`lst.insert(iter, item)`	Inserts `item` into the list before the position denoted by `iter`. Returns an iterator value that points to the inserted item
`lst.insert(iter, count, item);`	Inserts `count` copies of `item` into the list before the position denoted by `iter`. The return type is `void`
`lst.push_front(item);`	Inserts `item` at the front of the list
`lst.push_back(item);`	Appends `item` to the back of the list
`lst.pop_back();`	Removes the item at the back of the list
`lst.pop_front();`	Removes the item at the front of the list
`lst.remove(item);`	Removes all list elements equal to `item`
`lst.remove_if(pred);`	Removes all items for which the predicate `pred` returns `true`. The argument `pred` can be either the name of a Boolean function or a function object (defined later in this appendix)
`lst.erase(iter)`	Removes the item at the position denoted by `iter`. Returns an iterator value that points to the next item
`lst.erase(first, pastLast)`	Removes all items in the range [`first`, `pastLast`). Returns an iterator value that points to the next item
`lst.clear();`	Removes all items in the list

Table A.21 *list Assignment and Swap Operations*

`lst1 = lst2;`	After removing all items in `lst1`, copies all items from list `lst2` to `lst1`
`lst.assign(first, pastLast);`	After removing all items in `lst`, copies to `lst` all items in the range [`first`, `pastLast`) from another container of type `T` objects
`lst1.swap(lst2);`	Swaps the contents of lists `lst1` and `lst2`

Table A.22 *list Member Functions Related to Iterators*

list<T>::iterator itr;	Creates a bidirectional iterator for a list<T>
list<T>::reverse_iterator itr;	Creates a (bidirectional) reverse iterator for a list<T>
lst.begin()	Returns a bidirectional iterator value denoting the position of the first item
lst.end()	Returns a bidirectional iterator value denoting the past-the-end position
lst.rbegin()	Returns a reverse iterator value denoting the position of the first item of a reverse iteration (i.e., the last item in the container)
lst.rend()	Returns a reverse iterator value denoting the past-the-end position of a reverse iteration (i.e., the before-the-first position in the container)

Table A.23 *list Member Functions Related to Size and Comparisons*

lst.empty()	Returns true if lst contains no items. Returns same result as lst.size() == 0, but lst.empty() might be faster
lst.size()	Returns the number of items currently in the list
lst.resize(newSize);	If newSize > lst.size(), then append newSize - lst.size() instances of a default-constructed type T object to the end of the list. Otherwise, if newSize < lst.size(), erase the last lst.size() - newSize items from the list, else do nothing.
lst.resize(newSize, typeTobj);	If newSize > lst.size(), then append newSize - lst.size() copies of typeTobj to the end of the list. Otherwise, if newSize < lst.size(), erase the last lst.size() - newSize items from the list, else do nothing.
lst1 == lst2	Returns true if the lists have the same number of items and contain the same items in the same order, else returns false
lst1 < lst2 lst1 > lst2 lst1 <= lst2 lst1 >= lst2	Comparisons are in lexicographic order. (Successive pairs of items are compared. The order of the first unequal pair determines which order relations return true)

Table A.24 *Operations That Modify `lists`*

`lst1.splice(iter, lst2);`	Requirement: `&lst1` ≠ `&lst2`
	Effect: Inserts the contents of `lst2` into `lst1` before the position in `lst1` denoted by `iter`, and `lst2` becomes empty
`lst1.splice(position, lst2, iter);`	Removes the item at the position denoted by `iter` in `lst2` and inserts it before the position denoted by `position` in `lst1`.
`lst1.splice(position, lst2, first, pastLast);`	Requirement: If `&lst1` = `&lst2`, `position` must not be in the range [`first`, `pastLast`)
	Effect: Removes all items in the range [`first`, `pastLast`) of `lst2` and inserts them before the position denoted by `position` in `lst1`
`lst.sort();`	Sorts the list items into ascending order using the < operator to compare items
`lst.sort(cmp);`	Sorts the list items using the comparison function `cmp`, which can be either the name of a Boolean function or a function object (defined later in this appendix)
`lst1.merge(lst2);`	Requirement: The items in both lists are in sorted order (ordered by the < operator)
	Effect: Removes all items from `lst2` and merges them into `lst1` so that `lst1` is still sorted
`lst1.merge(lst2, cmp);`	Requirement: The items in both lists are in sorted order (ordered by the `cmp` function). The comparison function `cmp` can be either the name of a Boolean function or a function object (defined later in this appendix)
	Effect: Removes all items from `lst2` and merges them into `lst1` so that `lst1` is still sorted
`lst.unique();`	Removes all but the first in any sequence of consecutive items that are equal (satisfy the == relation)
`lst.unique(cmp);`	Removes all but the first in any sequence of consecutive items that satisfy the comparison function `cmp`, which can be either the name of a Boolean function or a function object (defined later in this appendix)
`lst.reverse();`	Reverses the order of the items in `lst`

The `deque<T>` Class

The third of the three STL sequence containers is the `deque`. The word *deque* (pronounced "deck," "deek," or "dee queue") is short for *double-ended queue*. The `deque` container, like the `vector`, provides fast random access into sequences of varying length. Unlike the `vector`, the deque provides fast insertion and deletion at *both* ends of the collection. This is accomplished by providing unused reserve not only at the start of the deque, as does the vector, but also at the end of the container.

The following are the primary differences between the deque and the vector:

- Insertion into a deque is fast (amortized time O(1)) at the front as well as the back. The vector is fast only at the back.
- Memory allocated to a vector is typically contiguous (that is, a built-in array), so vector iterators are usually C++ pointers. Memory allocated to a deque is not guaranteed to be contiguous, so iterators typically are implemented as class objects that mimic pointers. Therefore, accessing items in a deque tends to be slower than accessing items in a vector.
- Unlike the vector, no member functions are provided in the deque to control reallocation or capacity, so any insertion or deletion other than at the ends invalidates all iterators to the deque.

When should you choose a deque over a vector? If you require random access and frequent insertions at the front and the back, then the deque is the better structure.

Table A.25 displays a representative sample of the deque member functions.

Table A.25 *deque Member Functions*

Constructors, Assignment, and Swap Operations

`deque<T> d;`	Default constructor. Creates an empty deque object, d
`deque<T> d(otherDeque);`	Copy constructor. Creates a new deque d as a copy of otherDeque
`deque<T> d(count);`	Creates a deque of count items, each constructed by the default constructor for type T
`deque<T> d(count, typeTobj);`	Creates a deque of count items, each being a copy of typeTobj, an object of type T
`d = otherDeque;`	After removing all items from deque d, copies all items from otherDeque to d
`d.swap(otherDeque);`	Swaps the contents of d and otherDeque

Element Access and Insertion Operations

`d[index]`	Indexed access with no range checking. The element at index index may be fetched or stored
`d.at(index)`	Indexed access with range checking. Throws an out_of_range exception if index ≥ d.size()
`d.front()`	Returns the first item in the container. Same as d[0]

(continued)

d.back()	Returns the last item in the container. Same as d[d.size() - 1]
d.insert(iter, item);	Inserts item before the position denoted by iter. Returns an iterator value that points to the inserted item
d.insert(iter, first, pastLast);	Inserts before the position denoted by iter all items in the range [first , pastLast) from another container holding objects of type T
d.push_front(item);	Inserts item at the front of the deque
d.push_back(item);	Inserts item at the back of the deque

Deletion Operations

d.pop_front();	Removes the item at the front of the deque
d.pop_back();	Removes the item at the back of the deque
d.erase(iter)	Removes the item at the position denoted by iter. Returns an iterator value that points to the next item
d.erase(first, pastLast)	Removes all items in the range [first, pastLast). Returns an iterator value that points to the next item
d.clear();	Removes all items in the deque

Size-Related Operations

d.size()	Returns the number of items currently in the deque
d.empty()	Returns true if d contains no items. Returns same result as d.size() == 0, but d.empty() might be faster
d.resize(number);	Changes the size to number. If the deque grows, new items are constructed by the default constructor for type T

Iterator-Related Operations

deque<T>::iterator itr;	Creates a random access iterator for a deque<T>
deque<T>:: reverse_iterator itr;	Creates a (random access) reverse iterator for a deque<T>
d.begin()	Returns a random access iterator value denoting the position of the first item
d.end()	Returns a random access iterator value denoting the past-the-end position
d.rbegin()	Returns a reverse iterator value denoting the position of the first item of a reverse iteration (i.e., the last item in the container)
d.rend()	Returns a reverse iterator value denoting the past-the-end position of a reverse iteration (i.e., the before-the-first position in the container)

The Container Adapters stack, queue, and priority_queue

An **adapter** does not directly implement the structures that hold the data items. Rather, it provides a new interface between the user and an existing container. It "adapts" the interface of one of the sequence containers to provide the operations appropriate for a stack or queue.

The stack Adapter Any sequence container that provides members empty(), size(), push_back(), pop_back(), and back() is suitable as a container for the stack container adapter. All three sequence containers—vector<T>, deque<T>, and list<T>—satisfy these requirements. By default, deque<T> is the container used by the stack<T> adapter.

The stack operations shown in Table A.26 are familiar to anyone who has studied this book.

Table A.26 *Some stack Member Functions*

stack<int> stck;	Default constructor. Uses, by default, a deque<int> to hold items of type int
stack<float, vector<float> > stck;	Default constructor. Uses a vector<float> to hold items of type float. (Note the required space within "> >" to distinguish it from the built-in operator >>)
stack<string, list<string> > stck;	Default constructor. Uses a list<string> to hold items of type string
stack<char, vector<char> > stck(otherStck);	Copy constructor. Initializes stck to be a copy of otherStck, another stack of the same type (i.e., type stack<char, vector<char> >)
stack<char, vector<char> > stck(charVec);	Copy constructor. Initializes stck to be a copy of charVec, an object of the underlying container type vector<char>
stck.empty()	Returns true if stack contains no items. Equivalent to stck.size() == 0 but may be faster
stck.size()	Returns the number of items currently in the container
stck.push(item);	Pushes a copy of item onto the top of the stack
stck.pop();	Requirement: stck.size() > 0 Effect: Removes and discards the top item from the stack. The return type is void
stck.top()	Requirement: stck.size() > 0 Effect: Returns the top item on the stack without removing it.

(continued)

Table A.26 *(continued)*

`stck1 < stck2`
`stck1 > stck2`
`stck1 <= stck2`
`stck1 >= stck2`
`stck1 == stck2`
`stck1 != stck2`
	Two stacks are equal if they have the same size and all pairs of items are equal. Comparisons are made lexicographically. The first pair of elements that are unequal determines which relational operator returns `true`

The `queue` Adapter Any sequence container that has members `back()`, `front()`, `push_back()`, `pop_front()`, `empty()`, and `size()` can be used to hold `queue<T>` items. In particular, `list<T>` and `deque<T>` may be used. By default, `deque<T>` is the container used by the `queue<T>` adapter.

Notice in Table A.27 that the STL uses `push()` instead of `enqueue()` and `pop()` instead of `dequeue()`. Regardless of what we call the operation, we are still dealing with a queue—a FIFO (first-in, first-out) data structure—and `push()` and `pop()` mean insert and remove. The structure still returns the oldest item in the structure, just as a queue should.

Table A.27 *Some `queue` Member Functions*

`queue<int> q;`	Default constructor. Uses a `deque<int>` to hold items of type `int`. The `queue<T>` class supports the same variety of constructors shown in Table A.26 for the `stack<T>` class (except that `vector<T>` cannot be the underlying container)
`q.empty()`	Returns `true` if the queue is empty
`q.size()`	Returns the number of items in the queue
`q.front()`	Requirement: `q.size()` > 0 Effect: Returns the first item in the queue
`q.back()`	Requirement: `q.size()` > 0 Effect: Returns the last item in the queue
`q.push(item);`	Inserts `item` at the back of the queue
`q.pop();`	Requirement: `q.size()` > 0 Effect: Removes and discards the first item from the queue. The return type is `void`

`q1 < q2`
`q1 > q2`
`q1 <= q2`
`q1 >= q2`
`q1 == q2`
`q1 != q2`
	Two queues are equal if they have the same size and all pairs of items are equal. Comparisons are made lexicographically. The first pair of items that are unequal determines which relational operator returns `true`

The following program demonstrates how to declare and use a queue of string objects, using the default underlying container deque<string> to hold the strings.

```
// A queue example using the default (deque) underlying container

#include <iostream>
#include <queue>      // For queue<T> class
#include <string>     // For string class
#include <deque>      // For deque<T> class

int main()
{
  using namespace std;

  deque<string> deq;
  string str;

  // Build a list of words
  cout << "Type some words; 'quit' quits:" << endl << endl;
  cin >> str;
  while ( string("quit") !=  str )
  {
    deq.push_back(str);
    cin >> str;
  }

  // Create que1 by copying from an instance of a deque--the
  // underlying container
  queue<string> que1(deq);

  // Create que2 as a copy of que1
  queue<string> que2(que1);

  cout << "The number of strings entered is " << que1.size() << endl;
  cout << "que1.front() yields: " << que1.front() << endl;
  cout << "que2.back()  yields: " << que2.back()  << endl;

  cout << "The strings from que1 are:  ";
  while ( !que1.empty())
  {
    cout << que1.front() << " ";
    que1.pop();
  }
  cout << endl;
```

```
    cout << "The strings from que2 are:  ";
    while ( !que2.empty())
    {
      cout << que2.front() << " ";
      que2.pop();
    }
    cout << endl;
}
```

Execution of this program yields

```
Type some words; 'quit' quits:

now is the time quit

The number of strings entered is 4
que1.front() yields: now
que2.back()  yields: time
The strings from que1 are:  now is the time
The strings from que2 are:  now is the time
```

The `priority_queue` Adapter A `priority_queue`, whose declaration is located in the header file `<queue>`, has operations `empty()`, `size()`, `push()`, `pop()`, and `top()`. A `priority_queue` is like a `queue` in the sense that `push()` means enqueue and `pop()` means dequeue. However, the enqueued items are ordered by the < operator as follows. Whenever `push()` is called to enqueue an item, the item is inserted at the back of the sequence and then reordering takes place immediately to ensure that the item with the greatest value (the "highest priority") is at the front of the queue. Therefore, the `top()` operation always returns the highest priority item.

The `priority_queue<T>` adapter can use any of `vector<T>`, `list<T>`, or `deque<T>` as the underlying container. The default is `vector<T>`.

The Associative Containers

Earlier we said that the STL provides three kinds of containers: sequence containers, container adapters, and associative containers. We have looked at the first two and now give a brief overview of the third.

The associative containers are based on the concept of an *associative array* or *map*, a data structure that holds ordered pairs of the form *(key, value)*. For each key, there is an associated value in the map. The keys can be of one data type, and the associated values can be of another. Here is a code segment that uses the template class `map<K,T>`, where `K` means the key type and `T` means the value type:

```
#include <map>    // For map<K,T> class
  ⋮
map<int,float> m;
```

```
m[0] = 36.43;
m[1] = -15.9;
m[2] = 0.0;
```

As you can see, an associative array in which the key values are integers looks very much like an ordinary one-dimensional array. However, look at the following code:

```
map<string,int> age;

age["Mary"] = 18;
age["Bill"] = 22;
```

An associative array can be thought of as an array that allows indexes other than integers. By default, the contents of a `map` are ordered by key values using the < operator, and `map` iterators step through the container, delivering the items in ascending order of the keys.

The `<map>` header file declares two container types: `map<K,T>` and `multimap<K,T>`. In a `map`, the keys must be unique; in a `multimap`, duplicate keys are allowed.

The STL provides two other associative containers, `set` and `multiset`, which are available through the header file `<set>`. The `set` is an abstraction of a mathematical set. In the context of the STL, it is simply a special case of an associative array in which no value is associated with a key. Hence, the template class `set<K>` requires only one template parameter–the data type of its keys (hence, the data type of the set elements). The difference between the `set` and `multiset` containers is that all elements of a `set` must be unique (as in a mathematical set), whereas a `multiset` allows duplicate elements.

Space limitations prevent us from further exploration of the associative containers. For more information, see the references at the end of the appendix.

Algorithms

We have said that the Standard Template Library provides containers, iterators, and generic algorithms. In computer science terminology, an algorithm is a sequence of steps that solves a problem. In contrast, the term *algorithm* in the STL context means something much more specific: a template function that has iterators for its parameter types.

The STL supplies a large set of generic algorithms that operate on containers, whether they are STL containers or user-defined containers. The algorithms are *generic* because each algorithm is templated and the arguments in a function call are iterators, not containers. Therefore, a generic algorithm may operate on *any* data structure that provides an iterator type that meets the iterator requirements of that algorithm. Let's look at an example.

The STL supplies a `sort` algorithm with the following signature (the required header file and the function prototype):

```
#include <algorithm>
template <class RandomAccessIterator>
void sort( RandomAccessIterator first,
           RandomAccessIterator pastLast );
```

Given any container that supports random access iterators, the `sort` algorithm sorts the container elements into ascending order using the < operator. We know that the STL `vector` container supports random access iterators, so we could use `sort` as follows:

```
#include <vector>         // For vector<T> class
#include <algorithm>      // For sort() function
  :
vector<int> v;
  :
sort(v.begin(), v.end());  // Sort the entire vector
```

Because `sort` works on any container whose iterators meet its requirements, we can sort a built-in array as follows. (Recall that pointers into a built-in array meet the requirements of a random access iterator.)

```
int arr[100];
  :
sort(&arr[0], &arr[100]);  // Or  sort(arr, arr+100);
```

In this code, the call to `sort` passes as arguments the location of the first array element and the location of the imaginary past-the-end element (because `arr[99]` is the last valid array element).

Function Objects

With the STL `sort` algorithm in mind, what if we want to sort a container into descending rather than ascending order? The STL provides a second version of `sort` with the following signature:

```
#include <algorithm>
template <class RandomAccessIterator, class Compare>
void sort( RandomAccessIterator first,
           RandomAccessIterator pastLast, Compare cmp );
```

Here, the third argument in a call to `sort` is a user-supplied comparison operation on which the sorting is based. This argument can be either the name of a function or a **function object**. To demonstrate the first case, we could write a `greater_than` function as follows:

```
bool greater_than( int m, int n)
{
  return m > n;
}
```

and then use its name as an argument to the sort function so that we can sort a vector<int> container into *descending* order:

```
sort(v.begin(), v.end(), greater_than);
```

To deal with the second case, we introduce the general concept of a *function object*. Stated simply, a function object is a class object that acts like a function. More precisely, a function object is an object of a class that overloads the function call operator, which is (). Here is an example:

```
class Double
{
public:
  int operator() ( int i )
  {
    return 2 * i;
  }
};
```

Given class Double, we can create and use a function object f as follows:

```
Double f;
int n;

n = f(65);
```

The function call f(65) is equivalent to f.operator()(65) and returns the result 130. Thus, although f is used as if it were the name of a function, in reality it is the name of a class object.

Now back to our sorting problem. To sort a vector<int> into descending order, we can first write the following class:

```
class Greater
{
public:
  bool operator() ( int m, int n )
  {
    return m > n;
  }
};
```

and then proceed as follows:

```
Greater greater_than;          // Create a function object
                               // named greater_than
sort(v.begin(), v.end(), greater_than);
```

Of course, if we wanted to have a Greater-like class that compares float values and another that compares char values and so on, we'd have to write all these as different classes with different names. Fortunately, the STL provides a template class greater<T> that lets us supply the base type as a template parameter and keeps us from having to write our own comparison class:

```
#include <functional>     // For greater<T>
  ⋮
greater<int> greater_than;     // Create a function object
                               // named greater_than
sort(v.begin(), v.end(), greater_than);
```

Note that the template parameter in greater<T> must be a type T for which the > operator is defined.

In addition to greater<T>, the header file <functional> also defines the following template classes: less<T>, less_equal<T>, greater_equal<T>, equal_to<T>, and not_equal_to<T>. In all cases, type T must be a type for which the corresponding operator (<, <=, and so on) is defined.

Algorithm Classification

Some STL algorithms are read-only (they inspect but don't modify the items in a container), others change the values of the items, and yet others change the order of the items. The C++ Standard classifies generic algorithms into categories that are distinguished by their use.

- Non-modifying sequence operations
- Mutating sequence operations
- Sorting and related operations
- Merging
- Set operations
- Heap operations
- Numeric operations
- Complex numbers and numeric arrays

In the following sections, we focus on the first three of these categories and present only a small sample of the available algorithms. In the descriptions of these algorithms, the formal parameter lists include type names with the following meanings (where T is the type of the items to which the iterators point):

Predicate	A function or function object taking one argument of type T and returning a bool value
Compare	A function or function object taking two arguments of type T (in order to compare them) and returning a bool value
UnaryOperation	A function or function object taking one argument of type T and returning a value of type T
BinaryOperation	A function or function object taking two arguments of type T and returning a value of type T

`UnaryFunction` A function or function object taking one argument of type `T` and returning no value

Note: In the following descriptions, the use of iterator arithmetic to describe positions and ranges is *only* for descriptive purposes. We do not intend to imply that the iterator type supports pointer arithmetic.

Non-Modifying Sequence Operations

Algorithms in this category are called *non-modifying* because they do not modify the container elements pointed to by the iterators.

Algorithm: `count`, `count_if`

Synopsis: Counts the number of items in a container that match a certain value or that satisfy a predicate.

Signatures:

```
#include <algorithm>
template<class InputIterator, class T>
typename iterator_traits<InputIterator>::difference_type
count( InputIterator first,
       InputIterator pastLast,
       const T& value);

#include <algorithm>
template <class InputIterator, class Predicate>
typename iterator_traits<InputIterator>::difference_type
count_if( InputIterator first,
          InputIterator pastLast,
          Predicate pred);
```

Remarks on syntax: Conceptually, these two functions return integer values, but the `int` type might not be large enough to hold the result. So the return type is defined in terms of the difference between two iterator values. The keyword `typename` tells the compiler that what follows is the name of a type. `iterator_traits` is a struct that contains `typedef` statements for `difference_type` and other identifiers. The type `difference_type` is ultimately `typedef`'ed to `ptrdiff_t`, which is the integer type of the difference between two pointer values.

Requirement: For the `count` algorithm, `T` must be a type for which the == operator is defined.

Description: Each algorithm steps through the iterator range [`first`, `pastLast`). The `count` algorithm returns the number of items in the range that match the parameter `value`. The `count_if` algorithm returns the number of items in the range that satisfy the predicate `pred`.

Complexity: Each algorithm has a run time that is linear in the length of the range and has constant space complexity.

Algorithm: `find, find_if`

Synopsis: Locates the first item in a subrange of a container that matches a particular value. The predicate version, `find_if`, locates the first item that satisfies a predicate passed to the algorithm.

Signatures:

```
#include <algorithm>
template <class InputIterator, class T>
InputIterator find( InputIterator first,
                    InputIterator pastLast,
                    const T& value);

#include <algorithm>
template <class InputIterator, class Predicate>
InputIterator find_if( InputIterator first,
                       InputIterator pastLast,
                       Predicate pred);
```

Requirement: For the `find` algorithm, `T` must be a type for which the == operator is defined.

Description: `find` searches the range [`first`, `pastLast`) for the first item that matches `value`. `find_if` searches this range for the first item that satisfies the predicate `pred`. Both algorithms return an iterator value pointing to the item if it was found. If the item was not found, they return the value `pastLast`.

Complexity: Each algorithm has a run time that is linear in the length of the range and requires constant space.

Algorithm: `for_each`

Synopsis: Applies a function to every item in a range.

Signature:

```
#include <algorithm>
template <class InputIterator, class UnaryFunction>
UnaryFunction for_each( InputIterator first,
                        InputIterator pastLast,
                        UnaryFunction f);
```

Description: This algorithm applies the function `f` to every item in the range [`first`, `pastLast`). The return value of `f`, if any, is ignored. The return value of the algorithm is the value of `f` after it has been applied to each container item. (This return value is useful if `f` is a function object that has member data that it keeps track of—for example, how many times `f` has been called. If `f` has no such member data or refers to a function rather than a function object, the return value is typically ignored by the caller.)

Complexity: The algorithm run time is linear in the length of the iterator range. It has constant space complexity.

Mutating Sequence Operations

Algorithms in this category are described as *mutating* because they can change the objects pointed to by the iterators in their argument lists.

Algorithm: `copy`

Synopsis: Copies items from one range to another.

Signature:

```
#include <algorithm>
template <class InputIterator, class OutputIterator>
OutputIterator copy( InputIterator first,
                     InputIterator pastLast,
                     OutputIterator result);
```

Requirement: `result`, the starting point of the destination range, must not be in the range [`first`, `pastLast`). Also, there must be sufficient space at the destination to hold the copied items.

Description: The algorithm copies items from the range [`first`, `pastLast`) into the range [`result`, `result` + (`pastLast` - `first`)), starting from `first` and proceeding to `pastLast`. The function returns an iterator value denoting the past-the-last position in the destination range–that is, the position denoted by (`result` + (`pastLast` - `first`)).

Complexity: The algorithm is linear, performing `pastLast - first` assignments.

Algorithm: `fill`

Synopsis: Sets every item in a range to a specified value.

Signature:

```
#include <algorithm>
template <class ForwardIterator, class T>
void fill ( ForwardIterator first,
            ForwardIterator pastLast,
            const T& value );
```

Description: `fill` traverses the range [`first`, `pastLast`), assigning `value` to each item.

Complexity: The algorithm is linear in the length of the range.

Algorithm: `replace`, `replace_if`

Synopsis: `replace` traverses a sequence, replacing each specified value with another value. `replace_if` replaces values that satisfy a predicate.

Signatures:

```
#include <algorithm>
template <class ForwardIterator, class T>
void replace( ForwardIterator first,
              ForwardIterator pastLast,
              const T& old_value,
              const T& new_value );

#include <algorithm>
template <class ForwardIterator, class Predicate, class T>
void replace_if( ForwardIterator first,
                 ForwardIterator pastLast,
                 Predicate pred,
                 const T& new_value );
```

Requirement: For the `replace` algorithm, `T` must be a type for which the == operator is defined.

Description: `replace` replaces every occurrence of `old_value` with `new_value` in the range [`first`, `pastLast`). The algorithm `replace_if` replaces every item that satisfies `pred` with `new_value` in the range [`first`, `pastLast`).

Complexity: These algorithms are linear in the length of the range.

Algorithm: `reverse`

Synopsis: Reverses in place the relative order of items in a range.

Signature:

```
#include <algorithm>
template <class BidirectionalIterator>
void reverse( BidirectionalIterator first,
              BidirectionalIterator pastLast );
```

Description: The effect of `reverse` is to swap the first and last items in the range [`first`, `pastLast`), then the second and next-to-last items, and so on until the middle is detected, at which point the process stops.

Complexity: `reverse` processes all items once, so the time complexity is linear in the length of the range.

Algorithm: `transform`

Synopsis: Applies an operation to items from one or two ranges, placing the result in another.

Signatures:

```
#include <algorithm>
template <class InputIterator, class OutputIterator,
          class UnaryOperation>
```

```
OutputIterator transform( InputIterator first,
                          InputIterator pastLast,
                          OutputIterator result,
                          UnaryOperation op );

#include <algorithm>
template <class InputIterator1, class InputIterator2,
          class OutputIterator, class BinaryOperation>
OutputIterator transform ( InputIterator1 first1,
                           InputIterator1 pastLast1,
                           InputIterator2 first2,
                           OutputIterator result,
                           BinaryOperation binary_op );
```

Requirement: Unary operation `op` and binary operation `binary_op` must not have side effects.

Description: Applies a unary operation `op` to each item in the range [`first`, `pastLast`), or a binary operation `binary_op` to pairs of corresponding items in two ranges, [`first1`, `pastLast1`) and [`first2`, `pastLast2`), each storing the results in another sequence starting at the position denoted by `result`. For each version, the return value is an iterator value denoting the past-the-last position in the destination range.

Complexity: Each algorithm is linear. Exactly `pastLast - first` (or, for the second version, `pastLast1 - first1`) applications of either `op` or `binary_op` are made.

Sorting and Related Operations

Algorithm: `max_element`

Synopsis: Finds the largest item in a range.

Signatures:

```
#include <algorithm>
template <class ForwardIterator>
ForwardIterator max_element(ForwardIterator first,
                            ForwardIterator pastLast);

#include <algorithm>
template <class ForwardIterator, class Compare>
ForwardIterator max_element(ForwardIterator first,
                            ForwardIterator pastLast,
                            Compare cmp);
```

Requirement: For the first version, the items in the container must be of a type for which the < operator is defined. For the second version, `cmp` must be a Boolean function or function object whose semantics are "less than."

Description: `max_element` returns an iterator value denoting the position of the largest item in the range [`first`, `pastLast`). If there are several occurrences of the largest item, the position of the first one is returned. If [first, pastLast) is an empty range, the function returns pastLast.

The first version of max_element compares items using the < operator, and the second compares items using the function or function object cmp.

Complexity: Each algorithm is linear in the length of the range.

Algorithm: min_element

Synopsis: Finds the smallest item in a range.

Signatures:

```
#include <algorithm>
template <class ForwardIterator>
ForwardIterator min_element(ForwardIterator first,
                            ForwardIterator pastLast);

#include <algorithm>
template <class ForwardIterator, class Compare>
ForwardIterator min_element(ForwardIterator first,
                            ForwardIterator pastLast,
                            Compare cmp);
```

Requirement: For the first version, the items in the container must be of a type for which the < operator is defined. For the second version, cmp must be a Boolean function or function object whose semantics are "less than."

Description: min_element returns an iterator value denoting the position of the smallest item in the range [first, pastLast). If there are several occurrences of the smallest item, the position of the first one is returned. If [first, pastLast) is an empty range, the function returns pastLast.

The first version of min_element compares items using the < operator, and the second compares items using the function or function object cmp.

Complexity: Each algorithm is linear in the length of the range.

Algorithm: sort

Synopsis: Sorts items in a range using the quick sort. One version sorts by using the < operator, the other by using a user-supplied comparison function.

Signatures:

```
#include <algorithm>
template <class RandomAccessIterator>
void sort( RandomAccessIterator first,
           RandomAccessIterator pastLast );

#include <algorithm>
template <class RandomAccessIterator, class Compare>
void sort( RandomAccessIterator first,
           RandomAccessIterator pastLast, Compare cmp );
```

Requirement: For the first version, the items in the container must be of a type for which the < operator is defined. For the second version, `cmp` must be a Boolean function or function object whose semantics are either "strictly less than" or "strictly greater than."

Description: Both versions sort the items in the range [`first`, `pastLast`) into order using a recursive quick sort. The first version sorts items into ascending order. The second version sorts into either ascending or descending order, depending on the comparison function `cmp`.

Complexity: Average time complexity is $O(N*\log(N))$, and space complexity is $O(\log(N))$ because the routines are recursive. The worst-case time complexity is $O(N^2)$. If worst-case behavior is important, two other STL algorithms named `stable_sort` and `partial_sort` provide better worst-case guarantees, but with somewhat poorer average behavior.

We hope that this appendix has whet your appetite for the full range of features available in the Standard Template Library. We encourage you to consult the following references for further information.

References

1. *ISO/ANSI Standard 14882: Programming Languages—C++*, American National Standards Institute, 1998.
2. Niccolai Josuttis, *The C++ Standard Library*, Addison Wesley Longman, 1999.
3. P. J. Plauger was a principal member of the Standards committee. His company has a website, `www.dinkumware.com/refcpp.html`, that has substantial resources on the C++ standard library.
4. The Silicon Graphics website `www.sgi.com/tech/stl/` (or `www.sgi.com/`) provides many resources for information on the Standard Template Library.

glossary

abstract data type a data type whose properties (domain and operations) are specified independently of any particular implementation; a class of data objects with a defined set of properties and a set of operations that process the data objects while maintaining the properties

abstract step an algorithmic step for which some implementation details remain unspecified

abstraction a model of a complex system that includes only the details essential to the perspective of the viewer of the system; the separation of the logical properties of data or actions from their implementation details

abstraction (in OOD) the essential characteristics of an object from the viewpoint of the user

acceptance test the process of testing the system in its real environment with real data

activation record (stack frame) a record used at run time to store information about a function call, including the parameters, local variables, register values, and return address

actual parameter a variable, constant, or expression listed in the call to a function or procedure

adjacency list a linked list that identifies all the vertices to which a particular vertex is connected; each vertex has its own adjacency list

adjacency matrix for a graph with N nodes, an $N \times N$ table that shows the existence (and weights) of all edges in the graph

adjacent nodes two nodes in a graph that are connected by an edge

aggregate operation an operation on a data structure as a whole, as opposed to an operation on an individual component of the data structure

algorithm a logical sequence of discrete steps that describes a complete solution to a given problem, computable in a finite amount of time; a step-by-step procedure for solving a problem in a finite amount of time; a verbal or written description of a logical sequence of actions

ALU see *arithmetic/logic unit*

anonymous type a user-defined type that does not have an identifier (a name) associated with it

arithmetic/logic unit (ALU) the component of the central processing unit that performs arithmetic and logical operations

array data type a collection of components, all of the same type, ordered on *N* dimensions (*N* >= 1); each component is accessed by *N* indexes, each of which represents the component's position within that dimension

assembler a program that translates an assembly language program into machine code

assembly language a low-level programming language in which a mnemonic represents each of the machine language instructions for a particular computer

assertion a logical proposition that is either true or false

assignment expression a C++ expression with a value and the side effect of storing the expression value into a memory location

assignment statement a statement that stores the value of an expression into a variable

atomic data type a data type that allows only a single value to be associated with an identifier of that type

automatic variable a variable for which memory is allocated and deallocated when control enters and exits the block in which it is declared

auxiliary storage device a device that stores data in encoded form outside the computer's memory

base address the memory address of the first element in an array

base case the case for which the solution can be stated nonrecursively

base class the class being inherited from

batch processing a technique for entering data and executing programs without intermediate user interaction with the computer

big-O notation a notation that expresses computing time (complexity) as the term in a function that increases most rapidly relative to the size of a problem

binary expressed in terms of combinations of the numbers 1 and 0 only

binary search a search algorithm for sorted lists that involves dividing the list in half and determining, by value comparison, whether the item would be in the upper or lower half; the process is performed repeatedly until either the item is found or it is determined that the item is not on the list

binary search tree a binary tree in which the key value in any node is greater than the key value in its left child and any of its children (the nodes in the left subtree) and less than the key value in its right child and any of its children (the nodes in the right subtree)

binary tree a structure with a unique starting node (the root), in which each node is capable of having two child nodes, and in which a unique path exists from the root to every other node

binding time the time at which a name or symbol is bound to an address or to the appropriate code
bit short for binary digit; a single 1 or 0
black-box testing testing a program or function based on the possible input values, treating the code as a "black box"
block in C++, a group of zero or more statements enclosed in braces
body the statement(s) to be repeated within the loop; the executable statement(s) within a function
Boolean a data type consisting of only two values: true and false; `bool` in C++
Boolean expression an assertion that is evaluated as either true or false, the only values of the Boolean data type
Boolean operators operators applied to values of the type Boolean; in C++ these are the special symbols `&&`, `||`, and `!`
booting the system the process of starting up a computer by loading the operating system into its main memory
brainstorming the stage in an object-oriented design in which the first pass is made to determine the classes in a design
branch a code segment that is not always executed; for example, a *switch* statement has as many branches as there are case labels
branching control structure *see* selection control structure
bucket a collection of elements associated with a particular hash location
byte eight bits
call the point at which the computer begins following the instructions in a subprogram is referred to as the subprogram call
cancellation error a form of representational error that occurs when numbers of widely differing magnitudes are added or subtracted
central processing unit (CPU) the part of the computer that executes the instructions (program) stored in memory; consists of the arithmetic/logic unit and the control unit
chain a linked list of elements that share the same hash location
`char` a data type whose values consist of one alphanumeric character (letter, digit, or special symbol)
character set a standard set of alphanumeric characters with a given collating sequence and binary representation
circular linked list a list in which every node has a successor; the "last" element is succeeded by the "first" element
`class` an unstructured type that encapsulates a fixed number of data components with the functions that manipulate them; the predefined operations on an instance of a class are "whole assignment" and "component access"
class constructor a special member function of a class that is implicitly invoked when a class object is defined
class destructor a special member function of a class that is implicitly invoked when a class object goes out of scope
class member a component of a class; class members may be either data or functions

class object (class instance) a variable of a class type
clear- (white-) box testing testing a program or function based on covering all of the branches or paths of the code
client software that declares and manipulates objects (instances) of a particular class
clustering the tendency of elements to become unevenly distributed in the hash table, with many elements clustering around a single hash location
code coverage *see* clear- (white-) box testing
code walk-through a verification process for a program in which each statement is examined to check that it faithfully implements the corresponding algorithmic step, and that the preconditions and postconditions of each module are preserved
coding translating an algorithm into a programming language; the process of assigning bit patterns to pieces of information
collating sequence the ordering of the elements of a set or series, such as the characters (values) in a character set
collision the condition resulting when two or more keys produce the same hash location
communication complexity a measure of the quantity of data passing through a module's interface
compiler a program that translates a high-level language (such as C++, Pascal, or FORTRAN) into machine code
compiler listing a copy of a program into which have been inserted messages from the compiler (indicating errors in the program that prevent its translation into machine language if appropriate)
complete binary tree a binary tree that is either full or full through the next-to-last level, with the leaves on the last level as far to the left as possible
complete graph a graph in which every vertex is directly connected to every other vertex
complexity a measure of the effort expended by the computer in performing a computation, relative to the size of the computation
composite type a data type that allows a collection of values to be associated with an object of that type
composition (containment) a mechanism by which an internal data member of one class is defined to be an object of another class type
computer a programmable device that can store, retrieve, and process data
computer program a list of instructions to be performed by a computer
computer programming the process of planning a sequence of steps for a computer to follow
concrete step a step for which the implementation details are fully specified
conditional test the point at which the Boolean expression is evaluated and the decision is made to either begin a new iteration or skip to the first statement following the loop
constant an item in a program whose value is fixed at compile time and cannot be changed during execution
constant time an algorithm whose Big-O work expression is a constant

constructor an operation that builds new instances of an abstract data type (such as a list)

control abstraction the separation of the logical properties of a control structure from its implementation

control structure a statement used to alter the normally sequential flow of control

control unit the component of the central processing unit that controls the action of other components so that instructions (the program) are executed in sequence

conversion function a function that converts a value of one type to another type so that it can be assigned to a variable of the second type; also called transfer function or type cast

copy constructor a special member function of a class that is implicitly invoked when passing parameters by value, initializing a variable in a declaration, and returning an object as the value of a function

count-controlled loop a loop that executes a predetermined number of times

counter a variable whose value is incremented to keep track of the number of times a process or event occurs

CPU *see* central processing unit

crash the cessation of a computer's operations as a result of the failure of one of its components; cessation of program execution due to an error

CRC card (Class, Responsibility, Collaboration) a visualization technique that uses 4×6 cards to represent a class

cursor control keys a special set of keys on a computer keyboard that allow the user to move the cursor up, down, right, and left to any point on the screen

data information that has been put into a form a computer can use

data abstraction the separation of a data type's logical properties from its implementation

data coverage *see* black-box testing

data encapsulation the separation of the representation of data from the applications that use the data at a logical level; a programming language feature that enforces information hiding

data flow the flow of information from the calling code to a function and from the function back to the calling code

data representation the concrete form of data used to represent the abstract values of an abstract data type

data structure a collection of data elements whose organization is characterized by accessing operations that are used to store and retrieve the individual data elements; the implementation of the composite data members in an abstract data type

data type the general form of a class of data items; a formal description of the set of values (called the domain) and the basic set of operations that can be applied to it

data validation a test added to a program or a function that checks for errors in the data

debugging the process of removing known errors

decision *see* selection control structure

declaration a statement that associates an identifier with a process or object so that the user can refer to that process or object by name

deep copy an operation that not only copies one class object to another but also makes copies of any pointed-to data

`delete` a C++ operator that returns the space allocated for a dynamic variable back to the heap to be used again

delimiter a symbol or keyword that marks the beginning or end of a construct (e.g., statement, comment, declaration, and parameter list)

demotion (narrowing) the conversion of a value from a "higher" type to a "lower" type according to a programming language's precedence of data types. Demotion may cause loss of information

dereference operator an operator that when applied to a pointer variable denotes the variable to which the pointer points

derived class the class that inherits

deskchecking tracing an execution of a design or program on paper

development environment a single package containing all of the software required for developing a program

directed graph (digraph) a graph in which each edge is directed from one vertex to another (or the same) vertex

documentation the written text and comments that make a program easier for others to understand, use, and modify

doubly linked list a linked list in which each node is linked to both its successor and its predecessor

down a descriptive term applied to a computer when it is not in a usable condition

driver a simple dummy main program that is used to call a function being tested; a main function in an object-oriented program

dynamic allocation allocation of memory space for a variable at run time (as opposed to static allocation at compile time)

dynamic binding the run-time determination of which implementation of an operation is appropriate

dynamic data structure a data structure that can expand and contract during program execution

dynamic variable a variable created during execution of a program by the `new` operator

echo printing printing the data values input to a program to verify that they are correct

edge (arc) a pair of vertices representing a connection between two nodes in a graph

editor an interactive program used to create and modify source programs or data

encapsulation (in OOD) the bundling of data and actions in such a way that the logical properties of the data and actions are separated from the implementation details; the practice of hiding a module implementation in a separate block with a formally specified interface

enumeration data type a data type in which the formal description of the set of values is an ordered list of literal values

enumerator one of the values in the domain of an enumeration type

event counter a variable that is incremented each time a particular event occurs

event-controlled loop a loop that terminates when something happens inside the loop body to signal that the loop should be exited

exception a situation associated with an unusual, usually unpredictable event, detectable by software or hardware, which requires special processing
exception report a set of messages in a program that explains the actions taken when an invalid data item is encountered during execution
executing the action of a computer performing as instructed by a given program
execution summary a computer-generated list of all commands processed and any system messages generated during batch processing
execution trace a testing procedure that involves simulating by hand the computer executing a program
expression an arrangement of identifiers, literals, and operators that can be evaluated to compute a value of a given type
expression statement a statement formed by appending a semicolon to an expression
external file a file that is used to communicate with people or programs and is stored externally to the program
external pointer a named pointer variable that references the first node in a linked structure
external representation the printable (character) form of a data value
fetch-execute cycle the sequence of steps performed by the central processing unit for each machine language instruction
field a group of character positions in a line of output
field identifier (member identifier in C++) the name of a component in a record (`struct`)
field member selector the expression used to access components of a record variable; formed by using the record variable name and the field identifier, separated by a period
field of a record a component of a record data type
file a named area in secondary storage that is used to hold a collection of data; the collection of data itself
filtering the stage in an object-oriented design in which the classes determined during brainstorming are reexamined
finite state machine an idealized model of a simple computer consisting of a set of states, the rules that specify when states are changed, and a set of actions that are performed when changing states
flag a Boolean variable that is set in one part of the program and tested in another to control the logical flow of a program
flat implementation the hierarchical structure of a solution written as one long sequence of steps; also called inline implementation
floating point number the value stored in a type `float` variable, so called because part of the memory location holds the exponent and the balance of the location the mantissa, with the decimal point floating as necessary among the significant digits
flow of control the order of execution of the statements in a program
folding a hash method that breaks the key into several pieces and concatenates or exclusive-ORs some of them to form the hash value
formal parameter a variable declared in a function heading
formal parameter declaration the code that associates a formal parameter identifier with a data type and a passing mechanism

formatting the planned positioning of statements or declarations and blanks on a line of a program; the arranging of program output so that it is neatly spaced and aligned

free store (heap) a pool of memory locations reserved for dynamic allocation of data

full binary tree a binary tree in which all of the leaves are on the same level and every nonleaf node has two children

function a subprogram in C++

function call an expression or statement in the main program requiring the computer to execute a function subprogram

function definition a function declaration that includes the body of the function

function prototype a function declaration without the body of the function

function result the value computed by the function and then returned to the main program; often just called the result

function result type the data type of the result value returned by a function; often referred to simply as function type

function type *see* function result type

functional cohesion a property of a module in which all concrete steps are directed toward solving just one problem, and any significant subproblems are written as abstract steps

functional domain the set of valid input data for a program or function

functional equivalence a property of a module that performs exactly the same operation as the abstract step it defines, or when one module performs exactly the same operation as another module

functional modules in top-down design, the structured tasks and subtasks that are solved individually to create an effective program

functional problem description a description that clearly states what a program is to do

garbage memory locations that can no longer be accessed

general (recursive) case the case for which the solution is expressed in terms of a smaller version of itself

generic data type a type for which the operations are defined but the types of the items being manipulated are not

global a descriptive term applied to an identifier declared outside any function, so-called because it is accessible to everything that follows it

graph a data structure that consists of a set of nodes and a set of edges that relate the nodes to each other

hardware the physical components of a computer

hash function a function used to manipulate the key of an element in a list to identify its location in the list

hashing the technique used for ordering and accessing elements in a list in a relatively constant amount of time by manipulating the key to identify its location in the list

header node a placeholder node at the beginning of a list; used to simplify list processing

heap a complete binary tree, each of whose elements contains a value that is greater than or equal to the value of each of its children; *see also* free store
heuristics assorted problem-solving strategies
hierarchical implementation a process in which a modular solution is implemented by subprograms that duplicate the hierarchical structure of the solution
hierarchical records records in which at least one of the fields is itself a record
hierarchy (in OOD) structuring of abstractions in which a descendant object inherits the characteristics of its ancestors
high-level programming language any programming language in which a single statement translates into one or more machine language instructions
homogeneous a descriptive term applied to structures in which all components are of the same data type (such as an array)
identifier a name associated with a process or object and used to refer to that process or object
implementation phase the second set of steps in programming a computer: translating (coding) the algorithm into a programming language; testing the resulting program by running it on a computer, checking for accuracy, and making any necessary corrections; using the program
implementing coding and testing an algorithm
implementing a test plan running the program with the test cases listed in the test plan
implicit matching *see* positional matching
in place describes a kind of sorting algorithm in which the components in an array are sorted without the use of a second array
index a value that selects a component of an array
infinite loop a loop whose termination condition is never reached and which therefore is never exited without intervention from outside of the program
infinite recursion the situation in which a subprogram calls itself over and over continuously
information any knowledge that can be communicated
information hiding The practice of hiding the details of a function or data structure with the goal of controlling access to the details of a module or structure; the programming technique of hiding the details of data or actions from other parts of the program
inheritance a design technique used with a hierarchy of classes by which each descendant class inherits the properties (data and operations) of its ancestor class; the language mechanism by which one class acquires the properties—data and operations—of another class; a mechanism for automatically sharing data and methods among members of a class and its subclasses
inline implementation *see* flat implementation
inorder traversal a systematic way of visiting all the nodes in a binary tree that visits the nodes in the left subtree of a node, then visits the node, and then visits the nodes in the right subtree of the node

input the process of placing values from an outside data set into variables in a program; the data may come from either an input device (keyboard) or an auxiliary storage device (disk or tape)

input prompts messages printed by an interactive program, explaining what data is to be entered

input transformation an operation that takes input values and converts them to the abstract data type representation

input/output (I/O) devices the parts of a computer that accept data to be processed (input) and present the results of that processing (output)

insertion sort a sorting algorithm in which values are placed one at a time into their proper position within a list that was originally empty

inspection a verification method in which one member of a team reads the program or design line by line and the others point out errors

integer number a positive or negative whole number made up of a sign and digits (when the sign is omitted, a positive sign is assumed)

integration testing testing performed to integrate program modules that have already been independently unit tested

interactive system a system that allows direct communication between the user and the computer

interface a connecting link (such as a computer terminal) at a shared boundary that allows independent systems (such as the user and the computer) to meet and act on or communicate with each other; the formal definition of the behavior of a subprogram and the mechanism for communicating with it

internal file a file that is created but not saved; also called a *scratch file*

interpreter a program that inputs a program in a high-level language and directs the computer to perform the actions specified in each statement; unlike a compiler, an interpreter does not produce a machine language version of the entire program

invoke to call on a subprogram, causing the subprogram to execute before control is returned to the statement following the call

iteration an individual pass through, or repetition of, the body of a loop

iteration counter a counter variable that is incremented with each iteration of a loop

iterator an operation that allows us to process all the components in an abstract data type sequentially

leaf node tree node that has no children

length the actual number of values stored in a list or string

lifetime the period of time during program execution when an identifier has memory allocated to it

linear probing resolving a hash collision by sequentially searching a hash table beginning at the location returned by the hash function

linear time for an algorithm, when the Big-O work expression can be expressed in terms of a constant times N, where N is the size of the problem

linked list a list in which the order of the components is determined by an explicit link field in each node, rather than by the sequential order of the components in memory

listing a copy of a source program, output by a compiler, containing messages to the programmer

literal value any constant value written in a program

local variable a variable declared within a block; it is not accessible outside of that block

logarithmic order for an algorithm, when the Big-O work expression can be expressed in terms of the logarithm of *N*, where *N* is the size of the problem

logging off informing a computer—usually through a simple command—that no further commands follow

logging on taking the preliminary steps necessary to identify yourself to a computer so that it accepts your commands

logical order the order in which the programmer wants the statements in the program to be executed, which may differ from the physical order in which they appear

loop a method of structuring statements so that they are repeated while certain conditions are met

loop control variable (LCV) a variable whose value is used to determine whether the loop executes another iteration or exits

loop entry the point at which the flow of control first passes to a statement inside a loop

loop exit the point when the repetition of the loop body ends and control passes to the first statement following the loop

loop invariant assertions about the characteristics of a loop that must always be true for a loop to execute properly; the assertions are true on loop entry, at the start of each loop iteration, and on exit from the loop, but are not necessarily true at each point in the body of the loop

loop test the point at which the loop expression is evaluated and the decision is made either to begin a new iteration or skip to the statement immediately following the loop

machine language the language, made up of binary-coded instructions, that is used directly by the computer

mainframe a large computing system designed for high-volume processing or for use by many people at once

maintenance the modification of a program, after it has been completed, in order to meet changing requirements or to take care of any errors that show up

maintenance phase period during which maintenance occurs

mantissa with respect to floating point representation of real numbers, the digits representing a number itself and not its exponent

member selector the expression used to access components of a `struct` or `class` variable; it is formed by using the variable name and the member name, separated by a dot (period)

memory leak the loss of available memory space that occurs when memory is allocated dynamically but never deallocated

memory unit internal data storage in a computer

metalanguage a language that is used to write the syntax rules for another language

method a function declared as a member of a class object
metric based testing testing based on measurable factors
microcomputer *see* personal computer
minicomputer a computer system larger than a personal computer but smaller than a mainframe; sometimes called an entry-level mainframe
mixed mode expression an expression that contains operands of different data types
modular programming *see* top-down design
modularity (in OOD) meaningful packaging of objects
module a self-contained collection of steps that solves a problem or subproblem; can contain both concrete and abstract steps
module nesting chart a chart that depicts the nesting structure of modules and shows calls among them
name precedence the priority treatment accorded a local identifier in a block over a global identifier with the same spelling in any references that the block makes to that identifier
named constant a location in memory, referenced by an identifier, where a data value that cannot be changed is stored
named matching *see* explicit matching
named type a type that has an identifier (a name) associated with it
nested control structure a program structure consisting of one control statement (selection, iteration, or subprogram) embedded within another control statement
nested if an *if* statement that is nested within another *if* statement
nested loop a loop that is within another loop
`new` a C++ operator that returns the address of new space allocated for a dynamic variable
nodes the building blocks of dynamic structures, each made up of a component (the data) and a pointer (the link) to the next node
nonlocal a descriptive term applied to any identifier declared outside of a given block
nonlocal access access to any identifier declared outside of its own block
null statement an empty statement
nybble four bits; half of a byte
object class (class) the description of a group of objects with similar properties and behaviors; a pattern for creating individual objects
object program the machine-language version of a source program
object-based programming language a programming language that supports abstraction and encapsulation, but not inheritance
object-oriented design a building-block design technique that incorporates abstraction, encapsulation, modularity, and hierarchy
object-oriented programming a method of implementation in which programs are organized as cooperative collections of objects, each of which represents an instance of some class, and whose classes are all members of a hierarchy of classes united via inheritance relationships
observer an operation that allows us to observe the state of an instance of an abstract data type without changing it

one-dimensional array a structured collection of components of the same type given a single name; each component is accessed by an index that indicates its position within the collection

operating system a set of programs that manages all of the computer's resources

out-of-bounds array index an index value that, in C++, is either less than zero or greater than the array size minus one

output transformation an operation that takes an instance of an abstract data type and converts it to a representation that can be output

overflow the condition that arises when the value of a calculation is too large to be represented

overloading giving the same name to more than one function or using the same operator symbol for more than one operation; usually associated with static binding

overriding reimplementing a member function inherited from a parent class

parameter a literal, constant, variable, or expression used for communicating values to or from a subprogram

parameter list a mechanism by which functions communicate with each other

pass by address a parameter-passing mechanism in which the memory address of the actual parameter is passed to the formal parameter; also called pass by reference

pass by name a parameter-passing mechanism in which the actual parameter is passed to a procedure as a literal character string and interpreted by a thunk

pass by reference *see* pass by address

pass by value a parameter-passing mechanism in which a copy of an actual parameter's value is passed to the formal parameter

password a unique series of letters assigned to a user (and known only by that user) by which that user identifies himself or herself to a computer during the logging-on procedure; a password system protects information stored in a computer from being tampered with or destroyed

path a combination of branches that might be traversed when a program or function is executed; a sequence of vertices that connects two nodes in a graph

path testing a testing technique whereby the tester tries to execute all possible paths in a program or function

PC *see* personal computer

peripheral device an input, output, or auxiliary storage device attached to a computer

personal computer (PC) a small computer system (usually intended to fit on a desktop) that is designed to be used primarily by a single person

pointer a simple data type consisting of an unbounded set of values, each of which addresses or otherwise indicates the location of a variable of a given type; operations defined on pointer variables are assignment and test for equality

polymorphic operation an operation that has multiple meanings depending on the type of the object to which it is bound at run time

polymorphism The ability to determine which of several operations with the same name is appropriate; a combination of static and dynamic binding

positional matching a method of matching actual and formal parameters by their relative positions in the two parameter lists; also called *relative* or *implicit* matching

postconditions assertions that must be true after a module is executed
postfix operator an operator that follows its operand(s)
postorder traversal a systematic way of visiting all the nodes in a binary tree that visits the nodes in the left subtree of a node, then visits the nodes in the right subtree of the node, and then visits the node
precision a maximum number of significant digits
preconditions assertions that must be true before a module begins execution
prefix operator an operator that precedes its operand(s)
preorder traversal a systematic way of visiting all the nodes in a binary tree that visits a node, then visits all the nodes in the left subtree of the node, and then visits the nodes in the right subtree of the node
priming read an initial reading of a set of data values before entry into an event-controlled loop, in order to establish values for the variables
problem-solving phase the first set of steps in programming a computer: analyzing the problem; developing an algorithm; testing the algorithm for accuracy
procedural abstraction the separation of the logical properties of an action from its implementation
program validation the process of determining the degree to which software fulfills its intended purpose
program verification the process of determining the degree to which a software product fulfills its specifications
programming planning, scheduling, or performing a task or an event; see also *computer programming*
programming language a set of rules, symbols, and special words used to construct a program
pseudocode a mixture of English statements and C++-like control structures that can easily be translated into a programming language
quadratic probing resolving a hash collision by using the rehashing formula (HashValue $\pm I^2$) % *array-size*, where I is the number of times that the rehash function has been applied
queue a data structure in which elements are added to the rear and removed from the front; a "first in, first out" (FIFO) structure
radix the number of possibilities for each position; the digits in a number system
random probing resolving a hash collision by generating pseudorandom hash values in successive applications of the rehash function
range of values the interval within which values must fall, specified in terms of the largest and smallest allowable values
real number a number that has a whole and a fractional part and no imaginary part
record (`struct`) data type a composite data type with a fixed number of components called fields (members); the operations are whole record assignment and selection of individual fields by name
recursion the situation in which a subprogram calls itself
recursive call a subprogram call in which the subprogram being called is the same as the one making the call
recursive case *see* general case

recursive definition a definition in which something is defined in terms of a smaller version of itself

reference parameter a formal parameter that receives the location (memory address) of the caller's actual parameter

reference type a simple data type consisting of an unbounded set of values, each of which is the address of a variable of a given type. The only operation defined on a reference variable is initialization, after which every appearance of the variable is implicitly dereferenced

refinement in top-down design, the expansion of a module specification to form a new module that solves a major step in the computer solution of a problem

regression testing reexecution of program tests after modifications have been made in order to ensure that the program still works correctly

relational operators operators that state that a relationship exists between two values; in C++, symbols that cause the computer to perform operations to verify whether the indicated relationship exists

relative matching *see* positional matching

representational error arithmetic error caused when the precision of the true result of arithmetic operations is greater than the precision of the machine

reserved word a word that has special meaning in a programming language; it cannot be used as an identifier

responsibility algorithms the stage in an object-oriented design in which algorithms are written for each of the responsibilities outlined on the CRC cards

result *see* function result

return the point at which the computer comes back from executing a function

right-justified placed as far to the right as possible within a fixed number of character positions

robust a descriptive term for a program that can recover from erroneous inputs and other errors and keep running

robustness the ability of a program to recover following an error; the ability of a program to continue to operate within its environment

root the top node of a tree structure; a node with no parent

run-time stack a data structure that keeps track of activation records during the execution of a program

scenarios the stage in an object-oriented design in which the behavoir of each class is determined

scope the region of program code where it is legal to reference (use) an identifier

scope rules the rules that determine where in a program a given identifier may be accessed, given the point at which the identifier is declared

scratch file *see* internal file

secondary storage device *see* auxiliary storage device

selection control structure a form of program structure allowing the computer to select one among possible actions to perform based on given circumstances; also called a *branching control structure*

self the instance object (class) used in the invocation of a method

self-documenting code a program containing meaningful identifiers as well as judiciously used clarifying comments

semantics the set of rules that gives the meaning of instruction written in a programming language

semihierarchical implementation a modular solution implemented by functions in a manner that preserves the hierarchical design, except that a function used by multiple modules is implemented once, outside of the hierarchy, and called in each place it is needed

sentinel a special data value used in certain event-controlled loops as a signal that the loop should be exited

sequence a structure in which statements are executed one after another

shallow copy an operation that copies one class object to another without copying any pointed-to data

side effect any effect of one function on another that is not part of the explicitly defined interface between them

significant digits those digits from the first nonzero digit on the left to the last nonzero digit on the right (plus any zero digits that are exact)

simulation a problem solution that has been arrived at through the application of an algorithm designed to model the behavior of physical systems, materials, or processes

size (of an array) the physical space reserved for an array

software computer programs; the set of all programs available on a computer

software engineering the application of traditional engineering methodologies and techniques to the development of software

software life cycle the phases in the life of a large software project including requirements analysis, specification, design, implementation, testing, and maintenance

software piracy the unauthorized copying of software for either personal use or use by others

sorting arranging the components of a list in order (for instance, words in alphabetical order, numbers in ascending or descending order)

source program a program written in a high-level programming language

stable sort a sorting algorithm that preserves the order of duplicates

stack an abstract data type in which elements are added and removed from only one end; a "last in, first out" (LIFO) structure

stack frame *see* activation record

stack overflow the condition resulting from trying to push an element onto a full stack

stack underflow the condition resulting from trying to pop an empty stack

standardized made uniform; most high-level languages are standardized, as official descriptions of them exist

static binding the compile-time determination of which function to call for a particular object

static variable a variable for which memory remains allocated throughout the execution of the entire program

stepwise design *see* top-down design

stepwise refinement *see* top-down design

string a collection of characters that is interpreted as a single data item; in C++, a null-terminated sequence of characters stored in a `char` array
stub a dummy function that assists in testing part of a program; it has the same function that would actually be called by the part of the program being tested, but is usually much simpler
style the individual manner in which computer programmers translate algorithms into a programming language
subprogram *see* function
supercomputer the most powerful class of computers
switch expression the expression in a *switch* statement whose value determines which case label is selected; it cannot be a floating point expression
syntax the formal rules governing how valid instructions (constructs) are written in a programming language
system software a set of programs—including the compiler, the operating system, and the editor—that improves the efficiency and convenience of the computer's processing
tail recursion a recursive algorithm in which no statements are executed after the return from the recursive call
team programming the use of two or more programmers to design a program that would take one programmer too long to complete
template a C++ language construct that allows the compiler to generate multiple versions of a class type or a function by allowing parameterized types
temporary file a file that exists only during the execution of a program
termination condition the condition that causes a loop to be exited
test driver *see* driver
test plan a document that specifies how a program is to be tested
test plan implementation using the test cases specified in a test plan to verify that a program outputs the predicted results
testing checking a program's output by comparing it to hand-calculated results; running a program with data sets designed to discover any errors
testing the state of a stream the act of using a C++ stream variable in a logical expression as if it were a Boolean variable; the result is true if the last I/O operation on that stream succeeded, and false otherwise
text file a file in which each component is a character; each numeric digit is represented by its code in the collating sequence
top-down design a technique for developing a program in which the problem is divided into more easily handled subproblems, the solutions of which create a solution to the overall problem; also called stepwise refinement and modular programming
trailer node a placeholder node at the end of a list; used to simplify list processing
transfer function *see* conversion function
transformer an operation that builds a new value of an ADT, given one or more previous values of the type

traverse a list to access the components of a list one at a time from the beginning of the list to the end

two-dimensional array a collection of components, all of the same type, structured in two dimensions; each component is accessed by a pair of indexes that represent the component's position within each dimension

type cast *see* conversion function

type coercion an automatic conversion of a value of one type to a value of another type

type definition the association of a type identifier with the definition of a new data type

unary operator an operator that has just one operand

underflow the condition that arises when the value of a calculation is too small to be represented

undirected graph a graph in which the edges have no direction

unit testing testing a module or function by itself

unstructured data type a collection consisting of components that are not organized with respect to one another

user name the name by which a computer recognizes the user, and which must be entered to log on to a machine

value parameter a formal parameter that receives a copy of the contents of the corresponding actual parameter

value-returning function a function that returns a single value to its caller and is invoked from within an expression

variable a location in memory, referenced by an identifier, in which a data value that can be changed is stored

vertex a node in a graph

virtual function a function in which each invocation cannot be matched with the proper code until run time

virus a computer program that replicates itself, often with the goal of spreading to other computers without authorization, possibly with the intent of doing harm

visible accessible; a term used in describing a scope of access

void function (procedure) a function that does not return a function value to its caller and is invoked as a separate statement

walk-through a verification method in which a *team* performs a manual simulation of the program or design

weighted graph a graph in which each edge carries a value

word a group of 16, 32, or 64 bits; a group of bits processed by the arithmetic-logic unit in a single instruction

work a measure of the effort expended by the computer in performing a computation

workstation a minicomputer or powerful microcomputer designed to be used primarily by one person at a time

Index

Italicized page locators indicate a figure; tables are noted with a *t*.

Symbols

A

B

C

H

M

V

W

X

Z